The Prentice Hall Anthology of Latino Literature

Eduardo R. del Rio

University of Texas, Pan American

Prentice
Hall

Upper Saddle River, New Jersey 07458

Library of Congress Cataloging-in-Publication Data

The Prentice Hall anthology of Latino Literature [edited by] Eduardo del Rio.—1st ed.
    p. cm
    Includes bibliographical references and index.
    ISBN 0-13-026687-6
        1. American literature—Hispanic American authors. 2. Hispanic Americans—Literary collections. 3. Mexican Americans—Literary collections. 4. Cuban Americans—Literary collections. 5. Puerto Ricans—Literary collections. I. Rio, Eduardo del, 1960– II. Title.

PS508.H57 P74 2001
810.8'0868073—dc21

00-068811

VP, Editor-in-Chief: Leah Jewell
Acquisitions Editor: Carrie Brandon
Assistant Editor: Vivian Garcia
Editorial Assistant: Tom DeMarco
VP, Director of Production
and Manufacturing: Barbara Kittle
Senior Managing Editor: Mary Rottino
Production Editor: Randy Pettit
Prepress and Manufacturing
Manager: Nick Sklitsis
Prepress and Manufacturing
Buyer: Sherry Lewis
Director of Marketing: Beth Gillett Mejia
Marketing Manager: Rachel Falk
Cover Design Director: Jayne Conte
Cover Design: Robert Farrar-Wagner
Cover Art: © 1998 Jose Ortega
Director, Image Resources: Melinda Lee Reo
Image Specialist: Beth Boyd-Benzel
Manager, Rights and Permissions: Kay Dellosa

For Alexis

For permission to use copyrighted material, grateful acknowledgment is made to the copyright holders listed on page 523, which is considered an extension of this copyright page.

This book was set in 10/12 Galliard by Lithokraft II, and printed and bound by Courier-Westford. The cover was printed by Phoenix Color Corp.

Pearson Education LTD., London
Pearson Education Australia Pty, Limited, Sydney
Pearson Education North Asia Ltd, Hong Kong
Pearson Education Canada, Ltd, Toronto
Pearson Educacion de Mexico, S.A. de C.V.
Pearson Education - Japan, Tokyo
Pearson Education Malaysia, Pte. Ltd
Pearson Education, Upper Saddle River, New Jersey

Contents

Foreword

Why an anthology on U.S. Latino writers, some people may ask. U.S. Latinos now number more than 32 million Spanish speakers, and, according to the U.S. Census, demographers predict that Latinos will become the largest minority population in the United States sometime between 2005 and 2008. This demographic projection will only continue to increase the significance and the importance of Latinos as we move into the twenty-first century, and that is why *The Prentice Hall Anthology of Latino Literature* is appearing at a particularly auspicious moment in American literary history.

This is not to say that this is the only Latino literature anthology, but it is to say that I believe Eduardo del Rio's anthology is the most comprehensive one to date. Selecting passages that represent the work of an author is akin to writing a screenplay. Both endeavors require the anthologist and a screenwriter to choose from among the images, scenes, and incidents or events that writers create. The goal, then, is to choose the material that will be featured for reasons that viewers are encouraged to discern and discuss. In the latter case, the experience is similar to attempting to envision whether viewers will choose to pay and to take time from their lives to see a film based on the previews. Literature anthologies serve much the same purpose. From the passage chosen for inclusion, an anthologist hopes to whet appetites enough to encourage readers to seek out and to read the longer works which contain the featured selections.

In preparing the materials for this Latino literature collection, Eduardo del Rio has been motivated not only by the strength and quality of the individual selections, but by the desire to make this gathering comprehensively representative of the wide variety of Latino literature. The anthology for that reason is divided according to ethnic groups and by genre categories. Such an organizing principle is designed to allow readers to see the similarities as well as the differences among the various Latino literatures and cultures. This arrangement allows literature teachers and instructors to teach one, two, or several groups of Latino writers, according to the needs of a particular class. Thus, a Mexican American poem on, say, the school experience can then be compared to one by a Puerto Rican or a Cuban American poet.

The questions that accompany the selections are intended to improve critical thinking skills and to direct class discussions toward issues raised by the selections, should the instructor need some guidance in this area. The idea here is to provoke readers to think about the materials included in this text in order to help students understand how different Latino writers have written about their experiences and to encourage readers to interact with the selections in ways that are meaningful, relevant, and eye-opening to everyone.

—Marco Portales
Professor of English
Texas A&M University

Preface

When I started teaching Latino literature several years ago I had several goals I wanted to meet. The first one was simply to expose students to works by Mexican-American, Cuban-American, and Puerto Rican authors. I was always surprised to hear that most of my predominantly Mexican-American students had never been exposed to works by authors who shared some of their own backgrounds and experiences. More importantly, I wanted them to see that these works were valuable not simply because they were written by Latinos and Latinas, but because they were well crafted; in effect, because they were "good literature." Additionally, I wanted to show students that while there were some obvious differences within the works of various Latino groups, there were also some significant similarities. I hoped that aside from the linguistic connection, they could feel that they were part of a larger community by learning about the history, religion, and culture of other Latino groups.

Finding a textbook that accommodated these goals proved impossible. Anthologies containing selections by one particular Latino group were fairly easy to find. Mexican-American anthologies, for instance, were readily available. It was a bit more difficult to find books that included works by authors of different ethnicities, but a few existed. Unfortunately, they restricted themselves to only one genre. It was possible, for instance, to find an anthology of Latino poetry. At the time I started teaching Latino literature there was only one anthology that contained selections by authors of various Latino groups, which also provided offerings from different genres. While the books were well edited, it was arranged by theme rather than genre or ethnicity. Thus, I felt that it was not well suited to the goals that I wanted to achieve, and which I felt would prove most beneficial to my students. For a few years I struggled with individual works of fiction, poetry, and drama. This approach was not only expensive for students, but it also limited their exposure to a wider variety of texts and ideas. What was needed, I thought, was an affordable textbook that would aid both student and instructor by accentuating the differences and similarities present in the works of Latino and Latina authors.

In editing this anthology I have kept these goals in mind. For those who wish to study the works of only one Latino group this book is arranged so that it is possible to do so. However, the arrangement by ethnic group and genre is designed to allow instructors and students to explore the important differences and common traits present in these works. The questions that follow the selections incorporate this idea. I hope that it not only serves as a valuable classroom tool, but that it emphasizes the tremendous amount of quality literature being produced by Latino and Latina writers.

—Eduardo del Rio
University of Texas
Pan American

Introduction

The purpose of this anthology is to expose students to a field of literature that is growing rapidly. Latino studies, in fact, is no longer situated at the margins of literary studies. With a growing interest in culture, ethnicity, and gender, Latino studies is now a mainstay in many English departments, literary journals, professional societies, and scholarly conferences. In addition, the media's focus on the most rapidly increasing segment of our population makes it evident that the study of Latino literature will continue to play a vital role in students' education.

The design and structure of this anthology has been based on several considerations; however, foremost is the issue surrounding the very definition of *Latino/Latina literature*. Many critics have attempted to provide a coherent definition of the term, but there has been little agreement on a variety of issues. For instance, while it is clear that the authors classified as Latino/Latina should share a similar ancestry, scholars have disagreed on what that ancestry is. Additionally, while some scholars believe that Latino/Latina writers are those who were born in this country, others would argue that the term should include those who emigrated here and spent significant time in the United States. The question of language also plays a key role in determining this definition. Should the text under consideration have been written originally in English, Spanish, or some mixture of both? Others argue that content should play a role when deciding whether or not a writer is Latino or Latina. They claim that the subject matter, and more importantly, the thematic concern of the work, should explore certain key concepts. Finally, others feel that these factors should not be the determining guidelines, but instead choose to group the writers based on other categories, such as historical periods or genres.

The definition of *Latino literature* used as a basis when compiling this anthology is one that seeks to address all of these issues, and accommodate some of them. First, for the purposes of this anthology, *Latino literature* is defined as the work of writers whose ancestry can be traced to Spanish-speaking countries of the Americas. While there are clear variations of the Spanish language, and significant idiomatic and linguistic differences between the spoken and written word of Latinos and Latinas of various ancestries and backgrounds, this common bond serves as a unifying factor among them.

Second, the works of Latino literature should have been produced by authors who have lived in the United States for a significant period of time. Thus, whether or not the writer was born in this country or migrated here, it is crucial that his or her artistic consciousness be affected by the sounds, images, and experiences of life in the United States. This can only occur through an extensive exposure to those experiences.

Part of this experience involves a sense of duality regarding the English language. For some writers the Spanish language may be a mere memory, for others a periodic contact through familial bonds, and for some a direct confrontation with a new and confusing tongue. For all, however, whether born and raised here or newly arrived, linguistic consciousness includes a sense of both languages. Because of this tension, the body of Latino writers' works are written primarily in English. These writers seek to express this conflict in the language that is the embodiment of it.

Finally, the work of Latino and Latina authors should contain characteristics that are unique to the Latino experience. Some of these include an attention to family, a concern for home, an interest in historical formulations, and a focus on cultural components such as music, food, and religion. Above all, many of the works contain issues that pertain to identity formation, appropriation, and determination. This is not to say that each and every work should concentrate on dual identity as its principle focus, but the body of works of Latino authors should at some point consider it, especially as a function of ideology.

All of these factors should be considered when determining whether or not to classify a work as Latino literature. Because of this, this anthology does not include the work of such respected Latin American writers as Gabriel García Marquez and Octavio Paz. While these writers may be linked to one of these factors (Lorca wrote *Poeta en Nueva York,* for example, even though its focus is not Latinos) it would be difficult to link them to several of them. There are other significant writers who are not included in this anthology for similar reasons. Tomás Rivera, for instance, by all accounts a writer of great impact, is omitted because despite the fact that his greatest literary achievement *y no se lo trago la tierra* deals with the issue of dual identity, it was produced in Spanish and only through *other's* translations has it become accessible to an English-speaking audience. I emphasize this because some writers included in the anthology have written pieces in Spanish. However, there is often a crucial difference. While Rolando Hinojosa's works, for example, were written originally in Spanish, the translations (really reformulations) were done by Hinojosa himself. Lydia Cabrera, Matías Montes Huidobro, and Reinaldo Arenas are three Cuban writers among the numerous others who are omitted from this anthology for similar reasons. Likewise, while a sense of the historical evolution of Latino literature is crucial to its understanding, selections by figures such as Álvar Núñez Cabeza de Vaca and Jose Martí are also not included because of the parameters described here. The historical context of the works of some of these key figures will be discussed in the introductions to each particular section.

A few words should be said regarding the specific selections in this text. The anthology focuses only on writers of Mexican, Puerto Rican, and Cuban heritage. There are, of course, writers from other ethnic groups who are making their presence known. Julia Alvarez, for instance, a Dominican writer, is one notable example. While Alvarez has written a significant body of work and she clearly qualifies as Latina under the definition provided, she is among the few writers who are not connected to one of the three groups included here. There are other Latino/Latina writers from places such as El Salvador, Chile, and Perú who are contributing to this rapidly growing field, but at present the anthology includes only the three groups who form the majority in population and literary production.

This anthology is designed to highlight the similarities and differences between the culture and literature of these three different groups, while attempting to emphasize the unique qualities of each of them. Additionally, it strives to demonstrate the universal themes that many of these works display, while also showing their singularity. Because of this, some writers have regretfully been omitted from the text. Achy Obejas, Oscar "Zeta" Acosta, Alurista, Alberto Rios, and Cherrie Moraga are only a few examples of the writers whose works might have been included in an anthology such as this.

When considering the individual selections, as well as the book's structure, it was important that the overall effect of the anthology facilitate a student's ability to grasp how these literatures and cultures are both similar and distinctive. Thus, rather than a chronological survey, the text has been divided by ethnic group, and then further subdivided by literary genre. The questions that follow each reading are designed to facilitate those comparisons.

These statements may seem apologetic. They are not intended as such. They are merely an explanation of the book's scope. Additionally, the process of selection, by definition, involves exclusion, and with exclusion there will always be criticism. It is perhaps ironic that an anthology of Latino literature exclude certain authors and works, since the bulk of the work represented here focuses on matters relating to some type of marginalization. However, the fact that choices had to be made also speaks for the increase in production and recovery of works written by Latinos and Latinas, works whose aesthetic value goes hand-in-hand with some of their social, cultural, and political import.

LABELING

In general, there are two terms used to refer to people of Spanish descent, *Hispanic* and *Latino*. While some people use these terms interchangeably, for most, each carries specific cultural and/or political connotations.

The term *Hispanic* was first coined by the United States government, specifically the Department of Education and the Census Bureau, in the 1970s. The term seems to be a derivation of the Spanish word *hispánico,* which has various definitions, most of which have to do with either Spain or the Spanish language. Because of these factors, some people reject this term as it has specific political and geographic connections that they may not identify with. Since *Hispanic* is not a self-defining term, they argue, it has little or no validity. Furthermore, the fact that the term was created by the United States government to group people so that they may continue to subordinate them, in itself reveals its offensive nature. Additionally, the people who are considered *Hispanic* by others may not feel any connection to their European cultural heritage, and argue that the term reduces a varied people to only one common trait.

Latino, a term that has acquired more popularity in recent years, is more widely accepted in the academic community. The term is not connected to Spain, but to its colonies in Latin America. Thus, it encompasses people whose origins are in South and Central America, the Caribbean, and Mexico. Some people who use this term prefer it because it is intertwined with the racism and oppression of colonialism. Others prefer it simply because, unlike its counterpart, it is a term that was created as self-definition, and not imposed by others.

The complexity and confusion regarding the labeling of the people whose work is represented in this anthology is epitomized by LULAC—the League of United Latino American Citizens—established in 1929. While their acronym includes the word Latino, they bill themselves as "the largest Hispanic organization in the U.S."

Mexican-American Labels

There are several terms used by people of Mexican descent. *Chicano*, a term associated with the Civil Rights Movement of the 1960s, is still employed by writers today. There are two schools of thought regarding the origins of the word. The first is that it stems from the term the Aztecs used to refer to themselves, *Meshicas*. After combining this with *Mexican* and later further distorting it, it eventually evolved into the modern label. The other, perhaps even more difficult to support, is that it is a combination of the word *chico* (or small), a word some believe was often used by Europeans, and Mexican. *Mexican-American* is the preferred term for many people of Mexican origin who do not like the political implications associated with the term *Chicano*. While dual consciousness is not solely a result of linguistic difference, any hyphenated term such as this certainly underscores its importance.

Cuban-American Labels

The two most popular terms used by people of Cuban ancestry are Cuban-American and Cuban exile. The difference in the use of these two terms is mainly generational. Many of the people who arrived in the first two waves of Cuban immigrants in the 1960s continue, even to this day, to consider themselves Cuban. They prefer to be called Cuban exiles as it emphasizes their country of origin as well as the reason they abandoned it. In general, the children of these immigrants, who have been born or raised in the United States prefer the term *Cuban-American*.

Puerto Rican-American Labeling

Unlike their Mexican and Cuban counterparts, Puerto Rican-Americans rarely refer to themselves as hyphenated Americans. The most commonly used term for people who were either born on the island and emigrated to the United States is Puerto Rican. This perhaps has to do with geographic and cultural conditions which will be examined later. Nevertheless, the term *Puerto Rican,* when referring to those who were born or raised in the United States, clearly carries with it significant differences than when the term is applied to islanders who continue to live in Puerto Rico. Another popular term is *Nuyorican*. In general, this applies to people of Puerto Rican heritage who have some connection to New York. Many Puerto Ricans living in other parts of the United States, however, have no such connection.

It is important to point out that all of these hyphenated labels have come under attack as being a designation for second-class citizens. Additionally, the term *Puerto Rican-American* may seem redundant as Puerto Ricans are by definition U.S. citizens. However, to emphasize the focus of this text on Latino literature, and since part of the book's intent is to distinguish and differentiate, the hyphenated labels are used throughout.

CULTURAL AND LINGUISTIC CONSIDERATIONS

Clearly all these groups collectively share the use of the Spanish language. In fact, both Indian and Spanish words have often been incorporated into the English language and continue to thrive today. Just two examples are *hamaca* (hammock) and *tabaco* (tobacco). However, the influence that Spanish has had on each individual within the group varies. Thus, some authors rely heavily on Spanish words, for example, "Corky" Gonzalez and Ana Castillo. Sometimes Spanish and English words are combined and form new words that are often referred to as *spanglish*. Tato Laviera's poetry springs to mind. Often the writer may not rely on code-switching, but his or her work will explore the effects of the Spanish language on the English creative process and vice versa. Gustavo Pérez-Firmat's work is one example. However it may be expressed in their writing, either overtly or subtly, all these writers share a dual linguistic background.

However, all three groups represented in this anthology share more than the use of the Spanish language and a European cultural heritage. One of the things they share is a connection to indigenous and African roots. Many of the colonizers of the New World, often forcibly, engaged in sexual relations with African slaves and native Indians. The results of this interracial mixing were many *mulatto* (white/black) and *mestizo* (white/Indian) children. The cultural and linguistic dimensions of these bonds are evidenced in such things as modem spiritual beliefs and rituals. Called *espiritismo* by Puerto Ricans and *santería* by Cubans, the combination of African gods with Catholic saints, is one such example. For Mexicans, *curanderismo* offers a variety of healing treatments for ailments that modern medicine often can't resolve. The result of these interracial bonds is also visible in the music and dances of the peoples of these three groups. The *plena* and *son* of Puerto Ricans and Cubans have their equivalent in the *corridos* of Mexican-American folktale. The literatures of these groups, therefore, reflect the varied yet similar beliefs and customs of this multicultural heritage.

The racial dimension of their heritage is often explored in the writings of many of the authors of these three groups. While there is a different framework between the racial experiences of black Latinos (both Cuban and Puerto Rican) and Mexican-Americans, their works reflect similar notions of marginalization and a sense of racial difference. Some of the work of Martin Espada and Gloria Anzaldua explores this issue.

Although other literature often concerns itself with gender differences, Latino literature often deals with it in a unique way. Because many Latinas have the dual burden of being both Hispanic and female, much Latino literature focuses on exploring the cultural stereotypes associated with this group. *Machismo*, for example, is often examined as a paradigm of Latina identity and behavior. Many Latina writers create characters who both reinforce and shatter these stereotypes. Sandra Cisneros, Cristina García, and Esmeralda Santiago are just three examples of the new generation of Latina writers asserting their literary presence.

Another powerful element these cultures share is their interest in, and focus on, a sense of place. Sometimes this focus is displayed as a desire to return to a paradisal ancestral home. For Mexican-Americans, Aztlan, the mythical homeland of the Aztecs, is the embodiment of this idea. For Cuban-Americans a return to pre-revolutionary Cuba is often a source of nostalgic ruminations. For Puerto Ricans their tropical island, *Borinquen,* the name the native Taínos gave the land, may seem difficult to reach even though it is only a few miles away. Whether it be a mythical land, a nostalgic point in time, or a very real yet unattainable location, all of these peoples frequently share a longing to return to their origins. This shared yet distinctive interest is often displayed in the poems, stories, and plays of these writers. Sometimes it is depicted as an actual home, both real and symbolic, and at other times the home is merely in the imagination or memory of the speaker.

Perhaps the most important bond, however, is the concept of identity. All three groups have a shared past of having been, and some argue continue to be (as in the case of Puerto Rico), a colonized and oppressed people. Because of this, all three groups have developed a strong nationalistic sense while at the same time feeling the need to be accepted by their adopted home. Often this need comes as a result of being assaulted with images that reinforce the "American ideal." This dual consciousness manifests itself differently in all three groups. Because the forefathers of many Mexican-Americans were Mexicans before they were Americans, there is sometimes a lingering resentment expressed by some Mexican-American writers toward the dominant mainstream culture, while at the same time they are attempting to embrace it. Because of Puerto Rico's status as a Commonwealth, some Puerto Ricans view the United States as a continuing force of oppression. For many Puerto Ricans living in the United States, this duality is often expressed in terms of their allegiance to the island versus that of their adopted home. For many Cuban-Americans the United States is not their enemy, but rather their savior. Many Cuban refugees of the early 1960s were obviously grateful that the United States welcomed them with open arms. For their sons and daughters, however, who have grown up in the reality of a country where many social and economic inequalities exist, the view of their adopted home is often more problematic.

There are, of course, other political, social, and economic factors that influence the beliefs and attitudes of these Latino/Latina writers, and consequently their works, both individually and collectively. However, as exemplified by the selections in this anthology, the sense of "living on the hyphen" continues to be a shared experience for many of them.

MEXICAN-AMERICAN LITERATURE

A BRIEF SURVEY

The roots of Mexican-American literature begin with the arrival of the Spanish explorers in what is now the Southwest United States. Several of these have provided us with a detailed account of the life in the area's formative years. Alvar Nunez Cabeza de Vaca's *Adventures in the Unknown Interior of America* (1542), for example, provides useful insight into the lives of the Indian tribes of the area, as well as descriptions of the local flora and fauna. Gaspar Pérez de Villagrá's *Historia de la Nuevo México* (History of New Mexico) (1610) is the first record of poetry written in the area. In addition to the account of a long expedition through Mexico, this epic poem also includes a brief account of the first play ever written and performed in the Southwest. A young soldier named Farfán wrote a dramatic work thanking God for protecting the expedition in their travels, which the men performed on the banks of the Rio Grande River. In addition to these genres, others, based on oral traditions, were incorporated and/or created to add to the literary corpus. These include the ballad (or *romance*), couplets (*coplas*), and legends (*cuentos*).

During the nineteenth century individual works based on these traditions began to make their appearance. Among these are Lorenzo de Zavala's *Viaje a los Estados-Unidos de Norte America* (Journey to the United States of North America) (1834), and the anonymous historical drama *Los Tejanos* (The Texans) (1846). The century also saw a tremendous number of poems and short stories being published in periodicals across the country. Many of these have recently been recovered by the work of scholars working with the *Recovering the Hispanic Literary Heritage* project initiated by Nicolás Kanellos. Longer published works of the period include *The Squatter and the Don: Descriptive of Contemporary Ocurrences in California* (1885), now considered by many as the first Mexican-American novel, usurping José Antonio Villareal's *Pocho* from that spot. Regardless of its historical status, it is significant because it is one of the few pieces of extant literature by women of the period.

In the first half of the twentieth century, despite the spread of the English language, many writers continued to write in Spanish. Among these is Daniel Venegas, whose *Don Chipote o cuando los pericos mamen* (Don Chipote or when the parrots suckle) (1928) is a satiric work which criticizes the United States' exploitation of Mexican workers. Toward the end of the 1940s the Zoot Suit riots in Los Angeles signaled a shift in much of the writings of Mexican-Americans. The double standard of the U.S. government's contradictory treatment of Mexicans who served in World War II and the brutal treatment of those in the streets possibly prompted such works as Josefina Niggli's *Mexican Village* (1945), which traces the life of a young man of mixed heritage who travels to Mexico in search of his roots.

The latter part of the twentieth century saw an explosion of works in various genres by Mexican-Americans. In drama, the establishment by Luis Valdez of the *Teatro Campesino* which sought to highlight the plight of farm workers gave rise to informal skits, or *actos*. Later, more sophisticated works include *Zoot Suit* (1977). Other notable playwrights include: Estella Portillo Trample, Carlos Morton, Cherrie Moraga, and Denise Chavez. In fiction, beginning with Villareal's *Pocho* (1959), the corpus of Mexican-American literature has rapidly increased. Some notable authors and texts include Rudolfo Anaya's *Bless Me, Ultima* (1972), Rolando Hinojosa's *Estampas del valle y otras obras* (Sketches of the Valley and Other Works) (1972), and most recently Sandra Cisneros' *The House on Mango Street* (1991) and Ana Castillo's *So Far From God* (1994). In poetry the production by authors of Mexican descent has been both prolific and varied during this period. Some notable poets of the period are Alurista, Gary Soto, Pat Mora, and Lorna Dee Cervantes. From Rodolfo "Corky" Gonzales' battlecry in "I Am Joaquin" through Ana Castillo's commentary on gender inequality in "Women Are Not Roses," Mexican-American poetry demonstrates its diversity and wide range of subject matter.

Fiction

Sandra Cisneros

SANDRA CISNEROS was born in Chicago in 1954 to a Mexican-American mother and Mexican father. She received her B.A. in English from Loyola University. It was during her studies for an M.F.A. from the University of Iowa that she realized she wanted to write the kind of books she had never been exposed to growing up. She is the recipient of countless awards including a National Endowment for the Arts Fellowship in 1982 and 1988, a Lannan Foundation Literary Award in 1991, and a MacArthur Fellowship in 1995.

Cisneros's poetic works include Bad Boys *(1980), a collection of seven poems dealing with her childhood in Chicago;* My Wicked Wicked Ways *(1987), a series of autobiographical poems; and most recently* Loose Woman *(1995). In prose her most distinguished endeavor is* Woman Hollering Creek and Other Stories *(1991), a refashioning of the legend of* La Llorona, *which once again brought Cisneros a series of awards.* Hairs: Pelitos *(1994), a children's bilingual book, is her most recent endeavour.*

The selections that follow are taken from the work that thrust Cisneros into the limelight, The House on Mango Street *(1983). Winner of the Before Columbus American Book Award, the work is composed of a series of vignettes that ultimately form a coherent whole. While "My Name" appears towards the beginning of the story, and the other two at the end, they each touch upon the theme of belonging. We also have a glimpse of the development of the main character, Esperanza, as she attempts to resolve some of the issues the novel is concerned with.*

From The House on Mango Street

My Name (Esperanza)

In English my name means hope. In Spanish it means too many letters. It means sadness, it means waiting. It is like the number nine. A muddy color. It is the Mexican records my father plays on Sunday mornings when he is shaving, songs like sobbing.

It was my great-grandmother's name and now it is mine. She was a horse woman too, born like me in the Chinese year of the horse—which is supposed to be bad luck if you're born female—but I think this is a Chinese lie because the Chinese, like the Mexicans, don't like their women strong.

My great-grandmother. I would've liked to have known her, a wild horse of a woman, so wild she wouldn't marry. Until my great-grandfather threw a sack over her head and carried her off. Just like that, as if she were a fancy chandelier. That's the way he did it.

And the story goes she never forgave him. She looked out the window her whole life, the way so many women sit their sadness on an elbow. I wonder if she made the best with what she got or was she sorry because she couldn't be all the things she wanted to be. Esperanza. I have inherited her name, but I don't want to inherit her place by the window.

At school they say my name funny as if the syllables were made out of tin and hurt the roof of your mouth. But in Spanish my name is made out of a softer some-thing, like silver, not quite as thick as sister's name—Magdalena—which is uglier than mine. Magdalena who at least can come home and become Nenny. But I am always Esperanza.

I would like to baptize myself under a new name, a name more like the real me, the one nobody sees. Esperanza as Lisandra or Maritza or Zeze the X. Yes. Some-thing, like Zeze the X will do.

A House of My Own

Not a flat. Not an apartment in back. Not a man's house. Not a daddy's. A house all my own. With my porch and my pillow, my pretty purple petunias. My books and my stories. My two shoes waiting beside the bed. Nobody to shake a stick at. Nobody's garbage to pick up after.

Only a house quiet as snow, a space for myself to go, clean as paper before the poem.

Mango Says Goodbye Sometimes

I like to tell stories. I tell them inside my head. I tell them after the mailman says, Here's your mail. Here's your mail he said.

I make a story for my life, for each step my brown shoe takes. I say, "And so she trudged up the wooden stairs, her sad brown shoes taking her to the house she never liked."

I like to tell stories. I am going to tell you a story about a girl who didn't want to belong.

We didn't always live on Mango Street. Before that we lived on Loomis on the third floor, and before that we lived on Keeler. Before Keeler it was Paulina, but what

I remember most is Mango Street, sad red house, the house I belong but do not belong to.

I put it down on paper and then the ghost does not ache so much. I write it down and Mango says goodbye sometimes. She does not hold me with both arms. She sets me free.

One day I will pack my bags of books and paper. One day I will say goodbye to Mango. I am too strong for her to keep me here forever. One day I will go away.

Friends and neighbors will say, What happened to that Esperanza? Where did she go with all those books and paper? Why did she march so far away?

They will not know I have gone away to come back. For the ones I left behind. For the ones who cannot out.

Discussion Questions

1. In "My Name" what does Esperanza mean when she says she doesn't want to inherit her great-grandmother's "place by the window"?

2. Why does Esperanza want to change her name to "Zeze the X"?

3. What does the story say about the role of language in Mexican-American culture?

4. "A House of My Own" comments on the speaker's sense of identity and individuality. Why is it crucial that this house belong only to her?

5. Why does the author deliberately mix the grammatical structure in the last sentence of "Mango Says Goodbye Sometimes"? Who are those who "cannot out"?

6. Compare what Esperanza says about women in these stories to Ana Castillo's "Women Are Not Roses" on page 89.

7. Compare these poems to Nicholasa Mohr's description of her secret garden on page 365. In what different way do these speakers find their own space. What does that say about their identities?

Gary Soto

GARY SOTO's publications span over twenty years. He is as comfortable with poetry as with prose, and has produced an autobiography, essays, poems, and novels. In addition, for the last few years, he has produced films and children's literature. Soto has received numerous awards including a Guggenheim Fellowship (1979–1980); National Endowment for the Arts Fellowships (1981 and 1991); the Carnegie Medal (1993); and the National Book Award and Los Angeles Times Book Prize nominations (1995).

Soto was born in Fresno, California in 1952. He received an M.F.A. from the University of California, Irvine in 1976. His long list of publications include books of poetry: Where Sparrows Work Hard *(1981),* Black Hair *(1985),* New and Selected Poems *(1995), and* Junior College: Poems *(1997), as well as prose:* Small Faces *(1986),* Baseball in April and Other Stories *(1990).*

Living Up the Street perhaps best illustrates the varied interests of this prolific author: the innocence of childhood, the hardships of urban life, the importance of family; all these elements are constantly being juxtaposed with the reality of being Mexican-American and poor. Living Up the Street is deceptively simple, as Gary, often innocently, relates his encounters with prejudice without rancor or resentment. As he matures, however, his awareness of the difference between the depiction of the American Dream and his own life becomes increasingly evident.

From Living Up the Street

Black Hair

There are two kinds of work: One uses the mind and the other uses muscle. As a kid I found out about the latter. I'm thinking of the summer of 1969 when I was a seventeen-year-old runaway who ended up in Glendale, California, to work for Valley Tire Factory. To answer an ad in the newspaper I walked miles in the afternoon sun, my stomach slowly knotting on a doughnut that was breakfast, my teeth like bright candles gone yellow.

I walked in the door sweating and feeling ugly because my hair was still stiff from a swim at the Santa Monica beach the day before. Jules, the accountant and part owner, looked droopily through his bifocals at my application and then at me. He tipped his cigar in the ashtray, asked my age as if he didn't believe I was seventeen, but finally after a moment of silence, said, "Come back tomorrow. Eight-thirty."

I thanked him, left the office, and went around to the chain link fence to watch the workers heave tires into a bin; others carted uneven stacks of tires on hand trucks. Their faces were black from tire dust and when they talked—or cussed—their mouths showed a bright pink.

From there I walked up a commercial street, past a cleaners, a motorcycle shop, and a gas station where I washed my face and hands; before leaving I took a bottle that hung on the side of the Coke machine, filled it with water, and stopped it with a scrap of paper and a rubber band.

The next morning I arrived early at work. The assistant foreman, a potbellied Hungarian, showed me a timecard and how to punch in. He showed me the Coke machine, the locker room with its slimy shower, and also pointed out the places where I shouldn't go: The ovens where the tires were recapped and the customer service area, which had a slashed couch, a coffee table with greasy magazines, and an ashtray. He introduced me to Tully, a fat man with one ear, who worked the buffers that resurfaced the white walls. I was handed an apron and a face mask and shown how to use the buffer: Lift the tire and center, inflate it with a footpedal, press the buffer against the white band until cleaned, and then deflate and blow off the tire with an air hose.

With a paint brush he stirred a can of industrial preserver. "Then slap this blue stuff on." While he was talking a co-worker came up quietly from behind him and goosed him with the air hose. Tully jumped as if he had been struck by a bullet and then turned around cussing and cupping his genitals in his hands as the other worker walked away calling out foul names. When Tully turned to me smiling his gray teeth, I lifted my mouth into a smile because I wanted to get along. He has to be on my side, I thought. He's the one who'll tell the foreman how I'm doing.

I worked carefully that day, setting the tires on the machine as if they were babies, since it was easy to catch a finger in the rim that expanded to inflate the tire. At the day's end we swept up the tire dust and emptied the trash into bins.

At five the workers scattered for their cars and motorcycles while I crossed the street to wash at a burger stand. My hair was stiff with dust and my mouth showed pink against the backdrop of my dirty face. I then ordered a hotdog and walked slowly in the direction of the abandoned house where I had stayed the night before. I lay under the trees and within minutes was asleep. When I woke my shoulders were sore and my eyes burned when I squeezed the lids together.

From the backyard I walked dully through a residential street, and as evening came on, the TV glare in the living rooms and the headlights of passing cars showed against the blue drift of dusk. I saw two children coming up the street with snow cones, their tongues darting at the packed ice. I saw a boy with a peach and wanted to stop him, but felt embarrassed by my hunger. I walked for an hour only to return and discover the house lit brightly. Behind the fence I heard voices and saw a flashlight poking at the garage door. A man on the back steps mumbled something about the refrigerator to the one with the flashlight.

I waited for them to leave, but had the feeling they wouldn't because there was the commotion of furniture being moved. Tired, even more desperate, I started walking again with a great urge to kick things and tear the day from my life. I felt weak and my mind kept drifting because of hunger. I crossed the street to a gas station where I sipped at the water fountain and searched the Coke machine for change. I started walking again, first up a commercial street, then into a residential area where I lay down on someone's lawn and replayed a scene at home—my Mother crying at the kitchen table, my stepfather yelling with food in his mouth. They're cruel, I thought, and warned myself that I should never forgive them. How could they do this to me.

When I got up from the lawn it was late. I searched out a place to sleep and found an unlocked car that seemed safe. In the back seat, with my shoes off, I fell asleep but woke up startled about four in the morning when the owner, a nurse on her way to work, opened the door. She got in and was about to start the engine when I raised my head up from the backseat to explain my presence. She screamed so loudly when I said "I'm sorry" that I sprinted from the car with my shoes in hand. Her screams faded, then stopped altogether, as I ran down the block where I hid behind a trash bin and waited for a police siren to sound. Nothing. I crossed the street to a church where I slept stiffly on cardboard in the balcony.

I woke up feeling tired and greasy. It was early and a few street lights were still lit, the east growing pink with dawn. I washed myself from a garden hose and returned to the church to break into what looked like a kitchen. Paper cups, plastic spoons, a coffee pot littered on a table. I found a box of Nabisco crackers which I ate until I was full.

At work I spent the morning at the buffer, but was then told to help Iggy, an old Mexican, who was responsible for choosing tires that could be recapped without the risk of exploding at high speeds. Every morning a truck would deliver used tires, and after I unloaded them Iggy would step among the tires to inspect them for punctures and rips on the side walls.

With a yellow chalk he marked circles and Xs to indicate damage and called out "junk." For those tires that could be recapped, he said "goody" and I placed them on my hand truck.

When I had a stack of eight I kicked the truck at an angle and balanced them to another work area where Iggy again inspected the tires, scratching Xs and calling out "junk."

Iggy worked only until three in the afternoon, at which time he went to the locker room to wash and shave and to dress in a two-piece suit. When he came out he glowed with a bracelet, watch, rings, and a shiny fountain pen in his breast pocket. His shoes sounded against the asphalt. He was the image of a banker stepping into sunlight with millions on his mind. He said a few low words to workers with whom he was friendly and none to people like me.

I was seventeen, stupid because I couldn't figure out the difference between an F 78 14 and 750 14 at sight. Iggy shook his head when I brought him the wrong tires, especially since I had expressed interest in being his understudy. "Mexican, how can you be so stupid?" he would yell at me, slapping a tire from my hands. But within weeks I learned a lot about tires, from sizes and makes to how they are molded in iron forms to how Valley stole from other companies. Now and then we received a truckload of tires, most of them new or nearly new, and they were taken to our warehouse in the back where the serial numbers were ground off with a sander. On those days the foreman handed out Cokes and joked with us as we worked to get the numbers off.

Most of the workers were Mexican or black, though a few redneck whites worked there. The base pay was a dollar sixty-five, but the average was three dollars. Of the black workers, I knew Sugar Daddy the best. His body carried two hundred and fifty pounds, armfuls of scars, and a long knife that made me jump when he brought it out from his boot without warning. At one time he had been a singer, and had cut a record in 1967 called *Love's Chance*, which broke into the R and B charts. But nothing came of it. No big contract, no club dates, no tours. He made very little from the sales, only enough for an operation to pull a steering wheel from his gut when, drunk and mad at a lady friend, he slammed his Mustang into a row of parked cars.

"Touch it," he smiled at me one afternoon as he raised his shirt, his black belly kinked with hair. Scared, I traced the scar that ran from his chest to the left of his belly button, and I was repelled but hid my disgust.

Among the Mexicans I had few friends because I was different, a *pocho*[1] who spoke bad Spanish. At lunch they sat in tires and laughed over burritos, looking up

---

[1] a derogatory term for Mexicans living in the United States who have forgotten their cultural heritage.

at me to laugh even harder. I also sat in tires while nursing a Coke and felt dirty and sticky because I was still living on the street and had not had a real bath in over a week. Nevertheless, when the border patrol came to round up the nationals, I ran with them as they scrambled for the fence or hid among the tires behind the warehouse. The foreman, who thought I was an undocumented worker, yelled at me to run, to get away. I did just that. At the time it seemed fun because there was no risk, only a goodhearted feeling of hide-and-seek, and besides it meant an hour away from work on company time. When the police left we came back and some of the nationals made up stories of how they were almost caught—how they out-raced the police. Some of the stories were so convoluted and unconvincing that everyone laughed *mentiras*[2], especially when one described how he overpowered a policeman, took his gun away, and sold the patrol car. We laughed and he laughed, happy to be there to make up a story.

If work was difficult, so were the nights. I still had not gathered enough money to rent a room, so I spent the nights sleeping in parked cars or in the balcony of a church. After a week I found a newspaper ad for room for rent, phoned, and was given directions. Finished with work, I walked the five miles down Mission Road looking back into the traffic with my thumb out. No rides. After eight hours of handling tires, I was frightening, I suppose, to drivers since they seldom looked at me; if they did, it was a quick glance. For the next six weeks I would try to hitchhike, but the only person to stop was a Mexican woman who gave me two dollars to take the bus. I told her it was too much and that no bus ran from Mission Road to where I lived, but she insisted that I keep the money and trotted back to her idling car. It must have hurt her to see me day after day walking in the heat and looking very much the dirty Mexican to the many minds that didn't know what it meant to work at hard labor. That woman knew. Her eyes met mine as she opened the car door, and there was a tenderness that was surprisingly true—one for which you wait for years but when it comes it doesn't help. Nothing changes. You continue on in rags, with the sun still above you.

I rented a room from a middle-aged couple whose lives were a mess. She was a school teacher and he was a fireman. A perfect set up, I thought. But during my stay there they would argue with one another for hours in their bedroom.

When I rang at the front door both Mr. and Mrs. Van Deusen answered and didn't bother to disguise their shock at how awful I looked. But they let me in all the same. Mrs. Van Deusen showed me around the house, from the kitchen and bathroom to the living room with its grand piano. On her fingers she counted out the house rules as she walked me to my room. It was a girl's room with lace curtains, scenic wallpaper of a Victorian couple enjoying a stroll, canopied bed, and stuffed animals in a corner. Leaving, she turned and asked if she could do laundry for me and, feeling shy and hurt, I told her no; perhaps the next day. She left and I undressed to take a bath, exhausted as I sat on the edge of the bed probing my aches and my bruised places. With a towel around my waist I hurried down the hallway to the bathroom where Mrs. Van Deusen had set out an additional towel with a tube of shampoo. I ran the water in the tub and sat on the toilet, lid down, watching the steam

---

[2] lies

curl toward the ceiling. When I lowered myself into the tub I felt my body sting. I soaped a wash cloth and scrubbed my arms until they lightened, even glowed pink, but still I looked unwashed around my neck and face no matter how hard I rubbed. Back in the room I sat in bed reading a magazine, happy and thinking of no better luxury than a girl's sheets, especially after nearly two weeks of sleeping on cardboard at the church.

I was too tired to sleep, so I sat at the window watching the neighbors move about in pajamas, and, curious about the room, looked through the bureau drawers to search out personal things—snapshots, a messy diary, and a high school yearbook. I looked up the Van Deusen's daughter, Barbara, and studied her face as if I recognized her from my own school—a face that said "promise," "college," "nice clothes in the closet." She was a skater and a member of the German Club; her greatest ambition was to sing at the Hollywood Bowl.

After awhile I got into bed and as I drifted toward sleep I thought about her. In my mind I played a love scene again and again and altered it slightly each time. She comes home from college and at first is indifferent to my presence in her home, but finally I overwhelm her with deep pity when I come home hurt from work, with blood on my shirt. Then there was another version: Home from college she is immediately taken with me, in spite of my work-darkened face, and invites me into the family car for a milkshake across town. Later, back at the house, we sit in the living room talking about school until we're so close I'm holding her hand. The truth of the matter was that Barbara did come home for a week, but was bitter toward her parents for taking in boarders (two others besides me). During that time she spoke to me only twice: Once, while searching the refrigerator, she asked if we had any mustard; the other time she asked if I had seen her car keys.

But it was a place to stay. Work had become more and more difficult. I not only worked with Iggy, but also with the assistant foreman who was in charge of unloading trucks. After they backed in I hopped on top to pass the tires down by bouncing them on the tailgate to give them an extra spring so they would be less difficult to handle on the other end. Each truck was weighed down with more than two hundred tires, each averaging twenty pounds, so that by the time the truck was emptied and swept clean I glistened with sweat and my T-shirt stuck to my body. I blew snot threaded with tire dust onto the asphalt, indifferent to the customers who watched from the waiting room.

The days were dull. I did what there was to do from morning until the bell sounded at five; I tugged, pulled, and cussed at tires until I was listless and my mind drifted and caught on small things, from cold sodas to shoes to stupid talk about what we would do with a million dollars. I remember unloading a truck with Hamp, a black man.

"What's better than a sharp lady?" he asked me as I stood sweaty on a pile of junked tires. "Water. With ice," I said.

He laughed with his mouth open wide. With his fingers he pinched the sweat from his chin and flicked at me. "You be too young, boy. A woman can make you a god."

As a kid I had chopped cotton and picked grapes, so I knew work. I knew the fatigue and the boredom and the feeling that there was a good possibility you might have to do such work for years, if not for a lifetime. In fact, as a kid I imagined a dark fate: To marry Mexican poor, work Mexican hours, and in the end die a Mexican death, broke and in despair.

But this job at Valley Tire Company confirmed that there was something worse than field work, and I was doing it. We were all doing it, from foreman to the newcomers like me, and what I felt heaving tires for eight hours a day was felt by everyone—black, Mexican, redneck. We all despised those hours but didn't know what else to do. The workers were unskilled, some undocumented and fearful of deportation, and all struck with an uncertainty at what to do with their lives. Although everyone bitched about work, no one left. Some had worked there for as long as twelve years; some had sons working there. Few quit; no one was ever fired. It amazed me that no one gave up when the border patrol jumped from their vans, baton in hand, because I couldn't imagine any work that could be worse—or any life. What was out there, in the world, that made men run for the fence in fear?

How we arrived at such a place is a mystery to me. Why anyone would stay for years is even a deeper concern. You showed up, but from where? What broken life? What ugly past? The foreman showed you the Coke machine, the washroom, and the yard where you'd work. When you picked up a tire, you were amazed at the black it could give off.

Discussion Questions

1. What does Gary mean when he says on page 11 that "the woman knew"?
2. Discuss the symbolic significance of the chapter's title "Black Hair," as well as how it relates to the final lines of the excerpt.
3. What universal questions are raised in the final section of this excerpt?
4. On page 14 Gary refers to himself as a *pocho*. What differences and similarities do you see between his definition of a *pocho*, and Jose Antonio Villareal's? Look particularly at pages 19 and 24.
5. How is Gary's identity crisis in these same pages different than Piri Thomas's in the first excerpt of *Down These Mean Streets*?

José Antonio Villareal

Like many of the authors in this collection, José Antonio Villareal has had a variety of jobs throughout his life that have helped him effectively create vivid characters. He has been a public relations writer, a technical editor, and a delivery-truck driver. His three published novels are Pocho *(1959),* The Fifth Horseman *(1974), and* Clemente Chacón *(1984). While his output has not been as extensive as other Latino writers, few have had as much impact. Although no longer considered the first novel published in English by a Latino,* Pocho *is still well established as a forerunner of Mexican-American literature, and will perhaps always be considered the first work to introduce this literature into mainstream American culture.*

Pocho is loosely divided into two parts: the first describes the life of Juan Rubio, a tough veteran of the Mexican Revolution whose traditional beliefs and fierce loyalty effectively cause him to have to migrate to the United States. The second, and most intriguing, part of the work traces the life of Juan's son Richard, whose character is diametrically opposed to that of his father's.

From Pocho

Until now, Richard believed that someday they would live in México, and he fancied himself in that faraway unknown. He realized that it would be difficult for him in that strange place, for although he was a product of two cultures, he was an American and felt a deep love for his home town and its surroundings. So when he was certain the family would remain, he was both elated and sad. Glad that he would be raised in America, and sad for the loss of what to him would be a release from a life that was now dull routine.

Only through his books did he occasionally break the monotony, but the daydream they gave rise to were no longer enough. He was a man, for all his years, he refused to accept sexual satisfaction as the sublime effort of life. There must be more to it than just that. He was aware of his need for Zelda, but did not join his friends in every orgy, because once that bodily function was taken care of, he again felt a dissatisfaction with his existence, and so, instead, he began to spend more time away from them and from home. In his wanderings, usually into the neighboring San Jose, only Ricky sometimes accompanied him. His father was still unyielding in his old-country ideas, and did not allow him to keep late hours. The same frustration that came from what he considered an unjustly restricted life, which had made him spend more time with his friends, now made him stay out later every night. The first time it happened, his father was waiting for him.

"It is late," he said. "Where have you been?"

"Walking, Papá."

"Walking? You know you are not allowed to be out after nine o'clock, do you not?"

"Yes, sir. But I must live my life," answered Richard.

"Your life! Your life belongs to us, and will belong to us even after you marry, because we gave it to you. You can never forget your responsibility to the family." He was angry now that his son questioned his authority.

"Yes, Papá, but can you not see that I cannot stand living this way?" He knew he was doing wrong by every standard his father believed in, but he could not stop talking. "Listening every day to the girls and their silly talk is as bad as listening to you and your México and to Mamá talk about God! I am sick—sick. Can you not understand?"

"Understand? What is there to understand except the fact that my son is talking back to me! Is this the American learning you are receiving? To defy your father? It is like a grown person that you sound—an errant grown person!"

"You taught me to be a grownup. From the moment I first remember, you taught me that I was a man. I was never a niño to you but a macho, a buck, and you talked to me like a man, and you took me out into the fields from the time I was five years old. Why should I not talk like a grownup? I have spent most of my life with them."

"Are you sorry I have kept you by my side wherever I go?" The hurt in Juan Rubio showed in his voice.

"No, Father. For that I am happy. I am sorry only that you will not speak to me now, that you do not try to understand me as a man, because it pleases you to think of me as a child at this moment," said Richard. "But then it has always been that way. Always you and my mother frightened me into being good. If I misbehaved, the pointer-bitch would point me out, you said, and then its paw would come forth out of the blackness and take me away. You cannot imagine what horror it was for me to think of that paw coming through walls to get me—blood still fresh on it from its last victim, who had misbehaved, too. All those ghosts, whose only purpose in our world was to help parents discipline their children—you cannot know how real they were, because you laughed and called me a child for being afraid of the dark, for being afraid even to go to the back yard and make water . . . ."

Juan Rubio reached out and ran his hand lightly across his son's cheek. His voice was soft and tremulous as he tried to control his emotion. He knew now, for the first time, that his son was no longer a child, and the realization made him feel old. "That was a mistake, I see now, my son, but that is the way our people have always done," he said. "And you are right also, my son, in that you are a man, and it is good, because to a Mexican being *that* is the most important thing. If you are a man, your life is half lived; what follows does not really matter."

"But that is not enough for me, my father. I am what you say, not only because of what I carry between my legs but because I have put it to use. There must be more!"

"There is, my son. You have fulfilled but a part of your debt to your race, but you are young yet, and must fulfill the destiny of your God. When you are older, you will marry and have a family. Then you will know why you are here. That is God's will."

"No, father. That is what my mother says—I guess that is what all fathers and mothers say. We always must come back to that of the family, but if that is all there is to it, if one must marry and have a family and live like this, only working to eat and feed the family, not really living or having anything to live for, then I will never marry." His voice was pleading. "There is something inside, Father! Something I want and do not know!'"

"It is God's will that we live as we do. That we raise our children and they, in turn, raise their children. Families will follow families until the end. That is how God wants it."

"Then there is something wrong with God," said Richard.

"My son," said Juan Rubio, and he was crying. "You should not say such things, for as you are I once saw myself, and as you see me you will be. I learned long ago that one cannot fight the destiny, and stopped fighting. I gave up. I know you must fight also, but in the end you will understand. I but try to save you much heartbreak."

"And you are happy, Father?"

"Yes, my son, I am happy; except when I remember. Forgive me that I cannot help you. I feel your problem, but I am not an educated one."

And Richard knew that although his father was not one of the vanquished, as he claimed, there was little resistance left. He was disappointed, and suddenly afraid, that a man who had lived such a life as his father could call this existence happiness. And he cried in his fear of this thing—this horrible, inexplicable, merciless intangible—that held humanity in its power; that made such men as his father go out every morning before sunup to harvest tomatoes, spinach, peas, or fruit, with fingers stiff from the early-morning frost and bodies tortured by the midday heat, to return after dark and eat and, too tired to love, sleep. And in the winter months they wallowed in the mud, digging out dead trees with mattocks, and axes, or pruned, and, if unable to find jobs, they stood in line to claim a grocery order they had received from the State Relief Administration after having stood in another line, while all the while it rained. And they regained a portion of their longlost selfrespect, and were proud because they were feeding their families and their children would grow and raise their families.

This was happiness!

As the months went by, Richard was quieter, sadder, and, at times, even morose. He was aware that the family was undergoing a strange metamorphosis. The heretofore gradual assimilation of this new culture was becoming more pronounced. Along with a new prosperity, the Rubio family was taking on the mores of the middle class, and he did not like it. It saddened him to see the Mexican tradition begin to disappear. And because human nature is such, he, too, succumbed, and unconsciously became an active leader in the change.

"Silence!" roared Juan Rubio. "'We will not speak the dog language in my house!" They were at the supper table.

"But this is America, Father," said Richard. "If we live in this country, we must live like Americans."

"And next you will tell me that those are not tortillas you are eating but bread, and those are not beans but *hahm an' ecks.*"[1]

"No, but I mean that you must remember that we are not in México. In México—"

"*Hahm an' ecks,*" his father interrupted. "You know, when I was in Los Angeles for the first time, before your mother found me, all I could say in the English was *hahm an' ecks,* and I ate all my meals in a restaurant. Remember! What makes you think I have to remember that I am not in México? Why . . ."

"You were in the restaurant, Papá."

"Yes, well. . . . Every morning, when the woman came for my order, I would say *hahm an' ecks,* at noon *hahm an' ecks,* at night *hahm an' ecks.* I tell you I was tired, and then, one day, she did not ask, and brought me some soup and some meat. I do not know whether she felt sorry for me or whether they ran out of eggs, but I certainly was happy for the change."

---
[1] ham and eggs

"You are laughing at us," said Richard. "You yourself told me there are many Mexican restaurants in Los Angeles."

"Well, I was living in Hollywood at the time, working as an extra in the cowboy movies. There were no Mexicans to speak of in Hollywood." And he would smile in spite of himself, and the children would laugh.

"My teacher says we are all Americans," said one of the girls, who was in the first grade. She stood and began to recite, in a monotone, "I pledge allegiance to the flag—"

"You! Sit down!" said the father, in a loud voice, and laughed. "You are an American with that black face? Just because your name is Rubio does not mean you are really blond."

"It does not matter," said the little girl. "She told us we are all Americans, and she knows. After all, she is a teacher."

But all such scenes did not end with laughter, for Richard's mother was a different person altogether now, and constantly interfered when her husband was in the act of disciplining a child, and these interferences grew until they flared into violent quarrels. And Richard did not like himself, because he knew that many times he caused the disruption of family peace by playing one parent against the other in order to have his way. His mother now took to gossiping and to believing her neighbors, and Juan Rubio, who long ago had decided that he wanted nothing more out of life than to watch his children grow, saw this last vestige of happiness slipping from his grasp, and once more began to have women. Richard knew of it and was ashamed, but did not blame his father, and no longer blamed his mother, because everything was so wrong, and he was to blame as much as anyone else, and no one could do a thing about it.

So he watched the strong man who was his father; watched the raucous, infectious laugh disappear, so that he seldom saw the beautiful teeth again; watched the hair as it turned prematurely white, and the body as it lost its solidness and became flabby. Although he loved his mother, Richard realized that a family could not survive when the woman desired to command, and he knew that his mother was like a starving child who had become gluttonous when confronted with food. She had lived so long in the tradition of her country that she could not help herself now, and abused the privilege of equality afforded the women of her new country. She was not gay now; there was no gayness in her belief that her son was her world, and she proclaimed aloud that she lived only for her boy. For her, there were no songs left.

One day, Juan Rubio cooked his own breakfast, and soon after he moved into another room. Now there was no semblance of discipline whatever, and even the smallest child screamed at either parent, and came and went as she pleased. The house was unkempt and the father complained, but Consuelo, who had always been proud of her talents for housekeeping, now took the dirty house as a symbol of her emancipation, and it was to remain that way until her death.

That day, Richard saw clearly what he had helped create, and sought to repair the damage, but it was too late. What was done was beyond repair. To be just, no one could be blamed, for the transition from the culture of the old world to that of the new should never have been attempted in one generation.

It was not until the following year that Richard knew that his town was changing as much as his family was. It was 1940 in Santa Clara, and, among other things, the *Conscription Act*[2] had done its part in bringing about a change. It was not unusual now to see soldiers walking downtown or to see someone of the town in uniform. He was aware that people liked soldiers now, and could still remember the old days, when a detachment of cavalry camped outside the town for a few days or a unit of field artillery stayed at the university, and the worst thing one's sister could do was associate with a soldier. Soldiers were common, were drunkards, thieves, and rapers of girls, or something, to the people of Santa Clara, and the only uniforms with prestige in the town had been those of the CCC boys or of the American Legion during the Fourth of July celebration and the Easter-egg hunt. But now everybody loved a soldier, and he wondered how this had come about.

There were the soldiers, and there were also the Mexicans in ever-increasing numbers. The Mexican people Richard had known until now were those he saw only during the summer, and they were migrant families who seldom remained in Santa Clara longer than a month or two. The orbit of his existence was limited to the town, and actually to his immediate neighborhood, thereby preventing his association with the Mexican family which lived on the other side of town, across the tracks. In his wanderings into San Jose, he began to see more of what he called "the race." Many of the migrant workers who came up from southern California in the late spring and early summer now settled down in the valley. They bought two hundred pounds of flour and a hundred pounds of beans, and if they weathered the first winter, which was the most difficult, because the rains stopped agricultural workers from earning a living, they were settled for good.

As the Mexican population increased, Richard began to attend their dances and fiestas, and, in general, sought their company as much as possible, for these people were a strange lot to him. He was obsessed with a hunger to learn about them and from them. They had a burning contempt for people of different ancestry, whom they called Americans, and a marked hauteur toward México and toward their parents for their old-country ways. The former feeling came from a sense of inferiority that is a prominent characteristic in any Mexican reared in southern California; and the latter was an inexplicable compensation for that feeling. They needed to feel superior to something, which is a natural thing. The result was that they attempted to segregate themselves from both their cultures, and became truly a lost race. In their frantic desire to become different, they adopted a new mode of dress, a new manner, and even a new language. They used a polyglot speech made up of English and Spanish syllables, words, and sounds. This they incorporated into phrases and words that were unintelligible to anyone but themselves. Their Spanish became limited and their English more so. Their dress was unique to the point of being ludicrous. The black motif was predominant. The tight-fitting cuffs on trouserlegs that billowed at the knees made Richard think of some long-forgotten pasha in the faraway past, and the fingertip coat and highly lustrous shoes gave the wearer, when walking, the appearance of a strutting cock. Their hair was long and

---

[2] Peacetime conscription was inaugurated in the United States in September, 1940, with the passage of the Selective Training and Service Act.

swept up to meet in the back, forming a ducktail. They spent hours training it to remain that way.

The girls were characterized by the extreme shortness of their skirts, which stopped well above the knees. Their jackets, too, were fingertip in length, coming to within an inch of the skirt hem. Their hair reached below the shoulder in the back, and it was usually worn piled in front to form a huge pompadour.

The pachuco was born in El Paso, had gone west to Los Angeles, and was now moving north. To society, these zootsuiters were a menace, and the name alone classified them as undesirables, but Richard learned that there was much more to it than a mere group with a name. That in spite of their behavior which was sensational at times and violent at others, they were simply a portion of a confused humanity, employing their self-segregation as a means of expression. And because theirs was a spontaneous, and not a planned, retaliation, he saw it as a vicissitude of society, obvious only because of its nature and comparative suddenness.

From the leggy, short-skirted girls, he learned that their mores were no different from those of what he considered good girls. What was under the scant covering was as inaccessible as it would be under the more conventional dress. He felt, in fact, that these girls were more difficult to reach. And from the boys he learned that their bitterness and hostile attitude toward "whites" was not merely a lark. They had learned hate through actual experience, with everything the word implied. They had not been as lucky as he, and showed the scars to prove it. And, later on, Richard saw in retrospect that what happened to him in the city jail in San Jose was due more to the character of a handful of men than to the wide, almost organized attitude of a society, for just as the zootsuiters were blamed en masse for the actions of a few, they, in turn, blamed the other side for the very same reason.

As happens in most such groups, there were misunderstandings and disagreements over trivia. Pachucos[3] fought among themselves, for the most part, and they fought hard. It was not unusual that a quarrel born on the streets or backalleys of a Los Angeles slum was settled in the Santa Clara Valley. Richard understood them and partly sympathized, but their way of life was not entirely justified in his mind, for he felt that they were somehow reneging on life; this was the easiest thing for them to do. They, like his father, were defeated—only more so, because they really never started to live. They, too, were but making a show of resistance.

Of the new friends Richard made, those who were native to San Jose were relegated to become casual acquaintances, for they were as Americanized as he, and did not interest him. The newcomers became the object of his explorations. He was avidly hungry to learn the ways of these people. It was not easy for him to approach them at first, because his clothes labeled him as an outsider, and, too, he had trouble understanding their speech. He must not ask questions, for fear of offending them; his deductions, as to their character and makeup must come from close association. He was careful not to be patronizing or in any way act superior. And, most important, they must never suspect what he was doing. The most difficult moments for him were when he was doing the talking, for he was conscious that his Spanish was better than theirs. He learned enough of their vernacular to get along; he did not learn

---

[3] the street name associated with the Zoot Suiters of the 1940s in California.

more, because he was always in a hurry about knowledge. Soon he counted a few boys as friends, but had a much harder time of it with the girls, because they considered him a traitor to his "race." Before he knew it, he found that he almost never spoke to them in English, and no longer defended the "whites," but, rather, spoke disparagingly of them whenever possible. He also bought a suit to wear when in their company, not with such an extreme cut as those they wore, but removed enough from the conservative so he would not be considered a square. And he found himself a girl, who refused to dance the faster pieces with him, because he still jittered in the American manner. So they danced only to soft music while they kissed in the dimmed light, and that was the extent of their lovemaking. Or he stood behind her at the bar, with his arms around her as she sipped a Nehi, and felt strange because she was a Mexican and everyone around them was also Mexican, and felt stranger still from the knowledge that he felt strange. When the dance was over, he took her to where her parents were sitting and said goodnight to the entire family.

Whenever his new friends saw him in the company of his school acquaintances, they were courteously polite, but they later chastised him for fraternizing with what they called the enemy. Then Richard had misgivings, because he knew that his desire to become one of them was not a sincere one in that respect, yet upon reflection he realized that in truth he enjoyed their company and valued their friendship, and his sense of guilt was gone. He went along with everything they did, being careful only to keep away from serious trouble with no loss of prestige. Twice he entered the dreamworld induced by marihuana, and after the effect of the drug was expended, he was surprised to discover that he did not crave it, and was glad, for he could not afford a kick like that. As it was, life was too short for him to be able to do the many things he knew he still must do. The youths understood that he did not want it, and never pressed him.

Now the time came to withdraw a little. He thought it would be a painful thing, but they liked him, and their friendliness made everything natural. He, in his gratefulness, loved them for it.

I can be a part of everything, he thought, because I am the only one capable of controlling my destiny. . . . Never—no, never—will I allow myself to become a part of a group—to become classified, to lose my individuality. . . . I will not become a follower, nor will I allow myself to become a leader, because I must be myself and accept for myself only that which I value, and not what is being valued by everyone else these days . . . like a Goddamn suit of clothes they're wearing this season or Cuban heels . . . a style in ethics. . . .

Discussion Questions

1. What significant change is occurring in Richard's town? In his family? In his own identity?

2. How does Richard feel about Mexican nationals and how does he see himself in relation to them?

3. Compare Richard's feelings about Mexico to Pilar's for Cuba in the excerpts about her in *Dreaming in Cuban* on page 190.

Rudolfo Anaya

RUDOLFO ANAYA is considered by many critics as one of the premier authors of Latino literature. His many awards and honors, too numerous to mention and only briefly highlighted here, reflect the truth of that sentiment: the Premio Quinto Sol Literary Award (1971); the New Mexico Governor's Public Service Award (1978 and 1980); National Endowment for the Arts Fellowships (1979 and 1980); Before Columbus American Book Award (1980); Kellogg Foundation Fellowship, (1983–1985).

Anaya was born in New Mexico in 1937 and received a B.A. from the University of New Mexico in 1963, and two M.A.'s in 1968 and 1972. His long list of publications include novels, Heart of Aztlan *(1976),* Tortuga *(1979), and* The Legend of La Llorona *(1984); a collection of short stories,* The Silence of the Llano *(1982); two plays, an epic poem, and a screenplay. In addition he has edited and co-edited various collections and anthologies as well as contributed to dozens of journals.*

Bless Me, Ultima *(1972) is his most popular work. The novel is a bildungsroman about a young boy, named Antonio, who grows up in a small village in New Mexico around the time of World War II. The boy's relationship with the book's title character, a spiritual healer named Ultima, is the focus of the novel. The opening chapter selected here sets the stage for that relationship; one that, for Antonio, is both comforting and mysterious.*

From Bless Me, Ultima

Ultima came to stay with us the summer I was almost seven. When she came the beauty of the *llano*[1] unfolded before my eyes, and the gurgling waters of the river sang to the hum of the turning earth. The magical time of childhood stood still, and the pulse of the living earth pressed its mystery into my living blood. She took my hand, and the silent, magic powers she possessed made beauty from the raw, sunbaked llano, the green river valley, and the blue bowl which was the white sun's home. My bare feet felt the throbbing earth and my body trembled with excitement. Time stood still, and it shared with me all that had been, and all that was to come. . . .

Let me begin at the beginning. I do not mean the beginning that was in my dreams and the stories they whispered to me about my birth, and the people of my father and mother, and my three brothers—but the beginning that came with Ultima.

The attic of our home was partitioned into two small rooms. My sisters, Deborah and Theresa, slept in one and I slept in the small cubicle by the door. The

---

[1] the plain

wooden steps creaked down into a small hallway that led into the kitchen. From the top of the stairs I had a vantage point into the heart of our home, my mother's kitchen. From there I was to see the terrified face of Chávez when he brought the terrible news of the murder of the sheriff; I was to see the rebellion of my brothers against my father; and many times late at night I was to see Ultima returning from the llano where she gathered the herbs that can be harvested only in the light of the full moon by the careful hands of a *curandera*.[2]

That night I lay very quietly in my bed, and I heard my father and mother speak of Ultima.

"*Está sola*," my father said, "*ya no queda gente en el pueblito de Las Pasturas—*"[3]

He spoke in Spanish, and the village he mentioned was his home. My father had been a *vaquero*[4] all his life, a calling as ancient as the coming of the Spaniard to Nuevo Méjico. Even after the big *rancheros* and the *tejanos*[5] came and fenced the beautiful llano, he and those like him continued to work there, I guess because only in that wide expanse of land and sky could they feel the freedom their spirits needed.

"*Qué lástima*,"[6] my mother answered, and I knew her nimble fingers worked the pattern on the doily she crocheted for the big chair in the sala.

I heard her sigh, and she must have shuddered too when she thought of Ultima living alone in the loneliness of the wide llano. My mother was not a woman of the llano, she was the daughter of a farmer. She could not see beauty in the llano and she could not understand the coarse men who lived half their lifetimes on horseback. After I was born in Las Pasturas she persuaded my father to leave the llano and bring her family to the town of Guadalupe where she said there would be opportunity and school for us. The move lowered my father in the esteem of his *compadres*[7] the other vaqueros of the llano who clung tenaciously to their way of life and freedom. There was no room to keep animals in town so my father had to sell his small herd, but he would not sell his horse so he gave it to a good friend, Benito Campos. But Campos could not keep the animal penned up because somehow the horse was very close to the spirit of the man, and so the horse was allowed to roam free and no vaquero on that llano would throw a lazo on that horse. It was as if someone had died, and they turned their gaze from the spirit that walked the earth.

It hurt my father's pride. He saw less and less of his old compadres. He went to work on the highway and on Saturdays after they collected their pay he drank with his crew at the Longhorn but he was never close to the men of the town. Some weekends the llaneros would come into town for supplies and old *amigos*[8] like Bonney or Campos or the Gonzales brothers would come by to visit. Then my father's eyes lit up as they drank and talked of the old days and told the old stories. But when the western sun touched the clouds with orange and gold the vaqueros got in their trucks and headed home, and my father was left to drink alone in the long night. Sunday morning he would get up very *crudo*[9] and complain about having to go to early mass.

---

[2] a spiritual healer   [3] She is all alone, there are no people left in the town of Las Pasturas   [4] cowboy
[5] ranchers and Texans   [6] What a shame   [7] literally, someone who is a godfather or godmother to your children. Often used as a friendly term between close friends.   [8] friends   [9] with a bad hangover

"—She served the people all her life, and now the people are scattered, driven like tumbleweeds by the winds of war. The war sucks everything dry," my father said solemnly, "it takes the young boys overseas, and their families move to California where there is work—"

"Ave Mariá Purisima," my mother made the sign of the cross for my three brothers who were away at war. "Gabriel," she said to my father, "it is not right that *la Grande*[10] be alone in her old age—"

"No," my father agreed.

"When I married you and went to the Ilano to live with you and raise your family, I could not have survived without la Grande's help. Oh, those were hard years—"

"Those were good years," my father countered. But my mother would not argue.

"There isn't a family she did not help," she continued, "no road was too long for her to walk to its end to snatch somebody from the jaws of death, and not even the blizzards of the Ilano could keep her from the appointed place where a baby was to be delivered—"

"*Es verdad,*[11] my father nodded.

"She tended me at the birth of my sons—" And then I knew her eyes glanced briefly at my father. "Gabriel, we cannot let her live her last days in loneliness—"

"No," my father agreed, "it is not the way of our people."

"It would be a great honor to provide a home for la Grande," my mother murmured. My mother called Ultima la Grande out of respect. It meant the woman was old and wise.

"I have already sent word with Campos that Ultima is to come and live with us," my father said with some satisfaction. He knew it would please my mother.

"I am grateful," my mother said tenderly, "perhaps we can repay a little of the kindness la Grande has given to so many."

"And the children?" my father asked. I knew why he expressed concern for me and my sisters. It was because Ultima was a curandera, a woman who knew the herbs and remedies of the ancients, a miracle-worker who could heal the sick. And I had heard that Ultima could lift the curses laid by *brujas,*[13] that she could exorcise the evil the witches planted in people to make them sick. And because a curandera had this power she was misunderstood and often suspected of practicing witchcraft herself.

I shuddered and my heart turned cold at the thought. The *cuentos*[12] of the people were full of the tales of evil done by brujas.

"She helped bring them into the world, she cannot be but good for the children," my mother answered.

"*Está bien,*"[14] my father yawned, "I will go for her in the morning."

So it was decided that Ultima should come and live with us. I knew that my father and mother did good by providing a home for Ultima. It was the custom to provide for the old and the sick. There was always room in the safety and warmth of *la familia*[15] for one more person, be that person stranger or friend.

---

[10] a term of respect for Ultima   [11] it's true   [12] stories   [13] witches   [14] All right   [15] the family

It was warm in the attic, and as I lay quietly listening to the sounds of the house falling asleep and repeating a Hail Mary over and over in my thoughts, I drifted into the time of dreams. Once I had told my mother about my dreams, and she said they were visions from God and she was happy, because her own dream was that I should grow up and become a priest. After that I did not tell her about my dreams, and they remained in me forever and ever . . .

In my dream I flew over the rolling hills of the *llano*. My soul wandered over the dark plain until it came to a cluster of adobe huts. I recognized the village of *Las Pasturas* and my heart grew happy. One mud hut had a lighted window, and the vision of my dream swept me towards it to be witness at the birth of a baby.

I could not make out the face of the mother who rested from the pains of birth, but I could see the old woman in black who tended the just arrived, steaming baby. She nimbly tied a knot on the cord that had connected the baby to its mother's blood, then quickly she bent and with her teeth she bit off the loose end. She wrapped the squirming baby and laid it at the mother's side, then she returned to cleaning the bed. All linen was swept aside to be washed, but she carefully wrapped the useless cord and the afterbirth and laid the package at the feet of the Virgin on the small altar. I sensed that these things were yet to be delivered to someone.

Now the people who had waited patiently in the dark were allowed to come in and speak to the mother and deliver their gifts to the baby. I recognized my mother's brothers, my uncles from El Puerto de los Lunas. They entered ceremoniously. A patient hope stirred in their dark, brooding eyes.

This one will be a Luna, the old man said, he will be a farmer and keep our customs and traditions. Perhaps God will bless our family and make the baby a priest.

And to show their hope they rubbed the dark earth of the river valley on the baby's forehead, and they surrounded the bed with the fruits of their harvest so the small room smelled of fresh green chile and corn, ripe apples and peaches, pumpkins and green beans.

Then the silence was shattered with the thunder of hoofbeats; vaqueros surrounded the small house with shouts and gunshots, and when they entered the room they were laughing and singing and drinking.

Gabriel, they shouted, you have a fine son! He will make a fine vaquero! And they smashed the fruits and vegetables that surrounded the bed and replaced them with a saddle, horse blankets, bottles of whiskey, a new rope, bridles, chapas, and an old guitar. And they rubbed the stain of earth from the baby's forehead because man was not to be tied to the earth but free upon it.

These were the people of my father, the vaqueros of the llano. They were an exuberant, restless people, wandering across the ocean of the plain.

We must return to our valley, the old man who led the farmers spoke. We must take with us the blood that comes after the birth. We will bury it in our fields to renew their fertility and to assure that the baby will follow our ways. He nodded for the old woman to deliver the package at the altar.

No! the llaneros protested, it will stay here! We will burn it and let the winds of the llano scatter the ashes.

It is blasphemy to scatter a man's blood on unholy ground, the farmers chanted. The new son must fulfill his mother's dream. He must come to El Puerto and rule over the Lunas of the valley. The blood of the Lunas is strong in him.

He is a Márez, the vaqueros shouted. His forefathers were conquistadores, men as restless as the seas they sailed and as free as the land they conquered. He is his father's blood!

Curses and threats filled the air, pistols were drawn, and the opposing sides made ready for battle. But the clash was stopped by the old woman who delivered the baby.

Cease! she cried, and the men were quiet. I pulled this baby into the light of life, so I will bury the afterbirth and the cord that once linked him to eternity. Only I will know his destiny.

The dream began to dissolve. When I opened my eyes I heard my father cranking the truck outside. I wanted to go with him, I wanted to see Las Pasturas, I wanted to see Ultima. I dressed hurriedly, but I was too late. The truck was bouncing down the goat path that led to the bridge and the highway.

I turned, as I always did, and looked down the slope of our hill to the green of the river, and I raised my eyes and saw the town of Guadalupe. Towering above the housetops and the trees I of the town was the church tower. I made the sign of the cross on my lips. The only other building that rose above the housetops to compete with the church tower was the yellow top of the schoolhouse. This fall I would be going to school.

My heart sank. When I thought of leaving my mother and going to school a warm, sick feeling came to my stomach. To get rid of it I ran to the pens we kept by the molino to feed the animals. I had fed the rabbits that night and they had alfalfa and so I only changed their water. I scattered some grain for the hungry chickens and watched their mad scramble as the rooster called them to peck. I milked the cow and turned her loose. During the day she would forage along the highway where the grass was thick and green, then she would return at nightfall. She was a good cow and there were very few times when I had to run and bring her back in the evening. Then I dreaded it, because she might wander into the hills where the bats flew at dusk and there was only the sound of my heart beating as I ran and it made me sad and frightened to be alone.

I collected three eggs in the chicken house and returned for breakfast.

"Antonio," my mother smiled and took the eggs and milk, "come and eat your breakfast."

I sat across the table from Deborah and Theresa and ate my atole and the hot tortilla with butter. I said very little. I usually spoke very little to my two sisters. They were older than I and they were very close. They usually spent the entire day in the attic, playing dolls and giggling. I did not concern myself with those things.

"Your father has gone to Las Pasturas," my mother chattered, "he has gone to bring la Grande." Her hands were white with the flour of the dough. I watched carefully. "—And when he returns, I want you children to show your manners. You must not shame your father or your mother—"

"Isn't her real name Ultima?" Deborah asked. She was like that, always asking grown-up questions.

"You will address her as la Grande," my mother said flatly. I looked at her and wondered if this woman with the black hair and laughing eyes was the woman who gave birth in my dream.

"Grande," Theresa repeated.

"Is it true she is a witch?" Deborah asked. Oh, she was in for it. I saw my mother whirl then pause and control herself.

"No!" she scolded. "You must not speak of such things! Oh, I don't know where you learn such ways—" Her eyes flooded with tears. She always cried when she thought we were learning the ways of my father, the ways of the Márez. "She is a woman of learning," she went on and I knew she didn't have time to stop and cry, "she has worked hard for all the people of the village. Oh, I would never have survived those hard years if it had not been for her—so show her respect. We are honored that she comes to live with us, understand?"

"Sí, mamá," Deborah said half willingly.

"Sí, mamá," Theresa repeated.

"Now run and sweep the room at the end of the hall. Eugene's room—" I heard her voice choke. She breathed a prayer and crossed her forehead. The flour left white stains on her, the four points of the cross. I knew it was because my three brothers were at war that she was sad, and Eugene was the youngest.

"Mamá." I wanted to speak to her. I wanted to know who the old woman was who cut the baby's cord.

"Sí." She turned and looked at me.

"Was Ultima at my birth?" I asked.

"*¡Ay Dios mío!*"[16] my mother cried. She came to where I sat and ran her hand through my hair. She smelled warm, like bread. "Where do you get such questions, my son. Yes," she smiled, "la Grande was there to help me. She was there to help at the birth of all of my children—"

"And my uncles from El Puerto were there?"

"Of course," she answered, "my brothers have always been at my side when I needed them. They have always prayed that I would bless them with a—"

I did not hear what she said because I was hearing the sounds of the dream, and I was seeing the dream again. The warm cereal in my stomach made me feel sick.

"And my father's brother was there, the Márez' and their friends, the vaqueros—"

"Ay!" she cried out. "Don't speak to me of those worthless Márez and their friends!"

"There was a fight?" I asked.

---

[16] Oh my God!

"No," she said, "a silly argument. They wanted to start a fight with my brothers—that is all they are good for. Vaqueros, they call themselves, they are worthless drunks! Thieves! Always on the move, like gypsies, always dragging their families around the country like vagabonds—"

As long as I could remember she always raged about the Márez family and their friends. She called the village of Las Pasturas beautiful; she had gotten used to the loneliness, but she had never accepted its people. She was the daughter of farmers.

But the dream was true. It was as I had seen it. Ultima knew.

"But you will not be like them." She caught her breath and stopped. She kissed my forehead. "You will be like my brothers. You will be a Luna, Antonio. You will be a man of the people, and perhaps a priest." She smiled.

A priest, I thought, that was her dream. I was to hold mass on Sundays like Father Byrnes did in the church in town. I was to hear the confessions of the silent people of the valley, and I was to administer the holy Sacrament to them.

"Perhaps," I said.

"Yes," my mother smiled. She held me tenderly. The fragrance of her body was sweet.

"But then," I whispered, "who will hear my confession?"

"What?"

"Nothing," I answered. I felt a cool sweat on my forehead and I knew I had to run, I had to clear my mind of the dream. "I am going to Jasón's house," I said hurriedly and slid past my mother. I ran out the kitchen door, past the animal pens, towards Jasón's house. The white sun and the fresh air cleansed me.

On this side of the river there were only three houses. The slope of the hill rose gradually into the hills of juniper and mesquite and cedar clumps. Jasón's house was farther away from the river than our house. On the path that led to the bridge lived huge, fat Fío and his beautiful wife. Fío and my father worked together on the highway. They were good drinking friends.

"¡Jasón!" I called at the kitchen door. I had run hard and was panting. His mother appeared at the door.

"*Jasón no está aquí*,"[17] she said. All of the older people spoke only in Spanish, and I myself understood only Spanish. It was only after one went to school that one learned English.

"*¿Dónde está?*"[18] I asked.

She pointed towards the river, northwest, past the railroad tracks to the dark hills. The river came through those hills and there. were old Indian grounds there, holy burial grounds Jasón told me. There in an old cave lived his Indian. At least everybody called him Jasón's Indian. He was the only Indian of the town, and he talked only to Jasón. Jasón's father had forbidden Jasón to talk to the Indian, he had beaten him, he had tried in every way to keep Jasón from the Indian.

But Jasón persisted. Jasón was not a bad boy, he was just Jasón. He was quiet and moody, and sometimes for no reason at all wild, loud sounds came exploding from his throat and lungs. Sometimes I felt like Jasón, like I wanted to shout and cry, but I never did.

---

[17] Jasón's not here   [18] Where is he?

I looked at his mother's eyes and I saw they were sad. "Thank you," I said, and returned home. While I waited for my father to return with Ultima I worked in the garden. Every day I had to work in the garden. Every day I reclaimed from the rocky soil of the hill a few more feet of earth to cultivate. The land of the Ilano was not good for farming, the good land was along the river. But my mother wanted a garden and I worked to make her happy. Already we had a few chile and tomato plants growing. It was hard work. My fingers bled from scraping out the rocks and it seemed that a square yard of ground produced a wheelbarrow full of rocks which I had to push down to the retaining wall.

The sun was white in the bright blue sky. The shade of the clouds would not come until the afternoon. The sweat was sticky on my brown body. I heard the truck and turned to see it chugging up the dusty goat path. My father was returning with Ultima.

"¡Mamá!" I called. My mother came running out, Deborah and Theresa trailed after her.

"I'm afraid," I heard Theresa whimper.

"There's nothing to be afraid of," Deborah said confidently. My mother said there was too much Márez blood in Deborah. Her eyes and hair were very dark, and she was always running. She had been to school two years and she spoke only English. She was teaching Theresa and half the time I didn't understand what they were saying.

"Madre de Dios, but mind your manners!" my mother scolded. The truck stopped and she ran to greet Ultima. "Buenos días le de Dios, Grande," my mother cried. She smiled and hugged and kissed the old woman.

"Ay, María Luna," Ultima smiled, "*buenos días te de Dios, a ti y a tu familia.*"[19] She wrapped the black shawl around her hair and shoulders. Her face was brown and very wrinkled. When she smiled her teeth were brown. I remembered the dream.

"Come, come!" my mother urged us forward. It was the custom to greet the old. "Deborah!" my mother urged. Deborah stepped forward and took Ultima's withered hand.

"Buenos días, Grande," she smiled. She even bowed slightly. Then she pulled Theresa forward and told her to greet la Grande. My mother beamed. Deborah's good manners surprised her, but they made her happy, because a family was judged by its manners.

"What beautiful daughters you have raised," Ultima nodded to my mother. Nothing could have pleased my mother more. She looked proudly at my father who stood leaning against the truck, watching and judging the introductions.

"Antonio," he said simply. I stepped forward and took Ultima's hand. I looked up into her clear brown eyes and shivered. Her face was old and wrinkled, but her eyes were clear and sparkling, like the eyes of a young child.

"Antonio," she smiled. She took my hand, and I felt the power of a whirlwind sweep around me. Her eyes swept the surrounding hills and through them I saw for the first time the wild beauty of our hills and the magic of the green river. My nostrils

---

[19] may God give good mornings to you and your family

quivered as I felt the song of the mockingbirds and the drone of the grasshoppers mingle with the pulse of the earth. The four directions of the llano met in me, and the white sun shone on my soul. The granules of sand at my feet and the sun and sky above me seemed to dissolve into one strange, complete being.

A cry came to my throat, and I wanted to shout it and run in the beauty I had found.

"Antonio." I felt my mother prod me. Deborah giggled because she had made the right greeting, and I who was to be my mother's hope and joy stood voiceless.

"Buenos días le de Dios, Ultima," I muttered. I saw in her eyes my dream. I saw the old woman who had delivered me from my mother's womb. I knew she held the secret of my destiny.

"¡Antonio!" My mother was shocked I had used her name instead of calling her Grande. But Ultima held up her hand.

"Let it be," she smiled. "This was the last child I pulled from your womb, María. I knew there would be something between us."

My mother who had started to mumble apologies was quiet. "As you wish, Grande," she nodded.

"I have come to spend the last days of my life here, Antonio," Ultima said to me.

"You will never die, Ultima," I answered. "I will take care of you—" She let go of my hand and laughed. Then my father said, "*Pase, Grande, pase. Nuestra casa es su casa.*[20] It is too hot to stand and visit in the sun—"

"Sí, Sí," my mother urged. I watched them go in. My father carried on his shoulders the large blue-tin trunk which later I learned contained all of Ultima's earthly possessions, the black dresses and shawls she wore, and the magic of her sweet smelling herbs.

As Ultima walked past me I smelled for the first time a trace of the sweet fragrance of herbs that always lingered in her wake. Many years later, long after Ultima was gone and I had grown to be a man, I would awaken sometimes at night and think I caught a scent of her fragrance in the cool night breeze.

And with Ultima came the owl. I heard it that night for the first time in the juniper tree outside of Ultima's window. I knew it was her owl because the other owls of the llano did not come that near the house. At first it disturbed me, and Deborah and Theresa too. I heard them whispering through the partition. I heard Deborah reassuring Theresa that she would take care of her, and then she took Theresa in her arms and rocked her until they were both asleep.

I waited. I was sure my father would get up and shoot the owl with the old rifle he kept on the kitchen wall. But he didn't, and I accepted his understanding. In many cuentos I had heard the owl was one of the disguises a bruja took, and so it struck a chord of fear in the heart to hear them hooting at night. But not Ultima's owl. Its soft hooting was like a song, and as it grew rhythmic it calmed the moonlit hills and lulled us to sleep. Its song seemed to say that it had come to watch over us.

I dreamed about the owl that night, and my dream was good. La Virgen de Guadalupe was the patron saint of our town. The town was named after her. In my

---

[20] Please come in. Our house is your house.

dream I saw Ultima's owl lift la Virgen on her wide wings and fly her to heaven. Then the owl returned and gathered up all the babes of Limbo and flew them up to the clouds of heaven.

The Virgin smiled at the goodness of the owl.

Discussion Questions

1. Describe the relationship between Antonio and Ultima. What is Ultima's role in the household?

2. What is the significance of Antonio's dream, especially in connection with Ultima.

3. This excerpt contains symbolic elements, such as the owl. Find other symbols throughout this excerpt and try to identify their significance.

4. Compare the use of symbolism in this story with its use in Pablo Medina's *The Marks of Birth* on page 208. How are the ideas presented through those symbols representative of each culture? How are they similar to each other?

Ana Castillo

ANA CASTILLO was born in Chicago in 1953. She received a B.A. from Northern Illinois University in 1975 and an M.A. from the University of Chicago in 1979. She was a dissertation fellow at the University of California, Santa Barbara 1989–1990, and a professor of bilingual creative writing at Mount Holyoke College in 1994.

Castillo has received numerous awards including the American Book Award, Before Columbus Foundation (1986), a National Endowment for the Arts Fellowship for poetry (1990, 1995), and a Carl Sandburg Literary Award in Fiction (1993). She has published several books of poetry, including Zero Makes Me Hungry *(1975),* Otro Canto *(1977),* The Invitation *(1979),* Women Are Not Roses *(1984), and* My Father was a Toltec and Selected Poems *(1995). Her credits also include the novels* The Mixquiahuala Letters *(1986),* Sopogonía *(1990),* So Far From God *(1993),* Peel Me Like an Onion *(1999), and her latest rendition,* My Daughter, My Son, the Eagle, the Dove *(2000), a young adult novel. Additionally, she has published a collection of short stories titled* Loverboys *(1996), a much acclaimed series of essays titled* Massacre of the Dreamers: Essays on Xicanisma *(1994), and edited several books and anthologies.*

So Far from God is Castillo's most popular work. Heavily influenced by magical realism, a movement associated with such Latin American writers as Gabriel García Marquez, the novel almost haphazardly traces the lives of Sofí, the strong matriarch of the family; Esperanza, the eldest of Sofí's daughters; Caridad, the promiscuous one; Fe, who is crushed when her fiancé leaves her; and "La Loca," (The Crazy One) the youngest daughter whose real name everyone has forgotten. The plot of the novel has been compared by critics to a soap opera, as the reader is assaulted by a series of characters whose lives are anything but normal. The following selection reveals some of the characteristics of the five women.

From So Far from God

La Loca[1] was only three years old when she died. Her mother Sofí woke at twelve midnight to the howling and neighing of the five dogs, six cats, and four horses, whose custom it was to go freely in and out of the house. Sofí got up and tiptoed out of her room. The animals were kicking and crying and running back and forth with their ears back and fur standing on end, but Sofí couldn't make out what their agitation was about.

She checked the bedroom with the three older girls: Esperanza, the eldest, had her arms wrapped around the two smaller ones, Fe and Caridad. They were sleeping strangely undisturbed by the excitement of the animals.

Sofí went back into her own room where her baby, the three-year-old, had slept ever since Sofí's husband disappeared. Sofi put the baseball bat that she had taken with her when checking the house back under the bed—"just in case" she encountered some *tonto*[2] who had gotten ideas about the woman who lived alone with her four little girls by the ditch at the end of the road.

It was then that she noticed the baby, although apparently asleep, jerking. Jerking, jerking, the little body possessed by something unknown that caused her to thrash about violently until finally she fell off the bed. Sofí ran around to pick her up, but she was so frightened by her little daughter's seizure she stopped short.

The baby continued to thrash about, banging her little arms and legs against the hard stone floor, white foam mixed with a little blood spilling from the corners of her mouth; and worst of all, her eyes were now opened, rolled all the way to the top of her head.

Sofí screamed and called out "Ave Maria Purisimas," and finally her three other precious children came running in. "Mom, Mom, what happened?" And then, everyone was screaming and moaning because the baby had stopped moving, lay perfectly still, and they knew she was dead. It was the saddest *velorio*[3] in Tome in years because it was so sad to bury a child. Fortunately none had died since—well, if memory served right, doña Dolores's last son. Poor woman. Eleven children and one after the other passed on her until she was left with no one, except for her drunken foulmouthed husband. It seems all the babies were victims of a rare bone disease they inherited through the father's bloodline. What terrible misfortune for doña Dolores, suffering the pangs of labor through eleven births, all fated to die during infancy.

---

[1] literally "The Crazy One." Her nickname will be explained shortly.   [2] fool   [3] wake

Twelve years of marriage, eleven babies that did not survive, and to top it off, the husband drank up everything they owned.

A sad, sad story.

The day after the wake the neighbors all came out to accompany Sofí and the girls to the church at Tome, where Sofí wanted the little baby's Mass to be held before they lay her into the cold ground. Everyone Sofí knew was there: the baby's godparents, all of Sofí's *comadres* and *compadres*,[4] her sister from Phoenix, everyone except, of course, the baby's father, since no one had seen hide nor hair of him since he'd left Sofí and the girls.

That marriage had a black ribbon on its door from the beginning. Sofí's grandfather had refused to give the young lovers his blessing, the father had forbidden Sofí's *querido*[5] to step foot in their house during their three-year courtship, and the local parish priest joined the opposition when he refused to marry the couple in church.

Nobody believed that Domingo was good enough for little Sofí, not her sister, not her mother, not even her favorite teacher in high school, la Miss Hill, who had nothing but praise for Sofí's common sense and intelligence. Nobody thought el Domingo would make a good husband because of the fact that he liked to gamble.

Gambling was in the man's blood. And gambling is what Sofí did when she ran off with him, sheltered by the dark night of a new moon, and came back a *señora*.[6] And then, nobody could say nothing about it but wait for the inevitable failure of Sofí's marriage.

A month after he left, Sofí heard from her husband, a letter from El Paso with five ten dollar bills and a promise to send more whenever he could. No return address. And no more news from Domingo ever again after that. After a year, Sofia was so mad, she forbade anyone to even mention his name in her presence.

It was 118 degrees the day of Sofí's baby daughter's funeral and the two pallbearers, upon the instruction of Father Jerome, placed the small casket on the ground just in front of the church. No one was quite certain what Father Jerome had planned when he paused there in the hot sun.

Maybe some last-minute prayers or instructions for the mourners before entering the House of God. He wiped his brow with his handkerchief.

In fact, he was a little concerned about the grieving mother, who at that point was showing signs of losing it, trembling and nearly collapsing between two others. Father Jerome thought it perhaps a good idea to advise them all on funeral decorum. "As devoted followers of Christ," he began, "we must not show our lack of faith in Him at these times and in His, our Father's fair judgment, Who alone knows why we are here on this earth and why He chooses to call us back home when He does."

Why? Why? That's exactly what Sofí wanted to know at that moment—when all she had ever done was accept God's will. As if it hadn't been punishment enough to be abandoned by her husband; then—for no apparent reason and without warning,

---

[4] literally, someone who is a godfather or godmother to your children. Often used as a friendly term between close friends.   [5] lover   [6] literally, a woman who is married. Here it refers to a woman who is no longer a virgin.

save the horrible commotion of the animals that night—her baby was taken away! Oh, why? Why? That's all she wanted to know. "Ayyyyy!"

At that moment, while Sofí threw herself on the ground, pounding it with her rough fists, her compadres crying alongside her, saying, "Please, please, comadre, get up, the Lord alone knows what He does! Listen to the padre," Esperanza let out a shriek, long and so high pitched it started some dogs barking in the distance. Sofí had stopped crying to see what was causing the girl's hysteria when suddenly the whole crowd began to scream and faint and move away from the priest, who finally stood alone next to the baby's coffin.

The lid had pushed all the way open and the little girl inside sat up, just as sweetly as if she had woken from a nap, rubbing her eyes and yawning. "¿Mami?" she called, looking around and squinting her eyes against the harsh light. Father Jerome got hold of himself and sprinkled holy water in the direction of the child, but for the moment was too stunned to utter so much as a word of prayer. Then, as if all this was not amazing enough, as Father Jerome moved toward the child she lifted herself up into the air and landed on the church roof. "Don't touch me, don't touch me!" she warned.

This was only the beginning of the child's long life's phobia of people. She wasn't one of those afflicted with an exaggerated fear of germs and contagion. For the rest of her life, however, she was to be repulsed by the smell of humans. She claimed that all humans bore an odor akin to that which she had smelled in the places she had passed through when she was dead. Where she had gone she revealed from the rooftop that day within the limited ability of a three-year-old's vocabulary, in Spanish and English. Meanwhile everyone below was either genuflecting or paralyzed, and crossing themselves over and over as she spoke.

"¡*Hija, hija*!"[7] Father Jerome called up to her, hands clenched in the air. "Is this an act of God or of Satan that brings you back to us, that has flown you up to the roof like a bird? Are you the devil's messenger or a winged angel?"

At that point Sofí, despite her shock, rose from the ground, unable to tolerate the mere suggestion by Father Jerome that her daughter, her blessed, sweet baby, could by any means be the devil's own. "Don't you dare!" she screamed at Father Jerome, charging at him and beating him with her fists. "Don't you dare start this about *my* baby! If our Lord in His heaven has sent my child back to me, don't you dare start this backward thinking against her; the devil doesn't produce miracles! And *this* is a miracle, an answer to the prayers of a brokenhearted mother, ¡*hombre necio, pendejo* . . . !"[8]

"Ay, watch what you say, comadre!" one of Sofí's friends whispered, pulling Sofí from the priest, who had staved off her attack with his arms over his head. "Oh, my God!" others uttered, crossing themselves at hearing Sofí call the priest a pendejo, which was a blasphemy, crossing themselves all the more because although the verdict was still open as to whether they were witnessing a true miracle or a mirage of the devil, Sofí's behavior was giving way to the latter—after all, calling the holy priest a pendejo and hitting him!

---

[7] literally means daughter. Here it is being used as a "child" by a priest to one of his congregation.

[8] foolish and stubborn man

The crowd settled down, some still on their knees, palms together, all looking up at the little girl like the glittering angel placed at the top of a Christmas tree. She seemed serene and, though a little flushed, quite like she always did when she was alive. Well, the fact was that she *was* alive, but no one at the moment seemed sure.

"Listen," she announced calmly to the crowd, "on my long trip I went to three places: hell . . ." Someone let out a loud scream at this. "To *pulgatorio*[9] and to heaven. God sent me back to help you all, to pray for you all, o si no, o si no . . ."

"*O si no, ¿qué, hija?*"[10] Father Jerome begged.

"O si no, you, and others who doubt just like you, will never see our Father in heaven!"

The audience gasped in unison. Someone whispered, "That's the devil," but refrained from continuing when Sofí turned to see who it was.

"Come down, come down," the priest called to the child. "We'll all go in and pray for you. Yes, yes, maybe all this is really true. Maybe you did die, maybe you did see our Lord in His heaven, maybe He did send you back to give us guidance. Let's just go in together, we'll all pray for you."

With the delicate and effortless motion of a monarch butterfly the child brought herself back to the ground, landing gently on her bare feet, her ruffled chiffon nightdress, bought for the occasion of her burial, fluttering softly in the air. "No, Padre," she corrected him. "Remember, it is *I* who am here to pray for *you.*" With that stated, she went into the church and those with faith followed.

Once the baby was able to receive medical attention (although Sofí took her child this time to a hospital in Albuquerque rather than to rely on the young doctor at the Valencia County clinic who had so rashly declared her child dead), it was diagnosed that she was in all probability an epileptic.

Epilepsy notwithstanding, there was much left unexplained and for this reason Sofí's baby grew up at home, away from strangers who might be witnesses to her astonishing behavior, and she eventually earned the name around the Rio Abajo region and beyond, of *La Loca Santa.*[11]

For a brief period after her resurrection, people came from all over the state in hopes of receiving her blessing or of her performing of some miracle for them. But because she was so averse to being close to anyone, the best that strangers could expect was to get a glimpse of her from outside the gate. So "Santa" was dropped from her name and she was soon forgotten by strangers.

She became known simply as La Loca. The funny was (but perhaps not so funny since it is the way of *la gente*[12] to call a spade a spade, and she was called "La Loca" straight out), even La Loca's mother and sisters called her that because her behavior was *so* peculiar. Moreover, La Loca herself responded to that name and by the time she was twenty-one no one remembered her Christian name.

Her sisters, all born exactly three years apart from each other, had each gone out into the world and had all eventually returned to their mother's home. Esperanza had been the only one to get through college. She had gotten her B.A. in Chicano Studies. During that time, she had lived with her boyfriend, Rubén (who, during the

---

[9] purgatory   [10] Or if not, what my child?   [11] The Crazy Saint   [12] the people

height of his Chicano cosmic consciousness renamed himself *Cuauhtemoc*[13]. This, despite her mother's opposition, who said of her eldest daughter's nonsanctified union: "Why should a man buy the cow when he can have the milk for free?" "I am not a cow," Esperanza responded, but despite this, right after graduation Cuauhtemoc dumped her for a middle-class *gabacha*[14] with a Corvette; they bought a house in the Northeast Heights in Albuquerque right after their wedding.

Esperanza always had a lot of "spunk," as they say, but she did have a bad year after Cuauhtemoc, who was Rubén again before she recovered and decided to go back to the university for an M.A. in communications. Upon receiving her degree, she landed a job at the local T.V. station as a news broadcaster. These were transitional years where she felt like a woman with brains was as good as dead for all the happiness it brought her in the love department.

Caridad tried a year of college, but school was not for her and never had been, for that matter. She was the sister of the porcelain complexion, not meaning white, but as smooth as glazed clay. She had perfect teeth and round, apple-shaped breasts. Unlike the rest of the women in her family who, despite her grandmother's insistence that they were *Spanish*, descendants of pure Spanish blood, all shared the flat butt of the Pueblo blood undeniably circulating through their veins, Caridad had a somewhat pronounced ass that men were inclined to show their unappreciated appreciation for everywhere she went.

She fell in love with Memo, her high school sweetheart, got pregnant, and they married the day after graduation. But two weeks had not passed before Caridad got wind that Memo was still seeing his ex-girlfriend, Domitila, who lived in Belen; and Caridad went back home.

All in all, Caridad had three abortions. La Loca had performed each one. Their mother had only known about the first. They didn't tell anyone else about it but said to Memo and his family that Caridad had miscarried from being so upset about Memo's cheating on her. It was agreed by all that the marriage be annulled. It would have been a terrible thing to let anyone find out that La Loca had "cured" her sister of her pregnancy, a cause for excommunication for both, not to mention that someone would have surely had La Loca arrested. A crime against man if not a sin against God.

The occasions when La Loca let people get close to her, when she permitted human contact at all, were few. Only her mother and the animals were ever unconditionally allowed to touch her. But without exception, healing her sisters from the traumas and injustices they were dealt by society—a society she herself never experienced firsthand—was never questioned.

Caridad kept up with Memo for several years until he finally made his choice. It was not Domitila of Belen and it wasn't Caridad of Tome. It was the Marines. And off he went to be all that he never knew he was. For while it was said that the Army made men, the Marines' motto, he was told, was that they only took men.

Three abortions later and with her weakness for shots of Royal Crown with beer chasers after work at the hospital where she was an orderly, Caridad no longer

<hr />

[13] a name similar to many of the Aztec gods   [14] slang term for anglo-saxon. Often used in a derogatory manner.

discriminated between giving her love to Memo and only to Memo whenever he wanted it and loving anyone she met at the bars who vaguely resembled Memo. At about the time that her sister, who was definitely not prettier than her but for sure had more brains, was on the ten o'clock nightly news, you could bet that Caridad was making it in a pickup off a dark road with some guy whose name the next day would be as meaningless to her as yesterday's headlines were to Esperanza la newscaster.

Fe, the third of Sofí's daughters, was fine. That is, twenty-four, with a steady job at the bank, and a hard-working boyfriend whom she had known forever; she had just announced their engagement. With the same job since high school graduation, she was a reliable friend to the "girls" at work. Fe was beyond reproach. She maintained her image above all—from the organized desk at work to weekly manicured fingernails and a neat coiffure.

She and Thomas, "Tom," Torres were the ideal couple in their social circle, if one could call a social circle a group of three or four couples who got together on weekends to watch football on wide-screen television at Sadie's, or to go to a Lobos game at the university, or rent videos or once in a while got all dressed up and went to Garduño's for dinner.

Tom ran one of those mini-mart filling stations, sometimes working double shifts. He did not drink or even smoke cigarettes. They were putting their money away for their wedding, a small wedding, just for family and a few close friends, because they were going to use their savings for their first house.

As it was, while Fe had a little something to talk to Esperanza about, she kept away from her other sisters, her mother, and the animals, because she just didn't understand how they could all be so self-defeating, so unambitious. Although, by anyone's standards it was unfair to call her mother unambitious, since Sofí single-handedly ran the Carne Buena Carneceria she inherited from her parents. She raised most of the livestock that she herself (with the help of La Loca) butchered for the store, managed all its finances, and ran the house on her own to boot.

But as for Fe's antisocial sister, sometimes, when she came home from her job at the bank and saw La Loca outside the stalls with the horses, always in the same dirty pair of jeans and never wearing shoes, even in winter, she was filled with deep compassion for what she saw as a soulless creature.

She had only been six years old when La Loca had had her first epileptic seizure and her mother and community (out of ignorance, she was sure) had pronounced the child dead. She did not remember *"El Milagro,"*[15] as her mother referred to La Loca's resurrection that day in front of the church, and highly suspected that such a thing as her little sister flying up to the church rooftop had never happened.

Usually, Fe did not feel compassion for La Loca, however, but simply disappointment and disgust for her sister's obvious "mental illness," the fact that her mother had encouraged it with her own superstitions, and finally, fear that it was, like her own Indian flat butt, hereditary, despite everyone's protest to the contrary.

Fe couldn't wait until she got out—of her mother's home as well as Tome—but she would get out properly, with a little more style and class than the women in her family had. Except for Esperanza these days, whose being on television every night

---

[15] The Miracle

was lending some prestige to Fe at the bank. Although when Esperanza was in college, being a radical and living with that crazy Chicano who was always speeding on peyote or something, Fe hadn't known what to make of her older sister and certainly had no desire to copy Esperanza's La Raza politics.

Fe had just come back from Bernadette's Bridal Gowns, where she had had herself fitted for her dress, and the three gabachas (my term, not Fe's) she had chosen from the bank as her bridesmaids, instead of her sisters, had met that Saturday to have their pink-and-orchid chiffon gowns fitted too, when La Loca, sweeping the living room, pointed with her chin to the mail as soon as Fe came in.

"What? A letter for me?" Fe said cheerfully, recognizing Tom's neat, small printing on the square envelope. She smiled and took it to the bathroom to get a little privacy. La Loca had that look like she was going to stick close to her. Sometimes she did that. She had this sixth sense when she suspected something was amiss in the house and wouldn't let up until she uncovered it.

Dear Honey, it began, a short note on yellow paper from a legal pad. This was a little unusual, since Tom always sent cards, cards with lovers kissing, with irises and roses, with beautiful little sayings that rhymed to which he simply signed, "Your Tom." *Dear Honey.* Fe stopped. She heard a faint rap on the door. "Go away, Loca," she said. She heard her sister move away from the door. Fe read on: *I have been thinking about this for a long time, but I didn't have the nerve to tell you in person. It's not that I don't love you. I do. I always will. But I just don't think I'm ready to get married. Like I said, I thought about this a long time. Please don't call to try to change my mind. I hope you find happiness with someone who deserves you and can make you happy. Tom.*

When La Loca and Sofí—along with the help of Fred and Wilma, the two Irish setters that immediately joined in the commotion of the women's breaking down the bathroom door, and Fe's screaming and tearing the tiny bathroom apart—finally got to Fe, she was wrapped up in the shower curtain in the tub. "You're gonna suffocate, 'jita, get outa there!" Sofí called and with La Loca's help unwrapped the plastic from around Fe, who in her ravings had inadvertently made herself into a human tamale— all the while letting out one loud continuous scream that could have woken the dead.

Sofí shook her daughter hard, but when that didn't silence Fe, she gave her a good slap as she had seen people do on T.V. lots of times whenever anyone got like that. But Fe didn't quiet down. In fact, Fe did not stop screaming even when Sofí announced ten days later that she was going to get Tom. She decided to go personally to Tom's house when he did not return her calls.

"I got a daughter who won't stop screaming," she told Tom's mother, Mrs. Torres.

"I got a son who's got *susto,*[16]" Mrs. Torres replied.

"¿*Susto*? ¿*Susto*?" Sofí shouted. "*You* think that cowardly son of yours without *pelos on his maracas*[17] has *susto*? I'll show you *susto*! My daughter has been screaming at the top of her lungs for ten days and nights. She spent hundreds, maybe even a thousand dollars already on their wedding plans. She has people at work that she

---

[16] fright. Refers to a condition similar to the evil eye. In folklore it is thought that when a person undergoes a traumatic experience they are "frightened" and suffer both physical and emotional afflictions.

[17] hair on his testicles

can't even face no more. And let me tell you something, Mrs. Torres, don't think that I don't know that your son had her on the pill for a long time."

"Wait, just a minute, señora," Mrs. Torres cut in, holding up her hand. The two mothers, believe it or not, had never met before. Fe had been too ashamed of her family to bring Mrs. Torres over to her house. "My son . . . my son is a good boy. He hasn't eaten for days, he's just so upset about this breakup. But he said he had to do the honorable thing. He hasn't cost your daughter nothing he himself hasn't lost as well. What's money when in the long run he spared her from an unhappy marriage? I don't know why he changed his mind about marrying her. I keep out of my son's business. Just be glad he left your daughter when he did. You know how men are . . ."

"Ay!" Sofí moaned, because she knew full well that *that* last remark was meant to hit below the belt regarding her own marriage, and thanks to Fe, she knew next to nothing about Mrs. Torres to come back with a good rejoinder. But finally Tom came out of his room and she convinced him to come over so that he might make Fe stop screaming.

"What's that?" he asked, obviously spooked by Fe's shrill cries that were heard from outside the house. "Is that La Loca?" He had heard of her, but had never met Fe's so-called retarded sister. "Are you crazy?" Sofí said, unlocking the door. "That's *your* girlfriend! Why do you think I brought you here? If I know Fe, she'll snap out of it—maybe by you talking to her. We'll see."

But Tom stopped at the threshold. "I can't go in," he said. He looked nauseated. "I'm sorry, I just can't." And before Sofí could think of something to say to stop him, Tom was back in his car, smoking down the road. Damn, Sofí thought, seeing him speed away, maybe he *does* have susto.

Unfortunately, nothing and no one could quiet Fe down. She wanted her Tom back. And even when Caridad managed to get some tranquilizers from her hospital friends, Fe would only shut up for an hour or two at a time when she slept. She even screamed while she was being fed (because now it was Sofí and her daughters who took turns feeding, cleaning, and dressing poor Fe, who was truly a mess and who—if she were in any way capable of realizing it—would have been horrified at that thought).

Meanwhile, La Loca did what she could. She sewed a padded headband for Fe so that when she banged her head against the wall, as she increasingly did while she screamed, she wouldn't hurt herself as bad. She also prayed for her, since that was La Loca's principal reason for being alive, as both her mother and she well knew.

Above all, however, she prayed for Tom, because like so many *hispanos, nuevo mexicanos,*[18] whatever he wanted to call himself, something about giving himself over to a woman was worse than having lunch with the devil. Yes, he had susto. But no tea and no incantations by the *curandera*[19] his mother brought over to relieve him of it would ever cure him. The mere mention of Fe was enough to set him off into a cold sweat. So La Loca prayed for him because in a few years he would probably look for a new novia to marry while no one, not even Mrs. Torres, not even he himself, would know that he was still suffering from the inability to open his heart.

---

[18] Hispanics, new Mexicans   [19] a spiritual healer

Fe and her bloodcurdling wail became part of the household's routine so that the animals didn't even jump or howl no more whenever Fe, after a brief intermission when she dozed off, woke up abruptly and put her good lungs to full use. But it was Caridad who, being selfless would never have thought of becoming the center of attention, ultimately caused the entire household, including animals, to forget Fe when she came home one night as mangled as a stray cat, having been left for dead by the side of the road.

There was too much blood to see at the time, but after Caridad had been taken by ambulance to the hospital, treated and saved (just barely), Sofí was told that her daughter's nipples had been bitten off. She had also been scourged with something, branded like cattle. Worst of all, a tracheotomy was performed because she had also been stabbed in the throat.

For those with charity in their hearts, the mutilation of the lovely young woman was akin to martyrdom. Masses were said for her recovery. A novena was devoted to her at the local parish. And although Sofí didn't know who they all were, a dozen old women in black came each night to Caridad's hospital room to say the rosary, to wail, to pray.

But there are still those for whom there is no kindness, in their hearts for a young woman who has enjoyed life, so to speak. Among them were the sheriff's deputies and the local police department; therefore Caridad's attacker or attackers were never found. No one was even ever detained as a suspect. And as the months went by, little by little, the scandal and shock of Caridad's assault were forgotten, by the news media, the police, neighbors, and the church people. She was left in the hands of her family, a nightmare incarnated.

When Esperanza finally managed to get her mother to come home to try to rest a bit, they found Fe dozing off in her room and La Loca nowhere around. They didn't find her in the roperos, under the beds, not out in the stalls with the horses. The dogs would not reveal where she was, staring blankly at Sofí when she asked them about La Loca's whereabouts. Esperanza suggested calling the police. La Loca never left the house except to go out in the stalls, or walk down to the ditch, and though she rode, she never went out at night. Surely, the two women thought, after their having been gone for more than twelve hours, the two women thought, La Loca must have wandered off, not knowing what else to do.

But just as Esperanza was dialing the emergency number she heard a distinct clunk sound from inside the wood-burning stove in the living room. Sofí and the dogs heard it too and they all rushed at once to pull La Loca out. "Mom, is Caridad dead?" La Loca asked, soot-covered, arms around her mother's shoulders. She was crying. "*No, 'jita*, your sister is not dead. *Gracias a Dios*."[20]

Just then Fe woke up and the walls began to vibrate with her screaming and since everyone including the dogs and cats had been concentrating on La Loca for a moment, they gave a start, in unison. La Loca began to cry harder and Sofí, who couldn't take no more the reality of a permanently traumatized daughter, another who was more ghost than of this world, and a third who was the most beautiful child

---

[20] No daughter, Thank God

she had given birth to and who had been cruelly mutilated, let herself sink into the couch and began to sob.

"Mom. Mom. Please, don't give up," Esperanza called out, but she did not come to put her arms around her mother's hunched shoulders. "Aw!" Esperanza said, clearly trying not to give in to it all herself. Although this was far from the right moment to spring her news on her family, she found herself announcing, "I've just been offered a job in Houston. I don't know for sure if I should take it . . ."

No one heard her anyway. Being the eldest, she was used to her mother's preoccupation with her younger sisters. Caridad, because she was too beautiful; Fe, because her compulsions wound her up too tight; and the baby, La Loca, because she was kind of . . . well, *loca*. Esperanza threw her hands up in the air and went to bed.

The next day, Esperanza went straight to her boss and gave her notice. The staff was pretty excited for her since the job in Houston was definitely a step up and things were looking good for Esperanza in the way of career opportunities.

As it turned out, she got a message before the end of that week from a certain Rubén out of her past. *Lunch tomorrow?* the message read. Sure, why not? Esperanza thought. Enough time had passed so that she could almost say she bore no hard feelings against her college sweetheart. She was doing all right for herself and she was certain he had seen her on the nightly news, so he knew it, too. Soon she would be getting out of New Mexico, broadening her horizons, freeing herself from the provincialism of her upbringing, and Rubén with his blond wife and their three-bedroom house, coyote kid, dog, and minivan could just live happily ever after as far as she was concerned.

But as it turned out there was no more house in the Northeast Heights and no more minivan. Rubén was driving an old clunker, and Donna had split with their kid to *Houston.* (Apparently she too was intent on starting a new life, broadening her horizons, freeing herself from her provincial upbringing, and so on.)

"I have thought of calling you for a long time, Esperanza, Rubén told her. "I have gone back to the Native-American Church and everytime I go pray at a meeting at one of the pueblos or go to the sweat lodge, I think of us, and how it coulda been." He had put on a few pounds, well, more than a few, but to Esperanza, he still had that kind of animal magnetism she always felt toward him.

"You remember, *vieja*,[21] when we used to go to the peyote meetings together, when we sweat together at the lodge back in the days when we were in college?" he asked, giving her a nudge with his elbow. He was holding a mug of beer in his hand, and she saw as he waved his arms with great animation that he didn't spill any of it, but instead chugged it right down and grinned at her. No, he wasn't drunk, just feeling good. It was good to see him again, to be back together, and she ordered herself another beer too.

Esperanza didn't go back to work that day, but they ended up picking up where they left off, and to make a long story short, she didn't get to Houston that year, either. Every two weeks she was right there with Rubén, at the teepee meetings of

---

[21] literally means old woman. Often, as it is here, it is used as a term of affection by a man when referring to his wife or lover.

the Native-American Church, Rubén singing and drumming, keeping the fire, watching the "door," teaching her the dos and don'ts of his interpretation of lodge "etiquette" and the role of women and the role of men and how they were not to be questioned. And she concluded as she had during their early days, why not?

After all, there was Rubén with his Native and Chicano male friends always joking among themselves, always siding with each other, and always agreeing about the order and reason of the universe, and since Esperanza had no Native women friends to verify any of what was being told to her by Rubén about the woman's role in what they were doing, she did not venture to contradict him.

At this time a virtual miracle occurred in Esperanza's house and which eventually caused her to decide about her relationship with Rubén. Well, actually she had been thinking about it for a while. Every time they went to a meeting, which was maybe once every two or three weeks, everything was good between them. They went to the meeting. Sometimes they also did a sweat. Afterward, they went home and made love all day. The problem was that then she would not hear from Rubén again until the next time there was a meeting. She was beginning to feel like part of a ritual in which she herself participated as an unsuspecting symbol, like a staff or a rattle or medicine.

As the months went on, their separation between meetings and sweats had become unsettling. It completely closed her off from her other life, the life which Rubén referred to derogatorily as "careerist." She felt just plain sad and lonely about it. She wanted to share with him that part of her life. She needed to bring it all together, to consolidate the spiritual with the practical side of things. But whenever she suggested to Rubén that they have lunch again like they did that first time or to go out on a regular date in between meetings, he simply declined with no apologies, regrets, or explanations.

What was left of Caridad had been brought home after three months in the hospital. In addition to caring for Fe la Gritona (as her mother had begun to refer to her, although never to her face), it was Sofí's main job to care for Caridad, or as stated more accurately above, what was left of her.

It was La Loca who took care of the horses and the other animals as well as helped her mother with preparing meals for her sisters. One evening, right after one of La Loca's infrequent seizures, the miracle that Esperanza witnessed occurred. Sofí was tending to La Loca, who was on the living room floor, the tray with Fe's carne adovada and green chili all over her, Esperanza standing nearby, and of course, all the animals that had given their perfunctory warnings just beforehand stood nervously around as well. Then movement in the adjacent dining room caught their eyes at once. Dogs, cats, and women, twenty-eight eyes in all, saw *Caridad* walking soundlessly, without seeming to be aware of them, across that room. Before anyone could react she was out of sight. Furthermore, it wasn't the Caridad that had been brought back from the hospital, but a whole and once again beautiful Caridad, in what furthermore appeared to be Fe's wedding gown.

"Mom?" Esperanza said, hesitating, but eyes still fixed on the empty space where Caridad had passed.

"Dios mío," Sofí gasped. "Caridad."

"Mom," La Loca whispered, still on the floor, "I prayed for Caridad."

"I know you did, 'jita, I know," Sofí said, trembling, afraid to pull herself up, to go to the room where she suspected Caridad's corpse was now waiting to be taken care of.

"I prayed real hard," La Loca added and started to cry.

The dogs and cats whimpered.

The three women huddled together went to the bedroom where Caridad was. Sofí stepped back when she saw, not what had been left of her daughter, half repaired by modern medical technology, tubes through her throat, bandages over skin that was gone, surgery piecing together flesh that was once her daughter's breasts, but Caridad as she was before.

Furthermore, a calm Fe was holding her sister, rocking her, stroking her forehead, humming softly to her. Caridad was whole. There was nothing, nothing that anyone could see wrong with her, except for the fact that she was feverish. Her eyes were closed while she moved her head back and forth, not violently but softly, as was Caridad's nature, mumbling unintelligibly all the while.

"Fe?" said Esperanza—who was equally taken aback by Fe's transformation. She had stopped screaming.

Sofí, sobbing, rushed over to embrace her two daughters.

"I prayed for you," La Loca told Fe. "Thank you, Loca," Fe said, almost smiling.

"Loca." Esperanza reached over to place her hand on La Loca's shoulder. "Don't touch me!" La Loca said, moving away from her sister as she always did from anyone when she was not the one to initiate the contact.

Esperanza took a deep breath and let it out slowly. She had spent her whole life trying to figure out why she was the way she was. In high school, although a rebel, she was Catholic heart and soul. In college, she had a romance with Marxism, but was still Catholic. In graduate school, she was atheist and, in general, a cynic. Lately, she prayed to Grandmother Earth and Grandfather Sky. For good measure, however, she had been reading a flurry of self-help books. She read everything she could find on dysfunctional families, certain now that some of her personal sense of displacement in society had to do with her upbringing.

But nowhere did she find anything near to the description of her family. And now, Caridad's and Fe's spontaneous recoveries were beyond all rhyme and reason for anyone, even for an ace reporter like Esperanza. It was time to get away, Esperanza decided, far away.

"I'm going to call Rubén," Esperanza announced, but at that moment her mother was too overwhelmed by her two daughters' return to the living that she didn't hear Esperanza either.

"Rubén?" Esperanza said, when Rubén answered his phone.

"Yeah? Hey, how's it goin', kid?" he asked with his usual condescending manner, adding a little chuckle. Esperanza paused. He talked to her on the phone like she was a casual friend. A casual friend whom he prayed with and whom he made love with, but whom he could not call to ask on a given day how she was doing. When it was her moon-time the estrangement between them widened since she was not permitted to go to the meeting or to sweat, nor did he like to make love to her. A casual friend who accepted her gifts of groceries, the rides in *her* car with *her* gas, all up and down the Southwest to attend meetings, who called her collect the month he left on a "pilgrimage" to visit the Mayan ruins throughout southern Mexico, where she had not been invited to join him, who always let her pick up the tab whenever they stopped someplace for a few beers and burritos just before she left him—after the meetings, sweats, lovemaking, to go home so she could get herself ready for that job which he suspected her so much of selling out to white society for but which paid for all the food, gas, telephone calls, and even, let's admit it, the tens and twenties she discreetly left on his bedroom dresser whenever she went over, knowing he could use it and would take it, although he would never have asked her directly for it.

"It's my sisters," she started to say, but already something else was on her mind more pertinent than the recent recuperation of Fe and Caridad.

"Yeah, your sisters," Rubén said. "You got your hands full, huh, woman?"

"No," Esperanza responded with sudden aloofness. "As a matter of fact, they're taking good care of themselves. I just wanted to tell you that I'm accepting an offer in Washington. And that I think it's better if we just don't see each other anymore, Rubén."

"Well, uh . . ." Rubén was groping for a response that would reinstate the pride just demolished by Esperanza's abrupt rejection, when he was cut short by a *click*. Esperanza didn't mean to simply hang up on him but she had just caught sight of a man peering in through the kitchen window. What made it really eerie was that instead of barking the dogs were waving their tails. Just then the man opened the door and stepped in. She recognized him right away since she was already going on twelve when he had left. "Dad?"

Yes. It was their father, Sofí's husband, who had returned "after all those years" as they would say around Tome for a long time to come. Some say, *that* was the true miracle of that night. All kinds of stories circulated as to what had happened to him "all those years." Most of the rumors he would start himself, and when he would get tired of hearing them played back always with some new variation or detail of exaggeration added to them which did not quite suit his taste, he pretended to get angry about them, stopped them, and started a new story all over again.

For example, the favorite *chisme*[22] that went around about him was that he had been living down in Silver City, running a gambling operation and living the high life. After the story circulated awhile, the gambling operation became part of a house of ill-repute. Domingo found this addition to the story amusing, even something to boast about with his friends down at Toby's Package Liquors, or after Mass in the church courtyard. But when people started to say that Domingo had married the woman who owned and ran the brothel, Domingo got angry. He was many things, but a bigamist, nunca.

With regards to his own adventures, he quickly realized he had considerable competition with La Loca's life, which she herself didn't relate but which he invariably heard about from everyone else. When he tried to get her to fly to the roof or stick herself in the wood-burning stove, she simply stared at him as if such suggestions were absurd. However, the one thing she did confirm was her repulsion for

[22] gossip

human contact when ever he came close to her, unless she was the one who initiated it, which, believe it or not, once in a while she did.

She would approach him when he was eating or watching television and sniff him. Since he didn't want to scare her off, he'd remain still and pretend he didn't notice what she was doing.

"'Jita," Sofí asked her daughter one day when they were alone, "what is it that you smell when you smell your father?"

"Mom," La Loca said, "I smell my dad. And he was in hell, too."

"Hell?" Sofí said, thinking her daughter, who didn't have any sense of humor at all, was trying to make a joke.

But instead Loca replied quite soberly, "Mom, I been to hell. You never forget that smell. And my dad . . . he was there, too."

"So you think I should forgive your dad for leaving me, for leaving us all those years?" Sofí asked.

"Here we don't forgive, Mom," La Loca told her. And there was no question at that point in Sofí's mind that La Loca had no sense of humor. La Loca's voice empathized. "Only in hell do we learn to forgive and you got to die first," La Loca said. "That's when we get to pluck out all the devils from our hearts, that were put there when we were *here*. That's where we get rid of all the lies told to us. That's where we go and cry like rain. Mom, hell is where you go to see yourself. This dad, out there, sitting watching T.V., he was in hell a long time. He's like an onion, we will never know all of him—but he ain't afraid no more."

Discussion Questions

1. How does the name of each daughter relate to their characters?
2. Examine the relationship between Esperanza and Rubén. What does that relationship say about the role of women in Mexican-American culture, and does Esperanza conform to that role?
3. Compare the elements of magical realism present in this story to Anaya's *Bless Me Ultima* on page 25. What differences, other than tone, are present between Ultima and La Loca.
4. Compare the structure of this excerpt to Ed Vega's "The Barbosa Express" on page 411. While they both seem disjointed and surreal, they each come to a coherent conclusion. Explain how.

Denise Chavez

DENISE CHAVEZ's background in drama has allowed her to create characters that seem to come alive. After her high school education in Las Cruces, New Mexico, where she was born in 1948, she received a B.A. degree in drama from New Mexico State University in 1971. That was followed by an M.F.A. from Trinity University in

San Antonio in 1974, and later an M.A. from the University of New Mexico in 1984. Her many one-act plays focus on the characters' sense of belonging within a larger community, as well as depicting characters that seem ordinary but reveal a quiet heroism.

Her credits as a playwright span twenty years beginning with The Wait *(1970). She is best known for her fiction, however, and her latest work,* Face of an Angel *(1995) is her first novel. It centers on the life of a waitress named Soveida Dosamantes, and her relations with her friends and lovers in a small town in New Mexico. The Last of the Menu Girls (1986) is her finest achievement, as this collection of seven stories draws together all the themes that Chavez has been preoccupied with for her entire literary career. Rocio Esquibel, who works handing out menus in a hospital, is exposed to many different ordinary people and experiences. The following story masterfully manages to describe a backyard experience with a willow tree as both ordinary and memorable.*

From The Last of the Menu Girls

Willow Game

I was a child before there was a South. That was before the magic of the East, the beckoning North, or the West's betrayal. For me there was simply Up the street toward the spies' house, next to Old Man W's or there was Down, past the Marking-Off Tree in the vacant lot that was the shortcut between worlds. Down was the passageway to family, the definition of small self as one of the whole, part of a past. Up was in the direction of town, flowers.

Mercy and I would scavenge the neighborhood for flowers that we would lay at Our Lady's feet during those long May Day processions of faith that we so loved. A white satin cloth would be spread in front of the altar. We children would come up one by one and place our flowers on that bridal sheet, our breathless childish fervor heightened by the mystifying scent of flowers, the vision of flowers, the flowers of our offerings. It was this beatific sense of wonder that sent us roaming the street in search of new victims, as our garden had long since been razed, emptied of all future hope.

On our block there were two flower places: Old Man W's and the Strongs. Old Man W was a Greek who worked for the city for many years and who lived with his daughter who was my older sister's friend. Mr. W always seemed eager to give us flowers; they were not as lovely or as abundant as the Strongs' flowers, yet the asking lay calmly with us at Old Man W's.

The Strongs, a misnamed brother-and-sister team who lived together in the largest, most sumptuous house on the block, were secretly referred to by my sister and me as "the spies." A chill of dread would overtake both of us as we'd approach their mansion. We would ring the doorbell and usually the sister would answer. She was a pale woman with a braided halo of wispy white hair who always planted herself possessively in the doorway, her little girl's legs in black laced shoes holding back, sectioning off, craning her inquiry to our shaken selves with a lispy, merciless, "Yes?"

I always did the asking. In later years when the street became smaller, less foreign, and the spies had become, at the least, accepted . . . it was I who still asked questions, pleaded for flowers to Our Lady, heard the high piping voices of ecstatic children singing, "Bring flowers of the fairest, bring flowers of the rarest, from garden and woodland and hillside and dale . . . ." My refrain floated past the high white walls of the church, across the Main Street irrigation ditch and up our small street. "Our pure hearts are swelling, our glad voices telling, the praise of the loveliest Rose of the Dale . . . ."

One always came down . . .

Down consisted of all the houses past my midway vantage point, including the house across the street, occupied by a couple and their three children, who later became my charges, my baby-sitting reponsibilities, children whose names I have forgotten. This was the house where one day a used sanitary napkin was ritually burned—a warning to those future furtive random and unconcerned depositors of filth, or so this is what one read in Mr. Carter's eyes as he raked the offensive item to a pile of leaves and dramatically set fire to some nameless, faceless woman's woes. I peered from the trinity of windows cut in our wooden front door and wondered what all the commotion was about and why everyone seemed so stoically removed, embarrassed or offended. Later I would mournfully peep from the cyclopian window at the Carter's and wonder why I was there and not across the street. In my mind I floated Down, past the Marking-Off Tree with its pitted green fruit, past five or six houses, house of strangers, "*los desconocidos*,"[1] as my Grandmother would say, "*¿Y pues, quién los parió?*"[2] I would end up at my aunt's house, return, find myself looking at our house as it was, the porch light shining, the lilies' pale patterns a diadem crowning our house, there, at night.

The walk from the beginning to the end of the street took no longer than five to ten minutes, depending on the pace and purpose of the walker. The walk was short if I was a messenger to my aunt's, or if I was meeting my father, who had recently divorced us and now called sporadically to allow us to attend to him. The pace may have been the slow, leisurely summer saunter with ice cream or the swirling dust-filled scamper of spring. Our house was situated in the middle of the block and faced a triangle of trees that became both backdrop and pivot points of this child's tale. The farthest tree, the Up Tree, was an Apricot Tree that was the property of all the neighborhood children.

The Apricot Tree lay in an empty lot near my cousin's house, the cousin who always got soap in her nose. Florence was always one of the most popular girls in school and, while I worshipped her, I was glad to have my nose and not hers. Our mothers would alternate driving us and the Sánchez boys, one of whom my father nicknamed "Priscilla" because he was always with the girls, to a small Catholic school that was our genesis. On entering Florence's house on those days when it was *her* mother's turn, I would inevitably find her bent over the bathroom basin, sneezing. She would yell out, half snottily, half snortingly, "I have soap in my nose!"

---

[1] the unknown ones   [2] And so, who bore them?

Whether the Apricot Tree really belonged to Florence wasn't clear—the tree was the neighborhood's and as such, was as familiar as our own faces, or the faces of our relatives. Her fruit, often abundant, sometimes meager, was public domain. The tree's limbs draped luxuriously across an irrigation ditch whose calm, muddy water flowed all the way from the Río Grande to our small street where it was diverted into channelways that led into the neighborhood's backyards. The fertile water deposited the future seeds of asparagus, weeds and wild flowers, then settled into tufted layers crossed by sticks and stones—hieroglyphic reminders of murky beginnings.

Along with the tree, we children drew power from the penetrating grateful wetness. In return, the tree was resplendent with offerings—there were apricots and more, there were the sturdy compartments, the chambers and tunnelways of dream, the stages of our dramas. "I'm drowning! I'm drowning!" we mocked drowning and were saved at the last moment by a friendly hand, or, "This is the ship and I am the captain!" we exulted having previously transcended death. Much time was spent at the tree, alone or with others. All of us, Priscilla, Soap-in-her-Nose, the two dark boys Up the street, my little sister and I, all of us loved the tree. We would oftentimes find ourselves slipping off from one of those choreless, shoreless days, and with a high surprised "Oh!" we would greet each other's aloneness, there at the tree that embraced us all selflessly.

On returning home we may have wandered alongside the ditch, behind the Wester's house, and near the other vacant lot which housed the second point of the triangle, the Marking-Off Tree, the likes of which may have stood at the edge of the Garden of Eden. It was dried, sad-looking. All the years of my growing up it struggled to create a life of its own. The tree passed fruit every few years or so—as old men and women struggle to empty their ravaged bowels. The grey-green balls that it brought forth we used as one uses an empty can, to kick and thrash. The tree was a reference point, offering no shade, but always meditation. It delineated the Up world from the Down. It marked off the nearest point home, without being home; it was a landmark, and as such, occupied our thoughts, not in the way the Apricot Tree did, but in a subtler, more profound way. Seeing the tree was like seeing the same *viejito*[3] downtown for so long, with his bottle and his wife, and looking into his crusty white-rimmed eyes and thinking: "How much longer?" Tape appears on his neck, the voice box gargles a barking sound and the bruises seem deeper.

There, at that place of recognition and acceptance, you will see the Marking-Off Tree at the edge of my world. I sit on the front porch at twilight. The power is all about me. The great unrest twitters and swells like the erratic chords of small and large birds scaling their way home.

To our left is the Willow Tree, completing this trinity of trees. How to introduce her? I would take the light of unseen eyes and present the sister who lives in France, or her husband who died when he was but thirty. I would show you the best of friends and tell you how clear, how dear. I would recall moments of their eternal charm, their look or stance, the intrinsic quality of their bloom. You would see inside an album a black and white photograph of a man with a wide, ruddy face, in shirtsleeves, holding a plump, squinting child in front of a small tree, a tree too frail for

---

[3] little old man.

the wild lashes, surely. On the next page an older girl passing a hand through wind-blown hair would look at you, you would feel her gentle beauty, love her form. Next to her a young girl stands, small eyes toward godfather, who stares at the photographer, shaded by a growing-stronger tree. Or then you would be at a birthday party, one of the guests, rimmed in zinnias, cousins surrounding, Soap-in-her-Nose, the two dark boys (younger than in story time) and the others, miniaturized versions of their future selves. Two sisters, with their arms around each other's child-delicate necks, stand out—as the warps and the twinings of the willow background confuse the boys with their whips and the girls with their fans.

In this last photograph one sees two new faces, one shy boy huddled among the girls, the other removed from all contact, sunblinded, lost in leaves.

Next to us lived the Althertons: Rob, Sandy, Ricky and Randy. The history of the house next door was wrought with struggle. Before the Althertons moved in, the Cardozas lived there, with their smiling young boys, senseless boys, demon boys. It was Emmanuel (Mannie) who punched the hole in our plastic swimming pool and Jr. who made us cry. Toward the end of the Cardoza boys' reign, Mrs. C, a small breathless bug-eyed little woman, gave birth to a girl. Mr. C's tile business failed and the family moved to *Chiva* Town,[4] vacating the house to the Althertons, an alternately histrionically dry and loquacious couple with two boys. Ricky, the oldest, was a tall, tense boy who stalked the Altherton spaces with the natural grace of a wild animal, ready to spring, ears full of sound, eyes taut with anticipation. Young Randy was a plump boychild with deep, watery eyes that clung to Mrs. Altherton's lumpish self while lean and lanky Papa A ranged the spacious lawn year round in swimming trunks in search of crab grass, weeds, any vestiges of irregularity. Lifting a handful of repugnant weed, he'd wave it in the direction of Sandy, his wife, a pigeon of a woman who cooed, "You don't say . . ."

Jack Spratt shall eat no fat, his wife shall eat no lean, and between them both, you see, they licked the platter clean.

The Altherton yard was very large centered by a metal pole to which was attached the neighborhood's first tetherball. From our porch where my sister and I sat dressing dolls, we could hear the punch and whirr of balls, the crying and calling out. Ricky would always win, sending Randy racing inside to Mrs. A's side, at which time, having dispatched his odious brother, Ricky would beat and thrash the golden ball around in some sort of crazed and victorious adolescent dance. Randy and Mrs. A would emerge from the house and they would confer with Ricky for a time. Voices were never raised, were always hushed and calm. The two plump ones would then go off, hand in hand, leaving the lean to himself. Ricky would usually stomp away down the neighborhood, flicking off a guiltless willow limb, deleafing it in front of our watchful eyes, leaving behind his confused steps a trail of green, unblinking eyes, the leaves of our tree.

Every once in a while Randy would walk over to us as we sat dressing dolls or patting mud pies, and hesitantly, with that babyish smile of his, ask us to come play ball. We two sisters would cross the barriers of Altherton and joyfully bang the tetherball around with Randy. He played low, was predictable, unlike Ricky, who threw

---

[4] *Chiva* means goat. Here it refers to the poorer section of the city.

the ball vehemently high, confounding, always confounding. Ricky's games were over quickly; his blows firm, surprising, relentless. Ricky never played with my sister and me. He was godlike and removed, as our older sister, already sealed in some inexplicable anguish of which we children had no understanding. It was Randy who brought us in, called out to us, permitted us to play. And when he was not there to beckon us, it was his lingering generosity and gentleness that pushed us forward into the mysterious Altherton yard, allowing us to risk fear, either of Mr. Altherton and his perennial tan, or Ricky with his senseless animal temper. Often we would find the yard free and would enjoy the tetherball without interruption, other times we would see Ricky stalk by, or hear the rustling approach of clippers, signifying Mr. Altherton's return. If we would sense the vaguest shadow of either spectre, we would run, wildly, madly, safely home, to the world of our Willow where we would huddle and hide in the shelter of green, labyrinthine rooms, abstracting ourselves from the world of Ricky's torment or Mr. Altherton's anxious wanderings.

I have spoken least of all of the Willow Tree, but in speaking of someone dead or gone, what words can reach far enough into the past to secure a vision of someone's smiling face or curious look, who can tame the restless past and show, as I have tried, black and white photographs of small children in front of a tree?

The changes of the Willow were imperceptible at first. Mr. W, the Greek, through an oversight in pronunciation, had always been Mr. V. The spies became individualized when Mr. Strong later became my substitute history teacher and caused a young student to faint. She who was afraid of blood looked up into the professor's nose and saw unmistakable flecks of red. The two dark boys grew up, became wealthy, and my cousin moved away. The irrigation ditch was eventually closed. Only the Willow remained—consoling, substantial. The days became shorter and divided the brothers while the sisters grew closer.

Ricky, now a rampaging, consumed adolescent, continued his thoughtless forays, which included absently ripping off willow limbs and discarding them on our sidewalk. "He's six years older than Randy," said my mother, that dark mother who hid in trees, "he hates his brother, he just never got over Randy's birth. You love your sister, don't you?" "Yes, mother," I would say.

It was not long after Ricky's emerging manhood that the Willow began to ail, even as I watched it. I knew it was hurting. The tree began to look bare. The limbs were lifeless, in anguish, and there was no discernible reason. The solid, green rooms of our child's play collapsed, the passageways became cavernous hallways, the rivers of grass dried and there was no shade. The tree was dying. My mother became concerned. I don't know what my little sister thought; she was a year younger than I. She probably thought as I did, for at that time she held me close as model and heroine, and enveloped me with her love, something Randy was never able to do for his older brother, that bewildered boy.

It wasn't until years later (although the knowledge was there, admitted, seen) that my mother told me that one day she went outside to see Ricky standing on a ladder under our Willow. He had a pair of scissors in his hands and was cutting whole branches off the tree and throwing them to one side. Mother said, "What are you doing, Ricky?" He replied, "I'm cutting the tree." "Do you realize that you're killing it?" she responded calmly. It is here that the interpretation breaks down, where the photographs fade into grey wash, and I momentarily forget what Ricky's reply was, that day, so many years ago, as the limbs of our Willow fell about him, cascading tears, willow reminders past the face of my mother, who stood solemnly and without horror.

Later, when there was no recourse but to cut down the tree, Regino Suárez, the neighborhood handyman, and his son were called in.

Regino and his son had difficulty with the tree; she refused to come out of the earth. When her roots were ripped up, there lay a cavity of dirt, an enormous aching hole, like a tooth gone, the sides impressed with myriad twistings and turnings. The trunk was moved to the side of the house, where it remained until several years ago, when it was cut up for firewood, and even then, part of the stump was left. Throughout the rest of grade school, high school, and college—until I went away, returned, went away—the Willow stump remained underneath the window of my old room.

Often I would look out and see it there, or on thoughtful walks, I would go outside near the Altherton's old house, now sealed by a tall concrete wall, and I would feel the aging hardness of the Willow's flesh.

That painful, furrowed space was left in the front yard, where once the Willow had been. It filled my eyes, my sister's eyes, my mother's eyes. The wall of trees, backdrop of the traveling me, that triangle of trees—the Apricot Tree, the Marking-Off Tree, the Willow Tree—was no longer.

One day Ricky disappeared and we were told that he'd been sent to a home for sick boys.

As children one felt dull, leaden aches that were voiceless cries and were incommunicable. The place they sprung from seemed so desolate and uninhabited and did not touch on anything tangible or transferable. To carry pain around as a child does, in that particular place, that worldless, grey corridor, and to be unable to find the syllables with which to vent one's sorrow, one's horror . . . surely this is insufferable anguish, the most insufferable. Being unable to see, yet able, willing, yet unwilling . . . to comprehend. A child's sorrow is a place that cannot be visited by others. Always the going back is solitary, and the little sisters, however much they love you, were never really very near, and the mothers, well, they stand as I said before, solemnly, without horror, removed from children by their understanding.

I am left with recollections of pain, of loss, with holes to be filled. Time, like trees, withstands the winters, bursts forth new leaves from the dried old sorrows—who knows when and why—and shelters us with the shade of later compassions, loves, although at the time the heart is seared so badly that the hope of all future flowerings is gone.

Much later, after the death of the Willow, I was walking to school when a young boy came up to me and punched me in the stomach. I doubled over, crawled back to Sister Elaine's room, unable to tell her of my recent attack, unprovoked, thoughtless, insane. What could I say to her? To my mother and father? What can I say to you? All has been told. The shreds of magic living, like the silken, green ropes of the Willow's branches, dissolved about me, and I was beyond myself, a child no longer. I was filled with immense sadness, the burning of snow in a desert land of consistent warmth.

I walked outside and the same experience repeated itself; oh, not the same form, but yes, the attack. I was the same child, you see, mouthing pacifications, incantations . . . "Bring flowers of the fairest, bring flowers of the rarest. It's okay, from garden and woodland and hillside and dale. Our pure hearts are swelling. It's all right, our glad voices are telling, please, the praise of the loveliest rose of the dale."

Jack Spratt could eat no fat, his wife could eat no lean, and between them both, you see, they licked the platter clean . . .

My mother planted a willow several years ago, so that if you sit on the porch and face left you will see it, thriving. It's not in the same spot as its predecessor, too far right, but of course, the leveling was never done, and how was Regino to know? The Apricot Tree died, the Marking-Off Tree is fruitless now, relieved from its round of senseless birthings. This willow tree is new, with its particular joys. It stands in the center of the block . . . between.

Discussion Questions

1. Why is the destruction of the Willow Tree so memorable for Rocio?
2. How is Ricky's approaching maturity related to the tree?
3. How is the new tree at the end of the story related to the development of the main character? In particular, what does that relationship say about Rocio's identity. What does he mean when she says the tree is "between"?
4. Compare the feelings that Rocio has about herself at the end of the story with Marisol's feelings at the conclusion of the excerpt by Judith Ortiz Cofer on page 347.

Rolando Hinojosa

ROLANDO HINOJOSA SMITH was born in Mercedes, Texas, in 1929. He received his Ph.D. from the University of Illinois in 1969 and is a distinguished professor of English and creative writing at the University of Texas at Austin. He is a major force in Mexican-American literature and his Klail City Death Trip *series has become a staple of the Mexican-American literary canon.*

Hinojosa was the first Mexican-American author to receive a major international literary award, and his resume includes such honors as the Quinto Sol Literary Award (1972), for his novel Estampas del valle y otras obras. *Rather than translate his own work, Hinojosa rewrites each piece in the new language in order to fully capture the nuances that are unique to each. His focus, the relatively small area of the Lower Rio Grande of Texas, has led many critics to compare his work to Faulkner's creation of the characters in Yoknapatawpha County. Like Faulkner, Hinojosa's Belken County provides the reader with a diverse group of characters, whose lives are revealed through a series of anecdotes and dialogues.*

The Klail City Death Trip *series is composed of eight novels that have all been published in either Spanish or English, or both:* Estampas del valle y otras obras *(1972, published as* The Valley *in 1983),* Klail City y sus alrededores *(1976, published as* Klail City *in 1987),* Korean Love Songs from Klail City Death Trip *(1978),* Claros Varones de Belken *(1981, published as* Fair Gentlemen of Belken County *in 1987),* Mi Querido Rafa *(1981, published as* Dear Rafe *in 1985),* Rites and Witnesses *(1982),* Los amigos de Becky *(1990, published as* Becky and Her Friends *in 1990), and* The Useless Servants *(1993).*

The following selection is an excerpt from the seventh novel in the series: Becky and Her Friends. *After briefly abandoning the series to publish a murder mystery titled* Partners in Crime *in 1985, Hinojosa continues the saga of Belken County's inhabitants by providing a voice for twenty-six characters from the previous six novels. All of them are given a chapter to discuss Becky's divorce from Ira Escobar and her later marriage to Jehu Malacara. In the final piece Becky is allowed to speak for herself.*

From Becky and Her Friends

Becky

Years ago, Daddy decided to Mexicanize himself, and so much so that he's not an Anglo anymore, a *bolillo* as Jehu says.

As a kid, when I was with the Scholastics and later on at St. Ann's, we used English and nothing but . . . I spoke English to Mama, and she'd answer me in Spanish. That's pretty normal for Valley mexicanos. Besides, Mama prefers Spanish, and that's it.

Daddy is the sweetest, dearest thing there is. He's a good man in the good sense of the word. Oh, I know what people say, and I've heard it all my life: "All he does is hunt and fish." That's just talk. And Mama? She adores him, and I do too. He is something that people wish they were: kind, giving, and—a word not much in currency—virtuous.

People. People say Mama pushed me into marrying Ira. That's partly true, but I'm the one who made that mistake. I thought I loved Ira, convinced myself I did, and for a long time, too.

And what's the big to-do? Is there a mother who doesn't want her daughter well off? Comfortable? But it happens that I let myself, had placed myself there. I wanted to marry Ira. That I don't love him as a husband now, or that I don't want him to live with me and the kids, that is something I decided as well. I made a mistake a long time ago, and it was up to me to correct it.

Can't I be allowed to make a decision? Must I always accommodate myself, every time?

And I certainly didn't talk the divorce over with Mama and Dad beforehand. The difficulty, but difficult only in broaching the subject, was in talking to the kids.

Sarah was eight at the time, and Charlie going on eleven. They love their Father, as they should. I insist on it. But they can also see that this is another life, that their Mom has remarried. That Mom works, and that there's nothing wrong in it. As far as I know, the kids have not had the divorce thrown in their faces. If someone were to, old or young, the kids know what to say to that. Now then, that Jehu and I married a year and a half after the divorce is as much our business as it is Charlie's and Sarah's, but no one else's.

Jehu prefers straight talk. I do too, although I had to learn that for myself. It was hard going, but that wasn't Jehu's fault.

And this is what people must understand: Jehu is not the kids' Father; he's their Dad. There shouldn't be any mistake on that score, I don't think. They both love and respect Jehu, and he loves them. When they're not with me or when I can't take them to work with me, Jehu leaves the bank, takes them to the park, to Mom's house, or to see Rafe or Rafe's nephews out at the farm.

The first visits to Mom's house were strained. And why shouldn't they have been? But Time's a great leveler; it's like money, says Jehu. And he laughs when he says it; I do too. And in time, Mom's learned to come around. Mama is a snob, but is that a high crime? Aren't there worse things?

It seems almost a hundred years ago that Ira and I moved to Klail. And then, straight away, Noddy decided that Ira was to run for the Commissioner's post . . . even before we left Jonesville for Klail. Many things happened back then. Personal things.

Among them, I lied for Jehu. I lied to Mr. Galindo. To Noddy. To myself. But I didn't know Jehu then, and I had no way of knowing that Jehu was, is, capable of defending himself, from any quarter. But I lied because I already loved him, and so I sought to protect him from Ira, from Noddy. *That's* funny.

Ollie San Esteban. I do not, nor will I ever, speak ill of Ollie San Esteban or her memory. Never. I was a spoiled, silly, nattering little fool, but with all of that, I sensed somehow that changes had to be made. I knew I wanted Jehu. That's a difference. And we made love; he wanted to, and I wanted to. I wanted to see him, be with him, hold him. I was indiscreet, of course, but I wasn't a fool. All he saw in me was a pretty face. I knew that. But he had to know who I was, what I was.

As for those changes, I didn't have the nerve, the courage, or even the imagination to figure them out. But I learned. Now, alone or with Jehu, here, in our home, I think about what held me back from seeing the changes. It was fear. Finally, one day, I asked myself what it was I feared. The answers came tumbling out, hundreds of them. But then, at that time, I hadn't learned about ultimate questions . . . oh, yes. When I asked myself the ultimate question, and I answered yes to myself, and I knew I was dead serious. Fear, or whatever it was, flew out that front door, through the porch, and away from this house . . .

That day the kids came in from school, and I prepared some limeade for the three of us. Sarah brought the cookies, I remember, and Charlie set the table . . . He was about to go upstairs for his shorts and sneakers, ready to go out and play, but I asked them to sit. For a talk. I had no idea what they'd say, how long I would talk, but talk I did and all of us cried, too. And then we waited for Ira . . .

I sat there, I thought I'd done a selfish thing, that I was the same old Becky. And I cried. Just then, Sarah moved over and told me not to cry. And she was just eight-years-old, you understand. Charlie then ran upstairs and put on some long pants and a shirt. We waited. The car, the door, the front porch . . .

We were a long way from the first day we'd moved to Klail . . . I cut a ridiculous figure. And for a while there, I even pretended to myself that I wasn't Elvira Navarrete's daughter, as if Ira's mother had raised me. Denial, of course; nothing else but.

I had made myself into another person, and, too, I was such a fool I couldn't see Sammie Jo's friendship when it was offered.

And Sammie Jo and I are friends. She's something, *Es persona*. And that is how she saw me. As a person, but I couldn't see myself.

But getting back to Jehu. I was just one more conquest, but hardly that, since there'd been no resistance on my part. I went to him, even when I knew he loved Ollie San Esteban. And why shouldn't he love her, and yes, I also knew about him and Sammie Jo . . . And well, was I any better?

But I didn't love Ira. And there were the kids. And people. And Mom . . . And then the ultimate question . . . what would I do for Jehu to know me so that he would then love me. And so I told Ira that I'd decided he was not to live with us anymore.

That man Jehu . . . He called on the San Esteban family for over a year after Ollie's death. A man of responsibilities, you see. And then, twelve months to the very day of the decision, on a day like today, a bit gray and overcast, somewhat windy, hurricane weather, he showed up. There, on the porch.

We sat, and I couldn't stop talking. Poor Jehu. But I didn't care what he thought of me then and there. What I wanted to know, all I wanted to know, was did he love me, did he love me as I loved him? But thank God Jehu is the way he is. He nodded and looked at me for the longest time. I couldn't know, of course, but I felt it.

I don't know about you, but have you ever had someone look at you, up close, eye to eye? A clear, unclouded, an almost unblinking look at you? Jehu looked at me that way that afternoon.

I didn't ask him to say he loved me, I wasn't a kid. But he said it anyhow. One surprise after another, that man.

And then? He said to call the kids, to go out, for a walk, on the sidewalk, around the block. And Sarah, who'd never seen him, took his hand, hugged him. Sarah! Yes. And kissed him. Even the weather helped; the wind calmed down, as calm as the kids.

Charlie? Charlie ran up to his room and brought back a sketch he'd drawn at the Scholastics. When Jehu smiled, Charlie gave it to him: a present. I don't think they said a word between them.

Since much Spanish common property law prevails in Texas, the management and apportionment of property took time. It was Jehu who suggested that Romeo Hinojosa represent me. Jehu then said it would be better if he didn't call on me until after the divorce. He then explained this to the kids: clearly, simply, no embellishment. Well, Mr. Hinojosa made an excellent case for me and the kids, although I must say that Ira behaved like a pig in this. Kept bringing up the fact, his lawyer did, that Jehu had called on me. Poor Ira! He still doesn't understand a thing.

That's been two years now, and the trouble with Ira is that he can't see beyond tomorrow. The kids are growing up, and they may wind up not loving Ira because of Ira's behavior. Jehu, now, he will not allow the baby, Sarah, or Charlie either, for that matter, he won't allow them to speak disrespectfully about Ira. Jehu says that isn't done. He, too, never says a word against Ira, and so, the kids follow his example: no criticism.

Don't mistake what I say, though. Jehu knows Ira for the fool he is. And he knows that Noddy controls Ira, who doesn't know the first word about banking or little else. Jehu says Noddy knows this, and since Ira likes the easy way out of things, Noddy keeps him under wraps.

As for Noddy, he can throw both Jehu and Ira out of the banking business and into the streets any time he wants to. It's his bank. But Jehu doesn't care, and poor Ira does care. That's the difference.

And this is my new life, and it's the best one I could have chosen. There's no set routine to our lives . . . As I said earlier, Jehu comes home at noon, on a Wednesday, say, he'll call the bank and say he won't be back that afternoon. He'll drive to Klail Mid-School, sign out for the kids, and if I've got nothing pressing at the moment, we'll drive out to El Carmen Ranch and visit a while.

That's Jehu, impromptu. It's the same with the few parties we give at home. A few people we know, mostly family.

For Jehu it's always the family. Me. The children, that's the first family. And then the other family, Rafe, who's more than just a cousin. They're like kids, they call each other on the phone.

And speaking of Rafe, Jehu wanted to postpone the wedding, and I was for it. Rafe was recuperating from his eye trouble again, but Rafe wouldn't hear of it. Got me on the phone, "*No lo dejes,*"[1] is what he said.

People who don't know Rafe think he's reserved; that's the word I always hear. He's quiet, sure, and he's certainly that way in public. He's funny, though. Like Jehu, he laughs, he can tell a joke . . .

To me, Jehu is the reserved one. And patient? I think that's why the kids also love him. He's incredibly patient . . . and you know, it takes a good business head and sense to be patient. I learned that on my own.

I won't talk about my work or what I do at Barragán Enterprises. It's boring to talk about it, but it's something else to live it. It's my professional life; that's all there is to that.

Viola? I was wrong about her as I was wrong about many things. She loves me as if I were her own daughter, had she had one . . . I learned the business by watching her, by being there . . . and I remember my first important lesson in business: *Yes* means *yes,* and *no* means *no.* Negotiations are always preliminaries, but the yeas and nays are the finalities . . .

---

[1] Don't let him

I talked to few people about what I wanted to do . . . I talked to Mrs. Campoy, a hundred if she's a year, and bright and lucid . . . I also talked to Viola. Before I talked to Mama. See? And Viola? She cried. But do you see? We're talking about a fearless woman here. And she was the first to see what was in me, before I could even see for myself. Saw it before Jehu, too.

And that's it. I'm not a woman who was saved, redeemed. I saved myself. With help, of course. With love and good will, too, and all the rest. But if I couldn't save myself, if I couldn't save me from myself . . . But why go on?

Let's say I saved myself, and let it go at that.

Yes, the listener will also let it go at that.

Discussion Questions

1. Describe the relationship between Becky and her former husband.
2. How does Becky shatter the stereotypical attitudes about women in general, as well as about Latina women?
3. What similarities do you find between Becky and the speaker in Sandra Maria Esteves's poem "A La Mujer Borrinqueña" on page 437.

Roberta Fernandez

Originally from Laredo, Texas, Roberta Fernandez received a B.A. and an M.A. from the University of Texas, Austin, and a Ph.D. in Romance Languages and Literatures from the University of California, Berkeley, in 1990. She currently teaches at the University of Georgia in the Department of Romance Languages and Literatures and the Women's Studies Program.

She is the editor of an anthology of Latina writing: In Other Words: Literature by Latinas of the United States *(1994), and her work has appeared in many national and international literary reviews and anthologies. She has played an active role in the fine arts as well as literature, working at The Mexican Museum in San Francisco and later serving as curator of "Twenty-Five years of Hispanic Literature of the United States, 1965–1990," an exhibit presently being supported by the Texas Humanities Resource Center. Currently, she is preparing a book based on her doctoral dissertation on the life of Jose Mariátegui, and how his work affected the national identity and culture of Peru.*

Intaglio: A Novel in Six Stories *(1990), was chosen by the Multicultural Publishers Exchange as Best Fiction of 1991. It is a coming-of-age novel which sketches the lives of six different women along the Texas-Mexico border. "Esmeralda" is the fifth story in the sequence and its title is somewhat deceiving as the character is actually named Verónica. The reason for her nickname, as well as its possible symbolic significance, is developed throughout the story.*

From Intaglio: A Novel in Six Stories

Esmeralda

Esmeralda was the name they gave her, and for a long time no one seemed to care who she really might be. She had become a public figure of sorts, sitting for hours each day inside her rounded glass house. The crowds who routinely exchanged their coins for a new encounter with fantasy presumed she would be flattered by the exoticism they projected on her. Santiago Flores had been the first to refer to her as "*Esmeralda.*" In his daily flamboyant chronicle of local customs he had called attention to the "green-eyed beauty who greets the public at the Palace between one and six." For three days in a row he made reference to her, each time more exaggerated than before. "A beautiful jewel on display, one befitting the Museo de Oro which I had the pleasure of visiting on my recent trip to Bogotá." Finally, he had called her "*Una esmeralda brillante.[1] ¡Esmeralda!*" No name becomes her more." From then on, the public assumed a flattery that was more self-indulgent than well-intentioned towards the silent, bewildered young woman inside the glass enclosure. Throughout all the commotion she did not speak to anyone unless she was first persuaded that her reticence was a form of rudeness, a trait she tried to avoid at all cost.

II

When Verónica first started to work at the Palace Theater, before Santiago Flores had created the furor about her, she had walked home by herself in the early evening. Then the situation changed, and Amanda and Leonor had wondered if I would pass by the box office after my dancing class so that Verónica could be accompanied on her way home. After that, it was assumed I would meet her at the theater every evening promptly at six.

Verónica was five years older than I was; but, of the two, I had always moved about with more freedom. So, I was surprised she had gotten a job that required such direct contact with a large public. She surprised me further by explaining that the job had been her mother's idea. Since she was taking only morning classes to complete the credits she needed to graduate, her mother had suggested that she now get a full-time job in the afternoon. On the first day she looked for work, she was immediately hired at the theater.

In a sense, Verónica had always been working. Six years before, she had been brought to Leonor's house in a rather mysterious manner. At that time, the twelve-year-old girl had appeared unannounced at the door, accompanied by Isela—her mother—and her grandmother, Cristina Luna. I was sent home as soon as they

---

[1] A brilliant emerald

arrived, but from across the street I had watched as the driver of the pick-up truck brought in several suitcases. Soon after, he drove off. I waited a while, then was about to head on home when the truck pulled up again. This time Amanda stepped out and hurried inside. The next day I found out that after Cristina and Isela had consulted for a few hours with the other two Luna women, Verónica had been left behind. From then on she stayed with Leonor and Hugo, and each day after school she helped Amanda with her work.

From the beginning I sensed that Amanda made a special effort to insure I was never alone with her grand-niece. Several times after Verónica arrived, I also noticed that my mother and my aunt Zulema would cut off their conversation whenever any of us children were within hearing distance. So, even though I did not know anything about the new girl's background, I surmised there was something different about her and I withheld all my questions.

Verónica was soon under the tutelage of Amanda and Leonor. Amanda taught her to embroider with beads and in no time, Verónica assisted her aunt with most of her creations. Leonor too spent many hours teaching Verónica about the herbs and flowers in her garden and although the young visitor was not given to conversation she seemed to take in everything the aunts taught her. A little older than the rest of the children in the neighborhood, she was not paired off with anyone and spent most of her time alone, silently beading glass beads and sequins onto Amanda's garments.

Often Amanda's customers remarked on Verónica's beauty. "*Cara de ángel*[2] with a personality to match," was how several of them described her. I did not disagree with their evaluation; still, I wondered if her desire to remain unobtrusive played a role in how they viewed her. Why, I wondered, did she feel she had to be so obliging? What most perplexed me during all those years of observation was that she never ever went home. Even more intriguing was the fact that she did not seem to have the slightest interest in going back to Alfredo's ranch where she had lived for so many years.

III

"*Verde, que te quiero verde*!"[3] Orión recited in an insinuating tone, the minute Verónica and I got back from the theater.

"Orión, quit that," Leonor told him.

At the same time Verónica murmured, "Orión, that's mean. You have no idea how humiliated I am by what's happened."

"Come on," Orión insisted. "Secretly you're enjoying all the attention. You just don't want to admit it. This afternoon I passed by the theater and watched you for a while. These two guys—the Mondragones—were trying to get a smile out of you. But you were so high and mighty. Completely poker-faced. Come on, Ronnie, loosen

---

[2] face of an angel   [3] Green, I want you green. A provocative remark referring to her eyes.

up a bit. They just thought you were pretty and wanted to catch your eye. It was their way of complimenting you."

Verónica stiffened immediately. "I know who you mean and they don't strike me as harmless." Then she began to cry, softly at first, then uncontrollably.

"Ronnie, don't exaggerate. Why are you crying?" Orión asked in disbelief.

"Orión, I've already told you to hush up. Please leave the room immediately. I want to talk with Verónica in private."

As Orión was swaggering out of the room, I started to go with him but Leonor called me back. "No, Nenita, you don't have to leave. The three of us are going to have a long discussion."

I looked at Leonor rather doubtfully but she signaled for me to sit next to her. She then wove her fingers through mine and embraced Verónica with her other arm. I waited for someone to say something, then gave Verónica an uncertain sideways glance. Relieved, I saw that she had gotten hold of herself and I concentrated my attention on Leonor's face.

"Nenita, even though you're only thirteen, you're really much older than your years. You've been surrounded by people who have shared their affection with you in many ways. I know, already you've had some unhappy experiences but you're really a strong girl. In many ways much stronger than my Aurita. In fact, I don't want the two of you to discuss the conversation we are about to have. You and I are finally going to help Verónica take control of an unpleasant situation. You see, for many years we have forced a silence on her. It really weighs on me. After so long I'm ready to assume responsibility for my own remoteness in the matter." Leonor took a deep breath. Then she turned to Verónica.

"Tomorrow you're not going back to work. I'll talk to the manager myself. I'm also going to give Santiago Flores a piece of my mind. *Lo siento,*[4] Verónica. We should have made you quit your job as soon as the very first statement appeared in the paper. Like Orión just said, these men think they are doing women a favor by showering them with so-called compliments. *Piropos.* They think we should be grateful for the attention they give us whether we want it or not. It's really self-indulgence on their part."

She squeezed my hand. "Nenita, when Verónica was about your age, she had a problem. Something happened at Iris's and Alfredo's ranch where Verónica and her mother had been living for eight years."

Leonor paused. Then she looked at Verónica. "Let's see. Your father died in France in 1943. You were only five then. That's when you and your mother went to live at the ranch with Iris and Alfredo. Why don't you tell us what happened five years ago at the ranch? I've only heard other people's version of things. My sister Cristina has told me about it. Your mother, of course, always stuck up for you. So did Iris. That's why she sent her four children to live with Hugo and me shortly after you came." For a long time no one said anything. Then, Verónica inhaled deeply.

"His name was Omar," she began.

I looked at her as her eyes filled with tears once again.

---

[4] I'm sorry

"*Se llamaba Omar,*"[5] she repeated and looked straight out, trying to give shape to images she must have been struggling to forget in her recent past.

"He was from Sabinas Hidalgo, and he was only seventeen at the time. Slender. Like cinnamon tea with lemon and sugar. Sweet, very sweet. I didn't notice him at first but he made me take notice of him. Every night he would leave a present outside my window sill. The first time, he left something wrapped in newspaper. I opened it up and found a fresh prickly pear. The following morning I found another one, neatly sliced. It was ripe and sweet. That afternoon I was sitting on the porch. He came towards me. I didn't know who he was but then he extended his open hand, offering me half an orange and a slice of prickly pear. I smiled at him and accepted his gift. Then he disappeared without a word. The next morning I found a scarlet flower of the *ocotillo*[6] on my sill. Then, a nocturnal blossom of the tall *saguaro.*[7] Every night for two weeks he left a cactus flower.

"One morning I saw him heading to town with some of the other workers. I waited by the road for their return. Finally I saw the truck coming back. I pretended I was out for a stroll and waved as the truck passed by. Then, I turned back towards the gate. As I had hoped, he was standing there, waiting for me. I told him I also had a present for him, then I took off my locket and gave it to him. He opened it up, looked at the tiny picture inside, then read my name inscribed in the back of the locket. 'Ve-ró-ni-ca,' he said, almost to himself.

"Every night after that, I waited up for him by the window. He continued bringing me his usual presents and we would talk for about an hour, then he'd be on his way. One time I asked him to join me on the porch at dusk. He did, but Iris passed by and made him go away. 'You shouldn't be so friendly with the workers,' she said. Then she added, 'Besides, you're too young. People will start to talk.'

"From then on I wanted to be with Omar all the time. But we couldn't figure out where we could meet during the day without being seen. Then, one night as we were talking through the screen, I suggested that on the following night we wait until everyone was asleep and then meet on the porch. If we were very quiet no one would hear us.

"The next night we carried out our plan. Omar brought me another lovely cactus flower and we sat under the stars, smelling the pink jasmine, continuing to tell each other our life stories. We talked for a long time. Then I said I'd better go in. He put his arm around me and kissed me, softly, on my lips."

Verónica paused, then went on.

"I never found out where Alfredo came from that night nor how long he had been watching us. We had not heard him at all. But suddenly he was yanking at us, screaming obsenities. '*En mi casa no tolero puterías,*'[8] he yelled at me. Then he slapped Omar over and over and threw him off the porch. By then all the lights in the house had gone on. There was a lot of confusion and all I remember is my mother taking me to her room. Alfredo was right behind us. 'If she's going to act that way with my workers, why should I wait my turn? Get your *huila*[9]-daughter out

---

[5] His name was Omar   [6] a tall spinney cactus plant topped with vibrant red blooms   [7] a large cactus that can grow to enormous heights and can live for a hundred years   [8] I won't stand for indecencies in my house   [9] derogatory slang term for promiscuous woman

of my house at once or from now on I'll take her anytime I want,' he shouted at my mother.

"*Pobre mama.*[10] She slammed the door behind us, then tried to calm me down. It was about midnight but she called Mamá Cristina who sent someone to pick us up. We packed quickly. By the time the car arrived we were ready. I was terrified for Omar and wanted to see what had happened to him, but mother shoved me into the car ahead of her. Only when we were on our way out of the ranch did she begin to scold me. I was not trustworthy she kept saying. She'd have to figure out what to do with me. Now she'd have to get a job and think about where we were going to live. Mamá Cristina did not have room for two more people."

"You know the rest," she turned to Leonor. Mamá Cristina thought you might be able to keep me for a while."

"What happened to Omar?" I asked.

"I'm not sure. I never saw him again," Verónica replied. "I think Alfredo had him killed. Mother said Iris was unable to give her any definite information."

"Look, Verónica," Leonor said very seriously. "Alfredo may be given to bouts of violence but he'd never have anyone killed. I understand he called the *migra*[11] and had Omar deported. He also threatened him with loss of his masculinity if he ever got in touch with you."

"How come Alfredo interfered in Verónica's life?" I asked. "She wasn't doing anything wrong."

Leonor sighed. "That's just the way it is," was all she said. A moment later she added, "My poor Iris." She refuses to leave Alfredo. At least she had the good sense to get the children out of the house."

"You got the five of us because of him."

"I have no complaints as far as that goes." Leonor touched Verónica's cheek to reassure her.

"It's nice of you to say that, Leonor. It makes me feel better. As a matter of fact, I think I won't quit my job. I'm really being a big baby reacting to harmless comments like I have. Please don't call Santiago Flores either. I'll be able to handle things from now on."

"Are you sure?"

"Positive."

IV

The mystery around Verónica was gone. For the first time since I had met her I felt I no longer needed to be on my guard as we chatted on our way home together. Instead, I thought about the shame she must have felt, being exposed the way she had been, dragged from house to house. And for no reason at all. I was particularly preoccupied with the way she had lost Omar.

---

[10] Poor mother   [11] The Immigration Service

"Do you ever think about him?"

"All the time. But I'll never see him again. He was so different from Orión's and Orso's friends. They're always showing off, trying to outdo each other in everything. Omar was a gentle, giving person. It hurt me so much every time I thought about the way Alfredo hit him. Even now it hurts me. Some day I hope to meet someone else like him. But who knows what will happen?"

"It sounds like you're never going to be rid of him. Filomena says Martín will always be with her. She says if you lose the person you love when you're still in love, you never get rid of him. That's kind of nice, isn't it? Your mother probably feels the same way about your father."

"Probably. I've never thought about it before."

Verónica got very quiet. Then she looked at me. "I wonder what happens to a person like Iris. Why does she stay with Alfredo? She couldn't possibly love him anymore. I have the impression he hits her too."

"Aura says he does. She hates her father. He got violent with each one of the kids. My father's not like that. He's very good with me. I love him a lot."

"You're lucky. I barely remember my father. After he died, I used to pretend my teddy bear was my father. I always made him promise to watch over me. After the incident with Alfredo I realized I didn't have anyone to protect me. In the long run that was probably as bad as losing Omar, for it made me feel very vulnerable."

"So we'll all have to take care of you." I looked up and smiled at her. Then, I got very solemn. "But you have to protect yourself too. Especially if you feel as vulnerable as you say you do."

V

Violeta Aguilera had kept us rehearsing much later than usual. So when we were finally finished I did not even attempt to change out of my leotard but simply slipped on my pants and ran.

When I finally got to the ticket booth the person on the evening shift told me Verónica had already headed on home. "She'll probably be very glad to see you. Hurry," the woman said. "Hurry."

I followed our usual path. When I turned the third corner I spotted Verónica about two blocks ahead. I ran up one block, then noticed that a white Chevy with big wings was inching along behind her. As I got closer I heard the two guys in the car catcalling her, "¡*Esmeralda! ¡Esmeralda*!" Verónica was pretending not to pay attention. I ran faster and got to her side as the two were getting out of the car.

"It's the same idiots Orión mentioned the other day," she whispered. "I told him they weren't harmless."

"Well, come on. Let's get out of here," I said just as one of the guys grabbed her and started to drag her to the car. I hit him with my duffle bag and heard the cracking of the castanets against his ear. The other guy reached out for me but my dancer's foot hit him exactly at the spot where I had aimed at. He bent over, mumbling, "*Hijole*."[12] By then the first creep had pushed Verónica into the car. It was obvious they weren't concerned with me. The second one got in the car and they took off.

The street was deserted. I decided I was close enough to Leonor's to run there for help. When I burst in through the door I found Orso and Orión in the living-room. "They took her. They took her," I said as I tried to catch my breath.

"What are you talking about?"

"Those guys you said you watched at the theater the other afternoon. Remember you told Verónica they were just trying to give her a compliment. Those guys." I pleaded with Orión. "They dragged her into a brand new white Chevy and zoomed off with her."

"*Los Mondragón*. Come on, Orso. Let's go get them."

As the twins took off, I started to pick up the phone.

"What are you doing?"

I turned and saw Leonor and Hugo. They had been in the dining room all the time.

"I'm going to report a kidnapping to the police."

"No," Hugo said. "The police won't do anything. Let the boys take care of business."

VI

The next day Santiago Flores's column contained the following cryptic statement: "Last night one of my favorite jewels was stolen, then shattered. The perpetrators of the crime were brought to justice but the damage they have committed will be long-lasting. I am sorry for any negligence on my part which may have contributed to what so unexpectedly happened."

VII

For the next several weeks everyone took care of Verónica. Leonor meandered through her herbal patch, carefully selecting sprigs of different properties to prepare into teas and ointments. Blending either *yerba del oso* or *maravilla*[13] with baby oil, she'd pass the ointment on to Isela who would rub it for hours into her daughter's skin, inducing her to sleep profoundly for long stretches of time. After Verónica woke up, Cristina would soak her in hot minted baths, mixed with either *romerillo* or *pegapega*.[14] Amanda insisted on stating simply that "Verónica had experienced a great fright." To alleviate her from its effects, she ran palm leaves up and down Verónica's entire body, then burned creosote in clay urns next to her bed.

---

[12] a common expression. It can be used to signal bewilderment or pain, as it is here.   [13-14] all medicinal herbs used in home remedies by *curanderas,* or spiritual healers.

One Sunday morning I stopped by to see Leonor. As we talked, she prepared a pot of steaming chamomile tea and invited me to take it to Verónica. "Here are two cups. One for you and one for her. You can visit with her for a little while. I think it'll do her good to see you. All this time she's only been seeing us old ladies. Three weeks ago she was in a daze but all the massages and affection we've given her have paid off. She needs to start living again. In fact, Hugo thinks we should have a small dinner party soon. He's going to invite one or two of his colleagues from the college. It'll only be us, and Aura and Marina. You know the boys have gone to stay at the ranch for a while. You are most welcome to join us. *Ándale.* Go in there and perk her up a bit. *Anímala.*"

VIII

Verónica was sitting on a rocking chair looking out the window, her long dark hair and tawny skin glistening with the sunlight. I was surprised she looked as well as she did and told her so.

"Ay, Nenita. Every day Mamá and Leonor, and Mamá Cristina and Amanda have scrubbed me up and down. They've wrung me out, smoked me through, sprayed me from head to toe with so many different perfumes and ointments that I feel like Cleopatra or Bathsheba. All day long they've all forced me to concentrate on the moment. On the present. In the beginning they made me tell them in detail what happened that night, first to one, then to the other. I cried and cried with each telling. And they cried with me. In fact, one afternoon Leonor said we were all going to cry together for the sorrows of all the women in the family. A wailing session she called it *Lloronas, todas.*[15] She went first and talked about Iris, her favorite child. She said there was nothing she could do to help Iris out except care for her children. Since all of us had experienced a run-in with Alfredo at one time or another we all could empathize with Iris. Later we prayed for her to face up to her situation and to do something about it.

"Then Mamá Cristina spoke. Everyone else seemed to be aware of her affair but for me all this was a revelation. Apparently a lot of people know her 'secret', but it's better if you don't mention this to anyone. It seems she was never married and my mother was born out of wedlock. She would only refer to the man she loved—my grandfather I guess—as Victor X. She said she was engaged to him, then he went away to fight in the war. She wouldn't tell me which war—the Revolution or the First World War. At any rate Victor X did come back the year before my mother was born. Mamá Cristina claims she was madly in love with him and had her first real passionate experience with him. He didn't bother to inform her he had gotten married to someone else until she told him she was pregnant. Later, when her condition was becoming obvious, her brothers sent her to one of the aunts in another city. For many years, though, she continued seeing Victor X. Then one day he took his other family up north and Mamá Cristina never heard from him again. When she came back, my

---

[15] All criers.

mother was already six and Mamá Cristina did not try to explain her to anyone. The Luna brothers took care of the two for years and years. In fact, they are still supporting my grandmother.

"Mamá Cristina said she had no regrets for herself and she did not want any sympathy from us. But she did want us to lament for my mother. 'Isela,' she said, 'a child orphaned from a father who had not yet reached the Stygian shore.'

"My mother took her turn next. She started by emphasizing that wars are usually waged by men for dominance over other men. But their innocent victims turn out to be women and children. More specifically, she asked us to recall how one particular war, the Second World War, had left its mark on her, robbing her of a husband, a lover, a friend. Making her a widow and the mother of another fatherless child."

Verónica finally paused. "You know," she said, "I hadn't realized my mother felt as fragile and confused as she seemed to be that afternoon. It made me think I should help her somehow. But it also made me realize I don't ever want to get like her. Hearing her gave me the courage to take control of my own situation. So, when my turn came, I spoke in the name of all the women and girls who had experienced a sexual violation on the same day I did. On my own behalf, though, I insisted that the wailing stop. 'I do not want to become a victim,' I said and the others cried for me with relief. 'In the end, that is how we hoped you would feel,' Leonor said to me.

"Mamá Cristina raised her hands in triumph, saying we needed to switch moods altogether. It was time to describe sheer happiness, she said, 'even *picardía*,[16] our own or someone else's.'"

"This time she insisted on going first. She told us that a few years after Victor X had abandoned her she had thrown all caution to the wind and had gotten involved with someone else. To this day she considers herself in love with the same person. The confession seemed to take my aunts by surprise and they wanted more specific details. But she refused to tell us her lover's name and would only smile mischievously. 'But you never even go out,' Amanda told her. 'The only person, you ever go out with is your *comadre*[17] Celia Ortiz. Do you each have a secret lover somewhere? Oh, no! Don't tell me you're sharing a lover. Are you?' Mamá Cristina laughed so hard we completely forgot the sad mood we had worked so hard to get ourselves into. So then we told the good stories," Verónica paused. "The private ones," she finally said.

"Aren't you going to tell me any of them?" I asked, feeling I had been teased, then cheated of the bait.

"No. I'm not. We promised each other we wouldn't repeat those."

"Well, what was your own story?"

"You've already heard it. The one about Omar. But why am I the only one who gets to tell you both my own story and the stories I heard from the others? It's your turn to say something."

I paused for a moment.

---

[16] mischief   [17] literally, someone who is a godfather or godmother to your children. Often used as a friendly term between close friends.

Finally, I said, "Okay, I'm ready. This one is a salty story. First I have to ask you a few questions though. What's a *foca*?"

"A seal," Verónica replied rather puzzled.

"What's a *foco*?"

"A lightbulb."

"Right! But remember, you've just told me a foca is a seal. Let's just say a foca is a female seal and a foco is a male seal."

Verónica was giving me a dubious look.

"Remember, Verónica, you refused to tell me your good stories." I kept my eyes on her all the time I spoke.

"One morning Mrs. Foca was late to work. She waddled into her office half an hour late, swaying to her desk. All her friends noticed how clumsily she was moving but they pretended not to notice. Finally, when she was on her third cup of coffee her office mate turned to her.

"'What's the matter, Foca? It looks like you didn't get much sleep last night.'

"'That's right, Carmina. I was so tired when I got up this morning.'

"'¡*Caray*! Don't tell me you were working 'till late?'

"'It wasn't that. You're not going to believe me *pero anoche me pasé la noche entera con el Foco prendido*.'"[18]

Verónica burst out laughing as she grabbed a pillow and hit me on the head with it. Then she put her arms around me, squeezing me tightly. "Nenita, it's been a long time since I've laughed like this."

IX

Leonor explained that David Baca was Hugo's only colleague who could come for dinner on Wednesday.

David was new in town. A recent graduate from Houston, he was now associated with the program on international business at the local college. "David is teaching some business courses but his real love is *norteña*[19] music. That's what really brought him here," Hugo said as he introduced the young man to us. "In his spare time he's making the rounds, recording small musical groups on both sides of the border."

"Do you play a musical instrument yourself, David?" Leonor asked as we sat down to eat.

"Just the guitar. I like to sing the old songs and to strum along as I go."

David turned to Verónica. "What about you? Do you like music?"

"All kinds," she said. "But I don't sing or play an instrument."

"Verónica is an artist of a different sort," Leonor quickly chimed in. "Her embroidery is matched only by my sister's. And there's no one who's better at it than my sister Amanda."

"Will you show me some of your work?" David asked.

---

[18] I spent all of last night with the light on. The "salty" story relies on pun to convey its racy message.

[19] music typical of the northern part of Mexico. It usually involves instruments like the accordion.

It was obvious that throughout dinner, with subtle coaching from Hugo and Leonor, David made special efforts to involve Verónica in the conversation. Later, as he was about to leave, he thanked Hugo and Leonor for the invitation. "It's the first time I've had a chance to meet a local family," he said. Then, he added, "I think your niece Verónica is quite lovely."

"Well, David, why don't you ask her to accompany you the next time you go listen to music?" Hugo encouraged him, "I'm sure she'd love to join you. By the way, Flaco Jiménez will be in town tomorrow. Why don't you two take in his concert?"

X

David and Verónica went out every night after that. Since I was busy with school and dancing classes in the afternoons and Verónica was out in the evenings with David, several weeks passed by without our seeing each other. It was not until almost a month later, when Leonor invited me to join the entire family for a *merienda*[20] in the garden that I got to see Verónica. At first I thought she looked quite tired but soon she was all smiles as Leonor said Isela had an announcement to make. The following week, Isela stated, Verónica and David would be getting married in a small, private ceremony; after that, they would be going to Acapulco for a brief honeymoon.

The announcement did not come as a surprise, and everyone managed to look cheerful and to wish the couple well. When I finally got a chance to get close to Verónica, I asked her outright, "How do you feel about all this?"

"I'd like to think I'm happy," she replied.

XI

When the baby was born, Leonor claimed that Verónica had been lucky to have had such a healthy premature baby. "A bouncing six and a quarter-pounder," she told me when I went to see Verónica at the hospital.

"Let's go take a look at her," David suggested as he, Leonor and I headed to the nursery. "See if you can pick her out."

"That might get you into trouble," Leonor advised. Then she pointed to the infant in the third crib. "There she is. Verónica's little Destino."

"Is that going to be her name?" I asked in surprise.

"Verónica wants to name her Destino Dulce," Leonor chuckled.

"She's pretty set on calling her that. A girl named Destiny," David smiled. "I guess I'll just call her my little DeeDee."

He really thinks Destino is his baby, I thought. Suddenly, a strange feeling crept over me as I watched David. I realized then that he was very naive and I wondered what disappointments, if any, lay ahead for all three of them. Looking at the tiny

---

[20] light lunch

baby, I considered whether Verónica had willingly stepped inside an invisible, but nonetheless binding, wall of self delusion.

XII

That night I dreamed I was inside a green glass prison, holding Destino on my lap. Strangers were peering at us, waving bits of paper in their hands, their mouths forming sounds I could not hear. I looked at one face after another impassively, wondering who those people were, amazed that they felt compelled to convey a message, a wish perhaps, to Destino and me. Suddenly a space opened up among the crowd and Verónica was making her way through the path. As she crashed through the glass to get to us, the voice of the crowd rang out in a booming sound, "*¡Esmeralda! ¡Esmeralda!*"

"I'm taking my Destino with me. From now on, she will always be by my side," Verónica whispered as she picked up the baby, then made her way outside again. The crowds pushed against her but one way or another she made her way through them. Once she was out in the open, someone shouted, "She's gone!" And the masses ran after Verónica, trying in vain to catch up with her. "*¡Esmeralda!*" they called. "Don't leave us, *Esmeralda*. What will we do without you?"

Alone at last, inside the glass house, I was fascinated with the walls which slowly began to disintegrate in kaleidoscopic fashion. In place of the green glass, images of flowers and gems flashed past me. Before my eyes, sprigs of dazzling dahlias glided through rubied milk, and saffron-colored sunflowers twirled by on minted teas. I saw clusters of crape myrtle floating on melted jade; and slowly all traces of the glass prison disappeared. I found myself, instead, inside a house made of golden raffia and in the darkness a topaz presence began to glow. Sunbursts of volcanic warmth emanated from its center and all around me, copal and creosote burned in clay urns. Humming softly as nocturnal blossoms of the tall *saguaro* filled the room, I gave myself up to the energy of a powerful essence which began to breathe on me. Suddenly, a winsome face emerged out of the darkness and a cinnamon-colored stranger smiled at me as he offered me half an orange and a handful of freshly-cut cactus fruits. I smiled back, reaching out for his gifts.

Discussion Questions

1. Verónica is nicknamed Esmeralda because of her green eyes. What other connection do you see between that name and her character?

2. What is the significance of the baby's name in relation to the conclusion of the story?

3. Leonor's response to the narrator's question about Alfredo's behavior on page 65 is "That's just the way it is." Explain the significance of that statement.

4. Despite her trouble, at the conclusion of the story, Esmeralda embraces life. Compare that conclusion to the one in Helena Maria Viramontes's *Under the Feet of Jesus* on page 79.

5. In what ways are women treated by men in this story that are similar to those relationships in Dolores Prida's *Beautiful Señoritas* on page 268.

Helena María Viramontes

HELENA MARÍA VIRAMONTES was born in East Los Angeles in 1954. She received a B.A. from Immaculate Heart College and an M.A. from the University of California at Irvine. She currently teaches at Cornell University. She has received various awards for her short stories and has co-edited two collections of critical essays with Maria Herrera-Sobek.

Viramontes's collection of short stories The Moths and Other Stories *(1985) is a series of vignettes set mostly in the author's native Los Angeles. The various characters are confronted with discrimination and oppression and the tone is serious and often didactic. The stories are an avenue for social commentary on a male-dominated society and the ramifications of such dominance.*

The selection offered here is an excerpt from the conclusion of her novel Under the Feet of Jesus *(1995). This highly acclaimed work is narrated by a young female migrant worker, Estrella. By this point in the novel Estrella has defied the authority of the oppressive agricultural system by threatening a nurse whose lack of compassion for the plight of the workers is evident.*

From Under the Feet of Jesus

The children stood in the shade of the barn, a cathedral of a building. The twins' laughter curdled into whispers. The one twin, Perla, became frightened and scratched the divide where her two braids parted. The other twin, who went by Cookie though her name was Cuca, closed an eye and her gaze followed the slanted, splintery wood sheeting until she was staring at the glaring sky. Only Estrella studied the door with its flaked white paint, holding fast to keep the torn hem of her dress from fanning up with the wind.

Perla stopped scratching. She waited to see what her eldest sister would do.

—I'll tell Mama, Cookie dared.

Estrella offered her head first. The scent of dung and damp hay lingered thick and the motes of dust swirled. The barn seemed so strangely vacant; the absence clung heavy and the wind whistled between the planks. She noticed a chain suspended from the ceiling. Thick-linked, long and rusty, it swayed like a pendulum, as if someone had just touched it and ran off.

The barn door suddenly swung loose, squeaking worse than the brakes on Perfecto's wagon. The screech of the rusted hinge flushed out the owls and swallows roosting in the gable, a riot of feathers and fluttering that startled the twins. It happened so quickly. The swallows and owls shrieking in a burst of furious flight, feathers snowing down, the girls screaming.

Perfecto kicked at some pebbles with the toe of his shoe. The maggots appeared and he hadn't the energy to lift his boot and kill them. Think clearly. Remember, the nurse was not hurt, not really. Remember, they had taken only what belonged to them. If, in fact, she had called the authorities, they would've been hauled off to the police station by now. Of course. Of course.

He looked upon the moon's roundness like a quarter, bright as a new dime. Perhaps it wasn't as bad as it seemed. Perhaps the nurse simply reapplied her blood-red lipstick, then drove off just in time to pick up her sons and her sons were probably asleep in their beds right now. Perhaps the nurse was stirring cream into her de-caffeinated coffee, the spoon clinking on the cup while her husband watched the late night news. "You won't believe what happened to me today . . . ," she would probably say to him while he lay on the couch, because that is how Perfecto imagined people who had couches and living rooms and television sets and who drank coffee even at night.

Perfecto wanted to load up his tools, a few blankets, some peaches. He couldn't tell whether it was love or simply fear that held him back. His arms folded tighter across his chest, and he dug his hands deeper into his armpits so that they wouldn't move without his permission, so that they wouldn't begin to pack even before his decision was final. He could not wait for the barn and the money and tomorrow. If he left right this minute, without even turning back, pulled the arrow of pain from his belly, he would have a second chance. With four dollars to his name, a chestful of tools, some gasoline, and this old station wagon with a battery ready to die, he couldn't afford time.

Think. Think. Think, Perfecto, you *cabeza de burro chingado*[1]. The car had cooled and no longer warmed his back and he felt his skin goosebump. He had quit smoking in another life, when his hair was full and black and his children looked upon him as a man who could fix the axles of the world if he wanted to. He looked down at the loose swaying maggots. Perfecto was glad to have given up tobacco. He would have foolishly spent the last few dollars on a package of cigarettes, his desire was such, so overwhelming.

The planks of the floor creaked as they entered bearing the weight of children. The groan of their limp bodies, the comfort of sleeping in a reclining position, dusty blankets under their chins, muddied shoes slipped off their feet. Ricky's ankle red from not having worn socks, Cookie's toenails needed clipping. The buzz of children safely sleeping.

How long would it be before they came to arouse the children? Unleash the dogs? The authorities would come as they did for years, and pull their hearts inside out like empty pockets. How long? Throughout the car ride back to the bungalow, she had asked herself why hadn't she tried to stop Estrella or why hadn't she let Perfecto stop her. It simply came down to this: there was no stopping Estrella, no harnessing the climate of circumstances, no holding back the will of her body. How many times had her own mother warned her, pleaded with her not to get involved with a man like Estrella's real father?

Petra saw Perfecto slamming each car door. One. She stepped down the porch when she saw the stick leaning against the cooking pit and she clasped it like a

---

[1] a foolish person

weapon. She could barely see Estrella's tracings on the ground. Two. In several places, the circle had opened; trampled footsteps had left gaps. All the warnings in the world could not stop her. Three. The scorpions were known to be methodical predators and she scratched the ring with urgency until the ring was at least two inches deep in the soil. Four. When she first became pregnant with Estrella, her own mother blessed her with a kiss on her forehead, then slammed the door shut so final, it never opened again.

Perfecto's back was to her. He leaned on the hood of the car and she wanted to see his eyes. Trust me, she remembered Perfecto saying, but the only trust she had now was in Jesucristo. She palmed her coal black hair back. As she walked up the porch stairs, she let the stick slip from her fingers and fall to the ground. She would make an offering.

Petra had felt eyes all over her. The knot of eyes on the paneled wall glared at her as she slipped the shoes off her children. Then it was the tigereye stones of Jesucristo's eyes which followed her as she kneeled before the statue and lit each candle with a matchbook she kept near its base. The statue, draped in blue robes and crushing a green serpent with bare feet, stood on the elevated middle crate of the Holy Trinity. His removable hands were held out to display the red wounds of crucifixion and the two eyes, surrounded by the half moon of seven candles, gazed through the flames at her. The smoke rose and blackened the ceiling above her candles. Someone sneezed behind the day-blue sheet.

It was no use. She straightened the doily scarf bumpy from the envelope beneath it. The doily had been crocheted by Petra's grandmother and given to her as a gift. The doily was so special, Petra rested Jesucristo on it. She followed the diamond pattern of knotted thread with the tips of her fingers as if caressing a child's face, a jawbone and chin, as if she touched the doily for comfort.

They had whispered among them, las mujeres de la familia, about grandmother and how much of a nervous viejita she was. A curious little sparrow of a woman, with sharp jittery eyes that cut ice. The only thing which calmed her nerves was to sit by the lantern and crochet. When Petra's father was sick, tomorrow came and went and came and went until her father died and tomorrow still came and went and grandmother had crocheted perfect little diamonds, through it all. What thoughts had gone through her grandmother's mind as she crocheted, what threads looped and knotted and disguised themselves as prayers? And what had Petra learned from the trembling fingers which pulled a fine thread into the hook of the crocheting needle with such patience that the stitching was as intricate and as weather resistant as a spider's web? If only Petra was capable of crocheting, if only she could feel the threads slip in and out of her fingers like her grandmother once did, she wouldn't feel as if her own prayers turned into soot above her.

Under the doily lay the documents in the manilla envelope. She slipped the envelope out gingerly and poured out the contents onto her palm. Black ink feet on the birth certificates, five perfect circular toes on each foot, a topography print of her children recorded, dated, legal, *for future use to establish age to enter school, when applying for working papers, establish legal age for rights of franchise, for jury or military service, to prove citizenship, to obtain passports, to prove right to inheritance of property.*

Certificado de Bautismos[2]—five of them; a torn and mended Social Security card; Identification card—NOT A LICENSE—She had walked fourteen blocks to get to the DMV, and her picture looked flat and dull and pale as concrete, but the ID was a great relief. Petra often feared that she would die and no one would know who she was. "Remembrance of First Holy Communion" certificate (where was Ricky's—had she lost it?); a thick certificate award given to Estrella for an essay she wrote titled *My Blue Fat Cat*; "Authorization and Certificate of Confidential Marriage"—Personal Data of Husband: He tired quickly. Personal Data of Wife: She was four months pregnant and wanted to change the date, but the man behind the counter said not to worry, he would change it on the record. Married in the town of Santa Ana, county of Orange, state of California. They had to transfer buses twice. They got there five minutes before the office closed, and he held the door open while she went to the bathroom. All the warnings in the world could not stop her.

Petra folded the creases of the documents with the same care she folded a Phillips 66 map, and slipped the papers back into the envelope and placed it back on the altar. She raised herself but couldn't stand without struggling to brace her legs and so she leaned on the crate to support her weight, and the statue of Jesucristo wavered. Her reflexes were no longer fast enough to catch a falling statue; she could almost see the head splitting away from the body before it even hit the wood planks of the floor. The head of Jesucristo broke from His neck and when His eyes stared up at her like pools of dark ominous water, she felt a wave of anger swelling against her chest.

—You okay, Mama? Estrella whispered from the other side of the sheet.

—Go to sleep, she responded curtly.

Petra lifted the head and body of Jesucristo, from chips of white plaster on the ground. She was surprised by the lightness of the head, like a walnut in the palm of her hand, and nervously fumbled it upon the neck of the body. Unsuccessful, she replaced the headless statue on the long tread of crocheted doily, crossed herself and kissed Jesucristo's feet. She held onto the head.

Petra licked two fingers and sizzled out the wicks of each candle. She would have liked to keep the vigil burning but was afraid for her children. If one of the candles fell, the blankets would catch, as hungry as fire was, and her children would be incinerated like blazing piñon trees.

She walked to the porch and saw Perfecto leaning against the wagon with his arms folded. As usual, he had his back to her, and he looked into the distance, where the road intersected with the trees. She stared up at the cluster of clouds inching across the moon. The leaves of the top branches had the sheen of polished armor. If only she could crochet a row of diamonds to help her get through to tomorrow. She stared out into the beyond of the moonlight, where the darkness hung like a black sheet. The lima bean in her stomach felt like mesquite burning.

She glanced at the stick cast near the ground scrub. Was it too late to protect the children from the scorpions? Had they already entered the bungalow? Once a weapon, the stick now looked slight and feeble. How could she possibly think to protect her children if such a little clawing insect could inspire a whole midnight of fear? What made her believe that a circle drawn in the earth would keep the predators

---

[2] Certificates of Baptism

away? That was all she had: papers and sticks and broken faith and Perfecto, and at this moment all of this seemed as weightless against the massive darkness, as the head she held.

Petra's grasp tightened around the head of Jesucristo. Perfecto stood as quiet as the clouds drifting and she wanted to go see his eyes. If anyone could fix it, Perfecto could.

The smoke of the burning candles made Estrella sneeze and she forced open the window of the bungalow. With all her strength she loosened the swollen pane and the wood scraped against the pulley and she was able to sneak her fingers under and pry it open. The nocturnal air was brisk and welcome after the smothering mesquite-like incense of the room and she inhaled deeply. Not far from the cooking pit, from the unpaved road, she saw Perfecto hide his face with his hands, and his shoulders trembled as if he were crying.

In the hospital room where the vinyl couches were worn and darkened with the weight of people's hours, Alejo's lower lip had trembled and his eyes began to well and his tears caught her by surprise. *Please,* he begged. *Just stay with me for a while.* He was frightened beyond her capacity to comfort him. But the car ran outside, the white fumes rising from the exhaust pipe and the precious gasoline burned and her family waited, and he was where he should be. *Alejo,* she said sternly, *everything's gonna turn out all right. Just tell the doctors,* she said in a voice filled with a combination of tenderness and irritation. She believed it. He would be healed and return to work. It only now occurred to her that perhaps she would never see him alive again, that perhaps he would die.

She felt filthy, the coils of her neck etched with dirt and sweat. Estrella took off the muddied dress as if she wanted to discard the whole day like dirty laundry. Her muscles strained with every body movement and when she had reached for the hem of her dress or pulled her arms out of the sleeves of her muslin undershirt, she felt as if her body had been beaten into a pulp of ligaments and cartilage. She threw the dress in the corner of the room where the children were taught to put their clothes. In the distance, a dog barked then howled. There was a crate in the corner where she had placed her work trousers and she slowly slipped one foot then the other in to the pants. The candlelights glimmered a garland of light rays on the sheet which seemed as thin and as transparent as the ears of a desert jackrabbit.

Something shattered on the other side of the sheet, a thud no louder than her own shoe when she pounded it softly on the floor to make sure a spider had not crawled into it.

—You okay, Mama? she asked, opening up her laces and slipping one foot in. She sat near Rocky's pillow to strap on her shoes, tying the laces in double bows. The mother's voice ordered her to sleep and her silhouette moved to snuff out the candle flames with pinches of her fingers. The sheet went blank.

Estrella zippered her work trousers and buttoned up a clean flannel shirt. She stood and took hold of the lantern, and flipped the corner of the sheet and stepped onto the porch. The mother was already there, staring at Perfecto.

—Where do you think you're going? the mother asked. She held tight to Estrella's wrist. Estrella didn't know and didn't answer.

Then the mother embraced Estrella so firmly, Estrella felt as if the mother was trying to hide her back in her body.

When her eyes became accustomed to the dark and the moonlight paved a worn pathway toward the barn, Estrella knew what to do. The weight of night did not affect her eyesight; her eyes grew like the pupils of a cat to absorb every particle of light.

—Careful with the lantern, the mother yelled to her, The grass is real dry. She cupped her hand around her mouth and called louder to her: It can catch fire! but Estrella did not turn and the mother saw her figure walking unafraid into the darkness, a ball of gold ochre bouncing in the night.

The moon lay flat. Estrella's pace quickened until she realized she was running. She halted abruptly and held up her lantern. A gopher whipped by and disappeared with a rustle into the dry grasses. She could hear the howling of a coyote in the distance, the dogs responding with vicious barks and she continued at a slower pace. The barn loomed before her with its tall shadows and dented weathervane pointing downward. She heard the vane barely squeaking in the whispering breeze, then heard the hinges of the door.

She entered the barn. The inside was dark and dank like the cork of a wine bottle the men passed around on a Saturday night. The light of the lantern wrapped closely around her. At first she was startled by the ticking of the owls' claws above her, then by the sound of fluttering wings and nervous chirping of the swallows. She spoke to her shadow as if she were not alone.

—It's over there, she said and she directed her lantern for a better view of the chain. She tilted her head back. Way above her head, past the loft where some of the birds nested, was a trapdoor to the roof. She could barely see the lines of the moonlight squaring it.

She sat down in the small circle of yellow lantern light and removed her shoes, balled her socks, and tucked them in her shoes as the mother had taught them to do. She was about to turn off the lantern when she realized she had not brought the matchbook with her. She lowered its flame instead, enough to keep the kerosene burning. The blue pilot flame hesitated on its wick, until it wavered reassuringly. Estrella stood up. From her back pocket, she pulled out her bandanna and tied her long hair back with two knots. She spit into her palms, then rubbed her hands against the thighs of her trousers.

—Okay, she said to her other self.

Estrella clasped the chain and hoisted herself up.

There was no turning back now. She pulled her arms to raise her shoulders up until her feet could brace the chain better. The wood above her croaked and cracked slightly from her weight. Bits of splinter wood and dust as fine as ash showered on her and she closed her eyes before it was too late. For a moment the chain swung lightly and chinked against its hook and her grip tightened around the thick links. The taste of soil rolled in her mouth, and a speck watered her eye and she spit. The large thick loops of rust tinkled. The biceps in her arms strained until she was able to wrap her legs around the chain which gave her added support. Her ears hummed.

Her hands were callused and her grip became strong, but her bare feet seemed so vulnerable against the cool, wavering iron. There was no looking down. The coolness tickled her toes. She wrapped the chain between her thighs now and jerked down to raise herself up as if she were tugging on a cord of a bell. She stopped to re-lease one hand and wipe her sweaty palm against her trousers while she hugged tight the chain against her chest with her other. She glanced at the flicks of glow light below, then steered her attention upward to see the door square expanding much larger than she could have imagined it. The intensity of the climb soaked the back of her shirt collar with sweat.

The stench of bird droppings gave the loft a sharp acid smell which cut through the damp hay and alfalfa and dusty nests. The loft was leveled and she tenderly walked across the droppings and fodder which felt almost as brittle and sharp as specks of broken glass hidden under the soft feather down. Her fingers floated in midair and she searched for walls blindly, until she tore into a gossamer cobweb. Something scur-ried near her foot and she kicked it. By the way it sounded, a lopsided roll, it may have been a wine or Coke bottle, which rolled and flipped over the loft and fell straight down. It took some time before it shattered below, and she realized how high she had climbed. She looked down to see the specks of shattered glass just inches away from the lantern, and for a moment she imagined golden flaming eels danger-ously nipping at the straw on the ground. It was so hot up in the loft, her breath struggling against the thin, stale air and she felt her flannel blouse damp and sticky. Her shoes sat near the broken glass with their tongues hanging to the side like dogs panting. She did not stir. Her heart tolled in her chest. She waited for her eyes to be-come accustomed to the dark. Only after the outlines of walls and floors and ceilings surfaced, did she move toward the trapdoor.

Estrella tried pushing, palms up, but the door only moaned, and she heard the birds somewhere in the barn nervously protesting with incessant chirping. She felt around the edge of the square door to make sure there was no bolt to push out of its notch, no hook that had to be slipped out from its eye. She pressed her back like a shovel against the door and pushed up once again. Again and again until whatever resistance there was gave way to her back. She turned and pushed with her hands and the door swung open against the roof and the swallows flew out from under eaves of the cedar shakes like angry words spewing out of a mouth. Estrella stood bathed in a flood of gray light. The light broke through and the cool evening air pierced the stifling heat of the loft.

She was stunned by the diamonds. The sparkle of stars cut the night—almost violently sharp. Estrella braced her fingers over the rim of the door frame, then heaved herself up into the panorama of the skies as if she were climbing out of a box. The birds pumped their wings in the skies furiously like debris whirling in a tornado, and it amazed her that they never once collided with one another. Over the eucalyp-tus and behind the moon, the stars like silver pomegranates glimmered before an in-finity of darkness. No wonder the angels had picked a place like this to exist.

The roof tilted downward and she felt gravity pulling but did not lose her foot-ing. The termite-softened shakes crunched beneath her bare feet like the serpent under the feet of Jesus, and a few pieces tumbled down and over the edge of the barn. No longer did she feel her blouse damp with sweat. No longer did she stumble blindly. She had to trust the soles of her feet, her hands, the shovel of her back, and the pounding bells of her heart. Her feet brushed close to the edge of the roof and it was there that she stopped. A breeze fluttered a few loose strands of hair on her face and nothing had ever seemed as pleasing to her as this. Some of the birds began descending, cautiously at first, then in groups, and finally a few swallows flapped to their nests not far from where she stood. Estrella remained as immobile as an angel standing on the verge of faith. Like the chiming bells of the great cathedrals, she believed her heart powerful enough to summon home all those who strayed.

Discussion Questions

1. Why is it so important for Estrella to return to the barn?
2. What does her return say about her development and maturation. Specifically, what does it say about her identity as a migrant worker?
3. What is the symbolic significance of her name, especially when juxtaposed with her actions at the conclusion of the story?
4. What similarities can you find between the development of Estrella and Esperanza in Sandra Cisneros's story on page 9, and/or Negi in *When I was Puerto Rican* by Esmeralda Santiago on page 392?

Américo Paredes

The literary world lost a great chronicler of Mexican-American history and culture with the death of Américo Paredes in 1999. Born in Brownsville, Texas, in 1915, Paredes spent his entire life commenting on the inequities faced by Mexican-Americans, specifically the conflict of identity and culture experienced by people of his native area. This commentary most often took the form of a reconstruction and analysis of local folklore, beginning with the often anthologized With a Pistol in His Hand: A Border Ballad and its Hero *in 1958. Other works of the same genre include* Folktales of Mexico *(1970),* The Urban Experience and Folk Tradition *(1971),* A Texas-Mexican Cancionero *(1976),* Uncle Remus Con Chile *(1993), and* Folklore and Culture on the Texas-Mexican Border *(1993), which contains eleven of his most notable essays, was first published between 1958 and 1987.*

Paredes worked as a journalist for fourteen years before he received a B.A., M.A., and Ph.D. from the University of Texas at Austin. While there, he founded and served as the director of the Mexican-American Studies Program. His many prestigious awards span almost forty years and include a Guggenheim Fellowship in 1962 and a Charles Frankel Prize from National Endowment for the Humanities in 1989.

His best-known work is his reconstruction of the story of Gregorio Cortez. After a misunderstanding between the local sheriff and Gregorio and his brother Romaldo, the sheriff shot and killed Romaldo only to be shot himself in self-defense by Gregorio. After fleeing the area, a manhunt ensued that lasted ten days and culminated in Gregorio's capture when he was betrayed by a friend. Both the legend and the ballad, or corrido, *emphasize the nobility of Cortez as he is said to have surrendered to spare his people further suffering.*

George Washington Gómez (1990) traces the life of the title character whose immigrant father names him after the most famous American in the hopes that his son will become a great American too. Ironically, young George or Guálinto, *which is a Spanish version of his middle name, embraces the American ideal and in so doing betrays the memory of his father who was shot by Texas Rangers. The struggle that leads to this eventual transition is the focus of the excerpt that follows.*

From George Washington Gómez

In later years George W. Gómez would remember his childhood home as an enchanted place. The porch of the blue frame house was covered with honeysuckle vines that screened a comer of it entirely from view, forming a fragrant, shady cave. The front yard was full of rose bushes with flowers of many colors, which he scrupulously avoided for fear not only of the thorns but of his mother's wrath as well. Then there were the figs, the papayas, the guayabas growing by the sides of the house.

But it was the vast jungle of banana trees choking the backyard that fascinated him. Here he loved to wander in the cool sunny mornings and the drowsy silent afternoons when everybody else who was not at work slept the siesta. The green stalks, waving ten or twelve feet above the ground, looked like forest giants to him, and he would swear when he was a man that they were at least twenty-five feet high. Here Guálinto hunted tigers and engaged pirates. Here he became a lone Indian tracking the wounded deer. Here he was first startled by beauty in the brilliant red of a cardinal bird against the wet-green leaves and saddened by the cool, gentle whisperings of the evening breeze.

But night changed the world. With darkness the banana grove and the trees beyond it became a haunted wood where lurked demons, skeletons and white-robed women with long long hair. The city's stormy politics had thrown up a vomit of murders and gun battles. Guálinto's immediate neighborhood, being at the edge of town, had seen more than its share of bloodshed. By that tree a man was killed by his best friend. Politics. Over there a woman was attacked and murdered. On a big hackberry beyond the backyard fence was a cross made of big nails driven into the trunk. Nobody knew exactly why the cross was there, but there were many stories explaining it. Here, there, everywhere were memories of the unhallowed dead. They haunted the night. They made the darkness terrible. So Guálinto's nights were filled with delicious thrills and wide-eyed terror. His mother tried to calm his fears with religion. Everybody believed, with the possible exception of his Uncle Feliciano, who seemed to believe in nothing. However, he did not interfere with his mother's teaching religion to her son. So the boy learned a whole rosary of paternosters, aves and credos to protect him from evil.

He wore a tin likeness of the Virgin hung around his neck on a string, and he was taken to church on Sundays, where he learned more about Hell than about Heaven. And when he went to bed every night he said a prayer along with his mother:

"I must die, I know not when,
I must die, I know not where,
I must die, I know not how.
But this I do know:
If I die without the grace of God
I shall burn in Hell forever."

Then his mother put him to bed, satisfied she had done her duty toward making him an upright, God-fearing man. But after the lamp was blown out he feared sleep, for it might bring death silently on its wings. He hated God for being so cruel. That gave him a terrible sinking feeling and he started to pray, fervently and with trembling lips, for God had heard his thoughts and even now He was frowning in rage.

But sleep would take hold of him unawares. When he woke, the blessed sun was shining, and the only feeling in his stomach was hunger. "Mama," he asked one morning after breakfast, "why can't I remember things when I was little like you do? You can tell the prettiest stories about the time you were little."

"Because you are still little, *hijito*,"[1] his mother replied.

"Oh," he said, not understanding at all. After a short silence he came back to the question. "But Mama, why can you remember so many things while I can't? You can remember back to ten years ago."

"Ten years ago you weren't born yet." His mother was silent for a while. Then, "Ten years ago you were in Heaven with the little angels."

"But I don't remember."

"Of course you can't, silly. Nobody can."

He was silent, thinking. Thinking, thinking. If I was up there I ought to remember, just like I remember I was in the banana grove yesterday because I was. I was born but I don't remember that either. And she says I was up there. Was it me? With wings? How can Mama know? If nobody can remember. Maybe it wasn't me at all. Maybe it was somebody else. Maybe I'm somebody else!

A cold emptiness settled into his stomach. Familiar objects suddenly looked strange to him, as though he were out of his body and looking at himself and all other things from a distance. Strange, terrible questions surged inside of him, questions for which he had no words, no concrete form, so that they floated around in his head like little clouds. Why am I, I? Why am I not somebody else? This was as close as he could come to expressing them. Why is my mother my mother? Why are things things and how do I know that they are? Will they be the same when I die like the prayer says, and how will I know they will be the same when I am dead and can't see them any more? A numbing loneliness seized him and he felt like crying out. Then, for a moment, he almost grasped and put into solid thought the vague and desolating questions which floated inside his head. But as his mind reached out to hold on

---

[1] son

to them they dissolved like spots before his eyes. His mother was his mother again, and she was asking him if he wasn't feeling well.

"No, Mama," he replied. "I'm all right."

Thinking, remembering.

So, at eight years of age, after having finished low first with Miss Josephine, Guálinto passed to high second with Miss Huff, and in so doing entered American school at last. Under Miss Huff's guidance he began to acquire an Angloamerican self, and as the years passed, under Miss Huff and other teachers like her, he developed simultaneously in two widely divergent paths. In the schoolroom he was an American; at home and on the playground he was a Mexican. Throughout his early childhood these two selves grew within him without much conflict, each an exponent of a different tongue and a different way of living. The boy nurtured these two selves within him, each radically different and antagonistic to the other, without realizing their separate existences.

It would be several years before he fully realized that there was not one single Guálinto Gómez. That in fact there were many Guálinto Gómezes, each of them double like the images reflected on two glass surfaces of a show window. The eternal conflict between two clashing forces within him produced a divided personality, made up of tight little cells independent and almost entirely ignorant of each other, spread out all over his consciousness, mixed with one another like squares on a checkerboard.

Consciously he considered himself a Mexican. He was ashamed of the name his dead father had given him, George Washington Gómez. He was grateful to his Uncle Feliciano for having registered him in school as "Guálinto" and having said that it was an Indian name. He spoke Spanish, literally as his mother tongue; it was the only language his mother would allow him to use when he spoke to her. The Mexican flag made him feel sentimental, and a rousing Mexican song would make him feel like yelling. The Mexican national hymn brought tears to his eyes, and when he said "we" he meant the Mexican people. "*La Capital*"[2] did not mean Washington, D.C., for him but Mexico City. Of such matter were made the basic cells in the honeycomb that made up his personality.

But there was also George Washington Gómez, the American. He was secretly proud of the name his more conscious twin, Guálinto, was ashamed to avow publicly. George Washington Gómez secretly desired to be a full-fledged, complete American without the shameful encumberment of his Mexican race. He was the product of his Anglo teachers and the books he read in school, which were all in English. He felt a pleasant warmth when he heard "The Star-Spangled Banner." It was he it was who fought the British with George Washington and Francis Marion the Swamp Fox, discovered pirate treasure with Long John Silver, and got lost in a cave with Tom Sawyer and Becky Thatcher. Books had made him so. He read everything he could lay his hands on. But he also heard from the lips of his elders songs and stories that were the history of his people, the Mexican people. And he also fought the Spaniards with *Hidalgo,* the French with *Juárez* and *Zaragosa,* and the

---

[2] The Capitol

Gringos with *Blas María de la Garza Falcón* and *Juan Nepomuceno Cortina*[3] in his childish fancies.

In school Guálinto/George Washington was gently prodded toward complete Americanization. But the Mexican side of his being rebelled. Immigrants from Europe can become Americanized in one generation. Guálinto, as a Mexicotexan, could not. Because, in the first place, he was not an immigrant come to a foreign land. Like other Mexicotexans, he considered himself part of the land on which his ancestors had lived before the Anglotexans had come. And because, almost a hundred years before, there had been a war between the United States and Mexico, and in Texas the peace had not yet been signed. So in assembly, while others were singing, "We're proud of our forefathers who fought at the Alamo," Guálinto and his friends would mutter, "We're proud of our forefathers who killed Gringos at the Alamo."

In all this he was no different from other Mexicotexan school children in Jonesville. They came to school and were placed in "low" first and second grades. This, said the Gringo school board, is a pedagogical necessity. The little Latins must learn the English language before they can associate with the little Anglosaxons. But wouldn't they learn English quicker if they were in the same classes with English-speaking children? No, that is a pedagogical fallacy. So the Society for the Advancement of Latin American Voters makes an issue of it in the next elections and succeeds in electing their candidate precinct chairman. *Ya estaría*,[4] as Mexicans say.

Meanwhile, the little Latin, if he is lucky, has struggled through the highs and the lows of first and second grade and has fallen into the hands of one of those earnest young women from up north, too religious to join the CPA and too inhibited to become a vocal social reformer, but still entertaining some ideas about equality and justice. She gets a Bachelor's in Education and comes down to the Delta to teach little Latins at fifty dollars a month. Within a week she will declare she loves the little things and that their wide-eyed admiration touches her heart. She becomes the mother of the Mexicotexan's American self. She nurses that self along, shielding it from damaging influences as one would a sickly plant. She is gentle and understanding. She is patient with the struggling limitations of a new language and the barriers raised by different, customs and beliefs. She sets out optimistically to undo the damage done

---

[3] *Miguel Hidalgo y Costilla* (1753–1811) was a Mexican priest and revolutionary. On January 11, 1811, his army was completely routed near Guadalajara by a small force of Spanish soldiers. *Benito Pablo Juárez* (1806–1872) was a national hero and president of Mexico. Juárez became governor of the state of Oaxaca and was imprisoned when the Mexican general Antonio de Santa Anna seized the national government. He escaped to New Orleans, Louisiana, but returned to Mexico in 1855 to take part in the revolution that overthrew Santa Anna. General *Ignacio Zaragoza*, the leader at the battle at Puebla, Mexico, was born in Texas while it was still part of Mexico. Despite being outnumbered and underequipped the French were forced to retreat to Orizaba. Captain *Blas María de la Garza Falcón* (1712–1767) was the first settler of Nueces County, Texas. However, this reference may be to his father, General *Blas de la Garza Falcón*, twice governor of Coahuila. *Juan Nepomuceno Cortina* (1824–1894) was a Mexican folk hero who ignited the so-called Cortian Wars. When Cortina saw the Brownsville city marshall, Robert Shears, brutally arrest a Mexican-American who had once been employed by Cortina. Cortina shot the marshall in the impending confrontation and rode out of town with the prisoner. Early on the morning of September 28, 1859, he rode into Brownsville again, this time at the head of some forty to eighty men, and seized control of the town. Five men, including the city jailer, were shot during the raid as Cortina and his men raced through the streets shouting "Death to the Americans" and "Viva Mexico."
[4] roughly the equivalent of "mission accomplished" but in a sarcastic tone

by poverty and prejudice. She teaches him that we are all created equal. And before he knows it the little Latin is thinking in English, and he can feel infinitely dirty if he forgets to brush his teeth in the morning.

This is also the time when the little Latins come in direct contact with the little Anglosaxons. On the playground Gringo and Greaser have played in separate groups. But now they are in the same classes and they must mix because they are seated alphabetically. Out of this proximity, classroom friendships sometimes develop. But the Mexican soon learns that such friendships do not extend beyond the classroom door. He will see a classroom friend on the playground, surrounded by several other Anglos. When the dark-skinned boy approaches, the American boys stop talking, and not all of them return his greeting. They will resume their conversation, but guardedly now, without including him in it. The Mexicotexan learns to stay away; he makes them uncomfortable. And one day he learns at least one of the reasons why. He will be walking past a group of Anglo boys playing marbles, let us say.

"You're fudging!" one of them shouts.

"I'm not."

"You were!"

"I wasn't!"

They stand up and face each other, their red faces almost purple with rage, their hands balled up into fists. The Mexican stops; he has never seen a fight between two Americans. But the two just stand there, until one of them says, "You—German!"

The other answers, "You—Mexican!"

They see the Mexican standing close by. They smile, embarrassed, and go back to their game. The Mexicotexan walks away, thinking, "Gringos *sanavabiches.*"

No, the Mexicotexan is not as ignorant as Calvin Coolidge, who once said, "The Alamo? What's the Alamo?" The Mexicotexan knows about the Alamo, he is reminded of it often enough. Texas history is a cross that he must bear. In the written tests, if he expects to pass the course, he must put down in writing what he violently misbelieves. And often certain passages in the history textbook become subjects of discussion.

"Isn't it horrible what the Mexicans did at the Alamo and Goliad? Why are they so treacherous and bloody? And cowards too."

"That's a lie! That's a lie! Treacherous? That's you all over!"

"It's in our textbook. Can't you read?"

"Children, children. Let's get back on the subject."

"But he's saying things about us!"

"It's the book that says them."

The teacher smiles. "That was long ago," she says. "We are all Americans now."

"But the book, the book! It talks about us today! Today! It says we are all dirty and live under trees."

The teacher cannot criticize a textbook on Texas history. She would be called a Communist and lose her job. Her only recourse is to change the subject, telling a joke, something to make her students laugh. If she succeeds the tension is over, for the moment at least. Despite the textbooks, she does her best and that is often good enough. In her classes at least, democracy exists. There, often enough, the Mexicotexan is first instead of last. If the teacher is young and pretty he will fall in love with her, in such an obvious way that it embarrasses her. But if in some instances she represents for him Beauty itself, in many more she is for him Justice, Equality, Democracy. The embodiment of all that is supposed to be good in the American people.

It was in this kind of schoolroom environment that Guálinto Gómez approached puberty. Hating the Gringo one moment with an unreasoning hatred, admiring his literature, his music, his material goods the next. Loving the Mexican with a blind fierceness, then almost despising him for his slow progress in the world.

Discussion Questions

1. What is the tone of the beginning of the first excerpt? How does the idea of memory aid in providing that tone?

2. Describe Guálinto's identity crisis as set forth in the second excerpt.

3. Compare the thoughts Guálinto has at the end of the first excerpt to Gary Soto's in *Living Up the Street* on page 12.

4. On page 83, Guálinto describes his feelings when hearing the National Anthem. How are those feelings different and/or similar to the young boy's in Abraham Rodriguez Jr.'s *The Boy Without a Flag* on page 420?

Poetry

Pat Mora

PAT MORA's distinguished literary and academic career began as a high school teacher in her hometown of El Paso, Texas. From there she taught at both El Paso Community College as well as The University of Texas at El Paso, and most recently she has been a Distinguished Visiting Professor at the University of New Mexico. Her awards include the New America: Women Artists and Writers of the Southwest Poetry Award (1984), a Kellogg National Fellowship (1986-89), a National Endowment for the Arts Fellowship (1994), and a 1999 Premio Aztlan Literature Award.

Her poems, which have been translated into several languages, have been published in the following collections: Chants *(1984),* Borders *(1986),* Communion *(1991),* Agua Santa/Holy Water *(1995), and* Aunt Carmen's Book of Practical Saints *(1997). She has also published several illustrated books of poetry for children, a series of essays, a book of memoirs, as well as contributing to various literary magazines and journals. Mainly focusing on Mexican-American women, Mora's poems often explore the theme of alienation and the stark contrast between two cultures.*

Sonrisas

I live in a doorway
between two rooms. I hear
quiet clicks, cups of black
coffee, *click, click* like facts
budgets, tenure, curriculum,
from careful women in crisp beige
suits, quick beige smiles
that seldom sneak into their eyes.

I peek
in the other room señoras
in faded dresses stir sweet
milk coffee, laughter whirls
with steam from fresh *tamales*
sh, sh, mucho ruido,
they scold one another,
press their lips, trap smiles
in their dark, Mexican eyes.

Bilingual Christmas

Do you hear what I hear?
Buenos días and hasta luego[1]
in board rooms and strategy sessions.
Where are your grateful holiday smiles,
bilinguals? I've given you a voice,
let you in
to hear old friends tell old jokes.
Stop flinching. Drink eggnog. Hum along.

> Not carols we hear
> whimpering
> children too cold
> to sing
> on Christmas eve.

Do you see what I see

adding a dash of color
to conferences and corporate parties

---

[1] Good morning and see you later

one per panel or office
slight South-of-the-border seasoning
feliz navidad and próspero año nuevo,[2] right?
Relax. Eat rum balls. Watch the snow.

      Not twinkling lights
      we see but
      search lights
      seeking illegal aliens
      outside our thick windows.

The Grateful Minority

Why the smile, Ofelia?

Ofelia who?
Why the smile at lysol days
scrubbing washbowls, mop—
mopping bathrooms for people
who don't even know your name.
Ofelia who?
Dirty work you'll do again tomorrow,
mirrors you've polished twenty-five years.

Some days I want to shake you
brown women who whistle while
you shine toilets, who smile gratefully
at dry rubber gloves, new uniforms,
steady paychecks, cleaning
content in your soapy solitude.
Ofelia who?
Like desert flowers you bloom
namelessly in harsh climes.
I want to shake your secret
from you. Why?   How?

Discussion Questions

1. Who is the speaker in the first poem, and what two worlds does she feel trapped between? Which of those worlds would she feel more comfortable in?

2. How is contrast being used in the second poem? What two worlds are being compared? What is the implication behind the lines "adding a dash of color to conferences and corporate parties"? How does the speaker feel about her job?

---

[2] merry Christmas and happy new year

3. Why does the speaker in "The Grateful Minority" want to "shake" the women she describes?

4. Which of these poems focuses most on the concept of dual identity?

5. After reading Gustavo Pérez-Firmat's poem "Bilingual Blues" on page 000, try to determine which of the speakers in the poems feels more conflicted about their identity. Why?

Ana Castillo

ANA CASTILLO's poetry reflects the richness of the oral Mexican tradition. She has been writing poems since she was nine years old and she further developed her poetic skill while still in high school. Women Are Not Roses *is a collection of poems that analyzes the role of women in a patriarchal society.*

For more information on Castillo turn to page 000.

From Women Are Not Roses

Women Are Not Roses

Women have no
beginning
only continual
flows.

Though rivers flow
women are not
rivers.

Women are not
roses
they are not oceans
or stars.

i would like to tell
her this but
i think she
already knows.

Not Just Because My Husband Said

if i had no poems left
i would be classified *working class intelligentsia*
my husband said
having to resort to teaching or research
grow cobwebs, between my ears
if I had no poems left

if i did not sing in the morning
or before i went to bed, i'd be as good as dead
my husband said
struck dumb with morose silence or apathy
my children would distrust me
if i did not sing in the morning

if i could not place on the table
fresh fruit, vegetables tender and green
we would soon grow ill and lean
my husband said
we'd grow weak and mean and useless to our neighbors
if I could not place fresh fruit on the table.

Discussion Questions

1. What does the speaker in "Women Are Not Roses" mean by saying that women have "continual flows"?
2. Why did the poet choose the rose as a basis of the metaphor? What image does a rose usually convey?
3. What is the role of the wife in the second poem? How does she feel about her husband's words?

Sandra Cisneros

Published in 1987, the collection of sixty poems, My Wicked, Wicked Ways, *either is set in Cisneros's hometown of Chicago or reflects her travels throughout Europe. The title which contains the motif of guilt is probably a result of her conservative Catholic upbringing. Regardless of the setting or persona, however, the poetry in this collection often grapples with issues of defiance and rebellion, and thus frequently mirrors Esperanza's quest in* The House on Mango Street.

For a fuller biography on the author turn to page 000.

From My Wicked, Wicked Ways

My Wicked, Wicked Ways

This is my father.
See? He is young.
He looks like Errol Flynn.[1]
He is wearing a hat
that tips over one eye,
a suit that fits him good,
and baggy pants.
He is also wearing
those awful shoes,
the two-toned ones
my mother hates.

Here is my mother.
She is not crying.
She cannot look into the lens
because the sun is bright.
The woman,
the one my father knows,
is not here.
She does not come till later.

My mother will get very mad.
Her face will turn red
and she will throw one shoe.
My father will say nothing.
After a while everyone
will forget it.
Years and years will pass.
My mother will stop mentioning it.

This is me she is carrying.
I am a baby.
She does not know
I will turn out bad.

---

[1] an American movie star of the 1950s known for his dashing good looks

For All Tuesday Travelers

I am the middle-of-the-week wife.
The back-door sneak.
I wake the next-door neighbors
who wonder at who arrives so late,
departs so early.

Who yearn to know
the luxury of love delivered.
Love that comes and goes
without the ache,
without the labor.

It is a good life.
I would not trade it
for another wife's.

I who am the topic
of the Wednesday morning chatter.
Who in her lone society
politely sips the breakfast given her.

Correctly travels with a toothbrush,
her own comb. Says *thank you,*
please, goodbye, and runs along.

Discussion Questions

1. The speaker in the first poem suggests a reason for her behavior. What is it?
2. What kind of lifestyle does the speaker in the second poem lead?
3. Compare the attitudes toward women depicted in the second poem to those in Roberta Fernandez's "Esmeralda" on page 61.

Gary Soto

As he does in his fiction, in his poetry Soto manages to fuse innocence and experience in a very effective manner. Many of his poems reflect his childhood experiences, and insightful and powerful statements on discrimination and racism are often presented in very subtle ways. As we can see from the selections here, however, Soto also frequently moves away from the simplistic and mundane into the abstract and philosophical. These two poems show the range of his poetic abilities and are taken from two different texts. The first is the title poem to his book of verse of the same name. The second originally appeared in a special section of the Massachusetts Review.

Who Will Know Us?

for Jaroslav Seifert

It is cold, bitter as a penny.
I'm on a train, rocking toward the cemetery
To visit the dead who now
Breathe through the grass, through me,
Through relatives who will come
And ask, Where are you?
Cold. The train with its cargo
Of icy coal, the conductor
With his loose buttons like heads of crucified saints,
His mad puncher biting zeros through tickets.

The window that looks onto its slate of old snow.
Cows. The barbed fences throat-deep in white.
Farm houses dark, one wagon
With a shivering horse.
This is my country, white with no words,
House of silence, horse that won't budge
To cast a new shadow. Fence posts
That are the people, spotted cows the machinery
That feed Officials. I have nothing
Good to say. I love Paris
And write, "Long Live Paris!"
I love Athens and write,
"The great book is still in her lap."
Bats have intrigued me,
The pink vein in a lilac.
I've longed to open an umbrella
In an English rain, smoke
And not give myself away,
Drink and call a friend across the room,
Stomp my feet at the smallest joke.
But this is my country.
I walk a lot, sleep.
I eat in my room, read in my room,
And make up women in my head—
Nostalgia, the cigarette lighter from before the war,
Beauty, tears that flow inward to feed its roots.

The train. Red coal of evil.
We are its passengers, the old and young alike.
Who will know us when we breathe through the grass?

Moving Our Misery

If we peed into a canal,
If we added our youthful lash of salts to the water,
Misery would carry itself out of town.
I had been reading philosophy for World Religions
And concluded we were in big trouble.
Pericles[1] was long dead, *Socrates*[2] a rag in the earth,
And *Galileo*[3] the lunar grit under a farmer's thumbnail.
One day, when a girl said, No, I love you as a friend,
I took my sorrow and cried into this canal,
My Buddha-shaped tears falling like an ancient rain.
The canal moved, just slightly, stirred the dead water.
I unzipped there and it flowed—
The junk on the bottom, the sofas and tires,
A wagon wheel, fishing tackle, a telephone booth,
A yellow dish glove pointing toward heaven.
The water flowed, and right there I needed my brother,
Three of his husky friends, maybe one dog,
A circus elephant. What was philosophy
But youthful water on an ancient current?
We could count one,
Two, three, then unleash ourselves
Into the canal
Until it flowed like the Nile,
Flowed through yellowish vapors.
Then it would snow,
Maybe rain, and the fish would return,
An egret or a smirking duck, all of nature at our feet,
Some of it climbing into our hair—
The cricket kick starting the night in our left ear.
We are, my friend, looking at the Garden of Eden,
Where Man walked nobly in front of the lion,
But jumped a step when the beast roared at his tasty bottom.

---

[1] Pericles (circa 495–429 BC). Under his leadership Athens became a great center of literature and art.
[2] Socrates (470?–399? BC) was a Greek philosopher who profoundly affected Western thought.
[3] Galileo Galilei (1564–1642) was an Italian physicist and astronomer whose main contributions were the use of the telescope in the observation and the discovery of sunspots, lunar mountains and valleys, and the four largest satellites of Jupiter, and the phases of Venus.

Discussion Questions

1. In both of these poems, the speaker is concerned with establishing a connection with the past. Where and how does that occur in each poem?
2. What role does nostalgia play in the first poem?
3. According to the speaker in "Moving Our Misery," what has happened to the Garden of Eden?
4. How is the philosophical journey into the past similar to Lara's real journey into the past in Teresa Bevin's novel *Havana Split* on page 231? Look especially at the first three pages of the excerpt.

Bernice Zamora

BERNICE ZAMORA was born in Colorado in 1938 to working-class parents. At home she was encouraged to speak Spanish and adhere to traditional Catholic and Mexican-American customs. She returned to school several years after graduating from high school and earned a B.A. from University of Southern California, an M.A. from Colorado State, and ultimately a Ph.D. from Stanford in 1986.

While she has contributed to several anthologies and co-edited one herself, she became well known after the publication of Restless Serpents *(1976), which also contains poetry by Jose Burciaga. Like many Latina writers, Zamora's poetry explores the role of language, cultural traditions, and the place of women within a restrictive patriarchal society. These complex issues are explored with beauty and grace by the poet and the power and lyric quality of the language comes though in all of them.*

The republication of her 1976 work with an addition of new poems in 1994 retains the original title: Releasing Serpents. *While some critics have called her a feminist poet, Zamora herself contends that there are other issues, such as racial discrimination, that do not allow her to consider herself a traditional feminist writer. The following selection reminds us that like all good poets, Zamora does not restrict herself to one single issue. Rather than explore the enslavement of women, this selection, perhaps drawn from her own background (her father was a coal miner), examines a different kind of enslavement.*

Luciano

From the south coast I watched,
or tried to watch, this month's lunar eclipse.
Instead, a vision of Uncle Luciano
lying in a muddy street, looking at the moon,

appeared at 3:30 A.M. The eclipse was all
he wanted to see, he said, shaking
a liquid prism before my eyes.

When he was alive, he was a man of extraordinary traits:
        unhappiness
        integrity
        silence
        devotion.
He was a farmer, a coal miner and then a gravedigger.
A look of permanent shock stocked his face, stooped his
frame.
Life had lied to him and the truth he bore of that,
bored him into the ground, ground him into a silence,
silenced him with comprehension and incomprehension,
daily, to the end.

Discussion Questions

1. Why does Luciano have a "look of permanent shock" on his face? What had life lied to him about?

2. What does the author mean by "comprehension and incomprehension"?

3. What are the similarities between the life of Luciano and the lives of the characters depicted in Pedro Pietri's poem *Puerto Rican Obituary* on page 444?

Lorna Dee Cervantes

Cervantes was born in 1954 in the Mission District of San Francisco. While her mother cleaned other people's houses, the young Cervantes would read their books and thus acquired a taste for literature at an early age. She began writing her own poetry in high school and later published a small-press journal named Mango *which helped promote the works of other Mexican-American writers.*

Her two books of poetry Emplumada *(1981) and* From the Cables of Genocide: Poems of Love and Hunger *(1991) focus on a common theme in literature: the difference between appearance and reality.* Emplumada *is divided into three sections dealing with such issues as the social environment, the class status of women, and the creative process. Sometimes the conflict between appearance and reality is described as a difference between gender, as in the following selection.*

To We Who Were Saved by the Stars

Education lifts man's sorrows to a higher plane of regard.
A man's whole life can be a metaphor.

—Robert Frost

Nothing has to be ugly. Luck of the dumb
is a casual thing. It gathers its beauty in plain
regard. Animus, not inspiration, lets us go
among the flocks and crows crowded around
the railroad ties. Interchanges of far away
places, tokens of our deep faux pas, our interface
of neither/nor, when we mutter moist goodbye and ice
among the silent stars, it frosts our hearts on
the skids and corners, piles the dust upon our grids
as grimaces pardon us, our indecision, our monuments
to presidents, dead, or drafted boys who might have
married us, Mexican poor, or worse. Our lives could be
a casual thing, a reed among the charlatan drones,
a rooted blade, a compass that wields a clubfoot
round and round, drawing fairy circles in clumps
of sand. Irritate a simple sky and stars fill up
the hemispheres. One by one, the procession
of their birth is a surer song than change
jingling in a rich man's pocket. So knit, you
lint-faced mothers, tat your black holes
into paradise. Gag the grin that forms
along the nap. Pull hard, row slow, a white
boat to your destiny. A man's whole life
may be a metaphor—but a woman's lot
is symbol.

Discussion Questions

1. According to the speaker, how does destiny play a role in women's lives?

2. What is meant by the statement that "women's lot is symbol"?

3. How is a woman's life in this poem similar to that of the wife in Castillo's poem "Not Just Because My Husband Said" on page 90?

4. "Little Sister Born in this Land" by Elias Miguel Muñoz on page 264 is about the life of one particular girl. However, like "To We Who Were Saved by the Stars," Muñoz's poem comments on the role of destiny in a woman's life. What are the differences in the poems regarding that role?

Gloria Anzaldua

Anzaldua was born in 1942 on a ranch settlement in Texas called Jesus Maria of the Valley. She received her B.A. from Pan-American University in 1969, her M.A. from the University of Texas at Austin in 1973, and did post-graduate work at the University of California, Santa Cruz. Among her awards are the MacDowell Colony Fellowship, 1982; the American Book Award, Before Columbus Foundation, 1986; the fiction award, National Endowment for the Arts, 1991; and the Sappho Award, Astraea National Lesbian Action Foundation, 1992.

Her published works consist of This Bridge Called My Back: Writings by Radical Women of Color, *edited with Cherrie Moraga, 1981; a book of poems titled* This Way Daybreak Comes, *with Annie Cheatham and Mary Clare Powell, 1986;* Borderlands/La Frontera: The New Mestiza, *poetry and pose, 1987; two children's books,* Prietita Has a Friend—Prietita tiene un Amigo, *1991, and* Prietita and the Ghost Woman—Prietita y La Llorona, *1996; and a novel,* La Prieta, *1997.*

In Borderlands, *her most critically acclaimed work, Anzaldua shifts between poetry and prose as well as between languages to explore the relationship between the United States and Mexico. The selection provided is perhaps the epitome of the range of contradictory emotions and situations experienced by a resident of that border.*

To live in the Borderlands means you

are neither *hispana india negra española*
ni gabacha, eres mestiza, mulata,[1] half-breed
caught in the crossfire between camps
while carrying all five races on your back
not knowing which side to turn to, run from;

To live in the Borderlands means knowing
that the *india in you,* betrayed for 500 years,
is no longer speaking to you,
that *mexicanas* call you *rajetas,*[2]
that denying the Anglo inside you
is as bad as having denied the Indian or Black;

Cuando vives en la frontera[3]
people walk through you, the wind steals your voice,
you're a *burra, buey,*[4] scapegoat,

---

[1] hispanic indian spanish nor anglo, you are mestiza (Indian/white), mulata (black/white)   [2] someone who betrays their culture   [3] when you live on the border   [4] ass, ox

forerunner of a new race,
half and half—both woman and man, neither—
a new gender;

To live in the Borderlands means to
    put *chile* in the borscht,
    eat whole wheat *tortillas,*
    speak Tex-Mex with a Brooklyn accent;
    be stopped by *la migra*[5] at the border checkpoints;

Living in the Borderlands means you fight hard to
    resist the gold elixer beckoning from the bottle,
    the pull of the gun barrel,
    the rope crushing the hollow of your throat;

In the Borderlands
    you are the battleground
    where enemies are kin to each other;
    you are at home, a stranger,
    the border disputes have been settled
    the volley of shots have shattered the truce
    you are wounded, lost in action
    dead, fighting back;

To live in the Borderlands means
    the mill with the razor white teeth wants to shred off
    your olive-red skin, crush out the kernel, your heart
    pound you pinch you roll you out
    smelling like white bread but dead;

To survive the Borderlands
    you must live *sin fronteras*[6]
    be a crossroads.

Discussion Questions

1. As a whole, what does this poem conclude about the life of someone living on the border?

2. Compare the speaker's feelings about a person's African heritage to that of Martin Espada's speaker in his poem "Niggerlips" on page 456.

---

[5] The Immigration Service   [6] without borders

Jimmy Santiago Baca

JIMMY SANTIAGO BACA was born in New Mexico in 1952. His early life was tragic, as he was sent to an orphanage at the age of five after the death of his alcoholic father. He left the orphanage as often as he could and his life on the streets led him to a life of crime and drug abuse. He received no formal education and taught himself how to read while in prison. Despite this, his poetry is full of hope rather than despair or resentment.

In addition to contributing to anthologies and periodicals, Baca has published several books of poems including Immigrants in Our Own Land *(1979),* Swords of Darkness *(1981),* What's Happening *(1982),* Poems Taken from My Yard *(1986),* Martin and Meditations on the South Valley *(1987),* Black Mesa Poems *(1989), and most recently* Set This Book on Fire *(1999). His awards include the American Book Award for poetry, Before Columbus Foundation in 1988, the National Hispanic Heritage Award in 1989, and a Wallace Stevens Poetry Fellowship from Yale University.*

The three poems provided here from his Black Mesa Poems *are taken from roughly the beginning, middle, and end of the text, thus allowing us to trace the development of the speaker as he moves from childhood to maturity.*

Roots

Ten feet beyond the back door
the cottonwood tree
is a steaming stone of beginning time.
A battle-scarred warrior
whose great branches knock
telephone poles aside, mangle trailers
to meager tin-foil in its grasp,
clip chunks of stucco off my house
so sparrows can nest in gaps,
wreck my car hood, splinter
sections of my rail fence,
all, with uncompromising nostalgia
for warring storms.
I am like this tree
Spanish saddle-makers copied
dressing from.
The dense gray wrath of its bark
is the trackway
shipwrecked captains, shepherds, shepherdes

barn-burners, fence cutters followed.
Camped here at the foot of *Black Mesa*,[1]
beneath this cottonwood,
leaned muskets on this trunk,
stuck knife blades into its canyon valley bark
red-beaded tasseled arm sleeves clashing
with each throw, as the knife
pierced cattail or bamboo
pinched in bark.

I come back to myself
near this tree, and think of my roots
in this land—
Papa and me working in the field.
I tell Papa, "Look, here comes someone."
He rises, pulls red handkerchief from back pocket,
takes sombrero off, wipes sweat from brow.
You drive up to our field. Unclip briefcase
on the hood of your new government blue car.
Spread official papers out, point with manicured fingers,
telling Papa what he must do.
He lifts a handful of earth by your polished shoe,
and tells you in Spanish, it carries the way of his life.
Before history books were written,
family blood ran through this land,
thrashed against mountain walls and in streams,
fed seeds, and swords, and flowers.
"My heart is a root in this earth!" he said in Spanish, angrily.
You didn't understand Spanish, you told him,
you were not to blame for the way things must be.
The government must have his land.
The Land Grant Deed was no good.
You left a trail of dust in our faces.

I asked Papa how a skinny man like you
could take our land away.
He wept that night, wept a strong cry,
as if blood were pouring from his eyes,
instead of tears. I remember hearing his voice
coming through the walls into my bedroom,
"They twist my arms back and tear the joints,
and they crush my spine with their boots . . ."

---

[1] a region in south-central Arizona

In my mind's eye I looked into the man's face
for a long time. I stared at his car for a long time,
and knew as a child I would carry the image
of the enemy in my heart forever.

Henceforth,
I will call this cottonwood
Father.

Accountability

Who we are and what we do
appears to us
like a man dressed in a long black coat,
a bill collector
who offers a paper to sign
and says we have no choice
but to sign it.
In it,
we read who we are—
we should change this paragraph,
or the color of the hair,
or the time we took a trip,
or the woman we met in a coffeeshop,
it's not true,
or it didn't turn out quite that way.
"Sign it,"
he says,
"I have many others to see today."

A Daily Joy to Be Alive

No matter how serene things
may be in my life,
how well things are going,
my body and soul
are two cliff peaks
from which a dream of who I can be
falls, and I must learn

to fly again each day.
or die.

Death draws respect
and fear from the living.
Death offers
no false starts. It is not
a referee with a pop-gun
at the starting line
of a hundred yard dash.

I do not live to retrieve
or multiply what my father lost
or gained.

I continually find myself in the ruins
of new beginnings,
uncoiling the rope of my life
to descend ever deeper into unknown abysses,
tying my heart into a knot
round a tree or boulder,
to insure I have something that will hold me,
that will not let me fall.

My heart has many thorn-studded slits of flame
springing from the red candle jars.
My dreams flicker and twist

on the altar of this earth,
light wrestling with darkness,
light radiating into darkness,
to widen my day blue,
and all that is wax melts
in the flame—

I can see treetops!

Discussion Questions

1. In what way is heritage a significant factor in "Roots"?
2. Why is Accountability personified in the second poem? What role does he play?
3. Trace the development of the speaker in these three poems. How does his idea about his own roots change?
4. Compare the development of the speaker's identity in these poems to the same development in Pablo Medina's "Winter of a Rose" on page 256. Do both poems conclude in the same manner? How do each of the speakers feel about their past at the conclusion of each poem?

Drama

Estela Portillo Trambley

ESTELA PORTILLO TRAMBLEY was born in El Paso, Texas, in 1936 and died in 1998. She worked as a high school teacher, a college instructor, and a radio talk show hostess. She received an M.A. from the University of Texas-El Paso in 1977. While she has published both short stories and poems, her literary strength is in the area of drama. Her published plays include Days of the Swallows *(1971),* Sun Images *(1979), and* Sor Juana and Other Plays *(1983).*

Trambley's drama is much more structured than other Mexican-American works of the same genre. She is more interested in crafting a careful plot which, although it may contain some political ideology, is far removed from the experimental and informal acto *some of her peers have produced. For Trambley the experimentation lies within the production itself as the audience and players interact in a dynamic fashion.*

Sor Juana Inez de La Cruz, the subject of Trambley's story, was a seventeenth-century Mexican nun who is regarded by some as the first feminist of the New World. Sor Juana was a voracious reader and passionate poet and playwright, despite the fact that as a nun she was forbidden to write on secular subjects. Her Response, *for example, is her defense for having written a letter criticizing the sermon of a Jesuit priest for which she had been reprimanded by the Archbishop of Mexico. Instead of an apology, however, the* Response *is a defense of her literary career. Trambley's offering examines the existential conflicts of this unique woman.*

Sor Juana

CHARACTERS
(In order of their appearance)

Sor Juana Ines De La Cruz (at forty-two)
Sor Feliciana
Sor Catarina
Juana Asbaje (at eight)
Slave Juana (at nine)
Andres (at eleven)
Lady Leonor Maria De Carreto (Laura)
Lady Beatriz
Lady Margarita

Scholar
Altar Boy
Canon
Slave Juana (as adult)
Dr. Ignacio Pavon
Count De Paredes
Countess De Paredes (Lisi)
Bishop Miguel Fernando De
   Santa Cruz

Bernardo

Father Antonio Nuñez De Miranda

Marquis De Mancera

Father Juan Ignacio

Andres (as adult)

Priest

Sor Barbara

Sor Celestina

Note: To give validity to the historical sequences, a large cast is necessary. However, the play lends itself well to double casting. In my production I combined the roles of Canon, Father Juan Ignacio, and the Priest to be played by one actor. The noble ladies in Act One became the sisters in the final scene. Other double castings are possible.

ACT I

SCENE I

The Convent of St. Jerome, Mexico City, 1693: The near empty cell of SOR JUANA INES DE LA CRUZ. *It contains a cot, a chair, and some boxes containing the last few possessions of* SOR JUANA. *On top of one of the boxes are lighted votive candles, on another, a yucca whip.* SOR JUANA, *a slight, thin figure, forty-two years old, is dressed in a single white chemise. She kneels down center, holding a huge crucifix over her head.*

SOR JUANA: *(In prayer.)* Sweet Jesus, Jesús del alma mía, *me entrego a tu compañia. Perdóname mis pecados.*[1] Forgive my arrogance, my pride, my selfishness. Oh, Sweet Jesus, I have forsaken my vows. You, Who are all merciful, do not desert me in this, the hour of my need. Let your angels surround me. My strength has left me. My   5 mind has left me. I am empty. Oh, Divine Spirit, fill this sorrowful vessel with your compassion. Dear Christ, my body shall feel your pain, your wounds. *(She beats her breast, lowers head to floor, begins to unbutton top of her garment, rising. Kisses crucifix, crosses to box, lays crucifix on top, drops top of her garment down to her waist; back to audience, picks up whip.)*

The red haze, symbolic of the Misery, the penitence ritual of SOR JUANA, *begins to fade gradually.* SOR JUANA *blows out candles. Total darkness. There is the sound of a whip descending upon bare flesh, a suppressed groan. Another whip lash, the sound of suffering sobs.*

SOR JUANA: Oh, my God! Here's my soul! Take it from me! See? My blood runs free. I feel your presence. Touch my wounds. They are   10 your wounds. I shall not sleep—*el dormir es el ensayo del morir.*[2] *(Sound of the whip, a long, deep moan.)* My life! My life! All ashes.

---

[1] I give myself to you. Forgive my sins.   [2] Sleep is a rehearsal for Death.

Red haze gradually returns. SOR JUANA rises, lights candles. She covers exposed body, then takes candles down center, places them on both sides of her as she kneels and prays feverishly.

SOR JUANA: *Domine, non sum dignus.* Oh, Lamb of God! Cleanse my spirit. Soul of Christ, sanctify me. Body of Christ, save me. Blood of Christ, inebriate me. Water from the side of Christ, wash me clean. Passion of   15
Christ, strengthen me. Oh, Good Jesus, hear me. Within thy wounds, hide me. In the hour of my death, call me and bid me come to thee, that with thy saints I may praise thee and be thine, forever and ever . . .

BLACKOUT

SCENE 2

Sunrise. Two days later. SOR JUANA is asleep on the cot. SOR FELICIANA, her young niece, is sitting by her side. SOR CATARINA comes in quietly with a bowl of soup, crosses to bed, looks over SOR JUANA.

SOR CATARINA: She's so pale. She slept around the clock, though.
SOR FELICIANA: Fitfully, I'm afraid. She cries out in her sleep and tosses so.   20
SOR CATARINA: This soup will do her good. *(Places soup on top of one of the boxes.)* She hasn't eaten for days.
SOR FELICIANA: All those weeks of scourging herself. I'm glad you broke the lock.
SOR CATARINA: She was half dead when we found her. All that blood!   25
And that whip has got to go. Enough is enough. We should have interfered before. It's not natural, to whip yourself. Not for a *Hieronymite.*[3] She's sinking into some terrible darkness. We simply will not allow it anymore. I'll burn that infernal whip.
SOR FELICIANA: It's all because he's gone.   30
SOR CATARINA: Father Antonio?
SOR FELICIANA: Yes.
SOR CATARINA: It's much more than that. She's warring with herself. And with her capacity for passion . . . No. We shall put a stop to it.
SOR FELICIANA: When she wakes up she will force herself to go to San   35
Hipólito. You know how far she walks each day? Seven miles—in her condition.

---

[3] In seventeenth-century Spain, the religious orders were unrivaled in their patronage of the arts. Among the most important were the Hieronymites, whose white and brown habits are worn by these three saints: Paula, her daughter Eustochium, and Sophronius Eusebius Hieronymous, called Jerome in English. Under Jerome's spiritual direction, the two women founded a hospice and convent in the Holy Land that were regarded as the initial establishments of the Hieronymite Order.

SOR CATARINA: That seems to be her life now—worrying about those
        starving people in the barrios, taking whatever she can. Feed her the
        soup when she wakes up. Tell her Sister Sofia and Sister Magdalena   40
        will go to San Hipólito in her place. There is grain to give. I have
        written to Father Antonio. If he gets my letter he will come.

SOR FELICIANA: The Holy Company forbids it.

SOR CATARINA: After what's happened to Mexico City, to Sor Juana, *that*
        is of little importance. What we need now is a miracle. Father Antonio   45
        is our miracle. To have him back would raise her from the dead.

SOR FELICIANA: She loves him so!

SOR CATARINA: *(Crosses to door.)* I leave her in your care. Stay with her. I
        think she needs that soup more than sleep now. Wake her gently and
        make her understand God wants her well and strong.   50

SOR FELICIANA: Yes, Sister.

*SOR CATARINA exits. SOR FELICIANA goes to the bed, smooths SOR JUANA's
hair, takes her aunt's hand in hers.*

SOR FELICIANA: Juana . . .

SOR JUANA: Shhh . . . Listen—Do you hear the cowbell?

SOR FELICIANA: How are you feeling?

SOR JUANA: I heard the cowbell. Was it in my dreams?   55

SOR FELICIANA: Most likely. There is no cowbell.

SOR JUANA: The cowbell means Andrés will come along with his flute.

SOR FELICIANA: It was a dream. Andrés is d . . .

SOR JUANA: Is what?

SOR FELICIANA: Dead . . .   60

SOR JUANA: It must have been a dream. We were children again. We were
        climbing the cowpath, Juana. Andrés and I. To the rocks where
        Andrés found a cliff rose once, so long ago. Where's Juana?

SOR FELICIANA: You gave her her freedom. Don't you remember? She's
        living somewhere in the zambo barrio—with an aunt, I think.   65

SOR JUANA: Freedom? Juana is my sister. Andrés, my brother.

SOR FELICIANA: They were your mother's slaves, and when you came into
        the Order, your mother gave you Juana to attend you.

SOR JUANA: No. I'm not thinking clear . . .

SOR FELICIANA: You lost much blood . . .   70

SOR JUANA: Listen, I hear the cowbell . . . *(Blackout on stage area. Sound
        of cowbell as light comes up on flashback area. Time: 1659. JUANA
        ASBAJE is eight. JUANA, the zambo slave, is nine, her brother ANDRES,
        eleven. ANDRES is leading, playing his pito (flute). Suddenly he stops,
        takes a corn cake out of his pocket. Divides it in three parts, gives each lit-
        tle girl a piece.)*

SLAVE JUANA: You took it when Mamá Seya wasn't looking. I saw you.

ANDRES: *(Stuffing mouth.)* Mamá Seya doesn't mind. *(Turns to JUANA.)*
        Eat it, coya.

SLAVE JUANA: Tastes best when you're on a cowpath and the sky is blue.   75

ANDRES: *(Looks at sky.)* All blue—nothing but blue . . .

JUANA: All the way to Mexico City?

ANDRES: Sure. You see when you go there. Same sky.

JUANA: I wish you could go with me. That's what I wish.

ANDRES: Who would take the cows to pasture?   80

SLAVE JUANA: Who would feed the chickens and help Mamá Seya in the kitchen?

JUANA: I must go. I must show people how well I read and I will read my poems and sing my music.

SLAVE JUANA: People will go to see you like in the circus.   85

ANDRES: Like a dancing bear. People will come from all around.

JUANA: I'm not a dancing bear. *(ANDRES takes out his pito and begins to play a tune. SLAVE JUANA pretends she is a dancing bear. JUANA, eating her cake, dances too. Still playing his pito, ANDRES starts walking up the cowpath.)*

SLAVE JUANA: Wait for us! *(Starts after ANDRES.)*

JUANA: *(Following.)* You know that in Mexico City there are more books than in my grandfather's library? I've read all of those, you   90
know.

ANDRES: I cannot read.

SLAVE JUANA: All the books, could they make a mountain?

JUANA: Lots of mountains.

SLAVE JUANA: Will you forget about the sun?   95

ANDRES: And the river?

SLAVE JUANA: The bird songs?

ANDRES: The stars behind the mountain?

JUANA: Don't walk so fast.

ANDRES: *(Stops, takes cup from inside shirt, shows it to girls.)* Look!   100

JUANA: You're going to milk . . .

SLAVE JUANA: Let's catch a cow . . . *(All three run off as light fades, light comes up on cell area.)*

SOR FELICIANA: You're lightheaded. You've fasted too long. Sister Catarina brought some soup for you. *(Crosses to box, brings soup to SOR JUANA. Tries to feed her, but she is too absorbed in thought.)* Please drink   105
it, Tía. You need the strength. *(SOR JUANA takes some spoonfuls.)*

SOR JUANA: *(Pushing spoon away.)* Not too much. *(Looks at bruises and open gashes now cleaned.)* You washed it off, all the blood. How long did I sleep?

SOR FELICIANA: Around the clock. You needed it.   110

SOR JUANA: San Hipólito . . .

SOR FELICIANA: Don't worry. Sister Sofia and Sister Magdalena will give out grain today.

SOR JUANA: *(Tries to get up.)* I should go with them.

SOR FELICIANA: *(Stops her.)* No. You are to rest. We're not going to let   115
you have your way anymore, dear Tía.

SOR JUANA: And what is my way?

SOR FELICIANA: No more scourging, no more fasting, and the barrios in
San Hipólito can do without you for a few days. Sister Catarina took
the whip to burn it.   120

SOR JUANA: *(Pushes SOR FELICIANA away.)* No! *(She gets out of bed.)* I
must suffer the wounds of Jesus for what I made of my life . . . In a
windstorm, I stripped a yucca of its leaves, braided them, soaked them
in salt water—to make the whip flexible, to feel the sting of salt upon
my open wounds.   125

SOR FELICIANA: No more, Sor Juana. It is insane what you have done to
yourself. It is not you. Not a Hieronymite.

SOR JUANA: You forget—I was a *Carmelite*.[4] Their faith is pure—pure—
that is its strength, isn't it? That clean faith without doubt, without
words—I didn't have it then. I want it so now. I want it so. Faith—   130
Faith—Faith—Oh, Feliciana, what am I?

SOR FELICIANA: The most faithful, but you should be in bed.

SOR JUANA: I am not an invalid. I feel strong. This isn't the first time I've
spilled my blood or fasted. But with the coming of a new day, God
has always given me strength.   135

SOR FELICIANA: Please—you are forcing yourself. I can tell. I don't understand this delirium that has taken hold of you for so long.

SOR JUANA: *(Weak, shaking, with great effort crosses to chair, holds it for
support.)* There's nothing wrong with me. I'm—I'm fine.

SOR FELICIANA: You're so stubborn! *(Crosses to her aunt.)* Here, let me
help you back to bed. *(Touches her aunt's forehead.)* Why, you're burn-   140
ing up with fever. You must go back to bed.

SOR JUANA: There's so much to do. So much I've left undone. Let me
be. Go away.

SOR FELICIANA: Sister Catarina said I must stay with you.

SOR JUANA: Don't be foolish, my child. How can I make you understand   145
that all this pain, this confusion, this emptiness inside me, has to be
purged? It is between me and God. No one else. Go!

SOR FELICIANA: I wish I could help you . . .

SOR JUANA: You can help me by respecting my solitude.

SOR FELICIANA: Will you stay and rest—sleep some more? You're so frail.   150
You're body cannot take much more . . . Will you promise not to
leave your cell?

SOR JUANA: There are so many things to be done that I've left undone . . .

SOR FELICIANA: I will not let you walk off into the desert to follow the
moan of the wind as you did before. We couldn't find you! By the   155

---

[4] The word *Carmelite* takes its origin from Mount Carmel, the mountain of the Prophet Elijah, which
in the biblical and patristic traditions means fertility, beauty, generosity, and wealth of grace. All this,
adapted to the spiritual life, is realized in those who embrace the Carmelite monastic life. From 1400,
under the guidance of the friars, pious women who sought a deeper spirituality, have wanted to adapt
the spirit of Carmel and the Rule to their condition as women. Thus were born the cloistered Carmelite
nuns—officially in 1452 in Florence (Italy)—known as praying communities, completely dedicated to
meditation, prayer, work, and penance.

time we did, you were half-frozen. You might take it in your head to
go to San Hipólito after all. Your body cannot stand it! This energy
you have is not energy. It's some obsessive agony . . . Please, Sor
Juana, I understand your need to be alone, and I will go if you promise to stay.   160

SOR JUANA: The people in San Hipólito need coal. They need fires to
feed the children, to keep them warm.

SOR FELICIANA: (*Crosses to bed, picks up* SOR JUANA'*s only black habit at
the foot of the bed.*) Not today, Sor Juana.

SOR JUANA: What are you doing?

SOR FELICIANA: I'm taking your clothes with me.   165

SOR JUANA: No . . .

SOR FELICIANA: (*Crying softly.*) It's the only way. (*Goes to door with*
JUANA'*s only habit.*) I'm sorry. (*Exits.*)

SOR JUANA: (*Goes to door. Leans against it, turns, collapses to floor.*) No . . .
(*Tries to sit up with great effort; folds arms, rubbing.*) I'm shivering . . .   170
cold, cold, cold. Oh, God, do not forsake me! I'm so cold. (*Rises un-
steadily, goes to cot, takes blanket from bed, wraps herself in it; touches
forehead.*) I'm burning up. Why am I so cold? I think it's April. The
sun . . . (*Crosses to window.*) Ah, yes . . . warm, warm, warm. (*Stares
out into convent garden.*) Cornstalks! The flowers—where are they?
Where are my people? Laura? You died so long ago! Lisi? What's hap-   175
pened to Lisi? They loved me well . . . Oh, Father Antonio, I need
you so. Jesus, help me understand. Was I a willing bride? I remember
my own happiness so long ago—when I told myself, "I shall discover
God through knowledge, and the Church will let me learn. . ." Was
that good enough reason to become your bride? (*Crosses down center.*)   180
Sweet Jesus—love? Pure, clear, the flower of faith? That was not my
offering to you, Jesus. But I was so young, so hurt . . .

*Lights fade out on cell area, come up on flashback area. It's 1667, the Viceroy's
palace, Mexico City. The garden. One chair on a raised platform, appears
throne-like. The Marchioness, Lady Leonor Maria de Carreto, known as*
LAURA *to close friends, enters followed by* LADY BEATRIZ *and* LADY MAR-
GARITA. LAURA *crosses downstage, and with a sweep of the hand that holds an
open fan, she gestures to an area at a distance.*

LAURA: Over there—see them? Bronze, blue, green—aren't they superb?
Peacocks from my husband! How dear of him. Just what my garden
needs.   185

LADY MARGARITA: Such a garden! It's a woodland.

LAURA: One of the splendors of our new land.

LADY MARGARITA: We saw your Peacocks on the ship. Now, they're free.

LAURA: A safe arrival. Now you two are in my care for a little while. I
heard the ship was chased by English pirates. Infamous English! The   190
waters in the Gulf are infested with them.

LADY BEATRIZ: Fearful experience. Our ship fled against southerly winds.

LADY MARGARITA: With the help of God we arrived safely in Vera Cruz.

LADY BEATRIZ: And the help of Count Camborio. He kept our spirits up
all during the chase.   195

LADY MARGARITA: We stayed at his villa when we arrived in Vera Cruz.

LADY BEATRIZ: Marvelous place. He has twenty-four slaves—humble,
curious people. He told us slaves were abundant and your criollos
were good at civil work and the like. We are not so fortunate in Spain.
But tell me, Laura, why didn't Bernardo go to Vera Cruz to meet me?   200

LAURA: I don't know, really. I'm sure it was some pressing business.

LADY BEATRIZ: I shall be very angry with him. When we were first be-
trothed, he was so eager for an early marriage. Now that I've set a
date, you'd think he'd be anxious.

LAURA: Tell me, will you be married in Toledo?   205

LADY BEATRIZ: Yes. At the great *catedral*.[5] I shall take Bernardo back
with me. Oh, Laura, you must go back to Spain with us—you must
attend the wedding.

LAURA: Oh, I do long to see the Spanish sun again, but I cannot. The
building of the great *catedral*, here in Mexico City—it has been my   210
husband's dream. It is almost finished and we are preparing for a celebration. A sonnet will be written by Sor Juana Asbaje for the occasion
in honor of Diego de Ribera.

LADY MARGARITA: Isn't she the one who wrote that poem on the death
of our late King Phillip? I remember someone reciting it some years   215
back. They mentioned it was written by some child in your court,
some criolla. Is she still with you?

LAURA: Oh yes. In fact, it was that poem that brought her to my court. I
insisted on meeting her. She was thirteen at the time. She came from a
village called Amecameca, demanding that she be allowed to study at   220
the university. Amazing, precocious girl. Of course she was not allowed to enter the university. I took her under my wing.

LADY BEATRIZ: So you let her run loose in your garden.

LAURA: Come to think of it, she did go off this morning with your
Bernardo at her heels. They are good friends.   225

LADY MARGARITA: Ah, Lady Beatriz you came just in time.

LADY BEATRIZ: Don't be absurd, Margarita. *(To LAURA.)* I suppose you
keep her for the court's amusement.

LAURA: Oh, no. I love her dearly. I wish I could arrange a good marriage
for her, but unfortunately she is the illegitimate offspring of some   230
Spanish captain and a farm girl. She has no dowry. A great beauty,
though, and a brilliant mind.

LADY BEATRIZ: Not advantageous to a lady, I would say.

LADY MARGARITA: I agree with you. A woman with a mind is no more
than a curiosity to men.   235

LADY BEATRIZ: I am sure that is all she is to Bernardo.

---

[5] cathedral

LAURA: Tell me, will your uncle, the Bishop, perform the wedding?

LADY BEATRIZ: Yes. The whole Spanish court will attend.

LAURA: How exciting. *(Starts to leave, continuing conversation.)* I suppose Princess Mariana will attend.   240

LADY BEATRIZ: So will the young king.

LADY MARGARITA: He goes wherever she goes.

LAURA: So what I've heard is true . . .

LADY BEATRIZ: And what is that, M'Lady?

LAURA: It is really Princess Mariana who rules Spain. You must know all   245
the intrigues. Do tell me . . . *(They exit. JUANA ASBAJE enters, a slender,
tall girl of sixteen with wide-set eyes and chestnut hair, broad brow, quick
smile, straight nose, determined chin. BERNARDO catches up with her.)*

BERNARDO: Wait. You must understand.

JUANA: I do. She's come to fetch you back.

BERNARDO: It was arranged years ago—by our parents.

JUANA: You never told me. Why?   250

BERNARDO: I don't know—except that all I could see in the world was
you and I.

JUANA: You are mocking me.

BERNARDO: Please, Juana . . .

JUANA: Maybe you were just indulging yourself. A favorite pastime at   255
court—with you nobles.

BERNARDO: I love you, Juana Asbaje.

JUANA: You pretend to know about love?

BERNARDO: I know how I feel and how you feel.

JUANA: Don't presume, Sir! How inconsequent and variable is your reason. 260

BERNARDO: You have a right to be angry.

JUANA: I have no rights, Bernardo. In your game, only gentlemen with
titles and ladies with property have rights.

BERNARDO: I'd give anything in the world if I could change the conse-
quence of who I am, what I am committed to. What you and I feel is   265
beyond all measure . . .

JUANA: Your words burn in the sun. They will disappear with the wind,
ashes without voice. I am numb, Sir. I have no feeling. When you go,
what I shall feel for you, I do not know, but I've learned much from
this episode.   270

BERNARDO: Episode?

JUANA: What would you call it?

BERNARDO: Much, much more. It's not that simple.

JUANA: For both our sakes, it had better be.

BERNARDO: I wish . . .   275

JUANA: Your wishing could well cause harm.

BERNARDO: You're right. What I want and truly wish—they're not part of
the scheme that's planned for me. My obligations, loyalties . . . I'm
not free. Oh, I wish I were . . .

JUANA: How strange—the ways of enslavement. Please go . . .   280

BERNARDO: I feel like some kind of coward.

JUANA: No—don't feel that way. It's something much bigger than you. Marry your noble lady. Go, please go! (BERNARDO. *struggling with his feelings, hesitates a moment, then leaves. When* JUANA *senses him gone, she falls into* LAURA's *chair, crying.* SLAVE JUANA *enters, goes to her, kneels by chair.*)

SLAVE JUANA: *No llore, coya, el thielo sonlei.*[6]

JUANA: Oh, I'm glad you're here—even if it's for a little while. I'm so alone.   285

SLAVE JUANA: Dry your tears. Your mamá in San Miguel will not want to hear about your tears when I go back. You are so happy here! So many fine gentlemen and fine ladies! You say that all the time—how happy you are!   290

JUANA: Right now, I wish I were back home with all of you. Such happy years—reading my grandfather's books at Poanyán, listening to Mamá Seya's stories by the kitchen fire. Does your mamá still tell stories to the little ones?

SLAVE JUANA: All the little ones still come to her and sit in a circle at her feet like we used to do.   295

JUANA: And market day . . .

SLAVE JUANA: We would watch the tocotines dance and sing.

JUANA: Oh, how I long to hear the sweetness of the *Náhuatl*[7] tongue . . .

SLAVE JUANA: And the songs we used to sing. Remember? *(She stands.)*   300
Come, come . . . *(Begins to clap hands, snaps fingers, beats out a rhythm with her feet, begins to sing.)* Tumba, la, la, la—La tumba la, la, la . . .

SLAVE JUANA *takes* JUANA's *hands, pulls her to her feet, turns her around, continues singing and dancing.* JUANA *hesitates, then joins* SLAVE JUANA *in the song and dance.*

SLAVE JUANA and JUANA: La otra noche, con mi conga, tuvi sin durni. Pensaba—que no quele gente pliete—como aye so gente branca—   305
Tumba la, la, la—Tumba la, le, le. Y en este sueño facho[8] . . . *(SLAVE JUANA notices the entrance of* FATHER ANTONIO, *stops, puts hand on mouth, runs off.* JUANA *sees him, runs to him, attempts to kiss his hand. He gently withdraws it.* FATHER ANTONIO NUÑEZ DE MIRANDA *is a Jesuit, forty-eight years old. Behind his glasses are eyes that are intelligent, piercing, full of humor. There is an extraordinary aliveness about him. He is famous for practicing religious severities as a member of the* Inquisition Council[9]. *Yet, he is a simple man of peasant stock a man of the*

---

[6] *No llore*: Don't cry, child, the sky smiles upon you.   [7] The language of the ancient civilizations of the Toltecs, which lasted from the tenth to thirteenth centuries, and the Aztecs, which lasted from the fourteenth to sixteenth centuries, including the modern descendants of both.   [8] *La otra noche*: The other night, with my conga, I had a dream. I thought—that there will be no black people left—since there are so many white people . . . And in this strange dream . . .   [9] Churchmen, especially Dominicans, always functioned as the officers of The Supreme Council of the Inquisition.

*earth. Everything about him—his manner, his voice, his attitude, his
walk—suggests balance. He is known to be a man who measures realities
with great exactness.)*

FATHER ANTONIO: *(After withdrawing his hands.)* No need, my child.
    Who was the girl you were dancing with?

JUANA: One of the slaves from my mother's farm. She is like my sister.
    She will go back soon and I shall miss her so! At times like this I miss   310
    my valley. The slaves had songs for everything—joy, sadness, love . . .
    songs about the blueness of the sky, counting stars behind the moun-
    tain of *Anahuac*[10] . . .

FATHER: And what times are those?

JUANA: What?   315

FATHER: You said—at times like this . . .

JUANA: Sad times, I suppose . . .

FATHER: You've been crying.

JUANA: Doesn't matter anymore.

FATHER: Forgotten what you were crying about?   320

JUANA: I'm not a child anymore. It's not that easy.

FATHER: Would you like to talk about it?

JUANA: Oh, Father Antonio, tell me—what's to become of me? I don't
    belong here.

FATHER: You have always loved this life. Three years I've been your con-   325
    fessor—you have never said otherwise. And what's this about, "What's
    to become of me?" It should be—what do *you* want to become?

JUANA: It's not what I want to become, but what I want, Father. . .
    (Crosses to LAURA's chair and sits.)

FATHER: Is that what you want?

JUANA: What do you mean?   330

FATHER: To be a viceroy's lady, perhaps?

JUANA: I, who am the lowest of the low . . .

FATHER: Now, what caused that? Have you had a fight with your young
    man?

JUANA: He is not my young man. Never was.   335

FATHER: So that's it.

JUANA: His future bride, Lady Beatriz, daughter of the Duke of Airon
    and Marquis of Valero, has crossed the ocean to claim him. They will
    be married in a great *catedral* . . . Oh, Father, I'm so miserable . . .
    (Goes into his arms.)   340

FATHER: Just cry it out . . .

JUANA: I've already done that—and tears are silly, aren't they?

FATHER: They are not silly when you have something to cry about.

JUANA: Well, I won't cry anymore. What's inevitable is inevitable . . .

FATHER: And what is inevitable?

---

[10] *Anáhuac* (Aztec for "country by the waters") is the region consisting of the central plateau of Mexico
and the valley in which Mexico City is located.

JUANA: The closed doors. First, they refused to accept me at the university. Women, they informed me, should not attempt to seek the clearer eye, logic, wisdom. And today I discovered I don't belong here. My future has no certainty. I cannot hope for a good marriage like the noble ladies of this court. I have no dowry, no title . . . how dare I hope! I am no more than a curiosity at this court! 345 350

FATHER: Lady Laura loves you dearly. Everyone in this palace is fond of you, proud of you . . .

JUANA: Oh, Father, how can that give meaning to my life? Fond of me, proud of me . . . those are just vagaries. Am I to be at the mercy of such vagaries all my life? I must be something! Belong somewhere! 355

FATHER: The reputation of your brilliance grows . . .

JUANA: Another vagary!

FATHER: Go back home, then. Marry an honest man . . .

JUANA: No, I know now marriage is not for me. My greatest hunger is the need to know, to learn, to understand everything in the miracle of Creation. I want to read all the histories, all the poetry, learn all the sciences of the world. I need freedom for that, and freedom is hard to come by for a woman. 360

FATHER: Turn to God . . .

JUANA: I do not even know Him. 365

FATHER: You are pious.

JUANA: That is the way of women. God becomes a comfort early in our lives. Where men fail us, God doesn't. An expedient? No, I cannot believe in God through faith, or fear, or need. I must know Him through the intellect. Then I can say that I know God . . . 370

FATHER: The best way to serve God and men and thus find salvation is through humility and faith, the way to self-perfection.

JUANA: The principle of St. Ignatius of Loyola! You are humble! Your faith shines. That is your meaning. Oh, Father, I must get away from the frivolous passions in this court, from the superficial promises. You've warned me, again and again, and I never listened. Some time ago you told me my future would not be found at court. I didn't hear you. I was dreaming of a young man who promised me his love. Again you cautioned: April is no more than one month . . . The good face of a poor woman is a white wall where fools throw mud . . . Trampled flowers are wasted. Beauty, a man's love, all disappear on land, in smoke, in dust, with shadows . . . You told me all this, and I could not hear, for I was remembering the hot, demanding mouth of a lover . . . 375 380

FATHER: The answer is God . . . (*Light fades on flashback area; comes up on cell. JUANA, covering face with hands, is kneeling down center.*)

JUANA: (*Stands.*) No! I say no to You, God! They are right. No more whip! No more pain! No more vague, undefined guilt. I shall stand and reason with You, God, for it is through reason that I found You, gave myself to You and loved You. Oh, God reason and You shall give clarity to my guilt. (*Goes to window.*) I became Your bride without 385

really knowing You, Sweet Jesus. What took me to the Convent of San   390
José was some stubborn pride, a blind self-pity. Oh, I remember the
Mother Superior with her cadaverous, hollow-eyed face. Oh, the light
of her spirit and her face is still with me. She told me the convent was
a refuge for the frightened and the lost, and I was both. Becoming a
nun is another thing, she said. A struggle more fearful than the strug-   395
gle of Jacob and the Angel. I took the vows though the struggle was
dark and seething inside of me. I became a Carmelite. I could not find
You through faith. I wanted faith. I was jealous of the other sisters'
faith. You are so big to them. Prostrate before You, God, they are glorious forgotten queens, so sure of knowing You, loving You, living for   400
You . . . Faith burst forth fully developed like *Athena*[11] out of Zeus'
head, for them! for them! not me! I took to fevers and delusions. I left
the Order in delirium. What was my life? What is my life? *(Crosses to
box, begins to take out books.)* Back to the Viceroy's palace, to dear
sweet Laura, so full of sympathy. I went to the Marquis and begged   405
him to intercede once more with the university, to influence them.
Knowledge, I was certain, was going to be my salvation . . .

*Fade out on cell area, light goes up on flashback area. The audience room in
the Viceroy's palace. The Marquis De Mancera, Don Antonio Sebastian
De Toledo, is sitting by his wife, Laura, upstage right. Juana, seventeen,
stands by a podium, down left. In the audience are forty of the most learned
men from the university, classical men, theologians, philosophers, mathematicians, humanists. One of the Scholars rises.*

Scholar: Very well done, Juana Asbaje. You have proved your genius.
One last question: What is your definition of wisdom?
Juana: Wisdom is a delicate fabric within "being." For no other reason is   410
the angel more than man, and by the same token, the lack of wisdom
makes man brutish.
Scholar: Bravo! I am amazed. Not once have you faltered in your answers. I am sure that all the gentlemen with me are as impressed as I
am. All of us, the mathematicians, the philosophers, the scientists, are   415
full of admiration for the scope of your great knowledge. *(Applause.)*
Juana: I thank you, but I must be honest. I feel no gratitude for your
praise, for it is only praise. All of you have refused me entrance into
the university. The forty of you were asked to come here by my mentor and friend, the Marquis of Mancera, for the sole purpose of dis-   420
proving the belief that mine is only a smattering of knowledge. You
have witnessed that it is not; yet, if I were to beg you here and now to
voice approval for my entering the university, I know there would only
be silence. *(Pause.)* I am only a girl, you say . . . And all of you believe
that women should know only enough, for more than enough is   425

---

[11] Athena, the favorite daughter of Zeus, was primarily the goddess of the Greek cities, of industry and
the arts, and, in later mythology, of wisdom. She was also goddess of war.

harmful. It is not meant as an accusation against you. It is a sad, hopeless fact. But I, a woman, know better. A whole lifetime of striving to learn and know is not enough for man or woman, and in my struggle with self, with my own femininity, I know there is no difference between the mind of a man and the mind of a woman. Why the barriers? Why the fears?   430

MARQUIS: Now, Juana Asbaje, you have won the battle. Hasn't she, gentlemen? You stood before these prudent gentlemen like a royal galleon beating off the attack of a few enemy sloops, taking an all questions without task, replying to all arguments, to each in his own specialty.   435
You stand vindicated. My dear, I am proud of you. All of Mexico is proud of you . . . *(Applause.)* And now, gentlemen, if you will follow me, I will show you another marvel. This way. My herbarium is beyond. Come, come, gentlemen, you shall see no less than one hundred and fifty species, the largest collection of Indian herbs in the New   440
World. This way . . . *(MARQUIS exits. JUANA stands at podium, covers her face. She is crying in anger and defeat.)*

JUANA: *(Pounds on podium.)* It happens again, and again, and again!

LAURA: My dear, what on earth is the matter? You astounded them all. You've proven what you are.

JUANA: What I am? What am I? That's what's wrong. M'Lord says, "Another marvel . . ." You say I astound . . . Am I no more than a circus?   445
I thought I had found where I belonged at the convent, but I failed there too . . .

LAURA: You're so frail. Their way of life was repugnant to your nature—such rigid denials!   450

JUANA: Where do I belong then?

LAURA: You are making a name for yourself in the literary world.

JUANA: A name? One doesn't belong to a name! Father Antonio convinced me I belonged to Jesus. But did I? I was too rash, too eager to get away from here. This palace—the garden—even in the corridors I   455
would sense that Bernardo was behind me, at the turn, about to open a door. He was everywhere and my yearning for him was so painful. The jasmine outside my window, the soft wanting dark of spring, awakened every memory of what we were to each other. I wanted to forget. To put all those memories away forever. The only time I forget   460
the bittersweet hurt, the only time I do not feel the longing is when Father Antonio comes. I want so much to be like him.

LAURA: Oh, I know how faithless love can be. What woman doesn't? Many women have taken orders for similar reasons. There is no reason to reprimand yourself.   465

JUANA: How defeating for our kind! Oh Laura, I don't want to run away from anything in my life now. You and Father Antonio were by my side all during my illness. I remember the strength of his hands, the sweetness of your voice. I did not die, and somehow during my fever, when I was burning up, my mind was clear as crystal. I was one with   470

God. Then when I could again fill my lungs with pure air, when I
heard the calling of the Angelus, God became very real to me. I felt as
if I were a tiny flame struggling in the fire of His Love. It was something beyond faith, beyond intellect. I can't explain it.

LAURA: You want to be a nun.   475

JUANA: Yes, oh yes— but I have failed that.

LAURA: Father Antonio told me you had found your calling after the
crisis. How strange that he should know! He sat by your bed after a
whole night's vigil when they thought you would not live. He prayed
so for you, held on to you as if refusing death the gift of you. The   480
next morning when the doctors said the danger was over, Father
Antonio kissed your hand and turned to me and claimed, "She belongs to God."

JUANA: He was right. He's some kind of miracle in my life. I think I lived
because I could not bear to leave him.   485

LAURA: Juana, he has arranged it all. Father Antonio and I were going to
tell you later, but you need to know it now . . .

JUANA: Arrange what? Know what?

LAURA: Last week he came for me and we drove out to the border of the
city, south. To the Convent of St. Jerome.   490

JUANA: The Convent of St. Jerome! Most of the Hieronymites are
daughters of the very rich . . . I could never hope . . .

LAURA: It's all arranged! You have more friends than you think. Don
Pedro Velásquez did not allow my husband to pay your dowry. He insisted on being your mentor since he is your relative. And two knights   495
of the Order of Santiago, Don Antonio Mejía and Don Gaspar, have
purchased the property of your cell, gifting it to you.

JUANA: I don't understand . . .

LAURA: Father Antonio convinced all of us that it was the perfect order
for you. He told us St. Jerome wanted women to learn. It should be   500
wise women who teach young girls instead of men. The Hieronymites
are teachers. Their *locutorio* is a meeting place for learned people.
Now, with you there, it shall become the meeting place for the nobility. The Marquis and I and my court shall attend vespers at St. Jerome.

JUANA: Oh, Jesus be praised! St. Jerome, a lover of knowledge! A de-   505
fender of women! Oh, it *is* the place.

LAURA: Another surprise! My husband has convinced the Bishop to give
you certain privileges. You can have books and whatever you may need
to study and learn . . .

JUANA: I shall read Virgil, St. Augustine, St. Jerome, in the tongue of the 510
Church. I shall journey the whole world through my books . . .

*Fade on flashback area, light comes up on cell area. JUANA sits on one of the
boxes holding a book.*

JUANA: Oh, I know what You think of me, God! A hypocrite—is that
what You think I was? No, no, You simply loved me. And I? I forgot

about You! Do You hear? Not even in the silence of the church, kneeling before You, feeling my love for Jesus, did I doubt myself. How 515
funny it seems now—when I understand it all. St. Jerome was never a
haven from the world. I simply brought the world to St. Jerome. That
was another world, a world now lost. Father Antonio knew—from the
very first he warned me. During my novitiate, he was troubled by all
the gifts, the plans, the privileges given to me. The bookshelves that 520
were built for me right here in this cell, the fine furniture, the rugs, all
this bothered him so! But I was so full of joy because of the freedom I
now had to learn, to study, to write. I remember the afternoon, the
very eve before the taking of my vows. I remember . . . Oh, God! a
hypocrite and more. There was the joy, the excitement and then what 525
I felt that eve, that confused passion for that serious, earnest man. I
tell you now, if he had not been of the Faith—if I had not planned to
take the veil, I would have gone to the ends of the world with him. I
loved him fiercely and silently for so long. A love more than spiritual,
total, full of desire . . . I can still remember that eve . . . 530

*Lights fade on cell area, come up on flashback area. The foyer where the Regis-
ter of St. Jerome is kept. It lies on a small table.* JUANA, *dressed as a novitiate
(simple grey gown, white cloth covering hair) enters, leading* FATHER
ANTONIO *by the hand.*

JUANA: It's dark in here. So silent. *(Notices candle on table.)* We can light
that. I will need light to sign the register.
FATHER ANTONIO: *(Goes to table, lights candle.)* I still think you should do
this the proper way.
JUANA: No. The Mother Superior gave me permission. 535
FATHER: After the Marquis persuaded her. You are spoiled!
JUANA: Why should it be a festive affair, the signing of the register? Why
should there be others here? I only want you.
FATHER: You told me there was another reason.
JUANA: *(Goes to register, opens it, points to several places in the book.)*
Look—all of them, entries made by novitiates—I, so and so, legitimate 540
daughter of . . . I, so and so, legitimate daughter of . . . See—all of
them. I cannot claim the father who sired me. He never claimed me,
did not marry my mother . . . What shall I do?
FATHER: How you sign it is of little importance.
JUANA: Legitimate daughter of . . . a lie. 545
FATHER: Only the keeping of your vows matters. You shall vow to live in
poverty, to own nothing, to live in obedience . . . What I have seen—
gifts, privileges . . .
JUANA: Don't scold! I shall bring honor to St. Jerome.
FATHER: I do not doubt that. What about your own salvation? 550
JUANA: Knowledge will be my path to salvation. I do not have your hu-
mility. Your whole life—feeding the hungry, healing the sick. You love
the poor so!

FATHER: And you love the rich Spaniards so!

JUANA: They are my friends and I am grateful for what they've done for   555
me. Let's not quarrel. It is you I love the most. Look at you! *(Touches
his forehead to erase the frown on his face.)* There! That's better.

FATHER: I always give in to you, don't I? You are a beautiful bird, singing
as it flies. You do not touch the earth . . .

JUANA: Oh, Father, what's important is that you will never leave me. You   560
will help me be what you want me to be . . .

FATHER: What God wants you to be . . .

JUANA: At this moment—what you want me to be . . .

FATHER: Daughter . . .

JUANA: And you? More than father—brother, lover . . .   565

FATHER: Juana . . .

JUANA: I'm not saying sinful things. My heart says this and I merely
speak it. It says you are my other self—the one still unborn . . . *(She
embraces him, then goes to register, picks up pen and writes as she speaks.)*
I, Sor Juana Inés de la Cruz, legitimate daughter of Don Pedro de   570
Asbaje y Vargas Machuca and Isabel Ramírez, for the love of Our
Father, the Virgin Mary, and our glorious Pastor, St. Jerome, and Our
Mother, St. Paula, choose and promise God, Our Father, and His
Grace, Don Antonio de Cárdenas y Salazar, canon of this *catedral*,
provisional judge of the archbishopric in whose hands I profess in the
name of the Honorable Francisco Payo de Ribera, Bishop of   575
Guatemala, Archbishop of Mexico, and all his successors, living and
dying in my time, in the space of my life, to live in obedience, in
poverty, owning nothing, promising chastity and accepting perpetual
confinement, as is the rule of Our Father, St. Augustine and the rule
of our Order. I sign my name in Faith the 24th of February, 1669.   580
(Puts pen down, turns to FATHER ANTONIO.*)* Father . . .

FATHER: Yes, my daughter . . .

JUANA: One candle to light the darkness. So many shadows!

FATHER: Don't be afraid. Tomorrow, all will be light.

JUANA: How many days did you spend in the cellar making all those   585
luminaires?

FATHER: They line all the gardens and the path to the church and surround the church. They will light up the whole of Mexico City. This
very eve, they will be lighted. In all God's brightness, Satan cannot
come to tempt you!   590

JUANA: May God make me saintly . . . *(Blows out candle. Lights fade out
on flashback area. Total darkness. Singing begins.*

*[Baroque Spanish Mass.] Lights come up on flashback area again. A kneeling
pew covered by white cloth is at center. Music—the benediction. An* ALTAR
BOY *appears with cushion holding crown and ring. He is followed by the*
CANON. ALTAR BOY *crosses up center,* CANON *to right of kneeling pew.*
CANON *prays over crown and ring, blesses them.* JUANA, *dressed as a bride,*

enters, crosses to kneeling pew, kneels before CANON. *[For simple staging: procession could be included with convent nuns.] After* JUANA *kneels, the* CANON *holds the gold crown over her head.)*

CANON: Come, bride of Christ, and receive the crown that God prepared for you all through eternity.

JUANA: All my days I shall follow the angel of Our Father who is the Tabernacle of my body. I renounce the kingdom of the world and its vanities for the love of Jesus Christ whom I saw, whom I love, whom I believe, and whom I made the object of my predilection. I am His servant and I shall serve Him humbly. *(The crown is removed. The* CANON *places the ring of Fidelity on* JUANA's *finger.)* 595

CANON: On your finger I place the distinct pledge of the Holy Spirit. Thus you are named the wife of God. *(Choir voices rise in final benediction as lights dim at the end of Act I.)* 600

ACT II

SCENE I

The next evening. Rosary bell is heard. JUANA, *sitting cross-legged in bed, wearing a sackcloth wrapper, is playing a flute very softly, awkwardly, stopping every so often to touch it. She stops to listen to church bell, then covers face with hands. A tray of untouched food sits on one of the boxes.* SOR FELICIANA *enters, crosses to tray, inspects it.* JUANA *puts flute under pillow.*

SOR FELICIANA: You didn't touch your food.

SOR JUANA: I drank my tea. Stopped the shivering . . .

SOR FELICIANA: *(Crosses to bed, touches* SOR JUANA's *forehead.)* You're still feverish. Did you sleep?

SOR JUANA: I don't want to sleep—I don't want to dream. 5

SOR FELICIANA: *(Sits on bed next to* SOR JUANA.) I wanted to spend the day with you. We went out for wood and had such problems!

SOR JUANA: There's no more coal?

SOR FELICIANA: Supply wagons cannot get into the city. They're ambushed by the people up on the mountain. No fruits or meat . . . 10

SOR JUANA: They're starving, those people up on the mountain. They need the food more than we do. It's all so different, so terrifying. *(Crosses to window.)* Look, out there, the *locutorio*, silent, dark. Over a year now. Is the whole world like that now?

SOR FELICIANA: They're all dark now, all the *locutorios* of Mexico. Don't you remember? The Commissary of the Inquisition decided on that long before the burning of the city. I hear they are dark all over Spain too. 15

SOR JUANA: Sinful. Isn't that what the *locutorios* are supposed to be? And
            my plays? And all the festivals for the saints? I believe it now. My   20
            whole life was sinful . . .

SOR FELICIANA: That's not the truth, Sor Juana. The *locutorio* of St.
            Jerome; thanks to you, was the spiritual center for the devout. Great
            people, great minds, gathered out there. They all found a path to your
            door. You have always been faithful to the precepts of St. Jerome, to   25
            knowledge.

SOR JUANA: Faithful to knowledge, but not to my vows . . .

SOR FELICIANA: You're never going to get well with all that guilt inside of
            you. You never did anything wrong. You, of all people, the most gen-
            tle, the most wise.   30

SOR JUANA: I miss the garden so. Where there were flowers, there are
            turnips now. But we cannot eat flowers, can we . . .

SOR FELICIANA: After rosary services, I'm coming back with hot soup,
            and you're going to eat it. I'm going to make you. Food, rest will get
            you well . . .   35

SOR JUANA: You think so? I wonder where he is right now . . .

SOR FELICIANA: Who?

SOR JUANA: My confessor, my tormentor . . .

SOR FELICIANA: The last I heard, Father Antonio was leading a wagon
            train with food and medicine for the starving of Zacatecas. No harvest   40
            there.

SOR JUANA: Always with the poor, the sick, the hungry. But he knows
            how to gain Heaven, on earth as well. I didn't understand before, but
            now I wish I had spent my life the way he has. But he's so old. He
            shouldn't travel long distances any more. If only I could see him, talk   45
            to him one more time . . .

SOR FELICIANA: Oh, dear Aunt, you will see him. Sor Catarina has sent
            for him.

SOR JUANA: But he was forbidden to ever see me again.

SOR FELICIANA: That won't stop him if he knows you have been ill.   50

SOR JUANA: Oh, dear God, thank you for the hope! Days will be good
            again just waiting for him! *(Rosary bell rings again.)*

SOR FELICIANA: *(Kisses SOR JUANA, crosses to door.)* I must go now, but I'll
            be back after services. *(Exits.)*

SOR JUANA: *(Crosses to window.)* I miss the flowers so!   55

*Light fades on cell, comes up on flashback area. A table down right; a chair
with a flower basket full of bouquets next to it. SOR JUANA enters with a
handful of cut ribbons; SOR FELICIANA follows. St. Jerome has been the home
of SOR JUANA for seventeen years. She wears a tunic of white wool, blue-edged,
double-sleeved. Outside sleeve is bell-shaped, giving a certain elegance to the
habit. Over the tunic is a long black scapulary (two small slips of cloth almost
the length of the tunic underneath). The scapulary is six inches shorter than
the tunic. On the front piece of the scapulary is an image over the chest area.*

Emblem of the Annunciation, the Virgin Mary standing to the right of a re-cliner where a book lies open. The left hand of the Virgin lies on the book. Op-posite the Virgin, on the other side of the recliner, is the imprint of the Archangel Gabriel with folded white. wings. On her head, SOR JUANA wears a white toque and over that a long black veil. On her waist is a wide leather belt with a brass buckle. On her feet, plain black closed shoes and cotton stockings. Around her neck and failing parallel to the scapulary is a black rosary (fif-teen mysteries). The large gold cross of the rosary is adjusted high on the left sleeve of her tunic. The habit of the Order of St. Jerome. SOR JUANA and SOR FELICIANA put a ribbon around each of the bouquets. A children's choir begins to sing as they go about their labor.

> Aquella zagala
> Del mirar sereno
> Hechizo del soto
> Y envidia del cielo
>
> La que el mayoral   60
> De la cumbre excelso
> Hirió con sus ojos
> Hirió con sus ojos . . .[12]

Harmony without lyrics is heard.

SOR FELICIANA: The legend of the nymph. How beautiful, your words,
     your music.   65
SOR JUANA: My farewell gift for Lisi. The nymph that disappears in light.
     Oh, why must the people we love leave us . . .

> La ninfa del valle
> Donde nací
> Vuela, bailando   70
> La escala de luz
>
> En alta peñasca
> Donde tiembla el sol
> Canta la ninfa
> Canta, canta   75
> Con voz celestial.[13]

---

[12]That young maiden girl
Of the steady gaze
The enchantress of the woods
And the envy of the sky

The one the shepherd
From the high hills
Hurt with his look
Hurt with his look

[13]The nymph of the valley
Where I was born
Fly, dancing
the rainbow of light

On a high rock
Where the sun shakes
The nymph sings
Sings, sings
With celestial voice.

Sor Feliciana: There. All done. After they sing, each child will offer a bouquet to the Count and the Countess.

Sor Juana: Overwhelmed by flowers. My last festivity for them. They love this garden so, dear Count, dearest Lisi . . .   80

Sor Feliciana: Dr. Pavón is due any minute now . . .

Sor Juana: Oh dear, I forgot all about the interview. I suppose I must find the time since I said I would, but I do have so many preparations yet for the festivities tomorrow.

Sor Feliciana: Would you like to see him here in the garden?   85

Sor Juana: Yes, send him out here.

Sor Feliciana exits. Sor Juana notices her slave.

Sor Juana: There you are. Go tell Timoteo I would like the chairs set up this afternoon. A canopy over the Count and Countess' chair . . .

Slave Juana: Mistress . . .

Sor Juana: Let's see. I've taken care of the pastries, the chocolate came in from Chiapas. The Count's favorite wine must be chilled. And more flowers—of course, I must see to the flowers. *(Notices her slave.)* Go, girl, do as I say.   90

Slave Juana: You said I could go and see Andrés.

Sor Juana: What?   95

Slave Juana: You forgot about Andrés . . .

Sor Juana: Oh, I'm sorry. It did slip my mind. How is he? You saw him yesterday?

Slave Juana: He beat bad. He and Camila hide. I go take them food.

Sor Juana: You must be careful not to implicate yourself . . .   100

Slave Juana: He my brother.

Sor Juana: What he did is considered a most serious crime. He has run away from Don Martín many times before, but this time he turned on his master. That is a serious crime. Have you heard? Is Don Martín dead?   105

Slave Juana: Don Martín evil man. Good if he die.

Sor Juana: May God forgive Andrés . . .

Slave Juana: And you . . .

Sor Juana: Juana!

Slave Juana: I beg you buy Andrés away from Don Martín . . .   110

Sor Juana: You know I spoke to him about it, again and again. A stubborn man—a slave is a slave to him.

Slave Juana: The Count, the Countess, your friends—they could make him. They are important people. They could force Don Martín . . .

Sor Juana: You don't know what you're talking about. It's a delicate subject. There are certain unspoken rules about a master and his slaves. I cannot take sides.   115

Slave Juana: You forgot Andrés was like your brother long ago.

Sor Juana: I have not forgotten. But that was long ago. It's a different world.   120

SLAVE JUANA: You not love Andrés. You not care. Andrés and Camila go
    to mountain where people hide. Soon they will fight!
SOR JUANA: Fight? That is only fearful talk. It will not come to that.
SLAVE JUANA: You do not see because your nose in book all the time.
SOR JUANA: Enough. If only all men were equal. Perhaps some day this   125
    will be, through the help of God, knowledge . . .
SLAVE JUANA: Your head stuffed with words, Sister. Pretty, silly words, Sister.
SOR JUANA: How dare you. . .
SLAVE JUANA: You say I is like your sister.
SOR JUANA: You are also my slave.   130
SLAVE JUANA: Then why you say we is equal?
SOR JUANA: Go to Andrés. Help him as best you can. Tell him I will pray
    for him.
SLAVE JUANA: Many starve on mountain.
SOR JUANA: I will pray for them too.   135
SLAVE JUANA: That will not fill their bellies.
SOR JUANA: Prayer moves mountains . . .
SLAVE JUANA: Don't move mountain. Just give more food.
SOR JUANA: I said enough! Now go.
SLAVE JUANA: *(Turns to go, then stops.)* Andrés and Camila will not come   140
    back this time. They will not be caught. They have wagon and gun.
SOR JUANA: May God keep them safe. *(Watches SLAVE JUANA go, puts
    hand to forehead as if head hurts.)* Why must the world change so? I
    remember slaves singing at the plow. But I was a child then. I cannot
    bridge the years anymore. Oh my, I must see to those flowers . . .   145
    *(SOR FELICIANA enters with DR. IGNACIO PAVÓN, a Peruvian poet who
    has come from Lima to interview SOR JUANA.)*
SOR FELICIANA: Sor Juana, this is Dr. Ignacio Pavón. He has come all the
    way from Lima, Peru, just to interview you.
DR. PAVON: Sor Juana Inés de la Cruz, a great honor. *(Kisses her hand.)*
SOR JUANA: Dr. Pavón.
SOR FELICIANA: You'll forgive me. I have duties to attend to.   150
DR. PAVON: Thank you for leading me to this garden and to this great lady.
SOR FELICIANA: Goodbye, Dr. Pavón. *(Exits.)*
SOR JUANA: You have caught me in the midst of preparations—a farewell
    party for the Count of Paredes and his wife, Lisi.
DR. PAVON: I am intruding . . .   155
SOR JUANA: Oh, no, please! This is the perfect time. I need someone to
    cheer me up. A poet, you are!
DR. PAVON: A humble one in the light of your great fame. Beautiful
    place, St. Jerome.
SOR JUANA: My home for seventeen years.   160
DR. PAVON: Fruitful years.
SOR JUANA: They have not been idle. May I offer you some refreshment?
DR. PAVON: Not at the moment, thank you. I have come across an ocean
    to set eyes on the Tenth Muse.

SOR JUANA: So, I am pursued into pagan temples! My church is Christ's   165
church.

DR. PAVON: In your writings, you have given that Christian humanity to
the pagans. You cannot deny you love the Greeks.

SOR JUANA: The Greeks are the open door to our humanity. Tell me of
your work, your country.   170

DR. PAVON: What does a poet do? I'm a man coiled in his own passions,
unwinding, discovering, and sometimes, and mind you only sometimes, attempting to re-create with words some kind of energy lost in
my people. A sad attempt to remold our poor misguided civilization.

SOR JUANA: Unwinding passions—how beautifully you put it. We are   175
creatures of passion, are we not? Writers! What a lot we are!

DR. PAVON: All I've read by you, of you, is full of passion.

SOR JUANA: My greatest passion has been to learn and learn and learn.
My way to God.

DR. PAVON: There is, of course, your strong faith.   180

SOR JUANA: I shall share a secret with you.

DR. PAVON: A secret?

SOR JUANA: You journalists are always looking for something new. For a
long time now, I have come to believe that my love for knowledge is
much more than a passion. It's madness.   185

DR. PAVON: Madness? I don't understand . . .

SOR JUANA: Some time ago, a holy and candid abbess who was my superior forbad me to study. I was ordered not to read a single book. She
believed that knowledge was a form of inquisition. I did as I was told.
I did not study. I did not even take a book into my hands. A very dif-   190
ficult thing for me to do.

DR. PAVON: She had no right . . .

SOR JUANA: Oh yes, she did! She was a most holy abbess. She was true to
her vows. She lived by faith alone. Her path to God was different from
my own. Well, when I could no longer read, I found myself over-   195
whelmed by a curiosity. I studied the things that God created, all
around me—little things. One morning walking through the doorway
of my bedroom, I observed that though the lines of the two sides of
the hall were parallel and its ceiling was level, the eye pretended that
its lines leaned toward each other and that its ceiling was lower in the   200
distant part. I inferred that visual lines run straight, but not parallel,
forming a pyramid figure. I told myself that was the reason the ancients doubted that the earth was spherical. But then I told myself it
could be a trick of the eyesight. Thoughts came like this one, one after
another, day after day. It was like a fever consuming me. More than a   205
passion.

DR. PAVON: But such journeys of the mind are exciting.

SOR JUANA: My mind would not rest. I remember watching the little girls
we teach here at St. Jerome playing with a top one day. I noticed the
easy movement of the spherical form and how long the impulse lasted   210

once it was independent of its cause. I ran to the kitchen and took a
handful of flour. I sifted it on a table, then took the top and spun it
on the table. I spun it thus to see if the circles made by its movements
were perfectly circular or not. I discovered that only some spiral lines
lost their circularity as soon as they transmitted their impulse. Then to 215
my mind came the thought that in the study of music, harmony is circular. A spiral! Such thoughts invaded my mind, invade my mind still
these days, though I now spend long hours reading, experimenting.
God wants me to understand my universe. Did you know I had been
accused of heresy for doing what I do? The Bishop of Puebla does not 220
approve of me. They would like me to study more of the sacred theol-
ogy. Little do they know that both can be reconciled . . .

DR. PAVON: You have found a way . . .

SOR JUANA: Of course! Without Rhetoric, how could I understand the
figures, the tropes, the locution of the Holy Scripture? Or, without 225
Physics, how could I understand the many natural problems of the nature of sacrificial animals? Without Arithmetic, could I understand the
computations of days, months, hours, weeks as mysteries, as were
those of Daniel? How without Geometry could I measure the Holy
Chest of the Testament and even the Holy City of Jerusalem, whose 230
mysteries thus measured form a cube? All those dimensions! And the
marvelous distribution of all its parts! Without Architecture, how
could I understand the Great Temple of Solomon? God Himself was
the Architect who gave the disposition and plan. The Wise King was
only the foreman who executed it. They accuse me of loving knowl- 235
edge more than God.

Light fades out on flashback area, comes up on cell area. SOR JUANA *is still by
the window, looking out. She suddenly turns, crosses to bed, takes out flute
from under the pillow. Plays a few notes softly, then touches it tenderly.*

SOR JUANA: You gave this to me, Andrés. Your one possession. You and
Juana said goodbye forever. Yes, it was forever! We were children, free
. . . *(She plays a few more notes, then hugs flute, crosses to window
again.)* Oh, God, are You out there in the hovels where children cry
of hunger? Are You out there in the ashes that were the marketplace, 240
where the hanging tree sways with the wind? Are You here, with me
and my pain? No! I want to remember happy times. The garden full of
people and laughter . . . the last party we ever had in the garden. The
very last one. Even then the sounds of a wounded world, heavy with
pain, hung in the air . . . 245

*Light fades on cell area, comes up on flashback area. There are three chairs,
very ornate under a canopy. The center chair is raised slightly above the others.
A single ordinary chair is outside the canopy.* SOR JUANA *is seated on the
raised chair. The* COUNT DE PAREDES *sits to her right.* LISI, *his wife, sits to her
left.* DR. PAVON *sits on the single chair outside the canopy.*

LISI: I shall remember this day. The children were lovely, all our friends so kind! I hate to say goodbye to Mexico.

COUNT: I too shall miss Mexico, though I confess the Mexico outside these walls is not to my liking. The Indian, the sambo, has forgotten the good we have brought to this new world. We civilized a primitive people. Now they turn against us. 250

DR. PAVON: I equate civilization with violence, M'Lord. The white man has been less than a humanizing force.

COUNT: Did you hear about Don Rafael Martín? Attacked by one of his slaves. Found unconscious in the granary. 255

SOR JUANA: Will he die?

COUNT: He'll recover, but two slaves are gone, his wagon, his horse, and stores from his warehouse. Who is safe these days!

SOR JUANA: Humane masters, perhaps. Don Martín treats his slaves like animals. 260

COUNT: Do you condone the crime?

SOR JUANA: I don't condone crime, but all circumstances must be understood before the word "crime" is given to a single desperate act.

COUNT: Those runaway slaves have a good head start into mountain country. Don Martín's soldiers gave up the chase. I suppose you're glad the two slaves escaped. I'm afraid the mountains have their own merciless bondage. They may starve, freeze to death, become the prey of wild animals. 265

SOR JUANA: May God protect them and keep them safe.

COUNT: Would you say the same prayer for Don Martín? 270

SOR JUANA: There is no need. He is surrounded by comfort and care.

LISI: M'Lord, let's enjoy our last visit to St. Jerome. Oh, the memories I take with me—music, laughter, brilliant conversation. Sor Juana drawing, quoting her poetry, or passionate over a new scientific finding. Sor Juana, the center of our lives . . . I shall miss you so, dear friend. 275

COUNT: We should not be at odds, Sor Juana. I know you love us well. Ah, the peace of this place. Such flowers!

SOR JUANA: I shall miss you both. Six years. I've known you and loved you both for six years. And you have done so much good, M'Lord.

COUNT: I hope that during my reign I made the right decisions. I tried to. I pride myself in being a man in touch with the times. But dreams erode. The world is full of wolf packs and each great nation in time falls victim. 280

SOR JUANA: Ah, Dr. Pavón. There is much to say about His Excellency. He has been a compassionate ruler, just and right. as if he were born to be nothing less. 285

DR. PAVON: I have heard the like said of him. But you are right, dear Count, the wolf packs are growing. When I arrived in Vera Cruz, a French pirate ship had gone into Acapulco and carried off forty women. 290

COUNT: The Gulf is infested. Another problem for the new viceroy.

DR. PAVON: Ah yes! Count Monclova is a favorite of the Peruvian court. Has an arm made of silver. Lost it in a naval battle. For many years he was the companion of Her Excellency, the Vicereine of Peru. He carries a gold casket aboard his ship. It's said to be full of, gold and diamonds and a bone belonging to St. Rose of Lima. It is his protection against pirates. He will rule with a silver arm . . . preferable to ruling with an iron hand, eh? *(Laughs.)*   295

LISI: Alas, he has no wife. No one to lead him to this wonderful place. I daresay he will come to meet you, Sor Juana, and will attend one of your gatherings in the *locutorio*.   300

SOR JUANA: I fear it will not be so. There is the weight of too much criticism—of me, of St. Jerome, of *locutorios* in general. It can only get worse.

LISI: You have our protection even from across the sea.   305

SOR JUANA: I know it and I thank you.

LISI: Whatever happens, your work will be published. I'm taking all you have ever written to a publisher in Madrid.

SOR JUANA: They are the only children I have conceived. Imperfect, but they are yours . . .   310

LISI: They shall belong to the world . . . *(Light fades on flashback area, comes up on cell. SOR JUANA sits on bed and begins to play flute. Stage slowly darkens.)*

SCENE 2

The next afternoon. SOR JUANA and SOR FELICIANA are standing over the boxes.

SOR JUANA: I want all articles and letters in this small box. Books in the large one.

SOR FELICIANA: Are you up to doing this?

SOR JUANA: Of course I am. Look at me. You fed me last night. I ate   315
everything this morning. My fever's gone— and Father Antonio might come today. It's Wednesday, isn't it? He always came for tea on Wednesdays when he was in the city, remember?

SOR FELICIANA: Don't set your hopes too high . . .

SOR JUANA: It's a beautiful day, isn't it? Anyway, let's put all these things   320
away. Once everything is put away I shall feel that I have turned another page in my life, and the page is clean, waiting for new experiences. We shall bury these things deep in the dungeon of this convent . . .

SOR FELICIANA: There's no dungeon . . .   325

SOR JUANA: Very well. We shall store them somewhere dark where spiders can build their webs. I do not want my past.

SOR FELICIANA: I see your guilt did not disappear with the fever.

SOR JUANA: He will never recognize this place. I don't even have a table
to serve tea! I must have a table . . .   330

SOR FELICIANA: We'll find one if he comes . . .

SOR JUANA: Of course he's going to come. Let's start with this box. *(She
kneels on floor and starts taking books and papers from a box to sort
them. Comes across a copy of her love sonnets. She turns the pages.)*

SOR FELICIANA: What's that?

SOR JUANA: Poems . . .

SOR FELICIANA: May I? *(SOR JUANA hands book to her.)* Your sonnets!   335
How beautiful.

SOR JUANA: Not now . . .

SOR FELICIANA: Wait! *(She begins to read.)* "Love begins, a faint restless-
ness, a burning wakeful anxiety, growing in slopes, transsections, feeding on tears, entreaty . . ."   340

SOR JUANA: Ancient, ancient feelings.

SOR FELICIANA: Your feelings?

SOR JUANA: All mine. The pain of youth . . .

SOR FELICIANA: *(Continues reading.)* "Love, shadow of my scornful
good, bewitched image, fair illusion for which I'd gladly die, sweet   345
confection, for which I live in torment . . ."

SOR JUANA: They sound so awkward—such rash feelings.

SOR FELICIANA: Someone hurt you very much.

SOR JUANA: We suffer so when we are young. The howls of my pain.

SOR FELICIANA: Is that why you took the veil?   350

SOR JUANA: Who knows one's reasons for doing those things that
change one's life? What comes to mind is a childhood memory.
There was a mulatto on my grandfather's farm, a misshapen man,
an idiot, they used to say. Even as a child I could read the hurting
loneliness in his eyes by the way he walked and held his head. Poor   355
creature! One morning when the dark was dissolving, I followed
him out into the desert wondering what he did out there so early
in the morning. He ran to the middle of a sand hill. The wind
moaned and the dust curled under his feet. He held up his arms
as if pleading with the morning sky, then fell to his knees. Suddenly   360
he raised his head and howled. Just howled—long, sad, empty
sound that ran into the stillness of the sun. That was his loneliness,
his pain. He freed himself of the heavy cutting burden, to face
the day.

SOR FELICIANA: How sad. What happened to him?   365

SOR JUANA: He disappeared. I always imagined he had walked off into
the desert and found a place where he was like everyone else. Those
words are just the way I howl . . .

SOR FELICIANA: Your sensitive, beautiful words?

SOR JUANA: Why not? The writing of those sonnets washed me clean.   370
The anger, doubt. bitterness. all washed away.

SOR FELICIANA: Who was he?

SOR JUANA: A young nobleman, foolish and unwise, no different from myself.

SOR FELICIANA: It must have been so painful . . .   375

SOR JUANA: The grave agony that begins with desire, then that sudden rushing melancholy, evaporating contradictions. Those are the contradictions.

SOR FELICIANA: *(Reading through the pages.)* You speak of deception, again and again. *(Reads.)* "Triumph, my love, you who kills me with   380 disdain. And he who loves me, I myself, kill, for he loves in vain. I do not know if love is hate, or hate is love, for both are fires that prick the skin and move the heart and sweeten all the air . . ."

SOR JUANA: He will come today. I know he will. . .

SOR FELICIANA: It's not a certainty.   385

SOR JUANA: I am not at my best . . . my wool tunic, the blue-edged one—the embroidered scapulary, the one from Spain . . . Look at me—so disheveled . . .

SOR FELICIANA: All you have is what you're wearing.

SOR JUANA: How stupid of me! I forgot. Is there some tea left in the   390 kitchen? Just a little . . . *(Looks around room.)* He will be shocked, the way I look, the room—so empty, bare . . .

SOR FELICIANA: You sold everything. Do you regret it? All your beautiful things, your books, your instruments.

SOR JUANA: No! There's no regret. My empty cell will please Father   395 Antonio. It vexed him so, my having all those luxuries. May God for- give me! Is it three o'clock? He always came at three . . . so punctual!

SOR FELICIANA: It's closer to five.

SOR JUANA: Five . . . No! Sister Catarina sent for him. It's been two weeks now.   400

SOR FELICIANA: We have not received word as to his whereabouts. The fact that it's Wednesday doesn't mean . . .

SOR JUANA: I wanted him to come today. I need him to help me creep out of this darkness. Never mind the books. We'll see to them later. I'll watch for him at the window.   405

SOR FELICIANA: Do you want me to watch with you?

SOR JUANA: No. Go about your business. Thank you. I'd rather sit here by myself.

SOR FELICIANA: I'll check on the tea—just in case . . .

SOR JUANA: Yes, yes—do that.   410

SOR FELICIANA: *(Crosses to exit, turns.)* I'll stop by after supper. *(SOR JUANA, staring out into the garden, doesn't answer. SOR FELICIANA leaves.)*

SOR JUANA: I have cast off pride, possessions, so my flight to Heaven will not be cumbersome. Oh, Father, you were right! Knowledge more easily breeds arrogance than it does humility. Oh, Father Antonio, I know myself now! I've opened the door to the prison I created. It's   415 not a blind creature you will see before you . . . No more . . .

*Light fades on cell, comes up on flashback area. There is a statue of the Virgin
Mary backing a font of holy water. To the left is a confessional SOR JUANA
comes out of the confessional, crosses herself, goes to front, dips fingers in holy
water, crosses herself again. FATHER ANTONIO comes out of the confessional.
SOR JUANA turns, hands reaching out to welcome her confessor.*

SOR JUANA: My prayers of penitence can wait!

FATHER ANTONIO: You are forgiven, my child.

SOR JUANA: Trees are blooming, and the last time I saw you I was worried about the frostbite on your nose. *(Touches his face after looking at*   420
it intently.) There are tired lines around your mouth. You are too old
for long trips over mountains! Where were you?

FATHER: Manzana. I found a miracle there. *(Takes out folded printed sheet
from pocket, hands it to SOR JUANA.)* See . . .

SOR JUANA: *(Unfolding sheet.)* My mysteries! I wrote them a long time   425
ago. Where did you find them? Manzana—an Indian village, isn't it?

FATHER: Isolated, and now its people are dying of the plague like flies. I
exhausted all my energies, not fighting for peoples' lives, but preparing them for Heaven. The last rites become swollen ritual words in my
mouth. So many! One night, they forced me to rest and gave me a   430
fish for supper. I sat down at a table, too weary to protest, and unwrapped my fish. There it was—your mysteries.

SOR JUANA: Someone wrapped a fish with it?

FATHER: There it was, your name, your words, at a time like that! I forgot my hunger and fatigue. I read your prayer by a wavering flame in   435
the cold room—your fourth mystery to the Virgin Mary. It made me
new. I read it again and again and held it in my hand while I slept. A
miracle.

SOR JUANA: These were distributed in the *catedral,* thousands of them,
two years ago. This one fell into your hands . . . and all those months   440
I longed for you so, imagined you falling off a horse, or getting sick.
There was no more waiting at the gate for you, and somehow days became blurred and empty.

FATHER: When there is time to breathe or rest, you are in my thoughts
too.   445

SOR JUANA: But my prayers have been answered. I hear you were recalled
by the bishop. I heard the Tribunal had reprimanded you for neglecting your duties as an officer of the Inquisition. You have been ordered
to remain in Mexico City and I'm glad, glad, glad!

FATHER: I doubt that you are glad about my misfortune.   450

SOR JUANA: It isn't that to me! Someone younger, with more energies,
can take your place with those people.

FATHER: How little you understand. North of Coahuila—immolation—
anger against the God we gave them. Their most insane pagan god is
better to them than the God given to them by the Conquistadores.   455

SOR JUANA: They have lost the Way . . .

FATHER: I'm not so sure. I have been one of them for too long not to
          understand their anger and their fear.

SOR JUANA: All that I care about is that you're safe and that you're here
          and that I shall see you often.   460

FATHER: How blind you are, my daughter. The palace, the convent, that
          is not the world—nor those books that consume your life.

SOR JUANA: I know that these are rebellious times.

FATHER: How well you mouth the words of your masters.

SOR JUANA: My masters!   465

FATHER: For almost two decades you have spent your life writing, singing
          the praises of the masters. *Villancicos*[14] for a long parade of viceroys,
          vicereines—loas and sonnets about the Spanish great. Your praises
          have been bountiful for those who have conquered your people, ex-
          ploited them.   470

SOR JUANA: They are my friends. They are the only world I know . . .

FATHER: Have you forgotten your beginnings? You are mejicana!

SOR JUANA: I will not take sides! I dream, I hope for, I work for the
          brotherhood of all men. . . .

FATHER: What substance is there in the words you write, the ideas you   475
          express, when in this very city you hear the sad songs of the zambo
          slaves living in the hovels behind the rich man's house? The cry of
          women whose children are in pain because of hunger? Look upon the
          earth to find your Heaven, child. It is not in pretty words.

SOR JUANA: Why do I wait for you with such eagerness? There is no   480
          peace between us.

FATHER: Have you made peace with yourself?

SOR JUANA: I do not know what you mean. I just confessed my sins to
          you. You have absolved me . . .

FATHER: Oh, the triviality of your sins! You're not even aware of your sins! 485

SOR JUANA: You don't love me! You take such pleasure in trying to de-
          stroy what I believe . . .

FATHER: What you believe! It's what you *are* that's important. Look to
          your own people.

SOR JUANA: What would you have me be?   490

FATHER: In Fresnillo, where I was born, there is a dry, brittle shrub that
          clings ferociously to life. Its roots dig into the sand, the hostile sun
          violates. The tempestuous wind twists the shrub, strips it, wounds it,
          until it structures itself against its own nature, pulling away, pushing
          away, just to stay alive, just to survive. Its thorns, empty of the milk of 495
          hope, prick your finger. The shrub shrivels up against the violence
          around. That is the Mexican today—the Indian—the zambo slave. My
          spirit is like that shrub, my soul, my passions. I am a Mexican, so I
          fight! I beg money off the rich, I hide the fugitive, I scramble around

---

[14] Spanish songs of praise composed for religious services.

for food and medicine, because their hunger, their pain, their enslave-   500
ment, their deaths wound me, consume me . . .

SOR JUANA: I feel with you, but you must understand—I fight the same
struggle. My voice carries all over, my words of love, compassion,
brotherhood, peace . . .

FATHER: I'm speaking of human beings—not words!   505

SOR JUANA: You refuse to understand!

FATHER: And you refuse to see! *(Light fades on flashback area, comes up
on cell area.* SOR JUANA *is still by window.)*

SOR JUANA: He's not coming. He may never come. *(She crosses to a box
on the floor and rummages through it desperately until she finds a packet
of letters. She looks through them until she finds the one she is looking for.
It is a letter written to her by one Sor Filotea de la Cruz. She stares at it,
then crumbles it in her hand.)* They deceived me with this! Conspiracy!
The Holy Company against one lone woman. Cowards! *(She begins to*   510
sob.) They took him away from me . . . they took him away from
me . . . *(Light fades on cell area, comes up on flashback area. May 1691.
The Bishopric in the diocese of* BISHOP DON MIGUEL FERNANDO DE
SANTA CRUZ, *in Puebla.* BISHOP *is sitting behind desk, looking at three
documents. A published postulate written by a renowned Jesuit, Father
Antonio Vieira, an intellectual giant, entitled The Greater Good of Jesus.
The second document is a letter written by* SOR JUANA *as an answer to
the third document, supposedly a letter written by one Filotea de la Cruz,
Convent of the Holy Trinity.* FATHER JUAN IGNACIO, *the* BISHOP's *secre-
tary, enters.)*

BISHOP: We have a problem.

JUAN IGNACIO: You speak of Sor Juana Inés de la Cruz.

BISHOP: Precisely. Hostile forces within the Church and outside the   515
Church are shifting and changing to create dissension. As the Bishop
of Puebla, it is my duty to maintain some kind of balance.

JUAN IGNACIO: I understand, Your Holiness.

BISHOP: Don Francisco Aguiar y Seijas has changed the face of Mexico.

JUAN IGNACIO: Our esteemed Archbishop has seen to it that all comedies   520
in print be burned and has successfully replaced his most holy book
among the faithful, Consolations for the Poor . . .

BISHOP: You can imagine what he thinks of Sor Juana's pagan plays!
Mexico shall be well rid of impure customs, sinfulness. Sor Juana may
find herself in the Index one of these days. When our Archbishop first   525
came to Mexico six years ago, he found a country beset by vices, devoid of virtues . . . The time has come for great piety among the faithful. Festivities in the Church have been abolished, convent *locutorios*
are now closed. You would think Sor Juana would see the light, but
her pen has not stopped. And her latest—her criticism of Vieira—that   530
is too much for the Holy Company to endure. A hornet's nest . . .

JUAN IGNACIO: Of course! Her Athenagoric letter. It has caused a sensation. She claims it was not meant to be published.

BISHOP: I had it published. I also called it, appropriately, the Athenagoric
    Letter. Rather well titled, wouldn't you say?   535
JUAN IGNACIO: A clever insinuation on your part. She does love the
    Greeks. It's there, in all she writes. She is an Athena . . .
BISHOP: I assumed that if I had it published, she would be proved a fool!
    She is a fool! How dare she criticize the postulate of the most brilliant
    of Jesuits!   540
JUAN IGNACIO: There is no greater Catholic Predicator than Father
    Antonio Vieira.
BISHOP: The audacity of that woman! A man of the world! One who has
    mingled with great minds! To find himself opposed by this upstart—a
    nun with a parochial mind! He must be highly amused.   545
JUAN IGNACIO: A great part of the public is siding with Sor Juana.
BISHOP: I simply cannot believe—refuse to believe—that the ravings of a
    simple-minded maid should be preferred over the subtle discernment
    of the Holy Scripture in Vieira's argument. But then, Vieira's views are
    beyond common intelligence.   550
JUAN IGNACIO: A great man.
BISHOP: A man of action too! A long service as advisor to the king of
    Portugal, and later, standing before his Christian pulpit in Brazil, he
    gave voice to the abuses of the rich. He fears not! The powerful
    Brazilians used their influence at the Vatican to have him censored.   555
    But he went to Rome himself and pleaded a brilliant case before the
    Pope. Even the Pope gave in . . . Vieira went back to Brazil with a
    papal order in his pocket exempting him from the jurisdiction of the
    Grand Inquisitor. Vieira's postulate questions the old dogmas. So, no
    one agrees with him. They dare not! And many just simply cannot   560
    grasp the brilliance of his concepts. Then came Sor Juana with a re-
    hash of old stale beliefs—the kind that people cling to. That woman is
    a parrot. Oh, she praises with rhetorical passion. She loves, she dis-
    cusses, she reasons, she exalts . . . then, there's that curious humility in
    her words—so female. How dare she! A mere—mere . . .   565
JUAN IGNACIO: Woman. Your plan didn't work, then. When both argu-
    ments were published side by side, she was not discredited.
BISHOP: The public applauds her! This cannot be forgiven. That *gongo-
    rina* feeds the reading public the fare they prefer. I should have fore-
    seen it. Vieira's postulate on the "greater good of Jesus" makes people 570
    uncomfortable. The greater good, he forwards, is God's deliberate ab-
    sence from Mankind. That is a shocking idea to the ordinary layman
    or the ordinary churchman. Why didn't I foresee . . .
JUAN IGNACIO: Everywhere one goes, everything one hears—well, a bat-
    tle on church doctrine is well on the way.   575
BISHOP: She must be forced to put down her pen.
JUAN IGNACIO: I doubt that it is possible . . .
BISHOP: My dear Father, you give up too easily. I have found a way. I
    sent for Father Antonio Núñez de Miranda. She loves him well—too
    well, I'm afraid.   580

JUAN IGNACIO: I doubt that Father Antonio can persuade her.

BISHOP: His absence from her life might persuade her! I hear she is eager
for his visits. She relies and depends on him. Off and on, they have
been companions for almost a lifetime. He will come, to see me this
very day. In fact, I expect him now. *(Pause.)* Before he arrives, I would
like to take you into my confidence regarding a delicate matter.   585

JUAN IGNACIO: How can I be of service . . .

BISHOP: Remember the letter I dictated to you a month or so ago? *(Goes
to table, picks up letter from Sor Filotea and hands it to JUAN IGNACIO.)*

JUAN IGNACIO: I remember it well. At the time I thought it strange that
You did not sign your own name to it, but used the name, Sor Filotea,   590
Convent of the Holy Trinity, Puebla de los Angeles. I know you had
your reasons.

BISHOP: Very good reasons.

JUAN IGNACIO: It was a kind letter—praising Sor Juana's considerable talents, stating great affection for her.   595

BISHOP: I thought that if Sor Juana read the letter as from a fellow sister,
a woman, she would heed the soft current of advice I offered. In the
letter I urged she give up her worldly writings and return to her vows.

JUAN IGNACIO: Did she answer you?

BISHOP: Oh, yes. She sent the letter to the Convent of the Holy Trinity   600
addressed to Sor Filotea. It was turned over to me.

JUAN IGNACIO: How did she reply?

BISHOP: See for yourself.

*Crosses to table, picks up the answer to Sor Filotea written by SOR JUANA,
hands it to JUAN IGNACIO. As JUAN IGNACIO reads the letter, BISHOP paces
floor around his secretary.*

BISHOP: It's no use. She refused my advice. Look, pages and pages explaining her obsession—yes, I said obsession! Things of the mind con-   605
trol her. Oh, she is humble and apologetic. See? All a trick, I assure
you. A letter of merit, I agree, but one that reveals the stubbornness of
her nature. So this scheme failed. *(Pause.)* I shall ask a favor of you. Do
not mention this letter to anyone. It could prove an embarrassment . . .

*There is a knock at the door. JUAN IGNACIO opens it to FATHER ANTONIO.
JUAN IGNACIO leaves as FATHER ANTONIO enters.*

BISHOP: Ah! Father Antonio—it has been a long time.   610

FATHER ANTONIO: Your Holiness.

BISHOP: I hope you have had a taste of our hospitality here in Puebla.

FATHER: Yes. Thank you.

BISHOP: Come, sit down. I have brought you here all the way from the
capital for good reason.   615

FATHER: Your message said the "utmost urgency."

BISHOP: It is—and you are the only solution.

FATHER: I—am a solution?

BISHOP: The problem is Sor Juana Inés de la Cruz.

FATHER: That furor over her criticism of Viera? It's gotten out of hand. 620
    Her criticism was not meant for publication. It was her own private
    exercise . . .

BISHOP: She has said that of all her writing, yet it seems to get published
    in Madrid. Her words exercise a modesty that she does not truly have.

FATHER: I know her—and I do know her very well—to be a modest per- 625
    son. She has never considered what she calls her "scribblings" worthy
    of print.

BISHOP: You, who know her so well, believe her?

FATHER: It is not a matter of belief. Sometimes our own words belie us.
    What motivates her to write, to some extent, is an audience. It's a 630
    worn ritual in her life. She claims she is pressed by others to write. But
    her writing is her own search for God.

BISHOP: Absurd! When has this woman been true to her vows? That is
    the way to God!

FATHER: Hers is not an ordinary case. The world makes demands of her, 635
    the court . . . she has a genius, a talent.

BISHOP: Indeed! If this is foremost in her life, why even pretend piety?
    She serves not God, but the world! What happened to her vow of
    poverty? Where is her humility?

FATHER: The *locutorio* of St. Jerome has never made it possible. She has 640
    been a light, drawing to her the writers and intellectuals of her time.
    You cannot blame her for the circumstance of her fame. The church
    was very pleased by this not so long ago.

BISHOP: You, my dear Father Antonio, know that times have changed.
    The *locutorio* of St. Jerome is now closed as are all *locutorios* all over 645
    Mexico. Our Archbishop considers the frivolities that *locutorios* are fa-
    mous for a mark of shame in church history.

FATHER: I doubt that history will see it thus.

BISHOP: You are a member of the Inquisition Council. You know very
    well the severe austerity that cloaks the Church these days. Sor Juana's 650
    horizons differ greatly from those of our Archbishop. Now—this thing
    with Vieira.

FATHER: It was not of her own doing. She was urged to write it.

BISHOP: Who does she blame?

FATHER: She blames no one in particular. According to her—many peo- 655
    ple. Sor Juana does not run from any labor that gives her the exercise
    of reason. She admires Vieira greatly. She stands in awe of his intellect.

BISHOP: I know! I know! Nevertheless, what did she do? You must admit
    her postulate cannot compare with Vieira's. She says nothing that has
    not been said before. 660

FATHER: I will not judge either argument. Each has its merits.

BISHOP: There is the matter of her worldly possessions. Her cell is a lux-
    ury in itself—expensive gifts, fine furniture, thousands of books! The
    gardens of St. Jerome are a showplace . . .

FATHER: How am I a solution to all this?   665

BISHOP: She is very well aware of the Church's displeasure. She is aware
of her enemies, yet even after the Vieira episode, she wrote a silva for
the Viceroy, Count Galve. And those new *villancicos* in honor of St.
Catherine . . . She's very, very clever.

FATHER: You still have not answered my question . . .   670

BISHOP: In time. First, I must make you see why you are the last resort.
You have read her *villancicos* on St. Catherine?

FATHER: They are pure music and her most intimate convictions.

BISHOP: They are a weapon against her censors!

FATHER: I can't believe that you . . .   675

BISHOP: Wait! Hear me out first. Sor Juana has many persecutors, so she
claims. Did not St. Catherine suffer the great persecutions of Max-
imino? Sor Juana is accused of confusing the scholars of our day. Was
it not the same with St. Catherine? St. Catherine, as Sor Juana puts it,
was a martyr to Wisdom. Do you not agree that Sor Juana believes   680
herself to be the same? St. Catherine was condemned to a horrible
death, placed on a wheel of knives, then beheaded. But her wisdom
triumphed even over her death. The angels carried her up to Moses'
mountain to be buried. So our Sor Juana stands before us, the martyr,
the triumphant one. Do you think she would like her own Mt. Sinai?   685

FATHER: It's not fair! Your whole argument is a distortion . . .

BISHOP: Very well You do not see it my way, but on one thing you have
to agree: Everything she writes has the stamp of arrogance!

FATHER: I cannot help you if you think that way . . .

BISHOP: This is an order from the Inquisition Tribunal, Father Antonio.   690
I'm afraid it's not a matter of choice.

FATHER: What order?

BISHOP: You are forbidden to see her again. *(Lights fade on flashback
area, come up on cell area. SOR JUANA puts down the letter, crosses to
window again, looks out into the night.)*

SOR JUANA: They took you away from me. I did not believe that you
would do as they ordered. Ah, but you, the true Jesuit, must obey.   695
Why did they torture me by taking you away? That last time you
warned me that my words were my own prison. Words, I told you, are
all I have. Words caress me, fulfill me, warm me . . . not any more, not
any more, not any more! I must not write, you said. I cannot help it, I
said, I succumb, my fingers nervous, careless, to please others—imper-   700
fect scribblings. I'm only a woman incapable of changing worlds. You
warned me about what was happening outside the walls of this convent: missions abandoned in the province of Coahuila—Indian upris-
ing—multitudes hiding and starving in the mountains. I didn't want
to hear about the world falling apart! I had my compass, books, pen,   705
harp. I had conceived a world of my own in my mind. The mind
knows passions, feelings, beauty, order, I said. I listen only to the rea-
soning dimensions of scientific laws, human poetry, philosophy, the

words of God . . . a city had to burn, a brother had to die, and you
left me—before I could understand. My journey is at an end, my pur- 710
pose chills, but I wait. Oh, I wait for you, Father, and a tenderness
grows inside of me—the resurgent language of the heart. I dare not
open this window to breathe in the spring, for I would die of longing—for God? For you? It's grown so dark, I must have some light in
here. *(Goes to box where candle stands, lights it.)* Your single flame is 715
like my heart, impervious, waiting, like stars lost in the immense darkness of the sky. *(Crosses window, opens it; sounds of night birds are
heard, she looks at sky.)* How silent you are! How sweet is the night!
Oh, but I remember the bells! The bells that pierced the sanctuary of
my world . . . 720

*Light fades on cell, comes up on flashback area. The church bells of the whole
city are ringing. On the walk leading from the garden to the chapel of the
convent,* SOR JUANA *waits for* SOR FELICIANA *to catch up. From a great distance the muffled sounds of shouting and screaming and the sounds of gunfire
are heard. The red glow of a burning city inflames the skies. The* VICEROY's
palace, the marketplace in the Plaza Mayor, municipal buildings are on fire.

SOR FELICIANA: Where have you been?
SOR JUANA: I was down by the gate. The sacristan from San Angel came
    with the latest news.
SOR FELICIANA: Has the fire been contained?
SOR JUANA: Yes, but the marketplace was burned to the ground, and the 725
    Viceroy's palace suffered from the fire too.
SOR FELICIANA: Thousands came down from the mountains, from the
    starving pueblos. They headed for the palace, ragged Indians, women,
    children . . . they came down only to beg for food.
SOR JUANA: Is it true all the houses closed their windows so as not to 730
    hear them?
SOR FELICIANA: Even at the palace. The crowd screamed for the Viceroy,
    then someone picked up a stone and threw it at a window when no
    one answered. Soon, everyone was throwing stones. Some of the
    starving made their way to the warehouses behind the palace, broke 735
    down the doors and took the grain. Then someone threw a torch
SOR JUANA: And the Viceroy? His family?
SOR FELICIANA: They fled to the monastery of San Francisco, where they
    were given refuge.
SOR JUANA: The sacristan told me the Archbishop headed a procession 740
    out of the *catedral* to appeal to the crowds, calling among the faithful.
    They threw stones at the Archbishop, so he went back to the *catedral*.
SOR FELICIANA: The palace guard and the soldiers from the garrison
    opened fire on the people.
SOR JUANA: Fired among women and children? Those starving people 745
    have no weapons!
SOR FELICIANA: All the faithful in the city are being called to prayer.

SOR JUANA: Volumes and volumes and volumes of prayers.

SOR FELICIANA: Come, we must hurry . . .

SOR JUANA: The sky is red with anguish . . .   750

SOR FELICIANA: Come, we must not be late. *(SLAVE JUANA runs in greatly frightened, face stained with tears, falls to knees before SOR JUANA.)*

SLAVE JUANA: Sister. . .

SOR JUANA: What's wrong?

SLAVE JUANA: Andrés . . .

SOR JUANA: What about Andrés?   755

SLAVE JUANA: He is here, in the garden, hurt.

SOR JUANA: Blessed Mother! *(Motions for SLAVE JUANA to lead her to him.)*

SOR FELICIANA: Sor Juana . . .

SOR JUANA: Go on, go to prayer. I'll take care of this.

SOR FELICIANA: But, Sister . . .   760

SOR JUANA: Go on, I said.

SOR JUANA follows SLAVE JUANA to garden; SOR FELICIANA goes toward chapel. ANDRES lies prone on the ground. SOR JUANA kneels beside him, strokes his face.

SOR JUANA: Andrés, can you hear me?

ANDRES: Yes . . .

SOR JUANA: Where is your wound? Were you shot?

ANDRES: Yes . . . my leg.   765

SLAVE JUANA: He tired, Sister. Soldiers chase him. He got away. We got to hide him. *(SOR JUANA looks at wound, rips worn leg of cotton pants.)*

SOR JUANA: He's bleeding still. We need something to staunch the wound.

SLAVE JUANA: My poor brother! My poor brother!

SOR JUANA: Go get some clean cloth and some wine from the cupboard.   770
    (SLAVE JUANA is still crying.) Did you hear me?

SLAVE JUANA: I get them—I get them. Will my brother die?

SOR JUANA: Of course not. Stop crying and hurry. *(SLAVE JUANA exits.)*
    Juana says soldiers were chasing you. Did they see you come here?

ANDRES: I run fast—is dark . . .   775

SOR JUANA: Why were they chasing you?

ANDRES: I kill soldier . . .

SOR JUANA: Why?

ANDRES: He shot Camila—she with child. He shot her in the stomach.

SOR JUANA: Oh, my God, no! *(She kisses ANDRES' face and holds him   780
    close.)* I'm so sorry. They went straight to Heaven, Andrés, straight to
    Heaven. Oh my brother, your pain is my pain . . .

ANDRES: I killed him with his own gun.

SOR JUANA: May God forgive you.

ANDRES: You not know Camila . . .   785

SOR JUANA: I'm sorry. But she must have been beautiful. I wish . . .

ANDRES: What you wish?

SOR JUANA: Why didn't I go to you, to your family? I feel so badly about
    not . . .

ANDRES: No time to cry now. That was long ago. I remember like dream.   790
   You are the little girl?
SOR JUANA: Yes, my brother, I have your flute. I still play the song you
   taught me . . . Forgive me, Andrés!
ANDRES: Don't cry, coya, the sky is smiling.

SOR JUANA holds him close, crying. SLAVE JUANA returns with cloth and wine.
SOR JUANA puts bottle to ANDRES' lips. He drinks. She tears piece of white
cloth into shreds, uses one to staunch blood, then binds the wound. She uses
another piece to cleanse his face very tenderly.

ANDRES: *(Tries to raise himself)* I hide . . .   795
SLAVE JUANA: You hide him here, Sister.
SOR JUANA: Yes, yes . . . but where? I know! The main altar in the chapel.
   There's room there. After the service this evening we'll take you there.
   Now, you must stay in my room. Can you walk?
ANDRES: Yes. *(He holds on to SLAVE JUANA and SOR JUANA.)*   800
SOR JUANA: This way . . . *(There is pounding at the convent gate. The*
   sound of a soldier's voice: "Open this gate, in the name of the Viceroy!"
   Someone else calls out, "Break it down. He's in there. Break it down!"
   Sound of hacking on wood as the two women lead ANDRES away.)

Lights fade on flashback area. Slowly a red haze comes up on cell. The sound of
a flute is heard. SOR JUANA, sitting on the center of cot, crosslegged, is playing
the flute. She stops.

SOR JUANA: I am without illusion now—distrusting even stars. *(Leaves*
   bed and goes to window.) And dreams? Persuasions of the blood. *(She*
   plays flute as she crosses down center.) But dreams have freed me as faith
   has not. That dream, that first dream, where I was one with God. I   805
   still remember the terror of my smallness. A sleeping world—my spirit
   leaving the vegetative state of my body. I flew to the pyramidal
   shadow of the earth until it came to touch the lunar sky. Ah . . .
   through me poured a great silence. All things were purified. I became
   a whirlwind. Yes! a whirlwind penetrating the immensity of Heaven.   810
   My eyes saw thousands and thousands of things, variations that confused my understanding. And I hungered so to understand! Secrets
   beyond me . . . I felt the breath of God. I knew my smallness then.
   Suddenly, the terror! I felt Him, my God! *(She begins to play the flute*
   again.) Remember, Andrés? My brother . . . you taught me that song   815
   when I was but a child. They dragged you away from here and put a
   rope around your neck. Your eyes were dark with fear. I saw you dangling from the hanging tree. My eyes cannot erase it. My mind cannot
   erase it. A sovereign fact, this death of yours which was . . . a death of
   me. Oh, the raw concreteness of the world! The mind is not enough,   820
   is it? Oh, I have wept loudly in the dark and felt a copious guilt . . .
   And that dark, mysterious flow where no words exist—I found it,
   didn't I? Faith . . .

ACT III

SCENE I

1693: JUANA's cell. There is a small table with two chairs. On the table are cups, spoons and saucers. The boxes have been cleared away. SOR FELICIANA is straightening out the cot as SOR JUANA arranges cups and saucers on table. SOR CATARINA comes in with teapot containing steaming tea.

SOR CATARINA: Here you are. Mint tea. I wish it were some other kind . . .

SOR JUANA: Oh, it's fine. Thank you.

SOR CATARINA: I found a little sugar . . .

SOR JUANA: How wonderful of you!

SOR FELICIANA: *(Looks out the window.)* He's coming through the garden.   5

SOR JUANA: He's here? *(Goes to window.)* How old he looks!

SOR CATARINA: We'll leave you now so you can enjoy your visit. It's Wednesday and exactly three o'clock.

SOR FELICIANA: I'll be by for rosary . . .

SOR CATARINA: We must see to Sister Magdalena now. I'm afraid it's the   10
plague. We were hoping the convent would be spared. May God help us.

SOR JUANA: I should be helping you.

SOR CATARINA: There will be plenty for you to do—but not today. Enjoy
your afternoon.   15

SOR FELICIANA: He's here. He's finally here. *(Kisses her aunt on cheek. SOR CATARINA and SOR FELICIANA exit. SOR JUANA takes a small missal out of her skirt pocket and places it on the table. There is a knock at the door. SOR JUANA hurries to the door, then stops for a moment, her hand upon her heart. She takes a deep breath of joy, then opens the door to FATHER ANTONIO. They embrace without a word, then SOR JUANA takes his hand and leads him in.)*

SOR JUANA: This is a day I've waited for. Oh, my spirit's voice, angels
have brought you to me in brighter dreams. I saw your face so clearly.

FATHER ANTONIO: Juana . . .

SOR JUANA: You cannot imagine my life without you!   20

FATHER ANTONIO: You're thin. You've been so gravely ill.

SOR JUANA: My soul, my spirit. But I've made peace with myself.

FATHER ANTONIO: *(Looks around cell.)* Everything's gone.

SOR JUANA: The money I received was put to good use.

FATHER ANTONIO: You gave it to the poor.   25

SOR JUANA: It was not enough. There never is enough, is there? You've
helped such people all your life—did you ever feel it to be a hopeless cause?

FATHER ANTONIO: My hope has been tried many times.

SOR JUANA: Hope! Come, Father, sit down. There's tea. *(SOR JUANA and*   30
     FATHER ANTONIO sit at the table. SOR JUANA pours tea.)

FATHER ANTONIO: It's wonderful—the tea, sitting across the table from
     you. You were always in my thoughts.

SOR JUANA: To hear the sound of your voice again!

FATHER ANTONIO: I'm here to stay. I'm back at my old church.

SOR JUANA: I shall go help you sweep your church on Saturday morn-   35
     ings. You used to do that, remember?

FATHER ANTONIO: And wash my supper dishes on Tuesday nights . . .

SOR JUANA: As an offering to the Virgin Mary. Oh, Father, I bow my
     head each day at dusk in special prayer for the people who are part of
     me now . . . the people from the barrio in the gulch in San Hipólito.   40

FATHER ANTONIO: I know it well. I worked with the inmates of the asy-
     lum at the edge of the barrio.

SOR JUANA: I went to the asylum . . . remembering you. I stood by the
     door where you stood so many times, putting coins into wavering
     hands. All those people, lost forever—it's heartbreaking! I can do so   45
     little. These are times of desperation . . .

FATHER ANTONIO: But you never give up . . .

SOR JUANA: Never! My world has contracted to Tomasita, Carmela, the
     children . . .

FATHER ANTONIO: Who are they?   50

SOR JUANA: People who need me. Tomasita is old and blind, and she
     lives in one cold room. I keep a fire going for her and she holds my
     hand for hours. I take bread to Carmela, who has six children. She's
     so brave, so beautiful . . . the fierceness—to feed her children, to love
     them, keep them safe. Once a week I sit on a tree stump, with a comb   55
     in my hand and a can of kerosene. Mamas send their children for miles
     around to be deloused! But what the Sisters of St. Jerome do for the
     barrio is not enough. We need many more to help . . .

FATHER ANTONIO: I shall go with you.

SOR JUANA: Father, to have you by my side . . .   60

FATHER ANTONIO: It shall be so for the rest of my days.

SOR JUANA: I am content . . .

FATHER ANTONIO: And your quest—to find God through the intellect?

SOR JUANA: He is all the life around me . . .

FATHER ANTONIO: Amen.   65

SOR JUANA: The art of love—the art of finding God—lies not in words,
     does it? Having learned this so late in my life, I am now afraid . . .

FATHER ANTONIO: Because your name is in the world . . .

SOR JUANA: Yes. What I have written to be truth is not the truth I see
     before my eyes each day . . . except for love and dignity. I see that in   70
     the barrios every day. It embarrasses me to sound full of self-
     importance. They will say that all good things evaporated in Mexico
     with the coming of rebellion, that I was forced to give up my

possessions, my writing. They will make of me a martyr. I am not. I
simply faced myself and found myself wanting. My knowledge could
not dissolve the terror of death and violence. My books could not sus-
pend the suffering of so many! Words became only words; for that
reason I saw them as a form of deceit. It would be a prideful thing to
say such things with words. 75

FATHER ANTONIO: You do not write anymore? 80

SOR JUANA: During my time of trial, my penitence, some inner force
made me take up my pen. Once, when I was mad with guilt, I spilled
my blood and wrote out a legal petition for forgiveness. *(She goes to
missal, takes out one of the papers, hands it to FATHER ANTONIO.)* My
confession in blood, to wash away my sins . . . 85

FATHER ANTONIO: This is not you! Destroy it!

SOR JUANA: No. It shall be sent to the Divine Tribunal.

FATHER ANTONIO: There's no need.

SOR JUANA: Oh, I know the Holy Company! This legal petition is exactly
what they want. If my enemies want it, they can have it. The guilt belonged to another Sor Juana. In spite of all their accusations, perhaps
all they fear is my being so singular. Strange—that very singularity denied me myself! 90

FATHER ANTONIO: You have learned humility.

SOR JUANA: I do not mind being the lowest of the low . . . but that is
silly, isn't it? There's no such thing. Last Friday, before vespers, the air
was heavy with spring. Again, I picked up my pen. *(Goes to missal,
takes out another piece of paper, hands it to FATHER ANTONIO.)* I wrote
this . . . 95

FATHER ANTONIO: *(Reads it aloud)* "Oh mad Hope, green loveliness that
gives meaning to our lives, intricate delicate, dream of wakefulness,
vain treasure, heart of the world—imagined decrepit Spring, the 'now'
desired by the joyless, and for the joyful, the tomorrow . . . A mystery!
Let it follow your shadow when you search for the day, a day with
magic windows, windows where you paint what you desire to see. For
I, I have the measure of my fortune in my hand, my eyes, and see only
what I touch . . ." 100 105

SOR JUANA: *(Crosses to window.)* I must get up at sunrise and pick my
turnips tomorrow. Sister Catarina says I'm well enough to take the
wagon to San Hipólito. 110

FATHER ANTONIO: Will you stop by the church for me?

SOR JUANA: Yes.

SCENE 2

*Lights come up on flashback area. February 17, 1695. A room in the parish
house of San Angel. SOR JUANA kneels in the shadows, upstage right. She is
praying the Fifteen Mysteries on her rosary. Once she coughs, a harsh, deep,*

rasping cough, then returns to the prayers. In the center of area, on his deathbed, lies FATHER ANTONIO. A PRIEST is administering Extreme Unction. He holds a small vessel with olive oil. He dips his thumb into the oil, then makes the sign of the cross over FATHER ANTONIO's eyes, ears, nose, mouth, hands, and feet. As he anoints:

PRIEST: Through this holy anointing, and His most tender mercy, may the Lord forgive you whatever sins of sight, hearing, smell, taste, speech, touch, and steps . . . Amen. *(Continues praying in silence.* 115
Then he makes a sign of the cross, goes to SOR JUANA, touches her shoulder to console, and exits. SOR JUANA crosses to bed, kneels, takes FATHER ANTONIO's hand, kisses it, puts her head down on his chest, wanting to feel his last warmth. She raises her head, lovingly traces the outlines of his thin face.)

SOR JUANA: Oh, how the world has tired you! But you love it so, don't you? You will take that love with you to Heaven. But loving has always been so easy for you, my shepherd, my love . . . Can you hear me? Of course! You have always heard me, you will always hear me. You bent and twisted with the wind, my dear old shrub, and your roots are alive 120 and well in me and the many you have loved. I shall be so alone, so alone. No, you have filled my emptiness too well, for my days, all my days . . . they won't be many, I think, for all that is me will reach out for you . . . Oh, Sweet Jesus, Sweet Mother, hold him unto You. He is so precious . . . *(She strokes his head, then opens his shirt, listens to his* 125 *heart; then she kisses his chest and lays her head on it.)* You smell as sweet in death as you did in life! Do you think I can be upon this earth without you?

Lights come down on flashback area. A REQUIEM CHANT is heard as the lights begin to dim. It continues in the darkness. Suddenly the Chant is broken by the sound of a flute. The lights go up on cell area. SOR JUANA is sitting cross-legged on her cot, playing the flute of her childhood. Around her, sitting, standing, are SOR FELICIANA, SOR CATARINA, SOR BARBARA and SOR CELESTINA. The last two are very young. They have been nursing their ill sisters, for the plague has hit hard. All four wear work clothes and simple kerchiefs to cover their heads. Almost as if they have left all the cares of the world behind them, they seem like young girls, free of care as SOR JUANA plays her tune. She blows a wrong note. They all laugh. The laughter is broken by the knelling of the church bell, funeral bells.

SOR BARBARA: I can't stand them. All day long. Half of the sisters at St. Jerome gone. Death, death, all around us . . . 130
SOR JUANA: Shhh! Don't think about death. Think about being alive.
SOR BARBARA: That's hard these days.
SOR FELICIANA: Think of the nice dinner we had.
SOR CELESTINA: Chicken soup!
SOR CATARINA: Miracle of miracles. Where on earth did you get a 135 chicken, Sor Juana?

SOR JUANA: I was hoeing at sunrise, by the garden gate. Suddenly I had this feeling that I must open the gate. I did, and what did I see? A chicken stumbling over a mudhole, coming toward me.

SOR CELESTINA: An angel must have sent it.   140

SOR JUANA: *(To SOR BARBARA.)* There, you're smiling. Isn't it wonderful, to see the sunrise, to walk with the winds, to look up to the Heavens and know that God is watching over us?

SOR BARBARA: You're so brave.

SOR JUANA: And you, so young. How old are you?   145

SOR BARBARA: Nineteen.

SOR JUANA: And already you embrace God without misgivings. That's why you must think of being alive. I'm glad to be me. Aren't you glad to be you?

SOR BARBARA: Yes . . .   150

SOR FELICIANA: *(To SOR JUANA.)* All the guilts have melted away.

SOR CELESTINA: What guilts?

SOR JUANA: My guilts. You and Sor Barbara have been in the order, let's see, how long now . . .

SOR CELESTINA: Two years. To be part of St. Jerome, of Sor Juana!   155

SOR CATARINA: You are one of our shrines, Sor Juana. Long after the Order is gone, you'll still live!

SOR JUANA: Don't . . . don't kindle the old pride, It still lurks like a monster, waiting to take possession. Have pity on me!

SOR FELICIANA: I'm proud of all you have been all your life.   160

SOR JUANA: Like my guilts, my regrets of the last year are dispersing in the heat of our desert sun. Sometimes I feel . . . I feel almost weightless. *(She coughs.)*

SOR FELICIANA: You alright?

SOR JUANA: Of course. I'm feeling so whole these days. *(Begins to sing*   165
softly.) "Coya, coya, coya, *ja no Ilore ma', el thielo sonlei, el día lindo va* . . ."[15]

SOR BARBARA: I heard you sing that song, walking home from Father Antonio's burial I thought it was kind of strange . . .

SOR JUANA: I *am* strange. Andrés, my brother, sang that song when we   170
climbed the hill behind my grandfather's farm. Oh, memories are good *(crosses to window, traces thread of sunlight)* . . . like this thread of sunlight that holds all the mysteries of Creation. What's more wonderful, my mind does not question anymore.

SOR FELICIANA: But all the wonderful things you've written were written   175
because your mind questioned.

SOR JUANA: I'm not sorry for the old me. Even that I accept. It just took me longer to know my God. *(To SOR BARBARA and SOR CELESTINA.)* For you, there was the straight path of Faith.

---

[15] don't cry anymore, the sky smiles, and the day shall shine

SOR CATARINA: The old passions, they're still part of you.   180

SOR JUANA: Only this morning, before going out to hoe, I found this old letter I never mailed . . . *(Hands it to SOR CATARINA.)* To Father Kino.

SOR CATARINA: It's dated 1686, almost nine years ago.

SOR JUANA: Speaking of passions. He stood very much alone, defending   185
his concepts of comets against the censorship of our conservative Holy Fathers.

SOR CATARINA: *(Reads.)* "Dear Holy Father, I agree with you, comets are not omens from an angry God. They are just like any other heavenly body. My findings are most inferior compared to yours, Father Kino,   190
but I thoroughly agree, and cite from my own notes the position of the comet in relation to other celestial bodies, its magnitude, its distance from the earth, its velocity—all verify your concept of harmony in our Heavens . . . "

SOR JUANA: Stop! See, little sisters *(to SOR BARBARA and SOR CELESTINA),*   195
I was even stranger in earlier years.

SOR BARBARA: But it's wonderful, all your knowledge.

SOR JUANA: No, what is wonderful is the Faith that soars in my blood today. My memories of loving people, in my poor clumsy way. What is wonderful are the shadows in this room in the quiet of the after-   200
noon. What is joyous is being with you, playing this flute badly and remembering . . .

SOR FELICIANA: Oh, dear Aunt, you are growing wings, or becoming wind . . .

SOR JUANA: To the hill, to the hill! Run! Fly, my shepherd, quick! For   205
Our Blessed Virgin melts into the air . . .

SOR FELICIANA: Oh, I remember when you wrote those words . . . "Run! Fly! Quick! Quick! For She takes our heart and soul with Her, and taking the best of us, leaves the world desolate . . ."

SOR JUANA: I was wrong, so wrong! The world is never desolate! *(Picks*   210
up flute.) Now, I shall play the song without missing a note . . . *(The SISTERS laugh. SOR JUANA begins to play.)*

Curtain

Father Antonio Núñez de Miranda died February 17, 1695. Sor Juana Inés de la Cruz died April 17, 1695, two months to the day after the death of her beloved confessor.

Discussion Questions

1. Describe the conflict that Sor Juana experiences throughout the play.
2. How does Sor Juana shatter the stereotypical beliefs about women during the seventeenth century and about women in general?

Luis Valdez

LUIS VALDEZ was born in Delano, California in 1940. He received a B.A. from San Jose State University in 1964 and has been an actor, director, and writer. He has directed many of the plays he's written including Los Vendidos, Bernabé, La virgin del Tepeyac, La gran carpa de la familia Rascuachis, El fin del mundo, Zoot Suit, Bandito: The American Melodrama of Tiburcio Vasquez, *and* I Don't Have to Show You No Stinking Badges.

Valdez is considered by most critics as the father of Mexican-American theater, as he not only described the plight of his people, but also managed to create new theatrical forms. The mito,[1] *for instance, is a result of Valdez's belief that Mexican-American culture is rooted in Native American culture. Ironically, those beliefs are what led him to move away from the very movements he had helped establish. Nevertheless, Valdez's creation of a theater group called* Teatro Campesino *(Country Theater) will always maintain his place as one of the most powerful voices of the Mexican-American literary tradition.*

Bernabé *is the story of a village idiot who is in love with The Earth and wants to marry her. The Earth is portrayed as a* soldadera, *one of the women who followed and supported the troops during the Mexican Revolution of 1910. The play fuses both myth and history and while it depicts a town simpleton it explores metaphysical philosophy.*

Bernabé *

CHARACTERS

Bernabé	El Tío/El Sol
Madre	Torres/La Luna
El Primo	Consuelo/La Tierra

The action takes place in a rural town in the San Joaquin Valley of California. The time is the early 1960s. It is summer—not a cloud in the sky, not a breeze in the air. The crops lie majestically over the landscape, over the immensity of the fecund earth. The valley is sweltering under the heat. The sun is lord and master.

---

[1] *mito*: literally, myth. A type of short skit based on Native American dances.

Editor's Note: The text contains many Spanish words and phrases, often referred to as code-switching. Providing literal translations as the play progresses would be both cumbersome and awkward. More importantly, it would detract from the overall fluidity of the text. Thus, I have elected to provide the reader a glossary of terms, rather than a word-for-word translation. See pages 171–172.

Rising abruptly on the flatness of the land is Burlap, California—a small squat town not picturesque enough to be called a village, too large to be a labor camp—population 2,100, one of hundreds of similar tank towns that dot the long flat immensity of the valley, covered with dust and crankcase oil. The town has a Main Street, the commercial center of town, consisting of a gas station, general store, bank, hardware, cafe, Mexican show, and Torres Bar & Hotel. Amid these business establishments are empty lots littered with debris.

This is the world of Bernabé, a mentally-retarded farm worker in his early thirties touched with cosmic madness. The world of man he inhabits judges him insane but harmless a source of amusement and easy stoop labor. In his own world, however a world of profoundly elemental perceptions—he is a human being living in direct relationship to earth, moon, sun, and stars.

The set, then, is necessarily abstract—a design that blends myth and reality —the paradoxical vision of a cosmic idiot simply known as Bernabé. For he is a man who draws his full human worth not from the tragicomic daily reality of men, but from the collective, mythical universality of Mankind.

I

Midday: a scorcher in the San Joaquin Valley. Under an infinite pale blue sky, the dusty streets of Burlap, California are empty. No signs of life. Near Torres Bar & Hotel, BERNABE comes walking down the hot sidewalk at a steady clip. He is followed at some distance by his MADRE. Holding a transistor radio to his ear, BERNABE is listening to Tex-Mex music, oblivious to the heat.

MADRE: *(Stopping.)* Bernabé . . . *(BERNABE keeps going.)* Berna-BEH!
           (BERNABE stops with a sly grin.)
BERNABE: What?
MADRE: Wait . . . ¡Ay, Dios—this heat! *(MADRE waddles forward, sweat-
           ing and gasping for air—a wizened vision of old age in black, with a
           shawl wrapped tightly around her head.)*
BERNABE: *(Rudely.)* What do you want?
MADRE: Don't go so fast, hijo. You leave me behind.   5
BERNABE: Well, step on it, you old bag.
MADRE: *(Angered.)* Don't be ill-bred, hombre! I don't know why you
           have to get so far ahead of me. What if I fall down, eh? Is that what
           you want—to see me dead in the streets?
BERNABE: *(Grumbling.)* . . . always dying of something.   10
MADRE: *(Sharply.)* ¿Qué?
BERNABE: Nothing.
MADRE: *(Fiercely.)* Be careful how you speak to me, eh? I'm your madre!
           Do you want the ground to open up and swallow you? That's what
           happens to sons who don't respect their mothers. The earth opens up 15
           and swallows them alive, screaming to the heavens!

BERNABE: *(Looking down.)* La tierra? . . . Chale, not me. *(We hear a distant drone high above. Distracted,* BERNABE *looks up at the sky. Smiling.)* Look . . . an airplane. It's a crop duster.

MADRE: *(Hitting him.)* Aren't you listening to me, hombre? I'm getting too old to be out chasing you in the streets—and in this hot sun! Dios mío, you should feel this headache I'm suffering. ¿Sabes qué? You better go on to the store without me. Here. *(She pulls out a small money purse and turns away, digging out coins.* BERNABE *peeks over her shoulder.)* Get back. *(BERNABE *backs off.* MADRE *unfolds a ten dollar bill and hands it to him preciously.)* Take this. Buy some eggs, a pound of coffee, and a dozen tortillas. Do you think you can remember that?

BERNABE: *(Nodding.)* Eggs . . . coffee . . . tortillas. *(Pause.)* No pan dulce?

MADRE: No! And be careful with the change, eh? Don't let them cheat you. God knows what we're going to do till you find work. *(CONSUELO *comes down the sidewalk heading for the bar.* BERNABE *ogles her the moment she appears.* MADRE *scandalized.)* ¡Válgame Dios! Bernabé, turn around!

BERNABE: *(Grinning.)* ¿Por qué?

MADRE: ¡Qué importa! *(She turns him around.* CONSUELO *pauses for a second, smiling cynically, then exits into Torres Bar.)* Shameless viejas! ¡Descaradas! Don't ever let me catch you going into the cantinas, Bernabé—the shame would kill me! Andale, pues, get to the store. Go on . . . *(MADRE *starts to exit.* BERNABE *pauses and picks up an empty beer can on the street.)*

BERNABE: Oiga, can I buy me. . . *(Looks at the beer can and hides it.)* . . . an ice cream?

MADRE: *(Turning.)* No, no, no! Qué ice cream ni qué mugre! There's no money for sweets. And if you see Señor Torres, the labor contractor, ask him for work. Tell him your leg is fine now. Get going! *(BERNABE *starts to go, and* MADRE *exits in the opposite direction.* BERNABE *stops, once she is out of sight, and comes back to the bar. He crouches in the doorway looking in, as* EL PRIMO *and* TORRES *come down the sidewalk from the other side.)*

TORRES: So how was Tijuana?

PRIMO: A toda eme, boss.

TORRES: No problems, eh?

PRIMO: *(Cool and secretive.)* Chale. They had the carga waiting, I slipped them la lana, and I came back de volada. I got the stuff with me. . . fine shit, boss. The girls'll dig it.

TORRES: Let's go inside.

PRIMO: Orale.

TORRES: *(Spotting BERNABE.)* Well, well—look who's here. Your cousin! *(He kicks BERNABE *playfully.)*

BERNABE: *(Jumping.)* ¡Ay! Baboso, hijo de la . . .

TORRES: *(Laughing.)* Don't get mad, loco.

PRIMO: *(Feeling bad.)* He's only playing with you, primo.

TORRES: ¿Qué pues? Aren't you going to say hello?

BERNABE: *(Uneasy.)* Hello, Torres.   55
TORRES: *(In a joking mood.)* Say, Eddie, did you know Bernabé has him-
    self an old lady?
PRIMO: *(Humoring him.)* No, really, cousin?
BERNABE: *(Surprised.)* How do you know?
TORRES: The whole town knows. You've been sleeping with her.   60
PRIMO: No, really? *(BERNABE smiles mysteriously.)* Who is it, cousin? La
    Betty?
BERNABE: No.
PRIMO: La fat Mary?
BERNABE: *(Laughing.)* Chale.   65
PRIMO: Who, pues?
TORRES: Who else? The old lady who still gives him chi-chi. His mamá!
    (TORRES laughs boisterously.)
PRIMO: *(Offended.)* Orale, boss, you're laughing at my tía, man.
TORRES: Just kidding, hombre. ¿Qué traes? *(Getting back to business.)*
    Bueno, Bernabé, we got work to do. Let's go, Eddie.   70
PRIMO: Ahi te watcho, cousin. *(TORRES and PRIMO start to go into the bar.)*
TORRES: Está más loco . . .
BERNABE: *(Boldly.)* Hey, Torres!
TORRES: *(Stopping.)* What? *(Long pause. BERNABE searches for words.)*
PRIMO: What is it, primo?   75
BERNABE: *(Smiling slyly.)* I wanna be with my ruca.
PRIMO: Your ruca? What ruca?
BERNABE: The one that's right here.
TORRES: Here in my cantina?
BERNABE: No, here outside.   80
PRIMO: The sidewalk's empty, ese.
BERNABE: *(Insanely vague.)* The sidewalk's cement. She's over here . . .
    where the ground is . . . and out in the fields . . . and in the hills.
    (Looking up.) She loves the rain.
TORRES: *(Laughing.)* ¿Sabes qué? Something tells me this idiot wants to 85
    go upstairs.
PRIMO: *(Smiling.)* You mean—to visit Connie?
TORRES: He's got the itch. Isn't that it, Bernabé? You want one of my
    chamacas?
BERNABE: No!   90
TORRES: ¿Cómo que no? Your tongue's hanging out, loco. Look, if you
    tell me what you want, I'll get it for you. Compliments of the house.
BERNABE: With my ruca?
TORRES: The one you like.
BERNABE: *(Pause.)* I want a job.   95
TORRES: *(Puzzled.)* Job?
BERNABE: In the fields.
PRIMO: *(Laughs.)* He's got you now, Torres! You're gonna have to give
    him a chamba. The cousin's not as crazy as you think!
BERNABE: *(Laughs.)* Simón, I ain't crazy.   100

TORRES: *(Scoffing.)* You can't work with that crooked leg of yours.

BERNABE: It's okay now.

TORRES: And what about your head, loco? I can't have you throwing another fit and falling off the truck. Five men couldn't handle you.

PRIMO: Aliviánate, boss—it was only a heat stroke. Besides, Bernabé's the   105
best swamper you ever had. How many potato sacks did you load last
year, cousin? Two hundred, five hundred, mil?

BERNABE: Vale madre, mil!

PRIMO: A thousand sacos a day, man!

BERNABE: How about it, Torres?   110

TORRES: *(Shaking his head.)* Ni modo, Quasimodo. Tell your mother to
try the Welfare.

BERNABE: I need money to buy la tierra.

TORRES: What tierra?

BERNABE: This one. Here and there and all over.   115

PRIMO: *(Humoring him.)* You wanna buy a ranchito?

BERNABE: *(Emphatically.)* No, a big rancho—with lots of tierra! All the
tierra on earth. She's all mine.

TORRES: Yours?

BERNABE: My woman. We're gonna get married.   120

TORRES: *(Bursting out laughing.)* Pinche loco! Vámonos, Eddie. His
woman! What this idiot needs is a vieja. *(He exits laughing.)*

PRIMO: Llévatela suave, primo. *(PRIMO exits. Long pause. BERNABE kneels
on the earth.)*

BERNABE: *(Slyly.)* Tierra, they think I'm crazy. But you know I love you.
(Looks around.) See you tonight, eh? . . . like always. *(He kisses the   125
ground and exits.)*

II

*The scene is above and below the earth. Above, BERNABE's house, a small un-
painted shack, sits back from the street on a narrow lot. Below, BERNABE sits
in a hole in the ground covered with planks, lighting candles to a sexy Aztec
goddess pictured on a calendar from Wong's Market. MADRE emerges from the
house. It is sundown.*

MADRE: *(Calling.)* Bernabé? Bernabé, come and eat! Válgame Dios,
where is this hombre? BER-NA-BE! *(BERNABE ignores her. EL PRIMO
enters on the street.)*

PRIMO: Buenas tardes, tía. What's wrong? Lose Bernabé again?

MADRE: No, Qué lose! He hides just to make me suffer. Have you seen
him, hijo?   5

PRIMO: This morning, outside the cantina.

MADRE: *(Alarmed.)* La cantina?

PRIMO: I mean, the store, tía. The Chinaman's supermarket.

MADRE: *(Relieved.)* Pues, sí. I sent him to buy a few things for me. I
have a week now with a headache that won't go away. If you only   10
knew, hijo—how much I suffer and worry. Our rent is almost up, and
Bernabé without work. *(Pause.)* You do have a job, no m'ijo?

PRIMO: *(Nods.)* I'm working with Torres.

MADRE: Ay, pos sí, ¿no? They say that Señor Torres is rich. He always has
money.   15

PRIMO: Almost all the men in town are unemployed, tía. There won't be
any thing till the picking starts. Look, let me lend you ten bucks.

MADRE: *(Self-righteous.)* No, Eduardo. What would your mother say?
May God forbid it. I know my sister only too well. When it's about
money, she's an owl. No, no, no!   20

PRIMO: *(Holding out a ten spot.)* Here, tía.

MADRE: No, hijo, gracias.

PRIMO: Andele. Take it. *(He tries to put the money in her hand.)*

MADRE: *(Folding her arms.)* No, no—y no!

PRIMO: *(Shrugging.)* Well . . .   25

MADRE: *(Quickly.)* Well, okay, pues! *(MADRE snatches the ten dollars with
lightning reflexes and stuffs it in her bosom, hypocritically.)* And how is
your madrecita?

PRIMO: Fine, like always.

MADRE: Gracias a Dios. Bueno, if you see m'ijo, send him straight home,   30
eh? I don't know what will become of him. One of these days they'll
put him in the crazy house, then what will I do?

PRIMO: Try not to worry, tía. Adiós. *(MADRE exits into her house. PRIMO
starts to move on. EL TIO enters down the street.)*

TIO: ¡Oye, sobrino! Eddie!

PRIMO: Orale, tío—how you been?   35

TIO: Pos, ¿Cómo? Hung-over. Oye, you wouldn't happen to have two
bits? Un tostón—for the cure, you know? With 35 cents I can buy me
a mickey y ya 'stuvo. *(PRIMO gives him the money.)* N'ombre! That's a
real nephew. Say, I couldn't help notice you slipped some money to
my little sister, eh?   40

PRIMO: A few bolas. So what?

TIO: *(Scratching his head.)* No, nothing, but I bet you she didn't even
say gracias, right? Sure, don't deny it! Don't be a sucker, Guaro—
haven't I told you? That old dried prune don't appreciate nothing.
Look at me. How many years did I bust my ass in the fields to sup-   45
port her, her idiot son, and your own sweet mother who I love more
than anybody? You know, when I go over to your house, your 'amá
never fails to offer me a cup of coffee, a plate of beans—vaya, whatever, no? But this other miserable sister I got won't even give me a
glass of water. Instead she tells me to get the hell on my way, because 50
she has to feed Bernabé, and she don't like nobody to watch him eat!
(PRIMO laughs.) Isn't that so? That's how she is.

PRIMO: Orale, pues, tío. And speaking of the primo, you seen him?

TIO: *(Suspiciously.)* ¿Por qué? Is that old coyota looking for him? ¡Qué caray! *(Pause.)* Look, you know where the, poor loco is? but don't tell his madre, eh? . . . he's right there, in the field by his house.

PRIMO: The empty lot?

TIO: Sí, hombre, the little llano where the kids play. He's got a hole there he dug into the ground, see? That's where he crawls in and hides. At first he used to get into rock fights with the snot-noses, but lately he's been waiting till dark to go down there, so nobody bothers him.

PRIMO: *(Puzzled.)* How do you know all this, tío?

TIO: I've seen him. He disappears like a gopher and don't come out for two or three hours.

PRIMO: What does he do?

TIO: ¡Sabrá Judas! I even went and got into the hole myself once—when he was downtown with his madre, but I didn't see nothing . . . except for the dirt, soft and warm—like he crawls in and squirms around it.

PRIMO: In the dirt?

TIO: What else is there?

PRIMO: *(Pause.)* Chale. It can't be.

TIO: ¿Qué?

PRIMO: Forget it. He's not that crazy.

TIO: Sure he's crazy. Completely nuts.

PRIMO: Can he be that far gone?

TIO: Cracked and eaten by burros! What's on your mind?

PRIMO: Just something he told me and Torres this morning.

TIO: *(Pause.)* What?

PRIMO: Nothing much. It's impossible.

TIO: *(Exasperated.)* Well, what is it, hombre? You got me standing on my toenails!

PRIMO: *(Pause.)* He said he has a girlfriend.

TIO: Girlfriend?

PRIMO: La Tierra.

TIO: You mean the dirt?

PRIMO: *(Nods.)* And that they're gonna get married.

TIO: *(Pause.)* And you think he . . . ? No, hombre! He can't be that crazy!

PRIMO: Didn't I tell you?

TIO: *(Pause.)* A hole in the ground? *(Angered.)* Pos, mira qué loco tan cochino, hombre! How can he be doing such a dirty thing? Fucking idiot!

PRIMO: Easy, tio.

TIO: It's disgusting, Guaro. He's not your nephew.

PRIMO: He's a cousin.

TIO: Pos, ¡ahi 'ta! He's disgracing the whole family. We got the same blood, hombre. Chihuahua! What's his madre going to say if she finds him out? I bet you she suspects something already.

PRIMO: Chale.

TIO: Sí, señor. You think I don't know my own sister?

MADRE: *(Offstage.)* Berna-beh!

TIO: Listen! Here she comes again. (PRIMO *and* TIO *hide in the shadows, as* MADRE *re-enters. She spots* BERNABE'S *hole in the ground and approaches it suspiciously. Lifting a plank, she suddenly spots him.*)

MADRE: (*Gasping.*) Bernabé? Por Dios, come out of there!

PRIMO: She's got him.

TIO: ¡Pobre loco! He's going to get it now. (MADRE *starts tearing off the planks, as* BERNABE *cowers in his hole.*)

MADRE: ¡Ave Maria Purísima! ¡Virgencita pura, ayúdame! (PRIMO *and*   105
TIO *rush to the hole.*)

TIO: Quihubo pues, sister? What's the matter?

MADRE: Don't bother me now, Teodoro! I've got too many troubles.

TIO: Huy, pos—what's new?

MADRE: Don't even talk to me, hombre! You can be a disgraceful wino if   110
you want, but I have to look out for m'ijo!

PRIMO: Did you find Bernabé, tía?

MADRE: Sí, hijo! Look where he is—in a filthy hole! Come out of there,
Bernabé!

BERNABE: (*Refusing to come out.*) CHALE!

MADRE: ¡Sal de ahi te digo!   115

BERNABE: (*Cursing.*) ¡Vieja cabrona, píntese!

MADRE: (*Shocked.*) What? ¡Bendito sea Dios! Did you hear what he called
me?

TIO: (*Smiling.*) What's he doing?

MADRE: (*Pushing him back.*) None of your business! You up here—stag-   120
gering in the streets, and my son down there risking death, verdad?

TIO: What death? Stop exaggerating.

MADRE: (*Fuming.*) Exaggerating? Exaggerating! And if the ground falls
on top of him, what can happen, eh? Dios mío he'll suffocate! Do you
hear me, Bernabé? Come out of that dark, ugly hole!   125

PRIMO: The tía's right, primo. Come on out.

MADRE: Talk to him, Eduardo. Please! Before I die of the . . .

TIO: Exaggeration.

MADRE: (*Lashing at him.*) ¡Cállate el hocico! Just get out of here, sabes?
Leave!   130

TIO: You leave! Pos, mira, qué chirrión.

MADRE: Come out, Bernabé! ¡Ahorita mismo!

PRIMO: (*Reaching in.*) Come on, primo.

BERNABE: (*Shaking his head.*) What are you going to do to me?

MADRE: Nothing. Just come out.   135

PRIMO: Grab my hand, ese. (BERNABE *grabs* PRIMO'S *hand and slowly
emerges from the pit.*)

BERNABE: (*Fearful.*) Are you going to hit me, oiga?

MADRE: Come on, Bernabé!

BERNABE: (*Coming out.*) If you lay a finger on me, I'll kick your ass.

MADRE: (*Gasps.*) ¡Válgame Dios, Bernabé! (*She grabs him.*) Now I am   140
going to hit you, for your filthy mouth! ¡Malcriado! (*She beats him.*)

BERNABE: (*Cowering.*) Ay! ¡No! No, mamá!

TIO: That's enough, let him alone!

PRIMO: Don't hit him, tía.

MADRE: *(Incensed.)* Stay out of this—both of you! Bernabé's my son and   145
    I have the right to punish him. *(She hits him again.)*

TIO: But he's a man. Not a kid! *(Stopping her.)*

MADRE: I don't care! I'm his madre. And so long as God gives me life,
    I'll go on punishing him when he does wrong! Let go of me!

BERNABE: *(Weeping like a child.)* I didn't do nothing!   150

MADRE: Sí, nothing! You think I'm blind, eh? What were you doing in
    that hole? You think I don't know what dirty things you do in there? I
    can just imagine! But one of these nights the moon is going to come
    down and swallow you alive—¡por cochino!

BERNABE: *(With fear.)* No, 'amá, la luna no.   155

MADRE: Yes, you'll see! ¡Vamos, ándale! Into the house! ¡Ave María San-
    tísima! *(MADRE exits with BERNABE, pulling him by the hair. PRIMO and
    TIO look at each other sorrowfully.)*

TIO: Pobre loco.

PRIMO: She treats him like a kid.

TIO: That's what he is. You saw him—he really believes the moon can   160
    come down and swallow him. But I know what you mean. In a few
    weeks, he'll be in the fields, working and sweating like an animal. And
    do you think my sister appreciates it? No, hombre, she rents him like a
    burro!

PRIMO: Say, Tío—how old is Bernabé?   165

TIO: Pos, lemme see . . . thirty four? No, wait. . . thirty seven!

PRIMO: And how many girlfriends has he had?

TIO: Are you serious?

PRIMO: Simón. *(Pause.)* None, am I right?

TIO: Ninguna.   170

PRIMO: ¡Orale! Then it's not craziness.

TIO: What?

PRIMO: All the funny stuff about la tierra and the hole and everything,
    Tío. Figure it out. *(Pause.)* Look, will you help me do the cousin a
    favor?   175

TIO: Like what?

PRIMO: Pos, ya sabe. You know Consuelo, the hot momma that works
    over in Torres Club?

TIO: ¿La p . . . ?

PRIMO: ¡Simón, la chavalona!   180

TIO: No, Guaro, I don't get into those things no more.

PRIMO: So what? Look, go to the club and tell her to wait for me in one
    hour. Tell her Eddie wants to talk to her. Understand?

TIO: And why don't you go?

PRIMO: Because I'm bringing the primo.   185

TIO: *(Scoffing.)* Oh, sure. His madre's gonna let him go straight to the
    cantina! Forget it, sobrino. You're a bigger fool than I thought.

PRIMO: *(Smiling.)* You just leave the tía to me. She and I get along fine. If I tell her I'm taking Bernabé to see Torres about a job, no hay pedo. I'll have him there. ¿Juega?   190

TIO: Pos, qué caray, okay pues. ¡Juega!

PRIMO: *(Taking out money.)* Then here—have a few cold beers while you wait for us.

TIO: *(Taking the money eagerly.)* ¡Ay, chirrión! You mean I have to wait?

PRIMO: Don't you want to see your nephew happy?   195

TIO: What nephew? That pitiful idiot?

PRIMO: He's not such an idiot, tío. You'll see. Bueno, trucha pues. Torres Club, eh? Around nine. *(PRIMO and TIO start to go in opposite directions.)*

TIO: *(Stopping.)* ¡Epa! And what's the name of the . . . ?

PRIMO: Consuelo. She's got the big chamorrotes (thighs).   200

TIO: Pos, you ought to know. I don't.

PRIMO: *(Laughing.)* Orale, pues, ahi nos watchamos later. I'm going to eat with the tía. *(Starts to go again.)*

TIO: *(Stopping again.)* ¡Oye! And if Bernabé doesn't want to . . . tú sabes . . .   205

PRIMO: Then the favor's for you, tío. *(Exits.)*

TIO: *(Starts to exit.)* Ha! For me . . . *(Stops. Reconsiders, tilts head, smiles.)* Consuelo, eh? *(He exits.)*

III

Torres Club. Outside in the back alley. BERNABE comes out of the cantina with a beer can. The moon is bright.

BERNABE: *(Looking down.)* Tierra? It's me. . . out here in this alley. See, that's Torres' cantina . . . Look—a cerveza. You know what? My primo went and covered the hole where we get together. Mi 'amá sent him. But who cares, huh? It's just some boards. Tomorrow I'll take 'em off! Anyway, you're here, and over there, and way over there. And   5 right, right here. We're always together! *(Laughs and kisses the earth. TORRES enters. Sees BERNABE, laughs to himself, shaking his head. BERNABE scoops up a handful of dirt.)*

TORRES: Oye, oye, stop feeling her up!

BERNABE: *(Startled.)* Uh?

TORRES: *(Laughs.)* Don't get scared, loco. It's me. How's the girlfriend, okay?   10

BERNABE: Simón, okay. *(He rises.)*

TORRES: Nice and cool, eh? Pos, Qué suave. Chihuahua, it's hot, hombre! The sun went down and the night stayed hot. What are you doing here so late?

BERNABE: Nothing. *(Hiding his handful of dirt.)*   15

TORRES: And that beer?

BERNABE: My primo bought it for me. We came to look for work.

TORRES: So where's Eddie? Inside?

BERNABE: *(Nodding.)* Talking to Torres.

TORRES: Oh sí, eh? And who am I? La Luna?   20

BERNABE: *(Startled.)* Chale.

TORRES: *(Laughs.)* No, ¿verdad? There's the moon up there. Look how
    big she is! I wonder if she's jealous? The moon's a woman too, eh? Or
    maybe not. Maybe he's the brother of your ruca. Watch it, Bernabé,
    he's gonna take her away!   25

BERNABE: ¡Pura madre! Nobody can take her away!

TORRES: Well, don't get pissed.

BERNABE: She's mine. *(Looks at his handful.)*

TORRES: *(Tongue in cheek.)* Then tell that to the gabachos. See if they
    give her back.   30

BERNABE: What gabachos?

TORRES: The landowners, manito. Banks, corporations.

BERNABE: They ain't nobody.

TORRES: *(Pause.)* Hey—and if I wanted the land too, Bernabé? What do
    I do?   35

BERNABE: *(Laughs.)* Aguántate. You just wait!

TORRES: But she's my mamá.

BERNABE: ¿La tierra?

TORRES: Sure. She's your momma too.

BERNABE: Up yours! She's not my mother.   40

TORRES: Bueno, your hot momma, then. But look how the ranchers treat
    her, hombre. They sell her whenever they feel like it—to the highest
    bidder! See those fields over there? I just bought 'em yesterday. I own
    the ground under your feet too. All the lots on this street. And I got
    more on the other side of the barrio. Check it out. But you know   45
    what, loco? I'll rent her to you. *(Laughs.)* Give me a few bucks, and
    I'll let you have her—for the night! *(BERNABE is genuinely puzzled. He
    finds TORRES's reasoning totally nonsensical.)*

BERNABE: Say, Torres, you're even crazier than me! *(Laughs.)* ¡Ah, qué
    Torres!

TIO: *(Entering.)* ¡Oye tú! Where you been?   50

BERNABE: Right here.

TIO: What are you up to, hombre? Why did you leave the bar? *(Spots
    TORRES.)* Oh, buenas noches, Señor Torres.

TORRES: Buenas . . . *(Suspicious.)* What's up, Teodoro?

TIO: *(Nervous.)* No, nothing, this burro . . . I don't know why I got into   55
    this! Eddie brought him here . . . to do him a favor . . . *(Barking at
    BERNABE.)* Let's go inside, ándale! Your cousin already went up with
    the vieja. He said to get ready.

TORRES: No, hombre! He's going in with Connie?

TIO: Pos sí, if she lets him in.   60

TORRES: *(Smiles.)* Sure she'll let him. She does what I tell her.

TIO: My nephew's already talking her into it.

TORRES: So you're going to get laid, eh Bernabé?

BERNABE: *(Getting scared.)* I want another beer.

TIO: There's no more. Go do your duty!   65

TORRES: Don't rush him, hombre. This is an occasion. Come on in. So you're finally going to get married, eh loco?

TIO: ¡Qué pinche vergüenza! *(Exits.)*

IV

Torres Club—interior. The upstairs hallway of a cheap hotel. PRIMO *enters, his arm around* CONSUELO.

PRIMO: Orale, Connie, gracias for doing me this favor, eh?

CONSUELO: It's no favor, man. You gotta pay me.

PRIMO: Simón, but the vato's muy especial, you know?

CONSUELO: Who is this jerk?

PRIMO: My cousin.   5

CONSUELO: Who?

PRIMO: Bernabé.

CONSUELO: *(Nonplussed.)* You mean . . . el loquito del
pueblo? Sorry, Eddie, I'm sorry, but no dice.

PRIMO: ¿Por qué no?   10

CONSUELO: Because, porque no. How do I know what he's gonna do? Because he's crazy, that's why!

PRIMO: He's not that loco, chula. He just needs a little break.

CONSUELO: Well, it's not me, man.

PRIMO: Look, it's no big deal. I'm asking you to do the vato a favor.   15
He's my primo—sure he's missing a few marbles, but so what? He's got everything else. Andale, chula—just for a little bit. I promised him—it's his birthday.

CONSUELO: *(Pause.)* Give me fifteen bucks and he's on.

PRIMO: Fifteen bolas? What are you—gold-plated down there? *(CONNIE*   20
starts to go.) No, look, Connie—don't be that way. Besides, all I got are nine bills, see? Here. *(Gives her the money.)*

CONSUELO: *(Takes it reluctantly.)* Bueno, okay. But just one turn on the merry-go-round and that's it. Where's the loco at?

PRIMO: He's coming with el tío—they had a beer first.   25

CONSUELO: Tío?

PRIMO: Teodoro.

CONSUELO: That winito's your tío?

PRIMO: Simón, and also Bernabé's.

CONSUELO: And is his mamá here too?   30

PRIMO: Chale, what's with you?

CONSUELO: Naranjas, corazón. Okay, send him in, pues. (CONSUELO *exits into her room.*)

TIO: (*Offstage.*) Guaro?

PRIMO: Orale, tío—up here.

TIO: (*Offstage.*) Here comes Lover Boy . . . Drooling in his shorts! Is she ready?   35

PRIMO: And set to go.

TIO: (*Enters puffing.*) Híjole, la chicharra, hombre! It took long enough to get up here. Where's the bride?

PRIMO: In her room.   40

TIO: (*Looking.*) Ah, pos sí, I recognize the place.

PRIMO: Just like old times, eh tío?

TIO: Huy, what can I say, sobrino? I personally broke in this hotel. Every payday, I couldn't keep my nose out of here. They had some big fine things up here in those days.   45

PRIMO: And Bernabé?

TIO: (*Turning.*) He was right behind . . . Adiós, where did he go? There he is! See? ¡Andale, oyes! Don't hide. Come on up.

BERNABE: (*Offstage.*) For what?

TIO: For what? Pos—what do you think? It's payday. Are you scared?   50

BERNABE: (*Offstage.*) NO!

PRIMO: All right, ese, the ruca's waiting for you.

BERNABE: (*Entering.*) Where?

PRIMO: In there. It's la Connie, the one who was at the bar? La watchates? The fine buns and the big legs? (BERNABE *laughs.*) Simón   55
qué yes, verdad? She's ready, she's willing, and she's able, carnal. So get in there. Go get it!

BERNABE: (*Playing dumb.*) What?

PRIMO: You know, loco. (BERNABE *laughs lasciviously. He looks at his* PRIMO *and* TIO, *then hesitantly starts toward* CONSUELO's *room. He reaches the door and is about to go in, when he stops suddenly and turns grinning idiotically.*)

BERNABE: (*Backing off.*) Chale.   60

PRIMO: Nel, primo—don't chicken out, man. She's all set. Andale!

BERNABE: (*Shaking his head.*) No, she'll swallow me.

TIO: Swallow you!

BERNABE: La Luna. For being dirty.

PRIMO: That's bullshit, primo. Come on, you saw Connie. You liked   65
what you saw, right?

BERNABE: Yeah.

PRIMO: Well then? Go see it all.

BERNABE: Not now.

PRIMO: Why not?   70

BERNABE: I don't feel like it.

TIO: You felt like it downstairs.

BERNABE: (*Turning.*) I want another beer first.

TIO: Later—afterward.

PRIMO: You have to go in now, primo. She's waiting for you. Besides, I   75
   already paid her. . . twenty bucks. Okay?

BERNABE: I don't think so.

TIO: But didn't you hear, hombre. He already paid the vieja!

BERNABE: I don't give a shit. I don't want that vieja!

TIO: Bueno, if he's not going in . . . *(Pause.)* He's not going in. Take   80
   the idiot home, and that's it.

CONSUELO: *(At her door.)* Eddie? Oye, Eddie? ¿Qué pasó, pues?

PRIMO: Hold it a second.

CONSUELO: Hold it yourself! Tell him to hurry. *(She retreats into her room.)*

PRIMO: You see? She wants you to go in.   85

TIO: And to hurry.

PRIMO: Come on, ese. I know you want to.

TIO: Sure, he wants to. ¡Está buenota, hombre! I wouldn't hold back.

BERNABE: Then, you get in there.

TIO: Don't be an idiot! Qué caray, I would if I could, but I can't no   90
   more. She's more than I can handle. Here, have a drink—to give you
   strength. *(Gives him a swig of his beer.)*

PRIMO: Okay, pues, get in there, cuz!

TIO: Be a man, m'ijo. *(BERNABE starts to move toward CONSUELO's door
   again. Cautiously, he is about to enter, but he stops and beats a retreat.)*

BERNABE: *(Backing off again.)* Chale, I can't!   95

TIO: *(Cursing.)* ¡Me lleva la . . . que me trajo! This is a jackass without a
   rope, hombre.

PRIMO: *(Giving up.)* Simón, let's go, pues.

BERNABE: Where we going?

PRIMO: Home to your chante.   100

BERNABE: Nel, I wanna booze it up.

TIO: We already boozed it up.

BERNABE: Just one.

TIO: *(Exasperated.)* N'ombre! This fool don't want a puta, he wants a
   peda, Better take him home, Guaro. Before he gets drunk.   105

BERNABE: I'm not going to get drunk, oiga!

PRIMO: Let's go, Bernabé.

BERNABE: No! I wanna stay here.

TIO: Your madre's waiting for you.

BERNABE: ¡Me importa madre! They're waiting for me here too.   110

TIO: *(Shoving him toward the door.)* Then, get in there!

BERNABE: *(Pause.)* No . . . she'll swallow me.

PRIMO: *(Tries to pull him.)* Let's go, ese.

BERNABE: No!

TIO: ¡Andale! Grab him! *(PRIMO and TIO grab BERNABE.)*   115

BERNABE: *(Resisting.)* No! Nooo! I wanna drink! I wanna viejaaa! I want
   la tierraaa! *(CONSUELO comes out of her room in a nightgown.)*

CONSUELO: Oye, oye, what's happening, Eddie?

PRIMO: Nothing. We're going.

CONSUELO: ¿Qué pasó? Isn't he coming in?   120

PRIMO: Chale.

TIO: He's crazy. *(CONSUELO comes up to BERNABE, mockingly wanton, sultrily flaunting her body before his gaping eyes.)*

CONSUELO: ¿Qué pasó, Bernabé? You don't want to come with me? You know me, ¿qué no? I'm Consuelo—la Connie. Come on, gimme a little hug. *(BERNABE retreats.)* Andale, hombre—don't back away! Eddie tells me you like las chavalonas. Is that true, eh? Mira—gimme your hand like this . . . and now we put it here. *(She wraps his arm around her. BERNABE opens his fist—the handful of earth falls to the floor.)* Like novios, see? Do you want to dance? I have a record player in my room. Come on, let's go to the baile . . . *(She takes him to the door of her room.)* ¿Y ustedes? What are you gawking at? Get lost! Can't you see we're going on our honeymoon? *(CONSUELO laughs and closes the door, pulling in BERNABE with her. PRIMO approaches the dirt on the floor.)* 125 130

TIO: ¿Qué es, eso? What did he drop?

PRIMO: Tierra . . . *(They look at each other.)* Come on, tío. I'll buy you a beer. 135

TIO: Let's go. This idiot nephew's driving me crazy! *(They exit.)*

V

CONSUELO's room: darkness. A brief erotic silence, slowly punctuated by CONSUELO's moans and the pounding of BERNABE's heartbeat.

CONSUELO: *(In the dark.)* Ay, papasito . . . Ay, ay, ¡Ay!

BERNABE: *(Screaming.)* ¡AYYY!

CONSUELO: *(Pause.)* Bernabé?

BERNABE: ¡Quítate! ¡AYYYY!

CONSUELO: Shut up, hombre! ¿Qué tienes? 5

BERNABE: No, mamá, yo no hice nadaaaa!

CONSUELO: Are you going nuts on me?

BERNABE: Mamá! Mamááááá! *(Strobe light effect, slow to fast. BERNABE is backing away from CONSUELO—or at least the MADRE dressed in CONSUELO's clothes. The effect is nightmarish.)*

MADRE: *(As CONSUELO.)* ¿Qué tienes, papasito?

BERNABE: *(Backing off.)* No, nooooo! 10

MADRE: Naranjas, corazón. Don't you want to be with me? I'm your girlfriend . . . tu novia. *(Changing into MADRE.)* ¡Pero también soy madre y te voy a pegar! ¡Por cochino! ¡Vente! ¡Vámonos pa' la casa! *(She grabs him by the hair.)*

BERNABE: *(Like a child.)* No, mami, noooo! *(MADRE changes into CONSUELO and strokes BERNABE's head and face calming him down.)*

MADRE: *(As CONSUELO.)* Pero, ¿por qué no, bonito? You know me, que no? I'm Consuelo, La Connie. Eddie tells me you like las chavalonas. 15

Don't you want me? Soy tu novia . . . *(Back to MADRE.)* ¡Y por eso te
voy a pegar! Soy tu madre, y tengo derecho de castigarte mientras Dios
me preste vida. You want la tierra to swallow you alive? Come with me!

BERNABE: *(Shoving her back.)* No, noo, no quierooo! Tierraaaa! *(BERN-*   20
ABE runs out into the hallway. Lights up. Strobe effect disappears. PRIMO,
TORRES, and TIO come running.)

PRIMO: What's the matter, primo?

TORRES: ¡Oye, Connie! What the hell's going on, pues? *(CONSUELO comes*
out of her room, as herself. BERNABE screams.)

CONSUELO: Torres! Get this baboso out of here! ¡Sáquenlo!

PRIMO: What happen, chula?

CONSUELO: I don't know what happen. Está loco, ¿qué no ves?   25

BERNABE: *(Terrified.)* ¡Yo no hice nada!

TORRES: Did he go in at least?

PRIMO: Sure he went in.

TIO: Se metió bien contento.

CONSUELO: I told you, Eddie! ¡Te dije!   30

PRIMO: Come on, primo. Let's go home.

BERNABE: *(Cries out in horror.)* No! Nooo! ¡Me pega! She'll hit me!

PRIMO: Who'll hit you?

BERNABE: *(Points at CONSUELO.)* ¡Mi 'amáááá!

TIO: This isn't your mother, suato!   35

CONSUELO: See what I mean. *(BERNABE screams.)*

TORRES: *(To CONSUELO.)* Don't talk to him, stupid! Keep your mouth shut!

CONSUELO: You bastard. This is all your fault! You think I like to do this?

TORRES: ¡Cállate el hocico!

CONSUELO: And you keep the money!   40

TORRES: Get into your room! *(He pushes her.)*

CONSUELO: *(Defiantly.)* Tell them! Tell 'em how you use the girls! And
for what? Your pinche drugs?

TORRES: *(Slapping her around.)* I said shut your fucking mouth!

BERNABE: *(Reacting.)* No, nooo! MAMA! *(Rushes TORRES.)*   45

PRIMO: ¡Bernabé, cálmala!

TIO: Settle down, hombre!

TORRES: *(BERNABE on his back.)* Get him out of here!

PRIMO: We're trying, boss!

CONSUELO: Kick his ass, Bernabé!   50

TORRES: *(Pushing CONSUELO.)* I'm gonna get you!

BERNABE: *(Pounding on him.)* No, ¡déjala! Leave her alone! *(PRIMO and*
TIO struggle to take BERNABE off TORRES.)

PRIMO: Primo!

TIO: Bernabé

BERNABE: She's mine! My woman is mine!   55

TORRES: ¡Quítenlo! Get him OFF OF ME! *(He falls. CONSUELO laughs.*
BERNABE is hysterical, totally out of it. PRIMO and TIO succeed in pulling
him off TORRES.)

BERNABE: ¡Lo maté ¡LO MATE! I KILLED TORRES! *(BERNABE runs out. TIO starts to run after him. PRIMO helps TORRES on his feet. CONSUELO is still laughing.)*

TIO: *(Calling.)* Bernabé! Come back here, you idiot!

PRIMO: You okay, boss?

TORRES: ¿Pos, luego? Let me go.   60

TIO: ¡Oye, Guaro! The loco ran outside! What if he goes and tells his madre?

PRIMO: I don't understand what happened to him. What did you do?

CONSUELO: Don't ask me, man! It's not my fault if he thinks I'm his pinche madre!   65

TIO: *(To PRIMO.)* ¡Vámonos, hombre! We're gonna lose him!

PRIMO: Orale, let's go. Sorry, Torres. *(They exit. CONSUELO and TORRES are left behind. CONSUELO looks at TORRES and starts laughing. A deep bitter laugh, not without a certain satisfaction. She exits into her room.)*

TORRES: Goddamn whore! *(He exits.)*

VI

El llano: night. There is a full moon, unseen, but casting an eery light on the earth. BERNABE is at his hole, pulling off the boards. Suddenly, from the sky comes music.

BERNABE: *(Crying out.)* ¡Tierraaa! I killed Torres! ¡Hijo 'e su tiznada madre! ¡LO MATE! *(Pause. He hears the danzón music.)* What's that? *(Stops. Fearfully looks at sky, sees moon.)* ¡La Luna! It's coming down! ¡Mamá, la lunaaa! *(Sobs like a child. Moonlight gathers into a spot focussed on him. LA LUNA enters, dressed like a Pachuco, 1942 style: Zoot suit, drapes, calcos, hat with feather, small chain, etc.)*

LUNA: Orale, pues, ese vato. No te escames. Soy yo, la Luna.   5

BERNABE: *(Wrapping himself into a ball.)* ¡No, chale!

LUNA: Control, ese. Ain't you Chicano? You're a vato loco.

BERNABE: *(Looks up slowly.)* I ain't loco.

LUNA: Oh, simón. I didn't mean it like that, carnal. Te estaba cabuliando. Watcha. If they don't like you the way you are, pos que tengan   10
que, ¡pa' que se mantengan! ¡Con safos, putos! Shine 'em on, ese. Inside you know who you are. Can you dig it?

BERNABE: *(Feeling better.)* Simón.

LUNA: Pos a toda madre. *(Pause. Reaches into his pocket.)* Oye, like to do a little grifa? A good reefer will set you straight. You got any trolas?   15
(Finds match, lights joint for BERNABE.) Alivian el esqueleto, carnal. Me and you are going to get bien locos tonight. Ahi te llevo. *(Grabs joint from BERNABE.)* No le aflojes. *(BERNABE gets joint again.)* Ese, you see them stars way up there?—some of them got some fine asses . . . *(BERNABE laughs.)* Say, I saw you go into Torres Club   20
tonight. How was it?

BERNABE: *(Guilty.)* Okay.

LUNA: Simón, that Connie's a real mamasota, carnal. But tell me—a la bravota—why didn't you put it to her? Chicken? *(BERNABE throws the joint down.)* No, chale, don't tell me, pues. None of my beeswax. Here, no te agüites. *(Gives him back the joint.)* Oye, Bernabé, ¿sabes qué? I got a boner to pick with you, man. It's about my carnala. 25

BERNABE: Your carnala?

LUNA: Mi sister, loco. What you up to?

BERNABE: Nothing. 30

LUNA: Don't act pendejo, ese! I've been watching you get together almost every night. You dig me? She asked me to come down and see what's cooking. You just wanna get laid or what? She wants to make it forever, loco.

BERNABE: Forever? 35

LUNA: With you. Me la rayo. Watcha, let me call her. *(Calls.)* Oye, sister, come on! Somebody's waiting for you. *(Music accompanies the entrance of LA TIERRA. She emerges from the hole dressed as a soldadera [soldier woman of the Mexican Revolution, 1910] with a sombrero and cartridge belts. BERNABE is spellbound the moment he sees her. She stares at BERNABE, amazon and earth mother.)*

TIERRA: ¿Quién es?

LUNA: Pos, who? Your vato loco. Bernabé, this is my carnala. La Tierra.

TIERRA: Buenas noches, Bernabé. *(BERNABE makes a slight grunt, smiling idiotically.)* You don't know me? *(BERNABE is speechless and embarrassed.)* 40

LUNA: Orale, pues, carnal, say something. Don't tell me you're scared of her? *(BERNABE struggles to say something. His mind tries to form words. He ends up starting to laugh moronically, from helplessness.)*

TIERRA: *(Sharply.)* No, hombre, don't laugh! Speak to me seriously. Soy la tierra. *(BERNABE stares at her. A sudden realization strikes him and turns into fear. He screams and runs.)* 45

LUNA: ¡Epale! Where you going, loco? *(Stops BERNABE with a wave of his arm.)* Cálmala—be cool! There's nothing to be scared of. *(Pulls him toward TIERRA.)* Look at my carnala, see how a toda madre she looks in the moonlight. . . She loves you, man. Verdad, sister?

TIERRA: If he is a man. *(BERNABE is caught in a strange spell. He and LA TIERRA look at each other for a long moment. LA LUNA gets restless.)* 50

LUNA: Bueno, le dijo la mula al freno. You know what? I'm going to take a little spin around the stars—check up on the latest chisme. Oye, Bernabé, watch it with my sister, eh? Llévensela suave, pues. *(Exits.)*

TIERRA: *(Softly.)* What are you thinking, Bernabé?

BERNABE: *(Struggling to say something.)* I killed Torres. 55

TIERRA: *(Pushing him down.)* H'm, ¡qué pelado este! Weren't you thinking about me? Don't pride yourself. Torres isn't dead.

BERNABE: He's still alive?

TIERRA: Pos, luego. How were you going to kill him? With your bare hands? Right now, he's in his bar laughing at you! 60

BERNABE: ¿Por qué?

TIERRA: Because he knows I belong to him. Not to you.

BERNABE: *(Incensed.)* Chale, you're mine!

TIERRA: And how am I yours, Bernabé? Where and when have you stood
up for me? All your life you've worked. in the fields like a dog—and   65
for what? So others can get rich on your sweat, while other men lay
claim to me? Torres says he owns me, Bernabé—what do you own?
Nothing. *(Pause. BERNABE's head is down.)* Look at me, hombre! Soy
la Tierra! Do you love me? Because if your love is true, then I want to
be yours. *(BERNABE reaches out to embrace her.)* But not so fast, pelado!   70
I'm not Consuelo, sabes? If you truly love me, you'll have to respect
me for what I am, and then fight for me—¡como, los machos! Don't
you know anything? Many men have died just to have me. Are you capable of killing those who have me . . . and do not love me, Bernabé?

BERNABE: You want me to kill?   75

TIERRA: To set me free. For I was never meant to be the property of any
man—not even you . . . though it is your destiny to lie with me. *(She
extends her hand. BERNABE goes to her. She pulls him down, and they lay
down. He is almost going to embrace her, when LA LUNA comes back.)*

LUNA: Orale, stop right there! *(BERNABE sits up.)* ¿Qué, pues, nuez?
Didn't I tell you to watch it with my sister? What were you doing, eh?

BERNABE: *(Rises.)* ¿Qué te importa, buey? *(LA TIERRA rises and stands to*   80
one side, observing silently but with strength. BERNABE seems more
self-possessed.)

LUNA: Oye, so bravo all of a sudden?

BERNABE: You'd better leave, Luna!

LUNA: I'd better not, carnal!

BERNABE: Get out of here!

LUNA: Look at him, will you? Muy machote. What did you do to him, sis?   85

BERNABE: ¡Lárgate! *(Pushes LUNA.)*

LUNA: Hey, man, watch the suit. I'm your camarada, remember? Almost
your brother-in-law.

TIERRA: *(With power.)* Luna! Leave us in peace. He means me no harm.

LUNA: Pura madre, how do you know?   90

TIERRA: Because I know him. Since the very day of his birth, he has been
innocent, and good. Others have laughed at him. But he has always
come to my arms seeking my warmth. He loves me with an intensity
most men cannot even imagine . . . for in his eyes I am woman . . . I
am Madre . . .   95

LUNA: Simón —¡pura madre!

TIERRA: Yet I'm forever Virgin. So leave us alone!

LUNA: Nel, sister. Qué virgen ni que madre. I know what you two are up
to. Are you going to get married or what? Is this a one night stand?

TIERRA: That's up to Bernabé.   100

LUNA: What do you say, loco? Is this forever?

BERNABE: *(Pause.)* Simón.

LUNA: Pendejo.

TIERRA: Satisfied?

LUNA: Chale. You still need Jefe's blessing.   105

TIERRA: He'll grant it.

LUNA: Pos, you hope. First he's gotta meet Bernabé. You ready for Him, ese?

BERNABE: Who?

LUNA: El Mero Mero, loco. Su Papá. Mi Jefito. ¡EL SOL!   110

BERNABE: ¡¿Sol?!

LUNA: *(Turning.)* He's coming—watcha. It's almost dawn. ¿Sabes qué, ese? You better let me do the talking first. Me and the Jefe get along real suave. I'll tell Him you're Chicano, my camarada.

TIERRA: No, Luna.   115

LUNA: What?

TIERRA: He has a voice. Let him speak for himself

LUNA: *(Shrugging.)* Orale, no hay pedo. But you know the Jefito.

TIERRA: You will have to face him, Bernabé. If you truly love me, then you should have no fear of my father. Speak to him with respect, but with courage. He has no patience with cowardly humans.   120

LUNA: ¡Al alba! Here he comes! Don't stare at his face too long, ese! He'll blind you! *(LA TIERRA and LA LUNA kneel before the place. where the sun is rising. Indigéna music: majestic flutes and drums. EL SOL rises in the guise of Tonatiuh, the Aztec Sun God. He speaks in a resounding voice.)*

SOL: Buenos días, mis hijos.

TIERRA: Buenos días, Papá.   125

LUNA: Buenos días, Jefe.

SOL: Luna! How goes my eternal war with the stars? ¿Cuidaste mi cielo por toda la noche?

LUNA: Simón, Jefe, the heavens are fine.

SOL: ¿Y tu hermana? Did you watch over her?   130

LUNA: Si, señor. ¡Cómo no!

SOL: ¿Pues cómo? . . . ¡CALLATE!

TIERRA: ¿Apá?

SOL: *(Gently.)* Sí, m'ija, ¿cómo estás?

TIERRA: Bien, Papá.   135

SOL: And all your humanity, that plague of miserable mortals you call your children? Do they still persist in their petty greed and hatred and fear of death?

TIERRA: Sí, Tata. *(To BERNABE.)* Go.

BERNABE: ¿Señor? *(Pause.)* ¿Señor de los cielos?   140

SOL: ¿Quién me llama?

BERNABE: It's me, Señor. Down here.

SOL: ¿Quién eres tú?

BERNABE: Bernabé.

SOL: ¿Qué? ¡LOOK AT ME¡   145

BERNABE: *(Shielding his eyes.)* Bernabé . . . I come to tell you something, Señor . . . de mi amor . . .

SOL: *(Disdainfully.)* ¿Amor?

BERNABE: Por la Tierra.

SOL: ¡¿M'ija!?   150

BERNABE: *(Humbly.)* Con todo respeto, señor.

SOL: *(Pause.)* Many centuries have passed, Bernabé, since men remembered who is el padre de la tierra. En verdad, very few have ever had
the courage to face me, como es debido. Why have you come?

BERNABE: I am a man, Señor.   155

SOL: ¿Y esó qué me importa a mí?

BERNABE: I love her.

SOL: *(Scoffing majestically.)* Ha! Billions of men have loved her. Do you
think you are the first? Look at her, Bernabé, this is la Tierra who has
been all things to all men. Madre, prostituta, mujer. Aren't you afraid?   160

BERNABE: *(Bravely.)* No, Señor, of what?

SOL: ¡De su PADRE, desgraciado! ¡¡¡EL SOL!!! *(There is a terrifying
flash of light and thunder.* BERNABE *runs and hides.)* Look at him running like a coward! ¡MALHORA! I should kill you for what your kind
has done to m'ija!   165

BERNABE: It wasn't me, Señor!

TIERRA: *(Stepping forward.)* ¡Por favor, Tata! ¡Es inocente!

LUNA: Es cierto, Jefe. The vato's a Chicano. He's never had any tierra!

SOL: *(Pause, calms down.)* What is your work, Bernabé?

BERNABE: I work in the fields.   170

SOL: You are dirt poor, then?

BERNABE: Sí, Senior.

SOL: Then, how do you intend to take care of my daughter? You have no
money! You have no POWER!

BERNABE: *(Pause.)* Señor, I am nobody, that's true, In town people say   175
I'm only a loco. But I know one thing, that the rich people are more
locos than me. They sell la Tierra all the time, in little pedacitos here
and there, but I know she should never be sold like that . . . because
she doesn't belong to anyone. Like a woman should never be sold, ¿qué
no? Eso es lo que pienso, Señor. If anybody has hurt la Tierra, it's not   180
the pobres, it's the men with money and power. I can only love her.

LUNA: *(Sotto voce.)* ¡Orale, te aventates, ese! *(EL SOL silences LUNA with a
powerful glance.)*

SOL: Dices bien. *(Pause.)* Now I know who you are, Bernabé. Eres el úl-
timo y el primero . . . The last of a great noble lineage of men I once
knew in ancient times, and the first of a new raza cósmica that shall in-   185
herit the earth. Your face is a cosmic memory, Bernabé. It reminds me
of an entire humanity, de tus mismos ojos, tu piel, tu sangre. They too
loved la Tierra and honored su padre above all else. They too were my
children. They pierced the human brain and penetrated the distant
stars and found the hungry fire that eats of itself. They discovered   190
what today only a loco can understand—that life is death, and that
death is life. Que la vida no vale nada porque vale todo. That you are
one, so you can be two, two so you can be four, and then eight, and

then sixteen, and on and on until you are millions, billions!—only to   195
return once again to the center and discover . . . nada, so you fill up
the space with one again. ¿Me compredes, Bernabé? What power was
that?

BERNABE: El poder del Sol, Señor?

SOL: *(Pauses.)* Tienes razón. . . and that's why if you unite with m'ija,
you shall have that poder. And you shall be my Son! Tierra, do you   200
love this man?

TIERRA: Si, Papá.

SOL: Bernabé, ¿de veras quieres a la Tierra?

BERNABE: Con todo el corazón.

SOL: *(Ironically.)* ¿Corazón? No, hijo, not with your corazón. You may   205
love her with your body, your blood, your seed, but your heart belongs to me. ¿Estás listo para morir?

BERNABE: ¡Morir!

SOL: ¡Para vivir! *(BERNABE is momentarily stunned and confused. He looks
at LA LUNA and LA TIERRA. They say nothing.)*

BERNABE: Señor, I don't want to die.   210

SOL: Hijo, I offer you the power of the Sun. You have been nothing, now
you shall be everything. Yo soy el comienzo y el fin de todas las cosas.
Believe in me and you shall never die. Will you give me your corazón?

BERNABE: *(Pause.)* Si, Señor.

SOL: ¡Que sea así! *(Drums and flutes. BERNABE is sacrificed. LA TIERRA*   215
and LA LUNA lay his body out.)

SOL: ¡Bernabé levántate! *(BERNABE rises—a complete man.)* For here on
you shall be un hombre nuevo and you shall help me to conquer the
stars! *(BERNABE walks erect.)* Bernabé, la Tierra es virgen y tuya. Sean
felices.

TIERRA: ¡Bernabé! *(BERNABE and LA TIERRA embrace.)*   220

LUNA: ¡Orale! Congratulations, loco—I mean, ese. ¡A toda madre!

SOL: ¡SILENCIO PUES! *(Pause.)* The day is dying. The hour has come
for me to go. Mis hijos, I leave you with my blessings. *(Blesses them.)*
Luna, stand vigil over my cielo through the darkest night and give
light to your hermana, eh?   225

LUNA: Si, Jefe, like always.

SOL: Bueno, me voy pues. Bernabé, Tierra, tengan hijos . . . muchos
hijos. *(Starts to sink.)*

TIERRA: Buenas noches, Papá.

LUNA: Buenas noches, Jefe.   230

BERNABE: Buenas noches, Señor.

SOL: *(Sinking fast.)* Buenas noches . . . Bernabé! *(SOL is gone. There is a
silence. LA TIERRA shivers, then BERNABE and LA LUNA.)*

TIERRA: It's cold.

LUNA: Simón, the Jefito's gone. *(Looks up at the sky.)* Well, I better get
up to my chante también. Orale, novios—what kind of moonlight   235
would you like? Something muy romantic y de aquellas?

TIERRA: Never mind. Just leave.

LUNA: Mírala, mírala—just because you got married again! For the zil-   240
lionth time.

BERNABE: *(With a powerful calm.)* Mira, hermano, the time for insults is
over. If once I was a loco, now I am a man—and I belong to la Tierra,
as she belongs to me. So, good night.

LUNA: Okay, 'ta bien, pues. I gotta get to work anyway. *(Looks up.)* Fat-
assed stars! I bet you they're just itching to horn in on Jefe's territory.
I better go keep 'em in line. Buenas noches, pues, y don't be afraid to   245
get down and dirty, eh? ¡Orale! *(La LUNA, exits. La TIERRA turns her
back on BERNABE.)*

TIERRA: ¿Bernabé?

BERNABE: ¿Qué

TIERRA: Will you love me—¿para siempre?

BERNABE: Siempre.   250

TIERRA: ¡Hasta la muerte? *(She turns. Her face is a death mask.)*

BERNABE: Hasta la muerte. *(They embrace.)*

VII

*BERNABE's house. EL TIO comes in quickly, looking over his shoulder. MADRE is
at the door of her house.*

MADRE: Teodoro, ¿qué paso? Did you find m'ijo?

TIO: What are you doing in the street, hermanita? Get into the house,
ándale!

MADRE: ¿Pa' qué? To worry even more?

TIO: ¡El sol está muy caliente!   5

MADRE: I don't care if it's hot! What happen with m'ijo? *(Pause.)* ¿Qué
pasó, pues, hombre? Did they find him? Miserable wino, what good
are you? Bernabé's your nephew, but nothing worries you, verdad?
Did I tell you to go look in the pozo he made? *(Pause.)* You went,
verdad? You know something! ¿Qué pasó, hombre? *(She looks down the   10
street.)* Ay, Teodoro, some men are coming. Eduardo is with them!
They're bringing a body. ¡Válgame Dios! *(MADRE starts to run forward. TIO stops her.)*

TIO: Stay here, hermanita!

MADRE: *(Starting to get hysterical.)* NO, ¡déjame ir! ¡Déjame ir! It's
m'ijo. You know it is, ¿verdad? ¿Qué pasó? ¿Qué pasó?   15

TIO: Está muerto.

MADRE: ¡Ay! *(Gasps. Can't get breath.)*

TIO: We found him—buried in the earth. *(TORRES and PRIMO bring in
BERNABE's body. They lay him down, covered with a canvas. Now MADRE
releases a long, sorrowful cry as she leans over the body.)*

MADRE: M'ijo! M'IJITO!

PRIMO: It's all my fault, tío. Fue toda mi culpa.   20

TIO: No, hijo, don't blame yourself. You only wanted to help him. This was God's will. Fue por la voluntad de Dios. *(Drums and flutes. In the sky above and behind them, BERNABE and LA TIERRA appear in a cosmic embrace. He is naked, wearing only a loincloth. She is Coatlicue, Mother Earth, the Aztec Goddess of Life, Death, and Rebirth.)*

Discussion Questions

1. What is the nature of the relationship between Bernabé and La Tierra? What is the symbolic and historical significance of this character?
2. What aspects of Aztec mythology are present throughout the story? How do they relate to the play's central theme?
3. What is the relationship between Bernabé and his mother and between Bernabé and his other relatives? Why is his "Tio" also El Sol? In what way(s) are the real characters related to the mythical one(s)?
4. Like *Olú Clemente* on page 494, this play deals with death and renewal through the use of mythology. Compare and contrast how that idea is explored in both plays.

Glossary
Bernabé

agüites   be depressed

ahi te watcho   an example of what linguists call code-switching, or substituting words from one language to the other. "Watcho" = watch. Thus, the phrase means I'll see you later.

al alba!   watch it

amor   love

a toda eme   eme stands for the letter M. The phrase means "a toda madre"; it was great.

baboso   playful insult similar to calling someone a fool

bolas   dollars

bonito   pretty

buey   ox (a derogatory term for man)

cabuliando   teasing

caliente   hot

cállate   shut up

cantina   bar

carga   shipment

carnal   "brother"

castigarte   punish you

cerveza   beer

chale   no way

chamaca   young girl

chamba   work

chante   home

chisme   gossip

chula   pretty girl

cochino   pig

comienzo   start

cuidar   take care of

descarada   shameless

de volada   quickly

Dios   God

Dios mio   my God

escames   fearful

fin   end

hermana   sister

hijo   son

hombre   man

jefe   boss

lana   money

le dijo la mula al freno   said the mule to the brake

llévatela suave   take it easy
loco   literally means crazy but in slang often used as "dude" or "man"
luna   moon

madre   mother
malcriado   spoiled brat
mil   one thousand
muerte   death
mugre   junk

naranjas   literally "oranges" slang term for "nothing"
ni modo   no way
no hay pedo   no problem

oiga   listen
órale   alright

pan dulce   sweet bread
pedacitos   little pieces
pelado   guy (derogatory)
pinche   as a noun it means stingy, as an adjective means "damn"

pobre   poor
primo   cousin
pueblo   town

¿que?   what

ruca   slang equivalent of "chick"

sabes que   you know what
sabra Judas   who knows?
sangre   blood
siempre   always
simón   yes
sol   sun
suave   soft; smooth; easy

tierra   earth

válgame   similar to "oh my" when combined with Dios (God)
vato   guy
verguenza   shame
vieja   literally old woman, but often used as slang to simply mean woman

CUBAN-AMERICAN LITERATURE

A BRIEF SURVEY

While we usually think of the Castro era in relation to Cuban exile literature, the fact is that like the country itself, Cuban-American fiction and poetry has a rich and varied history. As early as 1823, for instance, a Cuban writer, José María Heredia, fled the island to America to avoid imprisonment. Employing two common symbols, the royal palm and the solitary star, Heredia's poetry sharply criticized the Spanish authorities and depicted a Cuba free of Spain's tyrannical grasp. Like Heredia, many other nineteenth-century writers found it impossible to live and write in Cuba, including Cirilo Villaverde and the incomparable José Martí, who fled to the United States, where they promptly wrote about their homeland. Writing in Spanish, Jose Martí's poetry reflects his sense of patriotism, and his book of poems *Versos Sencillos* (Simple Verses) (1891), echoes the sentiments expressed by Heredia.

The literature of Cubans in exile in the twentieth century also established early roots. Alejo Carpentier, for instance, chose to leave his native land in 1928 after having spent forty days in jail. Carpentier, who is considered by many as the father of Cuban novelists, has had his works translated into several languages. While Carpentier decided to return home in 1959 to show his support for the revolution, many other Cuban writers decided to leave Cuba, fearing what that revolution might bring. One of the first to seek asylum in the United States was Lino Novas Calvo. Exile renewed Calvo's interest in creative writing and he produced many stories, most dealing with aspects of prerevolutionary Cuba. Perhaps the best known Cuban writer of this century, however, is Guillermo Cabrera Infante. After supporting Castro's regime and even serving as Cuba's cultural attaché until 1965, Infante left Cuba never to return. His work has been compared to that of Hemingway and Joyce, and his most successful novel, *tres tristes tigres* (three trapped tigers) employs puns and extensive wordplay in an attempt to faithfully re-create the dialect of the work's setting: Havana in the 1950s.

For many of these early exiled writers, the focus of their work was on the land they left behind. Often, the text was replete with nostalgia. For others, the literature served as a vehicle to castigate Castro's regime. Among the latter may be included such writers as Emilio Fernandez Camus, Orlando Nuñez, Manuel Cobo Souza, and Luis Ricardo Alonso. In the last three decades there has been a definite shift in this two-dimensional portrait, however. Two key figures have changed the focus of Cuban-American literature. Celedonio González, beginning with his work *Los Primos* (The Cousins) (1971), concentrates on Cuban life and culture in the United States. Later in *Los Cuatro Embajadores* (The Four Ambassadors) (1973), Gonzalez not only examines culture shock and conflict between Cubans and Americans, but also depicts the U.S. economic system as an exploiter of Cuban workers, a subject considered taboo by many previous writers. The literature of exile as conflict is also explored by Matias Montes Huidobro in the award-winning novel *Desterrados al Fuego* (Exiled to the Fire) (1975). In this first-person narrative, a husband who has recently arrived in the United States is overwhelmed by the requirements of this alien culture. In an almost Chekovian fashion, the man's inability to adjust results in spiritual and physical deterioration.

Most recently many Cuban-American authors have further problematized the relationship between Cuba and the United States by using humor to further explore the linguistic and cultural confusion of exile. Additionally, authors have attempted to depict Cuban-Americans' feelings toward the United States as more than a simple either/or dichotomy. In fiction, Roberto Fernandez, Cristina García, and Virgil Suarez are notable examples. The poetry of figures such as Pablo Medina, Ricardo Pau-Llosa, and Elias Miguel Muñoz echo these views.

Cuban-American drama has also undergone a significant transformation. Through the end of the nineteenth century and the beginning of the twentieth, relocated Cuban cigar factory owners and workers in Tampa helped in the creation of a new type of Cuban theater. Many of the plays reflected their particular social situation; some of the plays' titles reflect their concerns: *Un tabaquero huelgista* (A Tabacco Striker) (1924), and *Huelga general* (General Strike) (1934). Many of the plays of the later writers such as Hilda Perera's *El Sitio de Nadie* (No One's Place) (1972), are political in nature and depict the brutality of Castro's regime. Marked by the establishment of *Areito*, a magazine mostly accepting and often supporting the Cuban revolution, Cuban-American theater underwent a definite change. As with fiction and poetry, Cuban-American drama reflects the varied beliefs of the children of Cuban exiles whose lives and identities were mostly formed in the United States. Among these writers are Dolores Prida and Omar Torres, whose works explore not only the contradictions of living on the hyphen, but whose works also discuss other significant elements in Latino literature related to gender, language, and culture.

Fiction

Cristina García

CRISTINA GARCÍA was born in Havana, Cuba in 1958, and she immigrated to the United States with her family two years later. She earned a B.A. from Barnard College in 1979, and an M.A. from Johns Hopkins University in 1981. She worked as a reporter, researcher, and correspondent for Time *magazine for several years during the 1980s. Her multiple awards include a Hodder Fellowship from Princeton University, a Cintas Fellowship, and a Whiting Writers Award.*

Her two published novels are Dreaming in Cuban *(1995) and* The Aguero Sisters *(1997). Despite her limited output thus far, García is one of the most critically acclaimed contemporary Cuban-American writers. Much of that acclaim is a result of the powerful characterization she develops in* Dreaming in Cuban. *The novel traces three generations of a Cuban family. The matriarch, Celia, who chooses to remain in Cuba after "El Liders's" revolution, firmly believing that the promise of an improved Cuba will eventually be realized. Her daughter Lourdes, raped by a revolutionary, decides to abandon her homeland and her past. She embraces the American Dream and opens two successful business, one of which she names "The Yankee Doodle Bakery," as a tribute to her new land and identity. Pilar, Celia's granddaughter and Lourdes's daughter is caught between these two opposing ideologies. She is drawn to her grandmother in an almost surreal way, yet she is undeniably American.*

Mainly through Pilar, the novel exhibits the characteristic blending of real and supernatural elements typical of magical realism. Nonetheless, this chaotic state does not extend into the everyday lives of the characters. García creates three women who have a strong sense of self despite the fact that they often find themselves in alien surroundings.

From Dreaming in Cuban

Celia

Celia del Pino, equipped with binoculars and wearing her best housedress and drop pearl earrings, sits in her wicker swing guarding the north coast of Cuba. Square by square, she searches the night skies for adversaries then scrutinizes the ocean, which is roiling with nine straight days of unseasonable April rains. No sign of *gusano* traitors. Celia is honored. The neighborhood committee has voted her little brick-and-cement house by the sea as the primary lookout for Santa Teresa del Mar. From her porch, Celia could spot another Bay of Pigs invasion before it happened. She would be feted at the palace, serenaded by a brass orchestra, seduced by El Líder himself on a red velvet divan.

Celia brings the binoculars to rest in her lap and rubs her eyes with stiffened fingers. Her wattled chin trembles. Her eyes smart from the sweetness of the gardenia tree and the salt of the sea. In an hour or two, the fishermen will return, nets empty. The *yanquis,* rumors go, have ringed the island with nuclear poison, hoping to starve the people and incite a counterrevolution. They will drop germ bombs to wither the sugarcane fields, blacken the rivers, blind horses and pigs. Celia studies the coconut palms lining the beach. Could they be blinking signals to an invisible enemy?

A radio announcer barks fresh conjectures about a possible attack and plays a special recorded message from El Líder: "Eleven years ago tonight, *compañeros,*[1] you defended our country against American aggressors. Now each and every one of you must guard our future again. Without your support, *compañeros,* without your sacrifices, there can be no revolution."

Celia reaches into her straw handbag for more red lipstick, then darkens the mole on her left cheek with a black eyebrow pencil. Her sticky graying hair is tied in a chignon at her neck. Celia played the piano once and still exercises her hands, unconsciously stretching them two notes beyond an octave. She wears leather pumps with her bright housedress.

Her grandson appears in the doorway, his pajama top twisted off his shoulders, his eyes vacant with sleep. Celia carries Ivanito past the sofa draped with a faded mantilla, past the water-bleached walnut piano, past the dining-room table pockmarked with ancient history. Only seven chairs remain of the set. Her husband smashed one on the back of Hugo Villaverde, their former son-in-law, and could not repair it for all the splinters. She nestles her grandson beneath a frayed blanket on her bed and kisses his eyes closed.

Celia returns to her post and adjusts the binoculars. The sides of her breasts ache under her arms. There are three fishing boats in the distance—the *Niña*, the *Pinta*, and the *Santa María*. She remembers the singsong way she used to recite their names. Celia moves the binoculars in an arc from left to right, the way she was trained, and then straight across the horizon.

At the far end of the sky, where daylight begins, a dense radiance like a shooting star breaks forth. It weakens as it advances, as its outline takes shape in the ether. Her husband emerges from the light and comes toward her, taller than the palms, walking on water in his white summer suit and Panama hat. He is in no hurry. Celia half expects him to pull pink tea roses from behind his back as he used to when he returned from his trips to distant provinces. Or to offer her a giant eggbeater wrapped in brown paper, she doesn't know why. But he comes empty-handed.

He stops at the ocean's edge, smiles almost shyly, as if he fears disturbing her, and stretches out a colossal hand. His blue eyes are like lasers in the night. The beams bounce off his fingernails, five hard blue shields. They scan the beach, illuminating shells and sleeping gulls, then focus on her. The porch turns blue, ultraviolet. Her

---

[1] brothers; a term used by socialists to connote solidarity

hands, too, are blue. Celia squints through the light, which dulls her eyesight and blurs the palms on the shore.

Her husband moves his mouth carefully but she cannot read his immense lips. His jaw churns and swells with each word, faster, until Celia feels the warm breeze of his breath on her face. Then he disappears.

Celia runs to the beach in her good leather pumps. There is a trace of tobacco in the air. "Jorge, I couldn't hear you. I couldn't hear you." She paces the shore, her arms crossed over her breasts. Her shoes leave delicate exclamation points in the wet sand.

Celia fingers the sheet of onion parchment in her pocket, reads the words again, one by one, like a blind woman. Jorge's letter arrived that morning, as if his pre-science extended even to the irregular postal service between the United States and Cuba. Celia is astonished by the words, by the disquieting ardor of her husband's last letters. They seemed written by a younger, more passionate Jorge, a man she never knew well. But his handwriting, an ornate script he learned in another century, re-vealed his decay. When he wrote this last missive, Jorge must have known he would die before she received it.

A long time ago, it seems to her, Jorge boarded the plane for New York, sick and shrunken in an ancient wheelchair. "Butchers and veterinarians!" he shouted as they pushed him up the plank. "That's what Cuba is now!" *Her* Jorge did not re-semble the huge, buoyant man on the ocean, the gentleman with silent words she could not understand.

Celia grieves for her husband, not for his death, not yet, but for his mixed-up allegiances.

For many years before the revolution, Jorge had traveled five weeks out of six, selling electric brooms and portable fans for an American firm. He'd wanted to be a model Cuban, to prove to his gringo boss that they were cut from the same cloth. Jorge wore his suit on the hottest days of the year, even in remote villages where the people thought he was crazy. He put on his boater with its wide black band before a mirror, to keep the angle shy of jaunty.

Celia cannot decide which is worse, separation or death. Separation is familiar, too familiar, but Celia is uncertain she can reconcile it with permanence. Who could have predicted her life? What unknown covenants led her ultimately to this beach and this hour and this solitude?

She considers the vagaries of sports, the happenstance of El Líder, a star pitcher in his youth, narrowly missing a baseball career in America. His wicked curveball attracted the major-league scouts, and the Washington Senators were interested in signing him but changed their minds. Frustrated, El Líder went home, rested his pitching arm, and started a revolution in the mountains.

Because of this, Celia thinks, her husband will be buried in stiff, foreign earth. Because of this, their children and their grandchildren are nomads.

Pilar, her first grandchild, writes to her from Brooklyn in a Spanish that is no longer hers. She speaks the hard-edged lexicon of bygone tourists itchy to throw dice on green felt or asphalt. Pilar's eyes, Celia fears, are no longer used to the compacted light of the tropics, where a morning hour can fill a month of days in the north, which receives only careless sheddings from the sun. She imagines her granddaughter pale, gliding through paleness, malnourished and cold without the food of scarlets and greens.

Celia knows that Pilar wears overalls like a farmhand and paints canvases with knots and whorls of red that resemble nothing at all. She knows that Pilar keeps a diary in the lining of her winter coat, hidden from her mother's scouring eyes. In it, Pilar records everything. This pleases Celia. She closes her eyes and speaks to her granddaughter, imagines her words as slivers of light piercing the murky night.

The rain begins again, softly this time. The finned palms record each drop. Celia is ankle deep in the rising tide. The water is curiously warm, too warm for spring. She reaches down and removes her pumps, crimped and puckered now like her own skin, chalked and misshapen from the saltwater. She wades deeper into the ocean. It pulls on her housedress like weights on her hem. Her hands float on the surface of the sea, still clutching her shoes, as if they could lead her to a new place.

She remembers something a *santera*[2] told her nearly forty years ago, when she had decided to die: "Miss Celia, there's a wet landscape in your palm." And it was true. She had lived all these years by the sea until she knew its every definition of blue.

Celia turns toward the shore. The light is unbearably bright on the porch. The wicker swing hangs from two rusted chains. The stripes on the cushions have dulled to gray as if the color made no difference at all. It seems to Celia that another woman entirely sat for years on those weathered cushions, drawn by the pull of the tides. She remembers the painful transitions to spring, the sea grapes and the rains, her skin a cicatrix.

She and Jorge moved to their house in the spring of 1937. Her husband bought her an upright walnut piano and set it by an arched window with a view of the sea. He stocked it with her music workbooks and sheaves of invigorating Rachmaninoff, Tchaikovsky, and a selection of Chopin. "Keep her away from Debussy," she overheard the doctors warn him. They feared that the Frenchman's restless style might compel her to rashness, but Celia hid her music to *La Soirée dans Grenade* and played it incessantly while Jorge traveled.

Celia hears the music now, pressing from beneath the waves. The water laps at her throat. She arches her spine until she floats on her back, straining to hear the notes of the Alhambra at midnight. She is waiting in a flowered shawl by the fountain for her lover, her Spanish lover, the lover before Jorge, and her hair is twisted with high combs. They retreat to the mossy riverbank and make love under the watchful poplars. The air is fragrant with jasmine and myrtle and citrus.

A cool wind stirs Celia from her dream. She stretches her legs but she cannot touch the sandy bottom. Her arms are heavy, sodden as porous wood after a storm. She has lost her shoes. A sudden wave engulfs her, and for a moment Celia is tempted to relax and drop. Instead, she swims clumsily, steadily toward shore, sunk low like

---

[2] a person who practices *santeria*, a form of spirituality which combines Catholic saints with African pagan gods.

an overladen boat. Celia concentrates on the sky. Their messages jump from tree to tree with stolen electricity. No one but me, she thinks, is guarding the coast tonight.

Celia peels Jorge's letter from her housedress pocket and holds it in the air to dry. She walks back to the porch and waits for the fishermen, for daylight.

Later that night, Celia rocks in her wicker swing and considers the star-inscribed sky, as if its haphazard arrangements might reveal something to her. But tonight it is as formal and unilluminating as a tiara.

Celia enters her kitchen and warms a little milk on the stove, then sweetens it with a few lumps of sugar. How is it possible that she can help her neighbors and be of no use at all to her children? Lourdes and Felicia and Javier are middle-aged now and desolate, deaf and blind to the world, to each other, to her. There is no solace among them, only a past infected with disillusion.

Her daughters cannot understand her commitment to El Líder. Lourdes sends her snapshots of pastries from her bakery in Brooklyn. Each glistening éclair is a grenade aimed at Celia's political beliefs, each strawberry shortcake proof—in butter, cream, and eggs—of Lourdes's success in America, and a reminder of the ongoing shortages in Cuba.

Felicia is no less exasperating. "We're *dying* of security!" she moans when Celia tries to point out the revolution's merits. No one is starving or denied medical care, no one sleeps in the streets, everyone works who wants to work. But her daughter prefers the luxury of uncertainty, of time unplanned, of waste.

If only Felicia could take an interest in the revolution, Celia believes, it would give her a higher purpose, a chance to participate in something larger than herself. After all, aren't they part of the greatest social experiment in modern history? But her daughter can only wallow in her own discomforts . . . .

. . . Celia rummages through her nightstand drawer for her favorite photograph of her son. He is tall and pale as she is, with a mole on his left cheek identical to hers. Javier is wearing his Pioneers uniform, bright and new as the revolution, as his optimistic face. She cannot imagine him any older than he is in this picture.

Her son was almost thirteen when the revolution triumphed. Those first years were difficult, not because of the hardships or the rationing that Celia knew were necessary to redistribute the country's wealth, but because Celia and Javier had to mute their enthusiasm for El Líder. Her husband would not tolerate praise of the revolution in his home.

Javier never fought his father openly. His war was one of silent defiance, and he left for Czechoslovakia secretly in 1966, without saying good-bye to anyone.

Javier wrote her a long letter after his father died three years ago, and said he'd finally become a professor of biochemistry at the University of Prague, lecturing in Russian, German, and Czech. He didn't mention his wife, not even in passing, but he wrote that he spoke Spanish to his little girl so she'd be able to talk with her grandmother someday. This touched Celia, and she wrote a special note to Irinita encouraging her to keep up her Spanish and promising to teach her how to swim.

Over the years, her son had written her only sporadically, quick notes jotted down, it seemed to Celia, between his lectures. Rarely did he write anything of substance, as if only the most superficial news was suitable for her. What she learned most about Javier came from the family picture her daughter-in-law, Irina, dutifully sent every Christmas. Celia saw her son age in these photographs, watched his mouth acquire his father's obstinate expression. And yet there was something vulnerable in his eyes that heartened Celia, that reminded her of her little boy.

In bed, Celia adjusts her breasts so she can sleep comfortably on her stomach. Every morning she wakes up on her back, her arms and legs spread, the cover sheet on the floor. She cannot account for her inquietude. Her dreams seem to her mere sparks of color and electricity, cut off from the current of her life.

Celia closes her eyes. She doesn't like to admit to herself that, despite all her activities, she sometimes feels lonely. Not the loneliness of previous years, of a reluctant life by the sea, but a loneliness borne of the inability to share her joy. Celia remembers the afternoons on the porch when her infant granddaughter seemed to understand her very thoughts. For many years, Celia spoke to Pilar during the darkest part of the night, but then their connection suddenly died. Celia understands now that a cycle between them had ended, and a new one had not yet begun . . . .

Mom jumps from the taxi in her sling-back pumps and runs past the giant bird of paradise bushes, past the rotting pawpaw tree, and up the three front steps of Abuela Celia's house. I follow her. The cement shows through the floor where the tiles are missing. It's a patterned tile, with pastel buds and climbing vines. It hasn't been mopped for months. A faded mantilla, soft as a moth, is draped over the sofa. There's a chalk-white piano and a refrigerator, a bulk of rust, against the far wall.

My mother inspects the bedroom she used to share with Tía Felicia, vacant now except for a frilly party dress hanging in the closet. She crosses the hallway to Abuela's room. A lace tablecloth is spread on the bed. A photograph of El Líder is on the night table. Mom turns from it in disgust.

I find Abuela sitting motionless on her wicker swing, wearing a worn bathing suit, her hair stuck haphazardly to her skull, her feet strangely lacerated. I kneel before her and press my cheek to hers, still salty from the sea. We hold each other close.

"*Dios mío,*[3] what happened to you?" Mom screams when she finds us. She scurries about preparing a hot bath with water boiled on the stove.

Abuela is missing a breast. There's a scar like a purple zipper on her chest. Mom holds a finger to her lips and flashes me a look that warns, "Pretend not to notice."

We wash Abuela's hair and rinse it with conditioner, then we pat her dry with towels as if this could somehow heal her. Abuela says nothing. She submits to my mother like a solemn novitiate. Mom untangles Abuela's hair with a wide-toothed comb. "You could have died of pneumonia!" she insists, and plugs in a Conair dryer that blows out the lights in the living room.

I notice Abuela Celia's drop pearl earrings, the intricate settings, the fine gold strands looping through her lobes. There's a cache of blue shadows in the pearls, a coolness in the smooth surfaces. When I was a baby, I bounced those pearls with my fingertips and heard the rhythm of my grandmother's thoughts.

"I went for a swim last night," Abuela Celia whispers to me alone. She looks through the arched window above the piano as if searching the waves to find the

---

[3] My God!

precise spot. Then she squeezes my hand. "I'm glad you remember, Pilar. I always knew you would."

Lourdes Puente

"Lourdes, I'm back," Jorge del Pino greets his daughter forty days after she buried him with his Panama hat, his cigars, and a bouquet of violets in a cemetery on the border of Brooklyn and Queens.

His words are warm and close as a breath. Lourdes turns, expecting to find her father at her shoulder but she sees only the dusk settling on the tops of the oak trees, the pink tinge of sliding darkness.

"Don't be afraid, *mi hija*.[4] Just keep walking and I'll explain," Jorge del Pino tells his daughter.

The sunset flares behind a row of brownstones, linking them as if by a flaming ribbon. Lourdes massages her eyes and begins walking with legs that feel held by splints.

"I'm glad to see you, Lourdes. Thank you for everything, *hija,* the hat, the cigars. You buried me like an Egyptian king, with all my valuables!" Jorge del Pino, laughs.

Lourdes perceives the faint scent of her father's cigar. She has taken to smoking the same brand herself late at night when she totals the day's receipts at the kitchen table.

"Where are you, Papi?"

The street is vacant, as if a force has absorbed all living things. Even the trees seem more shadow than substance.

"Nearby," her father says, serious now.

"Can you return?"

"From time to time."

"How will I know?"

"Listen for me at twilight."

Lourdes arrives home with a presentiment of disaster. Is her mind betraying her, cultivating delusion like a hothouse orchid? Lourdes opens the refrigerator, finds nothing to her liking. Everything tastes the same to her these days.

Outside, the spring rains resume ill-temperedly. The drops enter through the kitchen window at impossible angles. A church bell rings, shaking down the leaves of the maple tree. What if she has exhausted reality? Lourdes abhors ambiguity.

She pulls on the shipyard bell that rings in Rufino's workshop. Her husband will assure her, Lourdes thinks. He operates on a material plane. His projects conduct electricity, engage motion with toothed wheels, react in concert with universal laws of physics.

---

[4] my daughter

Rufino appears, dusted with blue chalk. His fingernails, too, are blue, an indigo blue.

"He's back," Lourdes whispers hoarsely, peering under the love seats. "He spoke to me tonight when I was walking home from the bakery. I heard Papi's voice. I smelled his cigar. The street was empty, I swear it." Lourdes stops. Her chest rises and falls with every breath. Then she leans toward her husband, narrowing her eyes. "Things are wrong, Rufino, very wrong."

Her husband stares back at her, blinking rapidly as if he'd just awakened. "You're tired, *mi cielo,*"[5] Rufino says evenly, coaxing Lourdes to the sofa. He rubs her insteps with a cool lotion called Pretty Feet. She feels the rolling pressure of his thumbs against her arches, the soothing grip of his hands on her swollen ankles.

The next day, Lourdes works extraconscientiously, determined to prove to herself that her business acumen, at least, is intact. She sails back and forth behind the bakery counter, explaining the ingredients in her cakes and pies to her clients. "We use only real butter," she says in her accented English. "Not margarine, like the place down the block."

After her customers make their selections, Lourdes leans toward them. "Any special occasions coming up?" she whispers, as if she were selling hot watches from a raincoat. If they answer yes—and it's always a musical yes to Lourdes's ears—she launches into her advance-order sales pitch.

By two o'clock, when the trainee reports for work, Lourdes has cash deposits on seven birthday cakes (including one peanut-butter-and-banana-flavored layer cake topped with a marzipan Elvis); a sixty-serving sheet cake for the closing recital of the Bishop Lowney High School marching band; a two-tiered fiftieth-anniversary cake "For Tillie and Ira, Two Golden Oldies"; and a double-chocolate butter cream decorated with a wide high heel for the retirement of Frankie Zaccaglini of Frankie's EEE Shoe Company.

Lourdes's self-confidence is restored.

"See this," she announces to her new employee, Maribel Navarro, riffling her orders like a blackjack dealer. "This is what I want from you." Then she hands Maribel a bottle of Windex and a roll of paper towels and orders her to clean every last inch of the counter.

Lourdes spends the afternoon training Maribel, a pretty Puerto Rican woman in her late twenties with a pixie cut and stylishly long nails. "You're going to have to trim those if you want to work here, Lourdes snaps. "Unsanitary. The health department will give us a citation."

Maribel is pleasant with the customers and gives the correct change, but she doesn't show much initiative.

"Don't let them get away so easily," Lourdes coaches her. "You can always sell them something else. Some dinner rolls, a coffee ring for tomorrow's breakfast."

Nobody works like an owner, Lourdes thinks, as she places fresh doilies under the chiffon pies. She pulls out a tray of Florentine cookies and shows Maribel how to arrange them on overlapping strips of wax paper so they look more appealing.

---

[5] *Cielo* means sky, but the expression is an affectionate one roughly meaning "my dear."

"The Florentines are seven ninety-five a pound, two dollars more than the other cookies, so weigh them separately." Lourdes pulls a sheet of tissue paper from a metal dispenser and places it on the scale with a cookie. "See. This Florentine alone weighs forty-three cents. I can't afford to throw that kind of money away."

Business picks up after five o'clock with the after-work crowd stopping by for desserts. Maribel works efficiently, tying the boxes of pastries firmly with string just as she was taught. This pleases Lourdes. By now, she has almost dispelled the effect of her father's visitation yesterday. Could she have imagined the entire incident?

Suddenly Lourdes's wandering eye, like a wary spy, fixes on the quarters sliding across the counter to Maribel. It observes Maribel packing the two cinnamon crullers in a white paper bag, folding the top over neatly, and thanking the customer. It watches as she turns to the register and rings up fifty cents. Then, just as the eye is about to relax its scrutiny, it spots Maribel slipping the coins into her pocket.

Lourdes continues waiting on her customer, an elderly woman sizing up a mocha petit four. When she's done, Lourdes strides to the register, pulls out nine singles and a roll of pennies for the afternoon's work, and hands it to Maribel.

"Get out," Lourdes says.

Maribel removes her apron, folds it into a compact square on the counter, and leaves without saying a word.

An hour later, Lourdes walks home from the bakery as if picking her way through a mine field. The Navarro woman has shattered Lourdes's fragile peace of mind. Breezes from the sluggish river seem to inscribe her skin with metal tips. She crawls to an edge inside herself, longs to be insensate, a slab of brick. Lourdes thinks she detects the scent of her father's cigar, but when she turns there's only a businessman hailing a taxi, his hand waving a cigarette. Behind him, a linden tree drops a cluster of seeds.

When Lourdes was a child in Cuba, she used to wait anxiously for her father to return from his trips selling small fans and electric brooms in distant provinces. He would call her every evening from Camagüey or Sagua la Grande and she would cry, "When are you coming home, Papi? When are you coming home?" Lourdes would welcome her father in her party dress and search his suitcase for rag dolls and oranges.

On Sunday afternoons, after high mass, they went to baseball games and ate roasted peanuts from brown paper cones. The sun darkened Lourdes's skin to the shade of the villagers on the bleachers, and the mix of her father's cologne and the warm, acrid smells of the ballpark made her giddy. These are her happiest memories.

Years later, when her father was in New York, baseball became their obsession. During the Mets' championship season, Lourdes and her father discussed each game like generals plotting a battle, assessing the merits of Tom Seaver, Ed Kranepool, and Jerry Koosman. They glued transistors to their ears all summer, even during Jorge del Pino's brief hospital stays, and cheered when the Mets caught fire and the Cubs finally folded.

On October 16, 1969, Lourdes, her father, doctors, nurses, orderlies, patients, nuns, and a priest who arrived to administer last rites to a dying man crowded the television room of the Sisters of Charity Hospital for the fifth game of the World Series. When Cleon Jones camped under the final fly ball against the Orioles, all hell broke loose. Patients, bare-assed in their hospital gowns, streaked down the corridors chanting, "WE'RE NUMBER ONE!" Someone popped a bottle of champagne and tears streamed down the faces of the nuns, who'd prayed fervently for such a miracle.

At Shea Stadium, the crowd tore onto the field, ripping up home plate, pulling up fat clods of turf and raising them high over their heads. They set off orange flares and firecrackers and chalked the outfield fence with victory slogans. Across the river in Manhattan, on Wall Street and Park Avenue, Delancey Street and Broadway, people danced under showers of computer cards and ticker tape. Lourdes and her father laughed and embraced for a long, long time.

When she had first left Cuba, Lourdes hadn't known how long they'd be away. She was to meet Rufino in Miami, where the rest of his family had fled. In her confusion, she packed riding crops and her wedding veil, a watercolor landscape, and a paper sack of birdseed.

Pilar ran away in the Miami airport, her crinoline dress swinging like a tiny bell through the crowd. Lourdes heard her daughter's name announced over the loudspeaker. She couldn't speak when she found Pilar, sitting on the lap of a pilot and licking a lime lollipop. She couldn't find the words to thank the uniformed American who escorted them to their gate.

After several days, they left Miami in a secondhand Chevrolet. Lourdes couldn't stand Rufino's family, the endless brooding over their lost wealth, the competition for dishwasher jobs.

"I want to go where it's cold," Lourdes told her husband. They began to drive. "Colder," she said as they passed the low salt marshes of Georgia, as if the word were a whip driving them north. "Colder," she said through the withered fields of a Carolina winter. "Colder," she said again in Washington, D.C., despite the cherry-blossom promises, despite the white stone monuments hoarding winter light. "This is cold enough," she finally said when they reached New York.

Only two months earlier, Lourdes had been pregnant with her second child back in Cuba. She'd been galloping through a field of dry grasses when her horse reared suddenly, throwing her to the ground. The horse fled, leaving her alone. Lourdes felt a density between her breasts harden to a sharp, round pain. The blood bleached from her fingernails.

A large rodent appeared from behind an aroma tree and began nibbling the toes of her boots. Lourdes threw a rock at it, killing it instantly. She stumbled for nearly an hour until she reached their dairy farm. A worker lent her his horse and she rode at a breakneck pace back to the villa.

Two young soldiers were pointing their rifles at Rufino. His hands circled nervously in the air. She jumped from her horse and stood like a shield before her husband.

"Get the hell out of here!" she shouted with such ferocity that the soldiers lowered their guns and backed toward their Jeep.

Lourdes felt the clot dislodge and liquefy beneath her breasts, float through her belly, and slide down her thighs. There was a pool of dark blood at her feet.

Rufino was in Havana ordering a cow-milking machine when the soldiers returned. They handed Lourdes an official sheet of paper declaring the Puentes' estate the property of the revolutionary government. She tore the deed in half and angrily dismissed the soldiers, but one of them grabbed her by the arm.

"You're not going to start that again, are you, *compañera?*" the tall one said.

Lourdes heard the accent of Oriente province and turned to look at him. His hair, tamed with brilliantine, grew dense and low on his forehead.

"Get out of my house!" Lourdes yelled at the men, more fiercely than she had the week before.

But instead of leaving, the tall one increased the pressure on her arm just above the elbow.

Lourdes felt his calloused palm, the metal of his ring clapping her temple. She twisted free from his grip and charged him so abruptly that he fell back against the vestibule wall. Lourdes tried to run past him but the other soldier blocked her way. Her head reverberated with the clapping palm.

"So the woman of the house is a fighter?" the tall soldier taunted. He pressed his face close to Lourdes's, pinning her arms behind her back.

Lourdes did not close her eyes but looked directly into his. They were unremarkable except for the whites, which were tinged with the filmy blue of the blind. His lips were too full for a man. As he tried to press them to Lourdes's mouth she snapped her head back and spat in his face.

He smiled slowly and Lourdes saw a stained band along his front teeth, like the watermarks on a pier. His gums were a soft pink, delicate as the petals of a rose.

The other soldier held Lourdes down as his partner took a knife from his holster. Carefully, he sliced Lourdes's riding pants off to her knees and tied them over her mouth. He cut through her blouse without dislodging a single button and slit her bra and panties in two. Then he placed the knife flat across her belly and raped her.

Lourdes could not see but she smelled vividly as if her senses had concentrated on this alone.

She smelled the soldier's coarse soap, the salt of his perspiring back. She smelled his milky clots and the decay of his teeth and the citrus brilliantine in his hair, as if a grove of lemons lay hidden there. She smelled his face on his wedding day, his tears when his son drowned at the park. She smelled his rotting leg in Africa, where it would be blown off his body on a moonless savanna night. She smelled him when he was old and unbathed and the flies blackened his eyes.

When he finished, the soldier lifted the knife and began to scratch at Lourdes's belly with great concentration. A primeval scraping. Crimson hieroglyphics.

The pain brought a flood of color back to Lourdes's eyes. She saw the blood seep from her skin like rainwater from a sodden earth.

Not until later, after the tall soldier had battered her with his rifle and left with his lumpy, quiet friend, after she had scoured her skin and hair with detergents meant for the walls and the tile floors, after stanching the blood with cotton and gauze and wiping the steam from the bathroom mirror, did Lourdes try to read what he had carved. But it was illegible.

Seven days after her father's visitation, Lourdes looks out her bakery window. The twilight falls in broad violet sheets. In the corner store, the butcher closes out his register. Bare fluorescent tubes and a rack of ribs hang from the ceiling, obscuring his profile. The florist rattles shut his gate next door, securing it with a fist-sized lock. Across the street, the liquor store is open, a magnet to the wiry man in the sagging tan suit cajoling people for spare change.

Lourdes recognizes a passerby, a heavyset woman with a veiled pillbox hat who praised her Boston cream pies. She is dragging by the hand a little boy in short pants and knee socks. His feet barely touch the ground.

On her way home, Lourdes passes a row of Arab shops, recent additions to the neighborhood. Baskets of figs and pistachios and coarse yellow grains are displayed under their awnings. Lourdes buys a round box of sticky dates and considers the centuries of fratricide converging on this street corner in Brooklyn. She ponders the transmigrations from the southern latitudes, the millions moving north. What happens to their languages? The warm burial grounds they leave behind? What of their passions lying stiff and untranslated in their breasts?

Lourdes considers herself lucky. Immigration has redefined her, and she is grateful. Unlike her husband, she welcomes her adopted language, its possibilities for reinvention. Lourde's relishes winter most of all—the cold scraping sounds on sidewalks and windshields, the ritual of scarves and gloves, hats and zip-in coat linings. Its layers protect her. She wants no part of Cuba, no part of its wretched carnival. Floats creaking with lies, no part of Cuba at all, which Lourdes claims never possessed her.

Four blocks from her home, Lourdes smells her father's cigar behind a catalpa tree.

"*Mi hija,* have you forgotten me?" Jorge del Pino chides gently.

Lourdes feels her legs as if from a distance. She pictures them slipping from their sockets and moving before her in a steady gait, still wearing their rubber-soled shoes, their white-ribbed stockings. Cautiously, she follows them.

"You didn't expect to hear from me again?"

"I wasn't even sure I heard you the first time," Lourdes says tentatively.

"You thought you'd imagined it?"

"I thought I heard your voice because I wanted to, because I missed you. When I was little I used to think I heard you opening the front door late at night. I'd run out but you were never there."

"I'm here now, Lourdes."

There's a ship leaving the harbor, its whistle resigned as an abbot in prayer, fracturing the dusk.

Lourdes recalls the plane ride to Miami last month to pick up Pilar. The airport was congested and they circled the city for nearly an hour before landing. Lourdes could smell the air before she breathed it, the air of her mother's ocean nearby. She imagined herself alone and shriveled in her mother's womb, envisioned the first days in her mother's unyielding arms. Her mother's fingers were stiff and splayed as spoons, her milk a tasteless gray. Her mother stared at her with eyes collapsed of expectation. If it's true that babies learn love from their mothers' voices, then this is what Lourdes heard: "I will not remember her name."

"Papi, I don't know what to do anymore." Lourdes begins to cry. "No matter what I do, Pilar hates me."

"Pilar doesn't hate you, *hija*. She just hasn't learned to love you yet."

They would join the army reserve or the auxiliary police like her, and protect what was theirs. In Cuba nobody was prepared for the Communists and look what happened. Now her mother guards their beach with binoculars and a pistol against Yankees. If only Lourdes had had a gun when she needed it.

It's Thursday, just after nine. There's a full moon out. It hangs fat and waxy in the sky, creased with shadows.

"Every loony in New York comes out of the woodwork on nights like this," the regular beat cop had warned her.

But so far everything's been quiet. It's too cold for loiterers. Lourdes suddenly remembers how her daughter had ridiculed Armstrong's first words on the moon. "He had months to think up something and that's all he could say?" Pilar was only ten years old and already mocking everything. Lourdes slapped her for being disrespectful, but it made no difference to her daughter. Pilar was immune to threats. She placed no value on normal things so it was impossible to punish her. Even now, Pilar is not afraid of pain or of losing anything. It's this indifference that is most maddening.

The last of the Jews have moved out of the neighborhood. Only the Kellners are left. The others are on Long Island or in Westchester or Florida, depending on their ages and their bank accounts. Pilar thinks Lourdes is bigoted, but what does her daughter know of life? Equality is just another one of her abstractions. "I don't make up the statistics," she tells Pilar. "I don't color the faces down at the precinct." Black faces, Puerto Rican faces. Once in a while a stray Irish or Italian face looking scared. Lourdes prefers to confront reality—the brownstones converted to tenements in a matter of months, the garbage in the streets, the jaundice-eyed men staring vacantly from the stoops. Even Pilar couldn't denounce her for being a hypocrite.

Lourdes feels the solid ground beneath her solid black shoes as she walks. She breathes in the wintry air, which stings her lungs. It seems to her as if the air were made of crystal filaments, scraping and cleaning her inside. She decides she has no patience for dreamers, for people who live between black and white.

Lourdes slides her hand up and down her wooden nightstick. It's the only weapon the police department will issue her. That and handcuffs. Lourdes has used the stick only once in her two months of patrolling, to break up a fight between a Puerto Rican kid and three Italians down at the playground. Lourdes knows the Puerto Rican's mother. She's the one who worked at the bakery for an afternoon. Lourdes caught her pocketing fifty cents from the sale of two crullers, and threw her out. No wonder her son is a delinquent. He sells plastic bags of marijuana behind the liquor store.

Lourdes's son would have been about the same age as the Navarro boy. *Her* son would have been different. He wouldn't have talked back to her or taken drugs or drunk beer from paper bags like the other teenagers. *Her* son would have helped her in the bakery without complaint. He would have come to her for guidance, pressed her hand to his cheek, told her he loved her. Lourdes would have talked to her son the way Rufino talks to Pilar, for companionship. Lourdes suffers with this knowledge.

Down the street, the trees are imprisoned equidistantly in square plots of dirt. Everything else is concrete. Lourdes remembers reading somewhere about how Dutch elm disease wiped out the entire species on the East Coast except for a lone tree in Manhattan surrounded by concrete. Is this, she wonders, how we'll all survive?

It became clear to Lourdes shortly after she and Rufino moved to New York that he would never adapt. Something came unhinged in his brain that would make him incapable of working in a conventional way. There was a part of him that could never leave the *finca*[6] or the comfort of its cycles, and this diminished him for any other life. He could not be transplanted. So Lourdes got a job. Cuban women of a certain age and a certain class consider working outside the home to be beneath them. But Lourdes never believed that.

While it was true that she had grown accustomed to the privileges that came with marrying into the Puente family, Lourdes never accepted the life designated for its women. Even now, stripped of their opulence, crowded into two-bedroom apartments in Hialeah and Little Havana, the Puente women clung to their rituals as they did their engraved silverware, succumbing to a cloying nostalgia. Doña Zaida, once a formidable matriarch who ruled her eight sons by a resolute jealousy, spent long afternoons watching *novelas*[7] on television and perfuming her thickening wrists.

Lourdes knew she could never be this kind of woman. After her honeymoon, she got right to work on the Puente ranch. She reviewed the ledgers, fired the cheating accountant, and took over the books herself. She redecorated the musty, coffer-ceilinged mansion with watercolor landscapes, reupholstered the sofas with rustic fabrics, and discarded the cretonne drapes in favor of sliding glass doors that invited the morning light. Out went the ornate bric-a-brac, the austere furniture carved with the family crest. Lourdes refilled the mosaic-lined fountain with sweet water and built an aviary in the garden, stocking it with toucans and cockatoos, parrots, a macaw, and canaries that sang in high octaves. Sometimes at night, she could hear the cries of the quail doves and solitaires interspersed with the songs from the aviary.

When a disgruntled servant informed Doña Zaida about the changes in her country house, she descended on the ranch in a fury and restored the villa to its former state. Lourdes, who defiantly rebuilt the aviary and restocked it with birds, never spoke to her mother-in-law again.

Lourdes misses the birds she had in Cuba. She thinks of joining a bird-watching society, but who would take care of the bakery in her absence? Pilar is unreliable and Rufino can't tell a Danish from a donut. It's a shame, too, because all Lourdes ever sees in Brooklyn is dull little wrens or those filthy pigeons. Rufino has taken to raising pigeons in wire-mesh cages in their backyard the way he saw Marlon Brando do in *On the Waterfront*. He prints messages on bits of paper, slips them through metal rings on the pigeons' legs, then kisses each bird on the head for good luck and lets it

[6] farm   [7] soap operas

loose with a whoop. Lourdes doesn't know, or care what her husband is writing, or to whom. By now, she accepts him the way she accepts the weather. What else can she do?

Rufino has stopped confiding in her. She hears secondhand snippets about his projects from Pilar, and knows he's trying to develop a super carburetor, one that will get two hundred miles to the gallon. Lourdes knows, too, that her husband is still brooding about artificial intelligence. She is not sure what this means although Rufino explained to her once that it would do for the brain what the telephone did for the human voice, take it farther and faster than it could go unassisted. Lourdes cannot understand why this is so difficult. She remembers seeing robots at the World's Fair ten years ago. She and Rufino and Pilar ate in a restaurant observatory shaped like a spaceship. The food was terrible. The view was of Queens.

These days, Lourdes recognizes her husband's face, his thinning reddish hair, and the crepey pouches under his eyes, but he is a stranger to her. She looks at him the way she might look at a photograph of her hands, unfamiliar upon close inspection.

Lourdes is herself only with her father. Even after his death, they understand each other perfectly, as they always have. Jorge del Pino doesn't accompany Lourdes on her beat because he doesn't want to interfere with her work. He is proud of his daughter, of her tough stance on law and order, identical to his own. It was he who encouraged Lourdes to join the auxiliary police so she'd be ready to fight the Communists when the time came. "Look how El Líder mobilizes the people to protect his causes," Jorge del Pino told his daughter. "He uses the techniques of the Fascists. Everyone is armed and ready for combat at a moment's notice. How will we ever win Cuba back if we ourselves are not prepared to fight?"

Pilar makes fun of Lourdes in her uniform, of the way she slaps the nightstick in her palm. "Who do you think you are, Kojak?" she says, laughing, and hands her mother a lollipop. This is just like her daughter, scornful and impudent. "I'm doing this to show you something, to teach you a lesson!" Lourdes screams, but Pilar ignores her.

Last Christmas, Pilar gave her a book of essays on Cuba called *A Revolutionary Society*. The cover showed cheerful, clean-cut children gathered in front of a portrait of Che Guevara. Lourdes was incensed.

"Will you read it?" Pilar asked her.

"I don't have to read it to know what's in it! Lies, poisonous Communist lies!" Che Guevara's face had set a violence quiverring within her like a loose wire.

"Suit yourself," Pilar shot back.

Lourdes snatched the volume from under the Christmas tree, took it to the bathroom, filled the tub with scalding water, and dropped it in. Che Guevara's face blanched and swelled like the dead girl Lourdes had seen wash up once on the beach at Santa Teresa del Mar with a note pinned to her breast. Nobody ever came to claim her. Lourdes fished Pilar's book out of the tub with barbecue tongs and placed it on the porcelain platter she reserved for her roasted pork legs. Then she fastened a note to the cover with a safety pin. "Why don't you move to Russia if you think it's so great!" And she signed her name in full.

All this she left on Pilar's bed. But it did not provoke her daughter. The next day, the platter was back in the cupboard and *A Revolutionary Society* was drying on the clothesline.

Lourdes's walkie-talkie crackles as she works her way along the length of river that forms the western boundary of her territory. The night is so clear that the water reflects every stray angle of light. Without the disruptions of ships and noise, the river is a mirror. It reminds Lourdes of a photograph she saw once of the famous Hall of Mirrors in the Palace of Versailles with its endless ricocheting light.

At the edge of her vision, the darkness shifts. Her spine stiffens and her heart is audible deep inside her ears. She turns and squints but she cannot make out the figure, crouched and still, by the river. Lourdes grips her nightstick with one hand and pulls on her flashlight with the other. When she looks up again, the figure springs across the low fence and jumps into the river, shattering the light.

"Stop!" she shouts, running toward the spot as if chasing a part of herself. Lourdes turns her flashlight on the river, penetrating its rippled surface, then hoists herself over the fence. "Stop!" she shouts again at nothing at all. Lourdes pulls her walkie-talkie from its holster and screams too close to the speaker. She cannot remember what to say, the codes she had carefully memorized. A voice is talking to her now, calm and officious. "Tell us your location," it says, . . . "your location." But Lourdes jumps into the river instead. She hears the sirens wailing as the cold envelops her, numbing her face and her hands, her feet in their thick-soled shoes. The river smells of death.

Only one more fact is important. Lourdes lived and the Navarro boy died.

Pilar

I was only two years old when I left Cuba but I remember everything that's happened to me since I was a baby, even word-for-word conversations. I was sitting in my grandmother's lap, playing with her drop pearl earrings, when my mother told her we were leaving the country. Abuela Celia called her a traitor to the revolution. Mom tried to pull me away but I clung to Abuela and screamed at the top of my lungs. My grandfather came running and said, "Celia, let the girl go. She belongs with Lourdes." That was the last time I saw her.

My mother says that Abuela Celia's had plenty of chances to leave Cuba but that she's stubborn and got her head turned around by El Líder. Mom says "Communist" the way some people says "cancer," low and fierce. She reads the newspapers page by page for leftist conspiracies, jams her finger against imagined evidence and says, "See. What did I tell you?" Last year when El Líder jailed a famous Cuban poet, she sneered at "those leftist intellectual hypocrites" for trying to free him. "They created those prisons, so now they should rot in them!" she shouted, not making much sense at all. "They're dangerous subversives, red to the bone!" Mom's views are strictly black-and-white. It's how she survives.

The family is hostile to the individual. This is what I'm thinking as Lou Reed says he has enough attitude to kill every person in New Jersey. I'm at a club in the Village with my boyfriend, Max. I figure I have enough attitude to kill a few people myself, only it never works on the right ones.

"I'm from Brooklyn, man!" Lou, shouts and the crowd goes wild. I don't cheer, though. I wouldn't cheer either if Lou said, "Let's hear it for Cuba." Cuba. Planet Cuba. Where the hell is that?

Max's real name is Octavio Schneider. He sings and plays bass and harmonica for the Manichaean Blues Band, a group he started back in San Antonio, where he's from. They do Howlin' Wolf and Muddy Waters and lots of their own songs, mostly hard rock. Sometimes they do back-up for this crazy bluesman, the Reverend Billy Hines, who keeps his eyes shut when he sings. Max says that the reverend was a store-front preacher who played the Panhandle years ago and is attempting a comeback. Max himself had a modest hit in Texas with "Moonlight on Emma," a song about an ex-girlfriend who dumped him and moved to Hollywood.

I met Max at a downtown basement club a few months ago. He came over and started speaking to me in Spanish (his mother is Mexican) as if he'd known me for years. I liked him right away. When I brought him around to meet my parents, Mom took one look at his beaded headband and the braid down his back and said, "*Sácalo de aquí.*"[8] When I told her that Max spoke Spanish, she simply repeated what she said in English: "Take him away."

Dad was cool, though. "What does your band's name mean?" he asked Max.

"The Manichaeans, see, were followers of this Persian guy who lived in the third century. They believed that hedonism was the only way to get rid of their sins."

"Hedonism?"

"Yeah, the Manichaeans liked to party. They had orgies and drank a lot. They got wiped out by other Christians, though."

"Too bad," my father said sympathetically.

Later, Dad looked up the Manichaeans in the encyclopedia and discovered that, contrary to what Max claimed, the Manichaeans believed that the world and all matter were created by nefarious forces, and that the only way to battle them was through asceticism and a pure life. When I told Max about this, he just shrugged and said, "Well, I guess that's okay, too." Max is a tolerant kind of guy.

I just love the way Lou Reed's concerts feel—expectant, uncertain. You never know what he's going to do next. Lou has about twenty-five personalities. I like him because he sings about people no one else sings about—drug addicts, transvestites, the down-and-out. Lou jokes about his alter egos discussing problems at night. I feel like a new me sprouts and dies every day.

I play Lou and Iggy Pop and this new band the Ramones whenever I paint. I love their energy, their violence, their incredible grinding guitars. It's like an artistic form of assault. I try to translate what I hear into colors and volumes and lines that confront people, that say, "Hey, we're here too and what we think matters!" or more often just "Fuck you!" Max is not as crazy about the Ramones as I am. I think he's more of a traditionalist. He has a tough time being rude, even to people who deserve

---

[8] Get him out of here.

it. Not me. If I don't like someone, I show it. It's the one thing I have in common with my mother.

Neither of my parents is very musical. Their entire record collection consists of *Perry Como's Greatest Hits,* two Herb Alpert & the Tijuana Brass albums, and *Alvin and the Chipmunks Sing Their Favorite Christmas Carols,* which they bought for me when I was a kid. Recently, Mom picked up a Jim Nabors album of patriotic songs in honor of the bicentennial. I mean, after Vietnam and Watergate, who the hell wants to hear "The Battle Hymn of the Republic"?

I used to like the Fourth of July okay because of the fireworks. I'd go down by the East River and watch them flare up from the tugboats. The girandoles looked like fiery lace in the sky. But this bicentennial crap is making me crazy. Mom has talked about nothing else for months. She bought a second bakery and plans to sell tricolor cupcakes and Uncle Sam marzipan. Apple pies, too. She's convinced she can fight Communism from behind her bakery counter.

Last year she joined the local auxiliary police out of some misplaced sense of civic duty. My mother—all four feet eleven and a half inches and 217 pounds of her—patrols the streets of Brooklyn at night in a skintight uniform, clanging with enough antiriot gear to quash another Attica. She practices twirling her nightstick in front of the mirror, then smacks it against her palm, steadily, menacingly, like she's seen cops do on television. Mom's upset because the police department won't issue her a gun. Right. She gets a gun and I move out of state fast.

There's other stuff happening with her. For starters, she's been talking with Abuelo Jorge since he died. He gives her business advice and tells her who's stealing from her at the bakery. Mom says that Abuelo spies on me and reports back to her. Like what is this? The ghost patrol? Mom is afraid that I'm having sex with Max (which I'm not) and this is her way of trying to keep me in line.

Max likes Mom, though. He says she suffers from an "imperious disposition."

"You mean she's a frustrated tyrant?" I ask him.

"More like a bitch goddess," he explains.

Max's parents split up before he was born and his mother cleans motel rooms for minimum wage. I guess Mom must seem exotic by comparison.

But she's really not. Mom makes food only people in Ohio eat, like Jell-O molds with miniature marshmallows or recipes she clips from *Family Circle.* And she barbecues anything she can get her hands on. Then we sit around behind the warehouse and stare at each other with nothing to say. Like this is it? We're living the American dream?

The worst is the parades. Mom gets up early and drags us out on Thanksgiving Day loaded with plastic foam coolers, like we're going to starve right there on Fifth Avenue. On New Year's Day, she sits in front of the television and comments on every single float in the Rose Parade. I think she dreams of sponsoring one herself someday. Like maybe a huge burning effigy of El Líder.

Max flatters me but not in a sleazy way. He says he loves my height (I'm five feet eight inches) and my hair (black, down to my waist) and the whiteness of my skin. His mouth is a little sauna, hot and wet. When we slow-dance, he presses himself against me and I feel his hardness against my thighs. He says I would make a good bass player.

Max knows about Abuela Celia in Cuba, about how she used to talk to me late at night and how we've lost touch over the years. Max wants to go to Cuba and track her down, but I tell him what happened four years ago, when I ran away to Florida, and my plans to see my grandmother collapsed. I wonder what Abuela Celia is doing right this minute.

Most days Cuba is kind of dead to me. But every once in a while a wave of longing will hit me and it's all I can do not to hijack a plane to Havana or something. I resent the hell out of the politicians and the generals who force events on us that structure our lives, that dictate the memories we'll have when we're old. Every day Cuba fades a little more inside me, my grandmother fades a little more inside me. And there's only my imagination where our history should be.

It doesn't help that Mom refuses to talk about Abuela Celia. She gets annoyed every time I ask her and she shuts me up quickly, like I'm prying into top secret information. Dad is more open, but he can't tell me what I really want to know, like why Mom hardly speaks to Abuela or why she still keeps her riding crops from Cuba. Most of the time, he's too busy referring the fights between us, or else he's just in his own orbit.

Dad feels kind of lost here in Brooklyn. I think he stays in his workshop most of the day because he'd get too depressed or crazy otherwise. Sometimes I think we should have moved to a ranch in Wyoming or Montana. He would have been happy there with his horses and his cows, his land, and a big empty sky overhead. Dad only looks alive when he talks about the past, about Cuba. But we don't discuss that much either lately. Things haven't been the same since I saw him with that blond bombshell. I never said anything to him, but it's like a cut on my tongue that never healed.

"So tell me how you want to be remembered," I tease Abuela Celia. It's very early in the morning and the light is a transparent blue. "I can paint you any way you like."

"You don't have to do that, *hija*. I just want to sit here with you." She settles into her wicker swing and pats the cushion by her thigh. Abuela is wearing her faded jade housedress and a brand-new pair of sneakers with thick cotton socks. Suddenly she leans toward me. "Did you say any way I like?"

"*Sí,* Abuela. You name it."

"Even younger? Much younger?"

"Or older, if you prefer." I laugh. She laughs, too, and her drop pearl earrings dance from her lobes.

"Well, I've always envisioned myself in a flared red skirt like the flamenco dancers wear. Maybe with a few carnations."

"Red ones?"

"Yes, red ones. Many red ones."

"Anything else?" I joke around, feigning a flamenco. But Abuela doesn't laugh. There's a sadness in her expression tempered by hope.

"Are you going to stay with me, Pilar? Are you going to stay with me this time?"

I paint a series of watercolor sketches of my grandmother. I'm out of practice, though. Abstract painting is more up my alley. I feel more comfortable with it, more directly connected to my emotions. In a few of the sketches, I paint Abuela Celia just the way she wants—dancing flamenco with whirling red skirts and castanets and a tight satin bodice. Abuela likes these paintings best, and even ventures a few suggestions. "Can't you make my hair a little darker, Pilar? My waist a little more slender? *Por Dios,*[9] I look like an old woman!"

Mostly, though, I paint her in blue. Until I returned to Cuba, I never realized how many blues exist. The aquamarines near the shoreline, the azures of deeper waters, the eggshell blues beneath by grandmother's eyes, the fragile indigos tracking her hands. There's a blue, too, in the curves of the palms, and the edges of the words we speak, a blue tinge to the sand and the seashells and the plump gulls on the beach. The mole by Abuela's mouth is also blue, a vanishing blue.

"These are very beautiful, Pilar. But do I really look so unhappy?"

Abuela talks to me as I paint. She tells me that before the revolution Cuba was a pathetic place, a parody of a country. There was one product, sugar, and all the profits went to a few Cubans, and, of course, to the Americans. Many people worked only in winter, harvesting the sugarcane. In the summer it was the *tiempo muerto,* the dead time, and the *campesinos*[10] barely escaped starvation. Abuela says she was saved because her parents sent her to live with her great-aunt in Havana, who raised her with progressive ideas. Freedom, Abuela tells me, is nothing more than the right to a decent life.

Mom eavesdrops on Abuela and me then lambastes us with one of her sixty-odd diatribes when she doesn't like what she hears. Her favorite is the plight of the *plantados,* the political prisoners who've been in jail here almost twenty years. "What were their crimes?" she shouts at us, pushing her face close to ours. Or the question of retribution. "Who will repay us for our homes, for the lands the Communists stole from us?" And religion. "Catholics are persecuted, treated like dogs!" But Abuela doesn't argue with Mom. She just lets her talk and talk. When Mom starts to go too haywire, Abuela gets up from her swing and walks away.

We've been in Cuba four days and Mom has done nothing but complain and chain-smoke her cigars late at night. She argues with Abuela's neighbors, picks fights with waiters, berates the man who sells ice cones on the beach. She asks everyone how much they earn, and no matter what they tell her, she says, "You can make ten times as much in Miami!" With her, money is the bottom line. Mom also tries to catch workers stealing so she can say, "See! *That's* their loyalty to the revolution!"

The Committee for the Defense of the Revolution has started hassling Abuela about Mom, but Abuela tells them to be patient, that she'll only be here a week. I want to stay longer, but Mom refuses because she doesn't want to give Cuba any more hard currency, as if our contributions will make or break the economy. (Mom is apoplectic because she has to pay for a hotel room and three meals a day even though we're staying with relatives.)

---

[9] My God   [10] peasants

"Their pesos are worthless! They let us visit because they need us, not the other way around!" Why did they let my mother in here, anyway? Don't these Cubans do their homework?

I keep thinking Mom is going to have a heart attack any minute. Abuela tells me it's been unusually hot for April. Mom is taking several showers a day, then rinsing her clothes in the sink and putting them on damp to cool herself off. Abuela doesn't get any hot water at her house. The ocean is warmer than what comes out of her pipes, but I'm getting used to cold showers. The food is another story, though, greasy as hell. If I stay much longer, I'll need to get a pair of those neon stretch pants all the Cuban women wear. I have to admit it's much tougher here than I expected, but at least everyone seems to have the bare necessities.

I wonder how different my life would have been if I'd stayed with my grandmother. I think about how I'm probably the only ex-punk on the island, how no one else has their ears pierced in three places. It's hard to imagine existing without Lou Reed. I ask Abuela if I can paint whatever I want in Cuba and she says yes, as long as I don't attack the state. Cuba is still developing, she tells me, and can't afford the luxury of dissent. Then she quotes me something El Líder said in the early years, before they started arresting poets. "Within the revolution, everything; against the revolution, nothing." I wonder what El Líder would think of my paintings. Art, I'd tell him, is the ultimate revolution.

Abuela gives me a box of letters she wrote to her onetime lover in Spain, but never sent. She shows me his photograph, too. It's very well preserved. He'd be good-looking by today's standards, well built with a full beard and kind eyes, almost professorial. He wore a crisp linen suit and a boater tilted slightly to the left. Abuela tells me she took the picture herself one Sunday on the Malecón.[11]

She also gives me a book of poems she's had since 1930, when she heard Garda Lorca read at the Principal de la Comedia Theater. Abuela knows each poem by heart, and recites them quite dramatically.

I've started dreaming in Spanish, which has never happened before. I wake up feeling different, like something inside me is changing, something chemical and irreversible. There's a magic here working its way through my veins. There's something about the vegetation, too, that I respond to instinctively—the stunning bougainvillea, the flamboyants and jacarandas, the orchids growing from the trunks of the mysterious ceiba trees. And I love Havana, its noise and decay and painted ladyness. I could happily sit on one of those wrought-iron balconies for days, or keep my grandmother company on her porch, with its ringside view of the sea. I'm afraid to lose all this, to lose Abuela Celia again. But sooner or later I'd have to return to New York. I know now it's where I belong—not *instead* of here, but *more* than here. How can I tell my grandmother this?

Discussion Questions

1. Discuss the conflict of identity each of the three characters experiences in relation to their connection to Cuba.

---

[11] *Malecón*—boardwalk. The one in Havana was extremely popular; similar to the one in Atlantic City.

2. What are these women's strengths and weaknesses? Apply these to their relationship to each other.

3. What is the role of memory in the excerpts? Look especially at pages (177, 183–187 and 190). How are memories and reality juxtaposed?

4. In what way is Celia similar to the mother in Jose Yglesias's "The Place I Was Born" on page 241? Consider how they each feel about their home.

5. How is Pilar's self-realization at the conclusion of the excerpt similar to that of Marisol's at the conclusion of Judith Ortiz Cofer's novel? See pages 346–347.

Oscar Hijuelos

OSCAR HIJUELOS was born in New York City in 1951. His published novels are Our House in the Last World *(1983), which traces the lives of a Cuban family in the 1940s;* The Fourteen Sisters of Emilio Montez O'Brien *(1993), told from different female perspectives; and his most recent offering* Empress of the Splendid Season *(1999).*

It is Hijuelos' Pulitzer Prize-winning novel The Mambo Kings Play Songs of Love *(1989), however, that thrust him into the spotlight. The novel tells the story of two brothers, Cesar and Nestor Castillo, who leave their native Cuba for New York in the 1950s. Their rise culminates in an appearance on the "I Love Lucy" show before they fade from public view. After the death of Nestor, Cesar, the older brother, ends his days in the Hotel Splendour, reminiscing about the past through an alcoholic haze.*

From The Mambo Kings Play Songs of Love

So why had The Mambo King started playing music again, after losing so much of his heart? It had to do with the family in Cuba, his brothers Miguel and Eduardo writing him letters and asking for money, medicine, and clothes. This had become his "cause." Even if he had never given a shit about politics before, what could he do when someone in the family asked him for help? At first he took on any kind of extra work, plastering and painting apartments to make more money, but then after being urged on by his old bassist Manny, he started accepting pickup jobs here and there around the city. (The first job back? Hilarious, a wedding out in Queens in 1961, a Cuban fellow who got caught by his bride pinching the bridesmaid's ass. Later, while they were packing up their instruments, out into the parking lot spilled bride and groom, the bride slapping and kicking at him.) The money that survived his generous and spendthrift ways went into buying food and medicine which he'd ship to Cuba. With Delores's *Webster's Dictionary* open before him, he would carefully draft letters to the government, inquiries as to the procedure for getting his family out, and then show these to one of the smarter tenants, a certain Mr. Bernhardt, who had once been a college professor. Reading through bifocals, Bernhardt, a portly and distinguished-looking fellow, made the proper corrections and then he'd redo the letters carefully on an antique British typewriter. (And Cesar would look around his living room. Bernhardt had worked as some kind of history teacher and his tables were covered with papers and books in Latin and Greek and clumps of photographs of archaeological sites, as well as a collection of thick, impossibly old books on witchcraft, and file folders containing pornographic photos.) The replies to his letters said that it all came down to getting permission from the Castro government; but those letters to Cuba seemed to go floating from office to office, rotting in bins filled with thousands of others. In the end, it would take them five years to get out.

There was more to it. On some nights, while listening to music, he'd remember his childhood in Cuba and how he'd go out to the sugar mill to hear the famous orchestras that toured the island: orchestras like Ernesto Lecuona's Melody Boys. In 1932, admission to hear Lecuona cost one dollar and everybody in Las Piñas would go, that being the grandest cultural event of the year. Families would make their way to the sugar mill in carriages, automobiles, and wagons, and the roads would be jammed with travelers from nearby towns. Some made the journey on horseback. Conversations cutting through the night, the chirping of the crickets, and the clop-clop-clop of horses. The stars humming like delicate glass bells. In the sugar-mill concert hall, there was a high-ceilinged ballroom with chandeliers and arched windows with great pleated drapes, Moorish wainscoting, and floors so polished they glimmered as if in sunlight. One night, nearly fifty years ago, Ernesto Lecuona came out onto the stage and Cesar Castillo, then a boy, was there to hear and see him. He was not a tall man and resembled, at first glance, a more thickset Rudolph Valentino. He wore a black tuxedo, a pearl-buttoned shirt, a bright-red bow tie. He had dark, penetrating eyes and long, slender hands. Seated before the piano, his face serene, he played the first, ebbing chords of his famous composition *"Malagueña."*

Later, during the intermission, the revered Lecuona came down off the stage to mingle with his audience. That night, as he saw Lecuona moving through the crowd, Cesar Castillo, fourteen years old, pushed forward to shake that grand gentleman's hand. That was the evening when Cesar introduced himself, saying, "My name is Cesar Castillo, Mr. Lecuona, and there's something I've written that I'd like you to hear. A ballad."

And Lecuona sighed, giving off a scent of lemon cologne. Although he seemed a little weary, he politely nodded and told the boy, "Come and see me afterwards in the parlor."

After the concert, in a large parlor adjoining the ballroom, the young Cesar Castillo sat down before a piano, nervously playing and singing his *canción*.[1]

Lecuona's reaction was honest and gentle: "You have a good singing voice, your verses are monotonous, but you have written a good chorus."

The name of the song? Nothing that he could remember, just that one of the verses mentioned "wilting flowers."

---

[1] song

"'Thank you, Mr. Lecuona, thank you,'" Cesar remembered saying, "thank you," as he followed him back toward the crowd, that image fading almost instantly, but not the desire to slip back inside that music which had sounded so beautiful.

In time, he was working joints like the Sunset Club and the 146th Street Latin Exchange (A cabdriver: "You know who I took up there one night? *Perez Prado*!")[2] on Friday and Saturday nights, dispensing with the hard business of running a band and just taking jobs as they came along. He didn't charge very much, twenty or twenty-five dollars a night, and this tended to get him work, because (whether he realized it or not) he was still something of a name.

He just never knew it.

Even took work as a strolling guitarist and singer in restaurants like the Mamey Tree and the Morro Castle in Brooklyn.

Of course, it was a pleasure to perform for the people again. Got his mind off things. And it always made him happy when someone would come along and ask him for an autograph ("*Ciertamente*!")[3]. It felt good when he'd go walking along the 125th Street markets on a Sunday afternoon and some guy in a sleeveless T-shirt would call out to him from a window, "Hey! Mambo King, how's it going?"

Still he felt his sadness. Sometimes when he played those jobs with Manny, he would get a ride back home. But most often he rode the subways, as he didn't like to drive at night anymore. Having scrapped his DeSoto, he had bought a '54 Chevrolet, but whenever he took it out, he would feel like jerking the car into a wall. Now he took it for occasional spins up and down Riverside Drive on nice days, washed it on Sundays, playing its radio and using it like a little office, to greet pals. Mainly, it was a pain in the ass; he was always paying parking tickets and lending it out to friends. That's why he'd sell it in '63, for $250. In any case, he liked to drink, and taking the subway meant that he didn't have to worry about wrecking the car or hurting anyone. The only setback was that he sometimes felt nervous waiting on the platforms late at night—New York had started to get bad in the early 1960s; that's why he would walk all the way to the end and hide behind a pillar and wait there for the train.

Anonymous in a pair of sunglasses and with his hat pulled low over his brow, guitar or trumpet case wedged between his knees, the Mambo King traveled to his jobs around the city. It was easy to get home when he worked restaurants in the Village or Madison Avenue bars, where he would serenade the Fred MacMurray-looking executives and their companions ("Now, girls, sing after me, 'Babalooooo!'"), as those jobs usually ended around eleven at night. But when he'd play small clubs and dance halls out on the edges of Brooklyn and the Bronx, he'd get home at four-thirty, five in the morning. Spending many a night riding the trains by himself, he'd read *La Prensa* or *El Diario* or the *Daily News*.

He made lots of friends on the trains; he knew the flamenco guitarist from Toledo, Spain, a fellow named Eloy García, who played in the Café Madrid; an accordionist with a tango orchestra in Greenwich Village, named Macedonio, a roly-poly fellow who'd go to work in a gaucho hat. ("To play the music of Matos Rodriguez is to bring Matos back," he'd say.) He knew Estela and Nilda, two

---

[2] Dámaso Pérez Prado (1916–1989) is considered by many to be the "king of mambo."   [3] Certainly

zarzuela[4] singers who would pass through matronhood with wilting carnations in their hair. He knew a black three-man dance team with conk hairdos, friendly and hopeful fellows, resplendent in white tuxedos and spats, who were always heading out to do auditions. ("These days we're hoping to get on the Ed Sullivan show.") Then there were the Mexicans with their oversized guitars, trumpets, and an accordion that resembled an altar, its fingerboard shiny with hammer-flattened religious medals of the Holy Mother, Christ, and the Apostles, bloody with wounds, hobbling on crutches, and pierced through with arrows to the heart. The men wore big sombreros and trousers that jangled with bells, and high, thin-heeled cowboy boots, leather-etched with swirly flowers, and traveled with a woman and a little girl. The woman wore a mantilla and a frilly dress made of Aztec-looking fabric; the little girl wore a red dress and played a tambourine on which an enamel likeness of John the Baptist had been painted. She'd sit restlessly, unhappily during the rides, while Cesar would lean forward and speak quietly to her mother. ("How is it going with you today?" "Slow lately, the best time is during Christmas, and then everybody gives.") They'd ride to the last stop downtown, to the Staten Island Ferry terminal, where they would play *bambas, corridos, buapangos,* and *rancheras*[5] for the waiting passengers.

"*Que Dios te bendiga.* God bless you."

"The same to you."

There were others, a lot of Latin musicians like himself on their way to weary late-night jobs in the deepest reaches of Brooklyn and the Bronx. Some were young and didn't know the name Cesar Castillo, but the old-timers, the musicians who had been kicking around in New York since the forties, they knew him. Trumpet players, guitarists, and drummers would come over and sit with the Mambo King.*

Still, there were the tunnels, the darkness, the dense solitude of a station at four in the morning, and the Mambo King daydreaming about Cuba.

It made a big difference to him that he just couldn't get on an airplane and fly down to Havana to see his daughter or to visit the family in Las Piñas.

Who would ever have dreamed that would be so? That Cuba would be chums with Russia?

It was all a new kind of sadness.

Sitting in his room in the Hotel Splendour (reeling in the room), the Mambo King preferred not to think about the revolution in Cuba. What the fuck had he ever cared about Cuban politics in the old days, except for when he might play a political rally in the provinces for some local crooked politician? What the fuck had he cared when the consensus among his musician pals was that it wouldn't make any difference

---

[4] a form of Spanish operatic music   [5] all musical forms originating in Spanish and/or indigenous traditions   *Always a nice hello and sometimes a reunion, the fellows inviting each other out to jam sessions. In the Hotel Splendour he remembered that one of his favorite jam sessions took place when Benny the conga player invited him over to the Museum of Natural History, where he worked, in his reincarnated life, as a guard. Around nine one night; when it was really dead, Cesar showed up with a few other musicians and they ended up playing in a small office just off the Great Hall of Dinosaurs, Benny playing the drums and a fellow named Rafael strumming a guitar and Cesar singing and blowing the trumpet, this music echoing and humming through the bones of those prehistoric creatures—the Stegosaurus and Tyrannosaurus Rex and Brontosaurus and woolly mammoth, breathing heavy in the vastness of that room and click-clacking onto the marble floors melodies caught in their great hooked jaws and in the curve of their gargantuan spinal columns.

who came to power, until Fidel. What could he have done about it, anyway? Things must have been pretty bad. The orchestra leader René Touzet had fled to Miami with his sons, playing the big hotels there and concerts for the Cubans. Then came the grand master of Cuban music, Ernesto Lecuona, arriving in Miami distraught and in a state of creative torpor, unable to play a note on his piano and ending up in Puerto Rico, "bitter and disenchanted," before he died, he'd heard some people say. Bitter because his Cuba no longer existed.

God, all the Cubans were worked up. Even that *compañero*[6]—who never forgot the family—Desi Arnaz had scribbled a little extra message on one of his Christmas cards: "We Cubans should stick together in these troubled times."

What had a friend called the revolution? "The rose that sprouted a thorn."

The great Celia Cruz would come to the States, too, in 1967.

(On the other hand, Bola de Nieve—the musician "Snowball"—and the singer Elena Burke chose to remain behind.)

When his mother had died in 1962, the news came in a telegram from Eduardo, and a funny thing, too, because he had been thinking about her a lot that week, almost a soft pulsing in his heart, and his head filled with memories. And when he first read the line "I have bad news," he instantly thought "No." After reading the telegram, all he could do for hours was to drink and remember how she would take him into the yard as a child and wash his hair in a tub, again and again and again, her soft hands that smelled of rose water scrubbing his head and touching his face, the sun down through the treetops, her hair swirling with curls of light . . .

The man cried for hours, until his eyelids were swollen, and he fell asleep with his head against the worktable.

Wished he had seen her one more time. Told himself that he would have gone back the previous year, when he'd first heard that she had gotten sick, if it hadn't been for Castro.

Sometimes he got into big arguments with Ana María's husband, Raúl, about the situation down there. A long-time union man, Raúl kept himself busy organizing union shops in factories in the West Twenties, where most of the workers were immigrants from Central America and Puerto Rico. They were still friends, despite their differences of opinion. But Raúl kept trying to persuade the Mambo King about Castro. On a Friday night he went so far as to bring him down to a club on 14th Street where old Spanish and Portuguese leftists held meetings. He sat in the back listening as the old Spaniards, their expressions and politics shaped by beatings and jail terms in Franco's Spain, gave long, heartfelt speeches about "what must be done," which always came down to "*Viva el socialismo!*"[7] and "Viva Fidel!"

Nothing wrong with doing away with the world's evils. He had seen a lot of that. In Cuba there had been rotting sheds made of cardboard and crates, skeleton children and dying dogs. A funeral procession in a small town called Minas. On the side of the plain pine coffin, a sign: "*Muerto de hambre.*"[8] On the street corners where the handsome *suavecitos*[9] hung out talking, some guy who'd lost a limb while working at the sugar mill, in the *calderas*,[10] begging. When he pictured suffering, he

---

[6] partner   [7] Long live socialism!   [8] Starved to Death   [9] smooth talkers   [10] the huge pots used to ferment the cane

thought of a dead dog he'd found lying on the cobblestone road near the harbor of Lisbon: a tiny hound, with a sweet face and pleasantly cocked ears, stiff on its back, with its belly torn open, its dark purple stomach bloated to the size of a fifteen-pound melon.

He had no argument with wanting to help others, Raúl. Back in Cuba, the people took care of their own. Families giving clothing, food, money, and, sometimes, a job in the household or in a business.

"My own mother, Raúl, listen to me. My own mother was always giving money to the poor, even when we didn't have very much. What more could anyone ask?"

"More."

"Raúl, you're my friend. I don't want to argue with you, but the people are leaving because they can't bear it."

"Or because they haven't the strength."

"Come on, let's have a drink."

A letter, dated June 17, 1962:

To my dear brother,

We may have been apart these years, but you have never lost our hearts. The truth is that the situation down here has become bad. Pedrito is the only one of us who has any sympathy for the Castro government. I feel so depressed just writing those words. just a year ago I was able to help the others out with the money I was making from the garage, but the government's taken that away, chained up the doors, and informed me that I was welcome to work there if I wanted, but to forget about being the owner. The bastards. That's Communism. I refused to go back and [crossed out]. I know that you've prospered and hope that you can see your way to sending us whatever you can. Bad enough that we've had to endure the tragedy of losing Nestor, but now all this seems to just make things worse. I wouldn't ask you if I didn't think you had the money. If you could send us fifty or a hundred dollars a month, that would be enough to help us live decently until our applications for exit visas are approved—if ever. But that is a whole other matter. May God bless you. We send you our love.

Eduardo.

So he raised money for his brothers and also sent money and gifts to his daughter, Mariela, even though she didn't really seem to need them. A headmaster during the days of the revolution, Mariela's stepfather had edited an underground pro-Castro newspaper and, after the revolution, was rewarded with a good post in the Ministry of Education. Living in an airy apartment on Calle 26 in the Vedado section of Havana, the family thrived, enjoying the privileges of his position, while she studied ballet.

(Among the photographs which the Mambo King had taken with him into the Hotel Splendour, a favorite picture of his daughter in leotards and tutu, beneath an arched window in a room with pilastered walls and ornate tiles. This was at her ballet school in Havana. The picture, taken in 1959, shows a thin, genteel girl with large brown eyes and a teaspoon-shaped face, lively and elegant, in ballet slippers and with a dreamy expression, as if listening to beautiful music. Another picture, taken in 1962, shows her dancing during a rehearsal of *Giselle*; watching her, Alicia Alonso and her ballet teacher, a pretty Cuban woman named Gloria.)

Sometimes he found himself hanging around the bars and *cantinas* of Washington Heights and, on occasion, Union City, New Jersey, where in the early sixties many of the feverish Cubans had settled. Sipping his *tacita of café negro,*[11] he would listen quietly to the political chitchat. The newly arrived Cubans, bitter and forlorn; the old, established Cubans trying to figure out what was going on in Cuba: a man with a shaking right hand whose older brother, a jeweler, had committed suicide in Havana; a man who had lost a good job as a gardener on the Du Pont estate; a man whose cousin had been sent to prison for walking down the street with a pound of sugar hidden in his shirt. A man who lost his farm. A man whose uncle was sentenced to twenty years for shouting "Fuck Castro!" at a town-hall meeting. A man whose precious and beautiful niece was abducted to frigid Moscow, where she married a humorless, barrel-chested Russian. A man who had been shot through the elbow during the Bay of Pigs invasion.

Voices:

"And they call us 'worms.'"

"Castro came to the island owning ten thousand acres of land and now he has the whole thing!'"

"I smuggled arms for that son of a bitch."

"Who thinks he would have succeeded had we known he was a Communist?"

"They say the reason Castro was released by Batista in '54 was because they castrated him."

"They reduce our discontent to our stomachs. They say we have left because we can't find a good meal in Havana anymore. That's the truth, because all the Russians are eating the food. But there's more. They have taken our right to sit with our families in peace, before tables bountiful with the fruit of our labors."

"So we left, *hombre,* and that Castro, *mojón guindao,*[12] can go to hell!"

"He's like Rasputin."

"Let them eat cake is his attitude."

"He made a deal with the devil."

"We've been betrayed all around."

"Yes, I know it," the Mambo King used to say. "I have three brothers and my father still living in Oriente, and they all say the same thing, they want to get out." Sip of coffee. "Except for my father. He's very old, in his seventies, and not well."

And he couldn't resist: "I have a daughter in Havana. It's my opinion that her thoughts have been tampered with."

The Mambo King would walk up the hill of La Salle Street, head bowed, back slightly stooped, belly hanging over his belt, and thoughts clouded with Cuba. In the clutter of his basement workroom, he would read the anti-Castro pamphlets that his friends gave him. Stuck between the pages of his younger brother's book,

[11] cup of black coffee   [12] shithead

Forward America! ("For whatever your problems may be, remember where there is fortitude and determination there is a way!"), this portion of a pamphlet from 1961–62, circled in red ballpoint ink and set on the table in that room in the Hotel Splendour:

> . . . We cannot deny that in the era of republican government we had political leaders who did not always, through honesty and patriotism, implement the just and splendid laws of our Constitution. Yet we could not have known or even imagined the kind of tyranny unleashed by Fidel Castro and his hordes. Former comic-opera dictatorships at least tried to seek democratic solutions to their moral failings. Their methods only became dictatorial when provoked by Communists, who disturbed the public peace and drove innocent, stupid, and fanatical young people out into the streets, using them as cannon fodder. Some people say Cuba is going to flourish anew under Fidel Castro, that malnutrition, prostitution, illiteracy, corruption, and poverty are going to be stamped out forever, that the island will become a paradise of equality, with a truly humanitarian government. Ask those who have been brutally tortured and lie dead in unmarked graves if this is so. The truth is different: Fidel Castro and his gang of robbers and murderous convicts, like the odious Argentine Che Guevara, the Spanish criminals Lister and Bayo, and expert torturers and killers like Raúl Castro and Ramiro Valdés, the head of G-2, have traded off Cuba to Euro-Asiatic powers. Powers that are geographically, spiritually, and historically far removed from everything Caribbean and that have turned Cuba into a tropical colony and military base for Russia. Since January 1, 1959, Cuba has become a miserable pauper state without resources or freedom and the sincere, happy spirit of Cubans has become replaced by tragic gloom. The gaiety of everyday Cuban life and commerce with its rum and good cigars and its bounty of sugar and all that springs from sugar has been reduced by a severe rationing in the name of Soviet-Cuban trade relations. The average Cuban citizen must brace himself stoically for the bleak future while Fidel himself smokes only the best twenty-dollar Havana cigars, drinks rum, and stuffs his gut with Russian caviar. While thousands of Cubans have begun to live in exile, one hundred thousand others rot in prisons for political crimes. The remaining population is divided up between the Cuban traitors who support the tyranny and those who have chosen to remain behind for personal reasons or cannot leave because the government will not allow them to. Let us not forget them! Long live Jesus Christ and long live freedom!

Inspired by the fiery prose of these pamphlets and by news from Cuba, the Mambo King would hole up in his basement workroom, drink beer, and write to Mariela—letters which over the years became more imploring in their tone.

The heart of them said this: "From what I hear about Cuba, I can't believe that you are happy there. I am not one to tell you what to do, but the day you want to leave and come to the United States, let me know and I will do everything I can, and do it willingly, because you are my flesh and blood."

He'd sign them, "Your lonely father who loves you."

Never receiving acknowledgment of these offers, he thought, Of course the letters are, intercepted and cut to ribbons before she can read them! Instead, her letters spoke about her dance training—"They say I am one of the more promising students"—and about high-toned cultural events, like a performance of Stravinsky's *Firebird* by the Bolshoi Ballet on the stage of the opera house (which left him blinking, because the only ballets he had ever attended were the pornographic ballets at Havana's notorious Shanghai Theater).

Sometimes (daydreaming, nostalgic) he believed that he would feel some new happiness if Mariela came up from Cuba to live with him, escaping by boat, or miraculously with the permission of the government ("Yes, the poor thing wants to be with her true father. Give her our blessing to leave.") Then she'd look after him, cook his meals, help keep house, and, above all, would receive and give him love, and this love would wrap around his heart like a gentle silk bow, protecting it from all harm.

In a way, thinking about Mariela helped him to understand why Nestor used to sit on the couch and torment himself for hours singing about his "Beautiful María," even if it was all a pipe dream. Something about love and the eternal spring, time suspended—so that the Mambo King daydreamed about himself sitting in his living room by the sunny window, head set back and eyes closed while his daughter, Mariela, cut his hair, the way his mother used to, Mariela's lovely voice (he imagined) humming into his huge ears, her face radiant with happy love for him. Now and then he would feel so inspired by all this that he would take the train to Macy's and, guessing at Mariela's size, buy her a half-dozen dresses and blouses, lipsticks, mascaras, and rouge, and, on one occasion, a long silk scarf, yellow like the sunlight in old paintings—rushing hurriedly through the store as if the right choice of gift would make things different. With these items he would enclose a note: "Just to let you know that your father loves you."

And for each November 17, Mariela's birthday, he'd put together a package of goods generally unavailable to Cubans, things that he thought a teenager would like: chocolate bars, cookies, jam, chewing gum, potato chips, sure evidence of the diversity and abundance of life in America.

She never came running into his arms.

Discussion Questions

1. What kind of picture is painted of Cuba by Cesar in his role as narrator? How does he feel about his home?

2. There are two characters mentioned in the excerpt, Mariela, his daughter, and María, his dead brother's lifetime love. Both of these characters have a symbolic significance in terms of Cesar's relationship to Cuba. What is it?

3. In what way are the musical references in the excerpt similar to those in Sandra Maria Esteves's poem "In the Beginning" on page 436?

Virgil Suarez

In addition to Spared Angola: Memories of a Cuban-American Childhood *(1997), a collection of essays, poems, and short stories, Virgil Suarez has published four novels, a book of short stories, and has edited three anthologies of Cuban-American poetry and prose. He received an M.F.A. from Lousiana State University in 1987 and currently teaches creative writing at the University of Miami in Coral Gables, Florida.*

Born in 1962, Suarez arrived in the United States from Cuba when he was twelve years old. Thus, he retains vivid childhood memories of his homeland, many of which are recounted in his book. The following selections provide two perspectives of Cuba by the narrator. The first examines the title of the book by presenting the mature character who is reunited with a relative he barely remembers. The second is a description of one of the many memories that the meeting described in the first selection brings forth.

From Spared Angola: Memories of a Cuban-American Childhood

After a twenty-year absence, my grandmother, Donatia, flies from Havana to Miami for a visit. Waiting for her in the crowded and noisy lobby of Miami International Airport, I am struck by memories of my childhood in the arms of this woman who, except for vague moments, is a perfect stranger. To my mother she is Tina of the constant aches and headaches, of the bouts with rheumatism, of the skin disease that spotted her face and neck with pink blotches, of the hair the color of smoke and straw. *Abuela*[1] Tina. Twenty years before this moment caught in the restless humdrum of waiting, this woman about to visit showed me many things: how to feed left-over rice to chickens, tie my shoelaces, brew the kind of watery coffee I like to drink with toasted bread. She kept my behind from feeling the wrath of my father's belt on numerous occasions; she stayed with me while I took a shower in the room by the side of the clapboard house because I was terrified of the bullfrogs that sought the humidity trapped there. She told me stories, most of which I've forgotten, except for the one about the old hag who would wait for a man to come by on horseback to cross the old bridge. The hag would jump on the horse and spook the animal and the rider. The horsemen knew never to look back or risk spooking themselves crazy. "Never look back," she said, "as you cross your bridges." The flight arrives and the waiting intensifies. My mother sinks her nails into my flesh as she holds my hand. My

---

[1] grandmother

father every so often retrieves a handkerchief from his back pocket (he's never used one) and wipes his forehead and under his eyes. The first few passengers come out the glass doors of Customs and are greeted by relatives who have never forgotten these tired and worn faces, frail bodies. Parents, sisters, brothers, sons, daughters, all now looking thirty-six years older. "Time," my father says, "is a son of a bitch." Finally, I spot my aunt (I have not seen her for as long as I have not seen my grandmother), my father's sister who'd gotten cancer. She is holding on to my grandmother, and I realize my memory has served me better than I am willing to admit. Grandmother Tina looks the same except for the patches of the skin disease which have completely taken over her face. My mother screams and lets go of my hand and runs to the arms of her mother. My father to his sister. I stand back and brace myself. After the hugs and the kisses, my mother says, "There he is! Your grandson, Mamá!" She walks toward me and I find I cannot move, for I cannot believe in movement; I am still stuck in time. She comes toward me. "*¿No te acuerdas de mí?*"[2] she says, her Spanish the necessary tug. I lean into her arms, for she is small and frail, and we stand there in the middle of the lobby. I tell her that I do remember. I remember everything. Slowly now we make our way out of the terminal to the parking lot, into the car, onto the freeway, home to my parents', up the stairs and into the living room of an apartment in which I've spent so very little time. All this time everybody has been talking except me; I've been driving and listening, bewildered by all the catching up. In the living room now, waiting for refreshments, my grandmother comes over to where I sit and she holds my face between her hands.

She looks into my eyes. Can I? Can I remember this woman? My grandmother Donatila. She's an apparition, I think, but don't say it. She says, "You must tell me about you, all that the distance has taken from us." I tell her I am happy to see her, after so much time. "*¿Sabes?*"[3] she says. "You are a lucky young man. Your parents did the right thing. When they took you out of Cuba, your parents spared you. Yes, you were spared. Spared Angola."

La Ceiba: Tree of Life

We children played within the folds of its elephant-skin roots, lost to the outside world, no politics here, no parents, only us and the sounds of our pleasure howls. Here we lowered our pants and showed our penises to each other—none of us had the right size, for how could we at such an age? We peed against the tree trunk and watched as the urine ran down the trunk to disappear into the reddish dirt. We carved our names on the roots of this tree, along with the names of the girls we didn't yet like but whose names we knew and carved anyway. We played cowboys and Indians,

---

[2] Do you remember me?   [3] You know?

hide-and-seek, and sometimes we gathered the *centavos*[4] left as *brujería*[5] offerings to *Las Siete Potencias*.[6] Of course we didn't know about respect then, so we disturbed the amulet offerings. Sometimes, we found a dead chicken or a white dove, feathers gone ashen with the stain of dirt and tainted by spilled blood. This, of course, scared us and we ran away. Sometimes though, we stayed and watched as the ants helped with decomposition, as they carried bits and pieces in relay lines off to a nearby underground nest. So many mornings and afternoons we lived here, undisturbed, isolated, until the one day when lightning hit the tree and it died. Then we slowly became victims of our own mischief and undoing. Aimless became a new word in our vocabulary.

Discussion Questions

1. What does the speaker's grandmother mean when she says that he was "spared Angola"?

2. In "La Ceiba" why does the speaker say they were victims of our own mischief and undoing? Identify characteristics of Cuban-American culture present in this story.

3. Compare the feelings of loss that the speaker displays in these two stories to the feelings expressed by Juan in Himilce Novas's *Mangoes, Bananas, and Coconuts* on page 226.

4. How is the relationship between the speaker and his grandmother similar to that between Sonny and his godmother in Jack Agüeros' "One Sunday Morning" on page 385?

Pablo Medina

PABLO MEDINA has lived most of his life in the Northeast since he immigrated from Cuba when he was twelve years old. Unlike some of his compatriots, Medina has always written in English. His publications consist of Pork Rind and Cuban Songs *(1975),* Exiled Memories: A Cuban Childhood *(1990),* Arching into the Afterlife *(1991),* The Marks of Birth *(1994), and* The Floating Island *(1999).*

Like many Cuban-American writers, Medina's work shows his preoccupation with the double-edged sword of assimilation. While his characters often eventually undergo a redemption, the road to self-knowledge is treacherous. The chapter presented here from The Marks of Birth *summarizes the last few years of Antón's life, paying particular attention to his doomed marriage. His metamorphosis now complete, Antón muses over his new-found avocation, gardening. The reality of his unfulfilled life breaks into the reverie, however, and his birthmark signals dissatisfaction.*

---

[4] pennies   [5] witchcraft   [6] The Seven Powers: in santeria, a combination of Catholicism and pagan rituals, they represent the seven most powerful gods.

From The Marks of Birth

The Birthmark

Fifteen years later, in a small town in New Jersey, the name of which is insignificant, Antón turned over his vegetable plot in early spring. He had been gardening ever since his wife, Alice, suggested he take to the hoe and spade four years before. He had done so, skeptically at first, but the first year's results had astonished him: big tomatoes bursting with the blood of the earth, magical carrots that improved vision just by looking at them, and onions so pungent the neighbors wept when he cut them. The second year was good, too, but the third year's harvest had been meager at best. He had picked only ten green peppers, all but two of them covered with blotches of black rot, and five tomatoes with strange yellow growths on them. The lettuce had been devastated by slugs, creatures he detested beyond reason and which he attacked with every chemical weapon he could legally buy. This spring he was hoeing because it was the only thing he could do. Two days before, he had quit his job, and so far he had avoided telling Alice.

He worked carefully, driving the hoe half a foot deep and pulling it up and around, making sure that every inch of the black topsoil was exposed. He was heartened to see a few worms wiggling out of the clumps that broke on the surface, and he dug with special care to keep from harming them. It was early in the year and there were few weeds. Those that he found he pulled out mercilessly. He did not want any green in his garden, not yet, and weeding now would make planting and harvesting a lot easier.

He could do this forever, he thought. He could do this forever through success and through failure and never have to look beyond the flat rectangular world of his plantings for any of the things he had been told he needed. In the garden he did not have to answer to others; he did not have to look busy, productive, or involved. When the harvest was bountiful, it was his glory; if it failed, he could blame it on the weather, the insects, the poor soil, finally on fate. Here he could be himself, not somebody else's image of himself. Language and style were irrelevant, and his relationship to plants was purely functional: plant and water them and they would bear him fruit. In the garden was the true anonymity and total safety of the self.

In the seven years following his college graduation, Antón had wafted through sixteen jobs, but none had to do with the earth. He had worked as a truck driver, a journalist, a security guard. He had driven cars cross-country, sold encyclopedias to Marine recruits and worthless building lots in the Everglades to retirees. He had enrolled in school to become a commercial pilot, but had to give up the flying lessons because they engendered a recurring dream from which he woke instants before crashing into the ocean. There were also stints in graduate school that eventually led to a degree in ancient literature. At some point he had started writing, merely to distract himself at first, gradually taking it more seriously, to the point of beginning a novel about a character dimly like his grandmother.

Then came Alice and his job at a college, teaching composition, and he thought for sure his wanderlust was over. The college job, however, had been the worst. Where he expected to find the energy of youth, he came upon a Sargasso[1] of indifference, and where he anticipated torrents of intellectual exchange, he found the stagnant waters of academe. Every night he came home with his heart weighed down and his head ringing with the bickerings of two demons: the demon of self-doubt, low and obese-sounding, and the demon of mortification, shrill and implacable. When the two spoke in unison, he felt his birthmark burn like a prairie fire.

He had met Alice Winslow at a reception in a bookstore. He didn't have much to say to her then, but he looked through the guest book afterward and took down her phone number. He tried to remember what it was about her that had first attracted him: her hair the color of honey exposed to the sun, her well-set Anglo-Saxon jaw, the smell of honeysuckle and oranges she exuded as she passed. Perhaps, rather, it was her restraint and her impenetrability.

He called and they went out a few times. Sometimes Alice was warm and friendly, sometimes cold and stern, but she was always in control, even after they made love the first time, when she turned away coldly and asked him to leave so she could sleep, then phoned him the next morning full of cheer and good humor.

Thrown off-balance, Antón pursued her, thinking he had found the answer to his questions. In so doing, he had ignored the basic arithmetical axiom that if there are many questions, there must correspondingly be at least as many answers. Back then, however, he still believed that *amor vincit omnia*,[2] even death, the source of all questions. He saw Alice, with her ordered life and her pragmatism, as the Answer. He forgot himself and fell in love with the concept behind her, rather than with her person. Now he knew better: Virgil was a charlatan. The truth was that death, not love, conquers all.

Nevertheless, the pursuit of Alice charged his life and gave it the direction it had lacked. He called her daily and insisted on seeing her several times a week. He brought her books and wrote her love poems, which she did not understand but accepted anyway, on the off chance that Antón might become a famous writer someday.

Five years older than Antón, Alice had been married before and she felt that her possibilities, personal as well as professional, were diminishing. He was kind and bright and full of promise. With the right person next to him, he might make something of himself while she kept her emotions in control, she encouraged Antón just enough to keep him in the thrall of his illusions.

In six months they were married. The ceremony was an agnostic affair, officiated by a female Unitarian minister who yawned twice during the exchange of vows and who left the reception as soon as she was paid. Fernando, Rosa, and Felicia had attended—they had little choice in the matter—but they could not disguise the skepticism which kept their words guarded and their affections measured. Felicia, especially, saw something like ice in Alice's eyes—something only a grandmother could detect.

---

[1] Sargasso: a tract of still water in the North Atlantic Ocean.   [2] Latin for "love conquers all"

Alice's family treated the wedding as if this were her first marriage. Her younger sister kept bobbing in and out with her camera, recording the event for an uncertain posterity. The stepfather, a corset salesman, was the life of the reception, with his sideshow humor. Her mother, profile rigid and impeccable, made sure everything was in order and kept the caterers moving to her clipped commands.

The first year together was a glorious one for the newlyweds. All was put aside for the liberation of the bird of lust. Initially, it was all a fumbling and a stumbling, not knowing what to say, where to touch, how to kiss. He liked to watch her disrobe until her pubis flamed before him; then he pulled her to bed and devoured her fire while she deepened like a bowl only the sea could fill. On weekends when the weather warmed, they spent long hours in the garden, she planting her flowers, he sitting on the porch steps watching her work and listening to her sing the Protestant hymns she was so fond of, over and over, until he knew by heart the landscape of the Puritan spirit that was her legacy and her birthright: "'Tis a gift to be simple, 'tis a gift to be free . . ."

And confusing desire with possibility, he convinced himself that he belonged here with Alice, way up in el Norte—"'Tis a gift to come down where you ought to be . . ."—in order to transform himself into a suburban creature blessed by love and delight, till by turning and turning, he'd come out right.

He spread mulch on the soil and over that, five bags of fertilizer. He mixed everything well and evened it out, then hosed it down until the mixture glittered black and rich and pungent. By mid-month he would be able to plant radishes and onions. This harvest would be better than his first, he thought, and a sudden giddiness overtook him. He smiled inwardly and said aloud, "There is no God but green," and liking the statement very much, he repeated it, hoping to remember his discovery, but then he questioned the accuracy of his metaphor. If green was God, it followed that weeds were God, too. He made a note of the proposition, leaned on the hoe, and stretched his free arm upward. The giddiness had left him, but not the possibility that gardening was as admirable a human pursuit as he had known.

Full of purpose and the courage that the earth had given him, he put away the tools and went inside to tell Alice the news he had been keeping from her for two days. He found her in the bathroom, holding a wad of hair she had collected from the shower drain. Before he could speak, she said she had a sewer committee meeting and would not have time for dinner. She dropped the hair into the wastebasket and slipped past Antón down the stairs and out of the house.

That's when the itch started again. First, there was a burning sensation in the center of his birthmark, followed by random pricks that multiplied and spread to the edges, until the whole of the brown surface was alive. He had tried scratching before, but that had only drawn blood and, made the discomfort last through the night. The friction excited the itch and made him reach heights of pure but unbearable misery. Only a cataplasm of hot mustard and whiskey he had concocted one especially desperate evening brought any relief.

He prepared the mixture in the kitchen, fixing himself a healthy drink of whiskey as he worked. Brown mustard was best, but there was none left in the refrigerator. He had once tried Chinese mustard, but it had been so strong that, for days after, he felt a burning afterglow over his kidneys. Today, it was yellow American.

Antón returned to the living room and stood with his back to Alice's antique mirror. He undid his pants and pulled his shirt up. The birthmark appeared as healthy as ever. Roughly the shape of Iceland in the concave sea of his back, it was tipped fifteen degrees toward the cleave of his buttocks and transversed on its northeastern quadrant by the tropic of his waist. As he applied the paste, he felt a yellow solace spread over his lower back. His eyes teared, a sure sign that the cure was working, and he lay facedown on the couch.

He had first felt the itch the night his parents had received Felicia's letter announcing the death of Antonio. Dinner had tasted of decay and the dust of the grave, and he had gone to bed early. As he lay in his room waiting for sleep, he tried to imagine Antonio's last moments in a damp cell with no company other than the cockroaches scurrying along the floor. He thought of his uncle heaving for breath, trying to huddle against the stone wall for warmth and, failing, realizing where he was and where he was heading. Antonio must have brushed it all away, smiled through his cough and fever, and fallen into the siesta of eternity.

At that moment Antón felt an unmistakable pressure, as if a thousand pins were pushing against but not puncturing his birthmark, followed by a burning itch, the pins coming alive and jabbing through the skin repeatedly. The itch grew in intensity until it seemed his kidney would catch on fire, then ebbed as quickly as it had come, leaving behind a glow like that of embers just before they die.

His back was quiet now. He raised himself off the couch, reached for the drink on the coffee table, and took a long swallow. As darkness crept into the house, he thought that of all the people he had known, it was Antonio he had most admired and wanted to be like, undaunted as he was by duty or the appearance of duty and using the world, including his family, as the fountain where he slaked his multiple thirsts.

As such, Antonio was the antithesis of Felicia, who had drummed into her grandson that his family was his destiny and his responsibility. Much as Antón fought it, her attitude prevailed, even after he left the island. Everything he did in New York, from playing baseball to going to a dance to taking an exam to ogling a woman on the street, seemed governed by her strictures. Her voice, soft and loving but inscrutable, had become imprinted in his mind. The more he tried to drown it out, the more his birthmark itched. It became his obsession to eliminate Spanish from his consciousness and make English the language of his thoughts and dreams. He whittled away at his accent and toned down his mannerisms so that they were controlled and Anglicized. If he became another person, surely her voice would disappear.

Then Felicia came to live with them in New York, and she was no longer just a voice inside him but a real, live island grandmother, clumsy and underdeveloped, whom he had to take to the doctor, the grocery store, the beautician. "I have no senses in English," she would say to him as they left the house. Antón would feel a dark mood spreading over him, and he would hunch his shoulders and lower his head as he walked next to her. Out there for the world to see, Felicia was the mark of his foreignness.

"It hurts here," she said, grabbing Antón's hand and moving it up and down along her ribs as the stupefied doctor watched.

"She wants a body wave and be sure not to burn her hair," Antón, red as a beet, would have to tell the hairdresser, who stared invitingly at him.

Her stay was mercifully brief, made tolerable only by the canasta games they played every afternoon. As soon as she left, Antón breathed a sigh of relief. At last he could stop being a dutiful grandson and continue with his metamorphosis. By the time he entered college two years later, he was signing his name as A. G. Turner, speaking accentless English, and behaving as if he had never heard of the island, let alone been born on it. In so doing; he ignored Antonio's first lesson, "Never diminish yourself," as well as his seventh, "The Lesson of Quixote," which stated that you should never let a disguise dominate you.

It was during his college years that Felicia reappeared in his life, in the shape of Ester Oliva. Antón first noticed Ester in a political science class. The lecturer had delivered a lengthy defense of Nicolás Campión[3] as one of the great liberators of the century when a woman dressed in black sitting by the large French windows had stood up and challenged him. The woman spoke with such conviction and authority that the professor closed the discussion and continued with his lecture.

Antón was stunned. This was a woman of passion. He would have stood up against the professor, too, but he was carrying a C in the course and his statements would have lacked the force of hers. And so he had gone against Lesson 17, "The Lesson of Moses": "Whenever the option is presented, never take the petty road. Always go for the grand gesture."

After class Antón approached her. Ester Oliva immediately looked through his disguise and recognized him as a compatriot. When Antón asked her how she knew, she answered that only someone who was not American could be so American.

She was on her way to her next class, and they talked only briefly. She was a government major and was convinced of her mission to fight the Campión regime in every possible arena until it was toppled. Before leaving, she invited him to a meeting of her campus organization that night.

Antón remembered the gathering of the Student Alliance for Democracy as a blur of boredom and pomposity. Only Ester Oliva, who happened to be the president, stood out. Once again she was wearing dark clothes. Her hair was tied back in a bun, exposing a strong, heroic neck, and on that neck two blue veins bulged slightly and forked away from her right jaw when she spoke. Her rhetoric was restrained but convincing, and she had learned to use the first person plural *we* in a natural, magnanimous way. Though she was not a mesmerizing orator, of the sort favored among islanders, she nevertheless held the group's attention, if not their hearts, with her brilliant command of facts and her scalpel-sharp analyses.

Later, while he and Ester were walking home, Antón made a disparaging comment about the membership of SAD and Ester surprised him with her candor. She said that for most of them this was their entertainment. She said they would leave school and go on with their lives and be embarrassed that they ever joined a political organization, especially one led by a woman.

"Only Fico Brull is serious," she had said. "And he's dangerous."

---

[3] The leader of the Cuban Revolution in the novel. The fictional representation of Fidel Castro.

Antón asked her what she was interested in and she said, without hesitation, "My country." When she asked him the same question, he felt jealous that he could not answer as simply as she—my country—as if the island were still a reality and not a dream.

He could have said, but didn't, that he had turned away from his country because you cannot retrieve a fantasy and you cannot reconstruct the past. He had surged into a present that could be his only in proportion to how fully he erased his old self. Marina used to call the United States the land of answers, and she was right. Answers lead to the world of the Vibra Bed[4] but never the world of dreams. In the new land there could be no "my country," because that was an illusion, not an answer. In the new land "my country" became "my self." He did not say any of this because it was too complicated to know it simply and clearly in the same way that Ester knew and could formulate her response.

What was he interested in? The night, the city, the sunset, poetry, art, music, he said, sounding like a personal ad. He stopped.

She was smiling at him strangely. "You and the rest of the people on this campus. What moves you, truly?" she asked.

He wanted to say that she moved him, but that would have been melodramatic. Instead, he said he did not care about the island or democracy or liberation or Nicolás Campión. Antón told her where politics had landed his great-uncle Antonio, despite. his instincts and his intelligence. He said that the only political act worth anything came out of survival in the Darwinian sense, not from dogma. As such it had biological origins and had to be spontaneous and unplanned. The rest was Machiavellian manipulation and only the Fico Brulls of this world would succeed at it.

They kept walking in silence, and Antón worried that he had said too much, but when they reached her door, she asked if he would come to the next meeting.

Antón attended the next meeting of the Student Alliance for Democracy and every one that followed it. In their walks home, he wore his skepticism like an armor and lambasted every political organization that laid claim to the island. Ester defended political commitment and sacrifice and said that without it the island might as well sink into the ocean. He countered by saying that islanders had an overblown sense of their own importance. The island was a third-rate nation with third-rate problems. Maybe it deserved to sink. This upset Ester and he had to apologize and then said, half meaning it, half not, that if he could feel about the island the way he felt about her, he would be in the front lines fighting for the liberation.

"But I am the island," Ester said. "And so are you."

Antón grabbed Ester by the forearm and turned her to face him. He kissed her on the lips, which quivered at first, then softened and opened fully.

They held each other and kissed every week after that, and would have become lovers, Antón now thought, had her graduation not gotten in the way. At the time, however, he could not shake the feeling that her involvement with him was, first and foremost, a political act. In two months she went off to fulfill her destiny. He stayed behind with two more years to go and a hole in his heart that he eventually learned

---

[4] A symbol of the depravity of America.

to cover up but could never fill. It was thus that he came to understand his great-uncle's Lesson 23, "The Lesson of Marilyn Monroe": "Stigmata never heal."

Antón remained a member of the Student Alliance for Democracy even after Ester Oliva graduated from the university and Fico Brull succeeded her as president. She had been right about him: Fico was dangerous. In him we're all the elements of a dictator but one, intelligence. He always walked a step ahead of whoever was with him, leaning forward as if he were about to burst through a door, and he carried a revolver at all times, a fact that impressed and cowed the other members of the Alliance. Here was a leader of the old school, fearless and ready to do battle at a moment's notice with anyone who stood in his way.

The problem for Fico Brull was that there was no one to battle. As a result, much of the organization's energy was spent trying to find enemies for him, mostly unwitting professors and students who, eager to ally themselves to a third-world cause, had expressed their solidarity with the Campión regime. The organization attacked its enemies, real or imagined, in every form possible, from sending anonymous letters to the school newspaper describing a particular professor's sexual practices, to making catcalls during his lectures, to phoning his home and yelling obscenities at his wife and children. Caught by surprise and unprepared for such virulence, Fico Brull's opponents invariably cracked, lowered their heads, and went back to their books. In a matter of months, he had vanquished all his antagonists within the university and was hungry for larger game.

And so the insatiable Fico Brull organized a trip to the United Nations to participate in a demonstration against the Campión government. Antón agreed to go, not out of allegiance to the cause—by this point he was aware that the only cause SAD was pursuing was Fico Brull's aggrandizement—but because he knew there would be representatives from every major political group in exile, and he secretly hoped to run into Ester Oliva.

By the time they arrived at the United Nations, upward of one thousand people had gathered across the street. The demonstrators huddled in small clusters, and the SAD contingent joined one of the more vocal of these. For some time they stayed in place, but as the group grew, the people in the back pushed the front edge against the barricades. The ones in front pushed back, and the resulting motion gave the crowd a fluid, pulsating appearance.

Antón was distracted, searching for Ester, and he found himself next to Fico Brull. Fico was in his glory, waving a placard over his head and exhorting his compatriots always to attack, never to surrender, when the crowd surged forward and pushed the two of them within arm's reach of a mounted policeman posted behind a barricade. Fico dropped his placard, pulled out a machete from underneath his raincoat, and tried to hack off the police horse's head. Due to the weapon's dullness or Fico's lack of strength, the machete bounced off the horse's neck and Fico swung again. This time the horse reared backward and Fico missed completely, falling to the ground underneath the animal. Almost immediately a patrolman materialized out of the crowd and started beating him around the head with a nightstick until red started flowing and Fico's blood sprayed on the curb. Before Antón had a chance to react, he had a billy club across the back of his neck and his face was being pushed against the pavement.

It took Fernando the better part of a day to get his son out of police custody and all of that night to extract from him the promise never to get involved in such silliness again. "Why waste your time dreaming, when this land is like a lake of opportunity ready to be grabbed?" Fernando, told his son, mixing his metaphors.

Antón did not tell his father that what he saw before him was not the waters of opportunity but an ocean of longing, and the more he grabbed, the less he could hold. That was twelve years ago, before deception and dissatisfaction before marriage, before he had "a life."

As he basked in the memory of Ester Oliva, he heard the back door opening and smelled the dank air of New Jersey wafting through the house. The cure had worked. His birthmark had settled down. He was trying to button his pants when the light went on and Alice materialized in the doorway to the kitchen.

"What's going on here?"

Her voice was clipped and measured. Antón was defenseless.

"My cure," he answered.

"It smells terrible."

She let go of the switch and went upstairs.

He fell back on the sofa. It had started raining outside, a soft suburban drizzle that brushed against the window behind him and eased his way into sleep.

Alice's short-lived first marriage had taught her to place her independence above her emotional entanglements. She insisted that she and Antón have separate bank accounts, separate closets, and separate bookshelves. Alice chose the cars they drove and the house they lived in, and how often to make love: twice a month, she had determined, for she had read, and had decided to believe, that too frequent sex with an uncircumcised man was unhealthy for a woman. Sometimes they would skip a month altogether, for from their wedding night on, Alice was riddled with a host of female ailments that kept them sleeping with their pajamas on for extended periods of time.

When she was free of cystitis or yeast infections and in between her periods, which were spontaneous and unpredictable as tropical storms, her indifference got in the way. Had Antón bothered to count, he would have discovered that, in their years of marriage, they had made love forty-five times, and on at least five of those occasions, she had drunk enough wine not just to lower her inhibitions, which were as much a part of her as the bacteria that ravaged her womb and the flash flood of her menses, but also to make her barely conscious, so that he might as well have been violating a corpse.

In truth, Alice had never loved Antón, much as she tried to convince herself otherwise, and so it was easy for her to assume a commanding role and to treat her husband as an adjunct to her decisions. Her sense of fair play, instilled in her by well-meaning liberal parents, and a vestigial kindness, which bubbled to the surface in spite of her better instincts, had kept her in the marriage beyond any hope of its salvation. In the meantime, there were affairs with other men: a Polish official, a Russian student, an Iranian geologist, and a few others, all circumcised, with whom she had brief encounters. She chose her lovers carefully to avoid any long-term entanglements and to confirm further her sense that she was in complete control of her world.

Then the Argentinian came into her life. His name was Manuel Flores and Alice met him when she taught English to adult foreign students. She could not help but notice the handsome man with the brown hair whose eyes fixed on her all through the period. Before long they were meeting after class for brief chats. He was an arms merchant by profession and he brought her exotic gifts from distant places, which she hid from her husband in the attic of their house. Manuel Flores's manners, formal but never condescending, were irresistible, and soon Alice was charmed into love by this man, the likes of whom she had only read about in the stories of American women expatriates. When she found out he was married, there was a momentary twinge of jealousy, but subsequently she was glad, for it would further guarantee the temporary nature of the relationship.

They became lovers, meeting in hotel rooms or in her house while Antón was at the college, and they would make love the afternoon long. Manuel Flores was unquenchable and more than eager to satisfy every one of the fantasies Alice had been reluctant to reveal to her husband. He tied her up and sprayed whipped cream on her; he taunted her with juicy pears and rubbed her with ripe bananas, which they ate together in ecstasy; and when she asked, he slapped her buns until they turned red, then fed her vanilla ice cream from a dripping cone, just as her father had done when she was a girl.

The day came when she recognized that she would do anything for this Argentinian stuck to her by sweat, passion, and fructose: leave her job, abandon her husband, fly to Patagonia if he asked. That was the day Manuel made a dozen promises to her and that was the day that she told Antón she was leaving.

Antón had reacted unexpectedly. Instead of wrath, there had been indifference. He simply heard what she had to say and returned to his work in the garden. The thought that his wife was having an affair intrigued and excited him. For a few moments later that morning he entertained the possibility of allowing Alice to do as she pleased, and he fantasized about making love with her after she had been with her lover, but it was only a fantasy and not anything real or good.

His musings were interrupted by a phone call from his father telling him that his great-uncle Ruperto had died unexpectedly in Miami. Under different circumstances, Antón might have felt real sorrow at his great-uncle's death. As it was, he was glad for the opportunity to leave, and took a plane south that same night.

By the time he returned ten days later, Alice had moved into an apartment with lively, vibrant furniture she thought her lover would like and fresh flowers—zinnias and daisies—his favorites. She waited three months for Manuel to come. Then she received a letter in which he reneged on all his promises, declaring in his broken, euphemistic English that he could not throw his wife to the garbage, not now, not ever. Alice did not cry, nor did she allow herself the luxury of despair; instead, she burned the letter, threw away all the gifts Manuel had given her, and renewed the oath her mother had lived by: "The only man worth trusting has the shadow of a gravestone over him."

Alice returned to Antón, not contrite but disappointed. By then the marriage had begun to taste like one of his jobs. His birthmark flared as never before and his sweat acquired an acrid, nefarious smell. He forced himself to feel outrage. He wept, threw books at the wall, dishes at the floor, and cursed at her, calling her *cabrona*, that Spanish word bearing all the venom that the English "bitch" lacked. He left for three weeks, visiting friends, his parents, even his grandmother in Miami briefly. He would have stayed away for good had not a force he did not understand, perhaps a dim sense of hope commingled with inertia, interfered. The fact is that he had no way of knowing for certain that the marriage was over. Not having a cause or a lover to escape to, he did the only thing he could. He went back to New Jersey to face the truth: Alice, the pink-lipped, bottom-blue Unitarian maiden, had betrayed him.

The rain had intensified throughout the night and Antón. was awakened in the morning by the tinny drip of water on the gutter pipe. Outside the window, a male cardinal hopped from branch to branch on the lilac bush. Beyond the back yard, the Sourland Mountains sloped away into the eastern flatlands of the state. To the right, the wooden skeletons of new, expensive houses marked the edges of the farmland that had recently been sold to developers. In a few months, fifty sewer lines would be running into town, but for him this was not an important realization.

He rose from the couch, finally, compelled by the weight of a full bladder on his urinary tract, and went upstairs to the bathroom. The door was locked. The fullness had turned to pain, and standing only intensified it. He knocked several times and was shifting his weight from foot to foot when Alice opened the door.

She was naked, skin blushed from the shower and thighs smooth as a baby's. Without her clothes, she was as clean and white as a frozen continent, and every curve of her, from the arches of her feet to her full calves, to her lithe back and straight neck, seemed to lead with natural logic to her dusk-colored hair. She was the measure of his success and the mirror of his failure. She was the ice field, the blasting wind: she was *el Norte*.[5]

His bladder was calling. He went to the toilet and lifted the cover. It was sanity returning.

"What's with you?'" she asked, holding the hair curler in her right hand like a weapon.

"I had to go," he answered.

She resumed fixing her hair with the nonchalance of someone who knows the power of her station. It was her house they were living in, her town, her land, and her authority that dominated the household. It was, in short, her marriage, while he was a mere appendage, dangling in the breeze of her certainties. He hesitated a moment before flushing—she hated when the toilet was not flushed—then went downstairs to make coffee.

Discussion Questions

1. How is Antón's birthmark connected to the development of his life?

2. Describe the relationship between Antón and his wife, especially in terms of his quest to become more "Americanized."

3. What is Antón's relationship to Cuba in terms of his self-identity?

4. In what way are Antón and Pilar from Cristina Garcia's *Dreaming in Cuban* on page 175 similar?

---

[5] the North

Margarita Engle

*MARGARITA ENGLE was born in Pasadena, California in 1951. She holds
an M.S. from Iowa State University and did her doctoral work at the University of
California, Riverside. Her two published novels are* Singing to Cuba *(1993), and*
Skywriting *(1995). Her next work, a historical novel set in Cuba in the 1820s, is
scheduled to appear in 2001.*

In Singing to Cuba, *the narrator returns to Cuba after a thirty-year absence.
Her travels and conversations throughout the country are juxtaposed with the story of
her great uncles's imprisonment. As she visits Cuban relatives, the story chronicles the
internment of scores of Cuban peasants during the Castro regime into prison-cities
known as "Captive Towns." Remembering, and perhaps more importantly voicing, the
stories of her relatives allows the narrator to fulfill her role as a Cuban-American
writer whose mission is to speak for those who have been silenced.*

The following excerpt comes at the conclusion of Singing to Cuba *when the narrator returns home and ponders what she has seen and experienced. As they do throughout the novel, the past and present are fused as her uncle Juan arrives from New York
for a visit, and later a newly arrived exiled relative seeks shelter at her home.*

From Singing to Cuba

I embraced my great-aunt and, feeling embarrassed but satisfied, told her, "You
won't be forgotten." Soon after, while I was standing in the patio watching a battle
between angels and demons, a Cubatur guide caught up with me. She was furious,
scolding me for leaving my tour group. The pretty guide said I could have run into
problems, I should be careful in a place where I didn't know how things worked. She
said, "Didn't I tell you that as long as you're in Cuba, you're my responsibility?" She
was cordial, solicitous, protective. She told me the Cuban government had only my
best interests at heart. I was immediately ushered away from Trinidad, flown to Havana, and then, the next day, after receiving several hours of honeyed speeches by
smiling guides, I was sent away from the island on a plane which reminded me of
slave legends about flying.

They rushed me away, shut inside the roaring silver body of an old Soviet
Aeroflot jet. As I was deported, the green island grew smaller. It was an island I now
knew, with certainty, was truly enchanted, an island blessed and cursed and bewitched, an island shaped like a sleeping dragon.

The plane flew head-on into a storm, slamming against the clouds, battered by
wind. I thought my life was ending. Hours later, I arrived in Mexico City, alive, but
frantic with fear.

In their effort to keep my departure quiet and friendly, the guides hadn't
checked my luggage. I still had my grandmother's old photographs, even the big one

of my uncle Juan posing with his Olympic team, next to a smiling black-and-white image of the Maximum Leader. And I had Gabriel's[1] imperfect basket, and the stored-up fragments of his released memory and a few verses of Miguelito's[2] songs, a few gentle melodies. . . .

When I returned from Cuba, I tried to tell people what it was like but, my words sounded so strange and remote that nearly everyone stared at me blankly, as if I had chronicled a journey to Neptune or Saturn, as if I had tried to describe the colors of gaseous rings or the patterns of light and dark inside the craters of distant moons. I might as well have said I'd been hit by a meteor. Northerners said they couldn't imagine a land where people were afraid of their own brothers and cousins, where feeling unhappy was against the law, and wistful songs were considered dangerous. They said they couldn't imagine the fear, the silence, the constant search for food, the storm of melancholy sweeping across an entire island, the loss of one's own voice, the loneliness.

I became secretive. It was something I had learned on the island of sorcerers and seraphim. Nothing could be forgotten. I hoarded the memories like an escaped slave hiding pirate gold.

I asked myself questions that could never be answered. Had the guides followed me on their own or, had someone, a stranger, informed them that I wasn't an ordinary tourist, but a Cuban-American visiting relatives without the permission of Marazul? Perhaps it had been the cabdriver who'd appeared at my door during the darkest hours of the night, demanding and accepting bribes? Or perhaps the maid who claimed her name was Amparo, my grandmother's name. Or, although I dreaded the thought, perhaps some distant cousin seeking extra rations or career advancement? I would never know, and it would never matter. My message had been delivered. The treasures had been smuggled out. Now I was free. I could return to my safe, comfortable routine in that arid rural corner of a big world. I could think of Cuba as one of those places the mind creates inside the boundaries of its dreams. I could forget.

But I couldn't forget. I felt myself still immersed in the deep, all-consuming melancholy of Havana, the illusory serenity of Trinidad, even the unseen rhythm and melody of the lost farm.

I tracked the daily news for information about Cuba. One day I read that bus service was paralyzed by the fuel shortage and that carrier pigeons were transporting government messages. Oxen were plowing fields while tractors stood idle. Bicycles were so precious that at night thieves ambushed riders to seize their cycles. Streetlights were being turned off and even television viewing hours were being limited to conserve power.

A Los Angeles Times headline read, "Let them eat ice cream," telling how the sweet frozen treat was now the only abundant food in Cuba.

A soap delivery truck was hijacked for its precious cargo.

---

[1] Gabriel: narrator's great-uncle who was a political prisoner in Cuba for 27 years. While in a labor camp he wove baskets which always included one small imperceptible defect as a way to retain some of his individuality. [2] Miguelito: narrator's first cousin. Like his father Miguel, Miguelito's songs are perhaps a symbol of his defiance of Cuba's totalitarian system.

Catholic Bishops asked Fidel to legalize the public celebration of Christmas. They received no reply.

An observer from the United Nations Commission on Human Rights was denied entry to the island.

The Maximum Leader announced that the people were willing to die for their leaders.

Work crews were assigned the task of digging a network of tunnels under the city of Havana. The tunnels were intended as bomb shelters in case of an attack by the armies of the North.

I received a human rights bulletin documenting the consequences of a peaceful demonstration which had taken place in front of State Security Headquarters at Villa Marista in Havana. A coalition of dissident groups had convened to shout, "Liberty for political prisoners!" State Security's paramilitary Rapid Action Brigades swiftly disbanded the demonstrators, who were beaten, tried and sentenced without access to defense lawyers.

During the course of my safe and comfortable days, I tried to tell people about silence and fear on the island, but a pastor from one of the small country churches said, "No one gives a darn about Cuba," and a woman in the congregation said, "This is just totally depressing." And she walked away in disgust.

"But Cuba is so close!" I shouted. "What happened to 'Love thy neighbor'?" I demanded. The pastor shrugged. "Most people don't," was his matter-of-fact answer. As if to make amends, another more empathetic pastor wrote "Pray for Cuba" in his weekly church bulletin every week for a year.

So I started writing Miguelito's words and Daniel's words which had been inherited from Gabriel and, remembering my promise to Miguelito, I wrote under a false name, just as if the words were still trapped in a place where words are dangerous.

An acquaintance asked me how my life had been changed by my return to the island. At first the question perplexed me. Then I realized that the journey had made me see the North through Cuban eyes. In supermarkets I would stop and gawk at the abundance. On amusement park roller coasters I would notice the difference between the delight of simulated fear and the grim panic of true dread. I realized that the pilgrimage had changed me profoundly. Now I could truly believe the strangest statements made in the Bible. Plagues of frogs. Manna for breakfast. Burning bushes. Evil kings. Horned beasts. Detached human fingers writing prophecies on walls.

I realized that the journey had made me believe that truth exists and that it is absolute, even when kept secret.

I continued scanning the human rights bulletins. A coalition for democracy had convened in Havana's Church of the Virgin of Mercy to pray for the liberty of political prisoners. The leaders were arrested by State Security while thousands of worshipers continued praying.

Like the Cuban teenagers in their stripped-bare churches, I tried to pray for Fidel, for guidance for him from above. A repentant slave trader wrote the hymn "Amazing Grace." The blind see. The lost are found. Couldn't the evil king also be saved? Yet I continued to think of him as suicidal. Any day now he might leap into the sea, trying to drag nearly eleven million captives down with him. He was becoming a giant octopus, a sea serpent. I prayed for armies of angels.

Then I received the bulletin about the arrest and torture of Omar, cousin of my grandmother Amparo and of Gabriel, Miguel, Isabelita and Daniel. Omar, the brother of Alvaro who, even though his flesh was crawling with maggots when they pulled him out of the punishment cells, survived to tell his cousin Gabriel about the *Alzados*.[3] Omar, brother of Emilio and Adán who had risen up in arms so briefly and had been shot as examples, Emilio in the mountains, and Adán in the town square of Trinidad, a corpse left on the cobblestones for all the children to see.

All my life, questions of good and evil always appeared to be centered in Cuba. Was God like nature? Was Fidel an idealist gone mad or a madman gone evil or an ordinary *Santero* [4] who danced too well and became possessed by demons?

"We thought he was God," Gabriel had said of Fidel. But God is loving.

I bought a red mare and, every day, while my husband was at work in the fields and my children were at school, I cantered back and forth across dry slopes and irrigated orchards, thinking of Omar and of his arrest on charges of being in a "dangerous" state of mind. I felt that the word described my own state.

At night I dreamed of Cuban women standing awestruck in front of supermarket bins fitted with apples and guavas. I dreamed about Cuban teenagers singing along with wandering pastors, waving their hands toward God as if to say, "Look, here we are, down here!"

I dreamed I was roaming the countryside near Trinidad, and just when I was about to find the lost farm, the Maximum Leader, appeared wearing the flashy costume of a Las Vegas performer, smirking and smiling, claiming he would create a New Man who would live in paradise. In the dream, someone laughed and I awakened, certain that I had heard the devil.

I dreamed I was climbing down a steep cliff on the island, trying to reach the shore of the sea, intending to collect fragile seashells as they were washed onto the beach by shimmering waves. I was anticipating the cool smooth touch of pale yellow moon snails marked with delicate brown spirals, as if the shells had been painted by a careful hand.

Descending the cliff, I noted with alarm that the ocean was rising fast, surging against the cliff in great ominous waves. I clambered back up the precipice and, reaching the summit, I saw a panorama of the most exquisitely beautiful green farm imaginable—with hills, cane, cattle, flowers, butterflies, a *guajiro*[5] working in the fields, singing and waving his woven-palm hat toward the vibrant sky.

I felt like I was in heaven. For days after the dream of a rescued farm, I went about my ordinary tasks feeling thrilled, intensely hopeful and content, singing.

It was autumn, fire season. Seated on the back of my mare I galloped across the dry hills, savoring the dream-image of that free *guajiro* on his reclaimed land.

I wrote to Miguelito and Aurora, trying to describe the seasons, the fires, the roadrunners, bobcats and coyotes, the trap-door spiders and horned lizards, the turquoise sky.

At first I received cautiously self-censored notes. We are fine. Everyone is well. The weather is lovely.

---

[3] Alzados: name given to those who raised up (*se alzaron*) against the revolutionary forces of the Maximum Leader. They hid in the mountains but their cause was ultimately in vain as they were all killed or arrested.   [4] a person who practices *santeria*, a combination of Catholicism and pagan rituals.
[5] a peasant

If only we had agreed on secret code words to transport truths past the eyes and fingers of Cuban government censors!

Miguelito wrote asking for guitar strings, and as I packaged and sent them, I felt a sense of dismay. Why hadn't I thought of sending guitar strings without being asked? How could I be so oblivious?

The next letter I received from my cousin said, "I hope you feel like a human being," and from those secretive words I knew he must mean that he did not feel human. Another letter came and, from the bitter emptiness between cautious, self-censored words, I knew he had finally given up the masquerade, the daily routine of his government job. He was singing.

I searched the news information about the suffering of Cuban dissidents, the crackdown against protest, the repression of poetry and art. Other topics seemed to be occupying the minds of reporters from the U.S. who had drifted into the past. They wrote nostalgic pieces about the Missile Crisis. They reported that historians were arguing about Columbus, some vowing that he was a good man, a devout man, a man of vision. Others retorting that he threatened to slice out the tongues of his sailors if they denied that Cuba was Asia. They said that eventually he was recalled by the Spanish monarchs because he persisted in enslaving baptized Indians, defying the expressed orders of the rulers of Imperial Spain. Power had seeped into the man's soul, one historian insisted, corrupting him.

I began searching obscure libraries for clues to decipher Gabriel's memory. Through an interlibrary loan I found a list of Alzados killed in the Escambray Mountains and in Trinidad between 1960 and 1966. The list included the names of many of my distant cousins. Emilio and Adán. Nicomedes, Adonis, Elizardo, Ibrahím, Angel, Efraín, Noel.

Christmas came and, the Soviet Union was dissolved. Cuba stood trembling on the brink of rebellion. My husband and children surprised me with a kite-shaped pendant of polished lapis flecked with gold. It made me think of sailboats, of the sky and the tides.

We walked to a stable at a nearby feed store to enjoy a living Nativity Scene featuring shepherds from a local children's choir. The shepherds were dressed in bathrobes, with striped towels tied onto their heads. While Mary was still on her donkey, it bucked. The shepherds giggled. After she dismounted, the donkey turned and nipped one of the sheep on its rear end, starting a brawl. The animals butted each other. A baby goat chewed on Joseph's microphone as he sang, "Joy to the world, the Savior reigns, let men their songs employ." I started wondering how to employ songs. One of the three Kings tripped and, Joseph, grinning, continued, "While fields and floods, rocks, hills and plains, repeat the sounding joy, repeat the sounding joy, repeat, repeat the sounding joy." And here was God on earth, newborn, amidst all these distractions!

That night I dreamed again that he, the Maximum Leader, and I, were both wandering through the Cuban countryside. I tried to avoid him but, he found me and demanded my documents. Inspecting them, he informed me that my visa had expired, but that he considered himself a fair and generous New Man and was willing to let me stay. I was grateful until, walking away, across the green hills and red mud, I realized that he was laughing because he'd transformed me into a Cuban, and now I was trapped.

Araceli wrote, "We are having a dreadful time with this special period, but the Maximum Leader says we must resist. Imagine!"

Isabelita sent a message saying she was blind now and could no longer write.

Daniel wrote, "In Cuba this year, the winter is like spring!"

Two days after Christmas the Associated Press reported that Cuban authorities had seen a human figure clinging to the wheel carriage of a Marazul charter flight which was returning to Miami after one of the State-authorized visits of fifty Cuban-Americans to relatives on the island. Upon arrival in the U.S., the plane had been inspected by F.B.I. agents, who reported finding only traces of human blood.

The world seemed upside down. I rode my horse, and wrote down the hoarded words of Miguelito's silence and Gabriel's memory.

At night I dreamed I was inside my cousin's crumbling house with Miguelito and Aurora. Bullets came flying in through the open windows and demons were screeching.

I began to search the Bible for explanations, seeking a new message. I started at the beginning and worked my way forward. A parable in Judges 9 caught my attention. It was about the way trees went forth to choose a king to reign over them, but only the bramble would agree to take the job, threatening to explode into flame unless all the other trees would take refuge in its shade.

In Psalms I read, "I am but a pilgrim here on earth: how I need a map" and in Hebrews, "Don't forget about those in jail. Suffer with them as though you were there yourself."

I read all the way through to the end. The truth will set you free. A flaming star called Bitterness. A time when men will wish to kill themselves but will find themselves unable to carry out the act. Locusts with human faces wearing gold crowns, looking like horses and stinging like scorpions.

The human rights bulletins kept arriving. Finally I received one documenting the arrest and torture of soldiers on the tail of the alligator, near the Captive Town of Ciudad Sandino. The soldiers had been arrested by State Security after refusing to capture a man found hiding in nearby caves. The man had a homemade explosive device hidden in his pocket. He was convicted of terrorism and was executed by firing squad against the Big Wall of a medieval castle. I recognized his name as that of Gabriel's grandson, the one I'd always known simply as Taíno.

On New Year's Day, 1992, my uncle Juan traveled to the West from New York and visited us in our rural home.

"This is nice,'" he said to my husband, "very nice. You have electricity. You have plumbing. You have cable television and no one bothers you."

My husband, whose ancestors had lived in the U.S. for centuries, looked at me curiously and whispered, "Electricity? Plumbing? Is he really surprised?"

Suddenly I realized that, as a Cuban exile, my uncle Juan had assumed that any rural area would be like the Cuban countryside, primitive, dangerous, no witnesses.

"I will tell my mother how nice this is," Juan promised me. "She believes you live in a very small, very old cabin far back in the brush where it is very uncomfortable and all the houses need many repairs. *En el monte.*" In the mountains. Frogs. Worms. Soil the color of blood.

Suddenly I understood why they had reached the U.S. and headed straight for the biggest, most crowded and anonymous city they could find. Suddenly I knew why

I had been raised in Harlem. Now I could imagine how Northerners would feel if the U.S. Army came marching across Iowa or Arizona, arresting farmers and relocating them to captive towns, executing some as examples, torturing those who were known to be the cousins of troublemakers, leaving the bodies stumped against impromptu firing walls in downtown Ames or Prescott. . . .

"I would like to go to Hawaii on vacation," uncle Juan told me, "but my wife is afraid of islands. I have been told that Hawaii is something like Cuba. The same flowers. The same fruit trees. And green, very green. But my wife, she says once you are on an island, if something happens, there is no escape. Just like in Cuba."

Juan showed me a poem his teenage granddaughter wrote about her father Juanito who died young in the North, young and unexpectedly, of the worms he brought into exile from Cuban soil, worms which had crawled up inside his flesh and consumed his heart. The poem was very good, full of sorrow and joy, a. wistful poem about feeling accompanied by angels, about never being alone.

Together my uncle and I looked at the photographs I had smuggled out of Cuba. He laughed when he recognized himself smiling so proudly next to Fidel Castro Ruz, *Presidente de la República, El Líder Máximo,* The Maximum Leader.

"I have told the Americans I work with about this picture," Juan said, and they say they don't believe me. I have told them about the Olympic team, and they don't believe me. They don't know what it's like in a small country. Now they will believe me."

We looked at Havana, the sea wall, El Morro Castle, Miguel holding the baby Miguelito. My childhood self, relaxing in a homemade white cotton hammock in Isabelita's patio. My arm draped across the glistening copper neck of a colt. My childhood self on horseback, chasing Gabriel's sons as they rounded up the cattle. His small grandson Taíno, smiling shyly, a parrot perched on one outstretched finger. Gabriel standing in the corral, twirling a lariat above his head. Gabriel with an exultant smile raising his fist, shaking it at the devil.

I gave all the photographs to Juan for delivery to Amparo in New York. "These memories," he said, "will make your grandmother very happy. Sad, perhaps, but also happy."

After Juan left, I went cantering across the hills of my home, debating my same old questions of good and evil, wondering about suffering, feeling like I held, inside my mouth, a golden ball which could never be swallowed.

While my husband was in the fields and our children were at school, I listened to recordings of the passionate "Deep Songs" of Andalusian gypsies. Heels stamped, trees twirled, drums pounded, gourds rattled.

The newspapers reported that 34 Cubans escaped from the island in a hijacked military helicopter.

Three Cuban exiles floated back to the island in an inflatable dinghy loaded with explosives. They were arrested and one was shot against the firing wall. As an example, said the Maximum Leader.

A British political analyst announced that she could foresee no immediate prospects of a mass rebellion in Cuba, because everyone who could possibly lead such a movement had been arrested in advance.

Hollywood celebrities gathered in New York for a pro-Castro rally. I wondered if the famous singers and actors knew how swiftly they would lose their artistic freedom should they ever actually venture into real life on the Maximum Leader's alligator-shaped island.

I dreamed I'd received an urgent letter from Miguelito, delivered by carrier pigeon. "*Se ha quemado todo. Ya no existe.*" Everything has burned. It no longer exists.

I awakened feeling both glad and afraid, wondering exactly which part of everything had burned and when.

Then, the next afternoon, when the mail arrived, I really did receive a message from Miguelito which had somehow been smuggled out of Cuba and bore the postmark of a town in Louisiana. "Forgive us our silence," the message stated. "We love you very much." Crumpled up inside the folded message, I found a song, a ballad about Gabriel's grandson Taíno and Araceli's brother, during their moment of confrontation in the caverns, the moment when they recognized each other as cousins and Taíno decided not to light his homemade bomb, and Araceli's brother decided not to arrest him.

I felt like I held a massive golden ball inside my mouth. I felt Cuban.

Re-reading the Bible, this time from back to front, I leafed farther and farther back, until finally I found, in I Kings 19:11–12, the passage which answered my question:

"The Lord said, 'Go out and stand on the mountain in the presence of the Lord, for the Lord is about to pass by.'

"Then a great and powerful wind tore the mountains apart and shattered the rocks before the Lord but the Lord was not in the wind. After the wind there was an earthquake, but the Lord was not in the earthquake. After the earthquake came a fire, but the Lord was not in the fire. And after the fire came a gentle whisper."

After reading the answer to my question, I stepped outside into the light and, there, waiting patiently at my door was a sunburned young woman who spoke quietly in Cuba's rapid, golden-ball Spanish.

"I am the wife of your great-uncle Gabriel's grandson," she murmured. "I come from the Captive Town seeking shelter. This is my child in my arms, a boy born at sea. I call him Angel because an angel of the Lord carried us across the sea. First we floated across the water with sharks snapping at our legs. The sun scorched our skin. The salt consumed our flesh. Then we were lifted up, and we soared as if carried by wings. And now here we are, waiting."

And just as I was about to ask, "Waiting for what?" she swallowed her golden ball and answered, in a clear and penetrating sing-song voice, a voice like a bell, a wild-bird voice which read my silent thoughts and fears and joy, "Waiting for an end to the battle which was already won before it began."

Discussion Questions

1. What does the narrator's dreams reveal concerning her feelings about Cuba, its leader, its people, and her connection to the island?
2. What is the meaning of the paradoxical statement at the conclusion of the piece?
3. Compare the familial relationships in the story to those in Yglesia's "Celia's Family" on page 246.
4. What elements about the visit by her uncle Juan and her ruminations about that visit are similar to the description of the transition of the town in Jose Antonio Villareal's *Pocho* on page 22?

Himilce Novas

The daughter of renowned Cuban writer Lino Novos Calvo, Himilce Novas immigrated to the United States in 1960. In addition to being a talented writer, she is a gifted speaker who has a radio broadcast in her local hometown of Santa Barbara, California. Mangos, Bananas, and Coconuts: A Cuban Love Story *(1996) is her first novel. However, she previously published three works of nonfiction:* Everything You Need to Know about Latino History, *(1994),* The Hispanic 100: A Ranking of Latino Men and Women Who Have Most Influenced American Thought and Culture *(1995), and* Remembering Selena: A Tribute in Pictures and Words *(1995).*

Novas's novel, once described as a Latin fable, reads much like a printed version of a telenovela, *or soap opera. Similar to Castillo's* So Far From God, *however, the intricate plot is satiric in nature and reveals much about Latino culture. The story is of twins, a boy and a girl, who are separated at birth. The girl, Esmeralda, remains in Cuba with her father who sexually abuses her, and the boy, Juan, is raised by his affluent and loving grandparents. Despite their physical separation, they are drawn to each other, as each feels they are somehow not complete. Their eventual reunion ends in tragedy, however, not realizing their shared parentage, they engage in a love affair.*

From Mangos, Bananas, and Coconuts: A Cuban Love Story

There was a saying in Arnaldo's hometown, the one he thought he was waking up in every morning before his fully conscious state told him he was a refugee working as a janitor, cleaning latrines and separating plastic garbage bags for the sanitation men. The saying went like this: "For every south, there is a north, and even though the north may know nothing of the south or the south of the north, they need each other to be what they are." It was a saying that people usually cut short. "Like the south to the north" they would say, since everyone knew what they meant. They used it when referring to fate in a general way, such as there is bad because there is good, or there are rich people because there are poor people, or there are stupid people because there are smart people. No matter what you applied it to, though, whether it was fate or not, it would work as long as it involved duality—blondes because there are brunettes, short because there is tall, obnoxious because there is graceful, greedy because there is generous.

Juan Saavedra Ona, Arnaldo's son and Esmeralda's twin brother, called himself Juan Ona because his grandfather had adopted him at birth and hid from him the fantastic tale of his conception. He'd had a sharp feeling in his heart almost since the day Esmeralda had arrived as an infant in Key West that he existed because there was another—a south or a north to him—who was the exact otherness and yet exact image of himself.

If someone, a detective or a district attorney for instance, were to interrogate him as to when he first became aware of the existence of his other—the way he was interrogated later about Arnaldo and Esmeralda, mercilessly, cruelly, to the point of exhaustion, watching the vomit spout like a geyser from his mouth—he would have said he had always known it, the way he had known he had a perennial five-o'clock shadow and green eyes the brilliant and disturbing color of Brazilian emeralds.

But although this was so, that Juan had always sensed he had a north or a south living in another part of the world, this notion had not gripped his heart to the point of obsession until he and his twin sister turned nineteen under the same stars at different latitudinal parallels.

Before they turned nineteen, Juan's life seemed to be going in an opposite direction, in a direction away from Esmeralda, that is, and therefore on a path where it would seem unlikely they would meet.

A few months after Fidel arrived in the capital, his men began to confiscate every *ingenio*[1] and every little parcel of land that belonged to the ruling class from Pinar del Rio to Oriente Province. Don Mario Ona, who had stuffed his *guayabera*[2] pockets full of American dollars from the United Fruit Company, packed up his little grandson and his wife María and three servants and airlifted them to Miami, to Key Biscayne, to a red-tile Mizner mansion he had bought for himself and his Tropicana Night Club mistress before Carlos Prío Socarrás came to power—in the late forties, that is, since Prío came before Batista who came before Castro.

And so, while Esmeralda was growing up on One Hundred and Seventeenth Street, starring in school plays at PS 155 and being swaddled and fondled in their father's arms, Juan grew up in Miami as part of the Cuban community—they preferred to call themselves exiles. And he grew up in a manner not different from how he would have grown up in Cuba, except that in Miami, because of the culture at large and the language and the other forty-nine states, Juan would eventually find a route, an underground railroad, where he could leave his roots, even his transplanted roots, and work his own way to his north or to his south, whichever Esmeralda was.

For a boy, and then a young man of great privilege and extraordinary looks, Juan was a melancholy type, a poetic soul prone to bouts of depression and solitude that no one, not even his grandmother, whom he called *Mami*, for she was the only mother he knew, could save him from once they would start their whirly-gig in his mind. And these whirly-gigs, these pregnant clouds, these goblins that would overtake him as often as once a month just before he met his fate, would come upon him, it seemed, for no reason at all. And when they came, his relative world where he existed and did the ordinary things humans do, would have to stop.

If he was playing baseball in the junior leagues he'd quit before the dark cloud could betray him. If he was dating a virgin or having an affair with an older woman—as was his preference since he was twelve and his grandfather's mistress in Key Biscayne initiated him by cutting his fly open with a pair of scissors and reaching importunately for his member—he would announce he'd been overtaken by sudden inspiration and shut himself in his bedroom for days at a time, staring at the ceiling

---

[1] large farm containing some kind of processer   [2] a type of man's shirt often made of fine thread and popular in the Caribbean

with both hands on his chest and consuming large quantities of Coca-Cola and fried plantains.

His grandparents, whom he thought were his parents who had him late in life, right after his sister Patricia had fallen victim to the polio epidemic, were the only people fully aware of his fits of melancholy. But neither one had faith in doctors, nor did they suggest that he seek medical advice for his strange condition. The resurrection of Patricia at the hands of the voodoo man who dishonored her had contributed to his parents' disdain for the medical profession. Don Mario and Doña María only saw the outward symptoms and not Juan's hell each time the unclean spirits seized him. They regarded their grandson's melancholy as an incurable part of his character, as the south that went with the rest of his general north—meaning by his north, his genius as a portrait artist and his skill as a young architect, as well as his movie-star good looks.

If his south was hell to pay, Don Mario Ona had remarked on several occasions when Juan had been found by a servant hiding under the bed, his north more than made up for it.

The part that no one saw was what Juan called the wringing of his soul. He pictured himself like the shirts his grandmother still had the servants scrub and dry by hand and then hang in the walled courtyard so no one could see the washing on the line, which she said was the mark of the immigrant poor in this country.

This wringing of his soul had its own life span, a life span that once begun, Juan could do nothing but surrender to as both spectator and victim.

The first melancholy seizure came at age four, as far back as he could remember. The next occurred at eleven, the year Esmeralda began to menstruate, and from eleven on, several times a year. The black cloud, the fear, and then the tearful grip usually occurred at night, almost always at the same time Arnaldo was slipping naked into Esmeralda's bed up north on One Hundred and Seventeenth Street in East Harlem.

If Juan were to describe his melancholy to the detective or district attorney who questioned him years later about Arnaldo and Esmeralda, he would say that for no particular reason, and sometimes when his life was going great and he had either finished a commissioned portrait or had just taken a beautiful woman to bed, a sudden sadness would bathe his inner lining like a waterfall, like a long river of blood. Suddenly he would be a ghostly chrysalis sucked empty of his butterfly, an abandoned carcass the elephants had mauled and then forgotten by a riverbed.

And following this melancholic overtaking, he would reason he had nothing in particular to live for and would begin rehearsing in his mind the many ways he could extinguish his brief stay on this planet. It was during this stage, this stage of enumerating and depicting the different modes of suicide, that he would hide under the bed, pretending his room was already swept clean of any trace or remembrance of him.

But towards his nineteenth year something happened to Juan that, although it did not turn entirely his melancholy tide, provided a solace, a way station between his north and his south, and helped him to navigate among the living.

To describe what this way station was, it is necessary to first see Juan from the outside in, as the world of Cuban bankers and museum sponsors in Miami perceived him, as the admissions office at Yale saw him, as the famous senator who had commissioned him to do his portrait when he was only seventeen remembered him.

"A fine, tall, hell of an *hombre*" might be the way the senator would have described him, with a firm pat on the back while addressing a crowd. Or "a sportsman with the gift of Velázquez and Goya rolled into one" might have been the way the museum director might have perceived him. His art teacher, who basically had nothing to teach him because Juan had brought his talents with him from who knows where, would have agreed.

But none—not the senator nor the teachers nor the women who surrendered their hearts before he had a chance to ask—would have described him as he saw himself.

The women remembered him for his looks and would have spoken of his tall lean figure, his square jaw, his jet black hair, his hypnotic eyes. The men would have been struck by his virility and would measure themselves against it. But they would never mention it, except to say, of course, that he was one hell of a guy.

The Cubans in Miami would have said he looked more American than Cuban. And no wonder, because he was raised on hamburgers and very little yuca with rice and beans. The Anglos he knew at his private military schools would have said Juan was just a regular guy, disciplined, luckier than most, a talented artist and a devil with women.

But none would have seen him as Juan saw himself during his melancholy fits, or the way he felt the day his eyes, captured his north or his south, whichever Esmeralda happened to be.

He'd had inklings of it before, and when he finally met Esmeralda he understood completely. But that first day when he surprised himself in the mirror—only it wasn't himself—he had no idea what it meant.

At first Juan caught a brief glimpse on his way from the bathroom, where he had just thrown up, to his bed, where he'd planned to spend the next few days until the storm passed, if it passed. For while he was in the throes of it, he fervently believed the goblins would never leave. And, suddenly alarmed, he turned back and stood squarely in front of the mirror and examined every inch of his naked self, in horror and then, moments later, in incredulous glee.

For what he saw was not the handsome, well-endowed young man of nineteen with shiny, virile hair running down the length of him and exposing all the more those parts that women dreamed about long after he'd forgotten their names, but rather a pastoral beauty, a young goddess from the equatorial woods, with eyes as green as his and shoulder-length hair as black and shiny as an Arabian mane and small breasts as round and hard as brown coconuts with sweet, silvery flesh. This creature in the mirror, himself, his other hemisphere, looked and moved and assumed the poses he struck. Only she had a Duchess of Alba, Naked Maja smile on her thick pomegranate lips, and, overhead, instead of a dark cloud, there hung a halo comprised entirely of fluttering Ghost and Morpho butterflies.

Juan stood a long time in front of the reflection, wondering if the ghost would dissipate, questioning his sanity, calling himself a *pájaro,* a *maricón,* a queer, a fag, a repressed pervert and a transvestite—for he'd picked up such prejudices in military school and still subscribed to the *macho* view of bugger and buggee. The image in the mirror gradually began to fill every crevasse in his soul. He suddenly pictured himself as the image saw him and as he saw the image, and he then felt Esmeralda's gaze invade his thoughts like a cool, fresh stream seeping through the bones of his bones, dispossessing him and then possessing him completely. And from that moment on, Juan understood who his north, or his south, was (although he still didn't know where she was), and the image of Esmeralda never left him again. Nor did the picture of himself looking like her in the mirror, so that each time he found himself in bed with a woman, he surrendered that woman who lived inside him to the arms of the woman in bed with him.

Although his melancholy did not leave until the day he finally met his fate, Juan found a way to contain it by appearing in front of his full-length mirror as soon as sadness began to overtake him. He called out to Esmeralda—not yet knowing her name—and stood in prayerful attention before her until every last goblin was chased away like a cowardly satyr by the sylvan beauty in the glass before him.

Discussion Questions

1. Describe the relationship between Juan and Esmeralda, paying particular attention to their upbringing.

2. While Juan and Esmeralda are clearly two different characters, they may also be seen as two sides of the same person. How does this possibility relate to the issue of identity conflict present in much of Latino literature?

3. What is the similarity between the bouts of melancholy Juan experiences and those by Cesar in Oscar Hijelos's *Mambo Kings* on page 196?

4. How is the nostalgia, or sense of loss, experienced by Juan similar to the description of those feelings relating to Jesus Colon's Puerto Rican childhood in *A Puerto Rican in New York* on page 432?

Teresa Bevin

TERESA BEVIN's first novel, Havana Split, *contains some of the same plot elements and thematic concerns present in other Cuban-American fiction. The female narrator, Lara, returns to Cuba in search of her past. She finds a changed country, but unlike other novels of its kind there is little political commentary regarding that change. The novel contains elements of magical realism but overall the plot is straightforward and sincere.*

The excerpt that follows uses the tinajon, *or giant jar, as a touchstone for the Cuba of the past. Lara's return to her homeland culminates in her meeting with a woman whose life is tied to her own. The meeting is a commentary on Latino stereotypes such as* machismo, *as well as an opportunity for the author to examine the disparity between appearance and reality.*

From Havana Split

City of Giant *Tinajones*

Floating above the cracked, sun-baked roof tiles, I admire the glistening tree-tops. They burst out of square little patios in the midday sun. Laundry hung to dry here and there, is waving in a gentle breeze. From above the old city looks as it did decades ago, with only a few tall structures poking out in the horizon interrupting the flat skyline. They are the only signs of city growth among multiple signs of neg-lect. The newer buildings are uniformly drab, resembling jailhouses, their poured concrete walls already crumbling.

During this lazy time of day I'm free to glide without fear of being seen. Every-body is inside, taking shelter from the heat. Well, not quite everybody. An old woman shuffles along a narrow sidewalk. I hover above her watching her arduous progres-sion. The sun relentlessly punishes her back, which is fused in an arthritic arch. Her deformed toes push out of her homemade *alpargatas*,[1] and her dress is shapeless, worn thin, the hem frayed. Her image sends a needle of compassion that pierces through me, and I descend, approaching quietly, wishing I could do something for her. She senses my presence, and lifts her chin slowly, tilts her head, and looks for me through the haze of her mature cataracts. The creases on her cheekbones are dry river beds carved by a million tears. She can't see me. Her pointy chin returns to the dent it has made for itself on her collar bone, and she resumes her slow pace down the nar-row street, muttering something to herself.

My maternal ancestors were from Camagüey, but most of their history has been forever lost among generations of hard-working people who had little concern for their lineage. My paternal ancestors in contrast, were keenly aware of theirs. A diary written by my great-great-grandmother Fernanda de Gonzaga during the war for in-dependence from Spain was kept in San Venancio as a family relic. Though full of his-tory and the author's own stoic philosophy, its uniqueness was lost on the children, who were forced to sit through boring readings when they would rather be throwing mud balls at each other. Aunt Mariana read the diary to Paquito, Augusto[2] and me in the summer of 1958. Her voice cracked and she paused to dry her tears when she read Fernanda's account of the death of three of her children from disease and famine while the village was surrounded by the Spaniards.

As a small child I trembled when the diary was taken out of its place of honor in the living-room of the house in San Venancio. But I later came to admire the dedication with which those pages were written, amidst fire, blood, and desolation.

Our trips to Camagüey were always happy times of running, among palm trees, wading in ponds, collecting impressive bugs never seen in Havana, and most of all,

---

[1] sandals   [2] Paquito and Augusto—two of Lara's cousins who remained in Cuba.

spending time with my countrified cousins who spoke funny and laughed at my penchant for stepping on cow flops and sitting on ant hills.

The city of Camagüey itself had a somber air that settled over the mazes of narrow streets and quaint little plazas. Church bells rang seemingly at any time, and women in mourning rushed passed my relative's house covering their head with lacy *mantillas.*[3]

Now, as I drove past crumbling churches and neglected parks, my memories didn't fit the scenes. Just before noon, silence prevailed through the mazes, and Camagüey seemed a ghost town.

Leaving the car parked in front of a central hotel, Osvaldo[4] and I walked by city blocks of colonial houses in the final stages of deterioration, about to cave in. The traffic we encountered while we strolled southwest on Cristo Street toward the cemetery, consisted of bicycles and carts pulled by horses or mules. The bikers sped and zig-zagged recklessly, whistling when they approached a pedestrian, who quickly moved out of the way. The stench of sewer and stagnant water seemed to penetrate our pores and hang onto our hair and clothes.

As we approached the white walls of the cemetery, I recalled how my brother Hector and I used to play hide-and-seek among tombstones while Mami and Papi visited our grandparents' gravesites. Hiding behind statues and ornate gates, I read and re-read the historic family names and the mournful messages on black and white marble, and wondered about the remains rotting below, within the moist earth.

The cemetery was always crowded on Mother's Day, when flowers and butterflies merged into mesmerizing puffs of fluttering activity. At that time the site turned into a magical garden where soft cries and sobs merged with the breeze rustling through hundreds of flower wreaths. Now, as we crossed the gate, the white glow blinded us, but there were no flowers or butterflies, and only two visitors could be seen from the entrance, two women sitting on a stone, talking.

Down the narrow paths lined with rows of tombs, signs of looting and vandalism were obvious. Mausoleums had been taken apart, and entire marble slabs were gone. How anyone could have made away with them was mystifying to me. Where a statue had been, only part of a pedestal remained. Metal holders, hinges, and crosses had left only their ghostly outlines of rust behind. The resting places of the former upper class, which had boasted the fanciest ornaments and the most marble, were naturally hit the hardest. And in the middle of it all, a new mausoleum towered above the old rubble.

"This must be for the martyrs of the war in Angola," Osvaldo observed.

"This big?" I asked, my eyes lost in the rows of names.

"You should see the one in Havana."

"It's always bigger in Havana, right?" I tried to joke, while realizing the magnitude of the loss of young Cuban lives. Stung, I walked away with my eyes unfocused over the crumbling stones, searching without looking. Suddenly I found myself reading the faded names etched on my paternal family pantheon, dating back to *Doña Fernanda de Gonzaga, 1835–1888.* Uncle Gilberto, Aunt Mariana, and other

[3] a fine piece of cloth   [4] Osvaldo—Lara's lifelong friend. After she left Cuba they communicated through letters for twenty years. He is serving as a type of tour guide during her return visit.

relatives were also buried there. Nobody had visited in decades, and thick, tall weeds emerged from fragmented marble and cement. Osvaldo helped me clear an area that yielded more names and in minutes we had piled a mound of debris on the walkway.

"It seems so futile," I said, giving up, and sat on a neighboring stone. But Osvaldo didn't stop until the place was clean, and then took the debris in his arms a few meters away to deposit it unobtrusively by a group of shrubs.

We continued advancing through an area too crowded with stones for a walkway. The tiny monuments seemed stacked almost on top of each other. A taller structure called my attention. My maternal grandfather's name was hardly visible on what was left of the monument to the association of mailmen of the city.

"I thought he was a carpenter," Osvaldo said.

"And a mailman, a policeman, a construction worker, and a *chupamierda*."

"A what?"

"He drove a giant vacuum that sucked shit out of septic tanks about to overflow. I don't think there ever was a monument erected in their honor."

We left the mournful enclosure as a funeral began its entrance through the gate. About forty people followed the hearse on foot.

Back in the streets, teenagers in school uniforms walked around with nothing to do, nowhere to go. Apparently on recess, the youngsters gathered around a lone boombox, swaying with the music, or necking against a wall.

Two boys talked loudly in the center of a group. The darker one of the two said to the other, with conviction, "No way I'm going to hook up with a dark-skinned woman. I want a white one, so my race can advance."

"Oz, did you hear that?" I whispered. "I thought Castro had eradicated racism."

"Only in propaganda for international consumption. In reality we have what you may call institutional racism. Government officials at the highest levels are all white. You should watch the news on TV sometime."

"I think I'll pass."

We wandered toward the commercial center of town, passing at some point in front of Cousin Blasito's house. A barred bay window offered a view into the living room. The place seemed deserted at first, but then I saw something moving inside a wooden crate that sat on a coffee table. A tiny baby in a baggy cloth diaper lying in the crate on a folded blanket, was quietly gumming its toes. The baby was probably Blasito's son, or maybe even his grandson, and the thought made me acutely aware of the passage of time. Blasito, too, had once been one of my favorite cousins. Gregarious and funny, he was incapable of sitting still for more than two minutes. From within the house the sound of a woman humming emerged, and the rhythmic sweeps of a straw broom seemed to follow the humming somewhere toward the back of the house. Tempted to leave Blasito a message so he would know I remembered him, I motioned to reach the heavy knocker. But then, my eyes were powerfully attracted to a framed photo enlargement that sat on the TV set: Cousin Blasito in army uniform, smiling, standing to the left of Fidel Castro. The photograph was at least ten years old, and it occupied a prominent place in the living room. I hoped that its purpose was to shield and protect, not to display devotion. But regardless, I grabbed Osvaldo's hand, and we kept on walking.

El Encanto had once been the best department store of Camagüey in its day, where the latest fashions were on display and the wives of the powerful could buy on credit. The store was still as refrigerated inside as it always was, but nothing else resembled its past. Rows of completely empty counters lined the way to the back, where hair color was on display.

"Hmm. A delayed shipment," Osvaldo observed. The boxes were covered with Russian characters, and they were all one color, dirty blonde, totally inappropriate for olive or brown Cuban skin tones.

The few cashiers smoked and chatted idly, flicking ashes onto the floor as they watched our every move.

Next door to El Encanto was Camagüey Electric. On its window, a slogan in big, red letters declared: "There's an electrical appliance for each and every household need." I looked at Osvaldo, puzzled. There were no appliances to be had. None could be seen on the windows, and upon closer inspection, none could be found inside. With a smirk of superiority that mocked the mannerisms of the government elite in their meaningless jargon, Osvaldo explained the sign. "*Compañera,*[5] somewhere in the world, there must be an electrical appliance for each household need. Therefore the statement is not an exaggeration."

"*Compañero,* I believe there are no appliances for popular consumption situated in this establishment because there are no "needs" in any household of our nation. Is that a fair assessment, *compañero?*"

"Affirmative, *compañera.* You obviously have learned from our political training. Congratulations."

"The ideas of one are for the good of all. Or something like that."

"Agh! Enough already!" Osvaldo covered his ears, grimacing.

We stopped for lunch at a historical place, a former mansion of colonial times, and were seated by a patio fringed by moss-covered *tinajones,* giant earthenware jars used since colonial times to gather rain water. In the past, the larger the *tinajón,* the more affluent the family was said to be. So enormous *tinajones* abound in yards and patios of Camagüey.

We went into a state of lethargy that normally follows an abundant *caldo gallego,*[6] and couldn't move for a while.

"Well, now what?" Osvaldo interrupted my somnolence.

"I've seen enough, but we have one more stop to make." I reached into my pocket. The envelope read "Ofelia Vidal," followed by an address.

Having lost track of the distance we had covered, we walked many blocks back to the car under a blazing sun. Fortunately, Camagüey is completely flat, which reduces strain, and we could walk on a shady sidewalk. The car, however, had been under direct sun for hours, so we had to open the doors and wait close to a half-hour before we could sit in it. We decided to freshen up at the hotel before searching for my godmother's friend.

---

[5] Comrade   [6] a Spanish porridge containing sausage and vegetables

A message from Zenaida[7] paralyzed us at the front desk. "I will call back," it said. We packed in silence, both wondering what Zenaida could be calling about that required her tracking us down to our hotel. She hadn't been kidding when she said she would be in touch.

As Osvaldo was ready to walk out of the room to load our bags in the car, I was called to the lobby to take the call. Zenaida had forgotten to tell me to report to Emigration Headquarters. "But we were just leaving," I protested.

"Look, all they do is write your name and passport number in a ledger as a method of control. It's all very silly, but you've got to do it."

Zenaida gave me directions, we finished packing and left. Annoyed, I parked across from the building and started walking. My eyes met those of a woman who looked very familiar She was observing me from the opposite sidewalk. I smiled and walked past her to enter the building and report to the authorities while Osvaldo waited outside.

The officers were extremely polite and cordial, in contrast to the way emigration officials treated us in Havana at the time we were trying to leave the country back in the sixties. We were then treated with despotism, smirks, and insulting remarks. Once, an officer intentionally flicked the ashes of his cigar on my mother's white shoes. She looked the other way and said nothing. She didn't even shake the ashes off her shoes until the officer was out of view. Any gesture of annoyance on my mother's part could have been interpreted as a sign of open hostility, and could easily place us at the bottom of the list, or the bottom of a cell. But now, Cuban exiles were welcome because they brought badly needed currency into the country. A woman in uniform greeted me warmly and invited me to sit. She asked me a few questions and copied my passport number on a ledger.

"All done already?" Osvaldo asked, surprised to see me return in less than ten minutes.

"As Zenaida said, it was no big deal." I reached in my pocket for the letter Godmother Clemencia had asked me to deliver. "Look, Oz, this address is right on this street. Let's get this over with, shall we?"

"Wait. Your twin is by the lamppost, looking this way." Osvaldo pointed her out to me. "I think she's waiting for you."

I turned to face the woman whose gaze had followed me down and across the street. She began to move in my direction, and I, too, walked toward her, moved by a curious feeling of recognition. Was she a cousin? We were now facing each other, and I could see some of my own features on her face. I wanted to hear her voice, though I somehow knew what it would sound like. "Do I know you?" I asked.

"I don't know. I was going to ask you the same thing." Her eyes were luminous.

"I am Ofelia Vidal," she said.

My name is Lara Canedo." I took her hand in mine.

She opened her eyes wide. "Lara Canedo? The daughter of Santiago Canedo?" Her voice went up in pitch. "I knew it! Something told me—" She let go of my hand,

---

[7] Zenaida—Cuban government official assigned to assist Lara during her stay in Cuba.

seemingly frightened by the touch. Then she swallowed, and tried to compose herself.

Instinctively I reached into my pocket and handed her the letter.

"You've been to see her," she said after looking at the envelope. "She didn't tell you?"

"Tell me what?" I asked, feeling impatient.

"Wait," she said, ripping the envelope open and reading the short letter.

What could my godmother be writing about? I was intrigued, but not worried. Then Ofelia looked up at me, "You've got to prepare yourself for a shock."

"I'm prepared," I said, sure that whatever she had to say was of great importance to her, but probably not for me. I was too far removed from her reality.

"Your father and mine were the same man."

My jaw dropped. The scene didn't strike me at first as something even remotely real. I blinked and swallowed hard, trying to recover from the realization of what this could mean.

"This is not a joke, is it?"

"I'm afraid not."

Wishing to deny the possibility, I thought she was crazy. But suddenly, everything else around me disappeared. There was just this woman in front of me, and I felt something opening up deep inside. Aunt Paula was in the roundness of her cheeks, my cousin Adela in her mouth, the shape of her teeth, and my godmother in the sparkling eyes. Then my mind kicked in, and I understood everything in spite my shock. Ofelia again seemed to hesitate as to whether she should touch me, but she stretched her hand. I could find no words for her, so I hugged her.

"I can't expect you to understand," she spoke softly. "I have a lot to tell you. Aunt Clemencia says you're ready, so we have to come to my house right now." She turned to Osvaldo, introduced herself while I simply stood there, and then turned to me.

"You see, my mother's name was Leticia Vidal. I'd be really surprised if you've never heard the name."

"I have. But you said she was?"

"She died two years ago. Of cancer," she replied, somewhat distant from her own words.

"I'm sorry." I said. "My mother also died two years ago."

"Some coincidence."

"Probably no more coincidence than our encounter." We stood there, looking at each other. Minutes before, I had no inkling of her existence, and now I needed to know where she had been all along, all my life. Had I expected that something like this would happen?

Why was I so ready to accept this woman into my heart, just because of whom she said she was? Why hadn't my godmother told me?

Our family resemblance was obvious. She looked like me more than any of my other siblings did. It seemed odd that nobody I had met so far had taken pleasure in shocking me with the truth. No one had made a point of showing me the dirt in my father's double life. My godmother knew all along, Mario and Nena had to know, and probably even Paquito knew. Perhaps they hadn't wanted to cloud my father's pristine memory, or my mother's dignity. But neither was among us to lose face in my knowledge, and I had met my half-sister on my own, in the street, regardless of Godmother Clemencia's set-up.

Walking toward her house, we looked at one another, pausing on facial details, expectantly. She was real, and beautiful. How could I allow myself to be hurt by the past, when the present looked like this? But naturally, I was hurt.

For years my mother had been tormented by rumors about a woman named Leticia who lived in Camagüey. I had eavesdropped on some conversations between her and Aunt Beatriz, and the tone hadn't escaped me. My mother sometimes received long distance calls from Camagüey that left her preoccupied and irritable for weeks. Those calls invariably coincided with my father's trips to San Venancio. Even as a child, I knew that someone was reporting on his whereabouts, though I didn't know why. My mother could do nothing but endure the pain of knowing him with someone else, and wait for his return, like so many other Cuban wives did at that time. She may have even been reduced to some solace in the fact that she was, after all, the wife. Remembering a time when I began to sense her despair, I finally understood the main reason for her suicidal threats. Leticia wasn't a rumor, she was flesh and bones, and I felt my mother's anguish in retrospect. Both women were now in peace, untouched by worldly concerns, and this encounter had to be seen independently from the past. In the larger plan there had to be a reason for this improbable event. The idea that I had a sister other than Isabel, and that I felt resentful for her existence, was all too disorienting. It was too late for a retreat into the safety of denial.

Osvaldo and I quietly followed a chatty Ofelia who seemed intent on exposing me to her reality. She and her family lived in a large colonial house in the Avenida de la Libertad, where my father had lived as a child for a year or two. He eventually owned the house, and at some point he added Leticia's name to the title, so Ofelia inherited it.

Ofelia's husband, Rodolfo, worked for the tourist industry and was at that time on one of his frequent trips to Havana. Her daughter, Letis, was a polite and attractive sixteen-year-old. Ofelia introduced me to her as a distant relative who was visiting from the United States.

We sat in the living room and uneasily proceeded to get further acquainted. Ofelia immediately suggested that Osvaldo and I stay with her that night.

"This is already the sixth day of my visit and I've a lot yet to accomplish," I explained, internally fighting a mixture of dread and curiosity, but mostly thinking of Casilda.[8]

"Stay for dinner, then. I have lots of noodles and some pork. That'll do."

She had the advantage of previous knowledge of my existence, but I held back the urge to ask how she came to know.

I found my new sister to be highly intelligent and humorous, curious as most Cubans about a lifestyle outside her reach, but dignified and fulfilled in her own. After I assured her that I wouldn't be upset, she went into her bedroom and reemerged with a box of photographs. So far, everyone had shown me photographs to refresh my memory and share in the past. But this was a past I had shared without

---

[8] Casilda—lifelong friend of Lara's, who stayed in Cuba. They correspond throughout the years.

knowledge, and though I felt cheated and profoundly injured, my curiosity prevailed and I kept my serenity.

"This is going to be a bore for you, Osvaldo." Ofelia smiled.

"No way! I love to look at photographs." Osvaldo moved closer to me on the couch, rubbing his hands together. "Nothing bothers me if it doesn't bother Lara."

"You know everything about my life, Oz. Now we'll learn this part together. Isn't that special?"

Ofelia moved about the room with agility, dragging the coffee table toward us, and then sitting with a bounce, like a child who anticipates a great deal of attention focused on her.

Pictures of my father as the head of a family other than mine passed in front of my eyes, clouding them with deep sadness I was struggling to hide. In those photos he was Ofelia's father, not mine. Clearly in his element, judging by his relaxed postures and a special air of inner satisfaction, he beamed. Leticia wasn't beautiful, but her sweet, tender expression was the opposite one would expect from a vixen. My father wore his country clothes, no suits, no ties, as if on vacation.

One of the photographs showed him holding Ofelia, then about two, above his head like a trophy. Leticia, her arms around his waist, looked up at the baby, laughing. I felt a piercing pain inside seeing my father happier with Leticia than he ever seemed to be with my mother. I had always been aware of the tension between my parents. There were many moments of harmony within a comfortable routine, but I knew, we all knew something wasn't right.

In viewing the pictures, many questions were answered, and many more were formulated in my mind. I felt compassion for my mother, for all of us, but strangely, mostly for my father. On the surface, his may have seemed the ideal life. He was handsome, successful, loved by two women, capable of supporting two families without any financial struggle. But for my father it must have been torture to keep such a huge secret from so many. Society, the law, pressure from his family, and a sense of duty kept him in Havana, away from where his heart was.

Anger and disappointment soon replaced the sadness as I looked into my father's face in those photographs. Were there any more brothers or sisters for me to meet? Had he been honest about anything in his life? Aware of my discomfort, Ofelia took the album from my hands and sat next to me. I was too flattened to talk, full of conflicting feelings toward my father, resenting him for his happiness away from us, and his disloyalty toward my mother, while I felt profoundly sorry for him at the same time.

Before my final decision to travel to Cuba, I was held back by the fear of discovering that my memories were mostly lies. I had just found the first one, and its enormity had eclipsed any other fear I might have harbored prior to my trip.

During the time when my father was in his prime, mistresses had been a sign of prosperity and status. But those hadn't been Papi's motives in relation to Leticia. Those photographs didn't lie. He was happy, comfortable; he felt loved. His feelings were not for me to judge, in spite of my pain. Once we were protected with dishonesty, but the truth has a way of surfacing, and I had to learn to face the truth as it was. My father must have been aware that not only the family, but even Mami pretended she didn't know, in order to save face.

"My mother knew that she couldn't compete with the status quo," Ofelia addressed my thoughts. "I envied you all from afar since about age ten, when my mother told me the truth. I was especially jealous of Isabel, who's closest to my own age."

Ofelia said that he visited them once a month during the late forties, fifties and early sixties. His excuse to my Mother was that he had to tend to the *finca*,[9] since many relatives had moved to Havana, and Aunt Paula and Uncle Celso couldn't manage by themselves. Occasionally he would bring all of us to San Venancio, perhaps in an effort to dispel my mother's suspicions. He would then leave us with Aunt Paula and go into town. That was until his business was confiscated. Then he couldn't splurge on a trip every month.

"The separation must have been very hard on you," I said, attempting to be generous.

"It was, especially when he died. We didn't even receive the news until five days after his burial. Aunt Clemencia came to tell us before she went to the funeral, but we were at the beach."

"Did she always know about you?"

"No. She approached me in the street, because she thought I looked so much like you."

"Was she very shocked?" I asked.

"If she was, she hid it well."

Our conversation revealed many unknown details for Ofelia, but not as many as for me. Leticia had come into our father's life years before my mother did. He wanted to marry her, but family opposition was too much. He was the oldest male of his generation and the future patriarch, and Leticia was a young widow of humble background. When my father met my mother, who was perceived as "good stock," his family was delighted, and immediately began to plan the wedding. My father buckled under the pressure, but wouldn't leave Leticia. My mother got pregnant immediately, and Isabel came to further subjugate my father. Ofelia was born two years later.

"Tell me about your other siblings. What are they up to?"

"Gabriel is a scientist who researches plants for medicinal purposes. He has published several articles on nutritional and medicinal uses for different kinds of plants and mushrooms. He now lives in San Francisco with his wife, who gives voice lessons and coaches opera singers."

"That's fascinating!" Ofelia exclaimed.

"They're a bit strange, but interesting nevertheless, both of them."

"Do they have any children?"

"No, and it's just as well. Neither of them has any parental skills anyway.

"How about Hector?"

"He's a commercial pilot, always traveling. No wife, no kids. He's a playboy."

"But you have never married or had children either. What does that make you?"

"A lesbian."

Ofelia bravely withstood the shock, needing only a second to recover. "What about him?" She pointed at Osvaldo, who by now was sound asleep on the sofa.

"It's a long story. We had something in the past."

---

[9] *Finca*—farm.

"Then you changed?"

"And how!" I said, laughing, seeking to ease the tension.

"But being a lesbian is not all there is to you, is it?"

"No. I've worked hard. Now I'm relaxing a bit more. I studied to be a psychologist, but ended up writing textbooks."

Ofelia listened closely to my abbreviated history, asking few questions. She later told me about her husband, her daughter, and her work as a librarian. She and her husband wanted to leave the country. "Rodolfo constantly fantasizes about life somewhere else. He's obsessed with finding a way out, always in search of connections that may one day allow us to go on a trip outside the island together. He has worked hard to earn his superiors' confidence. But we both know that travel arrangements for the whole family would be impossible. So he cultivated the friendship of a pilot who flies tourists between Havana and the Isle of Youth on a daily basis. They have planned an escape very carefully to the last detail, but everytime they set a date, something always comes up and we have to postpone our dash across the Florida Strait."

"That's so dangerous!" I shuddered. "You shouldn't talk about it with anyone."

I don't. This is the first time I have told anyone. Not even Aunt Clemencia knows."

"Can't you leave legally?"

"Not a chance. Rodolfo can't even think about it. He fears a shakedown of the tourist industry. The regime is focusing on that sector to revamp the economy, and when a particular sector receives special attention from high above, a re-organization usually follows, and heads roll. What if he's let go? This is our only hope."

They were in a very tight spot, and I was compelled to help, whatever my feelings about the situation might be. Ofelia wasn't the situation. She was someone very easy for me to love. "What can I do?"

"Nothing," she said, lowering her head. "We're not officially related."

"Who appears in your birth certificate as your father?"

Your father," she said, and we both laughed.

"Then, we're officially related on paper somewhere. I can claim you as a sister."

"That's a start," she smiled broadly.

My encounter with Ofelia emotionally overwhelmed me. As a recourse, I was reduced to distancing myself from all that I had learned in only a few hours. I didn't know what to think or feel, so I saved most ruminations for my return home, when I would be in more solid ground. The lie I had just uncovered hurt me deeply, but it wasn't Ofelia's fault, and her predicament hurt me as well. I could recognize more of me in her than I had ever been able to see in Isabel.

When it was time for me to leave, we held each other tight.

"Do we part as sisters?" she asked, holding back tears.

"Sisters," I said, meeting her eyes.

Discussion Questions

1. What stereotypical beliefs about Latino men are being explored in this piece?

2. How does Lara's return home serve to accentuate the differences between appearances and reality?

3. How is the definition of a *tinajón* related to the historical events that shaped Cuba in the last forty years?

4. What is the difference in tone and thematic concerns between Lara's return to her homeland and the narrator's return in Margarita Engle's *Singing to Cuba* on page 218?

5. Compare the relationship between the newfound sisters in this excerpt and that of the sisters in Ana Castillo's *So Far from God* on page 35. What do these relationships say about the importance of family in Latino literature?

José Yglesias

Beginning with A Wake in Ybor City *published in 1963 to his death in 1995, José Yglesias chronicled the lives of Cubans in exile and at home with compassion and insight. He was a tremendously prolific writer whose body of works include seven published novels, three collections of short stories, three works of nonfiction, several translations, and countless magazine and newspaper articles and reviews. Yglesias did not limit himself to works related to Cuba, as he also documented the lives of other Latin Americans and Europeans. Of particular note are* Down There *(1970), a series of interviews of people in Brazil, Chile, and Peru, as well as Cuba, and* The Franco Years *(1977), a book depicting several of the author's acquaintances during the years of the Spanish dictator's regime.*

Yglesias was born in Tampa and worked as a dishwasher, stock clerk, and typist. He served in the Navy during World War II and received the Naval Citation of Merit. His many awards include a Guggenheim Fellowship in 1970 and 1976 and a National Endowment for the Humanities Award in 1974.

The Guns in the Closet *is a collection of stories that were previously published and reissued posthumously in 1996. The two stories excerpted here show Yglesias at his best, describing the subtle complexities of family relationships.*

From The Guns in the Closet

The Place I Was Born

I am sixty; my mother is eighty. I live in New York City; she lives in Tampa. Until last year she lived in the section called Ybor City where Spanish speaking cigar makers settled more than a century ago. She spent her entire life in the old house that my grandparents moved to from Key West. She never budged from Tampa—not even during the Depression when many cigar makers went North looking for jobs—and getting her out of the family house took my brother, Eddie, and me years. He lives in Boise and is a few years younger—four, I think. Mother was sixty-three when Father died, and that is when we first began to talk to her about moving: a good part of Eddie's and my lives were spent on the subject, when you think about it.

I used to take turns with Eddie (Mother calls him Edmundo) coming to Tampa every other year to keep up what we called our two-pronged campaign. He would report on his lack of success on the phone after each trip, and I would always end that conversation with: "I wouldn't listen to you either—anybody that moves to Boise from Tampa, man, you're a two-time loser!"

Now that she has finally sold the old house at what she thought was a fair price, he and I have come on a visit at the same time. A kind of celebration. (Our wives stay out of all this, particularly visiting Florida or one another or Mother.) Mother now lives with her sister, also a widow, in one of those apartment buildings for retirees sponsored by some Protestant denomination or the other, but the old house is as much on her mind as ever. Our first morning there and she wants to be taken to it, not the *Centro Asturiano*[1] Cemetery where our father is buried.

She considered it some sort of negligence that the young, black couple did not think to stay home that day. Not that she had called them: Latins believe it is bad manners to give advance notice that you are coming by, as if you were asking them to go to the trouble of entertaining them. Before she left the car, she looked at the unmowed lawn and her lips became thin.

"If I had a daughter," she said after circling the house on foot and finding other faults, "every last room in this house would have been filled and I would not have sold it . . ."

"Forget about it, Mom," Eddie said. "Let's go eat one of those Cuban mixed sandwiches—there's nothing else in Tampa."

"Forget about it?" she said.

The house began as a shotgun house, but a third bedroom was added, then a little back room that in time was called the TV room, and finally a wrap-around porch. During the war, the shed became a carport with what is called a utility room attached. The yards in front and in back of our house were a tiny bit larger than the rest on the block, but not much more. When I was a kid there were sweet banana trees along the back fence; later, orange or grapefruit; finally, a camphor tree. In front, two palm trees always.

She had kept everything in the house too clean for its own good. She wore out tile and linoleums and paint jobs from washing them with strong soaps, not from use. The annuals and the perennials were urged mightily to grow and bloom. She fertilized and mulched. She watered and trimmed, and she fought the holly which she felt grew at too fast and wild a pace. The moment a frond of either of the palm trees out front began to wither, off it went. She did all this herself. No one, of course, had ever been hired to come in and clean; no one was allowed either to mow the tiny lawn or to garden but she.

She also cooked and baked too much. All Spanish and Cuban dishes and desserts. And each time, of course, the oven had to be scrubbed clean. Eddie had

---

[1] Asturian Center: Asturias is a region in Spain.

bought her a dishwasher, but she did not trust it. Finally, she began to admit that washing down the big porch and its walls with scrub brush and hose was hard on her arthritic pains. Two years and a half ago, her sister was widowed, and she caved in: they would move in together. But neither would move into the other's house and that is how we got them to apply to the church-sponsored apartment building in the Hyde Park area. She was self-conscious about abandoning Ybor City for the good part of town where, as they used to say, the Americans lived, and did not tell many people about her move.

She called a realtor that a neighbor's relative had once used, and then the real struggle began. Whereas in the past it was Eddie and I who called her every other week or so, she now began to call us regularly to complain about the realtor, to make declarations about what she would do with the rooms full of furniture and linens and china, and to find fault with the people who came by to look at the house. Also, to question the motives of the younger cousins who now came by to visit her.

"I didn't like the way your cousin Yvonne was asking what I planned to do with the porch furniture," she once began a conversation, and ended up saying, "Everything is going to be for sale. I'm going to have one of those garage sales and pick up a penny or two. It's time I started thinking about myself."

That was during a call to me. Two days later, she called Eddie to tell him that she did not like the idea of a garage sale. It was mercenary and bothersome, she said. Eddie said she was not obliged to have a garage sale, and she hinted that I was expecting her to hold one instead of calling Goodwill and having them cart off everything.

"Anyway, I must give something or the other to each and every member of the family," she said. "I owe a lot of favors."

Eddie called me, and at first he seemed to believe that I had brought up the subject with her and urged the garage-sale solution on her. "Why would I?" I said to Eddie finally, and he came up with a laugh not an apology. That irked me.

"A garage sale would only prolong the agony," I said. "Think of all the phone calls about what to price each item!"

Mother had never been anything but straightforward and truthful in her ways, but we learned not to take any development in the sale of the old house at face value. Was the realtor as sneaky as she said? Did he practically force her to absorb closing costs for Damon Thigpen? Should she give Mrs. Thigpen the refrigerator and kitchen table and chairs as if it were part of the sale price?

"If I'm giving a gift," she said, "I'm giving a gift, not the realtor getting the credit for making it part of the sale price."

Eddie was on the whole laid-back about these matters, but I occasionally commented on her arguments, and it all eventually got reported to Eddie as *my* arguments.

"Part of the sale price?" I said to her. "People usually throw in the stove, but that's all."

Eddie called. "Why don't you let the old lady give them whatever she wants?" he began, and then laughed. "I fell for it! I fell for it! I owe you."

I reminded him of it that day when she stepped across the street to talk to Corona before going to La Tropicana. "You're paying for the sandwiches," I said.

Corona had known us most of our lives, so we had to greet her, too. She said, "They are in trouble. Not from anything they have said directly to me, but from what I hear."

Corona had a way of sounding mysterious about non-Latins. She would not admit that although she had come to Ybor City from northern Spain when she was sixteen, she still did not, forty years later, speak English. She consequently reported their doings and their conversations with a great deal of indirection, so as not to give herself away.

"More trouble," Mother said. "Ah, me. Let us not discuss it anymore."

Corona did not spare her: "It would not surprise me if they are selling it."

On the way to La Tropicana, Mother enumerated the things she had done for the couple. The closing costs she had paid at the realtor's suggestion; but giving them the kitchen set and the porch furniture was her own idea. "I would have given them the hanging plants, too, except his wife hinted about them and no nice person does that."

In the parking lot of La Tropicana, Eddie said, "It's their house now, Mom—how they keep it is their business.

"You never had a drop of sentiment in you," she said.

She took time off from worrying about the fate of the house to point out that the ham in her sandwich had not been glazed. "Do you see that old-fashioned iron they used to glaze it with? They always kept it right behind the counter by the big hams. Like the iron my mother used on clothes. They're too busy serving all these crackers who don't know any better."

She believed it was the wife who neglected the house. She had never really cared about it. "I do not think she would like any house," Mother said, "but he was different. It does not have anything to do with their being Negroes."

I said, "Who said anything about that?"

"And the real Cuban mixed sandwiches do not have lettuce and tomatoes," she said. "You are taking me back to the house when we finish here."

Mr. Thigpen was sitting on the porch steps, his head in his hands, as if posing for a picture of dejection. Eddie and I had never met him, but he hardly had the energy to respond to our self-introduction. Mother had not done it; she was eager to get on to what interested her.

"You going to sell the house?" she said.

"I can't keep up the payments," he said.

"It looks terrible," she said. "Nobody will buy it the way it looks now."

"I'm just going to let the bank take it over," he said, sounding angry himself. "I already missed the payment last month."

Mother threw a hand up, the way she used to when she was impatient with Eddie or me.

"Your wife ought to go out and get a job," Mother said.

He must have had a lot of complicated feelings about his wife: he did not say anything, only looked away.

Mother turned her back on him and headed for our car.

Eddie actually said, "Good luck, Mr. Thigpen."

Mother decided to speak to Corona first. Thigpen went back to sitting on the steps. Corona in turn walked her over to our car.

Corona said, "They are not frugal like us."

Without saying anything to us, Mother crossed the street again. We saw her open her pocketbook and take out her wallet. Thigpen got up and shook his head. She stared at him and stopped counting bills from the wallet. She said something emphatic and shook her head and came back to us.

She said, "Come, it is time to go."

Corona stepped back and then waved as I drove off.

At the corner, Thigpen's wife turned into the block driving an old pickup truck. The kids were in back.

"Maybe if I talked to her . . ." Mother said.

This time I said, "Forget it."

Mother did not let us take the freeway which takes you to Hyde Park in five minutes. We no longer argued about it; I stayed on the old city streets and I have to admit you see more that way. I said that to Eddie and he added, "If you want to see more of this town."

We were barely out of Ybor City when Mother said, "I know what I will do—I will buy the house."

"No, you won't," Eddie said.

I said, "What makes you think the bank will sell it to you at a reasonable price."

I saw Eddie disagreed but kept himself from saying so.

"Turn around," she said. "I want to go to the bank, and talk to them right now."

Eddie slowed down but kept heading west on Columbus.

"You buy that house and you won't have any money left for yourself," Eddie said, and accelerated without meaning to. "Tell her." He looked at me for support.

"How do you know?" Mother said to Eddie. "You do not know the state of my finances."

Eddie parked on a worrisome street. He said, "You don't have to go to the bank, you can buy it from him."

What the hell, it was the place I was born. I said, "We could buy it together. But you do not move back there."

"How do I explain it to my wife?" Eddie said.

"You talked her into marrying you," I said.

"I will leave it to you when I die," Mother said. "You can tell her it is a very good investment."

"You're never going to die," Eddie said, but he was already making a U-turn.

"You leave this to me," Mother said. "I will ask him what is a rental he can meet. And if it suits me, I will let him be the tenant. He knows he cannot fool around with me—one month he does not pay and he is evicted."

Eddie said, "I pity them," and I did not contradict him.

Still thinking ahead, Mother said, "Another day I'll show her how to wash down the porch and sides with the hose I gave them."

Celia's Family

Celia heard the phone begin ringing before she opened the door to her small apartment in the Tampa Episcopalian Bayshore House. Lydia, she announced to the empty living room. She took time to put down the basket of folded, clean clothes on the sofa and to sigh deeply. Only then, as if fortified, she picked up the phone.

Lydia said, "Where were you? I called two times—"

"I don't know," Celia, said. "Maybe I was downstairs doing the laundry—"

"Well, I called and called," Lydia said, "and there wasn't any answer every time."

"Okay," Celia conceded, but sounded critical.

No reply from Lydia. That was a plus. Lydia got it. She wasn't dumb; she knew she was being snubbed. At times like this—and Lydia called every morning and evening—Celia swore she could hear her cousin thinking during the pauses: casting about for something to ask, hoping for news, imagining there was some activity planned or going on from which she was being excluded.

And, of course, there always was: there were too many cousins in their family for Lydia to be up-to-date on their doings. Twenty-one first cousins, to be exact. And they had forty-nine children, none of whom were Celia's and all of whom consequently were like close nieces and nephews to her.

"Anything happened?" Lydia asked, as if that were her reason for calling. "I haven't heard from anybody."

"You didn't hear Bush lost? Celia said. "Thank God."

"I didn't mean that," Lydia said quickly. "I knew that happened."

"You wouldn't hear it from those Cuban refugees of yours," Celia said. "They are probably in mourning."

"They do not talk about politics," Lydia said, waited a moment, and then added, "very much."

Celia sighed. "Is that so?"

"Not to me," Lydia said. "Not to me."

Celia sighed again. "You called to talk about them?"

"Me?" Lydia said. "Me!"

"Calm down, Lydia," Celia said.

"They live across the street," Lydia said. "I cannot do something about that."

"Please," Celia said.

With an intake of breath, Lydia got to the point. "Are you and Lola going out to the Tropicana?"

Celia recognized her grasp for what it was—intrepidity—and tried to throw her off—or, at least, make her work harder for an answer. She said, "Today?"

"I think so," Lydia said. "From something she said I figured it must be today."

"You were talking to Lola today?"

Lydia confessed, "Yes. She happened to call."

Celia said, "She called you?"

"I think so," Lydia said. "Maybe I did. I don't stand on ceremony."

Celia said, "Then why didn't you ask her?"

"You know how Lola is . . . you wouldn't think she is a sister, sometimes. You and I are cousins, but you are more of a sister than her."

"If Lola and I are going to have a Cuban sandwich at La Tropicana, she ought to know about it," Celia said. She waited. "At least as much as me."

"I have not had a good mixed sandwich in—in, at least, a month," Lydia said. "That's how long. I have no way of getting over to La Tropicana. Or anywhere."

"It's only a week since your car got dented," Celia said. "To hear you talk, people would think you are in a wheelchair."

"More," Lydia said.

"More?"

"That's how long the car has been with the body man," Lydia said. "It was another week before that when the boy hit me in the Tampa Bay Mall."

"Two weeks," Celia said.

"Two weeks?"

Celia said, "One week and one week makes two weeks."

"In my situation—I can't stand it—it seems like forever," Lydia said. She sighed but sounded angry rather than poignant. "It's not like living in your building. All those nice ladies on every floor, you always have company."

Celia could say a lot about that, but decided not to. They had had that conversation before, too.

"Or you can go down to the lobby. There is always somebody there. Or go to the hobby room."

"Don't play on my sympathies," Celia said. "Just come right out and say it: Take me to the Tropicana with you, poor little me."

"Why do you always have to put things that way?" Lydia said. "We weren't taught—"

"What way? What way?"

"So rough," Lydia said. 'You wouldn't know we were brought up together. Your mother—she was as good as my mama, too, remember—she would not like it one bit. She was sweet."

"Mama always told the truth," Celia said. "Right out. And she wouldn't be friends with no Cuban refugees. They're not refugees, they're counter-revolutionaries."

"They are not friends, they are neighbors—"

"It doesn't sound like that to me."

"I come out the door and they are there. What am I to do? Front door, back door, it doesn't matter. Friends!"

"What do you want?"

"There, there! That's what I mean. You are so rough." There was a little squeak at the other end which meant Lydia was working herself up to a sob.

Celia waited a moment, but it was no use. She placed a hand over the phone and said a bad word.

"Celia, Celia!" Lydia called. "Are you there?"

Celia made a noise.

"Celia, are you gonna pick me up?" Lydia said. "Will you tell Lola I'm coming? Maybe you don't have to tell her. Why should you? We're all family. Just pick me up. You are so good."

"I'll call you back," Celia said. "Nothing was definite. Just be ready."

"I am ready, I am always ready," Lydia said. "I'll sit on the porch and wait for you. You are the only good one in the family."

"I'll call you first," Celia said. "Maybe nothing will happen. I don't know."

Celia began with Lola by saying Lydia had called, and Lola immediately screamed.

"I haven't slept all night!" Lola said. "It's her doing and I'm sure she slept like the angel she is not."

"What? What?" Celia said, and began to laugh; that was Lola's gift, laughter.

"She called Leslie!" Lola said. "Would you believe it?"

"In Miami?"

"She reported me to my own daughter!" Lola said. "She told Lola that I treat her very mean."

"She told Leslie—"

"My own daughter. And Leslie believed her. Think of that. Leslie believed her. Would you believe it?"

Celia said, "I believe it," and felt much better.

She added, "Lydia can put on an act. I tell everyone in our family when she makes trouble, but I don't think I have convinced . . ."

"I didn't sleep all night," Lola said. "I didn't convince Leslie either. On both counts—I didn't convince her it was treachery for Lydia to call her, and I didn't convince her I was not mean."

Celia laughed.

"You want to hear all the things I thought up last night? First, I thought I would shoot Lydia dead," Lola said. "Get Cuco's old gun, which must be all rusty now, and shoot her there in her yard among all the weeds."

The image of Lydia's unmowed yard—all the cousins deplored it—made Celia laugh louder.

"Second, shoot Leslie, too."

And again Celia laughed.

"Don't laugh too much," Lola said. "She is my daughter, after all. Even if she is dumb."

That last was true, but of course she would never have said so.

"It's about time that old gun got used," Lola said. "Poor Cuco, may he rest in peace. Always worrying about burglars and he never got to use it, thank God."

"What did she tell Leslie?" Celia said, not wishing to comment on Cuco either. As she had told herself many a time, Lola has really needed her sense of humor.

"That I am mean to her, that I have no sisterly feelings, that I didn't take her to the Westshore Mall—that was last week when I yelled at her—though she is the oldest and deserving of much respect. Oh, God, what else? Also about last Sunday— I didn't pick her up and take her to that Protestant church she goes to, like a fool. I shouldn't say that."

"She knows better than to ask me to take her to any church," Celia said. "She is always feeling sorry for herself. But she doesn't stop a moment; she is always out."

"And she watches the soap operas too much," Lola said. "That's what I think."

Celia added, "And it's ridiculous for her to be going to a Protestant church at her age—I don't know what's happened to people."

Lola interrupted. "No, I tell you what it is. She went over to live with your family when mama went to the TB sanitarium and she stayed on and then married, so after she was ten she never lived with us. Of course, I don't feel as close to her as my other sisters."

Lola laughed after a pause. "That's not true," she said. "I feel closer to you and we never lived under the same roof."

Celia said, "She's just a pain, let's face it."

"Poor thing," Lola said, and laughed again.

"I guess I better pick her up then," Celia said.

"Oh, God, would you?" Lola said. "I'll meet you at La Tropicana. If I pick her up, I am going to get into a fight despite all my resolutions. This way it will be in public and I can act like a lady."

"That's okay," Celia said.

"I decided I wouldn't say a word to her. I decided this after a whole night of thinking, while I was having my café con leche this morning. Rise above it. Be a lady."

Celia laughed.

"You know, like American women. Upper class not white trash. You know what I'm saying—Latins don't rise above anything. We're in there swinging all the time. I embarrass myself whenever—"

"You don't mean that," Celia said. "Our mothers—"

"Your mother, not mine," Lola said, and laughed and laughed. "My mother was always yelling she had too many kids. And she cursed."

"The things you say, Lola," Celia said, and forgave Lola for going to all those fashion shows at ten dollars a head just to socialize and gossip and for lunching with her silly friends as if they were all still in high school. "Your mother suffered a lot."

"Poor thing," Lola said. "But not another word or I'll ruin my mascara."

That had become a signal for laughter with them, although Lola did wear mascara and it was unthinkable that Celia should.

"Though I have to tell you," Lola continued, "that it's a good thing to curse. It's better than an aspirin. I do it all the time when I am alone and there's nobody to hear me. I got into the habit with Cuco; he didn't like women to talk like men."

Celia murmured, "Yes, yes," although she had heard Lola confess this often.

"Celia?" Lola said in a small voice. "It was me who called Lydia, after all. I let her get to me; I didn't act like a lady. I can't lie to you."

"She said you called her," Celia said, "and that's how she figured out we were going to La Tropicana."

"La Tropicana? I didn't say a word about La Tropicana. I said a lot of things about her, but not a word about La Tropicana." Lola screamed again. "I said I was going to shoot her if she ever called Leslie again."

"No, you're not," Celia said. "Nobody's ever going to shoot Lydia. Not you or me. In fact, we are going to take her to La Tropicana and God knows where else, want to bet?"

Still gurgling with laughter, Lola said, "You know that old expression the men had—you're going to be wearing your ass in a sling? That's what I said. I don't know how it came to me; I haven't heard it in years. I was going to tell you all about it at lunch."

Celia said, "The lunch is ruined."

"I'm going to eat all my dessert," Lola said. "That will frustrate her. And don't you leave anything on your plate either. Let her starve."

"It's curious," Celia said. "She never said a word to me that you had scolded her. She told me you had called her and I didn't believe her. I thought it was the other way round."

"I call her sometimes," Lola said, and fell quiet.

Neither said anything for a moment.

Celia said, "I don't see how you can stand to have lunch with her. Today, anyway. You want me to call it off?"

Almost simultaneously, Lola said, "You know what it is, don't you—she doesn't want to die alone."

"She'll never die; she'll bury us both."

Lola said, "She is eighty-four."

"Eighty-four?" And Celia could see Lola at the other end nodding in her pitying way.

Lola said, "Poor thing."

Celia said, "She always wins."

"I'm calm now," Lola said. "It's always so good for me to talk to you—I don't have any sense. You're the sensible one in the family."

"Oh, I don't have any sense either," Celia said, but she accepted the compliment—another of Lola's gifts.

She then said, "I'll call Lydia and, tell her to wait for me. If I can reach her—she's probably across the street being chummy with those refugees."

"Everyone talks to them now, Celia," Lola said. "You know, no one thinks about all that anymore."

Yes, but not she.

Celia sat down on the sofa after speaking to Lola, meaning to achieve some sort of calm herself before calling Lydia to say she would come by at twelve-thirty. Before she got comfortable, it occurred to her that she was the loser in all this: it was more out of the way for her than for Lola to pick up Lydia, and she would undoubtedly end up paying the whole bill at La Tropicana. Never mind why that's so, she said aloud to the wall across the room with all the family pictures she had so carefully framed over the years—uncles and aunts, parents and grandparents, and all the people of her generation and the next. It's too complicated to explain, she added, just take my word for it. If Lola has one fault of character, it's that she's tight.

Yes, tight, and she got up to shake off the thought. It was not a nice one.

She stopped a moment in the middle of the room and looked out the picture window. The undulating shore of the bay stretched out ahead towards Ballast Point. All through her childhood in Ybor City, the Latino section of town—even until four years ago when she moved in here—she had always seen the bayshore from the window of a car. With wonder and awe as a child.

With feelings of social inferiority as she grew older. With acceptance, finally, that the bayshore was where the rich live and not she.

And yet here I am, she said to the picture window, living on social security, and then turned back to the phone, ready now to call Lydia. After all, she said, and never finished the thought. The phone rang as she stretched her hand towards it. Oh, she said, startled, Oh, and it was a moment before she got it to her ear. Her cousin Elvira's voice was already in the middle of a greeting.

"Hello, hello," she replied happily: it was a good sign that Elvira was able to call.

Elvira said, "Who is this?" She sounded stern, but Celia knew better.

"This is Celia," she said. "It's good to hear from you, Elvira dear, I was meaning to call myself."

"Celia?"

"Yes?"

Celia did not know, at moments like this, whether to wait and let the wheels of memory click into place for Elvira—or to rush ahead with talk and make it easier for her.

She rushed ahead with talk. "The reason I was going to call is that next time we should do something, not just sit in your patio. I was thinking it would be nice if I came by and took you off to La Tropicana."

She waited for only a second when Elvira did not reply.

"Remember how we cousins used to get together and eat Cuban sandwiches until we burst? I ate as much as the boys. Now, I can hardly eat a whole one."

She waited a little longer for Elvira this time.

"How times goes by. No one lives in Ybor City anymore," she finally said to fill the void.

In a thin voice Elvira said, "Ybor City?"

Celia laughed a false laugh. "Where all the Latinos and the cigar factories were neck and neck. I mean, no one in our family lives there anymore, do you realize that? You can't tell us from regular crackers."

She laughed again and again, but it sounded false, and she did not hear her cousin hang up.

"Elvira?" she said. "Elvira, I got an idea—why don't I come right now and pick you up and we'll—"

Elvira, she said to the picture window when she was sure Elvira was no longer listening. I did something wrong. Why did I say, Do you realize that . . . It was the wrong thing to say to, one in her condition. Elvira is too sweet to hang up on me.

She also should not have said that about time passing by. She should have been smarter than that, been more thoughtful. Time was disappearing for Elvira.

And her time with Elvira was also disappearing, along with everything else in Elvira's mind. She stood in the middle of the room and swayed a little, feeling insubstantial. This evanescence was worse than death. Worse than her husband's death. With death, things ended, came to a stop, but they were there, they did not disappear. It was history, you referred to them, you said *May he rest in peace,* as she did about Julio every time she mentioned his name.

She held the phone to her ear for a long while, but Elvira had, indeed, disappeared. She placed the phone back on its cradle carefully, and walked over to the wall of photographs. Elvira was there—she and Elvira at age four sitting on the swing at Elvira's home on Ybor Street. They used to fly back and forth on it, madly pushing on the floor simultaneously on the downswing. *Let it rain, let it rain*! they sang in Spanish with shrill abandon, *The Virgin's in the cave*!

One rainy Saturday, on Lydia's first payday at the factory, they were shrieking on the swing and Lydia showed up and gave them a quarter each. A quarter!

What a terrible person I am, Celia said aloud. She walked with energy to the phone and rang Lydia. After three rings, she lost her eagerness to reach her and began to think that she had long ago repaid that quarter. She did not count the number of times she let Lydia's phone ring. She gave her enough time to walk in from the porch. Enough time to get home from the Cuban refugees, if the truth be told.

When she put the phone down, it rang immediately. It was Lola. She had thought it over and she hoped that Celia could come pick her up after she had picked up Lydia. "I don't trust myself to drive today," she said. "I'll sit in back and it won't be necessary to say anything and have a fight."

"Sure, sweetheart," Celia said. "I just called her and she was not there. If she's not on the porch when I come by, I won't wait. I'll just go on over to your house."

"Maybe I should call her?" Lola said.

"No, no, don't bother, she's given you enough trouble for one day," Celia said. "Life shouldn't be so complicated."

"Yes, let's hope she's not there and we can have a simple good time like we planned," Lola said, and laughed her infectious laugh. "Right?"

"Right," Celia said lightheartedly. She even laughed the laugh Lola always inspired, but as soon as she hung up and was left with her own self, she began to doubt. Now, she would be picking up both of them at each one's home and doing all the driving and paying for the whole lunch.

She looked at the wall of the family photographs and said, Being good doesn't come easy to me, and walked inside determinedly to select a cheery blouse to wear to lunch.

Discussion Questions

1. What details about Cuba are presented throughout the story "The Place I Was Born"? How do these details aid in our understanding of the mother's behavior regarding her house?

2. Describe the kind of world that Celia lives in. Pay particular attention to the conversation she has with Lola on pages (000–000). What does Lola mean when she says "Latins don't rise above anything"?

3. Compare the relationship between the narrator and his mother in "The Place I Was Born" and Nilda and her mother in the excerpt from Nicholasa Mohr's novel on page 000.

4. In what way is the mother's behavior regarding her house similar to Esperanza's in Cisneros's *The House on Mango Street* on page 000?

Poetry

Gustavo Pérez-Firmat

Author and literary critic Gustavo Pérez-Firmat was born in Cuba in 1949 and immigrated to the United States in 1960. He lived and taught in North Carolina at Duke University for many years in the Department of Modern Languages. He currently holds an endowed Chair at Columbia University in New York City. His many nonfiction publications include Literature and Liminality: Festive Readings in the Hispanic Tradition *(1982);* Idle Fictions; The Hispanic Vanguard Novel, 1926–1934, *(1993);* The Cuban Condition: Translation and Identity in Modern Cuban Literature *(1988);* Cuban Literature *(1989); and* Life on the Hyphen: The Cuban-American Way *(1994).*

Firmat's wit and intense interest in linguistic nuances is revealed in his poetry. Reminiscent of the seventeenth-century English metaphysical poets, Firmat employs pun and paradox, as he displays a command of both languages. The speaker in many of his poems, living life "on the hyphen," often grapples with the ambivalence of belonging to two seemingly disparate worlds. The following poems selected from Bilingual Blues *(1995) reveal the existential angst common to many Cuban exiles. Few writers, however, are able to express this crisis with such cleverness and fluidity.*

Bilingual Blues

Soy un ajiaco[1] *de contradicciones.*[2]
I have mixed feelings about everything.
Name your *tema,*[3] I'll hedge:
name your *cerca,*[4] I'll straddle it
like a *cubano.*

I have mixed feelings about everything.
Soy un ajiaco de contradicciones.
Vexed, hexed, complexed,
hyphenated, oxygenated, illegally alienated,
psycho soy, cantando voy:[5]
You say tomato,
I say *tu madre;*[6]
You say potato,

---

[1] a kind of beef stew   [2] contradictions   [3] theme   [4] fence   [5] I am psycho, I go singing   [6] your mother

I say *Pototo*[7]
Let's call the hole
un hueco, the thing
a *cosa,* and if the *cosa* goes into the *hueco,*
consider yourself at home,
consider yourself part of the family.
Soy un ajiaco de contradicciones.
un potaje de paradojas,[8]
a little square from Rubik's Cuba
que nadie nunca acoplará.[9]
(Cha-cha-cha.)

Dedication

The fact that I
am writing to you
in English
already falsifies what I
wanted to tell you.
My subject:
how to explain to you
that I
don't belong to English
though I belong nowhere else,
if not here
in English.

Discussion Questions

1. The speaker in "Bilingual Blues" calls himself a "porridge of paradoxes." About what and in what way does this phrase apply to the speaker?

2. What is the overall effect of the use of code-switching throughout "Bilingual Blues"?

3. What is the speaker in "Dedication" saying about the role of language in his life? Relate this to his life in a physical as well as a metaphysical way.

4. In what way is the speaker's thoughts in both of these poems about duality related to the little sister's life as opposed to his own in Elias Miguel Muñoz poem on page 264?

5. What are the similarities between "Dedication" and Tato Laviera's poem "my graduation speech" on page 441?

---

[7] a Cuban 1950s comic who specialized in wordplay   [8] porridge of paradoxes   [9] that no one will figure out

Pablo Medina

PABLO MEDINA'S poetry is much like his fiction: unassuming yet powerful.
Pork Rinds and Cuban Love Songs *(1975) was the first book of poetry originally written in English published by a Cuban-American writer. The two poems selected here only hint at the poetic abilities of this gifted writer. In "The Exile" the speaker's connection to the past, a staple of Cuban-American literature, is presented through powerful imagery; visual, auditory, and tactile. The longer "Winter of a Rose" traces the speaker's exile, disillusionment, and eventual renewal.*

The Exile

He returned to grass two feet tall
around the house, a rope dangling
from the oak, an absence of dogs.
The year had neither ended nor begun,
the sun had yawned away the rain
and worms were drying on the ground.

Memories floated down from the trees: cane fields,
the smokehouse and its hanging meats,
breeze of orange and bamboo, a singing at dawn.

"Will you be with me?"
The voice came from the river. The jasmine
bloomed in the garden, he hiding,
he sweating under the moon
wanting to say I will I will and more.

There were stones all over the yard smelling of time.
He picked a few, threw them down the well
and listened to the water swallowing.

It made him smaller. He walked out the gate
and closed it behind him, wiped the sweat from his
eyes, felt his feet settling on the road.

Winter of a Rose

1

Of America
record sprint through history
we talked and dreamed

racing down highways wider than oceans:
Buicks and apples,
high schools, phonographs,
super athletes and their women
sleek like cats;
suburbs young and green and open
where children tricycle
through dusk and housewives cook
slow steaming dinners as the sun goes down;

land of factories and lilacs
and locomotives churning through the snow
where bearded voices sing of everything growth
and the chest grows big with the self.

2

Five in the morning
New Year's my father charged
into the room his mouth
exploding with headlines:

"*Batista's*[1] fallen
and gone to Spain!"
By midmorning the whole city
was a hurricane,
the mountains bristled
with beards and young men
like olive gods.

For the first time there was talk of peace and island,
talk of palm trees,
fierce faces,
smiles of future
droning in on tanks
garlanded with women and children
who saw their games reeling before them.

3

Some looked cautiously out of windows.
Behind the shutters slow old angers
pumped themselves
into rock.
Wept diamonds cut glass
until it showed only the past:

---

[1] Fulgencio Batista was the Cuban dictator overthrown by Fidel Castro in 1959.

Baccarat, Limoges, the ballerina
twirling stiffly in the drawing room,
servants glistening like teacups,
the sweet melancholy of cognac,

delicate wrists misting gently
with the conversation of last fall's
European tour—and oh how brilliantly
they fear now and hide beneath their shawls.

4

There is a photograph
of my father, mother,
sister and me going up
the steps to the plane
all smiling, I holding
a book my great-uncle
had given me on Oriental art.

Be free to learn.
Only that is good.
He said.

It was cold in New York.
New words made dough in my car.
The sky closed over my head.

When I made it to school
they thought I didn't
have a mind in English and if
you don't have a mind in English
you have a mind in nothing

Secretly I read Poe in the ninth floor
of that hotel that smelled
of widows with their skirts up,
discovered dankness in closets,
tubed hands in a boring bathroom.

5

Winter of concrete and brick,
winter of cars rumbling
desperately for love,
winter of whores like houses
painted over twenty times,
winter of the tear turned ice,

winter of a thousand urinals
and a man in a corner
with the whirling eye of need,
winter of subways rolling home,
scream and crash, scream and crash,
winter of frowns,
winter of sweats,
winter of a rose
on a girl's coat
plastic
and safe.

6

As far as you can go
in any direction
it is the same.
As if distance kept pulling itself
inside out, you are bound
to find yourself
eating dinner crosstown
copied right down
to the mole in your check,
or sunning yourself in a beach
and your face bloops out of waves
the same way in the other direction
and soon you realize
everything leaves you behind, always
the same looking at yourself
going home with a shovel
to dig for roots.

This place is full of dark holes
with the same frightened creature in them.

7

Enter the church.
Belief in rock,
in the flame of knowledge,
singe of flesh.

Pleasures sink,
the flame flickers:

every morning I loved
the only flesh allowed,
wood over the silence of marble.

Alone I wanted
bread to turn
human on the tongue.

The nave answered only its size,
waft of incense clouding the downturned face,
prayers brittle and cracked on the floor,
voices in a hollow skull:

*Introibo ad altare mei.**

8

Hunger for warmth
hunger for cold
hunger for history of candies
and the breasts they silhouette
hunger for the veins of virgins
and their fillets and their sweats
hunger for the lyres of spring
and suburban houses where accountants sing
and the breath of widows with their swollen shins

hunger for blindness and bishops and pens
hunger for whispers hunger for scents
and the dreams of janitors on the graveyard shift
and the housewife with a groaning mate
hunger for clocks and bathrooms and navels
and magazines and lentils

hunger for pubic clouds and pubic rain
hunger for wind and lanceolate leaves
and evergreen forests
and lips
and tongues
and gullets.

The city roars
the sun retreats
a child next door is weeping

9

Leaning against the steel
and glass
insurance building

---

* Enter into my altar.

America
is the fluid
in that man's mind
that lusts
for elsewhere
and the trees wave their song
the girl chased
by her skirt
to where a wall stands
unclimbable and stark and
the trees wave their song
is a dark street
that clamps out hope
distance burgeoning
behind the wall
if she stops
the dress falls
naked and tender
and alone
the mind's man lusts
and the trees wave their song

10

I ran
to lips so soft they smelled of clouds,
to the blindness of touch,
the welcome of brine.

I became water,
I became shore
rivered in until I lost myself:

trees, grass, hills
defining distance,
insects that devour it,
rain and birds
somewhere green,

a silent beautiful body
smiles of me:
sweet gash,
bone in my throat,
the farther I reach the more
I discover your winds,
your rabid storms,

gush of warmth,
tropic word

furrowing urge in
a wing's flight to long continents,
after the blind wreck
we
cloak with sleep
backs curved
to resemble ripe fruit

bite between us.

11

Would it were definable this
weave past waves, this dolphin need
voyage home from a vast
stark solitude,
the vision straight
like the thin green edge
you sail to:
each discovery a gust of wind.

Let the night grow deep
like a church and see
the candle's wax in melting
pull the morning in

a word made a thin
fresh wafer on the lips

a landscape like a body
warming you:
morning
come window-crashing
on your loneliness.

Snuggle your shores
between oceans
stretch the tongue so
the sun never sets

on the island
like the arm of a lover asleep

on God who is light catechized

on the sea
that echoes back a dream:

I am alive

<h2 style="text-align:center">Discussion Questions</h2>

1. Who or what is the voice that comes from the river in "The Exile"?
2. Trace the development of the speaker in "Winter of a Rose." How does the speaker feel about his self-identity at its conclusion?
3. In what way is imagery used in "The Exile" that is similar to the way it is employed in Virgil Suarez's story "*La Ceiba*: Tree of Life" on page 206?
4. How does time function in "The Exile" in a way that is similar to the way it functions in Gary Soto's poem 'Moving Our Misery" on page 94? What are the differences in its use?
5. Compare the sense of alienation depicted in "Winter of a Rose" to the one in Martin Espada's poem "Thanksgiving" on page 455. How are the tones in the two poems different despite their similar ideas?

Ricardo Pau-Llosa

RICARDO PAU-LLOSA left Cuba in 1960, the same year as many of his countrymen, including Gustavo Pérez-Firmat. He received a B.A. from Florida International University in 1974, and an M.A. from Florida Atlantic University in 1976. He has numerous awards for his poetry and his books of verse include Sorting Metaphors *(1983),* Bread of the Imagined *(1991), and* Vereda Tropical *(Tropical Path) (1998). Pau-Llosa is also well known for his expertise in contemporary Latin American art. He has served as co-curator of two major national exhibits featuring the works of Latino and Latin American artists, as well as authoring several monographs on key Latin American painters.*

Because of his understanding of the visual arts, Sorting Metaphors *relies on images rather than coherent structure to produce its intended effect. "Foreign Language" is a perfect example of this non-linear approach as the words move from image to image in a haphazard trail. "Minas de Cobre" ("Copper Mines"), is also an attempt at fusion, but rather than images, this poem coalesces ideas. The past and the present, for example, are drawn together by the speaker as a commentary on historical events.*

Foreign Language

Every object is a room
you walk words into.
Take an apple, its windows peeling.

In your hands the apple's
door opens a crack
and the words barge through
like salesmen confident of a kill.
The gerund opens the mail,
the verb's hands rumble through
the refrigerator, an adverb
caresses the daughter's knee,
the noun, its feet on the sofa,
says everything is as it should be.
Teeth tear through the walls of the apple
like a plane crashing in the suburbs.
The mouth is full of a wet white word
you can't pronounce, a pronoun quietly
reading the newspaper in the living room.
When you bit, you never knew what hit you.

Minas de Cobre

Beneath the tobacco fields
of *Pinar del Río*[1] the map says
there is copper. Two men
bludgeon an ore clump with hammers.
The Spaniards never came this far
or deep, it seems. The miners
work between Cuba and Yucatán
on the sea *Cortéz*[2] conquered before the Aztecs.
Now they open the Cuban earth
for better metal. The times have changed

their clothing and instruments, lights
have replaced plumes on their helmets, ore

beneath their blows instead of natives' heads.
They dig into the map above
the Peninsula de Guanahacabibes,
a toppled question mark on the wrong
side of the glass, pointing to Mexico.

They dig in the azure space,
their bodies punctually curved to
lift while the other drops the sledge hammer.

---

[1] One of Cuba's provinces   [2] Hernan Cortéz (1485–1547) was the Spanish explorer and conqueror of
the Aztec Empire.

The thing becomes many, then more,
fragments, images, like fluids
which science says are made up of tiny solids.
Which reminds me that when you dig
and hit blood you know
you've gone beyond memory.

Discussion Questions

1. How is an apple used as a metaphor to describe the difficulty of adapting to a new language in the poem "Foreign Language"?
2. What two civilizations are being compared in "Minas de Cobre"? What is the basis of that comparison?
3. Compare the role of language as an empowering force in both "The Exile," Gloria Anzaldua's poem "To live in the Borderlands means you" on page 98, and "Bi-Lingual Education" by Victor Hernandez Cruz on page 439.
4. Compare "Minas de Cobre" to Jack Agüeros' "Sonnet for Ambiguous Captivity" on page 454, in terms of the effects of conquest and colonization on a people.

Elias Miguel Muñoz

ELIAS MIGUEL MUÑOZ was born in Camagüey, Cuba, in 1954 and left when he was fourteen years old. He received a B.A. from California State University in 1976, an M.A. from the University if California in 1979, and a Ph.D. from the same institution in 1984. He has taught at several community colleges and Wichita State University. His book Crazy Love *(1988) experiments with form; the work combines the epistolary, the immigration experience, and a coming-of-age story. In the* Greatest Performance *(1991) he combines two biographies into one persona in order to comment on the lives of Latinos living in the United States.*

Muñoz's book of bilingual poems En Esta Tierra/In These Lands *(1988) includes portraits of family members as well Cuban and American locales. "Little Sister Born in this Land" explores the generational gap that exists between many Cubans and their family members. Usually this conflict is presented in terms of grandparent, parent, and child (as in* Dreaming in Cuban, *see p. 175) but here Muñoz opts to present this issue by using two siblings.*

Little Sister Born In This Land

When you slip
slowly and lovingly
through my fingers

I cannot hold you
and explain a thousand things
Each time you smile
and show me your shoes with buckles
or tell me a story
of space flights
(How you would love to be a princess
in those absurd and bloody wars)
Each time you intrigue me
with your riddles
with your words
that will always be foreign
to our experience

It isn't a reproach
sister
Little sister born in this land
It's just that you will never know
of hens nesting
(Is there anywhere in your childhood
a similar feeling?)
Once upon a time
there was a boy
on paving stones so white
and excursions on foot
toys made of tin
There was also mystery
in the ravines
There were evil pirates
and brave corsairs
There were lessons
for carving men
out of stone
There was caramel candy
and sweet potato pudding

It isn't a reproach
sister
Little sister born in this land
It's just that you have only
the joy of Disney heroes
Because you will smile
when the ingenious man
behind the cartoons
makes of you
of every child

a little clown
plastic and ridiculous

When you slip away
slowly and lovingly
I cannot invent
another childhood for you
cannot offer you mine
also nourished by heroes
but tasting of palm leaf
and *mamoncillo*[1]
It did not suffer the mockery
of expensive toys
that the deceptive
ghost of December
brings to you

When you slip away
slowly and lovingly
we cannot bury together
in the backyard
(Thar warm and always
open earth)
the models
that will take hold of you

that already stalk you
from their cardboard boxes
and their printed letters
on a glass of milk
or Coca Cola

It isn't a reproach
Sister
Little sister born in this land

Discussion Questions

1. Why does the speaker say that his little sister will "slip away"?

2. If the speaker is not "reproaching" his sister, what exactly are his feelings about her and why does he feel the way he does? What is the tone of the poem?

3. Although the sister is present in "Little Sister Born in This Land" and the aunt in Carolina Hospital's "Dear Tia" (page 267) is not, there are similarities in the speaker's feeling about their relationships. How do these poems explore the idea of loss in both similar and distinctive ways?

---

[1] a small green fruit with a rough skin and a fibered interior

Carolina Hospital

CAROLINA HOSPITAL *was one of the first poets to collect the verse of young Cuban-American writers. Her collection,* Los Atrevidos *(The Daring Ones, 1988), is so named because the poets represented are writing primarily in English, thus making a conscious effort to leave their ancestral language, if not their culture, behind. Along with her own poems, Hospital included selections by Gustavo Pérez-Firmat, Elias Miguel Muñoz, Pablo Medina, and Ricardo Pau-Llosa, among others.*

Hospital immigrated to the United States in 1961 at the early age of four. She holds an M.A. from the University of Florida granted in 1984. Her work has appeared in various literary journals and magazines, and is represented here by a poem which is a snapshot of the speaker's aunt.

Dear Tia

I do not write.
The years have frightened me away.
My life in a land so familiarly foreign,
a denial of your presence.
Your name is mine.
One black and white photograph of your youth,
all I hold on to.
One story of your past.

The pain comes not from nostalgia.
I do not miss your voice urging me in play,
your smile,
or your pride when others called you my mother.
I cannot close my eyes and feel your soft skin;
listen to your laughter;
smell the sweetness of your bath
I write because I cannot remember at all.

Discussion Questions

1. What is meant by the paradoxical statement of "a land so familiarly foreign"?
2. How does the poem form a coherent whole despite its seemingly contradictory beginning and ending?
3. Compare the feelings the speaker has for her aunt to the ones described by Virgil Suarez for his Cuban grandmother in "Spared Angola" on page 205.
4. Compare how the speaker feels about writing as an instrument of power to the way Esperanza feels about it in "Mango Says Goodbye Sometimes" by Sandra Cisneros on page 10.

Drama

Dolores Prida

DOLORES PRIDA was born in the province of Las Villas, Cuba, in 1943. She immigrated to the United States in 1961 and studied at Hunter College in New York City. She has worked as an editor for both Spanish and English language periodicals, published two volumes of poetry, written documentary films and a screenplay, and opened seven plays. She has received local, national, and international prizes including the Cintas Fellowship Award for Literature in 1976. She has also been active in the Cuban-American community, traveling to Cuba and lobbying for the release of political prisoners in that country.

The thematic content of Prida's plays usually reveals her desire to correct the double stigmatization that Hispanic women are subjected to. Coser y Cantar *(Sewing and Singing, 1981), for instance, consists of the two personalities of a female Cuban immigrant's character debating the pros and cons of Hispanic heritage versus American influence. Initially it seems that there are two separate characters named* Ella *and* She, *but it quickly becomes clear that "Her" and "She" are Prida's symbolic representation of a bilingual, bicultural Cuban-American.*

Beautiful Señoritas (1980) is a musical which develops the motif of a beauty pageant as a traditional Latin chauvinistic ritual. The stereotyping of Latina women is explored throughout the play as the little girl at its center holds the plot together. Using humor, music, and satirical scenes, the play ultimately reveals a serious issue: a woman's quest for self-identity and self-discovery.

Beautiful Señoritas

CHARACTERS

Four Beautiful Señoritas who also play assorted characters: Catch Women, Martyrs, Saints and just women.
The Midwife, who also plays the Mother
The Man, who plays all the male roles
The Girl, who grows up before our eyes

SET

The set is an open space or a series of platforms and a ramp, which become the various playing areas as each scene flows into the next.

Beautiful Señoritas was first performed at Duo Theater in New York City on November 25, 1977 with the following cast:

The Beautiful Señoritas	Vira Colorado, María Norman Lourdes Ramírez and Lucy Vega
The Midwife	Sol Echeverría
The Girl	Viridiana Villaverde
The Man	Manuel Yesckas

It was directed by Gloria Zelaya. Music by Tania León and Victoria Ruiz. Musical direction, Lydia Rivera. Choreography by Lourdes Ramírez.

Beautiful Señoritas opened on the West Coast April 6, 1979 at the Inner City Cultural Center's Stormy Weather Cafe in Los Angeles with the following cast:

The Beautiful Señoritas	Roseanna Campos, Jeannie Linero Rosa Maria Márquez and Ilka Tanya Payán
The Midwife	Peggy Hutcherson
The Girl	Gabrielle Gazón
The Man	Ron Godines

It was codirected by Eduardo Machado and Ilka Tanya Payán. Musical direction by Bob Zeigler. Choreography by Joanne Figueras.

Editor's Note: The text contains many Spanish words and phrases. Since much of the play relies on the Latin musical forms such as *salsa*, entire songs are presented in Spanish. In some sections, providing literal translations as the play progresses would be both cumbersome and awkward. More importantly, it would detract from the overall tone of the text which relies on fluidity, especially during the musical numbers. Thus, I have elected to provide the reader with a glossary of terms, along with paraphrases of the musical numbers, rather than a word-for-word translation. See pages 290–291.

ACT I

As lights go up DON JOSE *paces nervously back and forth. He smokes a big cigar, talking to himself.*

DON JOSÉ: Come on, woman. Hurry up. I have waited long enough for this child. Come on, a son. Give me a son . . . I will start training him right away. To ride horses. To shoot. To drink. As soon as he is old enough I'll take him to La Casa de Luisa. There they'll teach him what to do to women. Ha, ha, ha! If he's anything like his father, in   5 twenty years everyone in this town will be related to each other! Ha, ha, ha! My name will never die. My son will see to that . . .

MIDWIFE: (MIDWIFE *enters running, excited.*) Don José! Don José!

DON JOSÉ: ¡Al fin! ¿Qué? Dígame, ¿todo está bien?

MIDWIFE: Yes, everything is fine, Don José. Your wife just gave birth to a   10 healthy . . .

Don José:　(*Interrupting excitedly*). Ha, ha, I knew it! A healthy son!

Midwife:　. . . It is a girl Don José . . .

Don José:　(*Disappointment and disbelief creep onto his face. Then anger.
　　　　　He throws the cigar on the floor with force, then steps on it.) A girl! ¡No
　　　　　puede ser! ¡Impossible! What do you mean a girl! ¡Cómo puede　　　　　15
　　　　　pasarme esto a mí? The first child that will bear my name and it is
　　　　　a . . . girl! ¡Una chancleta! ¡Carajo! (*He storms away, muttering under
　　　　　his breath.*)

Midwife:　(*Looks at* Don José *as he exits, then addresses the audience. At
　　　　　some point during the following monologue the Girl will appear. She looks
　　　　　at everything as if seeing the world for the first time.*) He's off to drown
　　　　　his disappointment in rum, because another woman is born into this
　　　　　world. The same woman another man's son will covet and pursue and　　　20
　　　　　try to rape at the first opportunity. The same woman whose virginity
　　　　　he will protect with a gun. Another woman is born into this world. In
　　　　　Managua, in San Juan, in an Andes mountain town. She'll be put on a
　　　　　pedestal and trampled upon at the same time. She will be made a saint
　　　　　and a whore, crowned queen and exploited and adored. No, she's not　　　25
　　　　　just any woman. She will be called upon to . . . (*The* Midwife *is inter-
　　　　　rupted by offstage voices.*)

Beautiful Señorita 1:　¡Cuchi cuchi chi-a-boom!

Beautiful Señorita 2:　¡Mira caramba oye!

Beautiful Señorita 3:　¡Rumba pachanga mambo!

Beautiful Señorita 4:　¡Oye papito, ay ayayaiiii!　　　　　　　　　　　　　　30

Immediately a rumba is heard. The four Beautiful Señoritas *enter dancing. They dress as Carmen Miranda, Iris Chacón, Charo and María la O.
They sing:*

"The Beautiful Señoritas Song"

We beautiful señoritas
With maracas in our souls
Mira papi ay cariño
Always ready for amor

We beautiful señoritas　　　　　　　　　　　　　　　　　　　　　　　　　　35
Mucha salsa and sabor
Cuchi cuchi latin bombas
Always ready for amor

Ay caramba mira oye
Dance the tango all night long　　　　　　　　　　　　　　　　　　　　　　40
Guacamole latin lover
Always ready for amor

One papaya one banana
Ay sí sí sí señor

Simpáticas muchachitas   45
Always ready for amor

Piña plátanos chiquitas
Of the rainbow el color
Cucarachas muy bonitas
Always ready for amor   50

We beautiful señoritas
With maracas in our souls
Mira papi ay cariño
Always ready for amor

Ay sí sí sí señor   55
Always ready for amor
Ay sí sí sí señor
Always ready for amor
¡Ay sí sí sí señor!

The SEÑORITAS bow and exit. MARÍA LA O returns and takes more bows.

MARÍA LA O bows for the last time. Goes to her dressing room. Sits down and removes her shoes.

MARÍA LA O: My feet are killing me. These juanetes get worse by the   60
minute. *(She rubs her feet. She appears older and tired, all the glamour
gone out of her. She takes her false eye lashes off, examines her face carefully in the mirror, begins to remove makeup.)* Forty lousy bucks a week
for all that tit-shaking. But I need the extra money. What am I going
to do? A job is a job. And with my artistic inclinations . . . well . . .
But look at this joint! A dressing room! They have the nerve to call   65
this a dressing room. I have to be careful not to step on a rat. They
squeak too loud. The patrons out there may hear, you know. Anyway,
I sort of liked dancing since I was a kid. But this! I meant dancing like
Alicia Alonso, Margot Fonteyn . . . and I end up as a cheap Iris
Chacón. At least she shook her behind in Radio City Music Hall. Ha!   70
That's one up the Rockettes!
BEAUTY QUEEN: *(She enters, wearing a beauty contest bathing suit.)* María
la O, you still here. I thought everyone was gone. You always run out
after the show.
MARÍA LA O: No, not tonight. Somebody is taking care of the kid. I'm   75
so tired that I don't feel like moving from here. Estoy muerta, m'ija.
(Looks BEAUTY QUEEN up and down.) And where are *you* going?
BEAUTY QUEEN: To a beauty contest, of course.
MARÍA LA O: Don't you get tired of that, mujer!
BEAUTY QUEEN: Never. I was born to be a beauty queen. I have been a   80
beauty queen ever since I was born. "La reinecita," they used to call
me. My mother entered me in my first contest at the age of two.
Then, it was one contest after the other. I have been in a bathing suit

ever since. I save a lot in clothes . . . Anyway, my mother used to read
all those womens magazines—*Vanidades, Cosmopolitan, Claudia,*   85
Buenhogar—where everyone is so beautiful and happy. She, of course,
wanted me to be like them . . . *(Examines herself in the mirror.)* I have
won hundreds of contests, you know. I have been Queen of Los Hijos
Ausentes Club; Reina El Diario-La Prensa; Queen of Plátano Chips;
Queen of the Hispanic Hairdressers Association; Reina de la Alca-   90
purria; Miss Caribbean Sunshine; Señorita Turismo de Staten Island;
Queen of the Texas Enchilada . . . and now of course, I am Miss
Banana Republic!

MARÍA LA O: Muchacha, I bet you don't have time for anything else!

BEAUTY QUEEN: Oh, I sure do. I wax my legs every day. I keep in shape.   95
I practice my smile. Because one day, in one of those beauty contests,
someone will come up to me and say . . .

MARÍA LA O: You're on Candid Camera?

BEAUTY QUEEN: . . . Where have you been all my life! I'll be discovered,
become a movie star, a millionaire, appear on the cover of *People Mag-*   100
azine . . . and anyway, even if I don't win, I still make some money.

MARÍA LA O: Money? How much money?

BEAUTY QUEEN: Five hundred. A thousand. A trip here. A trip there. Depends on the contest.

MARÍA LA O: I could sure use some extra chavos. . . Hey, do you think I   105
could win, be discovered by a movie producer or something . . .

BEAUTY QUEEN: Weeell . . . I don't know. They've just re-made "King
Kong" . . . ha, ha!

MARÍA LA O: *(MARÍA LA O doesn't pay, attention. She's busily thinking
about the money. BEAUTY QUEEN turns to go.)* Even if I am only third, I
still make some extra money. I can send Johnny home for the summer.   110
He's never seen his grandparents. Ya ni habla español. *(MARÍA LA O
quickly tries to put eye lashes back on. Grabs her shoes and runs after
BEAUTY QUEEN.)* Wait, wait for me! ¡Espérame! I'll go with you to the
beauty contest. *(She exits. The* MIDWIFE *enters immediately. She calls
after MARÍA LA O.)*

MIDWIFE: And don't forget to smile! Give them your brightest smile! As
if your life depended on it!   115

*The GIRL enters and sits at MARÍA LA O's dressing table. During the follow-
ing monologue, the GIRL will play with the makeup, slowly applying lipstick,
mascara, and eye shadow in a very serious, concentrated manner.*

MIDWIFE: Yes. You have to smile to win. A girl with a serious face has no
future. But what can you do when a butterfly is trapped in your insides and you cannot smile? How can you smile with a butterfly condemned to beat its everchanging wings in the pit of your stomach?
There it is. Now a flutter. Now a storm. Carried by the winds of emo-   120
tion, this butterfly transforms the shape, the color, the texture of its
wings; the speed and range of its flight. Now it becomes a stained

glass butterfly, light shining through its yellow-colored wings, which move ever so slowly, up and down, up and down, sometimes remaining still for a second too long. Then the world stops and takes a plunge, becoming a brief black hole in space. A burned-out star wandering through the galaxies is like a smile meant, but not delivered. And I am so full of undelivered smiles! So pregnant with undetected laughter! Sonrisas, sonrisas, who would exchange a butterfly for a permanent smile! Hear, hear, this butterfly will keep you alive and running, awake and on your toes, speeding along the herd of wild horses stampeding through the heart! This butterfly is magic. It changes its size. It becomes big and small. Who will take this wondrous butterfly and give me a simple, lasting smile! A smile for day and night, winter and fall. A smile for all ocassions. A smile to survive. . . *(With the last line, the* MIDWIFE *turns to the* GIRL, *who by now has her face made up like a clown. They look at each other. The* GIRL *faces the audience. She is not smiling. They freeze. Black out.)* 125

130

135

In the dark we hear a fanfare. Lights go up on the MC. He wears a velvet tuxedo with a pink ruffled shirt. He combs his hair, twirls his moustache, adjusts his bow tie and smiles. He wields a microphone with a flourish.

MC: Ladies and gentlemen. Señoras y señores. Tonight. Esta noche. Right here. Aquí mismo. You will have the opportunity to see the most exquisite, sexy, exotic, sandungueras, jacarandosas and most beautiful señoritas of all. You will be the judge of the contest, where beauty will compete with belleza; where women of the tropical Caribbean will battle the señoritas of South America. Ladies and gentlemen, the poets have said it. The composers of boleros have said it. Latin women are the most beautiful, the most passionate, the most virtuous, the best housewives and cooks. And they all know how to dance to salsa, and do the hustle, the mambo, the guaguancó . . . And they are always ready for amor, señores! What treasures! See for yourselves! . . . Ladies and gentlemen, señoras y señores . . . from the sandy beaches of Florida, esbelta as a palm tree, please welcome Miss Little Havana! *(Music from "Cuando Salí de Cuba" is heard. Miss Little Havana enters. She wears a bathing suit, sun glasses and a string of pearls. She sings.)* 140

145

> Cuando salí de Cuba
> Dejé mi casa, deje mi avión
> Cuando salí de Cuba
> Dejé enterrado medio millón 150

MC: Oye, chica, what's your name?

MISS LITTLE HAVANA: Fina de la Garza del Vedado y Miramar. From the best families of the Cuba de Ayer. 155

MC: *(To the audience.)* As you can see, ladies and gentlemen, Fina es muy fina. Really fine, he, he, he. Tell the judges, Fina, what are your best assets?

MISS LITTLE HAVANA: Well, back in the Cuba of Yesterday, I had a house
with ten rooms and fifty maids, two cars, un avión and a sugar mill.   160
But Fidel took everything away. So, here in the U.S. of A. my only
assets are 36-28-42.

MC: Hmmm! That's what I call a positive attitude. Miss Fina, some day
you'll get it all back. Un aplauso for Fina, ladies and gentlemen! *(MISS
LITTLE HAVANA steps back and freezes into a doll-like posture, with a
fixed smile on her face.)*

MC: Now, from South of the Border, ladies and gentlemen—hold on to   165
your tacos, because here she is . . . Miss Chili Tamale! *(Music begins.
"Allá en el Rancho Grande".)* Please, un aplauso! Welcome, welcome
chaparrita! *(MISS CHILI TAMALE enters. She also wears a bathing suit
and a sarape over her shoulder. She sings.)*

> Allá en el rancho grande
> Allá donde vivía   170
> Yo era una flaca morenita
> Que triste se quejaba
> Que triste se quejaabaaa
> No tengo ni un par de calzones
> Ni sin remiendos de cuero   175
> Ni dos huevos rancheros
> Y las tortillas quemadas

MC: Your name, beautiful Señorita?

MISS CHILI TAMALE: Lupe Lupita Guadalupe Viva Zapata y Enchilada,
para servirle.   180

MC: What good manners! Tell us, what's your most fervent desire?

MISS CHILI TAMALE: My most fervent desire is to marry a big, handsome, very rich americano.

MC: Aha! What have we here! You mean you prefer gringos instead of
Latin men?   185

MISS CHILI TAMALE: Oh no, no no. But, you see, I need my green card.
La migra is after me.

MC: *(Nervously, the MC looks around, then pushes MISS TAMALE back. She
joins MISS LITTLE HAVANA in her doll-like pose.)* Ahem, ahem. Now,
ladies and gentlemen, the dream girl of every American male, the most
beautiful Señorita of all. Created by Madison Avenue exclusively for   190
the United Fruit Company . . . ladies and gentlemen, please welcome
Miss Conchita Banana! *("Chiquita Banana" music begins. MISS CON-
CHITA BANANA enters. She wears plastic bananas on her head and holds
two real ones in her hands. She sings.)*

> I'm Conchita Banana
> And I'm here to say
> That bananas taste the best   195
> In a certain way
> You can put 'em in your hum hum

You can slice'em in your ha ha
Anyway you want to eat 'em
Its impossible to beat 'em 200
But never, never, never
Put bananas in the refrigerator
NO, NO, NO NO!

(She throws the two real bananas to the audience.)

MC: Brava, bravissima, Miss Banana! Do you realize you have made our
      humble fruit, el plátano, very very famous all over the world? 205
MISS CONCHITA BANANA: Yes, I know. That has been the goal of my
      whole life.
MC: And we are proud of you, Conchita. But, come here, just between
      the two of us . . . tell me the truth, do you really like bananas?
MISS CONCHITA BANANA: Of course, I do! I eat them all the time. My 210
      motto is: a banana a day keeps the doctor away!
MC: *(Motioning to audience to applaud.)* What intelligence! What in-
      sight! Un aplauso, ladies and gentlemen . . . *(MISS CONCHITA BANANA*
      bows and steps back, joining the other doll-like contestants. As each
      woman says the following lines she becomes human again. The MC *moves*
      to one side and freezes.)
WOMAN 1:   *(Previously MISS LITTLE HAVANA.)* No one knows me. They
      see me passing by, but they don't know me. They don't see me. They 215
      hear my accent but not my words. If anyone wants to find me, I'll be
      sitting by the beach.
WOMAN 2:   *(Previously MISS CHILI TAMALE.)* My mother, my grand-
      mother, and her mother before her, walked the land with barefeet, as I
      have done too. We have given birth to our daughters on the bare soil. 220
      We have seen them grow and go to market. Now we need permits to
      walk the land—our land.
WOMAN 3:   *(Previously MISS CONCHITA BANANA.)* I have been invented
      for a photograph. Sometimes I wish to be a person, to exist for my
      own sake, to stop dancing, to stop smiling. One day I think I will 225
      want to cry.
MC: *(We hear a fanfare. The MC unfreezes. The contestants become dolls*
      again.) Ladies and gentlemen . . . don't go away, because we still have
      more for you! Now, señoras y señores, from la Isla del Encanto, please
      welcome Miss Commonwealth! Un aplauso, please! *(We hear music*
      from "Cortaron a Elena." MISS COMMONWEALTH enters, giggling and
      waving. She sings.)

Cortaron el budget 230
Cortaron el budget
Cortaron el budget
Y nos quedamos,
Sin food stamps
Cortaron a Elena 235

> Cortaron a Juana
> Cortaron a Lola
> Y nos quedamos
> Sin na' pa' na'

MC: ¡Qué sabor! Tell us your name, beautiful jibarita . . .   240
MISS COMMONWEALTH: Lucy Wisteria Rivera *(Giggles.)*
MC: Let me ask you, what do you think of the political status of the
  island?
MISS COMMONWEALTH: *(Giggles.)* Oh, I don't know about that. La
  belleza y la política no se mezclan. Beauty and politics do not mix.   245
  (Giggles.)
MC: True, true, preciosa-por-ser-un-encanto-por-ser-un-edén. Tell me,
  what is your goal in life?
MISS COMMONWEALTH: I want to find a boyfriend and get married. I will
  be a great housewife, cook, and mother. I will only live for my husband and my children. *(Giggles.)*   250
MC: Ave María, nena! You are a tesoro! Well, Miss Commonwealth,
  finding a boyfriend should not be difficult for you. You have everything a man wants right there up front. *(Points to her breasts with the
  microphone.)* I am sure you already have several novios, no?
MISS COMMONWEALTH: Oh no, I don't have a boyfriend yet. My father   255
  doesn't let me. And besides, it isn't as easy as you think. To catch a
  man you must know the rules of the game, the technique, the tricks,
  the know-how, the how-to, the expertise, the go-get-it, the . . . works!
  Let me show you. *(The MC stands to one side and freezes. The doll-like
  contestants in the back exit. MISS COMMONWEALTH begins to exit. She
  runs into the GIRL as she enters. MISS COMMONWEALTH's crown falls to
  the floor She looks at the girl who seems to remind her of something far
  away.)*
WOMAN 4:   *(Previously MISS COMMONWEALTH.)* The girl who had never   260
  seen the ocean decided one day to see it. Just one startled footprint on
  the sand and the sea came roaring at her. A thousand waves, an infinite horizon, a storm of salt and two diving birds thrusted themselves
  furiously into her eyes. Today she walks blindly through the smog and
  the dust of cities and villages. But she travels with a smile, because she 265
  carries the ocean in her eyes. *(WOMAN 4 exits. Spot on the GIRL. She
  picks up the crown from the floor and places it on her head Spot closes in
  on the crown.)*

*As lights go up, the MAN enters with a chair and places it center stage. He sits
on it. The GIRL sits on the floor with her back to the audience. The CATCH
WOMEN enter and take their places around the man. Each WOMAN addresses
the GIRL, as a teacher would.*

CATCH WOMAN 1:   There are many ways to catch a man. Watch . . .
  (Walks over to the MAN.) Hypnotize him. Be a good listener. *(She sits*

on his knees.) Laugh at his jokes, even if you heard them before. *(To MAN.)* Honey, tell them the one about the two bartenders . . . *(The MAN mouths words as if telling a joke. She listens and laughs loudly. Gets up.)* Cuá, cuá, cuá! Isn't he a riot! *(She begins to walk away, turns and addresses the GIRL.)* Ah, and don't forget to move your hips.   270

CATCH WOMAN 2: *(CATCH WOMAN 1 walks moving her hips back to her place. CATCH WOMAN 2 steps forward and addresses the GIRL.)* Women can't be too intellectual. He will get bored. *(To MAN, in earnest.)* Honey, don't you think nuclear disarmament is our only hope for survival? *(The MAN yawns. To GIRL.)* See? When a man goes out with a woman he wants to relax, to have fun, to feel good. He doesn't want to talk about heavy stuff, know what I mean? *(CATCH WOMAN 2 walks back to her place. She flirts with her boa, wrapping it around the man's head. Teasing.)* Toro, toro, torito!   275

CATCH WOMAN 3: *(The MAN charges after CATCH WOMAN 2. CATCH WOMAN 3 stops him with a hypnotic look He sits down again. CATCH WOMAN 3 addresses the GIRL.)* Looks are a very powerful weapon. Use your eyes, honey. Look at him now and then. Directly. Sideways. Through your eyelashes. From the corner of your eyes. Over your sunglasses. Look at him up and down. But not with too much insistence. And never ever look directly at his crotch. *(She walks away dropping a handkerchief. The MAN stops to pick it up. CATCH WOMAN 4 places her foot on it. Pushes the MAN away.)* Make him suffer. Make him jealous. *(Waves to someone offstage, flirting.)* Hi Johnny! *(To GIRL.)* They like it. It gives them a good excuse to get drunk. Tease him. Find out what he likes. *(To MAN.)* Un masajito, papi? I'll make you a burrito de machaca con huevo, si? *(She massages his neck.)* Keep him in suspense. *(To MAN.)* I love you. I don't love you. Te quiero. No te quiero. I love you. I don't love you . . . *(She walks away.)*   280

                                                                    285

                                                                    290

ALL: *(All four CATCH WOMEN come forward.)* We do it all for him!

MAN: They do it all for me! *(MAN raps the song, while the CATCH WOMEN parade around him.)*

"They Do It All For Me"

(Wolf whistles.)

> Mira mami, psst, cosa linda!
> Oye muñeca, dame un poquito   295
> Ay, miren eso
> Lo que dios ha hecho
> Para nosotros los pecadores
> Ay mamá, don't walk like that
> Don't move like that   300
> Don't look like that
> 'Cause you gonna give me

A heart attack
They do it all for me
What they learn in a magazine   305
They do it all for me
'Cause you know what they want
Ay mamá, tan preciosa tan hermosa
Give me a piece of this
And a piece of that   310
'Cause I know you do it all for me
Don't you don't you
Don't you do it all for me

*(CATCH WOMAN 2 throws her boa around his neck, ropes in the MAN and
exits with him in tow.)*

CATCH WOMAN 1:   ¡Mira, esa mosquita muerta ya agarró uno!
CATCH WOMAN 3:   Look at that, she caught him!   315
CATCH WOMAN 4:   Pero, ¡qué tiene ella que no tenga yo! *(All exit. The
                 GIRL stands up, picks up the handkerchief from the floor. Mimes imita-
                 tions of some of the WOMEN's moves, flirting, listening to jokes, giggling,
                 moving her hips, etc. Church music comes on.)*

*The NUN enters carrying a bouquet of roses cradled in her arms. She stands in
the back and looks up bathed in a sacred light. Her lips move as if praying.
She lowers her eyes and sees the GIRL imitating more sexy moves. The NUN's
eyes widen in disbelief.*

NUN: What are you doing, creature? That is sinful! A woman must be re-
       catada, saintly. Thoughts of the flesh must be banished from your
       head and your heart. Close your eyes and your pores to desire. The
       only love there is is the love of the Lord. The Lord is the only lover!   320
NUN: *(The GIRL stops, thoroughly confused. The NUN strikes her with the
       bouquet of roses.)* ¡Arrodíllate! Kneel down on these roses! Let your
       blood erase your sinful thoughts! You may still be saved. Pray, pray!
       *(The GIRL kneels on the roses, grimacing with pain. The PRIEST enters,
       makes the sign of the cross on the scene. The NUN kneels in front of the
       PRIEST.)* Father, forgive me for I have sinned . . . *(The SEÑORITAS enter
       with her lines. They wear mantillas and peinetas, holding Spanish fans
       in their hands, a red carnation between their teeth.)*
SEÑORITA 1:   Me too, father!
SEÑORITA 2:   ¡Y yo también!   325
SEÑORITA 3:   And me!
SEÑORITA 4:   Me too! *(A tango begins. The following lines are integrated
              into the choreography.)*
SEÑORITA 1:   Father, it has been two weeks since my last confession . . .
PRIEST: Speak, hija mia.
SEÑORITA 2:   Padre, my boyfriend used to kiss me on the lips . . . but it's   330
              all over now . . .

PRIEST: Lord, oh Lord!

SEÑORITA 3:   Forgive me father, but I have masturbated three times. Twice mentally, once physically.

PRIEST: Ave María Purísima sin pecado concebida . . .   335

SEÑORITA 4:   I have sinned, santo padre. Last night I had wet dreams.

PRIEST: Socorro espiritual, Dios mío. Help these lost souls!

SEÑORITA 1:   He said, fellatio . . . I said, cunnilingus!

PRIEST: No, not in a beautiful señorita's mouth! Such evil words, Señor, oh Lord!   340

SEÑORITA 2:   Father, listen. I have sinned. I have really really sinned. I did it, I did it! All the way I did it! *(All the SEÑORITAS and the NUN turn to SEÑORITA 2 and make the sign of the cross. They point at her with the fans.)*

SEÑORITAS 1, 3, 4:   She's done it, Dios mío, she's done it! Santisima Virgen, she's done it!

PRIEST: She's done it! She's done it!   345

SEÑORITA 2:   *(Tangoing backwards.)* I did it. yes. Lo hice. I did it, father. Forgive me, for I have fornicated!

PRIEST: She's done it! She's done it! *(The NUN faints in the PRIEST's arms.)*

SEÑORITAS 1, 3, 4:   Fornication! Copulation! Indigestion! ¡Qué pecado y que horror! ¡Culpable! ¡Culpable! ¡Culpable! *(They exit tangoing. The*   350 *PRIEST, with the fainted NUN in his arms looks at the audience bewildered.)*

PRIEST: *(To audience.)* Intermission! *Black out*

ACT II

In the dark we hear a fanfare. Spot light on MC.

MC: Welcome back, ladies and gentlemen, señoras y señores. There's more, much much more yet to come. For, you see, our contestants are not only beautiful, but also very talented señoritas. For the benefit of the judges they will sing, they will dance, they will perform the most daring acts on the flying trapeze!   5

Spot light on WOMAN 3 swinging on a swing center stage. She sings:

"Bolero Traicionero"

Take me in your arms
Let's dance away the night
Whisper in my ears
The sweetest words of love

I'm the woman in your life   10
Say you die every time

You are away from me
And whisper in my ear
The sweetest words of love

Promise me the sky   15
Get me the moon, the stars
If it is a lie
Whisper in my ear
The sweetest words of love

Darling in a dream of flowers   20
We are playing all the greatest games
Lie to me with romance again
Traicióname así, traicióname más

Promise me the sky . . .

(During the song lights go up to reveal the other women sitting in various poses waiting to be asked to dance. The GIRL is also there, closely watched by the CHAPERONE, who also keeps an eye on all the other women. The MAN enters wearing a white tuxedo and a Zorro mask. He dances with each one. Gives each a flower, which he pulls out of his pocket like a magician. The GIRL wants to dance, the MAN comes and asks her, but the CHAPERONE doesn't let her. The MAN asks another woman to dance. They dance very close. The CHAPERONE comes and taps the woman on the shoulder. They stop dancing. The MAN goes to the woman singing, pushes the swing back and forth. At the end of the song, the singer leaves with the MAN. The other women follow them with their eyes.)

SEÑORITA 2:   I swear I only did it for love! He sang in my ear the sweetest   25
words, the most romantic boleros. Saturdays and Sundays he sat at the
bar across the street drinking beer. He kept playing the same record
on the juke box over and over. It was a pasodoble about being as
lonely as a stray dog. He would send me flowers and candies with the
shoeshine boy. My father and brother had sworn to kill him if they   30
saw him near me. But he insisted. He kept saying how much he loved
me and he kept getting drunk right at my doorsteps. He serenaded
me every weekend. He said I was the most decent woman in the
world. Only his mother was more saintly . . . he said.

SEÑORITA 3:   He said the same thing to me. Then he said the same thing   35
to my sister and then to her best friend. My sister was heartbroken.
She was so young. She had given him her virginity and he would not
marry her. Then three days before Christmas she set herself on fire.
She poured gasoline on her dress, put a match to it and then started
to run. She ran like a vision of hell through the streets of the town.   40
Her screams awoke all the dead lovers for miles around. Her long hair,
her flowing dress were like a banner of fire calling followers to battle.
She ran down Main Street—the street that leads directly to the sea. I

ran after her trying to catch her to embrace her, to smother the flames
with my own body. I ran after her, yelling not to go into the water.   45
She couldn't, she wouldn't hear. She ran into the sea like thunder . . .
Such drama, such fiery spectacle, such pain . . . It all ended with a
half-silent hiss and a thin column of smoke rising up from the water,
near the beach where we played as children . . . *(We hear the sound of*
drums. The women join in making mournful sounds.)

The mournful sounds slowly turn into the "Wedding Song."

"The Wedding Song"
("Where Have All the Women Gone")

WOMAN:
There, there's Juana   50
See Juana jump
See how she jumps
When he does call
There, there's Rosa
See Rosa cry   55
See how she cries
When he doesn't call

CHORUS:
Where have all
The women gone

WOMAN:
Juana Rosa Carmen go   60
Not with a bang
But with a whimper
Where have they gone
Leaving their dreams
Behind   65
Leaving their dreams
Letting their lives
Undone

CHORUS:
(Wedding March Music.)
Look how they go
Look at them go   70
Sighing and crying
Look at them go

Towards the end of the song the women will form a line before the CHAPERONE
who is holding a big basket. From it she takes and gives each woman a wig
with hairrollers on it. Assisted by the GIRL, *each woman will put her wig on.*

Once the song ends, each woman will start miming various housecleaning chores. sweeping, ironing, washing, etc. The MOTHER *sews. The* GIRL *watches.*

MARTYR 1:   Cry my child. Las mujeres nacimos para sufrir. There's no other way but to cry. One is born awake and crying. That's the way God meant it. And who are we to question the ways of the Lord?   75

MARTYR 2:   I don't live for myself. I live for my husband and my children. A woman's work is never done: what to make for lunch, cook the beans, start the rice, and then again, what to make for supper, and the fact that Juanito needs new shoes for school. *(She holds her side in pain.)*

MARTYR 3:   What's wrong with you?   80

MARTYR 2:   I have female problems.

MARTYR 3:   The menstruation again?

MARTYR 2:   No, my husband beat me up again last night. *(The* GIRL *covers her ears, then covers her eyes and begins to play "Put the Tail on the Donkey" all by herself.)*

MARTYR 3:   I know what you mean, m'ija. We women were born to suffer. I sacrifice myself for my children. But, do they appreciate it? No.   85
Someday, someday when I'm gone they'll remember me and all I did for them. But then it will be too late. Too late.

MAMA: Such metaphysics. Women should not worry about philosophical matters. That's for men. *(She returns to her sewing, humming a song of oblivion.)*

MARTYR 3:   The Virgin Mary never worried about forced sterilization or   90
torture in Argentina or minimum wages. True, she had housing problems, but I'm sure there was never a quarrel as to who washed the dishes or fed that burro.

MAMA: Such heretic thoughts will not lead to anything good, I tell you. It is better not to have many thoughts. When you do the ironing or   95
the cooking or set your hair in rollers, it is better not to think too much. I know what I'm saying. I know . . . *(Continues her sewing and humming.)*

MARTYR 1:   And this headache. We're born with migraine. And with the nerves on edge. It is so, I know. I remember my mother and her mother before her. They always had jaquecas. I inherited the pain and   100
tazas de tilo, the Valiums and the Libriums . . .

MAMA: You don't keep busy enough. While your hands are busy . . .

MARTYR 2:   . . . And your mouth is busy, while you run from bed to stove to shop to work to sink to bed to mirror no one notices the little light shining in your eyes. It is better that way . . . because I . . . I don't   105
live for myself. I live for my husband and my children, and it is better that they don't notice that flash in my eyes, that sparkle of a threat, that flickering death wish . . . *(The* GIRL *tears off the cloth covering her eyes. Looks at the women expecting some action. Mumbling and complaining under their breaths, the women go back to their chores. The*

GUERRILLERA enters. She is self-assured and full of energy. The GIRL gives her all her attention.)

GUERRILLERA: Stop your laments, sisters!

MARTYR 1:   Who's she?   110

GUERRILLERA: Complaining and whining won't help!

MARTYR 3:   That's true!

GUERRILLERA: We can change the world and then our lot will improve!

MARTYR 3:   It's about time!

GUERRILLERA: Let's fight oppresion!   115

MARTYR 3:   I'm ready! Let's go!

MARTYR 2:   I ain't going nowhere. I think she's a lesbian.

GUERRILLERA: We, as third world women . . .

MARTYR 1:   Third world . . . ? I'm from Michoacán . . .

GUERRILLERA: . . . Are triply oppressed, so we have to fight three times as   120
hard!

MARTYR 3:   That's right!

GUERRILLERA: Come to the meetings!

MARTYR 3:   Where? Where? When?

GUERRILLERA: . . . Have your consciousness raised!   125

MARTYR 2:   What's consciousness?

MARTYR 1:   I don't know, but I'm keeping my legs crossed . . . *(Holds her
skirt down on her knees.)*

GUERRILLERA: Come with me and help make the revolution!

MARTYR 3:   Let's go, kill 'em, kill 'em!

GUERRILLERA: Good things will come to pass. Come with me and rebel!   130

MARTYR 3:   Let's go! *(To the others.)* Come on!

MARTYR 2:   All right, let's go!

MARTYR 1:   Bueno . . .

ALL: Let's go, vamos! ¡Si! ¡Arriba! ¡Vamosl Come on come on!

*MARTYR 3 picks up a broom and rests it on her shoulder like a rifle. The others
follow suit. All sing.*

> Si Adelita se fuera con otro   135
> La seguiría por tierra y por mar
> Si por mar en un buque de guerra
> Si por tierra en un tren militar

GUERRILLERA: But first . . . hold it, hold it . . . but first . . . we must peel
the potatoes, cook the rice, make the menudo and sweep the hall . . .   140
(The WOMEN groan and lose enthusiasm.) . . . because there's gonna be
a fund-raiser tonight!

Music begins. The GUERRILLERA and WOMEN sing.

> GUERRILLERA:
> There's gonna be a fund-raiser
> The brothers will speak of change

CHORUS:
We gonna have banana surprise   145
We gonna cut yautías in slice
There's gonna be a fund-raiser
But they'll ask us to peel and fry

GUERRILLERA:
We say okay
We will fight not clean   150
But they say go dear
And type the speech

Anita is gonna make it
She's gonna make it

CHORUS:
María will sweep the floor   155
Juanita is fat and pregnant
Pregnant for what
No matter if we're tired
As long long long long
As long as they're not   160
Tonight tonight
Tonight tonight
Tonight tonight
Tonight tonight

GUERRILLERA:
Won't be just any night   165

CHORUS:
Tonight tonight
Tonight tonight
Tonight tonight
Tonight tonight

GUERRILLERA:
We'll be no more harrassed   170

CHORUS:
Tonight tonight
Tonight tonight
Tonight tonight
Tonight tonight

GUERRILLERA:
I'll have something to say   175

CHORUS:
Tonight tonight

GUERRILLERA:
For us a new day will start

CHORUS:
Today the women
Want the hours

GUERRILLERA:
Hours to be loving   180

CHORUS:
Today the women
Want the hours

GUERRILLERA:	CHORUS:
And still the time to fight	Boring boring
To make this endless	Boring boring
Boring Boring Boring	Boring boring 185
Boring Boring Boring	Boring boring
Flight!	Flight!

All end the song with mops and brooms upraised. A voice is heard offstage.

MAN: *(Offstage.)* Is dinner ready! *(The WOMEN drop their "weapons" and run away.)*

WOMAN 1:   ¡Ay, se me quema el arroz!
WOMAN 2:   ¡Bendito, las habichuelas!   190
WOMAN 3:   ¡Ay, Virgen de Guadalupe, las enchiladas! *(They exit.)*
GUERRILLERA: *(Exiting after them.)* Wait! Wait! What about the revolu-
tion! . . . *(Black out.)*

As the lights go up the MAN enters dressed as a campesino, with poncho and sombrero. The SOCIAL RESEARCHER enters right behind. She holds a notebook and a pencil.

RESEARCHER: *(With an accent.)* Excuse me señor . . . buenas tardes. Me
llamo Miss Smith. I'm from the Peaceful Corps. Could you be so kind   195
to answer some questions for me—for our research study?
MAN: Bueno.
RESEARCHER: Have you many children?
MAN: God has not been good to me. Of sixteen children born, only nine
live.   200
RESEARCHER: Does you wife work?
MAN: No. She stays at home.
RESEARCHER: I see. How does she spend the day?
MAN: *(Scratching his head.)* Well, she gets up at four in the morning,
fetches water and wood, makes the fire and cooks breakfast. Then she   205
goes to the river and washes the clothes. After that she goes to town
to get the corn ground and buy what we need in the market. Then
she cooks the midday meal.

RESEARCHER: You come home at midday?

MAN: No, no, she brings the meal to me in the field—about three kilo-   210
meters from home.

RESEARCHER: And after that?

MAN: Well, she takes care of the hens and the pigs . . . and of course, she
looks after the children all day . . . then she prepares supper so it is
ready when I come home.   215

RESEARCHER: Does she go to bed after supper?

MAN: No, I do. She has things to do around the house until about ten
o'clock.

RESEARCHER: But, señor, you said your wife doesn't work . . .

MAN: Of course, she doesn't work. I told you, she stays home!   220

RESEARCHER: *(Closing notebook.)* Thank you, señor. You have been very
helpful. Adiós. *(She exits. The MAN follows her.)*

MAN: Hey, psst, señorita . . . my wife goes to bed at ten o'clock. I can
answer more questions for you later . . . *(Black out.)*

*In the dark we hear the beginning of "Dolphins by the Beach." The DAUGH-
TER 1 and the GIRL enter. They dance to the music. This dance portrays the
fantasies of a young woman. It is a dance of freedom and self-realization. A
Fanfare is heard, breaking the spell. They run away. The MC enters.*

MC: Ladies and gentlemen, señoras y señores . . . the show goes on and   225
on and on and ON! The beauty, the talent, the endurance of these
contestants is, you have to agree, OVERWHELMING. They have
gone beyond the call of duty in pursuit of their goal. They have performed unselfishly. They have given their all. And will give even more,
for, ladies and gentlemen, señoras y señores, the contest is not over   230
yet. As the excitement mounts—I can feel it in the air!—the question
burning in everyone's mind is: who will be the winner? *(As soap opera
narrator.)* Who will wear that crown on that pretty little head? What
will she do? Will she laugh? Will she cry? Will she faint in my
arms? . . . Stay tuned for the last chapter of Reina for a Day! *(MC*   235
exits. All the women enter.)

DAUGHTER 1:   Mamá, may I go out and play? It is such a beautiful day
and the tree is full of mangoes. May I get some? Let me go out to the
top of the hill. Please. I just want to sit there and look ahead, far away.
If I squint my eyes real hard I think I can see the ocean. Mami, please,
may I, may I go out?   240

MOTHER: Niña, what nonsense. Your head is always in the clouds. I can't
give you permission to go out. Wait until your father comes home and
ask him. *(Father enters.)*

DAUGHTER 1:   Papá, please, may I go out and play? It is such a beautiful
day and . . .   245

FATHER: No. Stay home with your mother. Girls belong at home. You
are becoming much of a tomboy. Why don't you learn to cook, to
sew, to mend my socks . . .

WIFE: Husband, I would like to buy some flowers for the windows, and
that vase I saw yesterday at the shop . . .   250

HUSBAND: Flowers, flowers, vases. What luxury! Instead of such fuss
about the house, why don't you do something about having a child? I
want a son. We've been married two years now and I am tired of waiting. What's the matter with you? People are already talking. It's me
they suspect . . .   255

MOTHER: Son, I have placed all my hopes on you. I hope you will be
better than your father and take care of me . . .

SON: I'm going off to the war. I have been called to play the game of
death. I must leave you now. I must go and kill . . .

WIDOW: He gave his life for the country in a far away land, killing people   260
he didn't know, people who didn't speak his language. I'm with child.
His child. I hope it's a son . . . he wanted a son so much . . .

DAUGHTER 2:   Mother, I'm pregnant. He doesn't want to get married. I
don't want to get married. I don't even know whether I want this
child . . .   265

MOTHER: Hija . . . how can you do this to me?! How is it possible.
That's not what I taught you! I . . . your father . . . your brother . . .
the neighbors . . . what would people say?

BROTHER: I'll kill him. I know who did it. I'll wring his neck. He'll pay
for this! Abusador sin escrúpulos. . . . Dishonoring decent girls . . .   270
And I thought he was my friend. He'll pay dearly for my sister's virginity. ¡Lo pagará con sangre!

DAUGHTER 1:   But I read it in *Cosmopolitan*. It said everyone is doing it!
And the TV commercials . . . and . . .

MOTHER: Hijo, what's the matter? You look worried . . .   275

SON: Mother, my girlfriend is having a baby. My baby. I want to bring
her here. You know, I don't have a job, and well, her parents kicked
her out of the house . . .

MOTHER: Just like his father! So young and already spilling his seed
around like a generous spring shower. Bring her. Bring your woman to   280
me. I hope she has wide hips and gives you many healthy sons.
(*MOTHER and SON exit.*)

*The WOMEN make moaning sounds, moving around, grouping and regroup-
ing. Loud Latin music bursts on. The WOMEN dance frenetically, then suddenly the music stops.*

WOMAN 1:   Sometimes, while I dance, I hear—behind the rhythmically
shuffling feet—the roar of the water cascading down the mountain,
thrown against the cliffs by an enraged ocean.

WOMAN 2:   . . . I hear the sound of water in a shower, splattering against   285
the tiles where a woman lies dead. I hear noises beyond the water, and
sometimes they frighten me.

WOMAN 3:   Behind the beat of the drums I hear the thud of a young
woman's body thrown from a roof. I hear the screeching of wheels

from a speeding car and the stifled cries of a young girl lying on the   290
street.

WOMAN 4:   Muffled by the brass section I sometimes hear in the distance
desperate cries of help from elevators, parking lots and apartment
buildings. I hear the echoes in a forest: "please . . . no . . . don't . . ."
of a child whimpering.   295

WOMAN 1:   I think I hear my sister cry while we dance.

WOMAN 2:   I hear screams. I hear the terrorized sounds of a young girl
running naked along the highway.

WOMAN 3:   The string section seems to murmur names. . .

WOMAN 4:   To remind me that the woman, the girl who at this very mo-   300
ment is being beaten . . .

WOMAN 1:   raped . . .

WOMAN 2:   murdered . . .

WOMAN 3:   is my sister . . .

WOMAN 4:   my daughter . . .   305

WOMAN 1:   my mother . . .

ALL: myself . . .

The WOMEN *remain on stage, backs turned to the audience.*

We hear a fanfare. The MC enters.

MC: Ladies and gentlemen, the choice has been made, the votes have
been counted, the results are in. . . and the winner is . . . señoras y
señores: the queen of queens, Miss Señorita Mañana! There she is . . .   310
(Music from Miss America's "There She is . . ." the GIRL *enters followed
by* Mamá. *The* GIRL *is wearing all the items she has picked from previous
scenes: the tinsel crown, the flowers, a mantilla, etc. Her face is still made
up as a clown. The* WOMEN *turn around to look. The* GIRL *looks upset,
restless with all the manipulation she has endured. The* WOMEN *are dis-
tressed by what they see. They surround the* GIRL.)

WOMAN 1:   This is not what I meant at all . . .

WOMAN 2:   I meant . . .

WOMEN 3:   I don't know what I meant.

WOMAN 4:   I think we goofed. She's a mess. *(They look at Mamá re-
proachfully. Mamá looks apologetic.)*

MAMA: I only wanted . . .   315

WOMAN I: *(Pointing to the MC.)* It's all his fault!

MC: Me? I only wanted to make her a queen! Can we go on with the
contest? This is a waste of time . . .

WOMAN 2:   You and your fff . . . contest!

WOMAN 3:   Cálmate, chica. Wait.   320

WOMAN 4:   *(To MC.)* Look, we have to discuss this by ourselves. Give us
a break, Okay?

MC: *(Mumbling as he exits.)* What do they want? What's the matter with
them? . . .

WOMAN 1:   *(To* GIRL.*)* Ven acá, m'ija. *(The* WOMEN *take off, one by one,*   325
    all the various items, clean her face, etc.)

WOMAN 2:   Honey, this is not what it is about . . .

WOMAN 3:   I'm not sure yet what it's about . . .

WOMAN 4:   It is about what really makes you a woman.

WOMAN 1:   It is not the clothes.

WOMAN 2:   Or the hair.   330

WOMAN 3:   Or the lipstick.

WOMAN 4:   Or the cooking.

WOMAN 3:   But . . . what is it about?

WOMAN 4:   Well . . . I was 13 when the blood first arrived. My mother
    locked herself in the bathroom with me, and recited the facts of life,   335
    and right then and there, very solemnly, she declared me a woman.

WOMAN 1:   I was 18 when, amid pain and pleasure, my virginity floated
    away in a sea of blood. He held me tight and said "now I have made
    you a woman."

WOMAN 2:   Then, from my insides a child burst forth . . . crying, bathed   340
    in blood and other personal substances. And then someone whispered
    in my ear: "Now you are a real real woman."

WOMAN 3:   In their songs they have given me the body of a mermaid, of
    a palm tree, of an ample-hipped guitar. In the movies I see myself as a
    whore, a nymphomaniac, a dumb servant or a third-rate dancer. I look   345
    for myself and I can't find me. I only find someone else's idea of me.

MAMA: But think . . . what a dangerous, deadly adventure being a
    woman! The harassment of being a woman . . . So many parts to be
    played so many parts to be stifled and denied. But look at so many
    wild, free young things crying, like the fox in the story: "tame me,   350
    tame and I'll be yours!"

WOMAN 1:   But I'm tired of stories!

WOMAN 2:   Yes, enough of "be this," "do that!"

WOMAN 3:   "Look like that!" Mira, mira!

WOMAN 4:   "Buy this product!"   355

WOMAN 1:   "Lose 10 pounds!"

MAMA: Wait, wait some more, and maybe, just maybe . . .

WOMAN 1:   Tell my daughter that I love her . . .

WOMAN 2:   Tell my daughter I wish I had really taught her the facts of
    life . . .   360

WOMAN 3:   Tell my daughter that still there are mysteries . . .

WOMAN 4:   . . . that the life I gave her doesn't have to be like mine.

THE GIRL: . . . that there are possibilities. That women that go crazy in
    the night, that women that die alone and frustrated, that women that
    exist only in the mind, are only half of the story, because a woman   365
    is . . .

WOMAN 1:   A fountain of fire!

WOMAN 2:   A river of love!

WOMAN 3:   An ocean of strength!

WOMAN 4:   Mirror, mirror on the wall . . .   370

They look at each other as images on a mirror, discovering themselves in each other. The GIRL is now one of them. She steps out and sings.

"Don't Deny Us The Music"

Woman is a fountain of fire
Woman is a river of love
A Latin woman is just a woman
With the music inside

Don't deny us the music   375
Don't imagine my face
I've fought many battles
I've sung many songs
I am just a woman
With the music inside   380

I am just a woman breaking
The links of a chain
I am just a woman
With the music inside

Free the butterfly   385
Let the oceans roll in
Free the butterfly
Let the oceans roll in
I am only a woman
With the music inside   390

Discussion Questions

1. What does the play reveal about stereotypical attitudes toward women, and specifically toward Latinas. Ultimately, what does the play have to say about those attitudes?

2. Examine the role of the "Four Women" who appear toward the end of the play. What powerful message do they deliver regarding the "proper" behavior of women?

3. Where and how does the play reveal its thematic concern with Cuba? How do historical events in Cuba affect the lives of the women in the play?

Glossary

amor love
aplauso applause
arroz rice
ayer yesterday

buque ship

carajo! similar to "damn"
cariño tenderness; also used to mean dear, or honey
chancleta literally a slipper, but slang term to denote that a girl was born rather than a male.

chavos   money
chiquita   small
concebida   conceived
cosa linda   beautiful thing
culpable   guilty

encanto   delight

fuera   leave

guerra   war

habichuelas   beans
huevo   egg

isla   island

jibarita   Puerto Rican name for
   peasant girl
juanetes   corns

machaca   dried beef
mar   sea
masajito   massage
migra   The Immigration and Natural-
   ization Service

mosquita muerta   shy, coy girl
muerta   dead
mujer   woman

otro   another

pecado   sin
platano   plantain; banana

quemar   burn

reinecita   little queen

simpática   appealing
sonrisas   smiles
sufrir   suffer

tesoro   treasure
tierra   earth
tilo   a sweet tea to calm the nerves
traicionero   traitor
tren   train

ven acá   come here

Songs: "The Beautiful Señoritas Song": This first song introduces the female characters to the audience. Its theme is essentially that of love, or lust. The four young
women proclaim how much they enjoy making love as they are "always ready for
amor."

"Cuando Salí de Cuba" is a satire of the popular song by that name. In the original,
the singer proclaims he left his heart and soul in Cuba, in this version the speaker
left his house, his plane, and half a million dollars.

"Alla en el Ranch Grande" is a satire on the Mexican song by that name. In this version the girl claims that she had nothing to wear or eat back home, not even a couple of eggs, and that her tortillas were all burned.

"Cortaron el Budget" is a satire of a popular Puerto Rican song. In this version the
budget is cut by the government thus eliminating food stamps.

René R. Alomá

*RENÉ R. ALOMÁ was born in Santiago de Cuba in 1947 and immigrated to
Canada after the Cuban revolution. He received a B.A. degree from Wayne State
University in 1969 and three years later received an M.A. from the University of*

Windsor. His three produced plays are Once a Family *(1975),* Le Cycliste *(1977), and* A Little Something to Ease the Pain *(1979). In addition he has written five plays for children:* A Friend Is a Friend *(1979),* The Magic Box *(1977),* Pinnochio *(1977),* Red *(1979), and* Fit for a King *(1983).*

In 1980 Alomá re-titled his play The Exile *as* A Little Something to Ease the Pain. *He again revised the work shortly before his death in 1986. The story recounts the lives of two cousins, Carlos and Nelson Rabel, whose lives and ideologies are diametrically opposed to each other. Despite this, or perhaps because of it, each holds a secret desire to live the other's life, if just for a moment. The duality of Cuban-American life is characterized by a fervent revolutionary and a Cuban exile writer, neither character feeling completely comfortable with this life.*

A Little Something to Ease the Pain

CHARACTERS

Carlos Rabel (Paye), a visiting exile
Nelson Rabel (Tatín)
Doña Cacha (Abuela), their
   grandmother
Dilia (Tía), their aunt
Clara (Tía), their grand-aunt

Ana, Tatín's wife
Amelia, a student

Julio Rabel, a cousin
Fr. Ephraim*
Paco*

*The roles of Fr. Ephraim and Paco can be played by the actors who play Tatín and Julio.

PLACE

The action takes place in and around the Rabel's house in Santiago de Cuba during one week in July, 1979

Spanish Words:
Abuela, Abue: Grandmother
Tía: Aunt
Natilla: A custard dessert
Ay: all-purpose exclamation
Mar Verde: Green Sea, the name of a beach
Dulce Coco: coconut sweet

Mantilla: lace shawl
Compañera: Comrade
Doña: Madam, title of respect to elderly matrons
Señor: Mister, sir
Tío: Uncle

PROLOGUE

Stage in complete darkness. At the stage right hand corner we see a light that looks like the light that would be cast by a round stained glass window of an old church in the noonday sun. In the shadow there is a wooden chair in which Fr. Ephraim *sits wearing a white cassock. We should not see him clearly, but we should realize that he is an old man and he seems to be asleep.* Paye *enters and puts down a suitcase and shoulder-strap tape recorder. He looks at the darkness, steps into the light. He sees the old priest, but is afraid to wake him, so he waits.*

Ephraim:　*(Clearing his throat as he speaks.)* What is it?
Paye:　Startled. What?
Ephraim:　What can I do for you?
Paye:　I'm looking for the priest.
Ephraim:　You have found him.　　　　　　　　　　　　　　　5
Paye:　Father Ephraim?
Ephraim:　Yes?
Paye:　It's Carlos. Carlos Rabel. The one they called Paye. Carmela Santos and I were the ones who printed those fliers against the banning of sermons . . . ?　　　　　　　　　　　　　　　10
Ephraim:　My sister Carmela wanted to marry a colored man, but mother would not allow it. Later when Mama was blind she married him. Darkness is a great equalizer. *(Pause.)*
Paye:　I used to be an altar boy.
Ephraim:　*(Remembering suddenly.)* Once you were trying to light the　　15
top candles last and you set your sleeves on fire . . . !
Paye:　*(Delighted by the recognition.)* Yes, that was me!
Ephraim:　I'm sorry. I fell asleep on my meditation.
Paye:　I thought the church was empty.
Ephraim:　I was dreaming of dust. Everyone was dust and the wind was　　20
blowing us away. I was supposed to be meditating on the five glorious mysteries. *(Sighs.)* I fell asleep
Paye:　Maybe I could come back another . . .
Ephraim:　You're back?
Paye:　For a visit.　　　　　　　　　　　　　　　25
Ephraim:　Ah!
Paye:　I live in Toronto. Canada.
Ephraim:　Canada! *(Paye nods.)* The church hasn't changed any, has it?!

PAYE: It's too dark, Father. I can't really see.

EPHRAIM: It hasn't changed. La Placita has changed. It's changed a lot   30
since you left.

PAYE: Yes, and the new monument is . . .

EPHRAIM: I say Mass on that monument every thirtieth of November in
memory of your uncle. It's the most attended Mass. . . next to Palm
Sunday.   35

PAYE: Palm Sunday is still a favorite?

EPHRAIM: Everyone wants palms to hang behind their door. It's more of
a superstition than a holy rite, but it's nice to have church full.

PAYE: Not many people come to church anymore?

EPHRAIM: Not many people come to church ever. It's the perpetual mal-   40
ady of Catholicism in Latin America; devotion without participation.
(Off on a tangent.) When the Cardinal was here from Spain we had
the altar covered in jasmines. The smell of jasmines goes well with
mantillas and incense. I can't stand up anymore, you know. My knees
are too weak to hold me up.   45

PAYE: There's no priest to assist you?

EPHRAIM: I was praying you'd have a vocation, no? What do you do?

PAYE: I'm a playwright, but . . .

EPHRAIM: A playwright. Pity. I thought you might have had a calling.

PAYE: To the priesthood?   50

EPHRAIM: You might have been a Cardinal. Are you famous?

PAYE: No. Not at all. Not yet.

EPHRAIM: Carlos . . . Carlos Rabel. A Cuban writing plays in Canada.
(Laughs.) Canada, right?

PAYE: Yes, Father.   55

EPHRAIM: Tell me, Paye, have you written a play about us?

PAYE: No. I . . . I haven't.

EPHRAIM: You should. You should write a play about an old priest who's
resigned to the fact, that his church will be dark and dusty forever. I
would like to be in your play. *(Quotes.)* "The whole world is a stage   60
and the people are the players." Shakespeare, the bard of Avon.
(Coughs.) Is your mother still as beautiful?

PAYE: Yes.

EPHRAIM: Raphael is a good painter. You like Raphael?

PAYE: Yes.   65

EPHRAIM: Your mother was a convert, you know. *(Silence. PAYE comes
close to the priest and looks closely into his eyes. EPHRAIM does not see
him.)*

PAYE: Father?

EPHRAIM: Yes.

PAYE: Do they still censor your sermons?

EPHRAIM: *(As if not hearing.)* Tell me Paye, when you become famous,   70
will you be a famous foreign playwright or a famous Cuban in exile?

PAYE: I don't know.

EPHRAIM: *(Slowly.)* You must resign yourself to being either foreign or at best a Cuban *"in exile."* It is a title you will have to bear just as I wear my robes.   75

PACO: *(Entering.)* Father! Who's there? *(He stays out of the light.)*

EPHRAIM: Ah, Paco. I have a visitor. From Canada. Carlos Rabel. Paco Gómez. *(PACO and PAYE shake hands.)*

PACO: Julio's cousin?

PAYE: Yes.   80

EPHRAIM: Paco is the caretaker cum sacristan. But he thinks he is my guardian angel.

PACO: It's dark in here.

EPHRAIM: My friend will understand. You see, Carlos, my eyes have become sensitive to the light.   85

PACO: The truth is he prefers the darkness.

EPHRAIM: Darkness is a great equalizer.

PACO: You must excuse Father Ephraim, but he must take his siesta now.

PAYE: Yes, I . . . *(PACO picks up the priest in his arms.)*

EPHRAIM: Tell your mother that I still remember her as one of Raphael's madonnas.   90

PACO: Pleased to meet you, Rabel.

EPHRAIM: And put me in one of your plays. I would like that. *(PACO begins to exit with, EPHRAIM.)*

PAYE: Yes, I will.

EPHRAIM: Thank you for coming to see me. God bless you, Carlos.   95

PAYE: Yes, Father, goodbye. *(Looks around at the dimly lit stage, genuflects and exits.)*

ACT I

From the black after PAYE *has exited, the stage lights come up to reveal some pillars and railings to indicate a verandah, and four large archways through which we see a kitchen,* AMELIA's *bedroom,* CACHA's *bedroom and the rest of the house beyond. The stage floor should be painted so that these rooms seem to be around a small square patio. There are steps leading from the corner stage right onto the verandah. There we see a suggestion of a door which leads into the house.* PAYE *comes up the steps, feeling the heat, carrying the suitcase and shoulder-strap tape recorder. He looks through the open door, but does not go in. Instead he comes around to the corner of the verandah which will be down stage center. He looks to the left, to the rest of the verandah which stretches to the stage left corner. The walls between the verandah and house through which we see the patio and the rooms surrounding it are non-existent, but must be respected as walls and therefore there is another entrance at the stage left side of the verandah, which can be indicated by a hanging piece of tiled roof.* PAYE *looks at the house and speaks directly to the audience from the corner of the verandah center stage.*

PAYE: *(Addressing the audience.)* My grandparents' house is a big square
        house which they rented until the Revolutionary Government passed a
        law giving the deed to the property to tenants who had paid rent for a
        period longer than twenty years. It is an old house, a Spanish colonial
        house, one of the oldest in the city of Santiago de Cuba. I was born in   5
        this house and I spent my childhood riding a tricycle on this verandah
        with assorted cousins—all boys! My grandparents' house has seen
        weddings and wakes, nine children, twenty-six grandchildren, fires,
        earthquakes, hurricanes, revolutions, departures and reunions. Now
        behind the door there is a little plaque stating the ownership of the   10
        occupants with the headline "Thank You, Fidel." *(He picks up the suit-
        case and enters the house through the stage right door.)*
PAYE: Abue! Good morning! Abuela! *(PAYE moves into the patio. There
        are clothes on the line. A towel has fallen. He picks it up and is about to
        hang it when AMELIA enters. Alarmed by his presence, she grabs a mop
        and cocks it in mid air.)*
AMELIA: Drop it!
PAYE: *(Startled.)* What?!
AMELIA: *(Calling.)* Dilia! Cacha!   15
PAYE: I . . .
AMELIA: Somebody! Quick!
PAYE: Wait a minute!
AMELIA: Thief! Thief!
PAYE: No. You got it all wrong!   20
AMELIA: Dilia! *(Swings the mop at him.)*
PAYE: Wait! *(AMELIA throws the mop at him and as PAYE ducks, she grabs
        him from behind in a bear hug.)*
AMELIA: I got him! *(DILIA enters.)* I got him!!
DILIA: Amelia, let him go, he'll hurt you.
AMELIA: I'll kill 'im first!   25
PAYE: It's me.
AMELIA: Call somebody! *(Begins calling out "thief" repeatedly. From this
        point on everyone speaks at once, saying their respective lines without wait-
        ing for any cue. The effect should be a jumble of everyone screaming and
        shouting until CACHA screams "shut up." At that point everyone stops.)*
DILIA: Amelia, don't be crazy, let him go!
PAYE: I sent a cable . . . *(AMELIA bites him on the neck.)* Ouch!!
CACHA: *(Entering.)* What in the world . . .   30
ANA: *(Enters.)* What is it?!
DILIA: A thief!
PAYE: Abuela *(Breaks loose.)*
DILIA: Look out!
ANA: Amelia, are you sure he's a thief?   35
PAYE: It's me, Tía!
ANA: Let the man get out!
DILIA: Look out, Mama.

ANA: Here, Amelia. *(Gives* AMELIA *the bat.)*
PAYE: Listen, it's me, Paye. Abuela!   40
AMELIA: I'll knock 'im out!
ANA: *(Taking up* AMELIA'S *repeated cry of "thief")* Thief! . . .
PAYE: It's me. Paye!
CACHA: Paye? Shut up all of you! It's Paye!
DILIA: Paye? *(Rushes over to turn off the radio.)*   45
CACHA: It's Paye! *(Opens her arms to him.)* Paye, my Paye. *(They embrace.)*
AMELIA: *(After a long pause.)* Jesus, I nearly bashed his head in! *(Picks up her mop and exits.)*
VOICE: *(Off.)* Is everything okay, Doña Cacha?
CACHA: Yes, Beto. It's Tato's son, Paye; he's come home. *(Blackout. Afro-Cuban drums are heard. People chattering as they get into places. Laughter. As the lights come up we find* CACHA *seated in one of the rocking chairs.* PAYE *is seated on the arm of* CACHA'S *chair with his arm around her.* DILIA *and* ANA *are gathering the clothes off the line as they speak.)*
DILIA: But the carnival is not till next week!   50
ANA: You haven't changed a bit!
CACHA: Ay, Paye, what a surprise!
DILIA: The last we heard, you were coming for the carnival!
PAYE: They just changed my flight!
ANA: I would have picked you out in a minute!   55
DILIA: We weren't expecting you till next week.
CACHA: It doesn't matter. The main thing is that you're here. I thought that I would have to close my eyes for good and never see you again, Paye. *(PAYE kisses her.)* I've missed you and Tato and. . . all of you.
DILIA: You didn't recognize us, eh, Paye?   60
PAYE: Sure I did.
CACHA: Older. Much older!
PAYE: Abue, you look terrific.
DILIA: Huh, don't let her fool you.
CACHA: What are you trying to do, make me out an invalid? *(To* PAYE.)   65
    I'm over eighty years old, and I have my own teeth, I cut my own food, I bathe and dress myself, and I haven't lost control of my bowels. *(PAYE laughs.)*
DILIA: Ah, Mama, Paye's come hundreds of miles, he doesn't want to hear about your bowels! Ay, Paye, how long has it been?   70
PAYE: Seventeen years?
DILIA: I bet you miss it plenty.
PAYE: Yes.
DILIA: What's Canada like? Not like here, is it?
PAYE: No.   75
ANA: Nothing's like here, they say. Perucho's son, you remember Perucho?

DILIA: Who?

ANA: Long time ago. Perucho.

PAYE: I remember.   80

ANA: *(To DILIA.)* He used to sell corn fritters at La Placita.

PAYE: Greasy little blobs! He had a glass eye and wore a raincoat
regardless.

CACHA: Ay, what a memory!

PAYE: It's hard to forget a man with a glass eye.   85

DILIA: I did.

ANA: Well, his sister is a good friend of Gaetana, the lady that used to
sew for Mirta, next door to my sister Somalia. Anyway, Perucho's son
left for New York, and he had a terrible time with English and the
cold. He *hated* it there. So he moved to Miami because everyone told   90
him it was just like Cuba. But no. The place was crawling with
Cubans, sure enough, all pretending they were still in Havana. But
Havana's not Santiago, and it wasn't the same, not at all.

DILIA: Ay, Ana, this is taking too long.

ANA: Wait, I'm just getting to it. Paye knows what I'm talking about,   95
don't you, Paye?

PAYE: Yes. I guess.

ANA: Anyway, Paye, he moved from Miami to Puerto Rico because they
say that San Juan is *just* like here. But, no sir. His father got a letter
from him just last New Year's . . . he said that *nothing* was like Santi-   100
ago! Now he wants to come back!

DILIA: *(Totally disinterested in ANA's story.)* I wonder where Tatín's got
to?

ANA: He said he'd be home before lunch.

CACHA: Oh, he's going to be surprised!   105

ANA: He said he'd be home before lunch.

CACHA: Oh, he's going to be surprised!

ANA: He'll be glad we came to Santiago early this year.

DILIA: Ay, Ana, are the boys going to get here before Paye leaves?

ANA: I don't think so . . . we made arrangements for them to be here   110
next week . . . we thought that . . .

DILIA: Ay, Tatín'll be so disappointed.

ANA: So will the boys.

PAYE: Where are they?

ANA: Ernesto's got a scholarship to a special course . . .   115

DILIA: One of the best schools on the island!

ANA: And Adrián's at a boys' camp near Havana. It's on a farm. We
arranged for them to come for the carnival. They've asked a lot about
you and the rest of the family abroad.

CACHA: Adrián looks a lot like you when you were that age!   120

AMELIA: *(Enters more groomed.)* I hope I didn't miss anything important.

DILIA: Ay, here's the one who nearly broke his skull! *(Laughs.)*

CACHA: This is my grandson, Carlos. Paye, this is Amelia. *(They shake hands.)*

AMELIA: Pleased to meet you.

CACHA: Amelia's living here with us while she goes to school in Santiago.   125

PAYE: Where are you from?

AMELIA: Oh, you never heard of it. It's up in the hills. Near Baracoa. It's a village called Alan.

PAYE: Alan?

AMELIA: It used to be a coffee plantation and the American who owned   130 it named the village after himself.

CACHA: It's *way* up in the hills.

AMELIA: You can see the coast line when the clouds lift. Maybe you would like to go?!

DILIA: Ay, Amelia, Paye's not a tourist. He's here to see us!   135

CACHA: Ay, yes! And we want to see him. Wait till Clara sees you!

DILIA: You better run down to Tía Clara's or she'll accuse us of keeping him all to ourselves!

CACHA: Clara's waited seventeen years, a few more minutes won't hurt.

DILIA: You forget how Tía Clara is when it comes to Paye?   140

ANA: *(To PAYE.)* Your Godmother, no?

PAYE: Yes.

DILIA: Clara has two gods, Jesus and this one! *(AMELIA laughs.)*

PAYE: I should go and see her . . .

ANA: Why don't I go and tell her he's here. . . she'll come . . .   145

DILIA: Ana, tell her that he just arrived. This very second.

VOICE: *(Off stage.)* Hello, Doña Cacha.

CACHA: Hello Graciela.

DILIA: *(Under her breath.)* You should see Graciela. The girl's a cow!

CACHA: Alpidio's daughter, you remember her, Paye? I think she went   150 out with Tatín.

DILIA: Only one, Mama. Tatín was going out with Ana when Paye left.

CACHA: Dilia doesn't like her because she went out with Tatín.

DILIA: The girl was vulgar. She would cough and spit like a lizard.

PAYE: I'm glad Tatín married Ana.   155

CACHA: Oh, yes.

DILIA: She's all right.

CACHA: It's not easy being married to Tatín. Mr. Perfect!

DILIA: He has high standards, and that's good.

CACHA: Too high. Ernesto and Adrián are terrified of him. And Ana, she   160 lives trying to keep things smooth.

DILIA: Tatín hasn't been given everything on a silver platter and he expects everyone to strive just as hard . . .

CACHA: See, Paye, no one can say a word about Tatín in front of your Aunt Dilia.   165

PAYE: Has he . . .? *(Gets up.)* It's hot, isn't it?

CACHA: Paye, you all right?

DILIA: You want some water? *(DILIA motions to AMELIA who goes but looks puzzled.)* It's the heat. He's not accustomed to this heat.

CACHA: Paye?   170

DILIA: You hungry? I bet you haven't eaten.

PAYE: I'm fine, Tía.

DILIA: I'll go get lunch ready, right away! *(Exits.)*

AMELIA: *(Hands PAYE a glass of water.)* Here.

PAYE: Thanks. *(Drinks.)*   175

DILIA: *(Shouting from the kitchen.)* Amelia, will you give me a hand in
    here!

AMELIA: Coming!

PAYE: *(Giving AMELIA the glass.)* Thank you, Amelia. *(AMELIA exits.)*

CACHA: You all right, Paye?   180

PAYE: Abue, I'm not sure if I have forgotten my feeling against Tatín. He
    hurt me.

CACHA: You hurt him a lot too. You refused to speak to him even to say
    goodbye.

PAYE: Abue, you think that Tatín, that he still . . .   185

CACHA: *(Taking PAYE's hand.)* When I was a little girl, Paye, my mother
    had a friend, Nenita. She was a beautiful lady; always powdered and
    combed. She used to visit us often. Then suddenly she stopped com-
    ing, and I asked why. My mother told me that Nenita had been in a
    fire and that she had been badly scarred. I cried, and I burst into tears   190
    on the spot! But as time went on, one day she came to visit us again. I
    heard her voice from the other room and I knew it was Nenita. I got
    nervous. I was afraid to come out. But they called. When I walked
    into the room and I saw her, I burst into tears again. She looked so
    lovely, just as lovely as ever, though her dress was cut high around her   195
    throat and her sleeves were long. I felt like such a fool. You see, Paye,
    Nenita had learned to cover her scars for her friends. *(Pause.)* Tatín is
    your brother, and if he has scars, he's learned to conceal them. You
    must do the same, Paye. You see?

PAYE: *(Almost in tears.)* Yes, Abue, I see. *(They sit in a long silence.
    CLARA enters followed by ANA.)*   200

CLARA: Where is he? Where's . . . ay, my Paye.

PAYE: *(Meeting her)* Tía!

CLARA: Oh, look at you. Oh, my Paye. *(Covers PAYE's face with kisses.)*
    Let me look at you. *(Stands back.)* Oh, God in Heaven! *(Throws her-
    self at PAYE again.)*

PAYE: Tía, please. *(Comforts her.)*   205

CLARA: Isn't he beautiful, Cacha?

CACHA: All my grandchildren are beautiful.

CLARA: And look at me. I must be a fright!

PAYE: You look fine, Tía. Pretty as ever!

CLARA: Go on. I don't even have any face powder, and I'm all sweaty.   210
    And my hair! I was going to tint it this evening. I'm all grey you
    know, almost white! Ay, there was a time when I couldn't get a bottle

of dye even for American money. Everyone thinks I'm too vain for my
age, but I say they can all fart into the wind. But, look at me now.
I'm not even dressed and here you are! Oh, Paye. My little Paye, all   215
grown up! *(Cries.)*

DILIA: *(Entering.)* Ay, Tía, let him breathe!

CLARA: You shut up, you've had Tatín all these years. My Paye's here
    now, and I . . . *(Cries.)*

PAYE: Tía.   220

ANA: I wonder what's keeping Tatín?

CLARA: *(Blowing her nose on the hem of her dress.)* I'm so proud of you.
    Your father, he keeps us up to date on your plays and . . . things.

PAYE: Papa tends to brag a little . . .

CLARA: I've always known you were the one in the family with the real   225
    sentiment . . . *(Kisses PAYE.)*

DILIA: Did you know Tatín got a medal from the Hispanic Academy?

PAYE: Yes, yes.

CLARA: A writer needs real sentiment!

DILIA: First prize!   230

CACHA: First time a Cuban's held that honor since 1948.

DILIA: *(Correcting her.)* '38, Mama. He's been published in Mexico and
    Chile and . . .

CLARA: Will you stop talking abut Tatín! I want to hear about Paye!

CACHA: How's lunch coming?   235

DILIA: The rice is on.

CACHA: Tell me about Sylvia; how's your mother?

PAYE: Fine.

DILIA: Mama, if you want to bathe, you better go do it now before the
    water shuts off for the day.   240

CACHA: I'll bathe later.

DILIA: There won't be enough in the tanks later. If Amelia does the
    dishes! That girl refuses to realize that on the days the water shuts off,
    whatever is in those tanks is all we have for the rest of the day. I'm
    always running out.   245

CACHA: Well, talk to her.

DILIA: I can't talk to her. You invited her here.

CACHA: I'm not the one who keeps running out of water.

DILIA: Never mind. I'll see about getting the tanks fixed myself.

CLARA: What's the matter with them now?   250

DILIA: They don't fill up properly.

CLARA: They never did. Ever since I can remember, those tanks . . .

DILIA: And what am I supposed to do, climb up on the roof myself?! I
    asked Fito to have a look at them, and Roberto was supposed to have
    fixed them, and he couldn't be bothered to look at them again! And   255
    Nando's useless! Sometimes my brothers make me sick. They live only
    a few blocks away and they only come here to tell me what I'm doing
    wrong in the caring of their mother!

CLARA: Dilia, please!

DILIA: And Mama thinks they're all saints!   260

ANA: All right, Tía.

CLARA: Ay, Dilia, we don't want Paye to think that the whole family's falling apart.

DILIA: Who said anything about falling apart?!

CLARA: It's the way you complain about everyone.   265

DILIA: I have reason to complain, Tía.

CACHA: Enough!

DILIA: I don't know what Tía Clara's accusing me of. Paye knows the family. What are we supposed to do, pretend we always get along like nuns on a bus ride? (PAYE laughs.)   270

CACHA: (Getting up.) I'll go take my shower. . .

DILIA: (Exiting.) Lunch will be another twenty minutes. Hurry up, Mama! (CACHA follows DILIA off to the interior of the house.)

CLARA: You musn't pay your Aunt Dilia any attention. Age doesn't agree with her. (Looks around to see if they're alone.)

ANA: I'll go give Tía a hand with lunch. (Exits.)   275

CLARA: Come, let's sit and talk for a minute. (CLARA leads PAYE to the rocking chairs.) When I heard you were here, I couldn't believe it. My heart jumped to my throat. Ana couldn't keep up with me running up the hill. I kept walking out of my shoes. These lousy things! (Shows them.) Come from Rumania, or something. They melt in the heat!   280 Soles come right off on the sidewalk!! Ay, Paye, if we had only known back then that it would turn out like this. Everyone here at the house still thinks that Fidel is Christ our Saviour! If I open my mouth in front of anyone here, they'd have my head on a skewer! I don't say a word up here. Out of respect for Cacha. I'm not afraid of anyone! I've   285 put Tatín in his place a few times and good! Once I made a reference to the day he slapped you during lunch, and he said that he would do it again. And I said to him, "Thank God, Paye's not here because, if you did it again, I would slap you silly, Señor Tatín." I gave him such a piece of my mind . . . He's never said another word to me since.   290

PAYE: You and Tatín don't speak to one another?

CLARA: Yes, we do. But he knows just where to draw the line. In front of me, he doesn't even praise Fidel! But, Paye, don't you open your mouth, please! God in Heaven! If anything happened to you on this trip your mother would never forgive us.   295

PAYE: Nothing is going to happen, Tía.

CLARA: You remember Niko the Turk? (PAYE nods.) They picked him up about a month ago. He was saying atrocities about the committee!

PAYE: He's half mad anyway, no?

CLARA: Exactly! He's even worse since you left! Half the time he runs   300 around with a load of shit in his pants! Ay, Paye, you have no idea what it's like! Imagine a shortage of oranges in Cuba!

PAYE: Well, that's because of the trade with Russia.

CLARA: Oh yes, that's what they say, but all I know is that during capitalism we had oranges!

PAYE: *(Laughs.)* You haven't changed a bit, Tía!

CLARA: Now tell me, tell me all about Canada and . . . Oh your post-cards! I got your postcards from all over Europe. I keep them in an album. I feel as if I've been to all those places! But you're so thin, Paye. Don't you have anyone to cook for you? We'll have to fatten you up. You'll have to come down to my house. I'll make some natilla for you. But, here I'm talking and talking and you should be the one who should be talking.

PAYE: I'd rather hear about you.

CLARA: Me?! What's there to tell. I go from my house to church and from church to my house and that's it. A widow's life can be pretty desolate sometimes. Especially when she doesn't have any children. Your uncle and I . . . *(Makes the sign of the cross.)* . . . we never had any children. Of course you knew that. It would have been good to have a few children. But . . . I couldn't.

PAYE: Tía, I didn't know . . .

CLARA: Naturally no one speaks of it anymore. It doesn't come up in conversation or anything, but there was time when everyone in the family felt sorry for your uncle for having married a barren woman. Oh, but that was before donkeys learned to bray! Beside I have my Paye here with me again! Oh, we're going to have such fun! It'll be like the old days. Like when I used to celebrate your birthdays! You remember? *(PAYE nods. TATÍN enters from the street.)*

TATÍN: Ey, Tía!

CLARA: Tatín! *(TATÍN advances in their direction, eyeing PAYE.)* You'll never guess . . .

TATÍN: Paye? *(PAYE stands up.)*

CLARA: That's right! *(They stare at one another in silence.)*

TATÍN: Paye? Are you speaking to me now? *(PAYE advances tentatively. TATÍN wipes his sweat.)*

PAYE: *(Locked in TATÍN's embrace.)* Tatín. . . *(DILIA and ANA enter from inside and stand watching.)*

DILIA: He didn't recognize him!?

CLARA: He did. Right away!

TATÍN: Paye, you remember Ana.

ANA: Yes. He did.

DILIA: He got here by surprise!

PAYE: They got my visa all mixed up.

CACHA: *(Entering.)* Is Tatín here yet?

DILIA: Yes, Mama.

CACHA: Well, our Paye's here early!

CLARA: My Paye! *(PAYE and TATÍN try to speak at once. They laugh.)*

TATÍN: Paye-Paye!

PAYE: It's nice to be called Paye again!

DILIA: What do they call you . . .?

PAYE: My friends, Carlos.

CACHA: Ay!   350
TATÍN: Should we call you Carlos?
PAYE: No! No! Paye's fine. It's just fine. It's just that no one's called my
         Paye in so long. Even the family in Jamaica. Once when I was there
         for Christmas, Papa called me Paye by mistake and Alexandra nearly
         choked on her milk. She thought it was the funniest thing since Aunt   355
         Sophie fell into Uncle Solomon's grave. *(TATÍN looks puzzled.)* They
         were lowering him in. Oh, you should've been there! She had been
         wailing: "Solomon, take me with you! Don't leave me, Solomon!"
         Then as she fell, she started screaming, "Draw me out! Will you get
         me outta here!" *(Everyone bursts into laughter but TATÍN.)* Everyone   360
         was laughing so hard they didn't have the strength to get her out of
         the hole. And Uncle Elías, he slipped in the mud and fell in too!
         (More laughter.)
TATÍN: Why do you still make up these lies? *(A moment of tension.)*
CACHA: *(To DILIA.)* How's lunch coming?
PAYE: *(Softly.)* It's the truth, I swear.   365
DILIA: I was waiting for you to start frying. *(Exits.)*
PAYE: Ay, Tatín, I brought a tape recorder for you. *(Looks around for his
         suitcases.)*
CACHA: Amelia put your things in your room. Your old room.
PAYE: I brought something for you too, Abue, and for you, Tía. *(Starts
         to exit.)*
CLARA: *(Following him.)* What is it?   370
PAYE: *(Off.)* Your favorite! Yardley's Violets.
CLARA: *(Off.)* Ay!
ANA: *(To TATÍN.)* Don't be so hard on him.
TATÍN: *(Looking toward CACHA to see if she heard.)* Ana, please!
CACHA: Go see what Paye brought for you. *(CLARA gasps with delight.)*   375
         You've been wanting a recorder for a long time, no?
TATÍN: Yes. Don't you want to see what he brought for you?
CACHA: I'm old. I can wait. Go. Go on! *(ANA and TATÍN start off.)*
         Tatín. *(They stop.)* He's here for one week . . . I want everything to be
         nice for him . . .   380
TATÍN: Yes, Abue.
CACHA: Paye. *(ANA and TATÍN exit to PAYE's room. CACHA sits in her
         rocking chair and fans herself. She speaks to the audience.)* It's a funny
         thing with names! Take Tatín; when he was born Tato did not want to
         name him Carlos after himself. That was too much like everybody else.   385
         So he named him Nelson after the Englishman. *(Smiles and shakes her
         head.)* Well, since he didn't inherit his father's name, he ended up in-
         heriting even worse, his father's nickname, and from Tato he got
         Tatín. *(PAYE and TATÍN laugh off.)* When Paye was born the whole
         family was expecting a girl. Well, imagine, I already had . . . *(Counts.)* 390
         . . . five grandchildren, and all of them boys. Tato had an armful of
         girls' names picked out. All of them foreign; after some duchess in

Sweden or a lady writer from France. None that I would be able to pronounce. But when the midwife put him in my arms and said, "It's another boy," we were all stumped. So I named him Carlos, like his father and my husband. That's a sensible name. How he got to be called Paye is really quite a simple story. As a baby, Sylvia took him to visit her family in Jamaica, and there he learned to say "Bye-bye" and wave his little hand; in English! It was real cute. But his cousins who had no idea of what he was saying, started calling him "Paye-paye" and it stuck. *(Laughs.)* The third one was named Aramis after the Three Musketeers, *(Raises an eyebrow.)* and no nick-names were allowed. Well, Ari for short. *(Smiles.)* Tato's always been one for foreign airs! I believe he named his daughter after a Russian princess. Alexandra. *(Pause.)* I never met Alexandra. I never held her in my arms. I've held all my grandchildren at birth. They were all born in this house and the midwife passed them directly into my arms. All my grandchildren, except one. Tato sent us a cable when Sylvia had Alexandra, and I held it, the little piece of paper . . . I held it next to my cheek and I cried. *(Rocks gently in her chair, fans herself and is silent. After a long pause, AMELIA calls from the kitchen.)*

AMELIA: Lunch! Doña Cacha! Tatín, Paye. *(TATÍN, PAYE and CLARA laugh offstage.)* Lunch! *(Lights fade as CACHA gets up and exits. Lights up on TATÍN. The inside of the house is in darkness. He sits on the downstage railing. PAYE enters from the interior of the house wearing jogging shorts and an open shirt, bare feet, stands behind TATÍN and yawns.)*

TATÍN: Where do you think you are? Miami Beach? You don't wear things like that in Santiago.

PAYE: I couldn't sleep. *(Pause.)*

TATÍN: Me neither. *(Pause.)* The heat?

PAYE: Yea, the heat. *(Pause.)* Ana asleep?

TATÍN: I guess. *(Pause.)* Time?

PAYE: Almost five. Tatín. . . ? *(Pause.)* Want to talk some more?

TATÍN: Sure. What did I say?

PAYE: You told her I was a "noteworthy Cuban playwright" and . . .

TATÍN: Aren't you?

PAYE: I was surprised at the adjective.

TATÍN: Noteworthy?

PAYE: No, Cuban. *(Silence.)*

TATÍN: An orange is an orange because it comes from an orange tree. *(They look at one another.)* They get oranges in Canada, no? *(PAYE smiles. Silence.)* Very few of our writers write for the theater. At the last writer's conference I met a young woman who wrote plays, but they were really for television. I myself have a few scenarios that might be best served by dialogue, but between my radio broadcast and lecturing I hardly have enough time to write all the things I want. *(Smokes.)* Besides, I really felt more at home in prose. I don't have a flair for the dramatic. I'm working on a story about a man who's on trial because his neighbors accuse him of manufacturing butterflies out of thin air. I

440
want to finish it for an anthology. I'm really quite excited about it. *(Pause.)* And you, are you working on anything?

PAYE: *(Shaking his head)* I try. I sit at the typewriter with my finger perched. . . and nothing. I haven't written anything in nearly two years.

TATÍN: You're wasting time.

PAYE: You remember that poem I wrote when I was eleven? "Ode to the Triumphant Revolution." *(TATÍN nods. PAYE smiles.)* I remember when it came out in the paper, Tía Clara read it out loud, and everyone was so proud, even Tía Dilia . . . everyone. I remember, you took the newspaper, glanced at my poem, and without even looking up went on to read the news of the day. Why must you always put me down?

TATÍN: I don't always put you down.

PAYE: Yes, you do. You call me a liar. Because I'm having difficulty writing, you say I'm wasting time.

TATÍN: You are wasting time. The first act of the play you sent was light weight.

PAYE: I was trying to come up with a comedy. Serious plays don't sell. *(They are beginning to raise their voices.)*

TATÍN: Serious plays become literature.

PAYE: *(Shouts.)* I know the people in that play. I write about people I know.

TATÍN: Then you should denounce the people you know.

PAYE: *(Shouts.)* I don't want to write propaganda. *(DILIA enters wearing a light housecoat.)*

DILIA: *(To PAYE.)* Shhh! Do you want to wake up your grandmother? *(PAYE turns brusquely and walks into the house. DILIA walks to TATÍN and caresses his head.)* What's the matter? There's something the matter, isn't there?

TATÍN: No.

DILIA: I know you well, Tatín. There's something brewing inside of you. I'm hurt that you won't talk to me. *(TATÍN doesn't answer. Pause. She kisses him on the cheek.)* Come on. You should get some sleep. *(Lights fade as they enter the house. Cuban music comes up. Daylight comes up on ANA seated at the table. She cleans stones from a bowl of beans. The Rabel household is occupied by DILIA in the kitchen, PAYE and CACHA getting up from their respective beds. CACHA and PAYE go through the archway that goes to the interior of the house. PAYE is carrying a towel. CACHA is still in her nightgown. While ANA speaks, DILIA fixes a tray comprised of a large expresso coffee pot and a pot of hot milk. She enters the interior of the house shortly after PAYE and CACHA pass by. Music volume cuts to half.)*

ANA: The Rabel family is quite the important family. Cacha's youngest son died fighting for Fidel. The whole family was up to their eyeballs in the fight against Batista, and when Fidel took power, naturally the

Rabels took their place in the ranks of the revolutionary government. *(Music fades to nearly nothing.)* Paye turned against the revolution with a vengeance. The Jesuits really had their claws in him. But still, imagine what a shock it was when Tato Rabel, the eldest of the Rabels, decided to leave Cuba. No, no, no, it was unbelievable. *(Music has faded . . . Pause.)* I've heard a hundred times how in 1942. Tato Rabel came back from Jamaica married to Sylvia. He had been working in the consular office in the island, that's where he learned to speak English; and he came back married to a fifteen-year-old English Jewess, with the face of an angel! Sylvia had to convert to everything. To Catholicism. To Spanish. To pesos. To the Rabel family. She gave up everything for her husband and for twenty years she was more Cuban than sugar cane. But in '62, Tato and Sylvia took Paye and Aramis and went back to Jamaica. Tatín refused to leave. Paye was delighted to take his father away. *(Blackout. We hear a radio playing Cuban music. Lights come up on PAYE and TATÍN sitting on the patio in rocking chairs. No one else is seen. As lights come up, music fades to background.)* 470 475 480

PAYE: I was so surprised when your letter came, the first one. What made you sit down and actually write to me?   485

TATÍN: I don't know. *(Offers PAYE a cigarette.)*

PAYE: No. thanks.

TATÍN: *(Lighting up.)* I think it was a letter Papa wrote to Abue saying he was concerned with your involvement in the Anti-Vietnam movement in university.   490

PAYE: *(Smiling.)* And you figured there was hope for me yet?!

TATÍN: Something like that. *(They chuckle.)* And you, why did you write back?

PAYE: I don't know. But when your letters would come talking about your work and the family and the carnival . . . *(Sighs.)* You know, I 495 have your letters all filed by date and once in a while I go through them. My favorite is one you wrote around the time Adrián was born. You talked about every one of the cousins, what they were like, what they were doing . . . I read that one often. I've wanted to be here so many times. *(Looks up the street.)* I was really hoping to be here for the 500 carnival.

TATÍN: That would have been nice.

PAYE: Tatín. . . ? *(Pause.)* You ever think about going abroad?

TATÍN: Why? Should I want to?

PAYE: No. I suppose not. *(A persistent jeep's horn is heard from the street. JULIO enters from the jeep.)*   505

TATÍN: You remember your cousin Julio?

PAYE: Not looking like that.

JULIO: *(Shouting.)* Paye!

DILIA: *(Rushing out.)* What's going on?

JULIO: Paye, put it there!   510

DILIA: It's only Julio, Mama.

CACHA: *(Joining them.)* At this hour . . . ?!

PAYE: Julio! Jesus, look at you!

JULIO: *(Flexing his arm.)* Just a little exercise. You look good for an old man your age! Whiter than salt pork! I got the jeep to take you to the beach.   515

PAYE: The beach?

TATÍN: We haven't been to bed yet.

JULIO: *You* go to bed, who invited you?

DILIA: Don't say hello to us.   520

JULIO: Ooops! *(Kisses DILIA.)* Abuela. *(Kisses CACHA.)*

CACHA: How's the baby?

DILIA: Julio's wife just had a baby.

CACHA: A month ago.

JULIO: A boy.   525

CACHA: Eduardo.

JULIO: What about you? You married yet?

PAYE: No, not yet.

JULIO: Christ, I'm on my third.

CACHA: It's nothing to brag about.   530

JULIO: Why not? Not many men can get a really good looking woman, let alone three.

DILIA: Not many men can get two women to divorce him in such a hurry!

PAYE: You've been divorced twice?   535

JULIO: Sure, we're a modern nation.

AMELIA: *(Enters still dressing herself.)* Julio!

JULIO: Hey big mamma! *(JULIO takes AMELIA's face in his hands and shows it to PAYE.)* You ever seen anything as ugly as this anywhere?

AMELIA: Get out! *(AMELIA slaps JULIO around.)*   540

JULIO: *(Trying to pat her ass.)* Well, at least you have something to fall back on. *(Pats her.)*

AMELIA: Get your hands off.

JULIO: Only teasing.

AMELIA: See what I have to put up with at every rehearsal?   545

JULIO: See what Abuela saddled me with?

CACHA: And I intend you to watch out for her.

JULIO: You kidding! With that face who'd bother her?

CACHA: Ther're a lot of drunks in the carnival and . . . ?

JULIO: They'd have to be plastered! *(AMELIA hits JULIO.)*   550

DILIA: Did you hear. Paye can't stay for the carnival?

JULIO: That's what he thinks. You think you're getting on a plane before July 25th, you're even stupider than me!

PAYE: Well, the main thing was to see the family.

JULIO: This year's dance is going to knock the judges on their asses. It's   555
the best La Placita has ever done. One of the guys playing the bongos

just came back from Angola.

AMELIA: And he's got some rhythms that are going to make the conga
   hot!

PAYE: I wish I could, Julio.   560

JULIO: Well?

DILIA: His visa's only for one week.

JULIO: What the hell does he need a visa for?!

PAYE: Next time, Julio.

JULIO: So, you'll miss the carnival. We'll have to have a party AT LEAST.   565
   How about it, Tía? Let's roast a pig!

DILIA: Where are we supposed to get a pig from?

JULIO: I'll get a pig. How about Saturday?!

CACHA: *(Lowering her voice.)* Julio, I don't want you getting into any
   trouble . . .   570

JULIO: Don't worry, Abue. The pig's as good as roasted.

AMELIA: Ay, a party!

JULIO: Okay! Them that's going to the beach, let's go. I only got the
   jeep for a few hours.

DILIA: Before you go, Julio, I want you to look at the water tanks.   575

JULIO: Right now?

DILIA: Just look at them now; it'll only take a second . . . *(JULIO begins to
   exit with DILIA.)*

JULIO: Get your towels and wait for me in the jeep. These old women are
   going to drive me crazy!

AMELIA: That Julio!   580

PAYE: He's certainly changed. I remember Julio as a skinny little shrimp
   with no teeth and always scratching himself. *(AMELIA laughs and
   exits.)*

CACHA: I guess you all grow up. Are you going to the beach?

TATÍN: I don't know, I . . .

CACHA: Why not? You're young! *(Exiting.)* I'll get your towels and   585
   things. Ana!

PAYE: The beach! A party! A roast pig! This pig Julio's talking about;
   where's he going to get it?

TATÍN: I don't know. He probably knows a man who raises pigs.

PAYE: Is that allowed?   590

TATÍN: Raising pigs?

PAYE: No. Knowing a man.

TATÍN: This is still Cuba, Paye. Sure you're not tired?

PAYE: Of course I'm tired, but I couldn't sleep now.

ANA: *(Enters.)* Paye, Abue can't find your bathing suit.   595

PAYE: Oh, it's still in my duffle bag. I'll find it. *(Exits.)*

ANA: Are you really going to the beach?

TATÍN: Yes, why?

ANA: No, nothing. Remember you have to prepare two radio broadcasts
   for when you get back.   600

TATÍN: Have I ever needed reminding?

ANA: No . . . How are things going with you and Paye?

TATÍN: Fine.

ANA: You know, he reminds me of Adrián. *(TATÍN laughs cynically.)* What's the matter?   605

TATÍN: Nothing.

ANA: What did I say?

TATÍN: Now I know why I lose patience with Adrián. He is like Paye.

ANA: You didn't lose patience with Adrián until recently.

TATÍN: Well, he gets so vehement when anyone in the house complains   610
about shortages or anything like that. He doesn't respect me anymore.
He talks back.

ANA: That's true maybe. But it's also you. You have been in a foul mood
for months. And when I ask you what's the matter, you always say
nothing. Is it me? *(Moves after him.)* Are you unhappy with me?   615

TATÍN: *(Sharply.)* It's not you! It has nothing to do with you!

JULIO: *(Offstage.)* No sweat. I'll fix it Saturday. *(TATÍN moves away from
ANA. She stares at him silently.)* Here we go! Abue's packing us breakfast, we better get outta here before she decides to pack a bed!

CACHA: Here! *(To JULIO.)* Make sure they're back before lunch.   620

JULIO: *(Shouting over CACHA's line.)* To the beach! And don't anyone
fart in the jeep, the floor boards are real loose! *(They exit noisily.
CACHA waves. ANA stands perfectly still.)*

CACHA: You all right, Ana?

ANA: Yes. I just didn't sleep well. I worry when Tatín isn't in bed with
me.   625

CACHA: There's nothing to worry about. They'll get some sleep later on.
Now he's too excited to sleep. You can't imagine what Paye's visits
means to him, to all of us.

ANA: I don't know what to imagine, what to expect.

CACHA: There's nothing to worry about, you'll see. *(Exits. Blackout.
Music from the radio is heard. DILIA is busy in the kitchen stirring in a
double boiler. PAYE enters from the street, shouting.)*   630

PAYE: *(Entering.)* Abue!

DILIA: *(In lowered voice.)* She's resting.

PAYE: Oh. *(Stands there for a moment with nothing to say.)*

DILIA: I'm making something special for you. Natilla.

PAYE: For me?   635

DILIA: Don't you like it anymore?

PAYE: Yes, I love it.

DILIA: Used to be your favorite.

PAYE: Oh, yes!

DILIA: Good! I've been skimming the top of the milk every day when I   640
scald it. I wasn't going to say anything until I was sure I had enough.

PAYE: For the party?

DILIA: No, it's for you. I didn't want you to go back without something to remember me by. *(Silence.)* Where's Tatín?

PAYE: He went over to La Placita; someone called him over . . .   645

DILIA: He has quite a following here in Santiago; never comes often enough. *(Silence.)* How about something cold to drink? *(Pours him a glass of lemonade.)*

PAYE: It's hot, isn't it?

DILIA: Yes, unbearable.

PAYE: Doña Rosario said it was earthquake weather.   650

DILIA: Tch! What the hell does she know? Some people always have something to add to the confusion. As if it wasn't enough with the heat. *(DILIA watches PAYE drink.)* Tell me if it needs more sugar.

PAYE: It's fine Tía.

DILIA: We haven't had a chance to talk, you and me. I know you proba-   655
bly haven't thought kindly of me . . . *(PAYE tries to speak.)* No, no. It's only natural. I . . .

PAYE: Tía . . .

DILIA: I never had much time for anyone else but Tatín. *(Pause. The radio D.J. blurts out the word "carnival.")* It's a pity you couldn't stay   660
for the carnival.

PAYE: Do you still go out, Tía?

DILIA: Me. No! I'm too old for that. I like to watch . . . see them go by and wave and clap. There has to be someone to watch! *(Silence. Turns the radio down to almost nothing. Looking down.)* I don't know you've   665
noticed on this trip . . . Tatín and I aren't like we used to be. I find out things about Tatín's life by reading them in the papers. I'm . . . another aunt. Mama always said that I was a stupid, selfish woman. Sometimes when the stakes are very high, you have a good hand, but you end up playing the wrong card and losing everything. Why do   670
you live all the way up in Toronto?

PAYE: Because in Jamaica, there's very little theater.

DILIA: Yes, but you see your family only once a year.

PAYE: That's as much as I can afford. And Papa pays half.

DILIA: Is there anything else you would do instead?   675

PAYE: Than playwriting? I've thought about it often.

DILIA: Why don't you get married and have children?

PAYE: *(Laughs.)* I couldn't support a wife, let alone have children. Besides, knowing a playwright's income, no woman would marry me.

DILIA: I still think that you should move to Kingstown.   680

PAYE: If I could live under communism, I would live in Santiago.

DILIA: I am not a communist, Paye. I'm too old and too stupid to un-
derstand socialism. I'm a Fidelista because I am a Rabel. I'd never heard of Karl Marx. The fact of the matter is that my life hasn't changed that much one way or the other. I still get up at six-thirty   685
every morning to scald the milk, make the coffee, butter the bread, fry the bacon. The revolution was not for me. It was for Tatín. He and his sons will see the Cuba that Fidel is building . . . I'm not campaign-

ing. But that is why Tatín had to stay. Tato couldn't take him. I   690
begged him. Tatín's place was here. He *understands* the revolution.
He had a right to stay?! He was all I had.

PAYE: *(Putting his hand on* DILIA's *shoulder.)* Tía . . .

DILIA: Tatín's life here . . . is a good life. He's someone.

PAYE: Oh yes, Tía. Tatín has everything. I envy him, Tía , if you want to
know the truth.   695

DILIA: Do you? Really?

PAYE: Yes. Yes I do. *(They stare at one another.* DILIA *smiles.)*

DILIA: *(Stirring her mix.)* You have to keep stirring or it'll separate.
(Tastes it.) I think it needs more vanilla.

PAYE: *(Handing her the bottle.)* Here. You know, I love natilla!   700

DILIA: Good! I'll warn you, it's not as good as Mama's, but she's my
teacher, so it can't be too bad. *(Offers him a taste off the mixing
spoon.)*

PAYE: Hmmmmmmmm! It's delicious.

DILIA: *(Smiles.)* Stay, I'll let you lick the bowl. *(Music swells. Blackout.
Exit. Lights come up on* PAYE *in his room changing shirts.* AMELIA *stands
by the dresser dressed in a militia uniform. She reaches into the bottom
drawer and takes out a belt-holster.)*

PAYE: Thank you for giving me your room, Amelia.   705

AMELIA: It's your room.

PAYE: *(Laughs.)* Yea. *(*AMELIA *has put on the holster.)*

AMELIA: It's a good thing you got some sun?

PAYE: Why?

AMELIA: When you arrived you looked whiter than a Polish sailor. *(Slight   710
pause.* AMELIA *sits at the edge of the bed.)* Doña Cacha is so happy since
you arrived. She seems younger somehow. She doesn't even seem
tired. *(*PAYE *sits down, takes off his running shoes and socks.)*

PAYE: You are very good to her, Amelia. I've noticed.

AMELIA: Doña Cacha has been good to me. I was only little when the   715
revolution built the first schoolhouse in my village. It was named Tony
Rabel after your uncle. Doña Cacha came up and I was chosen to
present her with a bunch of flowers. She said that the future of Cuba
was in the hands of us children. She didn't let go of my hand. I was so
proud. I wrote to her often. I told her about the monument to her   720
son and how I polished the plaque. When I graduated, I wrote her
that I had been offered a scholarship to study in Santiago but that my
father didn't have the money to send me. Doña Cacha wrote to my father and told him that she would take me into her home while I studied in Santiago. *(She stands up.)* Doña Cacha has been good to me.   725
The revolution has been very good to me and my family. I work hard
and I study hard because I want to reflect the values of the revolution.
I know first hand that these values are good and true for our people.
(They are standing at either side of the bed.)

PAYE: *(Bursting into a rage.)* Bullshit! We've traded one tyrant for
another. *(*TATÍN *stands within earshot.)*   730

AMELIA: *(Shouting.)* Things have improved!

PAYE: Improved?! Improved from what? All we needed was an honest government—and a market for our sugar, coffee, tobacco and rum!

AMELIA: How about the literacy program?

PAYE: Yeah, sure, learn to read so that we can better indoctrinate you!   735
Read the news! It tells you how great Fidel is.

AMELIA: He is great! I would lay down my life for him.

PAYE: Well, I hate him, and I would gladly see him dead! *(Pause.)*

PAYE: When I left Cuba, I never dreamed it would be for good—an exile.
I thought Fidel wouldn't last. But he closed the borders. He decides   740
who can go and who has to stay. He stole my birthright to *my* country. He set up a dictatorship and taught you to say "Thank you,
Fidel." *(Pause.)* For what?! He sold us to the Russians for a chance to
stay in power forever.

AMELIA: Doña Cacha warned us not to discuss politics with you. She was   745
right.

PAYE: I'm sorry I blew up at you—it's not you I'm angry with.

AMELIA: *(Changing the topic abruptly.)* Is it true they have penguins in
Toronto?

PAYE: Sure. They have them as pets; walk them around on leads—a friend   750
of mine has one; bit me here, once. See!

AMELIA: I don't think I could live in a place that had penguins!

PAYE: No.

AMELIA: I've got to run now—or I'll be late! *(She exits.)*

PAYE: *(Angry at himself.)* Jesus Christ! *(He flops on the bed crying. Blackout—slow fade on* TATÍN. *Lights up as* TATÍN *is dragging both rocking
chairs onto the verandah.* CACHA *follows him slowly. A newspaper is on
one of the rocking chairs.* TATÍN *places the chairs near the railing and he
sits on the stage right chair.* CACHA *sits in the stage left chair. She is carrying her fan.* TATÍN *opens the newspaper and begins to read.)*   755

CACHA: Paye's quite the young man! *(Silence.)* It's nice to see you two,
you and Paye. *(Silence.)*

TATÍN: *(Reporting from the paper.)* They're going to make it easier for exiled Cubans to return for a visit. They are no longer being considered
as traitors. Fidel is urging everyone to treat the visitors with "greatest   760
respect" . . .

CACHA: Yes. I'm glad you spoke highly of Paye's work in front of Amelia.
Paye needed to hear you say all that. He's waited a long time for it.
(Sighs.) Now, whether you mean it or not . . . Paye will only be home
a few more days. *(Silence.* CACHA *rocks and fans herself.* TATÍN *reads*   765
the paper.) I miss your father. Don't you?

TATÍN: Yes. *(Silence.)*

CACHA: When your Uncle Tony died, I thought that I would never recover. But death is very final and . . . in time . . . *(Pause.)* Having a
son in exile never ends. A son. A father. A brother. Paye's missed too   770
much. Exile is a terrible punishment. For everyone. *(Pause.)*

VOICE: *(Off.)* Good evening, Doña Cacha.

CELIA: *(Off.)* Yes, I know. They say he weighs sixty-eight pounds!

CACHA: Paye?!

CELIA: No, the pig! *(CLARA and PAYE enter laughing. TATÍN gives his seat*   775
           to CLARA and sits on the railing reading.)

CACHA: What's so funny?

CLARA: *(Controlling her laughter.)* Just as we were walking up the hill,
           the Chinese couple that moved into Dr. Pera's house come running
           out into the street. The man came out followed by the wife beating
           him over the head with a half-plucked chicken and screaming in Chi-   780
           nese. And a herd of children running behind like Chinese New Years.
           (CLARA and PAYE laugh again.)

TATÍN: Tía , in the first place, they're not Chinese. They're Korean. Re-
           member Korea? Where the war took place in the fifties?

CLARA: Ay, no wonder there's war in the world. There was a time when a
           Chinaman was a Chinaman no matter where he came from! This heat!   785
           (Fans herself.) It doesn't get this hot in Canada, eh Paye?

PAYE: No.

CACHA: *(Under her breath.)* It snows.

PAYE: In winter.

CLARA: Don't stand there like a flag pole. I'll fan you. Come. *(PAYE*   790
           moves next to her.) Come, Paye, sit on my lap like when you were my
           little boy.

PAYE: Tía, I'm too heavy! *(He does.)*

CLARA: Ay, snow! What's in Canada, Paye? Is that where Canada Dry
           comes from? *(She fans PAYE. PAYE and TATÍN laugh. TATÍN closes the*
           paper and gives it to CACHA, who opens it.)   795

TATÍN: I've always had a rather picturesque image of Canada. Sort of like
           Peyton Place; leaves on the sidewalk, picket fences and always a neigh-
           bor named Billy, with freckles.

PAYE: Leaves on the sidewalk gets a definite yes, the picket fence is iffy
           and the neighbor kid is more likely to be called Enzio or Pasquale.   800

TATÍN: What do you like about Toronto?

PAYE: In twenty words or less?! Oh . . . Toronto is like a pubescent girl.
           It's got everything, but it doesn't know what to do with it. *(CLARA*
           laughs.)

CACHA: *(Putting the paper aside.)* Well, that's that.

CLARA: She can only read the headlines without her glasses.   805

PAYE: Can I get you your glasses, Abuela?

CACHA: No, no. I really don't need them. I only read the headlines any-
           way. If something is important enough, it'll come up in conversation.

CLARA: *(Whispering.)* She's too vain to wear her glasses.

CACHA: Nonsense! I don't like to wear them because they distort every-   810
           thing. I can see. I don't see as well as I used to, but it's gone gradually
           and I've become accustomed to how I see things. I know my world.
           Then they gave me those glasses and I didn't know what was what.
           One minute the wall's over there, the next minute it's closer. If I look
           up I see you, if I look down I see only your nose!   815

TATÍN: They're bifocals.

CACHA: They're infuriating! I like to see things equally. If I have to give
up reading little letters, it's a small price to pay to keep my world in
perspective. *(CLARA fans PAYE.)* I see you got a little color. *(PAYE looks
at his forearms.)* Maybe Julio can take you to Mar Verde again. I hear   820
it's really beautiful.

PAYE: It is. You've never been?

CACHA: *(Laughing.)* Me?! Your grandfather used to take me to the
beach. He used to go to Ciudamar on Saturday afternoons.

CLARA: Ay, yes!   825

CACHA: In those days, the beaches were not all public and there was a
section, fenced off so that Batista's military men could swim. A diving
board, a pavilion, lawn chairs and umbrellas. They had everything.
The rest of us had to share two showers and a stretch of sand no bigger than a sandbox. In the private part there were always matrons   830
looking like Eva Perón, covering their porcelain skin from the sun. No
negroes were allowed there. *(Laughs.)* But they say that when a black
man takes revenge, he does it with style. *(Giggles.)* You know what
they used to do? They used to wait for the current to be flowing from
the public section to the military and they'd swim over to the rope   835
fence that divided even the water, and they'd shit and wave their load
goodbye to the other side! *(Laughs.)* Once your grandfather was floating on his back out in the deep water, when the current suddenly reversed and all the turd kept coming back. He felt something bobbing
by his feet; a shark?! No! It was a turd the size of a sausage. *(They're*   840
all laughing. The lights start to change slowly into a sunset effect.) He
never went to the beach again. That was in nineteen. . . forty-four. I
haven't been to the beach since.

PAYE: You should come with us next time. The sea air will do you good!

CACHA: I'm afraid Mar Verde's not for me.   845

PAYE: Mar Verde's for everybody. It is paradise! It's beautiful. Abue, it's
so beautiful. *(He stands at the edge of the verandah. Silence.)*

CACHA: They say that when Columbus landed in Cuba he said: "This is
the most beautiful . . ."

PAYE: *(Finishing the quote.)* " . . . beautiful land that human eyes ever be-   850
held."

CACHA: No one is quite certain where Columbus landed, but wherever it
was, he certainly summed it up quite nicely. *(The sunset glows for a few
seconds. Blackout.)*

ACT II

*Lights come up on a barrel in the middle of the patio. JULIO sings "Quiéreme
Mucho" from inside the barrel. He stands up and reveals his bare chest. PAYE
enters. JULIO sings to him . . .*

JULIO: Remember that one?

PAYE: *(Applauding.)* I'm surprised *you* remember it.

JULIO: I always think of you when I hear that song. You sang it at
         Abuelo's sixtieth birthday. *(PAYE smiles, embarrassed. JULIO climbs out
         of the barrel.)*   5

PAYE: Is that it? Fixed?

JULIO: *(Wiping his chest and flexing his muscles.)* Yes. The outgoing pipe
         was jammed with dirt. Well, that ought to hold it for a while. Now,
         you gotta help me get this sucker back up on the roof!

PAYE: Okay, let's go.   10

JULIO: Wait a minute! Let me cool off a second at least. Where's Tatín?

PAYE: He's writing something for his radio broadcast. I'll get 'im.

JULIO: No, no. Leave him be. He doesn't have to get sweat on his back.
         Neither do you, really.

PAYE: In this heat you can't help but sweat.   15

JULIO: Not like this. You guys have brains. You guys don't ever have to
         exert your muscles. Not like me. All I got is muscles. *(Flexes with
         pride.)* Nice, no? It drives the women crazy. *(Flexes into another pose.)*
         I don't have any brains.

PAYE: I'm sure you do.   20

JULIO: No. None to speak of. You guys, you got the brains in the family.
         I'll cut sugar cane every season and work out with the militia, and
         that'll be it for the rest of my life.

PAYE: What would you rather do?

JULIO: You really want to know.   25

PAYE: Yeah, tell me.

JULIO: What I'd really like to do? I'd like to have a steady sit-down job in
         an office with a big window to stare out of, like in Havana. And drive
         a car; one of those little sports cars. Red.

PAYE: Julio, you're an aspiring playboy.   30

JULIO: What's that?

PAYE: A playboy? It's like a, gigolo, but independent.

JULIO: Oh, yes, I could live with that.

PAYE: Have you ever thought of leaving . . . ?

JULIO: No. If you don't have brains, no matter where you go, you still   35
         end up shoveling shit. *(PAYE laughs.)* You make lots of money?

PAYE: Me? No.

JULIO: *(Surprised.)* How come?

PAYE: Playwrights don't get to make lots of money.

JULIO: Is that right? *(Stretches his back muscles. Dries himself off once   40
         more.)* You don't mind not making lots of money?

PAYE: Me? Yeah, I mind. I'm miserable about it.

JULIO: You didn't want to be a doctor like Ari?

PAYE: No.

JULIO: And you're still outside?   45

PAYE: What do you mean?

JULIO: Well, if I was going to be something that didn't make lots of

money . . . if I was going to be miserable and broke, I'd rather do it
in Cuba. Now, you, you got brains. You could be rich! If I had brains,
I might consider going abroad and getting rich . . . but then I'd only   50
be miserable outside of Cuba. Twice as miserable. *(Thinks a moment.)*
I would have to be *very* rich. I can't understand being abroad and not
being rich. There isn't much consolation in that! *(Silence.)* You remember the time you set Tatín's bed on fire?

PAYE: And I threw a bucket of water on him! *(They laugh.)* I locked my-   55
self in the bathroom. And when I thought it was quiet enough and
everyone was back in bed, I came out . . . Papa was there, with the
belt. *(They laugh. Music. Blackout. Lights come up on AMELIA on the
verandah.)*

AMELIA: *(Shouting.)* Rosario! Ah, compaañera. Doña Cacha wants to
know if we could borrow some of your chairs for the party?   60

VOICE: Ay, yes, of course. I have six cane-back ones, four with the
chrome legs, the one from my vanity and . . .

AMELIA: How about the long bench?

VOICE: Ay, that's so tough!

AMELIA: It's tougher standing up! There's going to be such a crowd!   65

VOICE: I've been thinking about the pig all day!

AMELIA: *(Trying to exit.)* I got to run now, I got to run down to Clara to
borrow her tablecloths!

VOICE: Ay, Amelia! I only have five cane-backs. I forgot. Graciela busted
the other one last week!   70

AMELIA: She can stand up! *(Blackout. Lights come up on TATÍN sitting on
the railing center. Smoking. There are party noises in the background.
Dance music. Voices. He addresses the audience.)*

TATÍN: Paye's letters were always full of all the wonderful things that are
out there. He'd mention steaks he had when there were real shortages
here. He'd bring up his trip to Europe and things he'd seen there, and
remark too bad you couldn't see this or that. It was as if he wanted to   75
hurt me.

ANA: *(Enters.)* So here you are. *(TATÍN looks.)* It's cooler out here. *(Sits
beside him.)* The pork was good, wasn't it? *(TATÍN nods.)* I'm sorry
Tía. Cuca put sauce all over your rice. I know you don't like it that
way. *(There is a burst of laughter from inside.)* Listen to that! Too bad   80
the boys didn't get to come. They should have come, you know.
(Pause.) I suppose it, would have made it harder for you and Paye to
talk.

TATÍN: *(Butting a cigarette.)* You were dancing with Paye.

ANA: Yes. He was telling me about seeing Baryshnikov at an open air am-   85
phitheater. *(Pause.)* Did he tell you he was unhappy living in Toronto?

TATÍN: Why? Why do you ask?

ANA: I don't know. I always thought that . . . you know . . . but from the
way he speaks, I get the feeling he feels . . . dissatisfied.

TATÍN: He's having a bad time of it right now.   90

ANA: Did he tell you that?

TATÍN: In dribs and drabs.

ANA: He still manages pretty well.

TATÍN: He works at a lot of other things.

ANA: Ahh! *(TATÍN looks at ANA.)* You know the shirt he's wearing. It's   95
silk. Bought it in India. He spent three months in India.

TATÍN: Yes, I know.

ANA: He's been everywhere.

TATÍN: Yes I know. He gets the Sunday New York Times and he's met
Lillian Hellman. He has an electric typewriter, a private phone and   100
everything Paul Simon ever recorded. *(Pause.)*

ANA: You wish you were in his shoes?

TATÍN: I wish I were in anybody else's shoes.

ANA: Tatín. . .

TATÍN: What about you? Whose shoes do you wish you were in?   105

ANA: I . . . I don't know . . .

TATÍN: Come on, just off the top of your head.

ANA: *(Thinks.)* I guess I still wish that I was Kim Novak.

TATÍN: Kim Novak?

ANA: When I was a little girl I always wanted to look like Kim Novak.   110
Now, Paye tells me she's not even a star anymore.

TATÍN: You asked Paye about Kim Novak? *(Laughs.)*

ANA: Well, why not? *(TATÍN laughs heartily.)* You're making me feel stupid. *(Starts to smile.)*

TATÍN: Kim Novak!!! *(They both burst out laughing.)*   115

ANA: *(As laughter subsides.)* Tatín. . . I know what's the matter . . . why
you've been acting like you've been acting. *(TATÍN looks at her atten-
tively.)* I thought it had to do with Paye . . . His visit and memories
and . . . but, it really has to do with the radio broadcasts, doesn't it? It
does, doesn't it? *(Applause from inside. Voices. As DILIA and CACHA
enter TATÍN jumps to attention as if he'd been discovered.)*   120

DILIA: C'mon you two, the party's inside!

TATÍN: Abue! Tía! *(They walk up stage but sit at the patio.)*

CACHA: You should be inside dancing!

TATÍN: We were getting some air.

CACHA: Ah, yes, it's cooler out here.   125

DILIA: You should see Tía Clara!

TATÍN: She must be boiling over in that dress.

DILIA: *(To TATÍN as if gossiping.)* She's been trying to match up Amelia
with one of the Moreno boys. Manolo.

TATÍN: Is he the one with the gold tooth?   130

DILIA: No, he's the one with the warts. *(Points to her chin, her cheek, and
her eyebrow. Laughs.)* I think Tía Clara's had too much to drink.

TATÍN: You're not too sober yourself, Tía.

DILIA: Drunk? Me?!

TATÍN: I saw you swig back Tío Nando's beer at the table. More than once!   135

DILIA: Tch! That much won't even take the itch from a bee sting!

(*Laughter and cheers from inside.*)

CACHA: Listen to that! (*CLARA enters. She is wearing, an overly fancy 50's cocktail dress.*)

CLARA: Ay! The queen of the carnival is here! I've been dancing and dancing . . .

CACHA: You better sit . . .   140

CLARA: And I'm still in one piece! I'm putting the young girls to shame. (*She sits.*) Ay, to be eighteen again!

CACHA: Or fifty. (*All laugh.*)

CLARA: Ay, no! No, Cacha, not me; if I'm going to dream, I want it all beautiful: eighteen, technicolor, violins and blonde hair! I'm glad I   145
got all dressed up! (*Blows down the front of her dress.*)

ANA: Can I get you a drink, Tía?

CLARA: Ay, Anita, you know I don't drink. But be an angel and get me my fan. It's on the table by the gramophone. (*ANA exits.*) I'm just a little hot, but as soon as I cool off. . . Ay Cacha, I didn't take a break!
(*Laughs.*)   150

CACHA: Clara, remember Monday's wash day.

CLARA: I may not even wash this Monday. (*Music changes to a conga.*)

DILIA: Conga! (*DILIA exits dancing.*)

ANA: (*Entering.*) I think Julio's drunk, he keeps trying to lift Tía Carmen. (*Gives CLARA her fan and ice water.*)   155

CLARA: You'll know he's drunk when he tries to lift Graciela! (*TATÍN laughs.*)

CACHA: You should laugh, you used to go out with her.

ANA: Before he was married.

CLARA: Before she was fat!

PAYE: (*Off.*) Tía Clara! Conga!   160

CLARA: Ay, a request! A request!

CACHA: Slow down Clara, . . .

CLARA: (*Hurriedly trying to put on shoes.*) I'm fine Cacha . . . (*Suddenly screams.*) Ahhhh! My bunion! I can't get my shoes back on! (*All laugh.*)

ANA: Sit this one out, Tía.   165

CLARA: Not on your life! I'll have to dance barefoot.

CACHA: Clara, tomorrow, you'll . . .

CLARA: (*Getting up.*) Tomorrow, I don't care if they amputate! (*Hobbles off, waving her shoes in the air.*)

ANA: She's crazy!

CACHA: Ay, no, Anita. Clara's wearing her party dress, that's all. I'm glad   170
Julio got the pig—and that we've all made it like the carnival for Paye. (*DILIA laughs from inside.*) When your grandfather was alive, there'd be parties in this house till noon the next day. Your uncles . . . when they were young, they used to dance like they had an itch in their groins from the inside out. Your Uncle Pucho used to spend the three   175
days of the carnival dancing. Even when he came by for a clean shirt

in the afternoons, he'd be congaing through the house singing, "If I don't dance, I lose the beat, if I don't dance, I lose the beat," over and over and over.

DILIA: *(Entering.)* You should see Pave dancing. He hasn't forgotten that 180
he's Cuban! And Tía Clara! You know she's dancing barefoot? *(Takes CLARA's fan.)*

ANA: I've never seen Tía Clara like this.

DILIA: Two weeks ago, all she could talk about was her hemorrhoids! Poor Tía Clara! Having to do without Paye all these years.

CLARA: *(Enters.)* The room's spinning in there. 185

DILIA: Tired, Tía!

CLARA: No! I just wanted the young girls to have a crack at Paye. Give me my fan. *(Sits.)*

DILIA: You're going to have to give away that dress after tonight.

CLARA: It'll wash. 190

ANA: Tía, you should get a new one.

CLARA: And where is one supposed to get this kinda material in . . .

DILIA: Don't get her started, please. *(Cheers are heard from inside.)*

CLARA: Listen to that! It sounds like the old days. Ay, if Sylvia and Tato could only be here tonight. *(To ANA.)* Sylvia used to have such a good 195
time at these things. Once she had two drinks in her, she didn't know if she was talking English, Spanish or Jew. *(To DILIA.)* You remember the time she was trying to tell Father Ephraim that he hit the nail on the head and she wound up telling him that he really knew how to screw! *(All laugh.)* 200

PAYE: *(Enters holding a beer.)* So the party's out here.

DILIA: Look at him, he's soaking wet!

CACHA: Isn't he beautiful! Why don't you change your shirt, you'll . . .

PAYE: I just have the shirt I'm leaving with tomorrow.

CACHA: What did you do with the others? 205

TATÍN: He's leaving some to me.

PAYE: And Julio, and Roberto and so on and so on.

CACHA: What are you going to do, run around Canada naked?

PAYE: How's everybody doing out here? *(All mumble "fine" or "all right," except CLARA who is staring into space. PAYE stumbles.)*

DILIA: You're drunk, Paye. 210

CLARA: Everybody's drunk to you, Dilia. It's a pity you never had a husband, then you'd know what drunk really was.

DILIA: Let's not start on that one!

AMELIA: *(Enters wearing her full carnival costume.)* Where's Paye?

CACHA: Ay, Amelia! 215

DILIA: See, Tía, Amelia couldn't stand to see you the only one all dressed up.

CLARA: Turn around, let's see.

AMELIA: I promised Paye I'd try it on before he left.

PAYE: It's superb!

AMELIA: La Placita's going to take first prize this year. 220

DILIA: As always! *(AMELIA exits.)*
CACHA: Having a good time, Paye?
PAYE: The time of my life. *(Raises his drink.)* To La Placita!
CACHA: Tonight we're all happy, Paye.
DILIA: You'll have a lot to tell them when you get back.   225
CACHA: Ay, yes, look at him; he's even got some color. *(CLARA fans
    PAYE, who has put himself within reach of the breeze.)*
DILIA: A few more days at Mar Verde and he'd really start looking like a
    Cuban again!
PAYE: *(Suddenly standing up.)* I have something to say. *(A shrill scream
    from inside.)*
DILIA: I better go see . . .   225 230
PAYE: No, no, Tía, sit down. I want everyone to hear. *(Kisses her.)* You
    know, I used to be afraid of you. *(To all.)* Now I find out that Tía
    loves me after all.
DILIA: Ay, Paye, you're drunk!
PAYE: *(Raising his beer.)* To my Tía Dilia! *(Tries to stand on a chair.)*   235
ANA: *(To TATÍN.)* I think he's had too much to . . .
CLARA: Ay, yes, Paye, sit down.
PAYE: *(Kissing CLARA.)* No, no, Tía. Now that everyone is here. *(Looks
    around.)* Well, the main ones . . . my family (Pause.) I want to return
    to Cuba for good! *(There is a momentary silence.)*   240
TATÍN: He's drunk!
PAYE: No, I'm not. I want to come home. If you'll have me?!
TATÍN: You're crazy! *(There are voices raised from inside. A girl screams.
    PAYE and TATÍN shout over the voices.)*
PAYE: What's so crazy about it? It happens . . .
AMELIA: *(In a panic.)* Dilia, come quick. It's Julio; he's drunk!   245
TATÍN: You don't know what the hell you're saying! You couldn't live here!
VOICE: *(Off.)* Julio!
VOICE: *(Off.)* Get somebody, quick, get Dilia! *(DILIA exits.)*
TATÍN: It's not as simple as that!
VOICE: *(Off.)* What the hell is he doing?!   250
PAYE: What's the matter, don't you want me here?!
TATÍN: No!
PAYE: It's my home!
AMELIA: Dilia, hurry!
VOICE: *(Off.)* Don't let 'im! Grab him!   255
VOICE: *(Off.)* Go around!
VOICE: *(Off.)* Stop him!
TATÍN: You're thinking of no one but yourself! Well I got news for you.
    Life in Cuba isn't like you've seen here this week. There isn't always a
    party.   260
VOICE: *(Off.)* He's had too much to drink!
PAYE: And you think I have everything given to me on a silver platter!
VOICE: *(Off.)* Don't, Julio!

AMELIA: Dilia, he's taking off everything!

VOICE: *(Off.)* Stop it Julio! *(The voices from inside have increased in urgency. Screams. JULIO appears stark naked. AMELIA and DILIA run after him. DILIA stops at upstage door.)*   265

JULIO: Adiós, Abuela! *(PAYE and TATÍN ignore the chase and get into a screaming match of their own.)*

TATÍN: You wouldn't be happy here!

PAYE: Julio is!

TATÍN: You're not Julio!!! *(TATÍN climbs on the table.)* I have an announcement too. I'm leaving Cuba for good!   270

ANA: On what boat?

DILIA: That is the most preposterous . . .

ANA: What about us, your wife and your kids?

TATÍN: Why is it with the goddamned Cubans that they won't listen and they all want to speak at once?   275

PAYE: Well, you'll have to put up with me because I intend to apply to come back.

TATÍN: I will do everything in my power to stop you.

PAYE: You hateful son of a bitch, what power do you have?!

TATÍN: You don't think I heard what you said to Amelia! I'll report   280
that . . .

PAYE: You stinking commie bastard—you'd betray your brother to get your way . . . You hate me that much.

TATÍN: Bullshit!

PAYE: Yes, it's hate—and I hate you back. You have the heart of a cock-   285
roach. *(PAYE goes wild screaming.)* I hate you! I hate you! I hate you!!!
(TATÍN slaps PAYE. PAYE slaps him back. Silence. PAYE bursts into tears and falls into TATÍN's arms. DILIA notices that CACHA is having difficulty breathing.)

DILIA: Mama! *(To ANA.)* Water!

CLARA: Take mine. *(She does.)*

PAYE: Abuela?

CACHA: I'm okay. I'm okay.   290

DILIA: *(To ANA and CLARA.)* Help me get her to bed. *(PAYE goes to help.)*

TATÍN: No. Stay. *(Trying not to be heard.)* I don't hate you, Paye. I don't want you here because if I could I'd leave myself.

PAYE: *(Loudly.)* You! You want to leave Cuba! *(ANA and DILIA turn to look at TATÍN. PAYE sits.)*

TATÍN: If I could get my wife and my sons out—all at once—I'd take the   295
next plane, boat, raft out of here.

PAYE: What?

TATÍN: This is a mess. We're sending troops to Angola, we're buying arms from Russia. My radio show is being censored. My writing is being questioned . . .   300

PAYE: In the six days that I've been here, you've been leading me to believe . . .

TATÍN: You believed what you wanted to believe. *(ANA enters.)*

ANA: Is that what it is, Tatín?

TATÍN: Yes. *(ANA crosses to him and puts her arms around him in support.)*   305

PAYE: How is she?

ANA: All right. The shock, her age. She's breathing fine now.

TATÍN: Do you want to leave, Ana?

ANA: I'm not the one who's being censored.

TATÍN: Could you leave?   310

ANA: My needs are simple. A ballet bar and a bunch of kids doing demi-
plies—anywhere. But if we leave, Tatín, we all leave together. You, me,
the boys. All four of us. Paye, you have a plane to catch tomorrow.
I'm glad you came. It doesn't take much to live in Cuba. Just blind
faith. Either you have it or you don't. *(She hugs PAYE.)*   315

PAYE: *(Returning the embrace.)* Thank you. Ana. *(ANA exits. To TATÍN.)*
What are you going to do?

TATÍN: Leaving Cuba is a slow, tedious process at best.

PAYE: You know, Tatín, I never felt like I belonged anywhere as much as
I do here. I have been living in exile all these years. And you're right,   320
I'm not writing. And I don't care if I ever write again.

TATÍN: You don't mean that.

PAYE: Yes, I do. I only write because I'm lonely. Because I'm seeking approval from total strangers in the dark, because . . .

TATÍN: You have something to say. You have imagination.   325

PAYE: Up there, in the winter, people bundle up and cast their eyes on
the sidewalk. Ice is slippery. It's a way of life. You don't look up. You
don't see who you're passing on the street.

TATÍN: Here, the committees are becoming more powerful. Now that my
work is getting noticed abroad, what I write becomes scrutinized. I'm   330
asked what things mean by people who learned to read ten years ago.

PAYE: Surely you knew there'd be censorship?

TATÍN: Of course. It is understood that until stability is reached, censorship is necessary, and that under siege, the militia must be armed to
the teeth. Our neighbors must be watched. Our people must be in-   335
doctrinated so that they can learn to cope with the new way of life.
(He lights up a cigarette.) But, that has become the new way of life.
You see, Paye, I am a disillusioned man. And it makes me sad.

PAYE: So what will you do?

TATÍN: I have two sons who know nothing but this and who believe fer-   340
vently the lessons they've been taught. And in a few years, they'll be of
military age and won't be allowed to leave. *(There is long silence.)*
Paye, stay abroad. And write.

AMELIA: *(Enters.)* We found Julio! *(Giggles.)*

TATÍN: Shhh! Abuela's in bed.   345

AMELIA: *(Suppressing her laughter.)* He was sitting on the pitcher's
mound on a nest of red ants. *(She laughs.)*

TATÍN: It's not funny.

AMELIA: His balls are swollen like pineapples! *(She exits.)*

PAYE: I'll envy you the carnival.   350

TATÍN: *(Shrugging his shoulders.)* Euphoria for the masses, a little something to ease the pain. What time is your plane? *(Before PAYE can reply, DILIA enters.)*

DILIA: Paye, Mama wants to see you. She is afraid she'll fall asleep and you'll leave without seeing her. Tatín, you wouldn't leave, would you? *(Almost in tears.)* When Mama dies, what will I do? *(TATÍN bursts into tears in DILIA's arms. Lights fade. Lights come up in CACHA's room. PAYE is sitting on the edge of the bed under the mosquito net.)*   355

PAYE: Abuela?

CACHA: Paye?

PAYE: Tía said . . .

CACHA: I've been waiting for you. They gave me something, I think to make me sleep, but I've been waiting . . . I must talk to you, Paye.   360

PAYE: Yes, Abue.

CACHA: Here, sit close to me. *(PAYE moves closer.)*

CACHA: I'm not going to die, Paye. Not yet. I . . . I'm waiting for everyone to come home. They have to come. Because I'm waiting. *(Touches PAYE's hand lovingly.)* Tomorrow . . . I will have to speak to Julio. And   365 Tatín! Tell them. I will speak to them tomorrow.

PAYE: Yes, Abue. Now rest . . . *(Starts to get up.)*

CACHA: *(Holding him back.)* Tato is my son. You are my grandson. You were born in my arms! *(SILENCE.)* This is your home, Paye. No one can turn you away. You understand, Paye?   370

PAYE: Yes, Abue.

CACHA: Even after I'm dead . . . this is your home. You were born in my arms, Paye. In this house.

PAYE: Abue . . .

CACHA: You will come back, Paye. I know it. Maybe not soon, but you   375 will come back. You will all come back. *(Reaches out for him.)* My little Paye.

PAYE: *(Controlling his emotions.)* Sleep now, Abuela, tomorrow . . .

CACHA: Yes. Tomorrow. Tell Tato I'm fine. I'm not going to die. Tomorrow, Paye . . . Paye-Paye. *(CACHA is asleep. PAYE kisses her. Music comes up softly. Blackout. Lights come up on DILIA, ANA and TATÍN facing front on the verandah. CACHA joins them. They clap and wave as though the carnival were passing by. There is carnival music. On the stage right corner, a light comes up on PAYE. He is speaking into a tape recorder.)*   380

PAYE: It is coming around to winter again real soon. The trees all over the city are a carnival of color; though in my mind they'll never compare to the carnival I missed that time. I shall never stop missing it. It and everything else I left behind. No matter where I am, I guess a part of me will always be there. My home. *(Pause.)* I miss you, Tatín.   385 I think of you all the time. I think of what we said to one another and what we left still unsaid. *(Pause.)* I never quite managed to tell you that. . . that I love you, and that neither miles, nor long silences, will ever alter that. It's a pleasant thought that makes my exile less cruel, easier to bear. Enough said and not enough. Mama and Papa are trying all they can through the Jamaican Embassy. Mama knows the counsel well and she seems hopeful that he'll get you and your family out. A million warm and gentle kisses for you and the whole family . . . from your brother who awaits you, Paye. P.S. I am enclosing a copy of my play. I hope you like it. *(As he speaks the last few words, everything goes wild with color and light. The music swells and confetti pours from the sky. Suddenly the music stops and all freeze in a tableau as the confetti falls slowly as in a glass enclosed souvenir shaker. As the last of the confetti falls, lights fade to black.)*

390

Discussion Questions

1. Describe the relationship between the two brothers. How is that relationship related to their feelings about Cuba?

2. How does each of the brothers feel about his own life? What issues about their identity do they share?

3. On page 324 the title of the play is used in connection to the local carnival. Explain the significance of that connection as it relates to the immediate context as well as to the larger issues explored in the play.

PUERTO RICAN-AMERICAN LITERATURE

A BRIEF SURVEY

Like its Cuban and Mexican counterparts, Puerto Rican-American literature originated in its connection to Spain. At the end of the nineteenth century, prominent figures such as Emeterio Betances, Lola Rodriguez de Tió, and Eugenio María de Hostos wrote and disseminated their works in New York. Their political pamphlets and essays railed against the Spanish government in an effort to seek Puerto Rico's independence. The great number of Spanish-language journals and presses in Florida and New York during the final decades provided the impetus for the great body of works that were published at the beginning of the subsequent century.

Several authors and works of the early part of this century served as inspiration for the authors that would later focus on the experience of Puerto Ricans in New York. Most notable among these are Julia de Burgos and Clemente Soto Velez. By the 1950s, these early pioneers who documented the exile experience of Puerto Ricans in New York, were joined by writers such as Bernardo Vega and Jesús Colón. Colón's *A Puerto Rican in New York and Other Sketches,* for example, is the first book-length English language depiction of Puerto Ricans in New York. Because of this, it marks a transition from the literature of Puerto Ricans who were more concerned with what they left behind than what their future held.

The Puerto Rican literature produced in the last decades owes a great debt to Colón and Vega, as much of it explores the conflicts resulting from exile and migration. Piri Thomas's *Down These Mean Streets* (1967), Nicholasa Mohr's *Nilda* (1974), and Judith Ortiz Cofer's *The Line of the Sun* (1989), are three representatives of this type of fiction. Considering the relatively recent dates of these publications it seems clear that like much of contemporary Cuban-American and Mexican-American literature, the conflicts of exile and migration continue to shape Puerto Rican literature and culture.

In poetry this focus on the experience of migration and exile has been a source of inspiration as well. A rich oral tradition and an attention to African heritage, however, are also paramount in the verse of many of the writers in the last few decades. Modeled on Afro-Caribbean poetry, as well as on the *Negritude movement,* a term coined by the Martinican poet Aimé Césaire to describe a sense of black cultural and artistic pride, the work of poet Louis Reyes Rivera is one salient example. Adopting the name *Nuyorican,* as a reference both to the city and to their Puerto Rican origins, poets like Miguel Algarin and Jack Agüeros were part of the Beat Generation, which produced such figures as Allen Ginsberg and Jack Kerouac. The *Nuyorican* poets drew their experiences, as did the Beat poets, from bohemian city life. Unlike the poets of the Beat era, however, the *Nuyorican* writers were truly living a life of deprivation as the children of immigrants who spoke little English and were placed on the lowest rung of the socioeconomic ladder.

Similar to the Teatro Campesino created by Mexican-American writers, the works of Puerto Ricans playwrights in the 1960s and 70s were often performed in the streets. Some writers, like Miguel Piñero, drew their inspiration from their prison experiences and performed and staged them in prison settings. Piñero's *Short Eyes* (1975), for example, takes place in the dayroom of a prison and was staged during the author's incarceration at Sing Sing prison. Much of the recent theater, however, has shifted its focus away from these depictions, and instead deals with a variety of issues that are not always sociopolitical.

Judith Ortiz Cofer

JUDITH ORTIZ COFER was born in the small town of Hormigueros in 1952, and moved to the United States in 1955. She grew up and went to school in Paterson, New Jersey, until her family moved to Georgia in 1968. She has a B.A. from Augusta College, an M.A. from Florida Atlantic University and did additional graduate work at the University of Oxford. She has published four chapbooks: Latin Women Pray *(1980),* Among the Ancestors *(1981),* The Native Dancer *(1981), and* Peregrina *(1986). Her works also include books of poetry:* Reaching for the Mainland *(1987),* Terms of Survival *(1987), and* Silent Dancing: A Partial Remembrance of a Puerto Rican Childhood *(1990), which also includes several essays. Her published fiction consists of* The Line of the Sun *(1989),* The Latin Deli *(1993), which also includes verse,* An Island Like You: Stories of the Barrio *(1995), for young readers; and* The Year of Our Revolution: New and Selected Stories and Poems *(1998).*

The Line of the Sun, *nominated for a Pulitzer Prize, sets two parallel stories: one involves a Puerto Rico constructed mainly from myth, and the other involves a young girl growing up in a Latino household in Paterson, New Jersey. The first half of the novel is set in the poor village of Salud, Puerto Rico, and introduces the characters Rafael Vivente and his wild brother-in-law, Guzmán. The second part focuses on the life of the young narrator, Marisol, as she grows up in "El Building" in New York City, a tenement house inhabited by Puerto Ricans. The two sides of Marisol's cultural identity are at odds with each other throughout the course of the story. Her father encourages her to become more "Americanized," while her mother insists on following the traditions of her island home. The resolution to this dilemma culminates in the family's moving from the city to the suburbs of New Jersey.*

Fiction

From The Line of the Sun

Chapter Seven

Ramona says Rafael was a stranger again to her when she arrived at the airport in New York on a bitter cold November day. Because she was unable to find an adequate coat in Mayagüez for either one of us, we were wrapped like gypsies in shawls and scarves. Ramona was beautiful, and people stared. Or perhaps we looked to them like two sisters, orphaned in a war. She was eighteen years old and in full bloom. Rafael in his dark navy uniform looked like an American sailor on leave. They were shy with each other, and Ramona says that I would not let him pick me up or even take my hand. He looked like no one I knew.

Though he was stationed at the Brooklyn Navy Yard, Rafael had decided that New York City was not a safe place for his young wife and daughter. He had looked up a cousin on his father's side who lived in Paterson, New Jersey—just across the Hudson River. His cousin, also distanced from the Santacruz family, had married his mother's maid, a woman older than he by ten years. He had finally left the Island with Severa, that was her name, and the two girls and a boy they had managed to conceive one after the other. There, in an apartment building inhabited mainly by Puerto Rican families, we lived the first few years.

It was in *El Building,* as it was called by the tenants, that my brother was born three years after our arrival. As I became slowly aware of the world around me, my life became circumscribed by the sounds, smells, and barriolike population of the building and the street where we lived but were never fully assimilated. Though it was a Puerto Rican neighborhood with Jewish landlords, my father considered it only a place to land temporarily. He did not allow my mother to join the gossip circles of the women at the laundromat, or even to shop by herself at Cheo's bodega, a little general store just across the street from El Building where a little man named Cheo sold hard-to-find delicacies of Island cuisine such as green bananas, yuccas, and plantains. Instead, when Rafael came home on leave for the weekends we went shopping at the American supermarket. It was not snobbery on his part so much as fear for us. Two years in New York City had taught him that a street-tough Puerto Rican immigrant is not the same species as the usually gentle and hospitable Islander. He had escaped the brunt of racial prejudice only because of his fair skin and his textbook English, which sounded formal as a European's. His wife and daughter, both olive-skinned and black-haired, were a different matter altogether.

It was *la mancha,* that sign of the wetback, the stain that has little to do with the color of our skin, because some of us are as "white" as our American neighbors; and it was the frightened-rabbit look in our eyes and our unending awe of anything new or foreign that identified us as the newcomers.

It was easy for Ramona to become part of the ethnic beehive of El Building. It was a microcosm of Island life with its intrigues, its gossip groups, and even its own spiritist, Elba, who catered to the complex spiritual needs of the tenants. Coming in from shopping, my mother would close her eyes and breathe deeply; it was both a sigh of relief, for the city streets made her anxious, and a taking in of familiar smells. In El Building, women cooked with their doors open as a sign of hospitality. Hard-to-obtain items like green bananas from the Island, plantains, and breadfruit were shared. At the best of times, it was as closely knit a community as any Little Italy or Chinatown; the bad times, however, included free-for-all domestic quarrels in which neighbors were called in to witness for a scorned wife: "Estela, did you or did you not see my Antonio with that whore Tita at the pool hall on Saturday?" Of course, after the arguments were over, the third party would inevitably be scorned by one or the other as an interfering fool. It was difficult to hold grudges with other tenants because the hallways were shared and, there was one narrow staircase for all, and it was impossible to avoid El Basement, where the washing machines and dryers that several of the women had bought collectively were kept. The basement was a battleground where long-standing friendships could be dissolved in a matter of minutes if anyone trespassed on someone else's time to use the machines; or worse, if you were one of the deprived ones who did not own interest in the Sears *lavadoras*[1] and you were caught sneaking in a load—your fate would stop just short of public stoning. At some point someone got the idea of hiring kids to patrol the basement. This created a new hierarchy in the already gang-oriented adolescents of El Building because it encouraged behind-the-scenes negotiations, bribes, and occasional violence for control of El Basement.

Life was lived at a high pitch in El Building. The adults conducted their lives in two worlds in blithe acceptance of cultural schizophrenia, going to work or on errands in the English-speaking segment, which they endured either with the bravura of the Roman gladiator or with the downcast-eyed humility that passed for weakness on the streets—a timidity that mothers inculcated into their children but that earned us not a few insults and even beatings from the black kids, who knew better. With them it was either get tough or die. Once inside the four walls of their railroad flats, though, everyone perched at his or her level. Fortified in their illusion that all could be kept the same within the family as it had been on the Island, women decorated their apartments with every artifact that enhanced the fantasy. Religious objects imported from the Island were favorite wall hangings. Over the kitchen table in many apartments hung the Sacred Heart, disturbing in its realistic depiction of the crimson organ bleeding in an open palm, like the grocer's catch-of-the-day. And Mary could always be found smiling serenely from walls.

Year after year Rafael, my father, would try unsuccessfully to convince Ramona to move away from El Building. We could have afforded it. With our assured monthly check from the navy, we were considered affluent by our neighbors, but Ramona harbored a fear of strange neighborhoods, with their vulnerable single-family homes sitting like eggs on their little plots of green lawn. Ramona had developed the garrison mentality of the tenement dweller that dictates that there is safety in numbers. When Father came home on leave he would complain of the lack of privacy in the place, the loud neighbors, the bad influences on my brother and me. Mother would point out that with him gone so much of the time she was safe there among others of her kind. He would take us for rides to Fairlawn, an affluent community where the doctors, lawyers, and other Paterson professionals lived. There was so much space, and you could even hear the birds. Mother glanced at the cold façades of the houses and shook her head, unable to imagine the lives within. To her the square homes of strangers were like a television set: you could see the people moving and talking, apparently alive and real, but when you looked inside it was nothing but wires and tubes.

Since Father's homecomings were of short duration—he was then on continuous tours of duty with a fleet of cargo ships delivering supplies to military bases in Europe—his arguments about moving from El Building were always left to be resolved next time. The one thing he was adamant about, however, was the school my brother and I attended. He was convinced that Public School Number 15, where all the other children in our block went, was a haven for winos and hoodlums. The hoodlums were the students; the winos slept on the benches of the so-called campus,

[1] washing machines

a park that surrounded the gray prisonlike school building where drifters took naps on the benches and drugs were sold behind bushes. He enrolled us in Saint Jerome's, where the nuns were liberal and the academic standards high. We were the only Puerto Rican students. All the others were Irish and Italian kids several generations away from immigration, sons and daughters of established professional parents. At Saint Jerome's we were taught art appreciation, church history, and Latin. No home economics for the girls, no shop for the boys. And we wore uniforms with beanies. My brother and I walked the five blocks to and from Saint Jerome's in dread of the neighborhood children, who at the very least shouted imprecations at us "sissies," stole our beanies, or tried to push us into the dirty slush on the streets.

When we were very young, Ramona would walk us to school and pick us up in the afternoon. For her this was a risk and an adventure. She had been brought up to think of herself as sacred ground and of men as wolves circling her borders ready to pounce. She carried herself not humbly but like a woman who acknowledged her beauty. She looked only straight ahead and walked fast, dragging us with her. I felt her fear and her anxiety through her hand, which held my own in a painfully tight grasp. On the streets of Paterson my mother seemed an alien and a refugee, and as I grew to identify with the elements she feared, I dreaded walking with her, a human billboard advertising her paranoia in a foreign language.

All her activities were done in groups of women. Though Rafael despised the gossip societies of El Building, he could do little to prevent Ramona from forming close bonds with the other women while he was away. The ones who did not work in factories formed shifting cliques based on their needs and rarely ventured out alone. They went shopping together, patronizing only certain stores; they attended the Spanish mass at ten o'clock on Sundays to hear the youthful Father Jones struggle through the service in heavily accented lisped Castilian; and they visited each other daily, discussing and analyzing their expatriate condition endlessly. They complained of the cold in the winter, their fights with the "super" for more heat or less, the stifling building in the summer, and their homesickness; but their main topic after husband and children was the Island. They would become misty and lyrical in describing their illusory Eden. The poverty was romanticized and relatives attained mythical proportions in their heroic efforts to survive in an unrelenting world.

RAMONA: "They say Mamá Cielo nearly died giving birth to Guzmán. She bled rivers, and the little devil came out kicking and screaming. She was never the same, never as strong after he was born. Some say a child in middle age can suck up your life's energy like a tumor. I got my womb sewed shut after my son . . ."

NEIGHBOR: "Me too, *niña*.[2] One child was enough for me." In my town there was a woman who spewed one out every year; after the fifth or seventh they looked more like frogs than children. My own mother dried up like a coconut from nursing kids. That's not for me."

RAMONA: "How Mamá Cielo managed to raise all of us on nothing is a wonder to me. We always had plenty of food. She had a garden and kept chickens in the backyard. Here, if you don't have this (she'd rub her thumb and index finger together to indicate money) you don't eat."

---

[2] girl

NEIGHBOR: "Here you even have to pay to stay warm and trust that son-of-a-great-white-whore super to fire the furnace."

Every month Ramona received a thin blue airmail envelope with a letter from Puerto Rico. It always opened with a blessing and a brief statement of Mamá Cielo's, Papá Pepe's, and my young Aunt Luz's health. Then, after some lines concerning people in Salud whose names meant nothing to my brother and me, there was usually something about Guzmán. This part we listened to carefully, for we had heard many stories about the black sheep of the family. How he had left the Island ten years ago, and that it was six months before they heard from him. Mamá Cielo had nearly died of anxiety. Only Papá Pepe, who had had a vision in a dream of Guzmán in a cavern hiding from his enemies, was certain that his son was alive.

Because the old people had turned heaven and hell upside down trying to discover the fate of their son, the newspaper in Mayagüez had contacted the government office in charge of the lottery only to expose the fact that there was no record of the agent who had come to Salud, that the venture had been privately financed and was perhaps even a scam. The ensuing investigation took years, they say, and in the meantime hundreds of young men ended up in migrant worker camps such as the one in which Guzmán had been dumped after an arduous journey. Though in his first letter to his parents Guzmán didn't go into details, it was clear that once in the camp he was forced to labor in the strawberry fields for ten hours a day under the supervision of armed guards. For weeks he did hot even know that he was in the vicinity of Buffalo, New York, working for an absentee grower who took little interest in how his managers got a labor force. He got out only by getting to know the cook, a woman who commuted in from Buffalo to cook for the Ricans after the cook that had been drafted fell ill with a wet cough. The details of their relationship were apparently not brought up in Guzmán's letter home, just that he climbed in the trunk of her old Studebaker and rode out. Later, to escape from real or imagined pursuers, or maybe from her, Guzmán took a bus into New York City.

There he had somehow talked his way into a job as errand boy for the conductors in the subway system, buying cigarettes for them, catering to their needs in a way that he had learned from the cutters. It was strictly off the payroll. He depended on the tips. He slept on trains and ate from the vending machines. Guzmán feared that the people from the Buffalo farm were still after him, and rarely did he venture out into the city during the day, preferring to ride the line from one end to another. It was not a dull job, for on a subway he was able to observe and categorize the city's inhabitants and learn the language, but, most important, Guzmán acquired the skills necessary for street survival. He became a subway warrior, his senses attuned to the dark look in a pervert's eye, the nervous hands of the amateur mugger, and the deviousness of the pickpocket. It was his survival course.

All this, of course, we did not learn from letters. It had to be later inferred from *Guzmán's Adventures,* the ongoing narrative as told by my mother, enhanced and colored until Guzmán became in our imaginations the brown giant of Island legend. There would be several versions of Guzmán's story, each one suited to its audience. And there would be gaps that would never be filled in, holes into which he would fall in silence.

As long as he lived strictly in our imaginations, Guzmán could be given any dimensions we wanted. When Ramona spoke of his rebellious childhood, I secretly thrilled at his defiance of the adults, whom I was just beginning to resent. At thirteen, I was being counseled in humble acceptance of a destiny I had not chosen for myself: exile or, worse, homelessness. I was already very much aware of the fact that I fit into neither the white middle-class world of my classmates at Saint Jerome's nor the exclusive club of El Building's "expatriates."

When Rafael had first visited Paterson, searching for a "safe" place to bring Ramona and their child, the city was in the midst of an internal flux that was invisible to a stranger. The white middle classes were moving out to the fringes, West Paterson, East Paterson; the Jewish businessmen were buying up inner-city property and renting apartments to blacks and Puerto Ricans. Thousands of immigrants overflowed from New York City, now in its final throes as an industrial center. But it was better than Brooklyn to my father, who witnessed the confusion of the streets while stationed in the Yard. In his white navy uniform he looked like an angel to me when he made his rare appearances at home. On those days we'd come home from school to an apartment smelling of pine cleaner and Ramona nervously wiping surfaces and picking up after us. The conversations with neighbor women were often giggly and whispered on the eves of his homecomings.

"Did you bring your papers home from school as I told you, Marisol?" she would demand as soon as I came in the door.

One of the first things that Rafael asked his children was how they were doing in school. He would look through all the papers we were supposed to save for him, commenting on everything, including our handwriting, making pointed comments to make us see that the world judged by appearances and a sloppy hand meant a sloppy person.

Rafael's fastidiousness extended to everything in our lives. The apartment was painted so often the walls took on a three-dimensional look and feel, and when I leaned on a windowsill (and that was often) I could leave imprints of my fingers and nails, on the soft enamel. He inspected everything, including our clothes, and if any item began to look frayed or worn, he would instruct Ramona to replace it immediately. We shopped in stores our neighbors couldn't afford or feared to enter, and my mother had a charge account at Penney's. The only thing he couldn't get her to do was move out of the crowded barrio of El Building. But within the four walls of our flat he did everything possible to separate us from the rabble. He managed to do that. By dressing better and having more than any of the children in El Building, we were kept out of their ranks; by having less than our classmates at Saint Jerome's, we never quite fitted in that society, either.

Unlike Ramona, Rafael almost never spoke of his childhood or the Island. In fact, his silences were more impressive than his speeches. When he came home on leave, the neighbor women would not just drop by as they usually did when Ramona was alone; we would prepare for his homecomings as if for a visiting dignitary. After Ramona received a telegram, for we had no telephone, she would begin cleaning the apartment and incessantly warning us about our behavior during his stay. Growing up, I knew only a few things about my father. Ramona's stories about Don Juan Santacruz, the cruel patriarch of a tragic family, could hardly be connected with the distant stranger Rafael had become. After nearly fourteen years in the navy he had risen only to the rank of noncommissioned officer, petty officer they called it. His job on an old World War II cargo ship was to watch the boilers. He spent ten to twelve hours a day below the water line, watching dials, alone. He learned silence there. He practiced it for hours, days, and months until he mastered it. When he came home to us, he found conversation difficult, and the normal noise of life disturbing.

During the *Cuban missile crisis*[3] we did not hear from Rafael for months. Ramona still received a monthly check from the navy, but no letters, no sign of life from him. This was my initiation as her interpreter. For weeks we went from office to office at the Red Cross, where we were treated like victims of a natural disaster, given drinks in plastic cups, and asked to wait. Sometimes I would fill out forms for my mother. But there were never any real answers. Yes, he was on a ship. No, communication was not possible, please go home and wait, Mrs. Santacruz. I learned about waiting at that time, a woman's primary occupation. I watched my mother smoke cigarettes and drink coffee and wait. She never discussed her fears with me. She just told me what to do.

One day after we had watched President Kennedy make his speech on our grainy television screen, Rafael showed up with his duffel bag at our door. He had lost so much weight that he looked like a child wearing an oversized sailor suit. He was pale and feverish. Ramona took him into their bedroom, and when he came out the next day he was more a stranger to us than ever.

He stayed home longer than he ever had before, recuperating from the exhaustion of half a year at sea. Doing what? "Counting the days," I heard him say in a flat voice late one night to Ramona. The bedroom I shared with my brother, Gabriel, faced the tiny kitchen area, where Ramona sat with her cigarettes and coffee to talk to neighbors and wait for Rafael, to read her letters from the Island. Here Rafael and Ramona caught up with their individual lives. Their conversations were mainly questions softly phrased by him, answers emotionally delivered by her. Obviously concerned, this time Ramona pressed him for details of his absence.

"I was the captain's interpreter," he finally conceded, "the only one on board who knew Spanish, and I helped out." No more. Either he was under a military injunction to silence on the subject of the Cuban crisis, or he just did not want to talk about it; for whatever reason, he chose not to elaborate on his part in it. Ramona dropped the subject and fell back into the role of interviewee to his never-ending interrogation. It was as if, unable to share our lives, he needed a full report on all our activities, including the most trivial: to live our days vicariously, to make decisions, ex post facto. Listening from our bedroom I felt resentment at his intrusion into our lives and my sense of privacy violated as I had when I had to fill out all those questionnaires for strangers. One night, assuming that I was asleep, they discussed me.

"Marisol is a '*señorita*'[4] now, Rafael. I am sure she will begin menstruating soon."

"You were not much older than she when we got married, Ramona. We have to be very careful with her. Have you seen her with any boys? I don't want her mixing with the hoodlums in this place." This, of course, led to a familiar topic with my parents: moving out of El Building. But I was burning with shame under the sheets

---

[3] In October 1962 President Kennedy and Soviet Premier Nikita Khrushchev confronted each other over the deployment of ballistic missiles in Cuba.   [4] young woman

in my narrow bed. How dare she mention such private matters to him? Four feet away from me, my brother snored softly.

Rafael tried to show us he cared. He did this by taking Gabriel for long walks in the city, excursions which my brother hated, for he was an overweight, studious little boy whose idea of a good time was reading his adventure books while consuming an entire double-row package of fig cookies. He was a favorite target for El Building's bullies, and so, once safely inside our little apartment, he preferred to stay there. School was another matter: there he had been identified by his fifth-grade teacher as possessing an amazingly high intelligence quotient and had been adopted by the well-meaning nun as her privileged guinea pig, the basis for her master's thesis. He had little to say to Rafael, so once again Rafael had to resort to the interrogation method. He always spoke in English to us: a perfect textbook English, heavily accented but not identifiable as Puerto Rican. Most of his shipmates, he once mentioned, thought he was German.

"Why does he have to follow me to school?" I asked Ramona. Rafael had begun this practice after he heard some black kids shouting threats at us one day. What he didn't know was that this was not unusual. Gabriel and I got it from both sides. In our Catholic school uniforms and beanies we were fair targets for all the public school kids. We had long since learned the usefulness of passive resistance. Unless they physically attacked us, we pretended not to hear. Rafael's shadowing us only added to our humiliation.

"He is just making sure you get to school safely." Ramona clearly understood my resentment, but she would never contradict her husband in our presence. "Do not cause problems, Marisol."

"I am almost fourteen years old, Mamá, I can walk to school by myself."

"I think you should go into your room and do your school work now."

We had both heard the unmistakable sound of Rafael's footsteps coming up the stairs. He always wore the heavy navy-issue shoes with the thick rubber soles which made a sound quite distinct from the street shoes of the other people in El Building.

"I don't have any homework. It's Christmas vacation time, remember? Today was the last day of classes." He was at the door, we heard the jingle of keys. It was obvious Ramona did not want a confrontation.

"There is a basket of laundry on the bathroom floor. Take it down to El Basement."

"It's almost dark." I was making it as difficult as possible for her to get rid of me. There was an agreement among El Building's housewives that women did not do their laundry in the basement after dark. It was known to all the tenants that some of the men used the place for gambling at night, and the teenage boys often met there to smoke and pass the time.

"There is still time. Just start the wash. I'll send your father after it later. Go!"

I waited until my parents went into their bedroom and started for the basement. Through the window at the end of the corridor I could see my brother's back. He was sitting on the fire escape, reading. Bundled up in his heavy winter coat, hat, and gloves, he looked more like a pile of clothes than a little boy, except that it moved as he turned the pages and adjusted his position. That was his private place. The stairwell was dim, lighted by a yellow bulb at each landing. I could hear the sounds of people in each apartment as I passed, getting ready for their evening meal; I smelled the thick aroma of fried sweet plantains, boiling beans, and the ever-present rice. I wondered if my mother's Island smelled the same as El Building at dinner time. But the thought that occupied my mind most of all was that of Frank, the high school boy I had a crush on. He was Italian. His father owned the supermarket near my school. He was entirely unaware of my existence. Why should he notice a skinny Puerto Rican freshman at Saint Jerome's, when he could choose any of the beautiful, well-developed girls from his own class?

Preoccupied with these thoughts, I entered the dank, ill-lit basement. At once I sensed that I was not alone, but the only sound I heard was the hissing of the steam pipes at first. I set down the basket and held my breath. I was not afraid—my mother's washer was near the exit and I could run toward the door if I saw anyone emerging from the shadowy maze of machines and cement columns. Then I heard a sound like that of a cat caught in a machine. It had happened before; the bad boys would sometimes put a stray in a washer to scare the women. It was probably the only thing that could have made me wander into the increasingly dark and dangerous far end of El Basement. As I tiptoed toward the sound, it became clearer that there was either a whole litter of cats, or it was no animal at all. It was definitely a human voice making little animal sounds in Spanish, a woman speaking:

"This floor is cold. Wait . . . wait . . ." Then some more moaning sounds.

I crouched down behind a dryer, which was warm as if recently used. I cautiously peeked around the corner. There were two people on the floor right in front of the machine. They were practically naked, though the man was still wearing his pants, only around his knees rather than his waist. I recognized him as the husband of one of my mother's coffee friends. I did not know the naked woman, but she was not the neighbor's wife. She had bright red hair. Her skin was dark but she was not black. Her breasts, the largest I had ever seen, hung down like two deflated balloons over her stomach. She kept complaining of the cold floor.

"This is not going to work, José."

He just kept saying "Sí, sí . . ." and trying to push himself on top of her. He was skinny, and I was sure she could have thrown him off her easily if she had wanted to. When he finally managed to climb on top of her, she wrapped her big legs around his skinny rump, and they both started rocking and moaning together. She seemed to have forgotten her initial discomfort and the cold floor. I watched fascinated until I heard Rafael's voice calling my name softly from the other end of the basement. The couple froze in the middle of one of their contortions, turning their faces toward the sound of my father's voice. The terror in their eyes was as exaggerated as the faces of the actors I had seen on the horror movies they showed on late night television. Eyes wide open and glossy, mouths twisted into a grimace. Not wanting Rafael to see this ridiculous scene, I crawled back toward the door.

"What were you doing back there, Marisol?" I could tell Rafael was practicing his self-control. His voice was low, and he kept his hands inside his navy coat, but a thick furrow divided his forehead. I had to think quickly.

"One of my gold earrings fell off." I brought my hand to my ear, which was luckily concealed by a layer of thick black hair. He had sent the earrings to me from somewhere in Europe for my last birthday. "It rolled away." I pointed into the dark. There were no sounds except the ominous hissing of the pipes.

"You should not come down here after dark. Ramona should know better." The last statement was made under his breath. There would be another late-night discussion about moving away from El Building tonight.

"You go upstairs, now."

"But what about the clothes and my earring?"

"I'll bring them up. You can wash them tomorrow. Forget the earring."

I raced up the stairs to lock myself in my bedroom and think about what I had seen by myself. Unfortunately, Gabriel had already claimed his side of the room and was busy constructing some heavy machinery with the expensive erector set Rafael had bought him on one of their walks. I lay down on my bed and put the pillow over my head for a little privacy. Ramona came in without knocking.

"Marisol, is something the matter? What happened down there?"

"Nothing happened, Mamá. Rafael came down to get me. You know why. I have a headache. Can I please just close my eyes for a few minutes?"

"Fine, but you are acting a little strange these days, young lady. We are going to have a talk very soon." She slammed the door as she left the room, and an intricate bridge Gabriel had just balanced between two shoe boxes came apart in the middle and collapsed. He frowned at the disaster in the exact manner Rafael had frowned at me. I hadn't noticed before how much they resembled each other—not in looks, for neither my brother nor I had turned out blond and fair like Rafael, but in the intensity of his brown eyes. My father always looked as if he were trying to figure out a very difficult mathematical problem. That was why he hardly ever smiled or talked. He was busy concentrating on solving that problem.

In the week following the episode in El Basement I saw José several times. He seemed to be watching me. It frightened me in an exciting way to feel his rat eyes on me when I walked down to the supermarket, but I was not worried that he would approach me. There was a sort of code of honor in El Building that I understood in a rudimentary way: it held that respectable wives and their daughters could be looked over and, if unescorted, even verbally complimented in the outrageous piropos, the poems invented on the spot and thrown at passing women like bouquets from open windows, doorways, streetcorners, anywhere where Latin men loitered. That was the price you paid for going out without a chaperone. But it was strictly hands off; if that unspoken rule was violated, revenge was usually swift. The offended husband or his representative could start a vendetta that often ended in the violator's having to leave El Building. He would certainly at the very least never be invited into a decent home again. This was part of the reason Ramona felt safe in El Building. I was just beginning to notice the effects of her beauty on men when we went anywhere together. The "uncivilized" way of the men of El Building was the main reason brought up when Rafael insisted that before I got any older we had to move out of the place. José, I knew, feared that I would tell on him. He couldn't know that I was not about to share my most terrible secret with my parents.

As Christmas Day approached, El Building began to fill up with relatives of the tenants up from the Island. Their voices filled the hallways with laughter, exclamations over the frigid temperature, the television sets, the children who had grown so much since the last time. It seemed all the women were cooking at once, saturating the place with the smells of coconut candy and pasteles the luckier ones had received from mothers and grandmothers on the other side, frozen and carefully wrapped in banana leaves and tin foil and hidden in the depths of shopping bags. The partying would last until Three Kings Day on January 6, when the children received their presents.

In our house we went shopping at Sears and Penney's.

We had a Christmas tree with presents under it that we would open on the twenty-fifth of December. I had been allowed to accept an invitation for a dinner party at my friend's house on Christmas Eve. She was the doctor's daughter, and Rafael approved. He gave Ramona money to buy me a dress. He called me a taxi. The driver looked nervous as he pulled up to El Building, and I noticed he had to reach over and unlock a door for me.

"At what time did you say you would be home?"

I looked at Rafael, annoyed. He had asked me the same question several times before. "All I know is that they eat at seven. Do you want me to come home right after I finish?"

"No. Stay a little while. Here is the number for the taxi."

"Hey, are you gonna tell me where you're going, or what?" This was the taxi driver.

My father gave him one of his furrowed-brow stares and waved goodbye to me. He stood on the dirty snow on the street in front of El Building the whole time we sat at a traffic light, and for as long as he could see the car and I could see him.

That night, Christmas Eve, while I was sitting in a dining room as large as half our apartment at a table that sat eight with an immense chandelier over it, hovering over a large turkey, my uncle Guzmán showed up at El Building.

The evening at my friend's had begun almost perfectly. I had sat on her bed and talked with her while her parents received the dinner guests. Her room was done in eggshell colors: glossy white walls and matching drapes and bedspread of the softest pink hue. Everything in the room was hers. She didn't have to share the room with anyone. Her brother was eighteen, a freshman at Princeton. He had the same smooth Italian good looks as my love object, Frank.

Letitia's parents were carefully polite to me. Once, during dinner I noticed Mrs. Roselli staring at my hands. I had been eating a rice dish with a spoon: everyone else, I quickly surmised, was using a fork. She caught my eye and smiled quickly, but I was embarrassed enough to excuse myself from the table and run up to the bathroom. Foolish tears were in my eyes when I ran straight into the arms of the brother, who was coming out of his room. He had a date, I had been told, with the prettiest senior girl at Saint Jerome's. For whatever reason, we embraced. He pulled me into his darkened room and pressed his lips to mine. Instinctively I responded to his kiss up to the point when he tried to introduce his tongue into my mouth. Though I could have fainted with the warm sensations of pleasure mapping my body out in little currents, I suddenly panicked. I pushed him away and ran out of his room. In the bathroom mirror I saw my face streaked with tears, my cheeks red, and warm to the touch. My stomach hurt. Something had not agreed with me. And then—without warning—the dinner I had just enjoyed came back up in spasms. Mrs. Roselli knocked on the door and plied me with anxious questions.

I got through the dinner, managing even to raise my glass with the others in my first taste of wine. The doctor drove me home. It was beginning to snow, and Paterson seemed to me beautiful for the first time. The Christmas displays in the shop windows on Main Street looked less harsh and gaudy through the thin veil of snow. The names of the stores as we passed them blinked in and out of my vision like the words to a nonsense song: Franklin's, Woolworth's, Quackenbush.

"What?"

"Excuse me?"

"I thought you said something. Are you feeling all right?" Doctor Roselli reached over with his hand and felt my forehead. "You're warm. Take aspirin as soon as you get home." His tone was very professional and I perceived that his concern was automatic, but I wanted more than anything to believe that people like the Rosellis could accept me as one of their own.

We were getting close to El Building. I wished I could just ask him to drop me off a block away. I could see there was a crowd of men and boys gathered on the front steps, probably drinking. One of them had a loud radio: it was blaring salsa music. The doctor pulled up to the curb. He came around to open my door and a snowball thrown from the alley next to El Building hit him square in the back of his head. He almost lost his balance and had to hold on to the car. I reached for his arm but he yanked it back angrily.

"Just go on in. Are your parents home?"

"Yes." I felt so humiliated. There was laughter coming from the group of men. There would be comments for me when I passed them. I hated them all. I started walking toward the door as Doctor Roselli's car pulled away from El Building, its wheels screeching in his haste to get away.

By the time I had climbed the five flights of stairs to our apartment I was feeling dizzy. When Ramona opened the door I saw her face as if from a carousel. She pulled me into our tiny living room. Her eyes were bright with excitement.

"Marisol, come in here. Look! Your uncle Guzmán is here."

A short, dark man stepped forward. He was dressed all in black. His face looked familiar in an oddly disturbing way, as if I were looking into a mirror in a darkened room.

"Marisol?" My mother's voice had taken on a concerned tone. Guzmán came forward, opened his arms as if for an embrace, and I fell into them in a dead faint.

Chapter Twelve

If the place you live in is destroyed in a fire, your priorities arrange themselves before you as a checklist, with the corresponding emotional reaction like a dictionary definition following. The lives of your loved ones come first, with hysteria or terror prescribed by your brain now functioning under stress; once they are safe, then comes concern for possessions, accompanied by regret for their loss and anxiety over the need to replace them—the need for survival leads to the immediate desire to find a substitute shelter. The aftermath of all this activity seems to be a morbid dwelling on the idea that you were singled out for punishment. All this I realized while, watching Ramona go through her paces during the first few days after the fire at El Building.

The first few days after the three of us had ridden in the ambulance with Guzmán to the hospital, we stayed in a shelter provided by the Red Cross. We had used the same phone number that I had memorized during the Cuban crisis in trying to locate my father, and the nice lady with the gentle voice and persistently patronizing manner came to our rescue. We were first taken to the basement of their headquarters, where cots had been set up for providing temporary shelter. But when it became evident that it would take days to fly Rafael home, since he was somewhere in the middle of the Atlantic ocean on a ship heading for England, they moved us to a hotel in downtown Paterson. From there we could walk to Saint Joseph's Hospital, where Guzmán was being treated for smoke inhalation, minor burns, and an infected wound that would have to be cut open and sewn back together again like a ragged tear on a garment.

Once again I found myself in the role of interpreter of the world for my mother who, after all these years, still believed that it operated like an extended family: in times of need or tragedy people naturally came to your rescue. She never quite understood why I had to make ten phone calls before we got an appointment with the man from the navy office; she shook her head in disbelief when she was told it would be days before the paperwork was completed and Rafael could come home. I told her where to sign and answered most questions without consulting her. I learned something during those days: though I would always carry my Island heritage on my back like a snail, I belonged in the world of phones, offices, concrete buildings, and the English language. I felt truly victorious when I understood the hidden motives in my conversations with adults, when they suddenly saw that I understood. Their acknowledgment of my insight was usually accompanied by either irritation at my presumptuousness or a new tone of respect in their voices.

The lady from the Red Cross office was very curious about the fire at El Building, and on the day when we were to move out of the Red Cross shelter to the hotel she asked me to come to her office alone.

"Honey, how did this happen? Every time we ask one of the residents, we get a different answer." She smiled her volunteer smile at me, the one that said *I am here out of the goodness of my heart to help the unfortunate and inferior.* I had learned to recognize this smile earlier in my life when for weeks we had tried desperately to get news of Rafael. It was a pleasant smile that also warned: *Don't ask for too much, or you'll get nothing.*

"Sit down, please, María."

"It's Marisol," I said politely.

"Pardon?" Still smiling, she pointed to a chair in front of her desk. Her name was Mrs. Pink, and there were objects in her office that paid tribute to her favorite color, such as the oil painting of pink roses that hung behind her desk. The walls were a pale rose, and there was a paddle hanging from a hook on the wall that had been painted pink and there was a pink bow wrapped around its handle. Mrs. Pink saw me looking at the paddle. "I am a retired teacher," she said with apparent pride. "Won't you sit down, María?" Her smile was fading as I continued to stand in front of her desk as if I had not heard her. She looked at me sternly. "Do you know what caused the fire? I understand there was a wild party going on in the tenement building where you and your family resided. Is it true?"

"I know nothing about it, ma'am. I think it was an accident that caused the fire." I spoke with my eyes lowered, my arms at my side, my feet together, in the posture of respectful attention taught to us by the nuns at Saint Jerome's.

"There were dozens of people drinking and carrying on like they do in a tenement building where the walls are thin as paper, and you didn't hear anything? You didn't know there was a party going on right next door? You look like a smart girl to me. You know there is going to be a big investigation. Is there something you are hiding? Remember we are here to help you."

Through my lowered lids I saw that she had put on the smile again. Her tone of voice, which had turned hard when I had refused to acknowledge her order to sit down, was once again condescending. I knew that her questions were nothing but curiosity about us and El Building. She was just a woman with time on her hands and had no right to insult me with her questions.

"I'm sorry, Mrs. Pink, but I have told you what I know. We are very grateful for your help, and when my father comes home I will tell him to come to see you. I'm certain he will be able to answer your questions after he speaks with my mother. I will tell him that you are investigating the fire."

Mrs. Pink got up from her chair so abruptly that a little stack of pink memo papers fell off, scattering all over the floor. She ignored it. I kept my eyes down.

"There is no need to tell anyone about our conversation. I just wanted to know a little more about your case so I can help you better. Here is the address of the hotel where you will stay until further notice." Flustered, she looked on her desk for the slip of paper, but apparently it had gotten mixed up with the mess on the floor.

Her face flushed an angry red, Mrs. Pink got down on her knees and gathered the wildly strewn notepaper, throwing it on her desk with an angry slap. "The truth will come out, that is all I've got to say," she mumbled as she dug through the pile. "One big eyesore removed in one fell swoop." She continued to mumble as if she had forgotten my presence while involved in her frantic little search. I had noticed teachers did that to children. It was as if they could shut us completely out of their perceptions for minutes at a time.

Finally, she looked up at me. "Don't you have some packing to do?" she said, as if offended that I was still there. "I know where to find you when I'm ready."

I don't know if she saw how my face struggled to remain impassive. I felt like laughing hysterically at this foolish woman. Pack? No, we didn't have much packing to do unless you counted the magazines Gabriel had salvaged in his terror and to which he clung these days as if they were his torn, smelly security blanket. He wanted to give them back to Rafael himself. And the nuns of Saint Jerome's had come through with clothing and coats straight from the homes of my tall classmates. Ramona and I looked more than ever like gypsies in our long skirts.

From the hotel we walked the few blocks to the hospital to see Guzmán. He was in a ward with five or six other men, and I could see that this made Ramona very uncomfortable. I encouraged her to sit in the waiting room and to read her Spanish romance novels or crochet while I visited with her brother. Gabriel had chosen to go back to school, though his teachers had volunteered to help us make up the work we missed. They understood that my mother needed my services as interpreter until Rafael arrived.

Guzmán had lost a lot of weight and looked like one of those South American children who appear in posters advertising their hunger and their need. At the Red Cross shelter, I had awakened in the night to look into those famished eyes staring down from the wall above my cot. I felt I had joined their club. Not a large man to begin with, Guzmán had now shrunk to the size of a twelve-year-old—either that or I had grown. Standing next to his bed, I felt that if necessary I could lift him and carry him. His dark eyes seemed immense in his cadaverous face. Pity overwhelmed me. He forced a smile pointing to the chair next to his bed.

"Is there anything I can get you? Anything you need?" I heard my new efficient voice with some surprise. But I felt that I could do anything he asked.

Very slowly Guzmán reached his hand to the night table next to his bed, but could not manage to pull the drawer out. I quickly laid my hand over his and pulled with him. He sighed deeply as he fell back on the pillows. He pointed to the drawer. "There is a wallet in there, and a bank book. Get them out for me."

"Anything else?" I did as he told me, laying the two items gently by his hand on the bed.

"That is all I need for now. Come closer, Marisol, I'm going to ask you to do something important for me."

I pulled my chair as close to the head of his bed as possible, and, leaning down to hear his weak voice better, I listened while Guzmán explained to me that he wanted to withdraw all his money from a bank in Paterson. He was going to call them and tell them that they were to give me or Ramona the money. As proof that I was his representative he provided me with all his identifying documents and a note (which I wrote in English, and he copied). Once I got the money I was to buy money orders with it and bring them to Guzmán. He did not explain what it was all about, and I did not want to ask, thinking that it was a sign of maturity not to question people when they asked you to do a favor. But I couldn't help saying something that I knew would lead to some kind of clarification:

"Your money will be safer in the bank, Guzmán. Are you sure you want it lying around while you're in the hospital?"

He turned to look at me. On his lips there was the hint of an amused smile. Even in his suffering he could read me better than anyone.

"I will tell you my plan after you finish this part of your mission." He touched my fingers with his. He was obviously exhausted. He allowed me to smooth the bed covers around him. I felt like bursting into tears when I saw the outline of his thin body with the thick bandage on his side.

"I'll be back tomorrow morning with the money." He didn't hear me. His eyes were closed.

Arriving back at the hotel Ramona and I were surprised to find Gabriel's schoolbooks thrown all over the floor. It wasn't time for him to be back; in fact, his bus was not due for another hour. Ramona, whose emotions were barely under control since the fire, burst into hysterical tears. Something had surely gone wrong. What would she tell Rafael? Her self-recriminations and tears made me feel resolute. I was about to dial the school's number to begin the process that I had by now mastered: putting into practice what I had learned about dealing with the world through words, persuasions, politely phrased threats.

Then the door burst open and Gabriel ran in shouting excitedly. His grin told us it was good news, whatever it was, though his words came out confused in his excitement. Rafael walked calmly in after my brother. He was wearing his white navy uniform and cap. For the first time in my life I felt a sense of relief at the sight of my father. His serious face, his immaculate appearance, brought light into the dim room that was our refuge. His voice was low and his words measured as he greeted Ramona, who threw her arms around him, still weeping. Gabriel held on to his hand as if glued to it. I stood by the phone waiting for my turn, but I meant it when I said to him as he kissed my cheek:

"I'm glad you're home, Father."

It was obvious by the new humble posture Ramona had fallen into, her easy tears and long silences, that there were many matters to be resolved between my parents. Rafael treated all three of us delicately, as if he feared we would break into pieces before his eyes. He and Ramona whispered to each other late into the night in the bed just a few feet from the one I shared with Gabriel. What I could hear from their intense conversations told me that our lives would never be the same. Rafael cursed El Building and its inhabitants, and Ramona wept quietly on and on for the friends she had lost: Elba was dead, the last to be taken out of the blazing shell that El Building had so quickly become; Santiago was fighting for his life in the hospital after rushing in to bring out a child whose mother had left him sleeping alone in their apartment while she went out. No one had known he was there until she came home screaming for her boy during the last stages of the fire. So many others were hurt, left out in the cold streets of Paterson with nothing but the silly costumes they had been wearing that night. What Ramona felt, what she wanted to be forgiven for, was her part in planning the meeting that led to the horrible disaster. Patiently, Rafael explained that she could not have known what would happen that night, but he also reminded her that she should never have left us alone. At the thought of what could have happened to Gabriel she sobbed so pitifully that in my bed, under my blankets, I also cried for the ones who had not been as lucky as we.

The day after he arrived, Rafael met alone with Guzmán for a long while. Then he told us what my uncle had decided. He wanted to go back to the Island as soon as he was discharged from the hospital. He had asked if Ramona could accompany him there. Rafael thought that this was a good idea. Easter vacation was coming up and he had decided to spend his month's leave looking for a house to buy. Ramona did not say anything. She seemed too sad for words these days. Not even the thought of seeing Mamá Cielo and Papá Pepe after all these years seemed to excite her. Knowing how she had resisted the idea of a house in the suburbs, I felt sorry for her.

"Guzmán asked me to take all his money out of the bank," I volunteered.

"I will take care of that now, Marisol." Rafael looked at Ramona kindly. "Part of that money is for Ramona. Your uncle wants her to buy herself some clothes and presents for the family." He looked at her expectantly, but she had nothing to say.

Rafael was like a golden angel whose presence assuaged our fears and brought hope for our future. Though his silences were as deep as ever, we fell into their rhythm in the enforced closeness of that hotel room, where even our breathing was audible. Ramona's grief had now settled into a quiet state of melancholy. It was a *tristeza*[5] that she would hold barely at bay for the rest of her life. The destruction of El Building had been her initiation, her rite of passage, and she was slowly accepting the fact that life would never be the same.

After the Easter holiday, I went back to Saint Jerome's, where I was treated with kindness by the nuns and my classmates. The parish raised money to help those left homeless by the fire, and since Gabriel and I were the only students to have been directly affected, we were the beneficiaries of Catholic hospitality, which left us perhaps richer in necessities such as clothing and household items than we had been before. The nuns collected and stored every contribution, while one of the priests advised Rafael about real estate. In the meantime, Guzman recovered from his ailments and wounds as much as he ever would and was discharged from the hospital. We all went to pick him up in a rented car.

I had to stifle a gasp when I first saw him out of bed. He was dressed in his favorite black, but he looked lost in his garments—a little boy, or a wizened old man in pants that were two inches too long, and a shirt whose winged collar swallowed his neck. He visibly leaned toward the side of his knife wound. It was this posture and all the weight he had lost that made him look so small. I saw Ramona's eyes mist over when she looked at him, and I prayed that she would not cry in front of him.

Rafael put his arm around Guzmán's shoulders and they walked slowly down the hall. The dark and the light. Their heads close together, they talked. I couldn't hear what they were saying, but I could imagine them together as boys, planning to sneak up to the American's Big House. I could see them whispering like this on the banks of the Red River where La Cabra lived. I saw them holding up old dying Don Juan Santacruz between them, and saying goodbye early that morning when Guzmán took the bus to the airport, when they had parted, not to see each other for the next fifteen years—my lifetime.

Guzmán had insisted on taking a plane to Puerto Rico with Ramona on the same day he was discharged from the hospital. We drove to New York on that bright early spring day. The two men sat in front, and Ramona sat between Gabriel and me in the back seat. Surprisingly, she did not give us endless instructions and warnings, though she would be away for almost a month. She drew Gabriel, tightly to her, and held my hand in hers. I felt her trembling. When we neared the terminal she turned to me and said simply, "Take care of your brother as if he were your child." I assured her that I would.

Watching Guzmán climb the steps into the Pan Am jet with Ramona close behind him, I felt a strange sense of nostalgia. It wasn't sadness really—I was still young enough to be excited by the prospect of moving into a real house, of starting a whole new life, but I think I would have liked to have been the one to take Guzmán back to the Island. In my mind I had made his life story mine. I had kept track of him

---

[5] a sadness

through my mother's stories, Mamá Cielo's letters, and all those late-night conversations I had stolen from my parents when they thought I was sleeping in my room. I had filled the gaps with my imagination until Guzmán had shown up at our door; then I had become his secret biographer, drawing excitement from all he represented to me.

This broken man taking one step at a time into the belly of the airplane had little to do with the wild boy I had created in my imagination, but I loved him too. He was a good man and brave, even if finally not the hero of my myth. In a way I was glad that he would no longer be around to confuse me. He and El Building would be gone, but not forgotten.

We waved to them from the terminal as they turned to look back before they entered the plane. They waved too, but I don't think they could see us from that distance.

In the next few weeks our world changed completely. Rafael, Gabriel and I entered the land of suburbia, first as tourists guided from house to house by cautious real estate agents who were obviously concerned about introducing the first Puerto Rican family into the middle-class Italian neighborhoods which they seemed to think were the best compromise. Rafael's navy uniform and his credit references calmed their fears, though, and soon we found ourselves committed to buy a little house in West Paterson. It was surrounded by a yard already turning green. It had an attic set up as a child's bedroom that I fell in love with for its privacy and for the desk built into the wall where a window faced an oak tree that would also belong to us. At present the tree was still mostly bare, its gnarled branches scraping the window panes like the hands of an old woman.

The day we decided on the house, I went up to this room I had already decided was mine, only to find Gabriel surveying it for his own purposes. It was late in the afternoon, and since there was no electricity, the room was soon in shadows. I pointed out the tree to my brother, showing him how the bony fingers of the witch came into the room as shadows. I dug into my memory for all the fairy tales I had consumed and made up for him the ultimate tale of darkness, and concluded with a rhetorical question: "Why do you think the previous owners of this house were trying so hard to get rid of it?"

By the time Rafael came up the stairs to tell us that we would be in this house before Ramona got back from the Island, Gabriel was more than eager to announce that he had chosen the little room across from the master bedroom as his. I was, of course, a little ashamed of what I had contrived to do, but in the years that followed, as I sat at the desk facing that window, watching the long arms of the witch change from brown to green to gold with the seasons, I knew that I had only done what I was destined to do all my life—I would always trade my stories for what I wanted out of life.

When Ramona came home, it was really spring. Rafael had used all of his leave time to set up the house for her. He had bought furniture and appliances on the installment plan, and he had given me the job of paying the bills so that Ramona could enjoy her new life in the suburbs without worry. With the help of a Sears catalogue, we had color-coordinated everything: curtains, sheets, throw rugs, and cushions matched in the best middle-class American taste. Though it was a pleasure for me to set up this house in the soothing hues that appealed to my father and to me, I had a feeling that Ramona would feel like a stranger in it. Where were her plaster saints, the ones who got her through the lonely, difficult times when Rafael was at sea? What about the brilliant reds and greens and yellows that reminded her of her lost Island paradise?

So it was with mixed feelings that I dusted and polished everything and opened windows and yelled unnecessarily at Gabriel to keep himself clean on the day Mother came home. Rafael pulled up in the driveway in the rented car, and when she stepped out, I could see that she was darker, her cinnamon skin several shades deeper. The white embroidered dress she wore accentuated her brown arms. I knew before she told me that it was Mamá Cielo's handiwork—I had heard about the old lady's magic touch with a needle all of my life. Ramona's long black hair gleamed in the cool white sunlight of the spring day. She wore sandals and carried a shopping bag. To our neighbors (and all of the years we lived there I always felt that their eyes were upon us) she must have looked like a new immigrant. Though she was lovelier than ever, it hurt me to see how easily Ramona had given herself back to the Island.

Though she smiled during the tour of the house, holding Gabriel's hand tightly as he chattered nonstop about his plans for a treehouse he would build in the summer and about his new friends in the neighborhood, there were no loud exclamations of joy like I had heard at the slightest provocation when we lived in El Building. She smiled and smiled, but she did not make plans with the rest of us. Since then I have confirmed this fact about human nature: that to live fully in the present your mind has to be always focused on tomorrow; happiness is the ability to imagine something better for yourself. Ramona's dreams of going back in style to her homeland had been her way of dealing with the drab reality of everyday life in a foreign land. Instead, she had lost what little she had and had come back from her real home to a place that threatened to imprison her. In this pretty little house, surrounded by silence, she would be the proverbial bird in a gilded cage.

Discussion Questions

1. What is the role of "El Building" in the lives of the characters in the story. Try to determine what the connection is between the building and Puerto Rico.

2. Trace the development of Marisol throughout these excerpts. Where does she describe her feelings of alienation because she is different from her friends? Does her view of herself as a Puerto Rican-American change at the conclusion?

3. Compare Marisol's sense of identity to Ramona's. Which of them has an easier time adjusting to their new life in Paterson? What does this suggest about the generational differences of immigrants?

4. What are the differences and similarities between the building where Marisol lives and the description of Nilda's home in Nicholasa Mohr's novel on page 348?

5. Compare Marisol's development regarding her identity as well as her ideas about a home to Esperanza's feelings in Sandra Cisneros's story on page 10.

Nicholasa Mohr

NICHOLASA MOHR has received numerous awards for her work throughout the years. They include an American Book Award, Before Columbus Foundation in 1981; a commendation from the Legislature of the State of New York in 1986; an honorary Doctorate of Letters from the State University of New York at Albany in 1989; an Annual Achievement in Literature Award from the National Hispanic Academy of Media Arts and Sciences in 1995, and a lifetime achievement award from the National Congress of Puerto Rican Women in 1996.

Mohr was born in Spanish Harlem in 1938 and raised in the Bronx, New York. She became interested in art at an early age and studied at the Arts Student League and the Brooklyn Museum of Art School. After working as an artist and teacher she became interested in writing and published her tremendously successful novel, Nilda, *in 1973. Works of her prolific career include:* El Bronx Remembered: A Novella and Stories *(1975),* En Nueva York *(1977),* Felita *(1979),* Going Home *(1986),* All for the Better: A Story of El Barrio *(1992),* Isabel's New Mom *(1993),* The Magic Shell *(1995),* Old Letivia and the Mountain of Sorrows *(1993),* The Song of El Coqui, and Other Tales of Puerto Rico *(1995),* I Never Even Seen My Father, *(1995),* Rituals of Survival: A Woman's Portfolio *(1985),* In My Own Words: Growing Up Inside the Sanctuary of My Imagination *(1994), and* A Matter of Pride and Other Stories *(1997).*

Nilda *was the first novel to describe the life of a Puerto Rican immigrant woman. It is semi-autobiographical, and it traces the life of a young girl as she grows conscious of the differences between her shielded home life and the culture of the streets. The following three excerpts explore different aspects of the novel. In the first Nilda comes into contact with two social workers; one overtly cold and uncaring, and another more subtle and restrained. Next Nilda describes her feelings when visiting a summer camp. And finally Nilda's mother, who is at death's door, offers her some important advice.*

From Nilda

Late November, 1941

Nilda looked at the big round clock on the wall facing the rows of benches in the large rectangular waiting room. They had left the apartment early that morning, taking the bus downtown to be at the Welfare Department by nine A.M., and it was now a quarter past eleven. The hands on the clock looked so still, as if they were never going to move on to the next number. She concentrated on the red second hand that jumped sporadically from black dot to black dot until it finally reached a number. Shutting her eyes, Nilda would open them quickly, hoping to catch the red second hand in action. At the beginning, she had lost almost every time, but after a while she was able to catch the second hand just as it landed on a dot. She began to figure out just how long it took the second hand to reach the next number, thereby causing the large black hand to move ever so slightly. The game was beginning to bore her and she lost interest. She leaned against her mother, who was shifting her weight from side to side, trying to find a more comfortable position on the hard bench.

"Mami," Nilda whispered, nudging her mother, "I'm tired. How much longer we gonna be?"

"Be still, Nilda," her mother answered quietly.

"I'm thirsty. Can I get another drink of water?"

"You been up to get water at least five times. Just be still; they'll call us soon. Everybody here is also waiting. You are not the only one that's tired, you know." Her voice was almost a whisper, but Nilda knew she was annoyed. Nilda hated to come to places like this where she felt she had to wait forever. Its always the same, she thought, wait, wait, wait! She remembered the long wait they'd had at the clinic last time. It was over five hours.

"Stop leaning on me, Nilda; you are not a baby. Ya basta! Sit up and be still!" This time her mother had turned to look at her and she knew she had better be still.

The only good thing is that I don't have to go to school, she thought. Her mother would give her an excuse note tomorrow, so she did not have to worry.

Nilda looked around the large room again; each long row of benches was filled with people sitting silently. There were no other children her age. Now and then someone new came in from the outside, walked up to the front desk and handed the clerk a card, then sat down on a bench, joining the silent group.

She looked at the grey-green walls: except for two posters, placed a few feet apart, and the big round clock, the walls were bare. She began to study the posters again; she knew them almost by heart. They were full of instructions. The one nearest Nilda had a lifelike drawing of a young, smiling white woman, showing how well she was dressed when she went to look for employment. The reader was carefully informed about proper clothing, using this figure as the perfect model. Her brown hat sat on her short brown hair. Her smiling face had been scrubbed clean, her white teeth brushed, and she wore very little makeup. Her brown suit was clean and her skirt was just about six inches below the knee. She carried a brown handbag, wore clean gloves and nicely polished shoes as she strolled along a treelined street, confident about her interview. She sure looks happy, thought Nilda. She must be a teacher or something like that.

The second poster was a large faded color photograph of a proper breakfast. The photograph showed fresh oranges, cereal, milk, a bowl of sugar, a plate of bacon and eggs, toast with butter and jelly. The reader was warned that it was not good to leave the house without having had such a breakfast first. Looking at the food, Nilda began to remember that she was hungry. She had eaten her usual breakfast of coffee with boiled milk, sugar, and a roll. It seemed to her that she had eaten a long, long time ago, and her stomach annoyed her when she looked at the bacon and eggs. I hope they call us soon, she said to herself.

The lady clerk at the front desk looked up and read a name aloud from a card. "Mrs. Lydia Ramírez," she called out.

"Come on," her mother said as she stood up and walked past the benches full of waiting people. Nilda followed her up to the front.

The lady clerk pointed and said, "Into the next room. You will see Miss Heinz." She then handed her mother a card. Nilda walked with her mother into another large room lined with rows of desks. A woman, seated at a desk across the room, raised her arm and waved to them.

"Over here, please." They walked quickly up to the woman and waited. The social worker, without lifting her head, pointed to the empty chair at the side of her desk. Her mother sat down. The woman continued to write something on a form sheet. Nilda stood next to her mother and looked down at the social worker as she went on writing. Her head was bent over and Nilda could see that her hair was very white and fine, with tiny waves and ringlets neatly arranged under a thin grey hair net. The tiny grey hairpins, which were carefully placed to hold each little lump of ringlets together, were barely visible. Her pink scalp shone through the sparse hair. Nilda had never seen such a brilliant pink scalp before. I wonder what would happen if I touched her head, she thought; maybe it would burn my finger. Finally, after a while, the woman lifted her head, nodded, and, still holding the pencil she had been writing with, asked, "Mrs. Lydia Ramírez?" Before her mother could answer, the social worker turned to Nilda and said, "My name is Miss Heinz. Does your mother understand or speak English?" Nilda turned to her mother with a look of confusion.

"I speak English," her mother replied quickly. "Maybe not so good, but I manage to get by all right."

"Let me have your card, please," Miss Heinz said, holding out her hand. Nilda's mother bent forward and gave Miss Heinz the card she had been holding. "Well, that's a help. At least you can speak English. But then," pointing to Nilda she continued, "why is she here? Why isn't she in school? This is a school day, isn't it?"

Nilda could see her mother turning red. Her mother never liked to go to these places alone; she always brought Nilda with her. Ever since Nilda could remember, she had always tagged along with her mother.

"She wasn't feeling too well so I kept her with me. She goes to school of course," her mother said. Surprised, Nilda looked at her mother. She had not been sick at all.

"Well, she should be home in bed, not here! Or are you alone?"

"No, I am not alone," her mother bit her lips and went on, "but there was no one at home this morning." Nilda knew Aunt Delia was home with her stepfather, and so were Sophie and the baby. Pausing, her mother went on, "My husband is resting; he is sick. So, I just thought—"

"This is not going to do her any good," interrupted Miss Heinz. Looking at Nilda, she asked, "What's wrong with you?" Nilda looked at her mother wide-eyed.

"She had an upset stomach," her mother answered.

Miss Heinz, blinking her eyes, heaved a sigh and picked up a folder with the name *Ramírez, Lydia.* "Now let's get on with this. I'm way behind schedule as it is, you know. Plenty of other people to see. Mrs. Ramírez, you have one married son and four children in school, three boys and a daughter. Your husband suffered two heart attacks, his second leaving him incapacitated, and you want us to give you public assistance. Am I correct?"

"Yes," her mother said in a voice barely audible. "He can't work no more."

"Well then, we'll have to ask you some questions. Now, are you legally married?"

"Yes."

"How long? I see that your boys have a different last name. They are named Ortega."

"I been married twelve years." Her mother wet her lips.

"Were you legally married the first time and, if so, are you a widow or a divorcée?"

"Divorce."

"In Puerto Rico or in this country?"

"I married in Puerto Rico, but I got divorced here."

"That was twelve years ago? Then is this your second husband's child?"

Her mother sat up straight and answered, "Yes." Nilda glanced at her mother. Surprised and confused, she knew that she had been almost three years old when her mother married her stepfather.

"Your oldest son, Victor, can he help out?"

"He goes to high school, but he gets something after, like a delivery boy sometimes, and he gives us what he can."

"You also have an aunt living with you. Does she help?"

"No, she's an older woman and she has a relief check, but it's very little, and she can only spare for food and medicine. You see, she's also hard of hearing and—"

"O.K.,'" she interrupted. "How is your health, Mrs. Ramírez?"

"I'm fine. O.K."

"Can't you find some employment?"

"I got a lot of people to care for and small children I cannot leave."

Nilda realized that she was tired of standing. Looking at the woman, Nilda saw her write something each time she asked another question. Her fine grey mesh hair net came down over her forehead and stopped abruptly at the spot where her eyebrows should be. Nilda carefully strained her eyes, focusing on that spot, looking for her eyebrows, but the woman didn't seem to have any. Her skin was very pink, with a variety of brownish freckles that traveled on her hands, arms, and neck, giving her skin the look of a discolored fabric. She wore a light beige dress with a starched white collar. On her right hand she wore a silver wristwatch and two silver rings. Nilda thought, She looks tightly sealed up. Like a package, only you can't see the wrapping because it's like see-through cellophane.

"How many rooms in your apartment?"

"We got six rooms." They went on talking and Nilda felt her legs getting heavy under her and a sleepiness begin to overtake her.

"Let me see your hands! Wake up, young lady! Let me see your hands!" Startled, Nilda saw that Miss Heinz was speaking to her. Extending her arms and spreading out her fingers, she showed the woman, her palms.

"Turn your hands over. Over, turn them over. Let me see your nails." Nilda slowly turned over her hands. "You have got filthy nails. Look at that, Mrs. Ramírez.

She's how old? Ten years old? Filthy." Impulsively, Nilda quickly pushed her hands behind her back and looked down at the floor.

"Why don't you clean your nails, young lady?" Nilda kept silent. "How often do you bathe?" Still silent, Nilda looked at her mother. She wanted to tell her to make the woman stop, but she saw that her mother was not looking her way; instead she was staring straight ahead.

"Cat got your tongue?" Miss Heinz asked. "Why doesn't she answer me, Mrs. Ramírez?"

Without turning her head, her mother said, "Nilda, answer the lady."

"I take a bath when I need it! And I clean my nails whenever I feel like it!" Nilda exploded in a loud voice.

"No need to be impertinent and show your bad manners, young lady."

"Nilda!" Her mother turned around and looked at her. "Don't be fresh! Stop it!" Looking at Miss Heinz she said, "I'm sorry."

"That's quite all right, Mrs. Ramírez, I understand. Children today are not what they used to be. Young lady, you are no help to your mother. I hope you're proud of yourself."

Bending over, Miss Heinz moved her head, shaking the lumps of ringlets as she opened the center drawer of her desk. She searched around, moving paper clips, pencils, index cards wrapped in a rubber band, and finally pulled out a small shiny metal nail file. Holding it up in front of Nilda, she said, "Now Miss, this is for you. I want you to take this home with you so that you have no more excuse for dirty nails. This," and she shook the small shiny silver file, "is a nail file. Have you ever seen one before?"

Still sulking, Nilda answered, "Yes, I know what it is."

"Good! Here, you may take it," she said, smiling as she handed the nail file to Nilda, who did not move.

"Take it!" her mother said. Nilda reached over and took the metal file. Miss Heinz looked at Nilda, who said nothing. "Nilda! What do you say?" her mother asked.

"Thank you," Nilda said in an irritated tone.

Miss Heinz turned away and, closing the folder, she said, "Before we can make any definite decision, we will have to have an investigator come out to your home for a visit. Since you have had public assistance before, you know the procedure I'm sure. It will take a little while, but we will let you know."

"Good-bye, Miss Heinz, and thank you very much."

"Not at all. Good-bye now," and she bent over her desk again. Nilda and her mother walked out of the room and out of the building.

Walking alongside her mother, Nilda could feel the cold sharp air of winter. She held the shiny cold metal nail file in her hand. That mean old witch, she thought. And Mama, she's mean too. Nilda felt her mother put her arm around her and she pulled away.

"What's the matter? You got a problem maybe, Nilda?"

"I don't have an upset stomach, Mama. Why did you let her talk like that to me? Why didn't you stop her?" Nilda felt the angry tears beginning to come down her face. "You should have done something. You don't care anything about me. You don't care."

"Nilda, stop it! I had to say what I did, that's all. I have to do what I do. How do you think we're gonna eat? We have no money, Nilda. If I make that woman angry, God knows what she'll put down on the application. We have to have that money in order to live."

"I don't care. I don't care at all!" Nilda screamed. Without warning, she felt a sharp pain going across the left side of her face, followed by a stinging feeling. Her mother was in front of her, looking at her furiously.

"I'll slap you again, only harder, if you don't shut up." Nilda began to cry quietly. They walked along silently to the bus stop.

Still holding the nail file, Nilda thought about Miss Heinz. Oh how I hate her. She's horrible, she said to herself. I would like to stick her with this stupid nail file, that's what. When no one was looking I would sneak up behind her and stick her with the nail file. Then she would begin to die. No blood would come out because she hasn't any. But just like that . . . poof! She, would begin to empty out into a large mess of cellophane. Everybody in that big office would be looking for her. "Oh, where is Miss Heinz?" they would all say. They would be searching for her all over. Poor Miss Heinz. Oh, poor Miss Heinz. First her eyebrows disappeared. Did you know that? She had no eyebrows. And now she's all gone. Disappeared, just like that! Poor thing. My, what a pity.

The bus pulled up. As Nilda climbed inside she felt the nail file slipping between her fingers and heard a faint clink when it hit the pavement.

January, 1942

It was time for the social worker to come to investigate. Everybody was jittery. Nilda had been coming home from school each day asking her mother if the investigator had come. It was already the middle of the week and they were still waiting. Nilda would look at her mother, searching for some reassurance that everything would come out all right, but the worried look on her mother's face seemed almost permanently fixed. All week her mother had been saying to Nilda, "Don't make noise; your papa is resting! Stop playing with the baby so much; he might throw up. Go on! Play someplace else. Stop being a nuisance."

Her mother had been telling everyone what to say to the investigator in case they were asked questions. Every day she would repeat herself, telling Sophie what to say about her situation and why she was living here. Nilda and her brothers were instructed to answer with polite yes-and-no answers and, when asked about personal family matters, to say only "I don't know" and not another word.

Nilda had just arrived from school and was quietly putting her things away so she could go play with Baby Jimmy. She heard her mother telling her to be quiet. Oh, I just wish she wouldn't tell me the same things every day, she thought. Always the same story. I know I have to be quiet. Washing up, she went over to Sophie's room and knocked softly on the door.

"Come in," said Sophie.

"Hi, Sophie. How's the baby?"

"All right. You wanna feed him?"

"Oh thanks, Sophie." She must be in a good mood, thought Nilda. Sophie very often gave the bottle to the baby herself or offered to let Frankie feed little Jimmy, even though she knew Nilda loved to feed him. Taking the blanket and the baby, Nilda settled down as Sophie handed her the bottle. "Hi, handsome! You are gonna get your bottle. Oh, I love you," Nilda said, hugging the baby. "You know what, Sophie? He got bigger in one day. Look, he's starving! Guess what? He smiled at me yesterday. He really did.'"

Sophie began to hum. Nilda looked at her, surprised to see her so happy.

Looking at Nilda, Sophie said, "Jimmy's coming."

"Really?"

"Yes. One of his friends came to us this morning. Jimmy is living in another state, in New Jersey. But he will be coming back to New York to get me and the baby."

"Are you gonna leave right away?" asked Nilda.

"Well, as soon as he gets here, I guess."

"Are you gonna live far away, Sophie?"

"I don't know, Nilda; it all depends on what Jimmy wants to do, or where he is. His friend said New Jersey so I guess that's where we'll go." Nilda felt a lump in her throat as she looked at the baby. She did not want Baby Jimmy to leave and wanted to say something, but she felt too miserable to speak. Sophie picked up a nail file and, humming, began to file her nails.

Nilda swallowed and finally asked, "Can I come to visit you and the baby?"

"Of course you can. All of you can come and, if we have an extra bed, you can stay overnight and baby-sit."

"Oh wow! Sophie, thanks! That's great," Nilda said, feeling happier.

The door opened and Frankie walked into the room. "Hi . . . oh, Nilda, you're feeding him. I'll take him when you finish."

"Get out! I'm going to hold him for a while. Right Sophie?"

"Let her hold him for a while; then you can play with him, Frankie."

"All right," he said. "Mama told me about Jimmy. That's great, Sophie."

"I can't wait. I want him to see the baby; it looks just like an Ortega," Sophie said.

"Yeah, man. He sure looks like a *spick*!"[1] Frankie said. They all laughed. He went on, "Aunt Delia calls him *la mancha de plátano*.[2] Man! Was she ever crying when you came home from the hospital." Sophie and Nilda began to laugh.

"He finished his whole bottle!" Nilda said proudly. Holding up the empty baby bottle, she went on, "See? He always finishes it with me. Don't he, Sophie?"

"He finished it with me too," said Frankie.

"He does it more with me," Nilda said, sticking out her tongue.

"Show-off!" said Frankie.

"Come on now. Stop it," said Sophie.

They heard the doorbell ring and all three of them quietly looked at each other. Soon muffled voices sounded and they knew a stranger was in the apartment.

---

[1] a derogatory term for Puerto Ricans; usually associated with Puerto Ricans with dark skin   [2] the stain of a banana; again, alluding to his dark skin

"Frankie, go see who it is," Sophie said. Quickly, Frankie left the bedroom. "Give me the baby, Nilda." Nilda handed Sophie the baby and walked out into the living room.

There was a tall woman standing with her mother in the living room. She had sandy brown hair, cut very short, a tan camel's-hair coat, belted in back, and brown oxford shoes. She carried a brown briefcase and handbag; both were almost the exact color of her shoes. "It certainly is a help that you can speak English," the woman smiled. "You would be surprised how hard it is to understand some of these people. How long have you been in this country, Mrs. Ramírez?"

"I been here about twelve years," her mother said. Won't you please sit down? I'll hang up your coat. Would you like a cup of coffee? I just made some fresh."

"Oh well, no, that's all right. I'll just put my coat right here on this chair and sit right down."

Her mother hesitated and then said, "'How about some nice hot coffee? Yes?"

"Oh no, don't bother."

"No trouble, Mrs. Wood. I got it all ready."

"No, thank you. I really have to get on with it, you know. I have many families to visit." She pulled out a manila folder. Then she took out a brown fountain pen and began to write something on a white sheet of paper. Nilda watched her and wondered if the ink was going to come out brown. She was disappointed when she saw that it was coming out blue, just like ordinary ink.

"How many rooms do you have?"

"Six.

"How many people living here?"

Her mother wet her lips and said, "Well, A got a married son . . . but, living here . . . we got three boys and my daughter, my husband, and my aunt. She's alone. She's a widow many years."

"Then that's seven people. Three adults and four children. Correct? How old are they? Are they all in school?"

"My older boy, Victor, is seventeen years old; Paul is fifteen, and Frankie, my youngest boy, is almost thirteen. My daughter, Nilda, is ten. They are all in school. My son Victor will be graduating high school this June," she said proudly.

"Does your aunt have children?"

"No, she married when she was very young and her husband died after they were married a short time; she never had no children."

"Does she do any sort of work?"

"No. She's sick and old. She has a small check from the Home Relief, but it's very little and just enough for food and medicine."

"Can't she help out?"

"Well, she gives if she got something, but she barely has anything for herself."

"You know we cannot pay rent for you if you have other people living here," the woman said, and jotted something down on the paper. "Does your aunt have her own room?"

"Yes," her mother said. "We don't use the dining room because we eat in the kitchen, and that way we can have an extra bedroom."

"Well, Mrs. Ramírez, she will have to pay, you know. Something, even if it's minimal."

"All right, she will give something, don't worry," her mother said anxiously. "She will."

Nilda thought, Wait till that lady sees Sophie and the baby. The two women went on talking. The social worker continued to ask questions.

Aunt Delia walked in with her newspapers folded and tucked neatly under her arm. Smiling, she looked at the woman and nodded her head courteously. Mrs. Wood looked up at Aunt Delia and returned the greeting with a slight nod.

"Oh, this here is my aunt, Mrs. Wood. She's a little hard of hearing and she don't speak English. She understands just very little." Her mother looked at Aunt Delia and said to her loudly in Spanish, "Delia, this is the investigator. Understand?" Then turning to Mrs. Wood, she said, "This is my aunt—Mrs. Rivera." Pausing, she went on, "Delia, this is Mrs. Wood."

"Who?" Aunt Delia asked.

"Mrs. Wood," her mother answered loudly.

"Nice to meet you, Mrs. Rivera," Mrs. Wood said pleasantly.

Aunt Delia gave her a broad friendly smile, exposing her gums. Then, with a serious expression, she said in Spanish, "It's a crime what's happening to the world today. Somebody is always getting raped. Listen," she went on rapidly, "it's a daily occurrence with the sex maniacs always attacking innocent women. They are the ones responsible for the war. Oh yes. They are! Would you like to see it right here in the paper? Let me—"

"Delia!" her mother interrupted. "This lady is not interested. She's the investigator! Not now. That's enough!"

"What did she say? What did you say, Mrs. Ramírez?" Mrs. Wood asked.

Before her mother could reply, Aunt Delia said, "She can read, can't she? She looked like an educated person. Lydia, let me show her here right here in this article. There's a picture even. Wait!" and the old woman started to open up the *Daily News*.

"What's that, Mrs. Ramírez? What is she saying in Spanish? What is she trying to tell me?" Mrs. Wood asked, perplexed.

Her mother smiled at Mrs. Wood. Making an effort to sound matter-of-fact, she said, "It's nothing, Mrs. Wood. My aunt can't hear too good." Walking over to Aunt Delia, her mother slowly picked up the *Daily News* and folded the paper, giving it to Aunt Delia. "Not now. Dear God!" She went on quietly but firmly in Spanish, "I have to talk to this woman. Please, Delia, go inside." Reluctantly Aunt Delia accepted the newspaper.

"Is she trying to tell me something, Mrs. Ramírez?" Mrs. Wood asked, very curious by this time. "I think I should know what it is."

"She's just nervous about the things she reads in the newspapers, that's all," her mother said softly to Mrs. Wood. Aunt Delia was still standing, holding the newspaper in her hand and frowning at the two women.

Turning toward Aunt Delia, so that Mrs. Wood could not see her face, her mother looked at Aunt Delia, opened her eyes wide, gritted her teeth, and said in Spanish, "Delia, get the hell outta here right now!" Turning back to Mrs. Wood, she said, "You see, Mrs. Wood, she's just a little nervous. You know how the newspapers are full of crime these days and all that. She's old and she worries about things like that."

Aunt Delia started to walk briskly out, but turned back just before leaving. Looking suspiciously at Mrs. Wood for a moment, she winked and said, pointing, "I'll bet you knew about it all the time, but wouldn't let on." Chuckling and mumbling to herself, Aunt Delia left the room.

"What's that?" Mrs. Wood asked.

"She just said it was nice meeting you, Mrs. Wood, and you should be careful in the streets."

"Oh yes, well, how sweet. You can't be too careful these days." There was a short pause and Mrs. Wood said, "Well now, you know, I have to see the apartment and look around. Just routine, I'm sure you understand."

Nilda looked at her mother, who didn't say anything, and wondered, When is she going to tell her about Sophie and Baby Jimmy?

"Mrs. Wood, this here is my daughter, Nilda. Nilda, this is Mrs. Wood, the lady from the Welfare Department."

"How are you, young lady?"

"Fine, thank you," Nilda said timidly.

"How old are you?"

"Ten."

"Oh, a nice big girl. Well. I'm sure you are a big help to Mother. Well. How do you like school? What grade are you in?"

"Yes. I am in the fifth grade. I go to P.S. 72 on 103rd Street."

"How nice . . . . Do you like it there?"

"Yes."

"Isn't that nice . . . . and you speak English so well."

"She's born here, Mrs. Wood," her mother said, offended.

"Oh . . . yes, that's right. Well I mean . . . that is, sometimes . . ."

Her stepfather walked into the room. Nilda noticed he had put on his good suit and his teeth, but did not have time to shave.

"This is my husband, Emilio Ramírez. This is Mrs. Wood."

"How are you?" he said, shaking her hand. "You know, Mrs. Wood . . . Mrs. Wood? That's the right name? O.K. Well, you know, this is only a temporary assistance. I have a good job, and we just got a union in my place, so that as soon as I get my ticker," he smiled and pointed to his heart, "in good shape again, I'll be able to go back to work."

Her mother looked at Mrs. Wood with a desperate expression; she had put down on the report that her husband would not be going back to work.

"Yes," the social worker said. "Well now, I have to look around and just fill out a few forms. If you don't mind, I really have to get on."

"Lydia, did you offer Mrs. Wood something?" her stepfather asked.

"Oh never mind, Mr. Ramírez; I really have to get going. It's all right."

"No," he said, "have something. Coffee? Tea maybe?"

"No. Really I couldn't but thank you anyway." Looking at her wristwatch, she added, "I must be getting on, you know; there are many other people on the list." Standing, she said to Nilda's mother, "Please, may I . . . ?"

"Oh sure, yes . . . this way please. . . . Listen, Mrs. Wood," she walked out into the hallway, "my daughter-in-law is just spending a few days here with my grandson

. . . You see my married son, James, is working in New Jersey, and he just sent them here, you know, to be here with me a little. . . . That way I can see my first grandson. . . . But they will be going back this week, by Friday." She knocked on Sophie's door. "Sophie? May we please come in?" Sophie opened the door, looking very worried. "This here is Mrs. Wood. She's come down from Welfare. . . . This is my daughter-in-law, Sophie Ortega."

"How do you do," Mrs. Wood said, and walked into the room. The baby was in the crib on his back, kicking, and chewing on a pacifier. "Isn't he adorable!" Mrs. Wood looked down at him. "Hi there. My, he has a lot of hair, and so black." Looking up at Sophie, who was fair and had light brown hair, she added, "He must look like his daddy."

"Oh yes! He looks just like Jimmy," Sophie said, and smiled proudly.

"How old is the baby?" She went on asking questions.

Nilda had been walking behind the women and now stepped around them and went up to the crib. Looking at the baby, Nilda leaned over and began to play with him, touching his hands and shaking his feet. Baby Jimmy began to coo and make noises.

"Nilda, that's enough!" her mother snapped.

"Mrs. Ramírez, you have a lovely grandson. Good-bye, Sophie," Mrs. Wood said.

Nilda followed as her mother showed Mrs. Wood the other bedrooms, the bathroom, and the kitchen. Frankie had been doing homework, and answered a few questions briefly and quickly. They walked back into the living room.

"Well, Mrs. Ramírez, you know we cannot pay rent for all these people."

"No people, just my aunt and my daughter-in-law who is leaving by Friday," her mother said, almost pleading.

"All right, I'll put that down. And we'll see. Now, we may be able to assist you with . . ."

They went on talking and Nilda heard her stepfather again. He walked into the room and said loudly, "You sure you won't have something, Mrs. Wood?"

"No thank you, Mr. Ramírez. I'm late as it is," she said.

"So late you can't have a glass of water? Have something!" he said, almost commanding.

"Emilio . . . por favor," her mother said.

"Capitalism puts us in this position. You know that, lady? I worked all my life; why do I have to ask for charity?"

"Please, Emilio . . ." her mother said. Mrs. Wood turned beet red and tried to smile.

"What are you going to give us, Mrs.? Gold perhaps? That you have to inspect everything here?" he said, raising his voice.

"Emilio! This lady is only doing her job. Now let us be," her mother said anxiously. "Please, Emilio . . . *cállate*!"

"All right, all right," he said, and sat down, glaring at Mrs. Wood.

Mrs. Wood stood up, quickly putting on her tan camel's-hair coat. "Well," she said smiling.

The front door opened and Paul came running in. "Hi, Ma. . . . Oh, hello," he said. Mrs. Wood looked at the boy.

"Mrs. Wood, this is my son Paul. Paul, this is Mrs. Wood, the lady from Welfare." Mrs. Wood opened her eyes wide, surprised as she looked at Paul.

"Hello," he said.

"This is your son?" she asked.

"Yes, this is my third child," her mother answered. Nilda had seen this happen many times before; Paul was so much darker than everyone else that people were always surprised. She hated it when they stared at Paul like this woman was doing. Mrs. Wood asked Paul the same questions she had asked Nilda and Frankie. Nilda couldn't wait for her to stop talking and leave. Leave Paul alone! she thought.

She stayed in the living room as her mother and Mrs. Wood went towards the door, and heard their voices.

"Good-bye and thank you, Mrs. Wood. You been very nice, and I appreciate whatever you can do for us. . . . You see, anything would be a help and . . ."

"Good-bye." Mrs. Wood's voice was far away.

"Good-bye. Thank you so much again," her mother called out.

"Shit! Bunch of capitalist bastards." She heard her stepfather as he marched down the hallway.

She looked at Paul and smiled. "Boy, Paul. I'm glad that's over. Now Mama won't be so cranky no more."

"Yeah, me too. That, lady seemed nice. Didn't she, Nilda?" asked Paul. Nilda looked at Paul and wondered, Didn't you see her looking at you that way? Maybe it's just me, she thought. "Don't you think she was nice, Nilda? Maybe she'll help us out."

"Yeah," she said, "maybe." They heard voices; her mother and stepfather were arguing.

"Emilio, por Dios . . . how could you? You think it's easy?"

"I'll go back to work . . . tomorrow! You think I can't support my family? What kind of shit does a man have to put up with?"

"You have to rest. . . . Please . . . you want me to go crazy?"

"Never mind. I'm calling the union right now, Lydia."

"Ay . . . Emilio, please just stop it."

Nilda heard the voices still arguing. "Jimmy is gonna come and get Sophie and the baby. I don't want the baby to leave, Paul," she said, almost crying.

"Don't be silly, Nilda. He gotta leave. He's gotta be with his mother, right? You gotta be with your mother, don't you?" Nilda nodded and swallowed, trying not to cry. "You'll visit them. Wait, you'll see. Probably see him more than if they were still staying here."

"Do you really think so, Paul?" she asked hopefully. "Sophie did say I could visit, and maybe stay over if they got room. You know, like to baby-sit and all that, since I know just how to take care of Baby Jimmy and he loves me so much. You know, he recognizes me already."

"You see? So there! What did I tell you?" Paul said, smiling at Nilda. She smiled back at Paul with a sense of reassurance. The voices had stopped arguing and it was quiet.

"Hey, we missed the radio programs. I'll bet 'The Lone Ranger' is over. What time is it?" She turned on the radio. The news was on. "Yes, this is a massive war effort by the entire nation. Americans are rallying to the call. Fathers, brothers, sons, uncles, and cousins, Americans and patriots all! These brave men are getting ready to leave their loved ones as the draft call gets under way. Young men are showing their patriotism by enlisting, and volunteer stations are being set up in each and every small town in the U.S.A. In Gillespie, Illinois . . .”

Nilda shut the radio off. “Oh shucks, we missed it.”

“Look for something else, Nilda,” said Paul.

“Naw, I’m going out to play,” she said. Getting up, she added, “Come on, Paul. Come out and let’s play a game of tag.”

“Go on, man. Nilda, I’m too old for that,” he said indignantly.

“I’m cutting out. See you, Paul.” Nilda left and got her coat. Running into the kitchen, she said to her mother, “Mama, I’m going out to play. *Bendición.*[3]”

“*Dios te bendiga,*[4] Nilda, get home in time for supper and homework.”

She jumped down the steps, taking them two at a time. Outside it was cold. Cars and buses sped by the avenue. She looked around her. Now, she thought, who’s around for a game of tag?

July, 1942

From Grand Central Station, like the first time, along with many other children, Nilda went off to camp again. It was an all-girls camp, nonsectarian, taking children from all areas of the Eastern states. Her mother told her that it would be different this time. Reassuring her, she had said, “Look, Nilda, I had to pay something for the camp. It’s not a free camp like the last time. I had to buy two pink jumpsuits for uniforms; everybody wears the same thing there. Everybody is the same. You see? Nobody is going to hit you, Nilda. There is not gonna be no nuns and none of that. I promise. O.K?”

She was going for a whole month. That’s like forever, she thought, feeling miserable. As the train sped out of New York City, leaving the Barrio and the tall buildings behind, Nilda became frightened, not knowing what was going to happen to her. Looking around her in the train car, she noticed that there were no dark children. Except for a couple of olive-skinned, dark-haired girls, she did not see any Puerto Rican or black children. She wondered if the two girls were Spanish.

Nilda thought about last summer and the nuns, and felt a sense of relief as she looked at one of the women counselors who was dressed in a light pink cotton suit. The woman caught Nilda’s glance and smiled at her. Nilda quickly looked away, hoping that the woman would not ask her any questions. She did not want to speak to anyone. She began to think of home and her family, making an effort to keep from crying.

She knew her brothers had gone to camp. Paul was big enough to work at his camp and make some money. Lucky thing! she thought. She remembered Victor was not going to be at home any more. Determined, despite his mother’s protests, he had

---

[3] Give me your blessing.   [4] God bless you. In Puerto Rican culture it is often used by a parent to a child before they part, or as a greeting when a close family member arrives.

joined the Army right after graduation. He had been gone two weeks already. She just couldn't imagine not having Victor at home any more. She had been very proud that her brother was going to be a soldier and had told Miss Langhorn all about it at school. "He is a good American," Miss Langhorn had said. "You and your family should be proud."

She remembered Victor's graduation party. Her mother had managed a small dinner for the family, and a cake. Aunt Rosario had come down from the Bronx with her husband, Willie, and her two children, Roberto and Claudia. Her mother and Aunt Rosario had been brought up together in Puerto Rico; they were first cousins. She was her mother's only relative in this country. Nilda saw Aunt Rosario and her cousins during holidays every year and on special occasions. She would travel with her family to the Bronx or Aunt Rosario would come to the Barrio to visit with them. Nilda didn't much like Roberto, but she enjoyed playing with Claudia.

Nilda smiled, thinking about all her family and Baby Jimmy. She remembered it had been a long time since she had seen him. He won't even know me any more when I see him again, she thought. Last winter they had received a card from Jimmy and Sophie postmarked somewhere in New York, not New Jersey, with no return address. She went on drifting into mental images.

A loud whistle sounded and the train began to slow down. "Bard Manor . . . Bard Manor . . . fifteen-minute stop," she heard a man's voice calling.

Outside they all lined up and marched over to several buses that were parked near the small railroad station. After a short ride, Nilda got off the bus with the rest of the girls. Nilda looked about her and saw no buildings; there were large areas of grass and trees. Off at a distance from the road she saw a group of cottages set among green hills.

They approached the cottages, which were made of unfinished logs with a dark rough bark. Nilda entered a cottage with her group; it was a large dormitory, simply furnished. There was a total of eight beds, four at either side of the room. A wooden bureau was placed next to each bed, with a small wooden bench at the foot. Each child automatically took a bunk.

"Hello, girls," said one counselor. "Let me introduce myself. I'm Miss Rachel Hammerman, and you can all call me Miss Rachel." Looking at the other counselor, she said, "Jeanette?"

"Yes," answered the other counselor. "Hi. I'm Miss Jeanette Pisacano. You can all call me Miss Jeanette."

Miss Rachel said, "Has everyone got a bunk? O.K. Then that will be your bunk for the rest of the time you are going to be here. In this section of Bard Manor Camp for Girls we have campers ages nine to twelve. The older girls live on the other side of the camp. We will visit them in time and they will visit us as well. In fact, we all eat together in the main house, which is about a ten-minute walk down the road. The pool is there with the tennis court, swings, and all the other goodies. Let's see . . . she paused. "Oh yes. Miss Jeanette and I also sleep here; I don't know if you noticed, but there is another entrance to the cottage; that is our entrance only. O.K.?" She waited, then asked, "Now, Jeanette, you wanna say something?"

"Yes," Miss Jeanette smiled. "We hope to really have a good time here. You all might complain about our early bedtime . . . seven-thirty we get ready."

"Awww. . . ." "Nawww," the girls complained.

"By eight o'clock we should be in bed," Miss Jeanette went on, smiling.

"Nooo. . . . Awww." "Awwww," the girls responded.

"You will be so tired," Miss Jeanette went on talking, "that you will be glad to get to bed when we finish with you." She paused and smiled. "You'll see." She laughed. "Anyway—" The girls interrupted, giggling and protesting. "Shhhh . . . shhhh." She continued, "Now listen, you all have two pink jumpsuits. They will be what you are going to wear most of the time that you are here. Just put on a pair of clean panties and your jumpsuits. At the end of the day you can put them in the large laundry cart in the shower room. Now, they will be laundered; you will always have a clean jumpsuit to wear. In the morning someone will put all the suits and panties on one camper's bunk. She will look at the name tags and distribute them. Every day another camper will distribute the jumpsuits, so that everyone will take a turn, rotating . . . ummm . . . and . . . " Looking at Miss Rachel, she asked, "What else, Rachel?"

"Oh well, we will make a list of chores for everyone. Every day each camper has a special chore to do. We will alternate the work."

"Too bad." "Yeah." "Aw shucks," said some of the girls.

Miss Rachel smiled. "Never mind; everybody works. Here we make our own beds and keep our cottage clean, as well as help in the dining room at mealtime, and so on."

Pausing, she asked, "Who's hungry?"

"Meeeee." "Me." "I'm starving," the girls yelled.

"O.K.," she said, "get your things put away and then wash up and make sure you all go to the toilet. Now, as soon as we finish, we go eat. All right? Make it snappy then," Miss Jeanette said.

"Wait, let's introduce ourselves."

"Oh, of course!" Miss Rachel looked around and said, "O.K., let's start." Pointing at Nilda, she said, "Your name is Nilda? Right? Tell us your full name."

"Nilda Ramírez," she said.

"Bernice White."

"Josie Forest."

"Evelyn Daniels."

"Stella Pappas." All the other girls called out their names.

Both women left the room and the girls started to put their things away. Nilda opened her suitcase and put her things away in the drawers. Then she set her bureau with her toothbrush, toothpaste, hairbrush, and comb. She picked up a pad of plain unlined paper and a small box of crayons, a present from Aunt Delia. She carefully wrote her name on them and placed them inside the top drawer.

All finished, she looked around at the other girls. She smiled at the girl in the next bunk.

The girl, smiling back, said, "Hello."

"Hi," said Nilda. "What's your name again?"

"Josie. What's yours?"

"Nilda. You been here before?"

"No. I've never been to camp before at all. This is my first time."

"Oh well," said Nilda, "I been to camp before. Not here, in another place, but I didn't like it; they were too strict." Looking around at the room she added, "This looks nice, don't it?"

"Yes," said Josie smiling. Some, of the other girls were going off to the bathroom. "I guess we'd better wash up if we wanna eat. You wanna come, Nilda?"

"O.K." Nilda walked along with Josie into a large bathroom with several sinks and toilets. There were clean towels and soap set out. Nilda saw that the toilets had doors. Good, she thought, I can make alone. She washed up and waited her turn to sit on the toilet.

Outside the sun was still out and the trees cast long shadows on the fields. She walked with the group, looking around her at the quiet woods. They walked along the road until they came to a large white two-story wood-frame house. A sign was over the entrance; gold letters trimmed in white on a black background read, BARD MANOR CAMP FOR GIRLS. Nilda saw a lot of outdoor equipment, swings, climbing bars, a tennis court, and a large swimming pool. There were also several small wood-framed buildings near the main house.

They went into a large dining room set with long tables and wooden folding chairs. Nilda saw that the chairs were exactly like the ones in Benji's church. Oh man, she thought. Turning to comment, she realized that there was no one who would know what she was talking about. Miss Rachel led them to a table set for ten persons and they sat down. The table was covered with a clean white tablecloth.

"Today we'll be served, but tomorrow we serve ourselves, as well as clear the table! So enjoy the service, ladies," she smiled.

They were served a vegetable soup, breaded chicken cutlets, carrots, hash brown potatoes, and a green salad. A large platter of bread with butter, dishes of jam, and pitchers of milk were on the table. Everyone passed them around. Dessert was an apple cake, which Nilda enjoyed. She ate everything.

The girls played outdoors for a little while after supper, running, and climbing on the equipment, Nilda began to play with a few of the girls in her group, chasing each other and tossing a large rubber ball around. Someone blew a whistle and the girls lined up.

As they walked back to their cottage, Nilda was feeling tired already. The counselors began to sing songs. At first, she barely opened her mouth, but then slowly she began to mouth a chorus, getting louder and louder. She heard herself singing clearly just like the rest of the girls.

That night in bed, Nilda pulled the covers around her, tucking in her feet. It was dark and quiet, except for the sound of the crickets. She could not fall asleep although she felt very tired. She thought of home again and the sounds and smells, so different. Sounds and smells she could understand. Footsteps on the hard sidewalk. A woman's high heels clicking, or a man's heavy shoes slapping the concrete as he ran to catch the bus late at night. Someone coughing. Someone whistling. All the traffic whizzing by. Summertime, everybody outside. The radios playing, people talking. Her mother making fresh coffee with boiled milk. The smell of the heat. Sometimes when it got unbearably hot, her mother let her sit on the fire escape with her pillow and blanket.

Suddenly the silence scared her and she wanted her mother; she wanted to go home. Nilda began to sob quietly and heard some of the other girls crying. She thought, They are crying too? Surprised, she listened to them cry for a little while, then remembered that tomorrow they were going to use the swimming pool. She had never been in a pool before. I wonder what that's gonna be like, she thought.

Everyone had stopped crying and she heard the heavy breathing of the girls fast asleep in the silent room. Outside the crickets continued chirping, occasionally changing their rhythm patterns slightly. Slowly Nilda became used to the new melody of sounds surrounding her.

July 14, 1942.

Dear Mami,

   I am fine. I'm haveing a real good time. I passed my swimming test. I am now advance beginner insted of only beginner that is a higher thing to be. We do a lot of art and crafts I am makeing you something and something for Papa. I received you letter. I told everybody about Victor that he is in Fort Bragg North Carolina. We had a cook out that is where you make a fire and cook the food outside and it tasted real good. We ate hot dogs and hambergers and milk and juice. We also toasted marshmellos. I like Miss Jenete she is really nice to me she is my counselor. I seen a lot of flowers like you told me about when you live in Puerto Rico. I hope you are fine and haveing a good time. Tell Titi Delia I made some drawings of the camp so she could see what it looks like here. I learn some songs. we really have a lot of fun it is swell here.

   Well that is it. Mami I love you and Papa and Aunt Delia and everybody. Bendicion Mama.

Love
Nilda xxxxxx

P.S. my friend Josie is nice and so is Stella they live in another state.

Nilda read the letter she had just written to her mother and, satisfied, folded it and put it inside an envelope. This was free time and she had finally decided that she had better answer her mother's letter. Most of the girls in her group were either writing, reading, or just sitting around. Getting up from her bunk, she decided to walk to the main house and put the letter in the mail basket. Looking for her two friends, she realized that they were probably at the main house anyway. Nilda started walking down the road; in the past two weeks she had gotten to know the camp quite well. She loved being able to recognize a large oak tree or a clump of bushes, a certain curve in the earth, a gentle slope in the horizon. All these familiar landmarks gave her a sense of security.

Nilda passed a trail off the side of the main road. They had all hiked through there one day; it was thick with trees and bushes. Stopping for a moment, she took the trail and started walking into the woods. She came to a fork in the trail. Taking the path on the right that seemed to climb, she continued along and came to a clearing where the landscape opened up into wide fields covered with wild flowers. The white Queen Anne's lace covered most of the fields, which were sprinkled with yellow goldenrod and clumps of tiny orange and purple flowers. The sky overhead was bright with the sun. Large white clouds glistened, rapidly moving across the horizon and out of sight.

Nilda remembered her mother's description of Puerto Rico's beautiful mountainous countryside covered with bright flowers and red flamboyant trees.

"There it was a different world from Central Park and New York City, Nilda," she could hear her mother saying. Looking ahead, she saw miles and miles of land and not a single sign promising to arrest her for any number of reasons. Signs had always been part of her life:

> DO NOT WALK ON THE GRASS. . . .
> DO NOT PICK THE FLOWERS. . . .
> NO SPITTING ALLOWED. . . .
> NO BALL PLAYING ALLOWED. . . .
> VIOLATORS WILL BE PROSECUTED.

No dog shit on my shoes, she laughed. And Mama always telling me to watch out for the broken pieces of whiskey bottles in the bushes. No matter where she was in Central Park, she could always see part of a tall building and hear the traffic.

Here there was not a building anywhere, she thought, no traffic and no streets to cross. She became aware of the silence again. The world of the Barrio and the crowds, was someplace else far away, and it was all right. Miles and miles away someplace, but she could still be here at the same time; that could really happen. Yes, it's true, she smiled to herself. She felt the letter to her mother still in her pocket.

Nilda went back towards the main road, drinking in the sweet and pungent smells of the woods. She listened to the quiet buzzing of insects and the rustling of the bushes as small animals rushed through, sometimes appearing and disappearing within a split second. She noticed that off to the side of the trail a few feet away was a thick wall of bushes. Curious, Nilda went towards it and started to push her way through. Struggling, she pushed away the bushes with her arms and legs and stepped into an opening of yards and yards of roses delicately tinted with pink. The roses were scattered, growing wildly on the shrubs. The sun came through the leaves, stems, and petals, streaming down like rows of bright ribbons landing on the dark green earth.

Breathless, she stared at the flowers, almost unbelieving for a moment, thinking that she might be in a movie theater waiting for the hard, flat, blank screen to appear, putting an end to a manufactured fantasy which had engrossed and possessed her so completely. Nilda walked over to the flowers and touched them. Inhaling the sweet fragrance, she felt slightly dizzy, almost reeling. She sat down on the dark earth and felt the sun on her face, slipping down her body and over to the shrubs covered with roses. The bright sash of warm sunlight enveloped her and the flowers; she was part of them; they were part of her.

She took off her socks and sneakers, and dug her feet into the earth like the roots of the shrubs. Shutting her eyes, Nilda sat there for a long time, eyes closed, feeling a sense of pure happiness; no one had given her anything or spoken a word to her. The happiness was inside, a new feeling, and although it was intense, Nilda accepted it as part of a life that now belonged to her.

After supper that evening, Nilda's group received a visit from the older girls. They wore jumpsuits as well, yellow with a brown trim, styled differently. Nilda was sitting alone at the side of the hill opposite the cottages. She was barefoot, reading a book. A tall dark-haired girl approached her. She was about fourteen or fifteen years old. Smiling, she looked at Nilda and asked, "Are you Nilda?"

"Yes," Nilda said, returning her smile.

"What's your last name?"

"Ramírez, Nilda Ramírez."

"Hi," she said, sitting down comfortably next to Nilda. "I'm Olga. Olga Rodríguez. This is my third summer here." Nilda nodded, impressed with the older girl. "Somebody told me about you. They said you are Spanish. Do you speak it?"

"Yes!" said Nilda. "I speak it at home to my mother sometimes, and all the time to my aunt; she don't speak English at all."

"O.K. then," said Olga, "let's talk. How are you?" she asked in Spanish, and continued, "How do you like camp? Tell me, how long have you been here?"

"Oh," Nilda responded excitedly in Spanish, "I been here since like about two weeks already. But I will be here a whole month. I like it very much here."

"Where do you live? In New York City?" asked Olga.

"Yes. I live near Central Park right off Madison Avenue—"

"In the Barrio?" interrupted Olga.

"Yes! Do you know it? Do you live there too? Maybe you go to my brother Frankie's school."

"I don't live in the Barrio," Olga answered. "I live downtown, on 14th Street between Seventh and Eighth Avenues."

"Oh, my mother took me there once. Is that where there is a big church? Our Lady of Guadalupe, I think. My mother and me took a subway there. That is a great big church."

"Yes, that is our church," responded Olga. In English she asked Nilda, "You are Puerto Rican, ain't you?"

"Yes," Nilda answered, reverting to English.

"You know Puerto Ricans ain't really Spanish. You shouldn't say that. That you are Spanish. I can't even understand you when you talk." Surprised, Nilda realized the older girl was cross. "It's very hard to understand what you say . . . like when you say . . . say the number five in Spanish." Olga paused. "Go on, say it; say five in Spanish."

"Five," Nilda said clearly in Spanish.

"There, that's all wrong! You are saying it all wrong! What kind of accent is that? In Spain they talk Castilian. That's what my parents talk at home. You probably never even heard of that," Olga said angrily. Nilda did not know what to say and looked at Olga. "Say shoes," Olga went on. "Go ahead, I'll prove it again; say the word 'shoes.'"

Nilda wanted to say something. She thought, perhaps I should tell her about Papa. He speaks like that. He sounds like her and he comes from Spain, so he must speak like she says. But the older girl's angry face left Nilda mute. She said nothing.

"Go on," Olga insisted. "Say shoes. I'm waiting."

"Say shoes!" Nilda repeated in English.

"Very funny," Olga said. "Well that proves what you speak is a dialect." Getting up, she went on, "Don't let me hear you calling yourself Spanish around here when you can't even talk it properly, stupid."

"You're stupid," Nilda answered.

"I'm leaving," Olga said. "We don't bother with your kind. You give us all a bad name."

Nilda watched Olga turn away and disappear over the next mound of grass. Picking up a single green blade, she popped it in her mouth and began to chew. It had a bitter taste at first, then she got used to it and she chewed slowly, imitating some of the cows she had seen eating in the countryside. She lay back, digging her heels into the soft ground, thinking about the older girl and what had just happened. Nilda stuck out her tongue, then looked at the sky, the trees, and the small birds that flew overhead. At that, moment she wanted to absorb all that was around her. Quickly, she began to let her body roll down the hill; faster and faster she went until her weight carried her to a full stop. Jumping up, she ran back to get her sneakers and her book. She didn't care about being Spanish; she didn't know exactly what that meant, except that it had nothing to do with her happiness.

May, 1945

Nilda waited in the corridor outside the ward, standing next to Victor, who was in uniform. He was to be discharged from the service in three weeks, but had arrived last night on special leave. Frankie walked back and forth nervously; once in a while he whispered something to Victor.

Everyone had been informed; telegrams had been sent to Jimmy and to Paul. Aunt Rosario had been at the hospital most of the night and, after going to the apartment briefly, had returned early this morning to summon a priest for Nilda's mother. Aunt Delia had not been allowed to come to the hospital this past week. Despite her persistent questioning, everyone had reassured the old woman that all was going well at the hospital.

Aunt Rosario stepped out of the ward, wiping her eyes. She looked at Nilda. "Nilda . . . go on inside now . . . but remember your mama is very, very sick, and I want you to try to compose yourself so that you don't make her too nervous." Aunt Rosario waited and Nilda did not move. "Go on . . . for heaven's sake," she said impatiently. "Lydia wants to see you alone for a little while . . . hurry up." Nilda nodded and slowly walked inside the ward and over to her mother's bed. This time the heavy green cloth curtains were pulled around the sides and front of the bed. Nilda extended her arm and pushed a section of the curtains aside, looking in. Recognizing her mother, she stepped in all the way, closing the curtains behind her.

Her mother was lying back with her eyes shut, her head slightly tilted forward. For an instant she felt her insides jump. Is Mama dead? she thought. But then she looked up and saw a metal stand supporting a bottle which hung upside down. An invisible liquid flowed out of the bottle and into a long thin tube; the tube was attached to a needle that was taped into her mother's right forearm. She went closer to her mother and heard her breathing. Then raising her hand, she lightly touched her mother's arm.

Opening her eyes, she looked at Nilda and smiled faintly. "Nilda?" Her voice was very hoarse and just above a whisper.

"Mama, how are you?" Nilda said shyly. She had not been to see her mother for a few days.

"Nilda . . . I'm very sick, nena." She paused and breathed heavily. Looking down, Nilda began to cry. Her mother watched her and slowly shook her head. Nilda buried her face next to her mother's on the pillow and cried uncontrollably for what seemed a long time. After a while she raised her head. "Take a tissue," her mother said. Nilda picked up a tissue, blew her nose, and wiped her eyes. "How's school?" her mother asked.

"Fine, Mama."

"You still drawing those wonderful pictures?"

"Yes."

"You are gonna stay in school . . . like a good girl and finish?" Her mother spoke very slowly. "You are not gonna be foolish and quit?"

"No, Mama." Nilda sat on a chair and was very still, her eyes fixed on her mother.

"Nilda, you have to promise me that you will stay in school, and that you will listen to Rosario." Nilda nodded. "You eating all right?"

"Yes." There was a long silence. This morning, at home, Nilda had planned to ask her mother about a whole lot of things, and to talk about some of the things that bothered her. Now, as she sat close to her mother, she was very frightened and felt almost like a stranger. She did not know what to say or what to do. "Mama?" Her mother looked at her. "Petra had a baby girl last Sunday." Her mother smiled. "She had a little girl; she named her Marianne."

"Marianne? Do you know, Nilda, that was my mother's name. Mariana. Yes, your grandmother. That's a pretty name. Have you seen the baby yet?"

"No, I just heard about it. Maybe I'll go visit them next week."

"What about Indio? Nilda, did they get in touch with that boy?"

"Well, I heard he is coming home on leave, and that his father already gave Mr. López his word that Indio would marry Petra. Even though they are Lutheran, they said he will marry Petra in the Catholic Church. Anyway, that's what I heard."

"Nilda, you must never do anything foolish like that. Never. Don't have a bunch of babies and lose your life."

"You had children, Mama, and you love them and—"

"Nilda," her mother interrupted, and reaching out with her free hand, took both of Nilda's hands and held them tightly. "Listen to what I say. I love you, Nilda, and I love your brothers, all of you, regardless who the father was, I don't care . . . you are all . . . still mine." She paused and closed her eyes, remaining silent for a while. Nilda wondered if she had fallen asleep, but she opened her eyes again. "You are a woman, Nilda. You will have to bear the child; regardless of who planted the seed, they will be your children and no one, else's. If a man is good, you are lucky; if he leaves you, or is cruel, so much the worse for you. . . . And then, if you have no money and little education, who will help you, Nilda? Another man? Yes, and another pregnancy. Welfare? Yes, and they will kill you in the process, slowly robbing you of your home, so that after a while it is no longer yours." She stopped speaking, and pushing her head back against the pillow, she stared at the ceiling, but continued to hold Nilda's hands.

"Mami?" Nilda whispered. "Aren't you happy? I love you, Mama. Aren't you happy with us? I want to be with you all the time, Mama."

Tightening her grip on Nilda's hands, and without looking away from the ceiling, her mother said, "I have no life of my own, Nilda." Her voice was very low and hoarse; Nilda had to lean closer to hear what she said. "I have never had a life of my own . . . yes, that's true, isn't it? No life, Nilda . . . nothing that is really only mine . . . that's not fair, is it? That's not right . . . I don't know what I want even. . . ."

She paused, and Nilda felt, her mother's body shaking; she was laughing without making any sound. "Do you know if I were to get well tomorrow . . . what I would do? Nilda? . . . I would live for the children I bore . . . I guess . . . and nothing more. You see, I don't remember any more what I did want. . . . Sometimes when I am alone, here in the hospital, I remember a feeling I used to have when I was very young . . . it had only to do with me. Nobody else was included . . . just me, and I did exist so joyfully in that feeling; I was so nourished . . . thinking about it would make me so excited about life. . . . You know something? I don't even know what it was now. How is that possible? That there is this life I have made, Nilda, and I have nothing to do with it? How did it all happen anyway?

"Do you have that feeling, honey? That you have something all yours . . . you must . . . like when I see you drawing sometimes, I know you have something all yours. Keep it . . . hold on, guard it. Never give it to nobody . . . not to your lover, not to your kids . . . it don't belong to them . . . and . . . they have no right . . . no right to take it. We are all born alone . . . and we die all alone. And when I die, Nilda, I know I take nothing with me that is only mine." She paused and said, "You asked me something, didn't you? . . . oh yes. . . . Am I happy? . . . I don't know. . . . But if I cannot see who I am beyond the eyes of the children I bore . . . then turning her head, she looked directly at Nilda for a moment ". . . it was not worth the journey . . . and I might as well not have bothered at all." Shutting her eyes once more, she lay back against the pillow.

Nilda began to cry again, this time quietly. After a bit, she said, "Mama, I don't understand you."

"Someday you will, you know . . . yes. Hold on to yourself, even if at times you have to let go some . . . but not all! No . . . Nilda . . . not ever. A little piece inside has to remain yours always; it's your right, you know. To give it all up . . . *entonces, mi hijita* . . . you will lose what is real inside you."

Discussion Questions

1. Compare the two social workers Nilda encounters. What are their beliefs about the people they deal with? Is there a significant difference between them regarding those beliefs?
2. Determine other instances where Nilda is made aware of her "difference." What do those instances say about the individuals who she deals with, and what do they say about mainstream society?
3. What does Nilda think about these instances? Is she fully aware of their significance?
4. How does Nilda feel during her trip to camp? Examine her discovery of a "secret garden." What is the symbolic significance of the garden in relation to Nilda's identity?
5. Compare the speech by Nilda's mother to Nilda on pages 367–69 to the thoughts of Petra Estrella's mother, in Maria Helena Viramontes's *Under the Feet of Jesus* on pages 74–77. In what way have these women's lives been affected by traditional beliefs and family obligations?

Piri Thomas

*PIRI THOMAS, born John Peter Thomas, was born in New York City in 1928.
In an attempt to remove young Piri from the lure of the streets, his family moved to
Long Island. Despite this, he was arrested in 1950 for his involvement in a shoot-out
with the police during the robbery of a nightclub. He was imprisoned for seven years
during which time he re-examined his life and decided to help others like himself rather
than continuing his life of crime. He has been doing just that ever since his release,
both through his writing and his personal involvement counseling gang members and
drug addicts.*

Thomas has written several plays, among them Las Calles de Oro *(The Golden
Streets), which was produced in New York in 1972. His other works include* Savior,
Savior, Hold my Hand *(1972),* Seven Long Times *(1974), and* Stories of El Barrio
(1978). He is currently working on a novel titled A Matter of Dignity.

Piri Thomas is best known for his autobiographical novel Down These Mean
Streets *(1967). Employing strong language and often shifting between Spanish and
English, the book traces the author's experiences with drugs and prison and culminates
in a spiritual awakening. The first excerpt is taken from roughly the middle part of the
novel. One of the novel's preoccupations, as it is for many works of Puerto Rican-
American authors, is the dual stigma involved in being both black and Puerto Rican.
The other chapter, where Piri decides to let go of the past, is taken from the conclusion
of the novel.*

From Down These Mean Streets

Hung Up Between Two Sticks

Not long afterward me and Louie got a little bit of that shit ourselves. Only we
didn't get no choice to cut out. We got hung up by a white clique from downtown
as we were coming out of the RKO flick on 86th Street. There were about eight paddies. We tried to cut out, but they got us tight inside their circle. Louie quickly
punched his way out and made it. It took me a little longer. I caught four belts for
every one I could lay on them. Finally I got out and started putting down shoe
leather. But the paddies were hot on doing me up real nice. One of them got so close
to me I saw his face over my shoulder. I stopped short and he ran right into a slap
with all my weight behind it. He went down on his ass and I told him cool-like,
"Motherfucker, I punch men and slap punks." His boys were too near for me to play
my grandstand to the most, so I started to make it. I heard him scream out from between his split lips: "You dirty, fucking shine! I'll get one of you black bastards."

I screamed back, "Your mammy got fucked by one of us black bastards." *One of us black bastards. Was that me?* I wondered.

It really bugged me when the paddies called us Puerto Ricans the same names they called our colored aces. Yet it didn't bother Louie or the other fellas who were as white as him; it didn't bother Crip, or the others, who were as dark as me or darker. Why did it always bug me? Why couldn't I just laugh it off with that simple-ass kid rhyme:

> Sticks and stones may break my bones,
> But words will never harm me.

I had two colored cats, Crutch and Brew, for tight *amigos*.[1] All the time I heard them talk about Jim Crow and southern paddies' way-out, screwed-up thinking. Crutch told me once that he was sitting on the curb down South where he used to live and some young white boys passed in a car and yelled out to him, "Hey, nigger, git outta that gutter and climb down the sewer where all you black niggers belong."

It really bugged me, like if they had said it to me. I asked Crutch if he knew any colored cats that had been hung. "Not person'ly," he said, "but my daddy knew some." He said it with a touch of sadness hooked together with a vague arrogance.

Crutch was smart and be talked a lot of things that made sense to any Negro. That was what bothered me—it made a lot of sense to me.

"You ain't nevah been down South, eh, Piri?" Crutch had asked me.

"Uh-uh. *Nunca*,[2] man. Just read about it, and I dug that flick *Gone with the Wind*."

"Places like Georgia and Mississippi and Alabama. All them places that end in i's an' e's an' a whole lotta a's. A black man's so important that a drop of Negro blood can make a black man out of a pink-asshole, blue-eyed white man. Powerful stuff, that thar white skin, but it don't mean a shit hill of beans alongside a Negro's blood."

Yeah, that Crutch made sense.

The next day I looked up at the faces of the people passing by my old stoop. I tried to count their different shades and colors, but I gave it up after a while. Anyway, black and white were the most outstanding; all the rest were in between.

I felt the fuzz on my chin and lazily wondered how long it'd be before I'd have one like Poppa. *I look like Poppa*, I thought, *we really favor each other*. I wondered if it was too mean to hate your brothers a little for looking white like Momma. I felt my hair—thick, black, and wiry. Mentally I compared my hair with my brothers' hair. My face screwed up at the memory of the jillion tons of stickum hair oils splashed down in a vain attempt to make it like theirs. I felt my nose. "Shit, it ain't so flat," I said aloud. But mentally I measured it against my brothers', whose noses were sharp, straight, and placed neat-like in the middle of their paddy fair faces.

Why did this have to happen to me? Why couldn't I be born like them? I asked myself. I felt sort of chicken-shit thinking like that. I felt shame creep into me. It wasn't right to be ashamed of what one was. It was like hating Momma for the color she was and Poppa for the color be wasn't.

---

[1] friends   [2] never

The noise of the block began to break through to me. I listened for real. I heard the roar of multicolored kids, a street blend of Spanish and English with a strong tone of Negro American.

"Hey, man," a voice called, "what yuh doing thar sitting on your rump? Yuh look like you're thinking up a storm." It was Brew, one of my tightest *amigos*.

"*Un poco,* Brew," I said. "How's it goin' with you?"

"Cool breeze," he said.

I looked at Brew, who was as black as God is supposed to be white. "Man, Brew," I said, "you sure an ugly spook."

Brew smiled. "Dig this Negro calling out 'spook,'" he said.

I smiled and said, "I'm a Porty Rican."

"Ah only sees another Negro in fron' of me," said Brew.

This was the "dozens," a game of insults. The dozens is a dangerous game even among friends, and many a tooth has been lost between fine, ass-tight *amigos*. Now I wanted the game to get serious. I didn't know exactly why. Brew and me had played the dozens plenty and really gotten dirty. But I wanted something to happen. "Smile, pussy, when you come up like that," I said. "I'm a stone Porty Rican, and—"

"And . . ." Brew echoed softly.

I tried to dig myself. I figured I should get it back on a joke level. What the hell was I trying to put down? Was I trying to tell Brew that I'm better than he is 'cause he's only black and I'm a Puerto Rican dark-skin? Like his people copped trees on a white man's whim, and who ever heard of Puerto Ricans getting hung like that?

I looked down at my bands, curling and uncurling, looking for some kinda answer to Brew's cool echo. "Brew," I finally eased out.

"Yeah."

"Let's forget it, Brew."

"Ain't nothin' to forget, baby."

I lit a butt. Brew offered me a whole weed. "Thanks. Nice day out," I said.

"So-kay," he said, and added: "Look, I ain't rehashin' this shit just went down, but—"

"Forget it, Brew. I'm sorry for the sound."

"Ain't nothin' to be sorry about Piri. Yuh ain't said nothin' that bad. Mos' people got some kinda color complex. Even me."

"Brew, I ain't said what I'm feeling. I was thinking a little while ago that if you could dig the way I feel, you'd see I was hung up between two sticks. I—"

"Look, Piri," interrupted Brew, "everybody got some kinda pain goin' on inside him. I know yuh a li'l fucked up with some kind of hate called 'white.' It's that special kind with the 'no Mr.' in front of it. Dig it, man; say it like it is, out loud—like, you hate all *paddies*."[3]

"Just their fuckin' color, Brew," I said bitterly. "Just their color—their damn claim that white is the national anthem of the world. You know?"

"Yeah."

"When I was a little kid in school," I said, "I used to go to general assembly all togged out with a white shirt and red tie. Everybody there wore a white shirt and red

___
[3] slang term for anglos

tie; and when they played the national anthem, I would put my hand over my heart. It made me feel great to blast out:

> My country, 'tis of thee,
> Sweet land of liberty,
> Of thee I sing . . .

And now when I hear it played I can't help feeling that it's only meant for paddies. It's their national anthem, their sweet land of liberty."

"Yeah, I knows, man," Brew said. "Like it says that all men are created equal with certain deniable rights—iffen they's not paddies. We uns thank you-all, Mistuh Lincoln, suh. Us black folks got through dat ole Civil War about fair, but we all havin' one ole helluva time still tryin' to git through the damn Reconstruction."

We both laughed. "That's pretty fuckin' funny if you can laugh," I said. "Let me try some of that creatin'. Be my straight man."

"What they evah do to yuh, Piri? Yuh ain't never been down South."

"'No, man, I ain't," I said, remembering that Crutch had said the same thing.

"So yuh ain't never run into that played-out shit of

> "If you white, tha's all right.
> If you black, da's dat."

"Yeah, Brew," I said, "it must be tough on you Negroes."

"Wha' yuh mean, us Negroes? Ain't yuh includin' yourself? Hell, you ain't but a coupla shades lighter'n me, and even if yuh was even lighter'n that, you'd still be a Negro."

I felt my chest get tighter and tighter. I said, "I ain't no damn Negro and I ain't no paddy. I'm Puerto Rican."

"You think that means anything to them James Crow paddies?" Brew said coolly.

"*Coño*,"[4] I mumbled.

"What yuh say, man?"

"I said I'm really startin' to almost hate Negroes, too," I shot back.

Brew walked away from me stiff-legged. His fists were almost closed. Then he came back and looked at me and, like he wasn't mad, said, "Yuh fuckin' yeller-faced bastard! Yuh goddamned Negro with a white man's itch! Yuh think that bein' a Porto Rican lets you off the hook? Tha's the trouble. Too damn many you black Porto Ricans got your eyes closed. Too many goddamned Negroes all over this goddamned world feel like you does. Jus' 'cause you can rattle off some different kinda language don' change your skin one bit. Whatta yuh all think? That the only niggers in the world are in this fucked-up country? They is all over this whole damn world. Man, if there's any black people up on the moon talkin' that moon talk, they is still Negroes. Git it? Negroes!"

"Brew," I said, "I hate the paddy who's trying to keep the black man down. But I'm beginning to hate the black man, too, 'cause I can feel his pain and I don't know that it oughtta be mine. Shit, man, Puerto Ricans got social problems, too. Why the fuck we gotta take on Negroes', too?" I dug Brew's eyes. They looked as

---

[4] a very common expression by both Cubans and Puerto Ricans. There is no literal translation for this word which is used for a variety of reasons. The closest term in this context is *dammit*.

if he was thinking that he had two kinda enemies now—paddies and black Puerto Ricans. "Brew," I said, "I'm trying to be a Negro, a colored man, a black man, 'cause that's what I am. But I gotta accept it myself, from inside. Man, do you know what it is to sit across a dinner table looking at your brothers that look exactly like paddy people? True, I ain't never been down South, but the same crap's happening up here. So they don't hang you by your neck. But they slip an invisible rope around your balls and bang you with nice smiles and 'If we need you, we'll call you.' I wanna feel like a 'Mr.' I can't feel like that just yet, and there ain't no amount of cold wine and pot can make my mind accept me being a 'Mr.' part time. So what if I can go to some paddy pool hall or fancy restaurant? So what if I lay some white chick? She still ain't nothin' but a white blur even if my skin does set off her paddy color."

"So yuh gonna put the Negro down jus' 'cause the paddy's puttin' yuh down," Brew said. "Ain't gonna bring nothin' from us exceptin' us putting you down too."

"Like you're putting me down?"

"I ain't put you down, Piri. You jus' got me warm with that 'I'm a Porty Rican' jazz. But I know where yuh at. You jus' gotta work some things out."

Brew shoved his big hand at me. I grabbed it and shook it, adding a slap of skin to bind it. I looked at our different shades of skin and thought, *He's a lot darker than me, but one thing is for sure, neither of us is white.* "Everything cool?" I said.

"Yee-ah. I ain't mad. I said I dig. Jus' got worried that you might turn to be a colored man with a paddy heart."

Like Poppa, I thought, and my eyes followed a fast-moving behind going up the stoop across the street.

"Nice piece of ass," Brew said.

"Naw, Brew, I—"

"You sayin' that ain't a nice piece of ass?"

"That wasn't what I was gonna say, you horny bastard. I meant that what I want out of life is some of the good things the white man's got. Man, what some of them eat for weekday dinner, we eat for our Sunday dinner—"

"'Tain't only Porty Ricans."

"Yeah, American Negroes, too."

"Thar's a lotta white people got it kinda bad, too," Brew said. "Some even worse."

"What you doing now, man, defendin' the paddies?" I asked.

"Jus' sayin' like it is."

I thought for a long while and finally said, "I'm gonna have everything good they have for living even if I gotta take it. Fuck it, I care about me a whole lot. Even the poor white people you're talking about are down on the Negro—more so than the paddy that got bread, 'cause since the poor paddy ain't got nothin', he gotta feel big some way, so the Negro's supposed to lie down and let the paddy climb up on his chest with his clodhoppers just so's he can feel three or four inches taller standing on another man's ribs."

"Yuh talking all this stuff, and yuh ain't evah been down South," Brew said disdainfully.

"Brew," I said with quiet patience, "you don't have to be from the South to know what's happenin'. There's toilet bowls wherever you go. Besides, I learn from you and Crutch and the others. I learn from what I read—and from the paddies."

"But it ain't exactly like being down South, Piri," Brew insisted solemnly.

"What's the matter, Brew?" I asked sarcastically. "A cat's gotta be hung before be knows what's happenin'?" I began to whistle, "Way Down Upon the Swanee River."

Brew went on like I hadn't said nothing, "So yuh can't appreciate and therefore you can't talk that much."

"That's what you say, Brew. But the same—"

"Yuh gonna jaw about the difference and sameness up here and down there," Brew broke in. "Man, you think these paddies up here are a bitch on wheels. Ha! They ain't shit alongside Mr. Charlie down thar. Down South, if one ain't real careful, he can grow up smilin' his ass off and showin' pearly whites till his gums catch pneumonia or workin' his behind off fo' nothin'."

"Yeah, but—"

"Let me say it like it is, Piri. It ain't as bad now as when my daddy was a kid, but it's bad enough. Though I guess bad is bad, a little or a lot. Now those Indians sure had some kinda hard way to go, but they had heart."

"Whatcha mean, man?" I asked, wondering what the hell Indians had to do with all this.

"My daddy use to say that

'The Indian fought the white man and died
An' us black folk jus' wagged ouah tails,
"Yas suhses," smiled and multiplied.'"

I cracked a smile and got up and yawned and stretched. "Brew," I said.

"Still here, man."

"Maybe it wasn't a bad idea to take it low when the weight was all on the other side. Dig it, man, the Indian fought the paddy and lost. And the Indian was on his own turf."

"We mighta won," Brew said.

"Yeah, we mighta, Brew," I said hollowly.

"Okay, man," Brew said, smiling.

"You know, Brew?" I said suddenly. "I'm going down South. Wanna come?"

"What fo', man?"

"It might just set me straight on a lotta things. Maybe I can stop being confused and come in on a right stick."

My man's face screwed up like always when he wasn't sure of something. "Ah don't know, Piri," be said. "'Down there it ain't like up here. You can do and say more, but down thar in some of them towns yuh jus' blow your cool and yuh liable to find yuhself on some chain gang or pickin' peas on some prison farm—or worse yet, gettin' them peas planted over yuh."

"That's okay, *amigo,* I still wanna make it. How 'bout it?"

"Ah dunno."

"Don't worry, Negro," I said. "I promise not to pull no Jim Crow act on you when we get there. Some of my best *amigos* are Negroes."

"It ain't that," Brew laughed. "It's jus' that bomb on your shoulder. We go down South and you start, all that Porty Rican jazz and we's liable to get it from both sides."

"Brew, I'm serious," I said.

"So am I, man, so am I. How yuh figure on goin'?"

"Merchant Marine's the big kick around here now. All we gotta do is make it down to the NMU."

"What's that?"'

"The National Maritime Union," I explained. "That's where we can take out some papers or something. Dickie Bishop works down there and we're tight, so no sweat."

"Okay, man," Brew said, "Ah'm with yuh. But only on the condition you cool your role."

"Till somebody starts something?"

"Till somebody else starts, not you. An' if trouble does start, don't go looking for too much police protection down there. Mos' of the fuzzes down there are cops by day and walkin' bed sheets by night."

"I won't look for it Brew," I said.

"Sometimes yuh don't hafta, Piri. Sometimes you don't hafta. When we gonna make it over to the NMU?"

"*Mañana,* man. First thing in the morning. You can meet me here around eight. Better yet, stay over my house tonight."

"On Long Island?"

"Yeah."

"You still go out there?"

"Once in a while," I said. "I still have my people there."

"Yeah, Ah know."

"Meet me about six o'clock," I said. "It's about two now."

"Tha's nice," Brew said. "It'll give me a couple hours with Alayce."

"Yeah, how is she?" I asked. "That's a nice woman."

"A-huh. She's awright. Gets me warm sometimes, but they don't come no motherfuckin' better, in or outta bed."

"Give 'er my regards."

"Sure will."

"Well, cool it, faggot," I smiled.

Brew grinned and said, "'Dozens? Evah notice bow your pappy walks?"

"Nope, I've been too busy diggin' how your mammy walks."

We laughed and slapped skin going away. I watched Brew make it and then walked off toward Penn Station. Some thoughts were still working in my mind. *Jesus, if I'm a Negro, I gotta feel it all over. I don't have the "for sure" feelin's yet.* I waved to one of the cats in front of El Viejo's candy store and kept on walking.

Hey, Barrio—I'm Home

The big day came at last, November 28, the day I would find out what was shaking. Once again I made it to the courtroom. My aunt and her pastor were there, their heads bowed in prayer.

My name was called and I rose, and the judge's voice came down from behind the big desk in that big paneled room.

"Have you been promised anything for accepting a plea of robbery in the second degree?" he asked.

"No, sir," I replied.

"Have you anything to say before sentence is passed?"

My Legal Aid court-appointed lawyer said something about six years in prison and rehabilitation. Then the district attorney, who's supposed to sink your lemon for you, opened his mouth and he talked better for me than my lawyer, saying be was willing to go along with leniency, a suspended sentence and probation. This shook me up inside, but my face still stood *cara palo*.

The judge said, "Can you keep your nose clean?"

"Yes, sir, I can."

"Okay, I'm going to let you go on probation for three years. Do right. You can go now."

Just like that, it was over. I was free. I turned and walked out through the swinging doors, my aunt and her pastor right behind me. We had to stop at the probation officer's desk, where I was given a card and told to report every week. The P.O. asked me if I had a job. I said no; he said get one fast. If I needed help I could get it, but if I messed up I'd be in trouble and back again. He told me I would have to report to him and to my parole officer, and if I screwed up on one I'd automatically screw up on the other. He warned me to stay away from my "old associates" and not to fuck anybody who wasn't my wife and said I could go.

I walked to the last door, the one that led to the street. One push and I was out. I stood there blinking at the bright sun. "I'm out! I'm out!" I said. Inside, the dizziness of being free was like a night that changed into day; all the shadows became daylight sharp. My first urge was to break out running as fast as I could, but I held myself down; I played cool and collected.

"You can thank God for all He's done," my aunt's pastor said.

"Yeah, Reverend," I said. But the thought of God was like having an obligation, and I didn't want any obligations, not after six years of obligations. I wanted to feel the street, and smell it and hold it between the fingers of my heart. The roar of a nearby elevated train drowned out all thoughts of God. I smelled the street and the people and the cold November air that meant freedom. I was gonna stay free, whether I made it to another country or whether I made it the right way. My head spun from the thought of having to go back to jail.

The next morning I went downtown with my aunt to make my first report to my parole officer. There were a lot of ex-cons in the office making their initial reports. A few of us knew one another. But each of us acted as though the other was a stranger, for one of the bad scenes of parole violation is associating with ex-cons or known criminals.

My P.O. didn't waste any time. He looked at his watch and told me, "You're thirty minutes late."

I nodded in agreement.

"It's a good way to start off, eh?" He was pretty insistent, but I wasn't gonna get mad, no matter what. I made my face stay the same, relaxed and soft. "You got a job?" he finally asked me.

"'No sir, not yet."

"Get one, fast."

"Yes sir."

He looked at my records, and after a long while he crossed his eyes at me and said, "If you do right, you're gonna stay out, otherwise you go back so fast it's gonna make your head spin."

I nodded.

"We're here to help you, and if you got any kind of problem we'll be glad to help you solve it."

I thanked him and he told me to report every Thursday. I stood up and he smiled for the first time, and I figured that all that crap he had blown on me was just to see if I would blow my top.

We left and took the Lexington Avenue subway back to Spanish Harlem. The rumbling and noise of the train made me nervous. I still wasn't used to city noise. The noise in prison is different; it's the sound of people who have a single frustration in common. But in the city, in Spanish Harlem, there is more of a choice of noise. I watched the walls of the tunnel whip by as the train lurched like a drunk along the rails. Finally, we pulled into the 110th Street station.

"Let's get off, *Tía,*"[5] I said.

"But it's only 110th Street, *hijo.*[6] We go one more stop."

But I didn't wait. I jumped through the closing doors, and waved her on, shouting, "I'll see you at home." My God! it felt good to be able to, leave when I wanted to. How many times at Comstock had I wanted to jump through the closing doors of my cell before they locked on me? And now I had jumped through some closing doors. It was such a little thing, but what a great feeling it produced. I ran up the subway steps to the street. The air felt great, and I ran over to my aunt's house and bounced up the stairs thinking about the job I hadda get for myself, my parole officer, and my probation officer.

The next day a rabbi and his brother-in-law gave me a job in their dress-and-shirt company as an all-around handyman and clean-up man. For $40 a week I ran errands, hung up dresses, put pins and tags on them, and delivered them.

I worked steadily and reported steadily and visited my aunt's church from time to time. I saw Pops and my brothers and sister on Long Island, but I lived with my aunt in stone-cool Harlem. It was great to be back in the street. A lot of my boys were either hollowed-out junkies or in prison, but a few of them were still making the scene, and after a few weeks I was making it with them. In the back of my mind, I was a little worried, but after all, I told myself, I had spent a lifetime in that fucking jail and I owed myself some ballin'.

The first rule I broke was the one about not fucking broads who weren't your wife. I shacked up with one of the homeliest broads I ever had seen, but she looked great after my long fast. Having broken one rule, I found it easier to break another,

---

[5] aunt   [6] my boy

and soon I was drinking again. Then I started smoking pot. This went on for some weeks; then, one morning, after a wild, all-night pot party, I crept into *Tía*'s apartment and dug myself in the mirror. What I saw shook me up. My eyes were red from smoke and my face was strained from the effort of trying to be cool. I saw myself as I had been six years ago, hustling, whoring, and hating, heading toward the same long years and the hard bit. I didn't want to go that route; I didn't want to go dig that past scene again.

I pulled away from the mirror and sat on the edge of my bed. My head was still full of pot, and I felt scared. I couldn't stop trembling inside. I felt as though I had found a hole in my face and out of it were pouring all the different masks that my *cara-palo* face had fought so hard to keep hidden. I thought, *I ain't goin' back to what I was.* Then I asked myself, *You remember all that crap you went through? What you want to do, go on for the rest of your life with your ass hangin'? Man, don't forget, you only get what you take. You can make a couple of yards a week and be cool about it. Just by the by, hustle a piece of junk and you're in. You don't use no more, so keep on not using and you're in like a mother. You can make cool bread now; why knock yourself out working? You ain't gonna live forever.*

The thoughts pressed on my brain. I grabbed my face with both hands and squeezed hard, pushing it all out of shape; I pulled my lips out and my face down. The reefer kick was still on, and I could feel the smallness of the room and the neatness of its humble furniture and the smell of its credit, which $1.50 a week paid off. I pushed my way to the window, pulled the light cord and hid from myself in the friendly darkness. Easing the noise from the old-time window shade, I pushed up the window and squeezed my hand through the iron gate my aunt had put in to keep the crooks out. I breathed in the air; it was the same air that I had breathed as a kid. The garbage-filled backyards were the same. Man, everything was the same; only I had changed. I wasn't the grubby-faced Puerto Rican kid any more; I was a grubby-faced Puerto Rican man. I am an *hombre* that wants to be better. Man! I don't want to be nuttin'. I want to be somebody. I want to laugh clean. I want to smile for real, not because I have to . . .

I peered through the darkness. My lips wanted to form words; I wanted to tell somebody I wanted to be somebody. I heard the squeaking of old bed springs, the scrounging of alley cats in overturned garbage cans. I saw the stars up there in God's pad and the gray-white outline of clothes swinging on the black morning breeze, and I leaned hard against the gate that kept crooks out and me in and looked at my dark, long fingers wrapped tightly around the cold black metal. I felt like I was back at Comstock, looking out, hoping, dreaming, wanting. I felt like I wasn't real, that I was like a shadow on a dingy hallway wall next to scribbled graffiti: "Joe loves Lucy," "Baby was laid underneath these stairs, 1947," "The super is a rotten motherfucker," "Piri is a Coolie," "Wait for me, Trina"—*Trina didn't wait* . . .

I felt a wave of loneliness smack over me, almost like getting high. "'Fuck it, fuck it," I said. The four-letter words sounded strange, dirty, like I shouldn't have been saying them. I said, "Motherfucker," and it sounded different, too. It didn't sound like long ago. It sounded not like a challenge thrown, at the world but like a cry of helplessness. I pressed my eyes hard in to the curve of my elbow. *I don't want to keep on being shit in a cesspool, squishing out through long pipes to hell knows where: I wanna be nice, all the way, for real* . . .

I remembered my aunt's church around the corner. *If God is right, so what if He's white? I thought, God, I wanna get out of this hole. Help me out. I promise if You help me climb out, I ain't gonna push the cover back on that cesspool. Let me out and I'll push my arm back down there and help some other guy get a break.*

The rest of my first year out drained away fast. I fought to keep from being swallowed up again by Harlem's hustles and rackets; I started to visit *Tía's* church on 118th Street; I got a raise from the rabbi and encouragement from my probation officers. But there was something missing and I knew what it was: Trina. I couldn't get her out of my mind. I couldn't walk through familiar streets without thinking, *There's where we used to go,* or *There's where we used to eat.* I tried to push her away from my mind but I knew I'd have to see her again. Her husband had turned out no good; I heard from here and there what a hard life he was giving her. I wondered if she had changed.

One night I met her cousin Ava on the street. She was married now and had two children. We talked about old times and she invited me up to her mother's house. "We're having a little get-together and all the family will be there," she said.

"All?" I asked.

"Yeah, all," she repeated.

"When?"

"Tonight. It's about seven o'clock now—say about nine.'"

"Great. I may just drop on by."

"May?"

"Yeah," I replied, "*may,*" but I knew I'd be there.

I went home thinking all the way. I tried to lay out the scene I'd pass through at nine o'clock that night.

I'd walk up the stairs at number 129 cool, oh so cool, wearing my best vines. Ava would answer the door.

"Hi, Piri."

I'd smile. "Hi."

"Come on in."

I'd step in and dig the scene. Ava's brothers would be on the sofa, her mother would be in the easy chair and Georgie, Trina's husband, would be sitting on the other chair. Trina would be standing by the window looking outside, her face in profile, sad-looking but bravely beautiful.

I'd walk into the parlor and there would be a breather silence, like if God walked in on a bunch of sinners. Ava and her brothers would look at each other knowingly and expectantly. Ava's mom would sit, still and quiet, and Georgie, that dirty rat, would turn pale and start shaking all over, smiling like a scared punk. I'd ignore him and look into Trina's eyes, and she'd whisper, "I've waited so long, Johnny Gringo, my Piri, I've waited so long."

I'd look, oh, so cool, so bad, so brave, and bold out my arms and say, "Come on, Marine Tiger, we're going home, baby. And bring your kid; it's my kid now."

Trina would melt into my arms and I'd bruise her lips and I'd crush her tight and we'd be like one Puerto Rican instead of two, and we'd turn and walk away toward the door. And Ava would shout, "Look out, Piri, he's gonna jump you!" and I'd feel the knife bite deep into my shoulder muscle, the pain going deep, and I'd hear screams from Trina's throat.

I'd lurch forward and with a great effort straighten up and face Georgie. His face would turn gray and splotchy with fear; he'd stand there paralyzed. I'd reach my arm behind me and grab the handle of the knife that is sticking in my back and, with a suave pull, squish it out of my back.

"*Don't kill me, please,*" Georgie would beg.

I'd look at him with contempt, fling the bloody knife away and start walking slowly toward him. Georgie would back away trap himself in a corner. I'd measure his face and crash my fist into it. He'd fight back weakly and I'd hit him with one fist and then another until he sagged slowly to the floor.

I'd feel blood in my mouth—the knife has punctured my lung; I maybe dying— and I'd lean on Trina. She'd kiss me, and we'd walk out the door and . . .

"Hey, Piri, wanna go to a flick tonight?"

"No, I'm sorry, I got some place to go tonight."

"Oh, okay."

Back in reality, I walked down the cold street and ran up the long, dingy steps to my aunt's apartment. Twenty minutes later I was in the bath, getting ready for I didn't know what.

At nine o'clock I stood in front of the apartment in number 129 and knocked and waited. The door opened. It was Ava's mom. "Come in, *hijo,* come in," she said, hugging me.

I stepped into the apartment. There was no one on the couch, no one in the parlor. I saw a stranger sitting at the kitchen table. *Georgie,* I thought. Ava was just coming out of the john. She hugged me and I looked past her into the bedroom, where Trina was standing at the door looking at me. Georgie smiled and I was introduced to him. He smiled and offered me a drink.

"No, thank you," I said, and as a chair was offered to me, I added, "Mind if I sit in the parlor?" I sat on the chair that I imagined Georgie would have been sitting in and I looked at Trina. There was nothing to say, nothing to do. I just sat there and made small talk. *Trina, say something,* I thought, *anything.*

But Trina didn't say anything, and after what seemed like many days, I heard myself saying, "Well, it's been nice visiting you all. I'm sorry, but I gotta go now, I, uh, got an appointment."

"Oh, I'm sorry you have to go, *hijo,*" said Ava's mom.

"We'll see you again, won't we?" Ava asked.

"Yeah, sure," I said. I looked at Trina. She smiled something at me, and I walked out the door and down the stairs and out into the cold street, thinking, *What a blank that was. I should have known, nothing is run the same, nothing stays the same. You can't make yesterday come back today.*

I Swears to God and the Virgin

I felt like walking and my walking got me to stop outside my old building at number 109 I wondered why I always looked at her like an old *novia.*[7] I looked around and the street was swinging. I stepped into number 109's dark hallway and

---

[7] girlfriend

made my way up the dirty marble steps, careful that I wouldn't step into long-ago memories of sodden dog piles of dogs' mess or slip on anybody's piss water. The mood was the same. I was gulping tired air by the time I reached the fifth floor and stopped to rest—and then I heard the hushed noise up on the roof landing. I looked up into a pair of eyes hollowed out like death, like a want, like a stone junkie. It was a junkie. It was no stranger.

"Hi, *panín*,"[8] I greeted. The eyes blinked, straining for some kinda recognition, and then knowing set in, and his voice curled down from his height:

"Damn, Piri! Is that you? Coño, ain't this a bitch? I'm fuckin' glad to see ya. What a blip, man; come on up. I thought you was the man. Them cats work on Sundays, too, Come on up, baby."

His voice didn't sound like Carlito's. It didn't sound like nothing at all.

"How ya been, Carlito? What's *nuevo*?[9]

I looked up at him and dug the sad answer.

"*Nada* new, 'side's being strung out."

He had a hand and the fist was tightly closed. It didn't have to open for me to know what was in it. "Schmack?" my face told him. His hand opened up and the five-cent bag was trembling there, with its li'l bit of "push back my troubles."

"I was jus' gonna shoot up, man, an' I heard you coming. I thought maybe you was the man. Them cats work on Sundays too."

I nodded: "Strung out, Carlito?"

"Twelve *bolsas*.[10] It's a bitch man, like at five cents a bag an' a bean for works, that's some bread."

I made mental figures and my junkie *panín* needed seventy-two dollars a day to keep from coming apart—to just stay normal. Something I was doing for nothing. I eased by and moved up to sit on the steps above him.

"You don't mind if I cook breakfast," Carlito laughed to himself. "Heh-heh, cook my breakfast." He pulled out a medicine bottle full of water, a bottle top made of metal. He pulled apart the five-cent bag and shook it into the bottle top, carefully, so-o-o-o carefully, brushing the paper to make sure be missed none of his 'breakfast.' I said nothing, I just watched as I had watched times I couldn't count, other guys, and other "me's."

Carlito pulled the paper match from its cover and it was almost an apologetic tear; he laid the book of matches down slowly and deliberately, almost like savoring the coming moment when the smack would bite deep into his tracked-up arm and slam into his heart with all the fury of despair. The match was lit, and Carlito placed, it under the bottle top.

"Oh, awh, haaaaa, this it, ahuh, gooood, right, bang." He blew the match out like a businessman after lighting up a dollar cigar. I thought, *Don't this bring me back a long time, don't I feel a yen for that kick? Don't I feel a something like him, like my eyes want to follow that fuckin' needle's thirst and trace the push and current of the* tecata *through the highways and byways of my man's coughing veins. Like I feel way*

---

[8] slang term for pal   [9] new   [10] bags of drugs

down deep somewhere the urge to put my arm down beside his in a humble-pie attitude and take my place among my boys who got beat not by the bop, but by . . .

"Want a jolt, Piri? I don't mind sharing with you. I can try for an *ángulo* soon as we get off. You're from the old boys and I don't really mind; I mean I won't do this for nobody, cause it ain't like the old days, when everybody shared the stuff with each other. Naw, not like that at all. You gotta be real tight with a stud. You don't share with everybody for nuttin'. If a guy does in with you or a couple of guys and you make up the five-cent bag, okay, then you share, but you don't give up the stuff for nuttin', not to just anybody. So don't worry Piri, I can hustle for us later. Say, man, how bad is your habit?" he asked.

I looked at Carlito and at the needle and at his arm, with his pants belt wrapped tightly around his suffering veins popped out at attention.

"I'm clean, Carlito, I'm not using." My voice dropped to a whisper. "I'm not using." And oh, God, I found my mind, thinking, *Wonder what it would be like again? Wonder what it would be like again? Wonder what it would be like again? Wonder . . .*

"I'm clean," I heard myself saying. My eyes watched the needle, pushed on to an eye dropper, poised—almost, I swear, licking its chops as it got nearer to Carlito's veins—and I watched and remembered as he toyed with his love and the drug came back out again, into the eye dropper, and it brought back some blood.

"I'm glad you're clean, Piri," I heard Carlito's voice soft and tender and harsh. His eyes closed and the needle still in his arm like it, didn't want to come out, like a lover who has loved and cannot find the way to withdraw. Carlito's fingers pulled out the needle and a juicy glob of dark, dark blood oozed out, a quick finger smeared the blood away, and more oozed out. Carlito opened a medicine bottle and poured a little water over the oozing hole where the lovers laid, and the blood stopped oozing. He pushed the needle into the water and sucked up plain old water and the works was washed, and the water was squirted out over the faintly blood-smeared arm and then was taken apart, ever so carefully. The works is a junkie's best friend after his smack.

I watched as the nod started to set in strong, and Carlito talked and I sat and listened.

"I'm glad you're clean; yeah, I mean it, man, I can be clean, too. In fact"—and I dig his low voice, muffled and full of hot-ashed talk of how he's gonna kick—"I'm gonna kick after I go in, yeah, baby, no more smack for me. Jesus, man, I got shame, I got self-respect, like anybody, like any fuckin' body else, and I can be clean too. Shit! I gotta quit, look at me." And I dug as be pointed to his face. It was lemon color—like jaundice.

"This junk gives all kinds of shit, I'm putrid like a motherfucker. I'm rotting; dig." And he pulls his shirt up and shows me his lower back and in between the crack of his behind are sores, healing and unhealed.

"I gotta give this up, and I swears to God and the Virgin, next time I quits for good, man. Man, I've been to Lexington and all them other places. I'm gonna kick this time for good. I can get clean."

Thoughts walked into each other through my mind—*Everything happened yesterday. Trina was yesterday. Brew was yesterday, Johnny Gringo was yesterday. I was a kid yesterday and my whole world was yesterday. I ain't got nothing but today and a whole lot of tomorrows.*

I don't think my boy saw me go past him. I couldn't stand seeing my man, I couldn't stand hearing him talk about what he was gonna do. His voice faded behind me.

"I got dignity, man. I got self-respect and ahhh . . ." I reached the second landing and heard him call, "Hey Piri, you making it?" I looked up through the stair well and I saw his little head with the big eyes.

"Yeah," I yelled back, and walked out into the street, past hurrying people and an unseen jukebox beating out a sad-assed bolero.

Discussion Questions

1. As a black-skinned Puerto Rican, Piri is often mistaken for an African-American. How does he feel about this mistake, and thus his own identity? Address this question by examining his descriptions and comments about his family.

2. What differences does Piri encounter when he returns home? What does the author suggest about the passage of time in connection to these differences?

3. Piri's drug use is related to his downfall and imprisonment. When he says at the conclusion that he's "making it," what does he refer to other than his rehabilitation?

4. How is Piri's African heritage portrayed in this excerpt as compared to the relationship between the speaker and his grandmother in Victor Hernandez Cruz's poem "African Things" on page 439?

5. How is the conclusion in this excerpt similar to the one in Rolando Hinojosa's *Becky and Her Friends* on page 56? What changes do Piri and Becky make in their lives? Why?

Jack Agüeros

Poet, playwright, scriptwriter, and fiction writer Jack Agüeros was born in New York City in 1934. He received a B.A. from Brooklyn College in 1964 and an M.A. in Urban Studies from Occidental College. His poems and stories have appeared in dozens of periodicals over the last twenty years. He has published two collections of poetry: Correspondence Between the Stonehaulers *(1991), and* Sonnets from the Puerto Rican *(1996). His collection of short stories,* Dominoes and Other Stories, *was published by Curbstone Press in 1993.*

Jack Agüero's plays are influenced by a literary genre of the Spanish Golden Age, the auto sacramental. *These morality plays, which had their inception in the Middle Ages, were refined and further developed by Calderón de la Barca in the seventeenth century. Different in scope than the* autos, *Agüeros uses allegorical allusions to discuss contemporary issues such as race, relations and intolerance.*

His short fiction also seems to contain a moral lesson, although it is not overt. Dominoes and Other Stories, *which took the author seven years to complete, re-creates the barrio of New York with its colorful characters and sometimes violent situations.*

The story presented here, however, focuses on the relationship between a young man and his godmother. The ability of one person to touch another and change their lives for the better is at the center of the story's subtly developed theme.

From Dominoes and Other Stories

One Sunday Morning

I

He knocked at the door marked 3A. A voice inside the apartment said, "Who?" and a dog barked and a cat meowed and a canary tweeted. "Me. Newspaper boy," he responded, adding "Sunday Daily News."

The woman, short and round, with a very beautiful face and long black eyelashes and long black hair, repeated, "Sunday News? You have all the sections?"

"*Si*," he said, "all of them."

"Including the radio programs?"

"Yes, for the whole week."

"Then come in."

This was the game they played every Sunday morning. He, Sonny, pretended he was a newsboy. His godmother, Titi, pretended not to know who was knocking.

He handed the newspaper to his godmother and said *Bendición*[1], got his kiss and benediction, and entered the long narrow corridor that went past the bathroom and opened into the living room. Beauty, the blondish little dog, wagged her tail and it banged along the wall of the corridor. Her tiny claws slipped on the linoleum and she fell, fell, and fell. When Beauty wagged her tail, she used her whole body, and she seemed hinged in her middle. Feeri, the Angora cat came out. He was nearly as tall as Beauty, and his great silky fur made him look nearly as round. Feeri came not to greet Sonny, but to be admired and stroked.

"Sonny, what are all the programs on WEAF this week?"

He knew them all, every program and at what time. All of his godmother's favorites not only on WEAF, but on the other stations as well. WJZ, too. On Sunday they had to listen to the Hartz Mountain Canary Hour.

II

His Godmother also had fish.
Fish in three tanks.

---

[1] In Puerto Rican culture it is often used by a parent to a child before they part, or as a greeting when a close family member arrives. Literally, "give me your blessing."

One kind called guppies; little tiny tiny fish. Some called Angelfish, others whose names he did not know, that had brilliant stripes along the thumbnail length of their bodies.

She loved animals.

She loved children.

She was godmother to many, many children. She had no children of her own.

They put the radio on. The Canary Hour began with many happy canaries singing, and the announcer would soon talk about why Hartz Mountain made the best canary feed in the United States. The other man, the host, conducted the canaries in their performances. Sonny would listen and let his eyes drift around the room.

Along the top of the wall about 12 inches from the ceiling there was wood moulding. The walls below were painted by a process called "Mickey Mousing." He had seen his father doing it many times. Paint the wall one color, let it dry, then dip a rag in another color and roll it over the first color. But his father never let him try it, never let him paint at all.

On the walls there were framed pictures of hunting dogs. There was a wooden cut-out elephant dancing on one leg. There was a framed black paper silhouette of a face, neck, and shoulders, with a real cloth dress. And as his eye drifted to the bedroom, beyond the open double doors, he saw the bedspread and the fish tanks next to the street windows.

The canaries sang; sometimes in chorus, sometimes in solos, sometimes in accompaniment with recorded music, sometimes without music at all. Sometimes somebody whistled to get the birds started, sometimes the somebody seemed to whistle the whole time. And while their cheerful voices filled the little apartment he stared at the bedspread.

He knew how it was made. The women saved every piece of cloth. His godmother was a blouse and skirt seamstress. His mother was a dress seamstress. Their best friend Carmen Nuñez did not work but also sewed at home. They all had Singer machines at home, "factory models" they called them, and made most of their own clothing and a lot for the children. They bought Simplicity Patterns at the Woolworth's, and cloth at *La Marqueta*.[2] And there were always odd pieces of cloth in a bin or box under or around the sewing machine. When enough of these odd pieces had accumulated, the women would sit in a circle and turn the cloth into little circles or hexagons. Each finished piece was only about 3 inches in diameter. Then they had to be sewn together, and the women decided what went well where. It was time consuming. By hand. No *whirr* and *whoom* of the machine motor starting, winding, and stopping. They called it "yo-yo" for reasons he did not know. Then the whole thing had to be lined. Each woman made one for herself, sharing advice and trading pieces of cloth.

His father forbid him to sew.

His Godmother said to him from the rocking chair, "Sonny it's time to feed the fish and Carlos." The Canary Hour was over.

"Titi, is it true that nightingales sing better than canaries? Papi says that God taught nightingales to sing, but canaries only learned from Angels."

---

[2] The Market; specifically the market located in El Barrio in New York City.

"Your father and his ideas. It's the only time he talks about God or Angels."

She would trail off then, change the conversation, never talk about his father.

The fish were by the front windows so that the sun would warm the water and "give them vitamins." He dusted some fish food from the box. For the canary, Carlos, he had to remove the white cups and take them to the kitchen table. There on an open shelf covered with oil cloth, he would find the Hartz Mountain Canary Food—the bright orange can, With its very yellow canary on the front. He would fill one porcelain cup with bird seed, and the other with water. And he would change the paper lining on the cage bottom.

III

His Titi also liked plants.

Titi also liked porcelain statues, and bisque figures, cut glass dishes and vases, chrome and glass martini shaker sets with matching glasses, blue-glass coffee tables, black iron and red marble smoking stands with ashtrays, carnival glass from the five and dime, ceramic candy and fruit dishes. He did not know what a martini was— neither did his Titi. But she had won the set at the movie house. And she had also gotten a whole set of china, one piece at a time at the local movie house, the Regun Theater on 116th Street.

"Junk." His father would say, "Your godmother likes to collect junk. Including godchildren," while he prepared cornmeal with milk, and sliced apples and raw pumpkin for his nightingale, Keero. "Any piece of junk I find I bring to our mother for your godmother, and she always takes it."

IV

Beauty was always pregnant. Feeri was always siring cats. Carlos found himself sharing the cage one day with a female canary named Libertad, and soon there were eggs in the nest and soon there was Chucho, Jacinto and Jose, in their own cage.

And the plants multiplied as if they were rooted in the Puerto Rican soil, with the Puerto Rican sun shining on them. And every available tin can had a plant in it from the Export Soda cracker can to the Danish butter tins. And the fish were multiplying also, and the prune juice bottles, which looked like round cookie jars, had fish in them, and now there were six tanks, even though the mother fish ate most of the babies. Titi had become an expert at predicting delivery and with a little fish net she scooped the newborn fish away from the mother's murderous tiny jaws. Soon one tank was only for pregnant fish, and one was the "nursery," where only babies swam.

Titi was playing her guitar in the rocking chair, when Sonny asked her, "Why didn't you get married and have children?"

She stopped playing and started rocking.

I got married. I married a very handsome boy named Billy. He was blond and strong and a hard working boy. He was seventeen, and I was only thirteen. But at thirteen I was a woman already, and I wasn't so fat, Sonny, I was slim and very beautiful. He played the guitar and I sang. He was teaching me to play and I was teaching him to sing. He loved music and he loved dancing. We were married about seven months when we went to a dance in Naranjito where your father is from—a little town in the mountains. We went dancing every weekend I and Billy had a Ford that we used to call *'de patitas,'* of little feet. I don't know why it was called like that. In the dance we got separated. I heard noises, there was a fight, there was gunfire, six or seven shots. When the room cleared Billy was laying on the floor dead. So was another man. They had nothing to do with the fight. But they were dead. I was a widow at thirteen. I was pregnant but I had a miscarriage. I lost my baby—do you know what it means?"

"Yes," he answered, not understanding.

"Here, let me show you a picture."

She got up and showed him a picture of a hospital room with her in the bed. There was a strangely tropical light coming in one window onto a white and black checkered, floor. Whether time, or the photographer had introduced a slight sepia quality to the photo, Titi did not know. "I think they always came out slightly brown," she said sadly, smelling the photograph. "It's time to listen to *The Shadow,* Titi." He turned the radio on and waited for it to warm up. And then he turned the dial pointer slowly as his father had taught him, and he worked it back and forth until he got the best reception on WEAF. Soon the radio was saying, "The makers of Blue Diamond Coal bring you—*The Shadow.*"

V

He had no coal.

He knew that it was better to buy anthracite than bituminous. Anthracite was hard coal, burned cleaner, gave off more heat. He could watch the delivery of anthracite to his building closely. He lived in apartment 2A, just over the *bodega,*[3] and just over the cellar below the store. And directly under his Titi. On the sidewalk there was a round iron cover about 15 inches wide. A coal truck would back up to the sidewalk, and the driver would jump out and pull away the iron cover. Then he would drop a shining metal chute from the truck, align it into the hole, and jump back into the driver's seat and the truck lifted upward, sending the coal down the chute. When he was done the driver jumped into the tipped up back of the truck and swept down the chute any pieces of coal that remained. Then back on the sidewalk, he swept around the hole and replaced the iron cover. Sometimes the super would come out and sweep again.

The front of his building had a three part stoop: under his apartment was the *bodega.* In the center was the entrance to the building and on the other side was

---

[3] the neighborhood grocery store

Suzi's Dry Cleaners. Beneath the *bodega,* was another flight of wooden steps laid over steel supports. He had been down to that basement once. It smelled terribly, was dark and dirty, and his father had been very angry, punishing him for going down there, making him kneel in one corner of their apartment for an hour. He had not gotten to see the coal bin. He had not gotten a piece of anthracite.

VI

"Sonny, it's very easy to do. You just grab the grey hair and pull it, that's all. Either with your fingers or with this."

"Doesn't it hurt?"

"No. It hurts more to have grey hair."

"I think it hurts."

"I'm telling you it doesn't hurt. It's my head and I ought to know. Now pull."

"Do I have to?"

"I'll pay you one penny for every one you pull. And I'll save the pennies here in this can. By the time a few years have passed you'll be rich."

"With all the money you owe me for the newspapers, too?"

"Yes, I'll put that in here too."

By the light of the window, next to the eight fish tanks, with the Spanish Hour playing on the radio, Sonny plucked his godmother's grey hairs. Through *tango* and *bolero,* he plucked away, disliking it very much. Sometimes he sang along with Libertad Lamarque, sometimes with Carlos Gardel, the two great singers the canaries were named after. He loved the tango that went:

La mujer que yo queria con todo mi corazon
Se me ha ido con el hombre que la supo seducir . . . [4]

He was not sure what the words meant.

"Titi, no more." He hated to pull them out, with or without the tweezer.

"Are you sure? You only took out ten."

"That's all I can find, I mean it."

"OK Let's feed the fish and the canaries."

While Sonny went to the kitchen to get the fish food, Titi started moving the glass tops of the tanks in preparation.

"Which one goes in here?"

"Here give me that box. That's the special one. Look out, Oh God! It went out the window!!"

A guppy had leapt out of the tank and through the open window. When they looked out the window they couldn't see the fish.

Titi ran to the kitchen sink. "Take this glass of water, run down to the basement and look around for him. He might still be alive. He can't be on the sidewalk—he didn't jump that far out."

---

[4] The woman that I loved with all my heart
   Has left with the man that knew how to seduce her

"Papi doesn't want me to go to the basement."

"Go on, this is an emergency. Get going."

Sonny ran out of the apartment and down the flight of steps, but his quick running was making him spill the water.

"Slow down a little—you need the water. And don't squeeze his body when you pick him up. Try to get him by the tail. Hurry up." Titi was yelling at the top of the stairs, and Beauty was barking, slipping and falling on the linoleum as she tried to make quick starts and tight turns, following Titi, who was running from the window to the hall, from the hall to the window. And the twelve canaries were all twittering in their four cages, making the cages swing, spilling water and Hartz Mountain seed all over the living room floor and onto the yoyo bedspread. The cages were hung in the bedroom doorway—the double doors long ago permanently pinned open by side tables.

By the time Sonny hit the street door he had about a half a glass of water, and he could hear his godmother yelling from the window "Hurry, hurry."

A few people had gathered on the sidewalk wondering who the lady in the 3rd floor window was yelling at. Sonny went down the stoop onto the sidewalk. He was concentrating on the glass of water, trying not to spill any more. He started down the stairs to the basement carefully, watching closely where he put his feet, in case the guppy was there. But then he saw the guppy lying on the next to the last wooden tread. He rushed down, gripped its tail and plunked it into the glass. The fish immediately began to swim.

He looked around for a piece of anthracite.

He saw none.

VII

When they had finished listening to the *Great Gildersleeves,* his godmother asked him to stay for a moment.

"Sonny, you know the little girl we call Tana, my godchild?"

"Yes, something happened to her mother."

"How do you know?"

"I heard Papi talking about it. Her mother jumped from the roof. Is it true?"

"That father of yours. How could he talk about such things to a child like you? Tana is coming to live here with me."

"Papi told me he was going to take me to the wake."

"He did! You are too young for a wake."

"Papi says I'm getting big now. That I have to learn about the world. That the world for a man is not these stories on the radio and singers like Carlos Gardel and Libertad Lamarque."

"Your father is wrong, Sonny. You're still little, and you have time to learn about the world—too much time. And I know more than your father—he thinks women don't know anything. Well, we work too, and hard and we talk, and we live, and we know, we know more than the men, believe me Sonny. I am your second mother. You are my favorite godchild, more, you are my son. I sat here rocking you in the night, feeding you a bottle. When you were born, I was there, and I have seen you every day of your life—every single day. Where was your father? What does he know about anything? When Tana comes to live here nothing will change between us. You hear me? I will still be your second mother, and you will still be my son. Understand? Just because Tana comes here, doesn't mean anything will change between us. Now give me a kiss."

"*Bendición,* Titi."

"May God accompany you, and the Virgin favor you."

He did not immediately move feeling that something else had to happen. Although he had just been told that nothing would change he already felt a change.

Then his godmother added, "Don't forget to deliver the paper on Sunday."

VIII

Tana came to live at his godmother's house.

Tana was skinny and took hours to chew her food.

Tana took so long to eat, that they were late for the radio shows. The food on Tana's plate would get cold and grey and it looked like the food in Feeri's bowl.

And Tana's father came to visit every night. Tana's father was nice, and now he fed the fish in the ten tanks, and changed the paper bottoms of the six canary cages, and tuned the stations.

On Saturday night they listened to Judy Canova.

One Sunday morning when Sonny came to deliver the paper, it had already been delivered by Tana's father.

Discussion Questions

1. This story explores the effect the life of one individual can have on the ordinary life of others. Describe Titi's life and how she affects the lives of Sonny, Tana, and Tana's father.

2. The story concludes with a subtle yet significant change. What does that change suggest about the passage of time, particularly as it applies to generational differences.

3. Compare the relationship between Sonny and his godmother and the son and mother in Jose Yglesias's "The Place I Was Born" on page 241. How is understatement used in both of the stories to accentuate the relationship?

Esmeralda Santiago

ESMERALDA SANTIAGO was born in Santurce, Puerto Rico in 1948. She completed her undergraduate work at Harvard in 1976, and received an M.F.A. from Sarah Lawrence College. She has published two volumes of memoirs When I Was

Puerto Rican *(1993), and* Almost a Woman *(1998). America's Dream, her first novel, tracing the life of a Puerto Rican woman trying to break out of the cycle of domestic violence, was published in 1996.*

When I Was Puerto Rican *is the story of Negi, a young girl who moves to the states with her family, and after coming to grips with discrimination triumphs by receiving a Harvard education. It begins with Santiago's description of growing up in several households, one centered in the rural barrio of Macun and the others closer to her mother's family in the author's native Santurce. After she moves with her mother and siblings to New York, Negi manages to gain entry into the New York High School of Performing Arts. While the book culminates in triumph evidenced by education and financial independence, it also suggests that those goals exact a price on the identity of the individual who achieves them.*

From When I Was Puerto Rican

Angels on the Ceiling

Mami smiled.

We were high over thick clouds, the sky above so bright it hurt my eyes. In the window seat, Edna pressed her face flat against the pane. She looked up, eyes shining. "There's nothing there!" She stretched over my lap and reached out her hand to Mami. "I'm hungry."

"They'll serve us dinner soon," Mami said. "Just wait."

The stewardesses brought us small trays fitted with square plates filled with sauce over chicken, mushy rice, and boiled string beans. It all tasted like salt.

The sky darkened, but we floated in a milky whiteness that seemed to hold the plane suspended above Puerto Rico. I couldn't believe we were moving; I imagined that the plane sat still in the clouds while the earth flew below us. The drone of the propellers was hypnotic and lulled us to sleep in the stiff seats with their square white doilies on the back.

"Why do they have these?" I asked Mami, fingering the starched, piqué-like fabric.

"So that people's pomade doesn't stain the seat back," she answered. The man in front of me, his hair slick with brilliantine, adjusted his doily, pulled it down to his neck.

I dozed, startled awake, panicked when I didn't know where I was, remembered where we were going, then dozed off again, to repeat the whole cycle, in and out of sleep, between earth and sky, somewhere between Puerto Rico and New York.

It was raining in Brooklyn. Mist hung over the airport so that all I saw as we landed were fuzzy white and blue lights on the runway and at the terminal. We thudded to earth as if the pilot had miscalculated just how close we were to the ground. A startled silence was followed by frightened cries and *aleluyas* and the rustle of everyone rushing to get up from their seats and out of the plane as soon as possible.

Mami's voice mixed and became confused with the voices of other mothers telling their children to pick up their things, stay together, to walk quickly toward the door and not to hold up the line. Edna, Raymond, and I each had bundles to carry, as did Mami, who was loaded with two huge bags filled with produce and spices *del país*.[1] "You can't find these in New York," she'd explained.

We filed down a long, drafty tunnel, at the end of which many people waited, smiling, their hands waving and reaching, their voices mingling into a roar of *hello*'s and *how are you*'s and *oh, my god, it's been so long*'s.

"Over there," Mami said, shoving us. On the fringes of the crowd a tall woman with short cropped hair, a black lace dress, and black open-toed shoes leaned against a beam that had been painted yellow. I didn't recognize her, but she looked at me as if she knew who I was and then loped toward us, arms outstretched. It was my mother's mother, Tata. Raymond let go of Mami's hand and ran into Tata's arms. Mami hugged and kissed her. Edna and I hung back, waiting.

"This is Edna," Mami said, pushing her forward for a hug and kiss.

"And this must be Negi," Tata said, pulling me into her embrace. I pressed against her and felt the sharp prongs of the rhinestone brooch on her left shoulder against my face. She held me longer than I expected, wrapped me in the scratchy softness of her black lace dress, the warmth of her powdered skin, the sting of her bittersweet breath, pungent of beer and cigarettes.

Behind her loomed a man shorter than she, but as imposing. He was squarely built, with narrow eyes under heavy eyebrows, a broad nose, and full lips fuzzed with a pencil mustache. No one would have ever called him handsome, but there was about him a gentleness, a sweetness that made me wish he were a relative. He was, in a manner of speaking. Mami introduced him as "Don Julio, Tata's friend." We shook hands, his broad, fleshy palm seeming to swallow mine.

"Let's get our things," Mami said, pulling us into a knot near her. "You kids, don't let go of each others' hands. It's crazy here tonight."

We joined the stream of people claiming their baggage. Boxes filled with fruit and vegetables had torn, and their contents had spilled and broken into slippery messes on the floor. Overstuffed suitcases tied with ropes or hastily taped together had given way, and people's underwear, baby diapers, and ratty shoes pushed through the stressed seams where everyone could see them. People pointed, laughed, and looked to see who would claim these sorry belongings, who could have thought the faded, torn clothes and stained shoes were still good enough for their new life in Brooklyn.

"That's why I left everything behind," Mami sniffed. "Who wants to carry that kind of junk around?"

We had a couple of new suitcases and three or four boxes carefully packed, taped at the seams, tied with rope, and labelled with our name and an address in New

---

[1] from the "old country"; i.e. Puerto Rico

York that was all numbers. We had brought only our "good" things: Mami's work clothes and shoes, a few changes of playclothes for me, Edna, and Raymond, some of them made by Mami herself, others bought just before we left. She brought her towels, sheets, and pillowcases, not new, but still "decent looking."

"I'll see if I can find a taxi," Don Julio said. "You wait here."

We huddled in front of the terminal while Don Julio negotiated with drivers. The first one looked at us, counted the number of packages we carried, asked Don Julio where we were going, then shook his head and drove along the curb toward a man in a business suit with a briefcase who stood there calmly, his right hand in the air as if he were saluting, his fingers wiggling every so often. The second driver gave us a hateful look and said some words that I didn't understand, but I knew what he meant just the same. Before he drove off, Mami mumbled through her teeth "*Chara-manbiche.*"[2] Don Julio said it was illegal for a driver to refuse a fare, but that didn't stop them from doing it.

Finally, a swarthy man with thick black hair and a flat cap on his head stopped, got out of his taxi, and helped us load our stuff. He didn't speak Spanish, none of us spoke English, and, it appeared, neither did he. But he gave us a toothy, happy smile, lifted Raymond into Mami's lap, made sure our fingers and toes were inside the taxi before he closed the doors, then got in with a great deal of huffing and puffing, as his belly didn't fit between the seat and the steering wheel. Tata and Don Julio sat in the front seat with the driver, who kept asking questions no one understood.

"He wants to know where we're from," Mami figured out, and we told him.

"Ah, Porto Reeco, yes, ees hot," he said. "San Juan?"

"Yes," Mami said, the first time I'd ever heard her speak English.

The driver launched into a long speech peppered with familiar words like America and President Kennedy. Mami, Tata, and Don Julio nodded every once in a while, uh-huhed, and laughed whenever the taxi driver did. I wasn't sure whether he had no idea that we didn't understand him, or whether he didn't care.

Rain had slicked the streets into shiny, reflective tunnels lined with skyscrapers whose tops disappeared into the mist. Lampposts shed uneven silver circles of light whose edges faded to gray. An empty trash can chained to a parking meter banged and rolled from side to side, and its lid, also chained, flipped and flapped in the wind like a kite on a short string. The taxi stopped at a red light under an overpass. A train roared by above us, its tiny square windows full of shapes.

"Look at her," Tata laughed from the front seat, "Negi's eyes are popping out of her head."

"That's because the streets are not paved with gold, like she thought," Mami teased.

The taxi driver grinned. I pressed my face to the window, which was fogged all around except on the spot I'd rubbed so that I could look out.

It was late. Few windows on the tall buildings flanking us were lit. The stores were shuttered, blocked with crisscrossed grates knotted with chains and enormous padlocks. Empty buses glowed from within with eerie gray light, chugging slowly from one stop to the next, their drivers sleepy and bored.

---

[2] Son of a bitch

Mami was wrong. I didn't expect the streets of New York to be paved with gold, but I did expect them to be bright and cheerful, clean, lively. Instead, they were dark and forbidding, empty, hard.

We stopped in front of a brick building. Here, too, battered trash cans were chained to a black lamppost, only these were filled with garbage, some of which had spilled out and lay scattered in puddles of pulpy hash. The door to the building was painted black, and there was a hole where the knob should have been.

Mami had to wake up Edna and Raymond. Tata picked one up, and Mami the other. Don Julio helped the taxi driver get our stuff.

"This way," Tata said.

We entered a hallway where a bare dim bulb shed faint blue light against green walls. Tata led us past many doors to the other end of the hall, where she pushed against another black door and led us into a cobblestoned courtyard with a tree in front of another, smaller building.

"Watch the puddles," Tata said, too late. Cold water seeped into my right shoe, soaking my white cotton socks. We went in another door without a knob, into a smaller hallway with steps leading up to a landing.

Tata pushed the first door on our left with her foot. We entered a small room with a window giving onto the courtyard. As we came in, a tall man got up from a cot near the window and weaved toward us. His long hair was gray. Round hazel eyes bulged from their sockets; the whites were streaked with red and yellow. He hugged Mami and helped her settle Raymond on the cot he'd just left. Tata lay Edna next to Raymond and tucked a blanket around them.

"So this is Negi," the tall man said.

"This is your uncle Chico, Tata's brother," Mami said. "You remember him, don't you?"

I remembered the name, but not this bony scarecrow with the stale smell of sweat and beer.

"She was just a little kid when I last saw her," he said, his hands on my shoulders. "How old are you now?"

"Thirteen," I croaked.

"Thirteen!" He whistled.

Don Julio came in. He took a key from a nail by the door and went out again.

"Give me a hand with this stuff, can you, Chico?"

"Oh, of course, of course." He shuffled off after Don Julio.

"How about something to eat?" Tata said. "Or a beer?" Mami shook her head. Tata took a Budweiser from the small refrigerator and opened it. She drank from the can.

"Are you hungry?" Mami asked me.

"Yes."

Tata put her beer down and turned on the hot plate next to the refrigerator.

"Chico made some *asopao*.[3] I'll make some coffee."

"Where's the bathroom?" Mami asked.

---

[3] a soup-like dish with rice and vegetables and either chicken or seafood

"Across the hall." Tata pointed to the door. Next to it there was a curtained-off area. On her way out, Mami peeked inside. The curtain hid a large bed and clothes on wire hangers lining the wall.

"That's our bedroom," Tata said. "Your apartment is upstairs. Two big rooms. And you don't have to share a bathroom like we do."

"I'll go take a look." Mami stepped out then turned around to find me right behind her. "Negi, you wait right here."

"But I want to see too."

"Have something to eat and keep still. You'll have plenty of time later."

I leaned against the door and watched Tata.

Even though she was quite tall, Tata was not cramped by the small room. Her hands, with long tapered fingers and wide nails, grasped pots and cooking spoons from shelves above the stove and placed them soundlessly on the glowing hot-plate burner. Her back was wide, straight, and she carried her head as if she had something on it that she couldn't let fall. Her hair was black streaked with silver, cut short and curled away from her face. Her large brown eyes were outlined with long black lashes under arched brows. She smiled mischievously as she put a bowl of *asopao* on the table opposite the cot and dragged one of the two chairs from its place against the wall.

"Here you are," she said. "Chico makes good *asopao,* but not as good as mine."

It was delicious, thick with rice and chunks of chicken, cubed potatoes, green olives, and capers. She tore off a chunk of bread from a long loaf on top of the refrigerator, spread it thick with butter, and put the bread on a napkin in front of me.

"Monín told me you like bread. This is fresh from the bakery down the street."

It was crunchy on the outside and soft on the inside, just the way I liked it.

Don Julio and Chico came back, followed by Mami, her eyes bright.

"What a great place! Wait till you see it, Negi. It's twice the size of this one, with windows in the front and back. And there's a huge bathtub, and a gas stove with four burners!"

"And your school is only five blocks from here," Don Julio said. "Just beyond *la marketa*."

"What's a *marketa*?" I asked. Everyone laughed.

"It's a big building with stalls where you can buy anything," Mami said.

"Like the plaza in *Bayamón*,"[4] Tata added.

"Only much bigger," Chico said.

"Look at her. She's excited about it already," Tata said, and they all stared at me with broad smiles, willing me to give in to their enthusiasm. I ran into Mami's arms, unable to admit that a part of me was looking forward to the morning, to the newness of our life, and afraid to let the other part show, the part that was scared.

There were angels on the ceiling. Four fat naked cherubs danced in a circle, their hands holding ivy garlands, their round buttocks half covered by a cloth swirling around their legs. Next to me, Mami snored softly. At the foot of the bed, Edna and

---

[4] a city close to San Juan, Puerto Rico (the capitol)

Raymond slept curled away from each other, their backs against my legs. The bedroom had very high ceilings with braided molding all the way around, ending in a circle surrounded by more braid above the huge window across from the bed. The shade was down, but bright sunlight streaked in at the edges. The cherubs looked down on us, smiling mysteriously, and I wondered how many people they had seen come in and out of this room. Slowly I crawled over Mami, out of bed.

"Where are you going?" she mumbled, half asleep.

"To the bathroom," I whispered.

The bed was pressed into the corner against the wall across from the window, next to a wide doorway that led into the next room. A long dresser stretched from the doorway to the window wall, leaving an aisle just wide enough to open the drawers halfway out.

It was six in the morning of my first day in Brooklyn. Our apartment, on the second floor, was the fanciest place I'd ever lived in. The stairs coming up from Tata's room on the first floor were marble, with a landing in between, and a colored glass window with bunches of grapes and twirling vines. The door to our apartment was carved with more bunches of grapes and leaves. From the two windows in the main room we could look out on the courtyard we had come through the night before. A tree with broad brown leaves grew from the middle of what looked like a well, circled with the same stones that lined the ground. Scraggly grass poked out between the cracks and in the brown dirt around the tree. The building across from ours was three stories high, crisscrossed by iron stairs with narrow landings on which people grew tomatoes and geraniums in clay pots. Our building was only two stories high, although it was almost as tall as the one across the courtyard. We, too, had an iron balcony with a straight ladder suspended halfway to the ground. It made me a little dizzy to look down.

The main room of our apartment was large and sunny and decorated with more braided molding. The whole apartment was painted pale yellow, except for the ceilings, which were smoky gray. The floor was covered with a flat rug whose fringes had worn away into frayed edges where they met the wood floor. A fireplace had been blocked up with a metal sheet. More cherubs, grapes, and vines decorated the mantel. One of the cherubs was missing a nose; another had lost both hands and a foot. Next to the fireplace there was a small stove with four burners close together, a narrow counter with shelves underneath, and a deep sink. A door next to the sink led to the toilet, which was flushed by pulling a chain attached to a wooden box on the wall above the seat. On the other side of the toilet room door, on the wall opposite the windows, there was a huge, claw-foot bathtub covered by a metal sheet. In the middle of the room was a formica table and four chairs with plastic seats and backs that matched the tabletop. A lopsided couch and lumpy chair covered in a scratchy blue fabric faced the tub as if bathing were a special event to which spectators were invited.

The windows and door were locked and Mami had warned the night before that I was not to leave the apartment without telling her. There was no place to go anyway. I had no idea where I was, only that it was very far away from where I'd been. Brooklyn, Mami had said, was not New York. I wished I had a map so that I could place myself in relation to Puerto Rico. But everything we owned was packed and stacked against the yellow walls. Not that there was a map in there, either.

There was nothing to do, nowhere to go, no one to talk to. The apartment was stifling. Inside the closed rooms, the air was still. Not even dust motes in the sunlight. Outside the windows, a steady roar was interrupted by sharp sirens or the insistent crash and clang of garbage cans, the whining motors of cars, and the faint sound of babies crying.

La marketa took up a whole block. It was much bigger and more confusing than the plaza in Bayamón, although it carried pretty much the same types of things. It was a red brick building with skylights in the high ceiling, so that whatever sun made it in lit up the dusty beams and long fluorescent light fixtures suspended from them. The floor was a gritty cement and gravel mix, sticky in places, spotted with what looked like oil slicks. Stalls were arranged along aisles, the merchandise on deep shelves that slanted down.

On the way to *la marketa* we had passed two men dressed in long black coats, their faces bearded. Ringlets hung from under their hats alongside their faces.

"Don't stare," Mami pulled on my hand.

"Why are they dressed so strange?"

"They're Jewish. They don't eat pork."

"Why not?"

"I don't know. They all live in the same neighborhood and only buy food from each other."

In *la marketa* almost all the vendors were Jewish, only they didn't wear their coats and hats. They wore white shirts and little round doilies on their heads. Many of them spoke Spanish, which made it easy for Mami to negotiate the price of everything.

"You never pay the first price they tell you," she instructed. "They like to bargain."

We went from stall to stall, arguing about every item we picked out. The vendors always made it seem as if we were cheating them, even though Mami said everything was overpriced.

"Don't ever pay full price for anything," Mami told me. "It's always cheaper somewhere else."

It was a game: the vendors wanting more money than Mami was willing to spend, but both of them knowing that eventually, she would part with her dollars and they would get them. It made no sense to me. It took most of the day to buy the stuff we needed for our apartment. Had she spent less time shopping around, she might have bought more. As it was, she only had half the things we needed, and we were exhausted and irritable by the time we got home. I had spent my entire first day in New York hunting for bargains.

The second day was no different. "We have to buy your school clothes, and a coat," Mami said.

Winter would be coming soon, Tata said, and with it, chilly winds, snowstorms, and short days.

"The first winter is always the worst," Don Julio explained, "because your blood is still thin from living in Puerto Rico." I imagined my blood thickening into syrup but didn't know how that could make me warmer.

"I can't wait to see snow," Edna chirped.

"Me neither," said Raymond.

Two days in Brooklyn, and they already loved everything about it. Tata cared for them while Mami and I shopped. She sat them down in front of a black-and-white television set, gave each a chocolate bar, and they spent the entire day watching cartoons, while Tata smoked and drank beer.

"What good kids they are," she complimented Mami when we came back. "Not a peep out of them all day."

Graham Avenue in Williamsburg was the broadest street I'd ever seen. It was flanked by three- and four-story apartment buildings, the first floors of which contained stores where you could buy anything. Most of these stores were also run by Jewish people, but they didn't speak Spanish like the ones in *la marketa*. They were less friendly, too, unwilling to negotiate prices. On Graham Avenue there were special restaurants where Mami said Jewish people ate. They were called delis, and there were foreign symbols in the windows, and underneath them the word *kosher*. I knew Mami wouldn't know what it meant, so I didn't bother asking. I imagined it was a delicacy that only Jewish people ate, which is why their restaurants so prominently let them know you could get it there. We didn't go into the delis because, Mami said, they didn't like Puerto Ricans in there. Instead, she took me to eat pizza.

"It's Italian," she said.

"Do Italians like Puerto Ricans?" I asked as I bit into hot cheese and tomato sauce that burned the tip of my tongue.

"They're more like us than Jewish people are," she said, which wasn't an answer.

In Puerto Rico the only foreigners I'd been aware of were *Americanos*. In two days in Brooklyn I had already encountered Jewish people, and now Italians. There was another group of people Mami had pointed out to me. *Morenos*.[5] But they weren't foreigners, because they were American. They were black, but they didn't look like Puerto Rican *negros*.[6] They dressed like *Americanos* but walked with a jaunty hop that made them look as if they were dancing down the street, only their hips were not as loose as Puerto Rican men's were. According to Mami, they too lived in their own neighborhoods, frequented their own restaurants, and didn't like Puerto Ricans.

"How come?" I wondered, since in Puerto Rico, all of the people I'd ever met were either black or had a black relative somewhere in their family. I would have thought *morenos* would like us, since so many of us looked like them.

"They think we're taking their jobs."

"Are we?"

"There's enough work in the United States for everybody," Mami said, "but some people think some work is beneath them. Me, if I have to crawl on all fours to earn a living, I'll do it. I'm not proud that way."

I couldn't imagine what kind of work required crawling on all fours, although I remembered Mami scrubbing the floor that way, so that it seemed she was talking

---

[5] dark-skinned   [6] blacks

about housework. Although, according to her, she wouldn't be too proud to clean other people's houses, I hoped she wouldn't have to do it. It would be too embarrassing to come all the way from Puerto Rico so she could be somebody's maid.

The first day of school Mami walked me to a stone building that loomed over Graham Avenue, its concrete yard enclosed by an iron fence with spikes at the top. The front steps were wide but shallow and led up to a set of heavy double doors that slammed shut behind us as we walked down the shiny corridor. I clutched my eighth-grade report card filled with A's and B's, and Mami had my birth certificate. At the front office we were met by Mr. Grant, a droopy gentleman with thick glasses and a kind smile who spoke no Spanish. He gave Mami a form to fill out. I knew most of the words in the squares we were to fill in: NAME, ADDRESS (CITY, STATE), OCCUPATION. We gave it to Mr. Grant, who reviewed it, looked at my birth certificate, studied my report card, then wrote on the top of the form "7–18."

Don Julio had told me that if students didn't speak English, the schools in Brooklyn would keep them back one grade until they learned it.

"Seven gray?" I asked Mr. Grant, pointing at his big numbers, and he nodded.

"I no guan seven gray. I eight gray. I teeneyer."

"You don't speak English," he said. "You have to go to seventh grade while you're learning."

"I have A's in school Puerto Rico. I lern good. I no seven gray girl."

Mami stared at me, not understanding but knowing I was being rude to an adult.

"What's going on?" she asked me in Spanish. I told her they wanted to send me back one grade and I would not have it. This was probably the first rebellious act she had seen from me outside my usual mouthiness within the family.

"Negi, leave it alone. Those are the rules," she said, a warning in her voice.

"I don't care what their rules say," I answered. "I'm not going back to seventh grade. I can do the work. I'm not stupid."

Mami looked at Mr. Grant, who stared at her as if expecting her to do something about me. She smiled and shrugged her shoulders.

"Meester Grant," I said, seizing the moment, "I go eight gray six mons. Eef I no lern inglish, I go seven gray. Okay?"

"That's not the way we do things here," he said, hesitating.

"I good studen. I lern queek. You see notes." I pointed to the A's in my report card. "I pass seven gray."

So we made a deal.

"You have until Christmas," he said. "I'll be checking on your progress," He scratched out "7–18" and wrote in "8–23." He wrote something on a piece of paper, sealed it inside an envelope, and gave it to me. "Your teacher is Miss Brown. Take this note upstairs to her. Your mother can go," he said and disappeared into his office.

"Wow!" Mami said, "you can speak English!"

I was so proud of myself, I almost burst. In Puerto Rico if I'd been that pushy, I would have been called *mal educada*[7] by the Mr. Grant equivalent and sent home

---

[7] misbehaved; spoiled

with a note to my mother. But here it was my teacher who was getting the note, I got what I wanted, and my mother was sent home.

"I can find my way after school," I said to Mami. "You don't have to come get me."

"Are you sure?"

"Don't worry," I said. "I'll be all right."

I walked down the black-tiled hallway, past many doors that were half glass, each one labelled with a room number in neat black lettering. Other students stared at me, tried to get my attention, or pointedly ignored me. I kept walking as if I knew where I was going, heading for the sign that said STAIRS with an arrow pointing up. When I reached the end of the hall and looked back, Mami was still standing at the front door watching me, a worried expression on her face. I waved, and she waved back. I started up the stairs, my stomach churning into tight knots. All of a sudden, I was afraid that I was about to make a fool of myself and end up in seventh grade in the middle of the school year. Having to fall back would be worse than just accepting my fate now and hopping forward if I proved to be as good a student as I had convinced Mr. Grant I was. "What have I done?" I kicked myself with the back of my right shoe, much to the surprise of the fellow walking behind me, who laughed uproariously, as if I had meant it as a joke.

Miss Brown's was the learning disabled class, where the administration sent kids with all sorts of problems, none of which, from what I could see, had anything to do with their ability to learn but more with their willingness to do so. They were an unruly group. Those who came to class, anyway. Half of them never showed up, or, when they did, they slept through the lesson or nodded off in the middle of Miss Brown's carefully parsed sentences.

We were outcasts in a school where the smartest eighth graders were in the 8–1 homeroom, each subsequent drop in number indicating one notch less smarts. If your class was in the low double digits, (8–10 for instance), you were smart, but not a pinhead. Once you got into the teens, your intelligence was in question, especially as the numbers rose to the high teens. And then there were the twenties. I was in 8–23, where the dumbest, most undesirable people were placed. My class was, in some ways, the equivalent of seventh grade, perhaps even sixth or fifth.

Miss Brown, the homeroom teacher, who also taught English composition, was a young black woman who wore sweat pads under her arms. The strings holding them in place sometimes slipped outside the short sleeves of her well-pressed white shirts, and she had to turn her back to us in order to adjust them. She was very pretty, with almond eyes and a hairdo that was flat and straight at the top of her head then dipped into tight curls at the ends. Her fingers were well manicured, the nails painted pale pink with white tips. She taught English composition as if everyone cared about it, which I found appealing.

After the first week she moved me from the back of the room to the front seat by her desk, and after that, it felt as if she were teaching me alone. We never spoke, except when I went up to the blackboard.

"Esmeralda," she called in a musical voice, "would you please come up and mark the prepositional phrase?"

In her class, I learned to recognize the structure of the English language, and to draft the parts of a sentence by the position of words relative to pronouns and prepositions without knowing exactly what the whole thing meant.

The school was huge and noisy. There was a social order that, at first, I didn't understand but kept bumping into. Girls and boys who wore matching cardigans walked down the halls hand in hand, sometimes stopping behind lockers to kiss and fondle each other. They were *Americanos* and belonged in the homerooms in the low numbers.

Another group of girls wore heavy makeup, hitched their skirts above their knees, opened one extra button on their blouses, and teased their hair into enormous bouffants held solid with spray. In the morning, they took over the girls' bathroom, where they dragged on cigarettes as they did their hair until the air was unbreathable, thick with smoke and hair spray. The one time I entered the bathroom before classes they chased me out with insults and rough shoves.

Those bold girls with hair and makeup and short skirts, I soon found out, were Italian. The Italians all sat together on one side of the cafeteria, the blacks on another. The two groups hated each other more than they hated Puerto Ricans. At least once a week there was a fight between an Italian and a *moreno,* either in the bathroom, in the school yard, or in an abandoned lot near the school, a no-man's-land that divided their neighborhoods and kept them apart on weekends.

The black girls had their own style. Not for them the big, pouffy hair of the Italians. Their hair was straightened, curled at the tips like Miss Brown's, or pulled up into a twist at the back with wispy curls and straw straight bangs over Cleopatra eyes. Their skirts were also short, except it didn't look like they hitched them up when their mothers weren't looking. They came that way. They had strong, shapely legs and wore knee socks with heavy lace-up shoes that became lethal weapons in fights.

It was rumored that the Italians carried knives, even the girls, and that the *morenos* had brass knuckles in their pockets and steel toes in their heavy shoes. I stayed away from both groups, afraid that if I befriended an Italian, I'd get beat up by a *morena,* or vice versa.

There were two kinds of Puerto Ricans in school: the newly arrived, like myself, and the ones born in Brooklyn of Puerto Rican parents. The two types didn't mix. The Brooklyn Puerto Ricans spoke English, and often no Spanish at all. To them, Puerto Rico was the place where their grandparents lived, a place they visited on school and summer vacations, a place which they complained was backward and mosquito-ridden. Those of us for whom Puerto Rico was still a recent memory were also split into two groups: the ones who longed for the island and the ones who wanted to forget it as soon as possible.

I felt disloyal for wanting to learn English, for liking pizza, for studying the girls with big hair and trying out their styles at home, locked in the bathroom where no one could watch. I practiced walking with the peculiar little hop of the *morenas,* but felt as if I were limping.

I didn't feel comfortable with the newly arrived Puerto Ricans who stuck together in suspicious little groups, criticizing everyone, afraid of everything. And I was not accepted by the Brooklyn Puerto Ricans, who held the secret of coolness. They walked the halls between the Italians and the *morenos,* neither one nor the other, but looking and acting like a combination of both, depending on the texture of their hair, the shade of their skin, their makeup, and the way they walked down the hall.

A Shot at It

Te conozco bacalao, aunque vengas disfrazao.
I recognize you salted codfish, even if you're in disguise.

While Francisco was still alive, we had moved to Ellery Street. That meant I had to change schools, so Mami walked me to P.S. 33, where I would attend ninth grade. The first week I was there I was given a series of tests that showed that even though I couldn't speak English very well, I read and wrote it at the tenth-grade level. So they put me in 9–3, with the smart kids.

One morning, Mr. Barone, a guidance counsellor, called me to his office. He was short, with a big head and large hazel eyes under shapely eyebrows. His nose was long and round at the tip. He dressed in browns and yellows and often perched his tortoiseshell glasses on his forehead, as if he had another set of eyes up there.

"So," he pushed his glasses up, "what do you want to be when you grow up?"

"I don't know."

He shuffled through some papers. "Let's see here . . . you're fourteen, is that right?"

"Yes, sir."

"And you've never thought about what you want to be?"

When I was very young, I wanted to be a *jíbara*.[8] When I was older, I wanted to be a cartographer, then a topographer. But since we'd come to Brooklyn, I'd not thought about the future much.

"No, sir."

He pulled his glasses down to where they belonged and shuffled through the papers again.

"Do you have any hobbies?" I didn't know what he meant. "Hobbies, hobbies," he flailed his hands, as if he were juggling, "things you like to do after school."

"Ah, yes." I tried to imagine what I did at home that might qualify as a hobby. "I like to read."

He seemed disappointed. "Yes, we know that about you." He pulled out a paper and stared at it. "One of the tests we gave you was an aptitude test. It tells us what kinds of things you might be good at. The tests show that you would be good at helping people. Do you like to help people?"

I was afraid to contradict the tests. "Yes, sir."

"There's a high school we can send you where, you can study biology and chemistry which will prepare you for a career in nursing."

I screwed up my face. He consulted the papers again.

"You would also do well in communications. Teaching maybe."

I remembered Miss Brown standing in front of a classroom full of rowdy teenagers, some of them taller than she was.

---

[8] someone from the mountains of Puerto Rico; a peasant, but in this context it carries with it a certain romanticism

"I don't like to teach."

Mr. Barone pushed his glasses up again and leaned over the stack of papers on his desk. "Why don't you think about it and get back to me," he said, closing the folder with my name across the top. He put his hand flat on it, as if squeezing something out. "You're a smart girl, Esmeralda. Let's try to get you into an academic school so that you have a shot at college."

On the way home, I walked with another new ninth grader, Yolanda. She had been in New York for three years but knew as little English as I did. We spoke in Spanglish, a combination of English and Spanish in which we hopped from one language to the other depending on which word came first.

"*Te preguntó el* Mr. Barone, you know, *lo que querías hacer*[9] when you grow up?" I asked.

"*Sí, pero,* I didn't know. *¿Y tú?*"[10]

"*Yo tampoco.* He said, *que* I like to help people. *Pero,* you know, *a mí no me gusta mucho la gente.*"[11] When she heard me say I didn't like people much, Yolanda looked at me from the corner of her eye, waiting to become the exception.

By the time I said it, she had dashed up the stairs of her building. She didn't wave as she ducked in, and the next day she wasn't friendly. I walked around the rest of the day in embarrassed isolation, knowing that somehow I had given myself away to the only friend I'd made at Junior High School 33. I had to either take back my words or live with the consequences of stating what was becoming the truth. I'd never said that to anyone, not even to myself. It was an added weight, but I wasn't about to trade it for companionship.

A few days later, Mr. Barone called me back to his office.

"Well?" Tiny green flecks burned around the black pupils of his hazel eyes.

The night before, Mami had called us into the living room. On the television "fifty of America's most beautiful girls" paraded in ruffled tulle dresses before a tinsel waterfall.

"Aren't they lovely?" Mami murmured, as the girls, escorted by boys in uniform, floated by the camera, twirled, and disappeared behind a screen to the strains of a waltz and an announcer's dramatic voice calling their names, ages, and states. Mami sat mesmerized through the whole pageant.

"I'd like to be a model," I said to Mr. Barone.

He stared at me, pulled his glasses down from his forehead, looked at the papers inside the folder with my name on it, and glared. "A model?" His voice was gruff, as if he were more comfortable yelling at people than talking to them.

"I want to be on television."

"Oh, then you want to be an actress," in a tone that said this was only a slight improvement over my first career choice. We stared at one another for a few seconds. He pushed his glasses up to his forehead again and reached for a book on the shelf in back of him. "I only know of one school that trains actresses, but we've never sent them a student from here."

---

[9] He asked you, what you wanted to be when you grow up   [10] Yes, but. And you?   [11] Me neither. But, I don't like people very much.

Performing Arts, the write-up said, was an academic, as opposed to a vocational, public school that trained students wishing to pursue a career in theater, music, and dance.

"It says here that you have to audition." He stood up and held the book closer to the faint gray light coming through the narrow window high on his wall. "Have you ever performed in front of an audience?"

"I was announcer in my school show in Puerto Rico," I said. "And I recite poetry. There, not here."

He closed the book and held it against his chest. His right index finger thumped a rhythm on his lower lip. "Let me call them and find out exactly what you need to do. Then we can talk some more."

I left his office strangely happy, confident that something good had just happened, not knowing exactly what.

"I'm not afraid . . . I'm not afraid . . . I'm not afraid." Every day I walked home from school repeating those words. The broad streets and sidewalks that had impressed me so on the first day we had arrived had become as familiar as the dirt road from Macún to the highway. Only my curiosity about the people who lived behind these walls ended where the façades of the buildings opened into dark hallways or locked doors. Nothing good, I imagined, could be happening inside if so many locks had to be breached to go in or step out.

It was on these tense walks home from school that I decided I had to get out of Brooklyn. Mami had chosen this as our home, and just like every other time we'd moved, I'd had to go along with her because I was a child who had no choice. But I wasn't willing to go along with her on this one.

"How can people live like this?" I shrieked once, desperate to run across a field, to feel grass under my feet instead of pavement.

"Like what?" Mami asked, looking around our apartment, the kitchen and living room crisscrossed with sagging lines of drying diapers and bedclothes.

"Everyone on top of each other. No room to do anything. No air."

"Do you want to go back to Macún, to live like savages, with no electricity, no toilets . . . "

"At least you could step outside every day without somebody trying to kill you."

"Ay, Negi, stop exaggerating!"

"I hate my life!" I yelled.

"Then do something about it," she yelled back.

Until Mr. Barone showed me the listing for Performing Arts High School, I hadn't known what to do.

"The auditions are in less than a month. You have to learn a monologue, which you will perform in front of a panel. If you do well, and your grades here are good, you might get into the school."

Mr. Barone took charge of preparing me for my audition to Performing Arts. He selected a speech from *The Silver Cord,* a play by Sidney Howard, first performed in 1926, but whose action took place in a New York drawing room circa 1905.

"Mr. Gatti, the English teacher," he said, "will coach you. . . . And Mrs. Johnson will talk to you about what to wear and things like that."

I was to play Christina, a young married woman confronting her mother-in-law. I learned the monologue phonetically from Mr. Gatti. It opened with "You belong to a type that's very common in this country, Mrs. Phelps—a type of self-centered, self-pitying, son-devouring tigress, with unmentionable proclivities suppressed on the side."

"We don't have time to study the meaning of every word," Mr. Gatti said. "Just make sure you pronounce every word correctly."

Mrs. Johnson, who taught Home Economics, called me to her office.

"Is that how you enter a room?" she asked the minute I came in. "Try again, only this time, don't barge in. Step in slowly, head up, back straight, a nice smile on your face. That's it." I took a deep breath and waited. "Now sit. No, not like that. Don't just plop down. Float down to the chair with your knees together." She demonstrated, and I copied her. "That's better. What do you do with your hands? No, don't hold your chin like that; it's not ladylike. Put your hands on your lap, and leave them there. Don't use them so much when you talk."

I sat stiff as a cutout while Mrs. Johnson and Mr. Barone asked me questions they thought the panel at Performing Arts would ask.

"Where are you from?"

"Puerto Rico."

"No," Mrs. Johnson said, "Porto Rico. Keep your r's soft. Try again."

"Do you have any hobbies?" Mr. Barone asked. Now I knew what to answer.

"I enjoy dancing and the movies."

"Why do you want to come to this school?"

Mrs. Johnson and Mr. Barone had worked on my answer if this question should come up.

"I would like to study at Performing Arts because of its academic program and so that I may be trained as an actress."

"Very good, very good!" Mr. Barone rubbed his hands together, twinkled his eyes at Mrs. Johnson. "I think we have a shot at this."

"Remember," Mrs. Johnson said, "when you shop for your audition dress, look for something very simple in dark colors."

Mami bought me a red plaid wool jumper with a crisp white shirt, my first pair of stockings, and penny loafers. The night before, she rolled up my hair in pink curlers that cut into my scalp and made it hard to sleep. For the occasion, I was allowed to wear eye makeup and a little lipstick.

"You look so grown up!" Mami said, her voice sad but happy, as I twirled in front of her and Tata.

"*Toda una señorita*,"[12] Tata said, her eyes misty.

We set out for the audition on an overcast January morning heavy with the threat of snow.

"Why couldn't you choose a school close to home?" Mami grumbled as we got on the train to Manhattan. I worried that even if I were accepted, she wouldn't let me go because it was so far from home, one hour each way by subway. But in

___
[12] a young woman

spite of her complaints, she was proud that I was good enough to be considered for such a famous school. And she actually seemed excited that I would be leaving the neighborhood.

"You'll be exposed to a different class of people," she assured me, and I felt the force of her ambition without knowing exactly what she meant.

Three women sat behind a long table in a classroom where the desks and chairs had been pushed against a wall. As I entered I held my head up and smiled, and then I floated down to the chair in front of them, clasped my hands on my lap, and smiled some more.

"Good morning," said the tall one with hair the color of sand. She was big boned and solid, with intense blue eyes, a generous mouth, and soothing hands with short fingernails. She was dressed in shades of beige from head to toe and wore no makeup and no jewelry except for the gold chain that held her glasses just above her full bosom. Her voice was rich, modulated, each word pronounced as if she were inventing it.

Next to her sat a very small woman with very high heels. Her cropped hair was pouffed around her face, with bangs brushing the tips of her long false lashes, her huge dark brown eyes were thickly lined in black all around, and her small mouth was carefully drawn in and painted cerise. Her suntanned face turned toward me with the innocent curiosity of a lively baby. She was dressed in black, with many gold chains around her neck, big earrings, several bracelets, and large stone rings on the fingers of both hands.

The third woman was tall, small boned, thin, but shapely. Her dark hair was pulled flat against her skull into a knot in back of her head. Her face was all angles and light, with fawnlike dark brown eyes, a straight nose, full lips painted just a shade pinker than their natural color. Silky forest green cuffs peeked out from the sleeves of her burgundy suit. Diamond studs winked from perfect earlobes.

I had dreamed of this moment for several weeks. More than anything, I wanted to impress the panel with my talent, so that I would be accepted into Performing Arts and leave Brooklyn every day. And, I hoped, one day I would never go back.

But the moment I faced these three impeccably groomed women, I forgot my English and Mrs. Johnson's lessons on how to behave like a lady. In the agony of trying to answer their barely comprehensible questions, I jabbed my hands here and there, forming words with my fingers because the words refused to leave my mouth.

"Why don't you let us hear your monologue now?" the woman with the dangling glasses asked softly.

I stood up abruptly, and my chair clattered onto its side two feet from where I stood. I picked it up, wishing with all my strength that a thunderbolt would strike me dead to ashes on the spot.

"It's all right," she said. "Take a breath. We know you're nervous."

I closed my eyes and breathed deeply, walked to the middle of the room, and began my monologue.

"Ju bee lonh 2 a type dats berry cómo in dis kuntree, Meessees Felps. A type off selfcent red self pee tee in sun de boring tie gress wid on men shon A ball pro klee bee tees on de side."

In spite of Mr. Gatti's reminders that I should speak slowly and enunciate every word, even if I didn't understand it, I recited my three-minute monologue in one minute flat.

The small woman's long lashes seemed to have grown with amazement. The elegant woman's serene face twitched with controlled laughter. The tall one dressed in beige smiled sweetly.

"Thank you, dear," she said. "Could you wait outside for a few moments?"

I resisted the urge to curtsy. The long hallway had narrow wainscotting halfway up to the high ceiling. Single bulb lamps hung from long cords, creating yellow puddles of light on the polished brown linoleum tile. A couple of girls my age sat on straight chairs next to their mothers, waiting their turn. They looked up as I came out and the door shut behind me. Mami stood up from her chair at the end of the hall. She looked as scared as I felt.

"What happened?"

"Nothing," I mumbled, afraid that if I began telling her about it, I would break into tears in front of the other people, whose eyes followed me and Mami as we walked to the EXIT sign. "I have to wait here a minute."

"Did they say anything?"

"No. I'm just supposed to wait."

We leaned against the wall. Across from us there was a bulletin board with newspaper clippings about former students. On the ragged edge, a neat person had printed in blue ink, "P.A." and the year the actor, dancer, or musician had graduated. I closed my eyes and tried to picture myself on that bulletin board, with "P.A. '66" across the top.

The door at the end of the hall opened, and the woman in beige poked her head out.

"Esmeralda?"

"*Sí*, I mean, here." I raised my hand.

She led me into the room. There was another girl in there, whom she introduced as Bonnie, a junior at the school.

"Do you know what a pantomime is?" the woman asked. I nodded. "You and Bonnie are sisters decorating a Christmas tree."

Bonnie looked a lot like Juanita Marín, whom I had last seen in Macún four years earlier. We decided where the invisible Christmas tree would be, and we sat on the floor and pretended we were taking decorations out of boxes and hanging them on the branches.

My family had never had a Christmas tree, but I remembered how once I had helped Papi wind colored lights around the eggplant bush that divided our land from Doña Ana's. We started at the bottom and wound the wire with tiny red bulbs around and around until we ran out; then Papi plugged another cord to it and we kept going until the branches hung heavy with light and the bush looked like it was on fire.

Before long I had forgotten where I was, and that the tree didn't exist and Bonnie was not my sister. She pretended to hand me a very delicate ball, and just before I took it, she made like it fell to the ground and shattered. I was petrified that Mami would come in and yell at us for breaking her favorite decoration. Just as I began to pick up the tiny fragments of nonexistent crystal, a voice broke in. "Thank you."

Bonnie got up, smiled, and went out.

The elegant woman stretched her hand out for me to shake. "We will notify your school in a few weeks. It was very nice to meet you."

I shook hands all around then backed out of the room in a fog, silent, as if the pantomime had taken my voice and the urge to speak.

On the way home Mami kept asking what had happened, and I kept mumbling, "Nothing. Nothing happened," ashamed that, after all the hours of practice with Mrs. Johnson, Mr. Barone, and Mr. Gatti, after the expense of new clothes and shoes, after Mami had to take a day off from work to take me into Manhattan, after all that, I had failed the audition and would never, ever, get out of Brooklyn.

Epilogue: One of These Days

El mismo jíbaro con diferente caballo.

Same jíbaro, different horse.

A decade after my graduation from Performing Arts, I visited the school. I was by then living in Boston, a scholarship student at Harvard University. The tall, elegant woman of my audition had become my mentor through my three years there. Since my graduation, she had married the school principal.

"I remember your audition," she said, her chiseled face dreamy, her lips toying with a smile that she seemed, still, to have to control.

I had forgotten the skinny brown girl with the curled hair, wool jumper, and lively hands. But she hadn't. She told me that the panel had had to ask me to leave so that they could laugh, because it was so funny to see a fourteen-year-old Puerto Rican girl jabbering out a monologue about a possessive mother-in-law at the turn of the century, the words incomprehensible because they went by so fast.

"We admired," she said, "the courage it took to stand in front of us and do what you did."

"So you mean I didn't get into the school because of my talent, but because I had chutzpah?" We both laughed.

"Are any of your sisters and brothers in college?"

"No, I'm the only one, so far."

"How many of you are there?"

"By the time I graduated from high school there were eleven of us."

"Eleven!" She looked at me for a long time, until I had to look down. "Do you ever think about how far you've come?" she asked.

"No." I answered. "I never stop to think about it. It might jinx the momentum."

"Let me tell you another story, then," she said. "The first day of your first year, you were absent. We called your house. You said you couldn't come to school because you had nothing to wear. I wasn't sure if you were joking. I asked to speak to your mother, and you translated what she said. She needed you to go somewhere with her to interpret. At first you wouldn't tell me where, but then you admitted you were going to the welfare office. You were crying, and I had to assure you that you were not the only student in this school whose family received public assistance. The next day you were here, bright and eager. And now here you are, about to graduate from Harvard."

"I'm glad you made that phone call," I said.

"And I'm glad you came to see me, but right now I have to teach a class." She stood up, as graceful as I remembered. "Take care."

Her warm embrace, fragrant of expensive perfume, took me by surprise. "Thank you," I said as she went around the corner to her classroom.

I walked the halls of the school, looking for the room where my life had changed. It was across from the science lab, a few doors down from the big bulletin board where someone with neat handwriting still wrote the letters "P.A." followed by the graduating year along the edges of newspaper clippings featuring famous alumni.

"P.A. '66," I said to no one in particular. "One of these days."

Discussion Questions

1. In what way(s) is Negi's strong character revealed? How is that character being reshaped by her teachers?

2. Why is it so important for Negi that she be accepted into the School of Performing Arts? What role does education play in Negi's life? What does that say about her ability (or lack thereof) to adjust to her new environment?

3. How are the images and lifestyles of New York City compared to those of Puerto Rico? What does that comparison reveal about Negi's identity?

4. Although the novel ends with Negi on her way to success, there is also a sense that something has been lost. What is it?

5. Compare Negi's comments about dark-skinned Puerto Ricans to those made by Brew and Piri in *Down These Mean Streets* on page 373.

Ed Vega

ED VEGA was born in the southern city of Ponce, Puerto Rico, in 1936. His family moved to the Bronx, New York, where Vegas attended public schools. He received a B.A. from New York University in 1963 and taught at several academic institutions in the New York area. He has also worked in a number of social service programs for inner-city youths. His stories have been published in several periodicals, and his published books include The Comeback *(1985), and* Casualty Report *(1991).*

Ed Vega's short stories often deal with prejudice on a subtle level. Many of his characters seem to have fully adapted to their environment, but eventually feel a certain loss that they cannot quite define. Other times ethnic differences are used to a character's advantage, as is the case with Mercury Gómez, a character in Vega's book Mendoza's Dreams *(1987). Gómez creates a successful messenger service by using the physical stereotyping of his ethnic group as an aid rather than a detriment.*

The book as a whole, however, consists of a series of stories connected through the narrator, a prominent writer named Mendoza. Mendoza chronicles the lives of the Puerto Rican people as a type of magician that might make their dreams a reality. "The Barbosa Express" is a perfect representative of these stories that often seem surreal but always have a realistic message.

From Mendoza Dreams

The Barbosa Express

Several years ago, at the tail end of the big snowstorm, I was in Florindo's Bar on 110th Street and Lexington Avenue when Chu Chu Barbosa walked in cursing and threatening to join the FALN and bomb the hell out of somebody or other. Barbosa's name is *Jesús* but nobody likes being called Gee Zoos or Hay Siouxs, so it's convenient that the nickname for *Jesús* is Chu or Chuíto because Barbosa was a motorman for the last seventeen years with the New York City Transit Authority.

Barbosa is your typical working class stiff, bitter on the outside but full of stubborn optimism on the inside. He has gone through the same kind of immigrant nonsense everyone else has to go through and has come out of it in great shape. In spite of ups and downs he has remained married to the same woman twenty-two years, has never found reason to be unfaithful to her, put one kid through college and has four more heading in the same direction. He owns a two-family home in Brooklyn and on weekends during the summer, he takes Bobby and Mike, his two sons, fishing on his outboard, "Mercedes," named after the children's mother.

Usually even tempered and singularly civic minded, he lists among his responsibilities his serving as treasurer of the "*Roberto Clemente*[1] Little League of Brooklyn," vice-president of the "Sons of Cacimar Puerto Rican Day Parade Organizing Committee," Den Father for the Boy Scouts of America Troop 641, Secretary of the "Wilfredo Santiago American Legion Post 387" and member of the Courtelyou Street Block Association.

That night Barbosa was out of his mind with anger. At first I thought it was the weather. The snowstorm was wreaking havoc with the city and it seemed conceivable Barbosa was stranded in Manhattan and could not get back to his family in Brooklyn. Knocking the snow off his coat and stamping his feet, Barbosa walked up to the bar and ordered a boiler-maker. He downed the whiskey, chugalugged the beer and ordered another one. I was right next to him but he didn't recognize me until he had finished his second beer and ordered another. Halfway through his third beer he suddenly looked at me and shook his head as if there were no reason for trying anymore.

---

[1] Roberto Clemente was a Puerto Rican major league baseball player who died in a plane crash on his way to help Nicaraguan earthquake victims.

"This does it, Mendoza," he said, still shaking his head. "It makes no sense, man. The whole town is sinking."

"Yeah, the snow's pretty bad," I said, but it was as if I hadn't even spoken.

"The friggin capital of the world," he went on. "And it's going down the d-r-a-drain. I mean, who am I kidding? I put on a uniform in the morning, step into my little moving phone booth and off I go. From Coney Island to 205th in B-r-o-Bronx. Fifteen years I've been on that run. I mean, you gotta be born to the job, Mendoza. And listen, I take pride in what I do. It isn't just a job with me. I still get my kicks outta pushing my ten car rig. Brooklyn, Manhattan and the Bronx. I run through those boroughs four times a shift, picking up passengers, letting them off. School kids going up to Bronx Science, people going to work in midtown Manhattan, in the summertime the crowds going up to Yankee Stadium. And that run from 125th Street to 59th Street and Columbus Circle when I let her out and race through that tunnel at sixty miles an hour. Did you know that was the longest run of any express train between stops?"

"No, I didn't," I said.

"It is," he said. "Sixty-six b-l-o-blocks."

"No kidding," I said, suddenly hopeful that Barbosa was pulling out of his dark mood. "That's amazing."

"You're damn right it's amazing," he replied, his face angry once more. "And I love it, but it's getting to me. How can they friggin do this? I mean it's their trains. Don't they know that, Mendoza? They don't have to shove it down my throat. But who the hell am I, right? I'm the little guy. Just put him in that moving closet and forget about him. Jerónimo Anónimo, that's me. I don't care what anybody thinks. For me it's like I'm pulling the Super Chief on a transcontinental run, or maybe the old Texas Hummingbird from Chicago to San Antonio along all that flat land, eighty, ninety miles an hour. I give 'em an honest day's work. It's 'cause I'm Puerto Rican, man. It's nothing but discrimination."

I could certainly sympathize with Barbosa on that account. I had met severe discrimination in the publishing world and had been forced to write nothing but lies about the people. I was curious to find out what had taken place to make Barbosa so angry.

"I know how you feel, Chu Chu," I said.

"I mean you're a writer and it might sound strange, Mendoza. But I'm not a stupid man. I've read, so I know about words. When I'm in my rig going along the tracks and making my stops, it feels like I'm inside the veins of the city down in those tunnels. It's like my train is the blood and the people the food for this city. Sometimes there is a mugging or worse down there, but I say to myself, hell, so the system ate a stale *alcapurria*[2] or some bad chittlins or maybe an old knish. Do you understand what I'm saying?"

"Of course I do," I said. "Subway travel as a metaphor of the lifeblood of the city."

"Right. It's the people, the little people that keep the city going. Not the big shots."

"Exactly."

"Then how can they do it? The trains belong to them."

---

[2] a food made of fried plantain filled with meat

"The grafitti's getting to you," I said, sympathetically.

"No, that's a pain in the ass but you get used to it. Those kids are harmless. I got a nephew that's into that whole thing. I wish the hell they'd find someplace else to do their thing, but they're nothing compared to the creeps that are running the system these days. Nothing but prejudice against our people, Mendoza."

I asked Barbosa exactly what had happened and he told me that nearly a thousand new cars had arrived. "They're beautiful," he said. "Not a spot on them. Stainless steel, colorful plastic seats and a big orange D in front of them for my line. Oh, and they also have this bell that signals that the doors are gonna close. Have you seen 'em yet?" I told him I had not since I avoid subway travel as much as possible, which he doesn't know nor would I tell him for fear of hurting his feelings. He then went on to tell me that even though he had seniority on other motormen, they didn't assign a new train to him.

"Why not?" I said.

"Discrimination," he said. "'Cause I'm Puerto Rican. That's the only reason, Mendoza. Just plain discrimination. Even *morenos*[3] with less time than me got new rigs and I got stuck with my old messed up train. I'm not saying black people are not entitled to a break. You know me. I ain't got a prejudiced bone in my body. Man, I even told them I'd be willing to take an evening trick just to handle one of the new trains, but they said no. I'm burnt up, Mendoza. I feel like blowing up the whole system is how I feel."

I immediately counseled Barbosa to calm down and not be hasty in his response. I said that there were legal avenues that he could explore. Perhaps he could file a grievance with his union, but he just kept shaking his head and pounding his fist into his hand, muttering and ordering one beer after the other. At the end of an hour he began laughing real loud and saying that he had the perfect solution to the problem. He patted me on the back and said goodbye.

Of course I worried about Chu Chu for three or four days because you couldn't find a nicer guy and I was worried that he would do something crazy. Every time I stopped by Florindo's Bar I'd ask for him, but no one had seen him around. Once, one of the bartenders said he had seen him in Brooklyn and that he was still working for the Transit Authority. I asked if he had gotten a new train, but the bartender didn't know. I didn't hear from Barbosa or see him again for the next six months and then I wished I hadn't.

About a week before the Fourth of July I received a call from Barbosa. He was no longer angry. In fact he sounded euphoric. This made me immediately suspicious. Perhaps he had taken up drugs as a relief from his anger.

"How you doing, Mendoza?" he said. "How's the writing going?"

"It's going, but just barely," I said. "My caboose is dragging," I added, throwing in a little railroad humor.

He let loose a big roaring belly laugh and, speaking away from the telephone, told his wife, Mercedes, what I'd said. In the background I heard his wife say, "that's nice," and I could tell she wasn't too pleased with Barbosa's condition.

"Your caboose, huh?" he said. "Well, I got just the right maintenance for that. Something to get your engine going again and stoke up that boiler with fresh fuel."

"What did you have in mind?" I said, fighting my suspicion.

---

[3] dark skinned

"A party, Mendoza. A Fourth of July party. We're gonna celebrate our independence."

This didn't sound too strange since Barbosa believed in the American Way of Life. He was a Puerto Rican, but he loved the United States and he wasn't ashamed to admit it. He didn't go around spouting island independence and reaping the fruits of the system. His philosophy was simple. His kids spoke English, were studying here and there were more opportunities for a career in the U.S. Whatever they wanted to do on the island was their business. "I don't pay no taxes there," he'd say. "I don't live there, I don't own property there, so why should I have anything to say about what goes on. Don't get me wrong. I love the island and nobody's ever gonna let me forget I'm from P.R., but it don't make no sense for me to be a phony about where I earn my rice and beans." I personally thought it was an irresponsible political stand, but I don't meddle in how people think or feel, I simply report on what I see.

"What kind of party?" I said.

"That's a surprise, but it's gonna be a party to end all parties. Music. Food. Drink. Entertainment. Fire works. You name it, we're gonna have it."

"At your house in Brooklyn?"

"Naw, too small. Up in the Bronx. Ralph, my nephew, can come pick you up."

"I don't know," I said. "I got a backlog of stuff and I'm not too good at celebrating the independence of this country," I found myself saying, even though I like to keep politics out of my conversations. He knew that and sensed that I was simply trying to get out of it.

"Aw, com'on, Mendoza," he said. "It's gonna be great. I wouldn't be inviting you if I didn't think you'd enjoy it. I know how hard you work and what your feelings are about this whole American and Puerto Rican thing, okay? Trust me. You'll never forget this. You're gonna be proud of me. Everybody's coming. The whole clan. You never seen my family together. I don't mean just my wife and kids, but my eight brothers and five sisters and their husbands and wives and their kids and my aunts and uncles and my parents and grandparents. And Mercedes' side of the family which is not as big but they're great. You gotta come."

I couldn't help myself in asking the next question.

"Where are you holding this party, Yankee Stadium?"

"That's funny," he said, and again laughed so loud my ear hurt. "No, nothing like that. You gotta come. My niece, Zoraida, can't wait to meet you. She's a big fan of yours. She's doing her, what do you call it, to become a doctor, but not a doctor."

"Her PhD? Her doctorate."

"That's it. She's doing it on your books. She's just starting out, so she wants to talk to you and get to know you."

All of a sudden I felt flattered, even though most of what I've written doesn't amount to much. I felt myself swayed by the upcoming adulation, but I truly wish I hadn't participated in what took place between early evening on the Fourth of July and some time around four o'clock in the morning when all hell broke loose on the elevated tracks near Coney Island.

"Where is she studying?" I said.

"Some college in Michigan," Barbosa answered. "I don't know. You can ask her yourself. Ralph'll pick you up about 6:30 on July 4th, okay?"

"All right," I said, suddenly experiencing a strange feeling of foreboding about the entire matter. "But I can't stay long."

"Don't worry," Barbosa said. "Once you get up there and the party starts you can decide that."

"What does that mean?"

Barbosa laughed and said he'd see me on the Fourth.

So on the Fourth of July I got ready. I put on white pants, polished to my white shoes, got out one of my *guayaberas*[4] and my panama hat and at 6:30 that afternoon Ralph Barbosa knocked on the door and down I went to one of my infrequent social activities.

I got into the car and off we went across the Willis Avenue Bridge into the Bronx. I asked him where we were going and he replied that his uncle had told him to keep it a surprise, but that it was up near Lehman College. I relaxed for a while, but still felt that feeling that something not quite right was about to take place. Some twenty minutes later we drove under the Woodlawn Avenue elevated line tracks and into the campus of Herbert H. Lehman College. Ralph parked the car, we got out and walked to a grassy area where a number of people were seated on blankets. Around them were boxes of food and drink, ice coolers, paper plates and cups, coffee urns and several other items that indicated we were to have a picnic.

I felt relaxed at once and as I was introduced to different members of the family I noticed that there were very few men. Out of the over 100 people gathered around several trees, most of them were women and children. I asked Ralph where I could find his uncle and I was informed that Barbosa was making final preparations. I was offered a beer, which I accepted gladly, was offered a beach chair which I also accepted, and then was introduced to Zoraida Barbosa, the PhD student, a lovely, articulate young woman with a keen intellect, and, unfortunately, a genuine interest in my work. So enraptured and flattered was I by her attention that more than an hour and a half passed. I then realized that the sun was going down and Barbosa still had not shown up. I once again began to worry.

Another half hour passed and now we were sitting in the dark and some of the younger children began to get restless. And then the word came that we were ready to move. "Move where?" I inquired. "It's all right, Mr. Mendoza," Zoraida said, taking my hand. "Just follow me." Such was her persuasiveness and her interest in me that I allowed her to take my hand and followed her as we crossed the grassy field. We walked for nearly a half mile until we were at the train yards. At that point I knew I was heading for a major catastrophe, but there did not seem to be any way of turning back.

I soon found out why the men had not been in attendance. I saw the plan clearly now. We were to descend into the train yards, a rather hazardous undertaking from the place where our crowd had stopped. The men, however, had constructed a staircase, complete with sturdy bannisters. This staircase went up over the wall and down some fifty feet into the floor of the train yard. I followed Zoraida and as we went I looked down on the nearly forty rails below, most of them with trains on them. This was the terminal of the Independent Subway System or IND as it is popularly known, a place where trains came to be cleaned and repaired or to lay up when they were not in use. Down we went and then guided by young men with flashlights

---

[4] a man's shirt usually made of fine thread, popular in Latino culture

we walked along, seemingly dangerously close to the ever present third rails until we arrived at an enclosure where a train had been parked. I suspected this was where trains were washed.

Again, utilizing a makeshift staircase I followed Zoraida as we climbed up into a train. Although the light of the flashlights being employed by the young men was sufficient for us to find our way, it was impossible to see what I had walked into. I was directed to a place on the train and asked to sit down. Expecting to find a hard surface when I sat down, I was surprised to find myself sinking into a plush armchair. Moments later I recognized Barbosa's voice asking if everyone was on board. Word came back that everyone indeed had boarded the train. Then quite suddenly the motors in the car were activated. I heard doors close and lights came on. I found myself in a typical New York Puerto Rican living room, complete with sofas, armchairs with covers, little tables with figurines, lamps, linoleum on the floor and curtains in the windows. I thought I would have a heart attack and began to get up from my chair, but at that moment the train began moving slowly out and a loud cheer went up.

I turned to Zoraida sitting on the arm of my chair and she patted my shoulder and said I shouldn't worry. A few moments later we were moving at fairly rapid rate and then the music came on, at first faintly but then as the volume was adjusted it was quite clear: Salsa, I don't know who, Machito, Tito Puente, Charlie Palmieri. I didn't care. This was outrageous. Moments later Barbosa came into our car and smiling from ear to ear greeted me.

"How do you like it?" he said, after I explained to him that my heart was nearly at the point of quitting. "It's pretty good, right? My nephew, Ernest, he's an interior decorator, did the whole thing. Wait till you see the rest of it. It's not a new train but it'll do."

I wanted to tell him that I had seen enough, but was too much in shock to protest. With an escort of his two brothers who, to my great surprise, were members of the police department undercover detective squad, we went forward as the train began picking up speed. I asked who was driving and Barbosa informed me that he had another nephew who was a motorman on the IRT Seventh Avenue line and he was doing the driving. From the living room car we moved forward into the next car, which was a control center laid out with tables, maps and computers. I was introduced to another nephew, a computer whiz working on his PhD in electral engineering. Several young people were busily working away plotting and programming, all of it very efficient. The next car, the lead one, was laid out as an executive office with a switchboard connecting the other cars by phone. There also were several television sets and radios, all tuned to the major channels and radio station. "We're gonna monitor everything that happens," Barbosa said, and introduced me to yet another nephew, an executive from AT&T, dressed in a business suit, seated at a big desk with wood paneling on the walls around him. Off to the side a young woman was transcribing from dictaphone onto an IBM Selectric. My shock was indescribable.

We retraced our steps through the train until we came out of the living room car into the bar car. How they had managed to get a thirty foot oak bar with matching wall length mirror on the train is beyond me, but there it was, stools riveted into the floor. I was introduced all around to the men and women at the bar, all of them relatives of Barbosa and all of them grinning from ear to ear about this adventure.

"I hope you're doing the right thing," I said.

"Don't worry, Mendoza," he said. "Everything's under control."

The next car was a kitchen with six different stoves, four refrigerators, two meat lockers, cutting boards, kitchen cabinets. Here I was introduced to Monsieur Pierre Barbosa, the chef for the Lancaster Hotel, on leave especially for this occasion. Dressed in white and wearing a tall chef's hat, he greeted me warmly and invited me to taste one of his sauces. I did so and found it quite agreeable, if somewhat tart. "Too tart?" he said. I nodded and he spoke rapidly in French to one of his assistants, another Barbosa nephew who moved directly to the sauce with several condiments.

In the next car there was a nursery with cribs and beds for the children and a medical staff headed by Dr. Elizabeth Barbosa, a niece who was a pediatrician in Philadelphia. There were also bathrooms for ladies and gentlemen in the next car. Two cars were devoted to dining tables with linen and candlesticks, each with its own piano. The last car was the most magnificent and modern dance establishment I've ever seen. The floor gleamed and there were lights beneath it and on the ceiling colored lights were going on and off and young people were dancing. "Our disco," Barbosa said, proudly. "With D.J. Mike, my son." His oldest son waved and Barbosa laughed. "I hope you know what you're doing," I said. "But I have to hand it to you. How did you do it?"

"This is a family, Mendoza," Barbosa said. "We'd do anything for each other."

Ten subway cars decked out for partying were moving now through the Bronx, making stops but not letting anyone on, the Latin music blaring from loud speakers above four of the central cars. Every stop we made, people laughed and slapped their thighs and began dancing and very few people seemed angry that they couldn't board the train. All of them pointed at the train. I asked Barbosa why they were pointing and he explained that the train was painted. He described it but it wasn't until the following morning when the escapade came to an abrupt end that I truly was able to see what he was talking about. Each of the cars had been sprayed a different color: orange, red, yellow, pink, green, several blues, white (I think that was the nursery) and the disco which was black and even had a neon sign with the letters *El Son de Barbosa*. All along the cars in huge graffiti letters each car said *The Barbosa Express* and each one, rather than having the Transit Authority seal had BTA or Barbosa Transit Authority on it. All of them were decorated with beautiful graffiti "pieces," as I learned these expressions were called when I was introduced to Tac 121, the master "writer," as these young men and women are called. Tac 121 was in reality Victor Barbosa, another nephew, studying graphic design at Boston University.

The party began in full and we kept moving through Manhattan and then into Brooklyn and the elevated tracks. Everyone had eaten by now and it was then that all hell began to break loose. It was now close to midnight. At this point one of the dining rooms was cleared and converted into a launching pad for a tremendous fire works display. I was introduced to yet another nephew, Larry Barbosa, who was a mechanical engineer. He had managed to restructure the roof of the car so that it folded and opened, allowing his brother, Bill, a member of Special Forces during the Vietnam War and a demolitions expert, to set up shop and begin firing colored rockets from the car so that as we made a wide turn before coming into the Coney Island terminal I could see the sky being lit up as the train made its way. The music was blaring and the rockets were going off in different directions so that one could see the beaches and the water in the light from the explosions.

I was exhausted and fell asleep while Zoraida was explaining her project and asking me very intricate questions about my work, details which I had forgotten with the passage of time. Two hours or so must have passed when I woke up to a great deal of shouting. I got up and went to the control car where Barbosa, dressed in his motorman's uniform, and some of his relatives were listening to news of the hijacking of a train, the announcers insinuating that the thieves had gotten the idea from the film "The Taking of Pelham 123." One of the television stations was maintaining continuous coverage with interviews of high officials of the Transit Authority, the Mayor, pedestrians, the police and sundry experts, who put forth a number of theories on why the people had commandeered the train. They even interviewed an art professor, a specialist on the graffiti culture, who explained that the creation of art on the trains was an expression of youths' dissatisfaction with the rapid rate at which information was disseminated and how difficult it was to keep up with changing developments. "Using a mode of transportation to display their art," he said, "obviously keeps that art moving forward at all times and ahead of change."

In another corner a couple of young men and women were monitoring the communications from the Transit Authority.

"We gotta a clear channel, Uncle Chu Chu," said one of the girls. "They wanna talk to somebody."

Barbosa sat down and spoke to some high official. I was surprised when the official asked Barbosa to identify himself and Barbosa did so, giving his name and his badge number. When they asked him what was happening, he explained how the hijackers had come to his house and kidnapped him, took him down to the train yards and forced him to drive the train or they would kill him.

"What do they want?" said the official.

"They wanna a clear track from here to the Bronx," Barbosa said. "And they want no cops around, otherwise they're gonna shoot everybody. They grabbed some women and children on the way and they look like they mean business."

"Can you identify them?"

"The women and children?"

"No, the perpetrators."

"Are you crazy or what!" shouted Barbosa, winking at me and the rest of the members of the family around him, most of whom were holding their sides to keep from laughing. "Whatta you wanna do, get me killed, or what? There's a guy holding a gun to my head and you want me to identify him?"

"Okay, okay," said the official. "I understand. Just keep your cool and do as they say. The Mayor wants to avoid any bloodshed. Do as they say. Where are you now?"

"Kings Highway," Barbosa said.

I was amazed. The train had gone to Coney Island, backed up, turned around and had made another trip to the end of the Bronx and back to Brooklyn. I looked above and saw news and police helicopters, following the train as it moved.

"Okay, we'll clear the tracks and no police," said the official. "Over and out."

"Roger, over and out," said Barbosa, clicking off the radio. He raised his hand and his nephew, leaning out of the motorman's compartment, waved, ducked back in, let go with three powerful blasts from the train whistle and then we were moving down the tracks at top speed with the music playing and the rockets going off and people dancing in every car.

"We did it, Mendoza," Barbosa said. "Son of a gun! We d-i-d-did it."

I was so tired I didn't care. All I wanted to do was go home and go to sleep. I went back in to the living room car and sat down again. When I woke up we were up in the Bronx and Barbosa's relatives were streaming out of the cars, carrying all their boxes and coolers with them. There were no policemen around. Zoraida Barbosa helped me out of the train and minutes later we were in Ralph's car. A half hour later I was in my apartment.

The next day there were pictures of Barbosa dressed in his uniform on the front pages of all the newspapers. The official story as it turned out was that graffiti artists had worked on the old train over a period of three or four weeks and then had kidnapped Barbosa to drive the train. Why they chose him was never revealed, but he emerged as a hero.

Unofficially, several people at the Transit Authority were convinced that Barbosa had had something to do with the "train hijacking."

A month later I was in Florindo's Bar and in walked Barbosa, happy as a lark. He bought me a beer and informed me that shortly after the train incident they had assigned him a new train and that in a year or so he was retiring. I congratulated him and told him that his niece had written again and that her dissertation on my work was going quite well. One thing still bothered me and I needed to find out.

"It doesn't matter," I said. "But who thought up the whole thing?"

"I thought up the idea, but it was my nephew Kevin, my oldest brother Joaquin's kid, who worked out the strategy and brought in all the electronic gear to tap into the MTA circuits and communication lines. He works for the Pentagon."

"He does what?!" I said, looking around behind me to make sure no one was listening.

"The Pentagon in Washington," Barbosa repeated.

"You're kidding?" I said.

"Nope," Barbosa said. "You wanna another beer."

"I don't think so," I said. "'I gotta be going."

"See you in the subway," said Barbosa and laughed.

I walked out into the late summer evening trying to understand what it all meant. By the time I reached my apartment I knew one thing for certain. I knew that the United States of America would have to pay for passing the Jones Act in 1917, giving the people automatic U.S. citizenship and allowing so many of them to enter their country.

As they say in the street: "What goes around, comes around."

Discussion Questions

1. What is the difference between the attitude of Barbosa and the narrator, Mendoza, about the relationship between the United States and Puerto Rico?

2. Explain what Mendoza means by his last comment in relation to the train ride he has just taken.

3. How is this story similar to Ana Castillo's *So Far from God* on page 35 both in structure and in the relationships among family members?

Abraham Rodriguez, Jr.

ABRAHAM RODRIGUEZ is a representative of the new generation of Puerto Rican-American authors. There is a span of thirty years between the publication of Piri Thomas's Down These Mean Streets *and Rodriguez's* Spidertown *(1993), and Rodriguez's brash attitude toward almost everything, including what he perceives as his predecessor's lack of involvement in the community, is reflected in his work. This young writer is not interested in understanding* why *Puerto Ricans are in the situation they are now, instead he attempts to come to grips with that situation.*

Rodriguez was born to Puerto Rican parents in the Bronx in 1961. He dropped out of high school at the age of sixteen, returning later to receive a G.E.D. He attended City College of New York for four years. His stories have appeared in several anthologies, and his collection of short stories, The Boy Without a Flag: Tales From the South Bronx, *was published in 1992. This opening story, perhaps reflecting the author's own rebelliousness, recounts a young high school student's refusal to salute the American flag. Triggered by his father's nationalistic comments, Rodriguez examines the ambivalence many Puerto Ricans feel as citizens of two distinct nations.*

The Boy Without a Flag

—To Ms. Linda Falcón, wherever she is

Swirls of dust danced in the beams of sunlight that came through the tall windows, the buzz of voices resounding in the stuffy auditorium. Mr. Rios stood by our Miss Colon, hovering as if waiting to catch her if she fell. His pale mouse features looked solemnly dutiful. He was a versatile man, doubling as English teacher and gym coach. He was only there because of Miss Colon's legs. She was wearing her neon pink nylons. Our favorite.

We tossed suspicious looks at the two of them. Miss Colon would smirk at Edwin and me, saying, "Hey, face front," but Mr. Rios would glare. I think he knew that we knew what he was after. We knew, because on Fridays, during our free period when we'd get to play records and eat stale pretzel sticks, we would see her way in the back by the tall windows, sitting up on a radiator like a schoolgirl. There would be a strange pinkness on her high cheekbones, and there was Mr. Rios, sitting beside her, playing with her hand. Her face, so thin and girlish, would blush. From then on, her eyes, very close together like a cartoon rendition of a beaver's, would avoid us.

Miss Colon was hardly discreet about her affairs. Edwin had first tipped me off about her love life after one of his lunchtime jaunts through the empty hallways. He would chase girls and toss wet bathroom napkins into classrooms where kids in the lower grades sat, trapped. He claimed to have seen Miss Colon slip into a steward's closet with Mr. Rios and to have heard all manner of sounds through the thick wooden door, which was locked (he tried it). He had told half the class before the day was out, the boys sniggering behind grimy hands, the girls shocked because Miss Colon was married, so married that she even brought the poor unfortunate in one morning as a kind of show-and-tell guest. He was an untidy dark-skinned Puerto Rican type in a colorful dashiki. He carried a paper bag that smelled like glue. His eyes seemed sleepy, his Afro an uncombed Brillo pad. He talked about protest marches, the sixties, the importance of an education. Then he embarrassed Miss Colon greatly by disappearing into the coat closet and falling asleep there. The girls, remembering him, softened their attitude toward her indiscretions, defending her violently. "Face it," one of them blurted out when Edwin began a new series of Miss Colon tales, "she married a bum and needs to find true love."

"She's a slut, and I'm gonna draw a comic book about her," Edwin said, hushing when she walked in through the door. That afternoon, he showed me the first sketches of what would later become a very popular comic book entitled "Slut At The Head Of The Class." Edwin could draw really well, but his stories were terrible, so I volunteered to do the writing. In no time at all, we had three issues circulating under desks and hidden in notebooks all over the school. Edwin secretly ran off close to a hundred copies on a copy machine in the main office after school. It always amazed me how copies of our comic kept popping up in the unlikeliest places. I saw them on radiators in the auditorium, on benches in the gym, tacked up on bulletin boards. There were even some in the teachers' lounge, which I spotted one day while running an errand for Miss Colon. Seeing it, however, in the hands of Miss Marti, the pig-faced assistant principal, nearly made me puke up my lunch. Good thing our names weren't on it.

It was a miracle no one snitched on us during the ensuing investigation, since only a blind fool couldn't see our involvement in the thing. No bloody purge followed, but there was enough fear in both of us to kill the desire to continue our publishing venture. Miss Marti, a woman with a battlefield face and constant odor of Chiclets, made a forceful threat about finding the culprits while holding up the second issue, the one with the hand-colored cover. No one moved. The auditorium grew silent. We meditated on the sound of a small plane flying by, its engines rattling the windows. I think we wished we were on it.

It was in the auditorium that the trouble first began. We had all settled into our seats, fidgeting like tiny burrowing animals, when there was a general call for quiet. Miss Marti, up on stage, had a stare that could make any squirming fool sweat. She was a gruff, nasty woman who never smiled without seeming sadistic.

Mr. Rios was at his spot beside Miss Colon, his hands clasped behind his back as if he needed to restrain them. He seemed to whisper to her. Soft, mushy things. Edwin would watch them from his seat beside me, giving me the details, his shiny face looking worried. He always seemed sweaty, his fingers kind of damp.

"I toldju, I saw um holdin hands," he said. "An now lookit him, he's whispering sweet shits inta huh ear."

He quieted down when he noticed Miss Marti's evil eye sweeping over us like a prison-camp searchlight. There was silence. In her best military bark, Miss Marti ordered everyone to stand. Two lone, pathetic kids, dragooned by some unseen force, slowly came down the center aisle, each bearing a huge flag on a thick wooden pole. All I could make out was that great star-spangled unfurling, twitching thing that looked like it would fall as it approached over all those bored young heads. The Puerto Rican flag walked beside it, looking smaller and less confident. It clung to its pole.

"The Pledge," Miss Marti roared, putting her hand over the spot where her heart was rumored to be.

That's when I heard my father talking.

He was sitting on his bed, yelling about Chile, about what the CIA had done there. I was standing opposite him in my dingy Pro Keds. I knew about politics. I was eleven when I read William Shirer's book on Hitler. I was ready.

"All this country does is abuse Hispanic nations," my father said, turning a page of his *Post,* "tie them down, make them dependent. It says democracy with one hand while it protects and feeds fascist dictatorships with the other." His eyes blazed with a strange fire. I sat on the bed, on part of his *Post,* transfixed by his oratorical mastery. He had mentioned political things before, but not like this, not with such fiery conviction. I thought maybe it had to do with my reading Shirer. Maybe he had seen me reading that fat book and figured I was ready for real politics.

Using the knowledge I gained from the book, I defended the Americans. What fascism was he talking about, anyway? I knew we had stopped Hitler. That was a big deal, something to be proud of.

"Come out of fairy-tale land," he said scornfully. "Do you know what imperialism is?"

I didn't really, no.

"Well, why don't you read about that? Why don't you read about *Juan Bosch*[1] and *Allende,*[2] men who died fighting imperialism? They stood up against American big business. You should read about that instead of this crap about Hitler."

"But I like reading about Hitler," I said, feeling a little spurned. I didn't even mention that my fascination with Adolf led to my writing a biography of him, a book report one hundred and fifty pages long. It got an A-plus. Miss Colon stapled it to the bulletin board right outside the classroom, where it was promptly stolen.

"So, what makes you want to be a writer?" Miss Colon asked me quietly one day, when Edwin and I, always the helpful ones, volunteered to assist her in getting the classroom spiffed up for a Halloween party.

"I don't know. I guess my father," I replied, fiddling with plastic pumpkins self-consciously while images of my father began parading through my mind.

When I think back to my earliest image of my father, it is one of him sitting behind a huge rented typewriter, his fingers clacking away. He was a frustrated poet, radio announcer, and even stage actor. He had sent for diplomas from fly-by-night companies. He took acting lessons, went into broadcasting, even ended up on the ground floor of what is now Spanish radio, but his family talked him out of all of it. "You should find yourself real work, something substantial," they said, so he did. He dropped all those dreams that were never encouraged by anyone else and got a job at a Nedick's on Third Avenue. My pop the counterman.

---

[1] Although Juan Domingo Bosch won the presidency in Santo Domingo in 1962 after years of opposing the dictator Trujillo, he was characterized as a communist sympathizer and overthrown by the army after seven months in office.   [2] Salvador Allende was the first socialist to be elected president of Chile in 1970.

Despite that, he kept writing. He recited his poetry into a huge reel-to-reel tape deck that he had, then he'd play it back and sit like a critic, brow furrowed, fingers stroking his lips. He would record strange sounds and play them back to me at outrageous speeds, until I believed that there were tiny people living inside the machine. I used to stand by him and watch him type, his black pompadour spilling over his forehead. There was energy pulsating all around him, and I wanted a part of it.

I was five years old when I first sat in his chair at the kitchen table and began pushing down keys, watching the letters magically appear on the page. I was entranced. My fascination with the typewriter began at that point. By the time I was ten, I was writing war stories, tales of pain and pathos culled from the piles of comic books I devoured. I wrote unreadable novels. With illustrations. My father wasn't impressed. I guess he was hard to impress. My terrific grades did not faze him, nor the fact that I was reading books as fat as milk crates. My unreadable novels piled up. I brought them to him at night to see if he would read them, but after a week of waiting I found them thrown in the bedroom closet, unread. I felt hurt and rejected, despite my mother's kind words. "He's just too busy to read them," she said to me one night when I mentioned it to her. He never brought them up, even when I quietly took them out of the closet one day or when he'd see me furiously hammering on one of his rented machines. I would tell him I wanted to be a writer, and he would smile sadly and pat my head, without a word.

"You have to find something serious to do with your life," he told me one night, after I had shown him my first play, eighty pages long. What was it I had read that got me into writing a play? Was it Arthur Miller? Oscar Wilde? I don't remember, but I recall my determination to write a truly marvelous play about combat because there didn't seem to be any around.

"This is fun as a hobby," my father said, "but you can't get serious about this." His demeanor spoke volumes, but I couldn't stop writing. Novels, I called them, starting a new one every three days. The world was a blank page waiting for my words to recreate it, while the real world remained cold and lonely. My schoolmates didn't understand any of it, and because of the fat books I carried around, I was held in some fear. After all, what kid in his right mind would read a book if it wasn't assigned? I was sick of kids coming up to me and saying, "Gaw, lookit tha fat book. Ya teacha make ya read tha?" (No, I'm just reading it.) The kids would look at me as if I had just crawled out of a sewer. "Ya crazy, man." My father seemed to share that opinion. Only my teachers understood and encouraged my reading, but my father seemed to want something else from me.

Now, he treated me like an idiot for not knowing what imperialism was. He berated my books and one night handed me a copy of a book about *Albizu Campos,*[3] the Puerto Rican revolutionary. I read it through in two sittings.

"Some of it seems true," I said.

"Some of it?" my father asked incredulously. "After what they did to him, you can sit there and act like a Yankee flag-waver?"

---

[3] Born at the close of the nineteenth century, Albizu Campos fought against the annexation of Puerto Rico to the United States arguing that it would destroy Puerto Rican identity. Because of this, he is considered as a symbol of liberty by many Puerto Ricans.

I watched that Yankee flag making its way up to the stage over indifferent heads, my father's scowling face haunting me, his words resounding in my head.

"Let me tell you something," my father sneered. "In school, all they do is talk about George Washington, right? The first president? The father of democracy? Well, he had slaves. We had our own Washington, and ours had real teeth."

As Old Glory reached the stage, a general clatter ensued.

"We had our own revolution," my father said, "and the United States crushed it with the flick of a pinkie."

Miss Marti barked her royal command. Everyone rose up to salute the flag.

Except me. I didn't get up. I sat in my creaking seat, hands on my knees. A girl behind me tapped me on the back. "Come on, stupid, get up." There was a trace of concern in her voice. I didn't move.

Miss Colon appeared. She leaned over, shaking me gently. "Are you sick? Are you okay?" Her soft hair fell over my neck like a blanket.

"No," I replied.

"What's wrong?" she asked, her face growing stern. I was beginning to feel claustrophobic, what with everyone standing all around me, bodies like walls. My friend Edwin, hand on his heart, watched from the corner of his eye. He almost looked envious, as if he wished he had thought of it. Murmuring voices around me began reciting the Pledge while Mr. Rios appeared, commandingly grabbing me by the shoulder and pulling me out of my seat into the aisle. Miss Colon was beside him, looking a little apprehensive.

"What is wrong with you?" he asked angrily. "You know you're supposed to stand up for the Pledge! Are you religious?"

"No," I said.

"Then what?"

"I'm not saluting that flag," I said.

"What?"

"I said, I'm not saluting that flag."

"Why the . . . ?" He calmed himself; a look of concern flashed over Miss Colon's face. "Why not?"

"Because I'm Puerto Rican. I ain't no American. And I'm not no Yankee flag-waver."

"You're supposed to salute the flag," he said angrily, shoving one of his fat fingers in my face. "You're not supposed to make up your own mind about it. You're supposed to do as you are told."

"I thought I was free," I said, looking at him and at Miss Colon.

"You are," Miss Colon said feebly. "That's why you should salute the flag."

"But shouldn't I do what I feel is right?"

"You should do what you are told!" Mr. Rios yelled into my face. "I'm not playing no games with you, mister. You hear that music? That's the anthem. Now you go stand over there and put your hand over your heart." He made as if to grab my hand, but I pulled away.

"No!" I said sharply. "I'm not saluting that crummy flag! And you can't make me, either. There's nothing you can do about it."

"Oh yeah?" Mr. Rios roared. "We'll see about that!"

"Have you gone crazy?" Miss Colon asked as he led me away by the arm, down the hallway, where I could still hear the strains of the anthem. He walked me briskly into the principal's office and stuck me in a corner.

"You stand there for the rest of the day and see how you feel about it," he said viciously. "Don't you even think of moving from that spot!"

I stood there for close to two hours or so. The principal came and went, not even saying hi or hey or anything, as if finding kids in the corners of his office was a common occurrence. I could hear him talking on the phone, scribbling on pads, talking to his secretary. At, one point I heard Mr. Rios outside in the main office.

"Some smart-ass. I stuck him in the corner. Thinks he can pull that shit. The kid's got no respect, man. I should get the chance to teach him some."

"Children today have no respect," I heard Miss Marti's reptile voice say as she approached, heels clacking like gunshots. "It has to be forced upon them."

She was in the room. She didn't say a word to the principal, who was on the phone. She walked right over to me. I could hear my heart beating in my ears as her shadow fell over me. Godzilla over Tokyo.

"Well, have you learned your lesson yet?" she asked, turning me from the wall with a finger on my shoulder. I stared at her without replying. My face burned, red hot. I hated it.

"You think you're pretty important, don't you? Well, let me tell you, you're nothing. You're not worth a damn. You're just a snotty-nosed little kid with a lot of stupid ideas." Her eyes bored holes through me, searing my flesh. I felt as if I were going to cry. I fought the urge. Tears rolled down my face anyway. They made her smile, her chapped lips twisting upwards like the mouth of a lizard.

"See? You're a little baby. You don't know anything, but you'd better learn your place." She pointed a finger in my face.

"You do as you're told if you don't want big trouble. Now go back to class."

Her eyes continued to stab at me. I looked past her and saw Edwin waiting by the office door for me. I walked past her, wiping at my face. I could feel her eyes on me still, even as we walked up the stairs to the classroom. It was close to three already, and the skies outside the grated windows were cloudy.

"Man," Edwin said to me as we reached our floor, "I think you're crazy."

The classroom was abuzz with activity when I got there. Kids were chattering, getting their windbreakers from the closet, slamming their chairs up on their desks, filled with the euphoria of soon-home. I walked quietly over to my desk and took out my books. The other kids looked at me as if I were a ghost.

I went through the motions like a robot. When we got downstairs to the door, Miss Colon, dismissing the class, pulled me aside, her face compassionate and warm. She squeezed my hand.

"Are you okay?"

I nodded.

"That was a really crazy stunt there. Where did you get such an idea?"

I stared at her black flats. She was wearing tan panty hose and a black miniskirt. I saw Mr. Rios approaching with his class.

"I have to go," I said, and split, running into the frigid breezes and the silver sunshine.

At home, I lay on the floor of our living room, tapping my open notebook with the tip of my pen while the Beatles blared from my father's stereo. I felt humiliated and alone. Miss Marti's reptile face kept appearing in my notebook, her voice intoning, "Let me tell you, you're nothing." Yeah, right. Just what horrible hole did she crawl out of? Were those people really Puerto Ricans? Why should a Puerto Rican salute an American flag?

I put the question to my father, strolling into his bedroom, a tiny M-1 rifle that belonged to my G.I. Joe strapped to my thumb.

"Why?" he asked, loosening the reading glasses that were perched on his nose, his newspaper sprawled open on the bed before him, his cigarette streaming blue smoke. "Because we are owned, like cattle. And because nobody has any pride in their culture to stand up for it."

I pondered those words, feeling as if I were being encouraged, but I didn't dare tell him. I wanted to believe what I had done was a brave and noble thing, but somehow I feared his reaction. I never could impress him with my grades, or my writing. This flag thing would probably upset him. Maybe he, too, would think I was crazy, disrespectful, a "smart-ass" who didn't know his place. I feared that, feared my father saying to me, in a reptile voice, "Let me tell you, you're nothing."

I suited up my G.I. Joe for combat, slipping on his helmet, strapping on his field pack. I fixed the bayonet to his rifle, sticking it in his clutching hands so he seemed ready to fire. "A man's gotta do what a man's gotta do." Was that John Wayne? I don't know who it was, but I did what I had to do, still not telling my father. The following week, in the auditorium, I did it again. This time, everyone noticed. The whole place fell into a weird hush as Mr. Rios screamed at me.

I ended up in my corner again, this time getting a prolonged, pensive stare from the principal before I was made to stare at the wall for two more hours. My mind zoomed past my surroundings. In one strange vision, I saw my crony Edwin climbing up Miss Colon's curvy legs, giving me every detail of what he saw.

"Why?" Miss Colon asked frantically. "This time you don't leave, until you tell me why." She was holding me by the arm, masses of kids flying by, happy blurs that faded into the sunlight outside the door.

"Because I'm Puerto Rican, not American," I blurted out in a weary torrent. "That makes sense, don't it?"

"So am I," she said, "but we're in America!" She smiled. "Don't you think you could make some kind of compromise?" she tilted her head to one side and said, "Aw, c'mon," in a little-girl whisper.

"What about standing up for what you believe in? Doesn't that matter? You used to talk to us about Kent State and protesting. You said those kids died because they believed in freedom, right? Well, I feel like them now. I wanna make a stand."

She sighed with evident aggravation. She caressed my hair. For a moment, I thought she was going to kiss me. She was going to say something, but just as her pretty lips parted, I caught Mr. Rios approaching.

"I don't wanna see him," I said, pulling away.

"No, wait," she said gently.

"He's gonna deck me," I said to her.

"No, he's not," Miss Colon said, as if challenging him, her eyes taking him in as he stood beside her.

"No, I'm not," he said. "Listen here. Miss Colon was talking to me about you, and I agree with her." He looked like a nervous little boy in front of the class, making his report. "You have a lot of guts. Still, there are rules here. I'm willing to make a deal with you. You go home and think about this. Tomorrow I'll come see you." I looked at him skeptically, and he added, "to talk."

"I'm not changing my mind," I said. Miss Colon exhaled painfully.

"If you don't, it's out of my hands." He frowned and looked at her. She shook her head, as if she were upset with him.

I re-read the book about Albizu. I didn't sleep a wink that night. I didn't tell my father a word, even though I almost burst from the effort. At night, alone in my bed, images attacked me, I saw Miss Marti and Mr. Rios debating Albizu Campos. I saw him in a wheelchair with a flag draped over his body like a holy robe. They would not do that to me. They were bound to break me the way Albizu was broken, not by young smiling American troops bearing chocolate bars, but by conniving, double-dealing, self-serving Puerto Rican landowners and their ilk, who dared say they were the future. They spoke of dignity and democracy while teaching Puerto Ricans how to cling to the great coat of that powerful northern neighbor. Puerto Rico, the shining star, the great lap dog of the Caribbean. I saw my father, the Nationalist hero, screaming from his podium, his great oration stirring everyone around him to acts of bravery. There was a shining arrogance in his eyes as he stared out over the sea of faces mouthing his name, a sparkling audacity that invited and incited. There didn't seem to be fear anywhere in him, only the urge to rush to the attack, with his arm band and revolutionary tunic. I stared up at him, transfixed. I stood by the podium, his personal adjutant, while his voice rang through the stadium. "We are not, nor will we ever be, Yankee flag-wavers!" The roar that followed drowned out the whole world.

The following day, I sat in my seat, ignoring Miss Colon as she neatly drew triangles on the board with the help of plastic stencils. She was using colored chalk, her favorite. Edwin, sitting beside me, was beaning girls with spitballs that he fired through his hollowed-out Bic pen. They didn't cry out. They simply enlisted the help of a girl named Gloria who sat a few desks behind him. She very skillfully nailed him with a thick wad of gum. It stayed in his hair until Edwin finally went running to Miss Colon. She used her huge teacher's scissors. I couldn't stand it. They all seemed trapped in a world of trivial things, while I swam in a mire of oppression. I walked through lunch as if in a trance, a prisoner on death row waiting for the heavy steps of his executioners. I watched Edwin lick at his regulation cafeteria ice cream, sandwiched between two sheets of paper. I was once like him, laughing and joking, lining up for a stickball game in the yard without a care. Now it all seemed lost to me, as if my youth had been burned out of me by a book.

Shortly after lunch, Mr. Rios appeared. He talked to Miss Colon for a while by the door as the room filled with a bubbling murmur. Then, he motioned for me. I walked through the sudden silence as if in slow motion.

"Well," he said to me as I stood in the cool hallway, "have you thought about this?"

"Yeah," I said, once again seeing my father on the podium, his voice thundering.

"And?"

"I'm not saluting that flag."

Miss Colon fell against the door jamb as if exhausted. Exasperation passed over Mr. Rios' rodent features.

"I thought you said you'd think about it," he thundered.

"I did. I decided I was right."

"*You* were right?" Mr. Rios was losing his patience. I stood calmly by the wall.

"I told you," Miss Colon whispered to him.

"Listen," he said, ignoring her, "have you heard of the story of the man who had no country?"

I stared at him.

"Well? Have you?"

"No," I answered sharply; his mouse eyes almost crossed with anger at my insolence. "Some stupid fairy tale ain't gonna change my mind anyway. You're treating me like I'm stupid, and I'm not."

"Stop acting like you're some mature adult! You're not. You're just a puny kid."

"Well, this puny kid still ain't gonna salute that flag."

"You were born here," Miss Colon interjected patiently, trying to calm us both down. Don't you think you at least owe this country some respect? At least?"

"I had no choice about where I was born. And I was born poor."

"So what?" Mr. Rios screamed. "There are plenty of poor people who respect the flag. Look around you, dammit! You see any rich people here? I'm not rich either!" He tugged on my arm. "This country takes care of Puerto Rico, don't you see that? Don't you know anything about politics?"

"Do you know what imperialism is?"

The two of them stared at each other.

"I don't believe you," Mr. Rios murmured.

"Puerto Rico is a colony," I said, a direct quote of Albizu's. "Why I gotta respect that?"

Miss Colon stared at me with her black saucer eyes, a slight trace of a grin on her features. It encouraged me. In that one moment, I felt strong, suddenly aware of my territory and my knowledge of it. I no longer felt like a boy but some kind of soldier, my bayonet stained with the blood of my enemy. There was no doubt about it. Mr. Rios was the enemy, and I was beating him. The more he tried to treat me like a child, the more defiant I became, his arguments falling like twisted armor. He shut his eyes and pressed the bridge of his nose.

"You're out of my hands," he said.

Miss Colon gave me a sympathetic look before she vanished into the classroom again. Mr. Rios led me downstairs without another word. His face was completely red. I expected to be put in my corner again, but this time Mr. Rios sat me down in the leather chair facing the principal's desk. He stepped outside, and I could hear the familiar clack-clack that could only belong to Miss Marti's reptile legs. They were talking in whispers. I expected her to come in at any moment, but the principal walked in instead. He came in quietly, holding a folder in his hand. His soft brown eyes and beard made him look compassionate, rounded cheeks making him seem friendly. His desk plate solemnly stated: Mr. Sepulveda, PRINCIPAL. He fell into his seat rather unceremoniously, opened the folder, and crossed his hands over it.

'Well, well, well," he said softly, with a tight-lipped grin. "You've created quite a stir, young man." It sounded to me like movie dialogue.

"First of all, let me say I know about you. I have your record right here, and everything in it is very impressive. Good grades, good attitude, your teachers all have adored you. But I wonder if maybe this hasn't gone to your head? Because everything is going for you here, and you're throwing it all away."

He leaned back in his chair. "We have rules, all of us. There are rules even I must live by. People who don't obey them get disciplined. This will all go on your record, and a pretty good one you've had so far. Why ruin it? This'll follow you for life. You don't want to end up losing a good job opportunity in government or in the armed forces because as a child you indulged your imagination and refused to salute the flag? I know you can't see how childish it all is now, but you must see it, and because you're smarter than most, I'll put it to you in terms you can understand.

"To me, this is a simple case of rules and regulations. Someday, when you're older," he paused here, obviously amused by the sound of his own voice, "you can go to rallies and protest marches and express your rebellious tendencies. But right now, you are a minor, under this school's jurisdiction. That means you follow the rules, no matter what you think of them. You can join the Young Lords later."

I stared at him, overwhelmed by his huge desk, his pompous mannerisms and status. I would agree with everything, I felt, and then, the following week, I would refuse once again. I would right him then, even though he hadn't tried to humiliate me or insult my intelligence. I would continue to fight, until I. . .

"I spoke with your father," he said.

I started. "My father?" Vague images and hopes flared through my mind briefly.

"Yes. I talked to him at length. He agrees with me that you've gotten a little out of hand."

My blood reversed direction in my veins. I felt as if I were going to collapse. I gripped the armrests of my chair. There was no way this could be true, no way at all! My father was supposed to ride in like the cavalry, not abandon me to the enemy! I pressed my wet eyes with my fingers. It must be a lie.

"He blames himself for your behavior," the principal said. "He's already here," Mr. Rios said from the door, motioning my father inside. Seeing him wearing his black weather-beaten trench coat almost asphyxiated me. His eyes, red with concern, pulled at me painfully. He came over to me first while the principal rose slightly, as if greeting a head of state. There was a look of dread on my father's face, as he looked at me. He seemed utterly lost.

"Mr. Sepulveda," he said, "I never thought a thing like this could happen. My wife and I try to bring him up right. We encourage him to read and write and everything. But you know, this is a shock."

"It's not that terrible, Mr. Rodriguez. You've done very well with him, he's an intelligent boy. He just needs to learn how important obedience is."

"Yes," my father said, turning to me, "yes, you have to obey the rules. You can't do this. It's wrong." He looked at me grimly, as if working on a math problem. One of his hands caressed my head.

There were more words, in Spanish now, but I didn't hear them. I felt like I was falling down a hole. My father, my creator, renouncing his creation, repentant. Not an ounce of him seemed prepared to stand up for me, to shield me from attack. My tears made all the faces around me melt.

"So you see," the principal said to me as I rose, my father clutching me to him, "if you ever do this again, you will be hurting your father as well as yourself."

I hated myself. I wiped at my face desperately, trying not to make a spectacle of myself. I was just a kid, a tiny kid. Who in the hell did I think I was? I'd have to wait until I was older, like my father, in order to have "convictions."

"I don't want to see you in here again, okay?" the principal said, sternly. I nodded dumbly, my father's arm around me as he escorted me through the front office to the door that led to the hallway, where a multitude of children's voices echoed up and down its length like tolling bells.

"Are you crazy?" my father half-whispered to me in Spanish as we stood there. "Do you know how embarrassing this all is? I didn't think you were this stupid. Don't you know anything about dignity, about respect? How could you make a spectacle of yourself? Now you make us all look stupid."

He quieted down as Mr. Rios came over to take me back to class. My father gave me a squeeze and told me he'd see me at home. Then, I walked with a somber Mr. Rios, who oddly wrapped an arm around me all the way back to the classroom.

"Here you go," he said softly as I entered the classroom, and everything fell quiet. I stepped in and walked to my seat without looking at anyone. My cheeks were still damp, my eyes red. I looked like I had been tortured. Edwin stared at me, then he pressed my hand under the table.

"I thought you were dead," he whispered.

Miss Colon threw me worried glances all through the remainder of the class. I wasn't paying attention. I took out my notebook, but my strength ebbed away. I just put my head on the desk and shut my eyes, reliving my father's betrayal. If what I did was so bad, why did I feel more ashamed of him than I did of myself? His words, once so rich and vibrant, now fell to the floor, leaves from a dead tree.

At the end of the class, Miss Colon ordered me to stay after school. She got Mr. Rios to take the class down along with his, and she stayed with me in the darkened room. She shut the door on all the exuberant hallway noise and sat down on Edwin's desk, beside me, her black pumps on his seat.

"Are you okay?" she asked softly, grasping my arm. I told her everything, especially about my father's betrayal. I thought he would be the cavalry, but he was just a coward.

"Tss. Don't be so hard on your father," she said. "He's only trying to do what's best for you."

"And how's this the best for me?" I asked, my voice growing hoarse with hurt.

"I know it's hard for you to understand, but he really was trying to take care of you."

I stared at the blackboard.

"He doesn't understand me," I said, wiping my eyes.

"You'll forget," she whispered.

"No, I won't. I'll remember every time I see that flag. I'll see it and think, 'My father doesn't understand me.'"

Miss Colon sighed deeply. Her fingers were warm on my head, stroking my hair. She gave me a kiss on the cheek. She walked me downstairs, pausing by the doorway. Scores of screaming, laughing kids brushed past us.

"If it's any consolation, I'm on your side," she said, squeezing my arm. I smiled at her, warmth spreading through me. "Go home and listen to the Beatles," she added with a grin.

I stepped out into the sunshine, came down the white stone steps, and stood on the sidewalk. I stared at the towering school building, white and perfect in the sun, indomitable. Across the street, the dingy row of tattered uneven tenements where I lived. I thought of my father. Her words made me feel sorry for him, but I felt sorrier for myself. I couldn't understand back then about a father's love and what a father might give to insure his son safe transit. He had already navigated treacherous waters and now couldn't have me rock the boat. I still had to learn that he had made peace with The Enemy, that The Enemy was already in us. Like the flag I must salute, we were inseparable, yet his compromise made me feel ashamed and defeated. Then I knew I had to find my own peace, away from the bondage of obedience. I had to accept that flag, and my father, someone I would love forever, even if at times to my young, feeble mind he seemed a little imperfect.

Discussion Questions

1. How do the father's comments about Puerto Rico affect the actions and beliefs of his son? Is there a difference at the end of the story between father and son regarding those beliefs?
2. What does the boy realize at the conclusion of the story about his dual identity? Does he come to grips with that duality?
3. In what way is the conflict the boy attempts to resolve similar to that of the speaker in Gustavo Pérez-Firmat's "Bilingual Blues" on page 353?
4. How is the conflict the boy confronts similar to that of Guálinto in Américo Paredes's *George Washington Goméz* on page 81?

Jesús Colón

JESÚS COLÓN *was born in the central mountainous town of Cayey, Puerto Rico, in 1901. He arrived in the United States as a stowaway in 1918. Lacking a formal education, Colón was nevertheless immersed in a literary milieu. In addition to his career as a newspaperman, Colón had other jobs to help meet his financial obligations. These included dishwasher, clerk, and longshoreman. He worked as a correspondent for newspapers in Puerto Rico as well as ones in the New York area. His keen ear allowed him to vividly re-create the sounds of the street in his newfound home.*

Colón's contribution to Puerto Rican-American literature cannot be overstated. He lived in and wrote of a time in history when the first immigrants from the island where establishing themselves in an alien world. His book, A Puerto Rican in New York and Other Sketches, *captures the voices of many of these newly arrived citizens. What distinguishes this book from others being published during the 1950s is that it was written in English. In fact, the book is the first of its kind; it is the first book-length English language depiction of Puerto Ricans in New York. Because of this, it marks a transition from the literature of Puerto Ricans who were more concerned with what they left behind than what their future held. Thus, most, if not all, of the Puerto Rican-American writers represented in this anthology owe him a tremendous debt.*

From A Puerto Rican in New York and Other Sketches

A Voice Through the Window

When I was a boy in Cayey, my hometown in Puerto Rico, we lived in a house in back of which was a big cigar factory. Every morning, starting around ten, a clear, strong voice coming from the big factory came through my window. It had a tinge of the oratorical in it.

One morning, my boyish curiosity was aroused beyond endurance. I went through the backyard to one of the ground floor windows of the cigar factory. There were about one hundred and fifty cigarmakers, each one sitting in front of tables that looked like old-fashioned rolltop desks, covered with all kinds of tobacco leaves. The cigarmakers with their heads bent over their work listened intently. In the vast hall of the factory, I looked for the source of the voice to which they were listening. There was a man sitting on a chair on a platform. The platform had a thin wooden railing around it, except for the opening where a short, steep and narrow wooden staircase connected the platform with the floor below.

Later, upon inquiring, I came to know that the man up on the platform was responsible for the clear, strong voice. He was called "El Lector"—the Reader. His job was to read to the cigarmakers while they were rolling cigars. The workers paid fifteen to twenty-five cents per week each to the reader. In the morning, the reader used to read the daily paper and some working class weeklies or monthlies that were published or received from abroad. In the afternoon he would read from a novel by Zola, Balzac, Hugo, or from a book by Kropotkin, Malatesta or Karl Marx. Famous speeches like Castelar's or Spanish classical novels like Cervantes' *Don Quixote* were also read aloud by "El Lector."

So you were amazed by the phenomenon of cigarmakers who hardly knew how to read and write, discussing books like Zola's *Germinal,* Balzac's *Pere Goriot,* or Kropotkin's *Fields, Factories and Workshops,* during the mild Puerto Rican evenings in the public square.

Yes, the Reader was a very important person in the cigar factory and in the general life of the cigarmakers. He was usually something of an orator and an actor ready to strike a pose at the least provocation. So through my early boyhood this voice of the Reader, coming defiant and resonant from the cigar factory through my window, used to enchant and instruct me in the style of these great French and Spanish novelists and the ideas of their various schools of thought. Frankly speaking, at that tender age I rather preferred the straight stories of Zola or Balzac to the ideological architecture of the thinkers, most of whose concepts went over my head.

But one thing is certain, my ear got accustomed to hearing the repetition of certain words and phrases which, as I grew up, I came to understand more clearly.

Sometimes, when I am in a meditative mood, I just close my eyes and isolate myself from my surroundings. Then I transport myself to my childhood in Puerto Rico. I can see that window and listen to that voice reading from the adventures of *Don Quixote* or the miseries and persecution suffered by Jean Valjean, books and characters that will be remembered many years after the latest "whodunit" has been read and forgotten.

The Cigar Factory Reader was something more. He was usually connected with the socialist movement. He was the town orator for the baptismal parties, weddings, ceremonies or eulogies when death took away one of the more or less prominent persons in the town. Sometimes the Reader joined the cigarmakers' conversations at one of the benches in the public square. On such occasions, everybody was waiting for any pearl of wisdom that might drop from his mouth. This would be favorably compared with the latest harangue from our town mayor or the sermon of last Sunday given by the priest at the Catholic church with the rose-colored dome, where most of us had been baptized.

Some of these readers became very famous throughout the cigar-manufacturing towns of Puerto Rico. There was one who at the very end of the days work used to close the book he was reading and continue to "read"' from memory to the workers. Some of the cigarmakers had taken the trouble of bringing a copy of the book to work in order to follow the reader from his closed book just to see if he left something out. The reader never did. These feats of memory encouraged many workers and even boys like myself to try memorizing well-known passages like the introductory paragraph of *Don Quixote,* with which we started to like and then to love literature and the enlightened thinkers of mankind.

I still hear this voice through the window of my childhood. Sometimes I listen to the same themes today. Sometimes in Spanish, most of the time in English, from the halls and squares of this New York of ours. Sometimes this voice comes through the radio, from Europe and Asia, crystallized now in pamphlets and books that have shaken the world to its foundations. But always the theme is the same, the same as the readers from the cigarmaker's factory, coming to my home in my childhood's past.

Always the same voice of the reader of my boyhood memories. But now clearer, stronger, surer, devoid of rhetoric, based on facts and history.

This voice seems to be saying now, as it said through the reader's mouth in my distant childhood: The confusions, misunderstandings, disillusions, defections and momentary defeats will be overcome. In the end, if we keep on struggling and learning from struggle, the workers and their allies will win all over the world.

Discussion Questions

1. Based on this excerpt, what can we conclude regarding the role of morality in literature?

2. Trace the development of the narrator from boyhood to maturity in relation to the reader he speaks of? What role does memory play in this development?

3. Compare the memories of Puerto Rico that the speaker describes with those of Lourdes in Cristina Garcia's *Dreaming in Cuban* on page 181.

Poetry

Miguel Algarin

MIGUEL ALGARIN was born in Santurce, Puerto Rico in 1941, and moved to New York with his family in the early 1950s. He grew up in the city's Lower East Side, a community that was rapidly growing with Puerto Rican immigrants. He received a B.A. from the University of Wisconsin in 1963, an M.A. from Pennsylvania State in 1965, and did doctoral work at Rutgers University. His poetry has been published in several books: Mongo Affair *(1978),* On Call *(1980),* Body Bee Calling from the XXI Century *(1982),* Time's Now/Ya Es Tiempo *(1984), and* Love is Hard Work *(1997).*

Drawing his inspiration from the oral tradition of poetry popular in the Puerto Rican countryside, Algarin began honing his craft during the late sixties and early seventies in New York City. Adopting the name Nuyorican, *as a reference both to the city and to their Puerto Rican origins, Algarin and other New York Puerto Rican writers were part of the Beat Generation which produced such figures as Allen Ginsberg and Jack Kerouac. The* Nuyorican *poets drew their experiences, as did the Beat poets, from bohemian city life. Unlike the poets of the Beat era, however, the* Nuyorican *writers were truly living a life of deprivation as the children of immigrants who spoke little English and were placed at the lowest rung of the socioeconomic ladder. Their work flourished, however, and eventually Algarin opened the Nuyorican Poets Café on East Sixth Street. Aided by popular figures as the playwright Amiri Baraka and the poet William Burroughs, the café prospered and now holds weekly poetry competitions which are broadcast to Tokyo, Chicago, and San Francisco.*

Algarin's latest book of poetry, Love is Hard Work, *is composed of four sections. The first, titled "Nuyorican Angels," consists of the speaker's re-creation of the voices of the street as angelic sounds. Thus, Mitch, as the poet calls himself, connects to everything he sees and hears in Whitman–like fashion. The second poem, "August 21," is taken from the third and pivotal section of the book. In it, the streets of* Loisaida *(a derivation of Lower East Side) come alive, as the poet chronicles daily events.*

Nuyorican Angel

Lines of fluid fire
shoot from the index finger
of the first angel,
his eyes penetrate emotional lead,
parting flesh woven time.
No, this Angel is not soft light—
he moves in compulsive, phlegmatic,
thick, muscular thrusts,
he enters pulsating,
kicking the mind apart,
rousing violent torrents
of liberating, sensual blood flows.
Swift, anxious yearning
fuels his desire to enter
the temple of live bodies,
no membrane can stop
his arrogant parting of the skin,
he scorches living flesh.

August 21

4:30 A.M. Lina calls,
"I've been raped, I called the police
now I'm calling you."
Coming to, I hear her cry and talk
till the police arrive and take her to the hospital
I didn't get an address from Lina so I sat and thought
and felt the ordeal, from house to precinct,
to hospital for penicillin
and the semen sample the rape squad
requires for charges to stick.
Called her at 9:30 in the morning,
she'd been back from the hospital since 8:30 A.M.,
penetration against desire,
sensual betrayal spewing unwanted seeds,
prying, wedging, invading her body.
Called Lina back at 2:30 P.M., Nellie was there
I was glad that she got there
but felt vulnerable for not getting to her first,
hung up and went to Brooklyn to fill Lina's prescription.

She was already walking down the street with Nellie
to get the anti-pregnancy pills herself,
she's walking slower today
as if to shed the hurt in her.

Discussion Questions

1. If the speaker in "Nuyorican Angel" is the poet, explain his desire to enter the body of his listeners in "rousing violent torrents."

2. Both poems describe violence in distinctive ways. Describe the violence described in the second poem and explain the simile in the last line.

3. Compare "August 21" to Jack Agüeros's "Sonnet: Waiting in Tompkins Square Park" on page 452. How are the descriptions of life on the streets of New York similar? Which of the poems assigns blame for that lifestyle? Explain.

Sandra Maria Esteves

SANDRA MARIA ESTEVES was born in the Bronx, New York, in 1948. Sheltered by her mother and her aunt who cared for her while her mother worked, Esteves was sent to a Catholic school for seven years. There, she was not allowed to speak the Spanish she would hear every weekend on her trips home. This duality of language caused Esteves to become more sensitive to the nuances of the spoken and written word, an ability which is reflected in her work.

She completed a B.F.A. at the Pratt Institute in Brooklyn, New York, and spent most of the decade of the 1970s writing, painting, and reading her work alongside others of her ilk such as poets Miguel Algarin and Tato Laviera, and artists like Jorge Soto and Marcos Dimas. Her awards include a New York State Creative Artists Public Service Fellowship for Poetry in 1980, and a Poetry Fellowship by the New York Foundation for the Arts in 1985. Her published volumes of poetry include Yerba Buena *(1981), which was selected as Best Small Press Publication that year,* Tropical Rains: A Bilingual Downpour *(1984), and* Bluestown Mockingbird Mambo *(1990).*

In the Beginning

In the beginning was the sound
Like the universe exploding
It came, took form, gave life
And was called Conga

And Conga said:
Let there be night and day
And was born el *Quinto*[1] y el *Bajo*[2]

And Quinto said: Give me female
There came *Campana*[3]
And Bajo said: Give me son
There came *Bongoses*[4]

They merged produced force
Maracas[5] y *Claves*[6]
Chequere[7] y *Timbales*[8]

¡Qué viva la música!
So it was written
On the skin of the drum

¡Qué viva la gente!
So it was written
In the hearts of the people

¡Qué viva Raza!

So it is written.

A la Mujer Borrinqueña

My name is Maria Christina
I am a Puerto Rican woman born in el barrio

Our men . . . they call me *negra*[1] because they love me
and in turn I teach them to be strong

I respect their ways
inherited from our proud ancestors
I do not tease them with eye catching clothes

---

[1] *quinto*: a guitar-like instrument with five strings   [2] *bajo*: bass   [3] *campana*: triangle
[4] *bongoses*: drums   [5] *maracas*: gourds with seeds that rattle   [6] *clave*: similar to a harpsichord
[7] *chequere*: an instrument made of a dried gourd wrapped with beads   [8] *timbales*: a percussion
instrument

---

[1] black woman

I do not sleep with their brothers and cousins
although I've been told that this is a liberal society
do not poison their bellies with instant chemical foods
our table holds food from earth and sun

My name is Maria Christina
I speak two languages broken into each other
but my heart speaks the language of people
born in oppression

I do not complain about cooking for my family
because *abuela*[2] taught me that woman is the master of fire
I do not complain about nursing my children
because I determine the direction of their values

I am the mother of a new age of warriors
I am the child of a race of slaves
I teach my children how to respect their bodies
so they will not o.d. under the stairway's shadow of shame
I teach my children to read and develop their minds
so they will understand the reality of oppression
I teach them with discipline . . . and love
so they will become strong and full of life

My eyes reflect the pain
of that which has shamelessly raped me
but my soul reflects the strength of my culture
My name is Maria Christina
I am a Puerto Rican woman born in el barrio
Our men . . . they call me negra because they love me
and in turn I teach them to be strong.

[1980]

Discussion Questions

1. Trace the story of creation described in "In the Beginning."

2. Describe the kind of woman being depicted in "A la Mujer Borrinqueña." What is her role as mother? As lover? As a Latina?

3. What are the similarities and differences between the woman being described in "A la Mujer Borrinqueña" to Sandra Cisneros's speaker in "For All Tuesday Travelers" on page 92?

4. Why does the author purposefully misspell Borinqueña?

---

[2] grandmother

Victor Hernandez Cruz

VICTOR HERNANDEZ CRUZ was born in Aguas Buenas, Puerto Rico, in 1949, and moved to New York with his family in 1954. He is essentially a self-educated man whose ear for music and language allows him to successfully describe the feeling of living between two cultures. He has published his poetry in several books: Papo Got His Gun *(1966),* Snaps *(1969),* Bi-Lingual Education *(1982),* Red Beans *(1991). He has taught at several academic institutions including Berkeley, San Francisco State, and the University of California at San Diego.*

Cruz's work often depicts his people's journey from a mostly agricultural setting to a highly urbanized one, as he documents what it must have been like to arrive in New York in the 1940s and 1950s with no experience in urban life, with very little money, and with no knowledge of the language. Add to these difficulties changes in climate, landscape, and social customs, and we confront a unique experience that may never be repeated in quite the same way. His additional interest in music, language, and his African heritage is evidenced in the selections provided here.

African Things

o the wonder man   rides his space ship/
brings his power through many moons
carries in soft blood   african spirits
dance & sing in my mother's house. in my cousin's house.
black as night can be/   what was Puerto Rican all about.
all about the
indios & you better believe it the african things
black & shiny
grandmother speak to me & tell me of african things
how do latin
boo-ga-loo sound   like you
conga drums in the islands   you know
the traveling through many moons
dance & tell me black african things
i know you know.

[1973]

Bi-Lingual Education

When things divide
the nature of this age
like 12 midnight when heaven

and hell slice
don't look in the mirror
lest you see yourself
your tongue hanging out
like a carpet
where two ladies
are sprawled   entwined
They come to eat you
in doubles
They chew you
till you are
a strong and perfect 1.

Discussion Questions

1. How does the speaker in "African Things" feel about his heritage?
2. According to the speaker in "Bi-Lingual Education," what are the effects of bilingual education?
3. Compare the speaker's feelings about his African heritage in the first poem to the same feeling in Martin Espada's "Niggerlips" on page 456, and also to Sandra Maria Esteves's "A la Mujer Borinqueña" on page 437.
4. Compare the issue of bilingualism in "Bi-Lingual Education" to that in Pat Mora's "Bilingual Christmas" on page 87.

Tato Laviera

TATO LAVIERA straddles both cultures in his poetry, and the title of one of his books, AmeRícan *(1986), is a reflection of his concept of himself as neither wholly American nor wholly Puerto Rican. He was born in Santurce, Puerto Rico, in 1951 and migrated to New York with his family when he was nine years old. Besides having taught writing at Rutgers University, he is deeply committed to helping the community. He has worked as director of the community services, served as chair of the board of directors of the "Madison Neighbors in Action," and sat on the board of directors of the "Mobilization for Youth, Inc."*

Several of Laviera's plays have been presented in New York, and he has published three books of poetry: Enclave *(1981),* Mainstream Ethics *(1989), and the one from which these poems are taken,* La Carreta Made A U-Turn *(1979). The book's title derives from Rene Marques's 1953 play* La Carreta *(The Oxcart), which describes the transition of the Puerto Rican people from the countryside into the urban areas of the capital and eventually to New York City. These immigrants' inability to adjust to their new environment is refashioned in Laviera's book. By employing code-switching and powerful imagery, he provides a vivid picture of a new immigrant whose two distinct identities have merged into one.*

my graduation speech

i think in spanish
i write in english

i want to go back to puerto rico,
but i wonder if my kink could live
in *ponce, mayagüez* and *carolina*[1]

tengo las venas aculturadas[2]
escribo en spanglish
abraham in español
abraham in english
tato in spanish
"taro" in english
tonto[3] in both languages

how are you?
¿cómo estás?
i don't know if i'm coming
or *si me fui ya*[4]

si me dicen barranquitas, yo reply,
"*¿con qué se come eso?*"[5]
si me dicen caviar, i digo,
"a new pair of converse sneakers."

ahí supe que estoy jodío
ahí supe que estamos jodíos[6]

english or spanish
spanish or english,
spanenglish
now, dig this:

hablo lo inglés matao
hablo lo español matao
no sé leer ninguno bien[7]

---

[1] three Puerto Rican cities located in the southern, western, and eastern regions of the island [2] my
veins (blood) are acculturated [3] fool [4] or if I already left [5] what do you eat that with
[6] that's when I knew we were screwed
  that's when I knew we were all screwed
[7] i speak broken english
  i speak broken spanish
  i can't read either one well

so it is, spanglish to matao
what i *digo*[8]
            ¡*ay, virgen, yo no sé hablar!*[9]

savorings, from piñones[1] to loíza

to combine the smell of tropical
plaintain roots *sofritoed*[2]
into tasty crispy platanustres
after savoring a soft *mofongo*[3]
with pork rind pieces, before
you cooked them into an *escabeche*[4]
peppered with garlic *tostones*[5]
at three o'clock in a piñones sunday
afternoon, after your body cremated
itself dancing the night, *madrugando*[6]
in san juan beaches, walking over
a rooster's cucu rucu and *pregonero's*[7]
offering of wrapped-up *alcapurrias*[8]
fried in summer sun . . .
hold yourself strong
ahead is the *Ancón,*[9] the crossing to loíza . . .
you have entered the underneath
of *plena,*[10] mi *hermano,*[11]
steady rhythms that constantly don't change
steady rhythms that constantly don't change
tru cu tú tru cu tú
tru cu tú tru cu tú
tu tu tu

against muñoz[1] pamphleteering

and i looked into the dawn
inside the bread of land and liberty

---

[8] what I say   [9] oh my God, i can't speak at all!

---

[1] *Piñones* is an area in the northern part of the island.   [2] *Sofrito* is the basic foundation for many Puerto Rican dishes. It is a mixture of crushed garlic, bell pepper, and onions which is then sauteed in olive oil with tomato sauce.   [3] *Mofongo* is made with fried green plantain.   [4] *Escabeche* is a meal made from fish.   [5] *Tostones* are fried green plaintains.   [6] staying up all night   [7] a street vendor   [8] *Alcapurria* is a fried food stuffed with meat   [9] The name the Tainos, the indigenous people of Puerto Rico, gave the river.   [10] *Plena* is a form of Afro-Caribbean music.   [11] brother

---

[1] Luis Munoz Marin was the first governor of the newly formed Commonwealth of Puerto Rico in 1952, a status he had sought for many years.

to find a hollow sepulchre of words
words that i admired from my mother's eyes
words that i also imbedded as my dreams.

now i awake to find that the underneath
of your beautiful poetry pamphleteering
against the mob of stars took me nowhere
muñoz, took me nowhere, muñoz, nowhere
where i see myself inside a triangle
of contradictions with no firm bridges
to make love to those stars.

inside my ghetto i learned to understand
your short range visions of where you led us,
across the oceans where i talk about myself
in foreign languages, across where i reach
to lament finding myself re-seasoning my
coffee beans.

your sense of
stars landed me in a
north temperate uprooted zone.

Discussion Questions

1. Why does the speaker in "my graduation speech" say he is a *tonto*, or fool, in both languages? Describe the feelings the speaker has about his limited proficiency in both languages.

2. Compare the imagery used in "Savorings" to that used in Sandra Maria Esteves's poem "In the Beginning" on page 436.

3. Why does the speaker in "against muñoz pamphleteering" cast blame on muñoz?

4. Compare the feelings of the speaker in "my graduation speech" and Gustavo Perez-Firmat's poem "Dedication" on page 254. How is pun used in both poems.

5. Compare the feelings of the speaker toward his adopted home and the life of Luciano in the poem by Bernice Zamora on page 95.

Pedro Pietri

PEDRO PIETRI *was born in Ponce, Puerto Rico, in 1943 and immigrated to the United States in 1945. He is the author of twenty-three plays, many of which have been presented in New York in various venues. They include* The Living-Room *(1978),* Jesus is Leaving *(1978),* The Masses Are Asses *(1984), and* Illusions of a

Revolving Door, *a collection of seven plays (1992). His poetry collections are* Puerto Rican Obituary *(1971) and* Traffic Violations *(1983).*

Pietri's appearance of a tough motorcycle club member, belies his personality. While he is exuberant, loud, and flashy, his words often convey a thoughtful carefully measured message. His poetry reflects this contrast. Puerto Rican Obituary *is by far his most popular work. It is an appeal to ethnic pride as a defense against the broken promises of The American Dream. The woes of discrimination and prejudice are countered by a call for defiance and nonconformity.*

Puerto Rican Obituary

They worked
They were always on time
They were never late
They never spoke back
when they were insulted
They worked
They never took days off
that were not on the calendar
They never went on strike
without permission
They worked
ten days a week
and were only paid for five
They worked
They worked
They worked
and they died
They died broke
They died owing
They died never knowing
what the front entrance
of the first national city bank looks like

Juan
Miguel
Milagros
Olga
Manuel
All died yesterday today
and will die again tomorrow
passing their bill collectors
on to the next of kin
All died

waiting for the garden of eden
to open up again
under a new management
All died
dreaming about america
waking them up in the middle of the night
screaming: *Mira Mira*[1]
your name is on the winning lottery ticket
for one hundred thousand dollars
All died
hating the grocery stores
that sold them make-believe steak
and bullet-proof rice and beans
All died waiting dreaming and hating

Dead Puerto Ricans
Who never knew they were Puerto Ricans
Who never took a coffee break
from the ten commandments
to KILL KILL KILL
the landlords of their cracked skulls
and communicate with their latino souls

Juan
Miguel
Milagros
Olga
Manuel
From the nervous breakdown streets
where the mice live like millionaires
and the people do not live at all
are dead and were never alive

Juan
died waiting for his number to hit
Miguel
died waiting for the welfare check
to come and go and come again
Milagros
died waiting for her ten children
to grow up and work
so she could quit working
Olga
died waiting for a five dollar raise

---

[1] Look, Look

Manuel
died waiting for his supervisor to drop dead
so he could get a promotion

Is a long ride
from Spanish Harlem
to long island cemetery
where they were buried
First the train
and then the bus
and the cold cuts for lunch
and the flowers
that will be stolen
when visiting hours are over
Is very expensive
Is very expensive
But they understand
Their parents understood
Is a long non-profit ride
from Spanish Harlem
to long island cemetery

Juan
Miguel
Milagros
Olga
Manuel
All died yesterday today
and will die again tomorrow
Dreaming
Dreaming about queens
Clean-cut lily-white neighborhood
Puerto Ricanless scene

Thirty-thousand-dollar home
The first spics on the block
Proud to belong to a community
of gringos who want them lynched
Proud to be a long distance away
from the sacred phrase: *Que Pasa*[2]

These dreams
These empty dreams
from the make-believe bedrooms

---
[2] What's Happening

their parents left them
are the after-effects
of television programs
about the ideal
white american family,
with black maids
and latino janitors
who are well train
to make everyone
and their bill collectors
laugh at them
and the people they represent

Juan
died dreaming about a new car
Miguel
died dreaming about new anti-poverty programs
Milagros
died dreaming about a trip to Puerto Rico
Olga
died dreaming about real jewelry
Manuel
died dreaming about the irish sweepstakes

They all died
like a hero sandwich dies
in the garment district
at twelve o'clock in the afternoon
social security number to ashes
union dues to dust

They knew
they were born to weep
and keep the morticians employed
as long as they pledge allegiance
to the flag that wants them destroyed
They saw their names listed
in the telephone directory of destruction
They were train to turn
the other cheek by newspapers
that misspelled mispronounced
and misunderstood their names
and celebrated when death came
and stole their final laundry ticket

They were born dead
and they died dead

Is time
to visit sister lopez again
the number one healer
and fortune card dealer
in Spanish Harlem
She can communicate
with your late relatives
for a reasonable fee
Good news is guaranteed

Rise Table Rise Table
death is not dumb and disable
Those who love you want to know
the correct number to play
Let them know this right away
Rise Table Rise Table
death is not dumb and disable
Now that your problems are over
and the world is off your shoulders
help those who you left behind
find financial peace of mind

Rise Table Rise Table
death is not dumb and disable
If the right number we hit
all our problems will split
and we will visit your grave
on every legal holiday
Those who love you want to know
the correct number to play
Let them know this right away
We know your spirit is able
Death is not dumb and disable
RISE TABLE RISE TABLE

Juan
Miguel
Milagros
Olga
Manuel
All died yesterday today
and will die again tomorrow
Hating fighting and stealing
broken windows from each other
Practicing a religion without a roof
The old testament

The new testament
according to the gospel
of the internal revenue
the judge and jury and executioner
protector and eternal bill collector

Secondhand shit for sale
Learn how to say *Como Esta Usted*[3]
and you will make a fortune

They are dead
They are dead
and will not return from the dead
until they stop neglecting
the art of their dialogue
for broken english lessons
to impress the mister goldsteins
who keep them employed
as lavaplatos porters messenger boys
factory workers maids stock clerks
shipping clerks assistant mailroom
assistant, assistant assistant
to the assistant's assistant
assistant lavaplatos and automatic
artificial smiling doorman
for the lowest wages of the ages
and rages when you demand a raise
because is against the company policy
to promote SPICS SPICS SPICS[4]

Juan
died hating Miguel because Miguel's
used car was in better running condition
than his used car
Miguel
died hating Milagros because Milagros
had a color television set
and he could not afford one yet
Milagros
died hating Olga because Olga
made five dollars more on the same job
Olga
died hating Manuel because Manuel
had hit the numbers more times

---

[3] How are you   [4] a derogatory term to refer to Puerto Ricans

than she had hit the numbers
Manuel
died hating all of them
Juan
Miguel
Milagros
and Olga
because they all spoke broken english
more fluently than he did

And now they are together
in the main lobby of the void
Addicted to silence
Off limits to the wind
Confine to worm supremacy
in long island cemetery
This is the groovy hereafter
the protestant collection box
was talking so loud and proud about

Here lies Juan
Here lies Miguel
Here lies Milagros
Here lies Olga
Here lies Manuel
who died yesterday today
and will die again tomorrow
Always broke
Always owing
Never knowing
that they are beautiful people
Never knowing
the geography of their complexion

PUERTO RICO IS A BEAUTIFUL PLACE
PUERTORRIQUEÑOS ARE A BEAUTIFUL RACE

If only they
had turned off the television,
and tune into their own imaginations
If only they
had used the white supremacy bibles
for toilet paper purpose
and make their latino souls
the only religion of their race

If only they
had return to the definition of the sun
after the first mental snowstorm
on the summer of their senses
If only they
had kept their eyes open
at the funeral of their fellow employees
who came to this country to make a fortune
and were buried without underwears

Juan
Miguel
Milagros
Olga
Manuel
will right now be doing their own thing
where beautiful people sing
and dance and work together
where the wind is a stranger
to miserable weather conditions
where you do not need a dictionary
to communicate with your people
Aqui Se Habla Español[5] all the time
Aqui you salute your flag first
Aqui there are no dial soap commercials
Aqui everybody smells good
Aqui tv dinners do not have a future
Aqui the men and women admire desire
and never get tired of each other
Aqui Que Pasa Power is what's happening
Aqui to be called *negrito*[6]
means to be called LOVE

[1973]

Discussion Questions

1. Explain what is meant by the statement that Juan and the others have died and "will die again tomorrow."

2. What is being suggested about the effects of "Americanization" on Puerto Ricans by the fact that they all died hating each other?

3. What, according to the speaker, is the most unfortunate aspect of the deaths of these workers?

---

[5] We speak Spanish here   [6] black

Jack Agüeros

Like his plays and short stories, Jack Agüero's poetry combines his interest in Renaissance forms and contemporary street situations and characters. The title of his latest collection of verse, Sonnets from the Puerto Rican, *is a perfect example of this seemingly incongruous combination. The book is divided into five sections: "Landscapes," "Five Sonnets for the Happy Land Social Club Fire," "Sonnets for the Four Horseman of the Apocalypse," "Love," and "Portraits." The sonnets included here show the wide range of the book's scope, despite its use of only one poetic form.*

Sonnet: Waiting in Tompkins Square Park

My father used to tell me about the Great Depression.
Long lines of men waiting in anticipation of soup.
Long lines of men waiting in anticipation of interviews.
Long lines of men; waiting; in anticipation; waiting.

What I do now is wonder as I see long lines of men
Waiting for food in Tompkins Square Park, and women
Cast about the landscape of benches, boxes, tottering
Tents, transient as leaves blown by the wind off Avenue B,

And long lines of bodies sleeping on the park bandshell
Neatly distributed in rows on the stage like cards in
Solitaire, or a supine chorus line choreographed for a
Busby Berkeley film routine. This, show my father never saw.

Or did my father see and censor, never mention to a child
That government was the Four Horsemen of the Apocalypse.

Sonnets for the Four Horsemen of the Apocalypse: Long Time Among Us

I. Sonnet for the Elegant Rider

The way I get it is, that when the world is about to end
Four horsemen will come thundering down from somewhere.

One will ride a red horse, and his name will be War.
One will ride a white horse and his name I don't get
since it's Captivity. Does that mean slavery? I don't
want to guess about these things, but translations can
be treacherous. One will ride a black horse and be named
Famine. I get that. Now here's another part that leaves
me scratching my head—one will ride a pale horse, and
since when is pale a color? He is named Death, and I
think this translator has him on the wrong horse. Death,
I know, rides the white horse, which symbolizes his purity.

You see, the future tense is wrong, since nothing is as now, or
as inevitable, or so personally elegant and apocalyptic as Death.

II. Sonnet for You, Familiar Famine

Nobody's waiting for any apocalypse to meet you, Famine!

We know you. There isn't a corner of our round world
where you don't politely accompany someone to bed each
night. In some families, you're the only one sitting
at the table when the dinner bell tolls. "He's not so
bad," say people who have plenty and easily tolerate you.
They argue that small portions are good for us, and
are just what we deserve. There's an activist side to
you, Famine. You've been known to bring down governments,
yet you never get any credit for your political reforms.

Don't make the mistake I used to make of thinking fat
people are immune to Famine. Famine has this other ugly
side. Famine knows that the more you eat the more you
long. That side bears his other frightening name, Emptiness.

III. Sonnet for Red-Horsed War

Obvious symbolism; let's call it blood-colored; admit
War jumped the gun on the apocalypse a long time ago.

Isn't it shy Peace that deserves free transportation?

What horse would Peace ride? Peace is usually put on a
Dove, but is so rare it ought to ride the extinct Dodo
of lost feathers we infer, and song we never heard.

War is vulgar, in your face, and favors harsh words.
Rides recklessly, and lately has even learned to fly;
drops pink mushrooms, enjoys ugly phrases like body
count and megacorpse. Generals love War, worship it by
sanctifying pentagons. When War shakes your hand, he
rips it from your arm; shoot and burn is his lullaby.

Like Kronos, War dines napkinless on his raw sons or
any burned flesh. Look, War is apocalypse all the time.

IV. Sonnet for Ambiguous Captivity

Captivity, I have taken your white horse. Punctilious
Death rides it better. Dubious, I try to look you in
your eye. Are you something like old-time slavery, or
are you like its clever cousin, colonialism? Are you
the same as "occupied," like when a bigger bird takes
over your nest, shits, and you still have to sweep? Or
when you struggle like the bottom fish snouting in the
deep cold water and the suck fish goes by scaled in his
neon colors, living off dividends, thinking banking is
work? Captivity, you look like Ireland and Puerto Rico!

Four horsemen of the apocalypse, why should anyone fear
your arrival, when you have already grown gray among us
too familiar and so contemptible? And you, Captivity, you

remind me of a working man who has to be his own horse.

Discussion Questions

1. What comment is being made about the state of modern society in "Sonnet: Waiting in Tompkins Park"?
2. What is the speaker's feeling about Death in "Sonnet for the Elegant Rider"? What does he mean that the "future tense is wrong"?
3. How is War being personified in "Sonnet for Red-Horse War?"
4. In the final sonnet, why does the speaker compare "Captivity" to Ireland and Puerto Rico?
5. In the last sonnet, compare "Captivity" in relation to Puerto Rico to the way the father is treated in "Roots" by Jimmy Santiago Baca on page 100.

Martin Espada

Attorney Martin Espada was born in Brooklyn, New York, in 1957. He is currently a professor of English at the University of Massachusetts, Amherst. In 1982 he published The Immigrant Iceboy's Bolero, *with photographs by his Puerto-Rican born father, Frank Espada. His other works include* Trumpets from the Islands of Their Eviction *(1987),* Rebellion Is the Circle of a Lover's Hands *(1990),* City of Coughing and Dead Radiators *(1993), and* Imagine the Angels of Bread *(1996). He has also published a translation of the poetry of Clemente Soto Velez, edited a book of contemporary Latino poetry, and most recently written a book of both poems and essays.*

In City of Coughing and Dead Radiators, *Espada uses humor to convey a serious message about prejudice and stereotypical attitudes. Both of the selections presented here explore racial tension in very dissimilar ways. In "Thanksgiving" the speaker's visit to his in-laws' home for the holiday meal leads to an uncomfortable situation. The tension in "Niggerlips" is much more acute, but the speaker's ethnic pride serves to diffuse it.*

Thanksgiving

This was the first Thanksgiving with my wife's family,
sitting at the stained pine table in the dining room.
The wood stove coughed during her mother's prayer:
Amen and the gravy boat bobbing over fresh linen.
Her father stared into the mashed potatoes
and saw a white battleship floating in the gravy.
Still staring at the mashed potatoes, he began a soliloquy
about the new Navy missiles fired across miles of ocean,
how they could jump into the smokestack of a battleship.
"Now in Korea," he said, "I was a gunner, and the people there
ate kimch'i, and it really stinks." Mother complained
that no one was eating the creamed onions. "*Eat, Daddy.*"
The creamed onions look like eyeballs, I thought,
and then said, "I wish I had missiles like that."
Daddy laughed a 1950s horror movie mad scientist laugh,
then told me he didn't have a missile, but he had his own cannon.
"Daddy, eat the candied yams," Mother hissed, as if
he were a liquored CIA spy telling military secrets
to some Puerto Rican janitor he met in a bar. "I'm a toolmaker.
I made the cannon myself," Daddy said, and left the table.
"Daddy's family has been here in the Connecticut Valley since 1680,"
Mother said. "There were Indians here once, but they left."

When I started dating her daughter, Mother called me a half-black,
but now she spooned candied yams on my plate. I nibbled
at the candied yams. I remembered my own Thanksgivings
in the Bronx, turkey with *arroz y habichuelas* and *plátanos*,[1]
and countless cousins swaying to bugalú on the record player
or roaring at my grandmother's Spanish punchlines in the kitchen,
the glowing of her cigarette like a firefly lost in the city. For years
I thought everyone ate rice and beans with turkey at Thanksgiving.
Daddy returned to the table with a cannon, steering the black
iron barrel. "Does that cannon go boom?" I asked. "I fire it
in the backyard at the tombstones," Daddy said, "That cemetery
bought all our land during the Depression. Now we only have
the house." He stared and said nothing, then glanced up suddenly,
like a ghost had tickled his ear. "Want to see me fire it?" he grinned.
"Daddy, fire the cannon after dessert," Mother said. "If I fire
the cannon, I have to take out the cannonballs first," he told me.
He tilted the cannon downward, and cannonballs dropped
from the barrel, thudding on the floor and rolling across
the brown braided rug. Grandmother praised the turkey's thighs,
said she was bringing leftovers home to feed her Congo Gray parrot.
I walked with Daddy to the backyard, past the bullet holes
in the door and the pickup truck with the Confederate license plate.
He swiveled the cannon around to face the tombstones
on the other side of the backyard fence. "This way, if I hit anybody,
they're already dead," he declared. He stuffed half a charge
of gunpowder into the cannon and lit the fuse. From the dining room,
Mother yelled, "*Daddy, no!*" Then the ground rumbled under my feet.
My head thundered. Smoke drifted over the tombstones.
Daddy laughed. And I thought: When the first drunken Pilgrim
dragged out the cannon at the first Thanksgiving—
that's when the Indians left.

Niggerlips

Niggerlips was the high school name
for me.
So called by Douglas
the car mechanic, with green tattoos
on each forearm,
and the choir of round pink faces
that grinned deliciously

---

[1] rice and beans and plantains

from the back row of classrooms,
droned over by teachers
checking attendance too slowly.

Douglas would brag
about cruising his car
near sidewalks of black children
to point an unloaded gun,
to scare niggers
like crows off a tree,
he'd say.

My great-grandfather Luis
was *un negrito* too,[1]
a shoemaker in the coffee hills
of Puerto Rico, 1900.

The family called him a secret
and kept no photograph.
My father remembers
the childhood white powder
that failed to bleach
his stubborn copper skin,
and the family says
he is still a fly in milk.

So Niggerlips has the mouth
of his great-grandfather,
the song he must have sung
as he pounded the leather and nails,
the heat that courses through copper,
the stubbornness of a fly in milk,
and all you have, Douglas,
is that unloaded gun.

Discussion Questions

1. Both of these poems describe forms of racism. Which of them does this in a more overt way?
2. Describe the use of contrast in "Thanksgiving."
3. Is there a difference in the way the speaker in "Niggerlips" feels about his heritage and the way his great-grandfather did? If so, explain the significance of this change.
4. Compare the feelings the speakers in these poems have about their skin color to that of the speaker in Esteves's poem on page 437.
5. How are Gloria Anzaldua's poem on page 98 and these poems by Espada similar?

---

[1] a black man

Miguel Piñero

MIGUEL PIÑERO was born in Puerto Rico in the small town of Gurabo in 1946 and came to the United States as a young boy. The violence and drug culture of the streets became a part of his life at an early age and he served sentences for drug possession and burglary. While in prison at the infamous Sing Sing facility, Piñero began to turn his life around. He had written some poetry in his cell, and then joined a prison repertory group known as "the Family." During the course of these experiences, Piñero wrote Short Eyes, *which eventually won the New York Drama Critics Circle Award for best American play of 1974. The play takes place in the dayroom of a detention center, where a group of mostly black and Hispanic prisoners waits out the pretrial period.*

Piñero's other plays include The Sun Always Shines for the Cool, Eulogy for a Small-Time Thief, *and* A Midnight Moon at the Greasy Spoon, *published together in 1983. Like all of his plays,* A Midnight Moon *centers on members of the underclass. It is set in a small twenty-four-hour luncheonette located in Times Square. It is owned and operated by Joseph Scott, a man in his late sixties whose acting career never took off the way he would have wanted. Throughout the course of the play we get glimpses into the lives of some of the diner's customers: a young Greek immigrant who marries a hooker so he may stay in the country, an aging actress whose life is a series of blown auditions, and a street hustler who owns a less than reputable massage parlor, among others. They all weave in and out of the play just as they weave in and out of American society. Similar in some ways to Miller's portrayal of a heroic yet tragic salesman, Piñero's play comments on the invisible lives of the people who most of us choose not to see.*

A Midnight Moon at the Greasy Spoon

CHARACTERS

Joseph Scott, *Late sixties, active, strong.*
Gerald Fisher, *Late sixties, active, strong.*
Dominick Skorpios, *Late thirties, Greek immigrant.*
Fred Pulley, *Early seventies.*
Night-Life, *Mid twenties.*
Joe the Cop, *Late fifties.*
Zulma Samson, *Late forties.*
Jake the Nigger, *Late forties.*
Reynolds, *FBI Man.*

Lockhart, *Bureau of Immigration.*
Man One, *Insurance Salesman.*
Man Two, *Record Company Executive.*
Hooker One, *On a string.*
Hooker Two, *Freelancer.*
Shopping Bag Lady, *Mumbles.*
Junkie Girl, *Far gone.*
Lost Man, *From out of town.*
Boy, *Songwriter, musician.*
Girl, *Singer.*

Plus as many miscellaneous customers as can be creatively accommodated.

ACT I

A small luncheonette in the Times Square area servicing the workers of the
New York Times *and whatever hungry people come in to eat. The place is
open all night. In half light frozen like the figures in Edward Hopper's
"Night Hawk,"* GERRY *is at the coffee urn,* DOMINICK *prepares to cut the pie,*
JOE *is poised at the cash register preparing to make change for a departing*
CUSTOMER, HOOKER ONE *is on the pay phone, A* BIKER *sits at the counter
waiting for his coffee, a* STUDENT *sits at a side counter reading a textbook.
After a moment the lights go to full and the action begins. General ad libs as*
GERRY *serves the* BIKER, *the* CUSTOMER *pays* JOE, DOMINICK *serves a piece of
pie to the* STUDENT. *Then . . .*

DOMINICK: There's not enough pies to last the night, Joe.

JOE: So what.

GERRY: So what? So what, he says, like if he don't like making money.

JOE: Listen, you were supposed to order the pies, right?

DOMINICK: I told you yesterday that I couldn't order the pies 'cause I   5
    was coming in late today . . .

JOE: You came in on time.

DOMINICK: Well the marriage was faster than I thought it was going to
    be like.

GERRY: Welcome to America, Dominick.   10

JOE: How was the wedding, Dominick?

DOMINICK: Very fast . . . very fast . . . I go into the place in the morning,
    we sign some papers, we go into a room . . . One, two, three, that's it.
    I bring my cousin Aristotle with us as a best man. She had some
    junkie girl with her as best woman.   15

JOE: Maid of honor.

DOMINICK: What honor, Joe . . . she had no honor, bring a girl like that
    to her wedding. She's crazy without honor, thank God I'm not going
    to live with her.

JOE: What do you mean you're not gonna live with her?   20

DOMINICK: You know why I married her.

JOE: Sure I know, but you got to get between them legs of hers at least
    once.

GERRY: Yeah, Dominick, after all the money you put out for her to marry
    you, you got to get laid at least once to make it legal, if you know   25
    what I mean Dominick?

DOMINICK: Sure I know what you mean, but this is strictly business.

JOE: It may be strictly business, Dom, but anytime you can get a piece of
    leg that looks like a piece of leg you ought to get that piece of leg be-
    fore she gets away . . . you know what I mean, Dominick.   30

DOMINICK: I don't know.

JOE: What do you mean, you don't know?

GERRY: She's your wife, you got a right to get a piece of leg.

DOMINICK: But this is strictly business . . .

JOE: Anytime, anywhere in America a man is the boss of his home. Your   35
     wife is bought and paid for, she's yours, Dominick.

DOMINICK: I don't know . . .

GERRY: What's there to know, all you got to do when she comes home . . .

DOMINICK: She ain't coming home.

JOE: You mean she isn't coming home . . . ? She's got to come home.   40

GERRY: Where else is a wife supposed to go but home?

DOMINICK: I mean there is no home to come home to.

GERRY: No home to come home to. That doesn't even sound right.

JOE: That's a great title for a song. *(Singing.)* There's no home to come
     home to, like no home that I know. What's a home without a piece of   45
     leg.

DOMINICK: Look, after the wedding she went her way, I came here.

GERRY: Ain't you gonna see her again?

DOMINICK: When the divorce papers come through.

JOE: But that's not gonna be for a long time.   50

GERRY: Yeah, that's right, and besides, you have to become a citizen first
     before you divorce her. Don't forget that.

JOE: Don't be stupid, Gerry, that's why he married her.

GERRY: I know why he married her . . .

DOMINICK: Joe, what if she doesn't . . .   55

JOE: She has no choice.

DOMINICK: . . . she can say, go fuck your own leg instead.

JOE: Don't be stupid, Dominick, she can't say that.

GERRY: Why not?

DOMINICK: Yeah, why not?   60

JOE: Because she can't say that.

GERRY: That doesn't make any sense to me.

DOMINICK: To me either, it makes no sense to me.

JOE: Why does everything have to make sense?

GERRY: Joe, if things don't make any sense, then you can't execute them.   65

JOE: Hey, Gerry, give me that cloth there.

GERRY: Catch.

JOE: No . . . oh shit, look at this. You got the thing inside the chocolate
     syrup, dummy.

GERRY: Here . . .   70

DOMINICK: What happened with what you were saying, Joe?

JOE: I'm thinking Dominick, let me think.

GERRY: You want maybe we should go outside in case you blow a fuse?

JOE: Oh, oh, oh . . . Dominick, how much you laid out to marry that
     broad?   75

DOMINICK: Close to three thousand dollars.

GERRY: That's a lot of money to become a citizen of the USA.

JOE: Yeah, with so many people trying to get out of the USA.

GERRY: As far as I'm concerned, I still go with the good old saying . . .
     love it or leave it. If you don't like it, get your ass out.   80

JOE: Boy, if people knew that people like Dominick work for years to save up enough money so that they can marry some broad and become a citizen . . .

GERRY: What are you doing, Joe? Campaigning for mayor?

JOE: I bet if I did campaign for mayor I'd win by a landslide, 'cause I know what this town needs, somebody strong that's not afraid to kick some ass in that mansion, who's not afraid of the mafia or the union bosses or doesn't have his hand out for kickbacks all the time. You know that's what this town needs. If I was mayor, the schools wouldn't be full of drugs and police and revolutionaries. I'd put them all up against the wall and shoot 'em, no trials. I'd arrest them and shoot them on the spot like Castro did in Cuba.

GERRY: How do you know what Castro did in Cuba?

JOE: Because that's what all them Communists do when they take over. They have a blood bath to clean out all the people that gave them a bad time.

GERRY: You sound like a communist.

JOE: I don't sound like a communist. Don't say things like that. You know the walls have ears. This place may be tapped.

DOMINICK: Hey Joe, have you thought about? . . .

JOE: What?

DOMINICK: What we were talking about.

JOE: I haven't thought of nothing as yet but I will. Just let the old noggin get to work and we'll have a brain storm.

GERRY: Yeah, maybe we should get an umbrella, hey.

JOE: Maybe we should get an umbrella. That's funny, real funny. You know the communists don't have a bad idea when they start out, you know. I mean it. I mean like they have a good idea when they start to throw out the rotten apple before it contaminates the whole barrel. That's their motto and like it or not, it's a good one. If we had in this country stopped all them spicks and niggers from going crazy protesting this and that, we would have been in a better more orderly country. We let all the foreigners come in and tell us what to do with our country. Ridiculous. That's why this country is falling apart now, you know that. Why I read in the *Daily News* yesterday that one of the top men in the Mayor's administration was arrested for being a crook. And look what happened to Kennedy and his brother. The poor kid didn't have a chance to get anywhere.

GERRY: You think he had a chance at being the President?

JOE: Are you kidding! With all the money his family has!

GERRY: Them Kennedys sure have had a bad time with their kids. All of them killed and running around, never being at home. Sure is hell of a family life they have, huh?

JOE: Now Joe Kennedy was one hell of a man. Let me tell you he was a real old timer. He was one of them old time pioneers.

DOMINICK: You mean he was with Wyatt Earp and Billy the Kid?

JOE: Naw, well, I bet he might have known them. I mean he had the
       guts to know them.

GERRY: He didn't know them.   130

JOE: What do you know! You know anything of the Kennedy family.

GERRY: No.

JOE: Well, I'm an expert on the Kennedy family. I know everything about
       them. I didn't vote for John because he was too young and wouldn't
       know how to handle a country the size of this one. If he had been   135
       running for Governor or Senator or maybe Mayor of the City, I might
       have voted for him. But for president, naw. I mean he was killed just
       in time.

GERRY: What a crazy thing to say, that the president was killed just in
       time.   140

JOE: What I mean is if he had lived, everybody would have seen how
       lousy a president this man was and he would have never gotten the
       chance to run for any office again.

DOMINICK: But Joe, he must have been a great president. I mean when I
       came here, I landed in Kennedy Airport. I read of a place that they   145
       call Cape Kennedy where they shot those rockets to the moon. I
       mean, that to me means that he was a great man.

JOE: Who's saying he wasn't a great man? He got killed didn't he?

GERRY: So what does that prove?

JOE: It proves that he was a great man. All great men get assassinated,   150
       right? What was the name of the colored guy that got killed in the
       south, you know, the guy who walked all over the place?

GERRY: King.

JOE: What?

GERRY: That was his name, King. They got some kind of center down   155
       here named after him, he said that . . .

JOE: Said what?

GERRY: That little black boys and little white boys would be holding
       hands.

JOE: If I caught my son skipping down the streets holding hands with   160
       some nigger boy, I'd break his arm.

GERRY: I don't care if he's black or white or yellow or red, if I caught my
       son holding another boy's hand, I'd do the same thing too. No son of
       mine is gonna hold any man's hand and skip down the street like
       some freakin' fairy.   165

DOMINICK: "I have a dream."

JOE: You have a dream?

DOMINICK: That was the thing he said.

JOE: Who said?

DOMINICK: Doctor Martin Luther King, Jr.   170

JOE: Who's that?

GERRY: That's the name of the guy who made the speech we were just
       talking about.

JOE: How do you know his name, Gerry? How'd you know his name, Dominick. 175

DOMINICK: I read about him in school. He was really a beautiful human being.

JOE: What do you know? Look, you're a foreigner here. . . . What do you know about the niggers in this country? Them spades can really turn on you. They have no manners. I had a spook working here a couple of years ago and he was really a nasty-mouth nigger. I mean he would cough in front of people who sat down to eat. He'd pick his nose in public, farted all the time and then would stink like a dead cat stinks. I think his stomach was rotten or something, you know. Everytime he went downstairs to the basement to shit, the smell would just fill this whole place. 180 185

GERRY: Joe please, I'm eating.

JOE: So go ahead and eat, who's stopping you?

GERRY: Never mind.

JOE: I had to let him go. After that I had a spick working in here and I had to keep my eye on him all the time. You know you can't trust a spick. They steal everything that's not nailed to the floor. I mean, he was a good worker, but like, I had to keep my eye on him all the time, you know. 190

DOMINICK: Did he steal? 195

GERRY: Who knows? But Joe's right; them spicks steal like if, you know what it is being a thief comes to them natural, like making money comes to us. It's a second nature to them.

DOMINICK: Did you see him steal anything?

JOE: That's what Gerry is saying. They are just like the Arab. They can steal the nails off Jesus Christ and still leave him hanging on the cross. I had a spick friend of mine who once told me that at an early age their parents teach them how to steal and lie and everything. It's like going to school I mean. 200

DOMINICK: Did you believe him? 205

JOE: Of course I believed him. He wouldn't lie to me.

DOMINICK: I don't know, Joe. Like this country is full of all different kinds of people, you know.

JOE: I know, I know, ain't that a fact, but that's because we're kind. We let all kinds of people in this country of ours. We're not selfish with our wealth. With the opportunities that are here for all people, what the hell. 210

GERRY: Yeah, you know the old saying, you can't keep it unless you give it away.

JOE: What'd you say, Gerry? 215

GERRY: You know, it's better to give than receive . . . or like them holy rollers tell you . . . can't get into heaven with all that money so give it to me? Like Holly Nel said, a camel can't pass anything if you put a needle in his eye. (*GERRY exits to back.*)

FRED: *(Entering.)* Hey, where's the bum?   220

JOE: Hey bum, how are ya?

FRED: Okay, how ya doing, bum? Where's the other bum?

JOE: He's in the back. Hey, Gerry.

GERRY: Yeah?

JOE: Fred's out here . . .   225

GERRY: Hey, bum.

FRED: That's right, you bum, stay back there and rot, you bum.

GERRY: Ah, you don't wanna see me 'cause you owe me some money!

FRED: Where do I owe money to a bum from? Oh yeah, that's right. You
   were begging on the subways and I told you I'd have to owe you . . .   230
   for a cup of coffee.

JOE: That's a great one.

FRED: Hey, Dominick, how are ya doing?

DOMINICK: Okay, Fred.

FRED: The name is Mister Pulley.   235

DOMINICK: Okay, Mr. Pulley.

JOE: Ain't you got no manners for senior citizens?

DOMINICK: I do, I'm sorry sir.

FRED: That's quite all right. Just don't let it happen again.

DOMINICK: No sir, I won't.   240

FRED: *(To Joe.)* Did you get tickets for the roller derby this Saturday?

JOE: I'm gonna watch it on TV.

FRED: Watch it on TV? You must be getting old, you bum. To watch it
   out there in person is the way to see roller derby. Let me tell you there
   is nothing like it. When Mike Gannon goes around that turn knocking   245
   everything and everybody out of his way . . . Let me tell you something, you bum, that's a sight to see. There's nothing like it and you
   can't tell me you really get the whole thing on TV because I know,
   I've watched the roller derby on TV and it is not the same thing as
   watching it out there with that crowd yelling for blood. And you   250
   don't get to see what really goes on when them Amazons get it on in
   a fisticuff action. Them torn clothes reveals a lot more than they show
   on TV. Can you know what I mean? Some of them girls are really
   built like brick shithouses. Some of them broads remind me of the
   battleship I was stationed on during the big one.   255

JOE: Yeah, I know, but I gotta lotta work to do around the house, you
   know.

FRED: Let me get a cup of coffee and a toasted muffin.

JOE: Hey, Gerry, get the bum his regular.

GERRY: Okay, a toasted English coming up. *(DOMINICK hands JOE a cup*   260
   of coffee for FRED.)

FRED: Hey, Dominick, you feel like making a couple' a bucks this
   weekend?

DOMINICK: I don't know if I have time this weekend.

JOE: Dominick just got married today.

FRED: Hey, congratulations, Dominick.   265

JOE: *(Handing FRED the coffee.)* He married a Puerto Rican.

FRED: A what?

GERRY: *(Entering with the English muffin.)* You heard him.

FRED: Hey, bum!

GERRY: Hey, bum!   270

FRED: So you married a Puerto Rican girl, huh? I hear tell they are some
        hot little number.

GERRY: That's what I hear too. I mean I never had me one of those.

FRED: You probably get a heart attack if one of them little numbers got
        on you, you bum.   275

JOE: They would sure do a number on him.

FRED: They sure would, thanks. Where's the Sweet and Low?

GERRY: Here ya are, service with a smile.

FRED: Your smile I don't need, hey.

JOE: Hey Dominick, you wanna pass a mop on the floor before they start   280
        coming in here.

FRED: Yeah, so Dominick got himself hooked up to a little Puerto Rican
        number, huh? Hey, Dominick, you got more brains than I thought
        you had. By the way, how old are you?

GERRY: How old are you, Dominick?   285

DOMINICK: Thirty-eight years old next month.

FRED: You gonna stay in this country now, Dominick?

DOMINICK: Yes.

JOE: Sure he is, that's why he married that spick!

FRED: How she look?   290

JOE: She's a looker, that's for sure.

GERRY: Yeah, she sure is. Three thousand dollars worth of looks.

FRED: Three thousand dollars, are you kidding?

JOE: Nope, that's what he paid to marry her.

FRED: Hell, for three grand I would have married him.   295

GERRY: You're not exactly his type, Fred.

FRED: I could be just like Jack Lemmon in that film with Marilyn Mon-
        roe. What was the name of that movie? I saw it three times with Jack
        Lemmon, a real funny guy. I seen all his movies you know.

GERRY: "Some Like It Hot!" . . .   300

FRED: That's it, "Some Like It Hot," a great film.

JOE: They don't make films like that any more, you know.

FRED: That's a darn shame, isn't it?

GERRY: It sure is.

DOMINICK: Can I still see it in the movies?   305

FRED: The late, late, late movie.

JOE: Fred, you're a riot.

JOE THE COP: *(Entering.)* Hey, Joe, how's tricks?

JOE: Tricks are for kids, want some corn flakes?

JOE THE COP: Hello, Dominick.   310

DOMINICK: Hello, Officer Joe.

JOE: Dominick, get some glasses.

GERRY: What'll you have?

JOE THE COP: Give me a pastrami on white, hold the mustard. Coffee
with no sugar.   315

GERRY: And an apple turnover, all traveling, right?

JOE THE COP: Right. So how's business?

JOE: Business is fine. How's business out there in the streets?

JOE THE COP: Same as always. Saturday night everybody is trying to kill
somebody else.   320

JOE: Things get bad some times out there, right?

JOE THE COP: You're damn right. Especially on nights, like this. The
weather isn't so bad, it's a good night for muggers. People wanna go
out and take walks. I wish people would just go home and lock themselves in until it's time to go to work the next day. That's what I do,   325
well not me, Joe, but my wife and kids I mean. If my kids aren't home
by eight o'clock, I go looking for them and when I find them they
know what's in store for them. Most parents nowadays don't wanna
hit their kids no matter what they do. If it was up to me every kid that
came into the station house would receive an ass whipping like my fa-   330
ther use to give me.

JOE: I know what you mean. My kids are all grown up now and all of
them with the exception of the oldest are hard working citizens making
their daily living. No charity crap for them. The oldest one went to
Vietnam and came back a . . . a . . . I don't know what to call him . . .   335
a communist junkie pinko fag creep. I threw the bum out of the house.

FRED: I fought in the big one and these kids go out to a little brawl like
Vietnam and they make a big stink out of it. They really think they
been to war. They come back talking life if they, they, they . . .

JOE: I know what you mean, Fred. I can't even begin to pinpoint the   340
problem of the chicken-livered shithead.

JOE THE COP: Well, they finally gave me a desk job now.

JOE: You got yourself a desk job at the station?

JOE THE COP: Yep, taking it easy.

JOE: What are you two doing there with Dominick?   345

GERRY: Wouldn't you like to know.

FRED: Just trying to help the young fella along with some marital hints,
you know what I mean?

JOE: Dominick just got married.

JOE THE COP: He did, huh? Dom old boy, you just made one of Amer-   350
ica's grave yet traditional human errors.

DOMINICK: I did? How?

JOE THE COP: Dropping the wings of bachelor freedom and donning the
yoke of marriage slavery, but nevertheless, I wish you health, wealth
and love . . .   355

JOE: I'll drink to that.

DOMINICK: Thank you . . . thank you very much . . . *(Enter ZULMA in a
rush)*

ZULMA: Hi, everybody . . . hot chocolate to go . . . extra milk . . . no
    sugar . . . is the phone working, Joe? My, Gerry, the years are taking
    their toll . . . potbelly, pretty soon. Stop drinking all that beer, right   360
    Fred? Hey, Dominick . . . hello . . . this is X-87 . . . nothing . . .
    What? No . . . but I will . . . well if that's the way you feel about it
    then okay. I'll just get me another answering service . . . goodbye . . .
    Chocolate ready? I was going to get me another service anyway . . . I
    was . . . really . . . oh well, Joe, you know how it is in the business,   365
    sometime you're up, sometimes you're down . . . but I guess I know
    what you're thinking once a person reaches a certain point in the
    struggle to reach some kind of notoriety and they don't get there then
    it's time to bid farewell to all that is a part of one's natural habit as is
    the habit to eat to breath to sleep. The nature of a prayer is to be   370
    heard by whoever is listening, I seem to have a bad connection to that
    certain ear wherever it is.

JOE: What are you talking about?

GERRY: Dominick here just got married.

JOE THE COP: Would you mind repeating what you just said, I didn't get   375
    it all.

ZULMA: What I'm talking about? I'm talking about David Merrick . . .
    Alex Cohan . . . Gower Champion . . . Joe Luggage and Frankie Suit-
    case, about all those guys who control the means and the manner of
    my existence on this planet, about *Show Business* and *Backstage* and   380
    Variety and all those casting notices that appear in the paper, about the
    Equity billboard, about the daydreams that rush through our heads as
    we climb the stairs to an audition, about the tears that flood out after
    being rejected once . . . twice . . . three times in one afternoon . . .
    and that's not counting the morning, or the telephone calls, the hun-   385
    dreds of pictures and résumés that hit the mailboxes . . . of course, I
    can't repeat what I said, I speak from the moment not from a script
    . . . as for you, Dominick who just got married, break a leg . . . well,
    time has it that I venture forth toward the unknown fate of a sacred
    audition. . . this hot chocolate will be cold by the time I reach my des-   390
    tination, but that's not the moment of truth . . . it comes later on in
    the day with the hot chicken soup that I heat in the naked cold of my
    lonely room . . . when the night finds me moaning over the uselessness
    of trying to survive in the path of glamor and beauty, for I have lost
    both of these elements during the course of the years, yet my talent   395
    has no end in sight and yet I am not judged by this but by the fullness
    of my breast. So long, guys, I will see all of you tomorrow if the lord
    is on my side . . . if not, send me no flowers . . . for I will venture to
    exploit all of me in that great casting office in the sky . . . bye . . .

DOMINICK: Who was she!   400

JOE THE COP: I don't know her name, but by the silver tongue that she
    left behind, she must be the stone ranger . . .

JOE: That's nice, Joe. See you next time.

JOE THE COP: Good night, Joe, Gerry, Mr. er, er???

FRED: Fred, Fred Pulley. Call me Fred.   405

JOE THE COP: Good night, Fred . . . and Dominick, don't do nothing I
wouldn't do. *(JOE THE COP exits.)*

JOE: So long, Joe. Nice guy. One of the really decent cops on the force.

GERRY: He's all right for a cop.

JOE: All cops are really all right. They have a tremendous job on their   410
hands when they become New York City cops.

GERRY: Don't I know it. Don't forget my oldest one is a cop.

DOMINICK: Why did Officer Joe say that to me?

JOE: Say what?

DOMINICK: That I shouldn't do nothing he wouldn't do. I don't know   415
what he wouldn't do, so how am I going to know if I am doing something that he wouldn't do?

JOE: You know, as crazy as that may sound, it makes sense. But even . . .
look, that's just an old American saying, Dom.

DOMINICK: It doesn't make any sense to me.   420

GERRY: You mean you never heard it said before, Dom?

JOE: If he had, would he be acting like he hadn't?

GERRY: Just surprised, that's all. *(Telephone rings.)*

DOMINICK: I got it.

JOE: I'll get it. City Morgue, you stab 'em, we slab 'em. Oh, hi Ruth.   425
Sorry, can't make no deliveries today. The boy didn't show. Yeah,
yeah, I know this is the second day in a row, but what can I tell you?
Listen, order from someone else. No, no hard feelings whatsoever,
okay, bye . . . the bitch.

GERRY: Who was that?   430

JOE: Ruth Singerton from up the street. She's really got a whole lot of
nerve, hasn't she?

GERRY: She has a whole lot of something else too.

JOE: She sure does. That woman has a future behind her.

FRED: Well, here you are, Joe.   435

JOE: Leaving already?

FRED: Yeah, got to get back to work. You know some people work while
others pretend to work, right, Gerry?

GERRY: I wouldn't know, I'm only here eight hours a day.

FRED: Aaah, you bum. Take it easy you bums.   440

JOE: You too, you bum.

DOMINICK: Good night, Mr. Pulley.

FRED: Hey, call me Fred.

DOMINICK: Right, Fred . . . bye.

GERRY: Get out of here already you bum.   445

FRED: Let me get a pack of Camels.

JOE: Here you are, on the house.

GERRY: Yeah, we like giving away coffin nails.

FRED: Ahhh, you bum. So long, see you tomorrow.

JOE: Okay, Fred. *(FRED exits.)*   450

GERRY: How old you think Fred is?

JOE: He's past sixty-five I think.

GERRY: He's a baby compared to you, heh Joe?

JOE: Blow that out your ass.

DOMINICK: What about the delivery boy, Joe?   455

JOE: What delivery boy? He's fired.

DOMINICK: My cousin, Aristotle, is looking for work. He's young and strong.

JOE: Bring him around tomorrow and I'll have a look at him.

GERRY: What are you now, a casting, director . . .   460

DOMINICK: What's a casting director, Joe?

GERRY: What do you wanna eat, Dominick? . . . I'll make it for you.

DOMINICK: Eggs and tomatoes.

GERRY: You want some coffee?

DOMINICK: Yes. No, today, tea with lemon.   465

JOE: A casting director, it's a job in the entertainment business.

GERRY: The entertainment business?

JOE: It's a business!

GERRY: Gee, Joe, I'm only kidding.

JOE: Well I don't take it as a joke.   470

GERRY: Okay, okay, sorry that I try to be human.

DOMINICK: What's wrong? Why are you two fighting?

GERRY: He was an entertainer most of his life.

DOMINICK: A what?

JOE: I was in show business. That's why I bought this place. Never   475
played Broadway, so when I got too old to make the rounds regularly
I decided, well I may never play Broadway, so let me work on Broadway. So me and three other friends of mine bought this here place
and settled down to relax our few years on this earth with the toil of
good, honest, hard work. I'm the only one left of the three. Gerry   480
just bought a share of the place, makes him a partner now. But he
worked in this place for a long time before he could make enough
money to buy a share of the place. Dominick, there's plenty of opportunity in America to make a decent living if you put your mind to
it. I mean don't think that it's been easy for anybody. When you get   485
right down to it, Dominick, there are very few people in this country
who were born with a silver spoon in their mouth. Most of us got to
where we are today by getting up every morning and reporting to
work and by saving a pretty penny here, a pretty penny there, until
you find that you have enough to make a lot of pretty pennies to   490
work for you. You should work hard for the dollar and then sit back
and relax and let the dollar work hard for you. That's the way to live
in America. I mean I really don't understand all this bitching that
goes on in the newspapers every day. The Negro and the Puerto Ricans and now the Cubans and Vietnamese, we let them in this coun-   495
try to do something for themselves and they expect the country to
feed them and clothe them and lead them by the hand until they can

find some type of education, looking for a handout. They don't want
to work.

DOMINICK: Do not ask what your country can do for you, ask what you   500
can do for your country.

JOE: Exactly. Hey that's pretty clever.

DOMINICK: John F. Kennedy said it in a speech.

JOE: He did, huh? . . . smart your man. I still think he was too young to
run a country like this one. Not enough experience in high political   505
office. There's a lot of sharpies up there. Dominick, you go to night
school right, and you read the papers, what's your opinion?

GERRY: Not that it matters any.

JOE: Come on, be serious. Soon this man is going to be a citizen of this
country and he should know that he can express his political, religious   510
and social views, without fear of persecution.

DOMINICK: Well you know, Joe, I lived over there and I lived in many
places that you call over there.

GERRY: *(Singing.)* Over there, over there. Tell 'em that the yanks are
coming. The yanks are coming over there.   515

JOE: That's un-American, Gerry. If you make fun of those songs that inspired men to fight for freedom of the world, you might as well spit
on the flag and curse the President.

GERRY: Damn, Joe, I was only kidding, you kid around, too.

JOE: Yeah, but when I do, it's different.   520

GERRY: What's so different about it?

JOE: Because when I do it, I do it as a showman. You're not a showman,
a stand-up comic; I was.

GERRY: Like you was not like you are.

JOE: Let me tell you how it was when we got to Paris during the big one.   525

GERRY: We know how it was, Joe.

DOMINICK: I read about it in school.

JOE: Yeah, but reading about it is not the same as hearing about it. Them
French girls, my God were they the horniest broads that I ever met in
my life. They rip your pants off if they caught you in the streets or in a   530
hotel room. Man, they were sure the horniest broads in my life. One
thing I can say for the French is that their women sure taught me a
mess of things about women.

GERRY: I have something to say about the French too. The French is a
wonderful race polly boo.   535

JOE: Ahahaha . . . the French is a wonderful race polly boo.

JOE and GERRY: *(Singing together to DOMINICK.)*
                  The French is a wonderful race polly boo . . .
                  The French is a wonderful race polly boo . . .
                  The French is a wonderful race
                  they fight with their feet   540
                  and fuck with their face.
                  Hinky, dinky, pollyyy booo.

JOE: I haven't sang that since Paris, my, my, how time has slipped right
        on by.

GERRY: What was the other Polly Boo song that we used to sing.   545

JOE: Oh, right, let me see, the first marine bought the beans.

GERRY: Polly boo . . . come Dominick, just say polly boo, okay?

JOE: The second marine cooked the beans.

GERRY and DOMINICK: Polly boo.

JOE: The third marine ate the beans and shitted all over the submarine.   550

JOE and GERRY and DOMINICK: Hinky dinky, polly boooo.

JOE: Let's stop it, too much.

GERRY: Joe, you all right?

JOE: Yeah, I'm all right.

GERRY: Joe, why don't you go to Paris?   555

JOE: It would be nice, wouldn't it.

GERRY: It'll be great. You and me, the kids are all grown up and they,
        well, you know they . . .

JOE: They don't need us anymore.

GERRY: Sometimes I think I'm in their way. They were talking about put-   560
        ting me in an old age home.

JOE: So that's why you moved away?

GERRY: Yeah, that's why. *(Telephone rings.)*

JOE: This is the house of the Lord, Moses is speaking. Oh hello,
        Ruth . . . it's that Singerton broad again. Yeah, Dominick, you feel   565
        like making a delivery?

DOMINICK: Sure, why not. Do I get a tip?

JOE: Yeah, don't bet on the horses . . . ahahahaha.

GERRY: What you want me to cook up, Joe?

JOE: The regular thing.   570

GERRY: Four coffees, two light no sugar, one black, one regular, two
        danishes, one neopolitan, one eclair, one french cruller and we'll
        throw in one corn muffin.

DOMINICK: What is the address?

JOE: Here ya are and don't stay there all night googling at her ass.   575

GERRY and JOE: *(Singing.)*

                Barney Google with the goo goo googly eyes
                Barney Google with a wife three times his size
                She sued Barney for divorce
                Then she ran off with his horse
                Barney Google with the goo goo googly eyes.   580

GERRY: Take the umbrella, it's drizzling out there.

JOE: Hey, Dominick, don't get wet.

DOMINICK: Thanks.

JOE: So that's why you moved out, heh?

GERRY: Yeah, I didn't understand their insistence on them putting me in   585
        a prison away from all the love and care that I can give them. I know
        that they mean well, but that kind of well meaning I can do without.

I'm not a cripple, Joe, I drive my own car. I supported them until
they were old enough to make it out here in the jungle by themselves. Like I did, I paved the road with education, the education that   590
I was not lucky enough to get. Sure they would come and see me
once or twice a week, maybe every day for a while and how long do
you think that would last? Have you ever seen a home for the aged?
It's a death life, all these living beings wrinkled and feeble and mumbling to themselves, holding on to the last postcard from other cou-   595
ples' children, imagining that they are their own grand kids. Decaying
photographs of themselves inside handmade frames, that helped for
awhile, too many homes, private ones, state owned, some of them
real fancy names with chandeliers and candles burning. Others were
brutal in themselves, home for the aged and the feeble. What can you   600
do, when you reach the point of fear, of helplessness? A little money
keeps you alive inside yourself. And then they want to take it all away
from you, for your own good, for their own sense of privacy is more
like it, Joe, for their sense of insanity that pushes them into being social workers rather than the children that you brought up and strug-   605
gled and fought for all your life. If I didn't put them in an institution
when they were young, why do they want to do it to me because I'm
old? They rate me obsolete, that's what it is, Joe, they rate us obsolete. We hold no more useful function in their lives. I wonder what
would happen if someday they come to that realization about all of us   610
. . . When they figure that keeping us in a home is very expensive,
would they just feed us into the gas chambers like Hitler did those
poor miserable Jews? Would they all leave and give us a piece of earth
to toil until we are dead? Maybe they will create dead end jobs that
serve the same function that we do, none. You know when Lyndon   615
Johnson retired to his ranch in Texas, I thought that he would be like
the rest of the retired presidents of this nation and die along with the
headlines in a garbage can. Then I saw a picture of him in the *Daily
News* riding a horse and wearing his hair as long as the very people
who protested his stay in office and his policies. What do you think   620
he was telling the world, a retired President of the greatest nation on
earth wearing his hair like that? It was almost like a sign of arrogance,
of protest, against the talk that he was old and ready to die any moment. Joe, I haven't seen my children or my grandchildren since
Martha and I moved out of the house to be on our own. They said   625
that I was insane and . . . oh shit, I miss the hell out of them, Joe. I
love my children like I never loved anything else in this world, and
watching and helping to take care of their children was like reliving
the past with them all over again. Me and Martha would take them
out and spoil the hell out of them, but it was a good kind of spoiling,   630
the good kind, and they used that to try to commit me. I miss them,
Joe, and I know that I'll never see them again, because 1, Joe, I have
made that decision myself. Joe, sometimes I feel like . . . *(He begins*

to sing.) Sometimes I feel like a motherless child . . . *(NIGHTLIFE, a young man of twenty, enters.)*

NIGHTLIFE: Hi, my it's getting cold out there. Hardly no people on the   635
streets . . . *(He pops a quarter in the jukebox.)* It's a good day for a
mugging. *(Stevie Wonder's "Living for the City" comes up on the
jukebox.)*

JOE: If that's your work I guess it is. What'll it be?

MAN: Give me a chocolate malted milk.

GERRY: *(Exiting to the kitchen.)* One chocolate malted, coming up.   640
(NIGHTLIFE begins to boogie to the music.)

NIGHTLIFE: Is that chocolate cream pie?

JOE: Yep, fresh chocolate cream pie.

NIGHTLIFE: *(Still boogying.)* How much a slice?

JOE: Forty-five cents.

NIGHTLIFE: Let me get those two pieces.   645

JOE: Both of them?

NIGHTLIFE: Yeah, both of them, do you mind?

JOE: You're paying for them. You're eating them, so why should I mind?
You want them now?

NIGHTLIFE: Yeah, now, thanks. *(NIGHTLIFE begins to stuff the pie into his*   650
mouth.)

JOE: You like pie, huh?

NIGHTLIFE: Yeah, I like pies.

JOE: Good, huh?

NIGHTLIFE: Good. *(After a beat.)* You happen to know what time it is?

JOE: The clock is on the wall behind you.   655

NIGHTLIFE: Man, I didn't know it was so early. I works late, they call me
Nightlife.

JOE: It's a name.

NIGHTLIFE: Can I read that paper until the malt is ready?

JOE: Sure, why not, here. *(As JOE folds up the paper, NIGHTLIFE boogies to*   660
the kitchen door and peers into the back.)

JOE: You expecting someone else?

NIGHTLIFE: Why?

JOE: Just that you keep looking around to see if anyone is there.

NIGHTLIFE: Maybe I'm trying to make sure that *no one* is there.

JOE: Maybe.   665

NIGHTLIFE: How's this business, you make a good dollar?

JOE: We do all right.

GERRY: *(Entering from the kitchen.)* Here's your chocolate malt, sonny.

NIGHTLIFE: Nightlife is my name.

GERRY: *(Putting the malt on the counter in front of NIGHTLIFE.)* I call   670
people by their names if they are my friends or are about to be my
friends.

NIGHTLIFE: Yeah, that's cool. *(He drinks the malt down in one long gulp.)*
You make a nice malted milk.

GERRY: Thanks, I try.   675

NIGHTLIFE: Don't we all.

JOE: *(Slapping a check in front of NIGHTLIFE.)* That'll be a dollar
   sixty-five.

NIGHTLIFE: I got eyes, I can see, thank you. *(The three of them stare at
   each other for a moment, then NIGHTLIFE takes out a cigarette, looks at
   JOE and GERRY with an exaggerated villainous smile. He gets up with
   one hand in his pocket and performs a whole silent movie bad guy routine
   of curling his mustache and giving the Richard Widmark crazy killer
   laugh. He then remains in total silence for a long moment, then yells out
   "BOO" slapping the counter with two dollars. JOE pulls out a large revolver and GERRY has a meat cleaver at the ready. NIGHTLIFE begins to
   laugh at them hysterically. JOE takes the money, gives NIGHTLIFE his
   change, refuses the tip. NIGHTLIFE leaves, laughing his way out the door.
   Two men, REYNOLDS and LOCKHART, enter the place along with JOE THE
   COP.)*

JOE: Hey, Joe, what brings you around?   680

GERRY: Hey Joe, what happened to the desk job?

JOE THE COP: This is business, Gerry.

JOE: Police business in our place?

GERRY: I told you they'd catch up with you sooner or later, Dillinger.

JOE THE COP: These two men are from the Government.   685

REYNOLDS: Reynolds, Federal Bureau of Investigation.

LOCKHART: Lockhart, Bureau of Immigration.

REYNOLDS: Joseph Scott, you own the place?

JOE: Yeah, that's right. We own the place. It's a legal business. There's
   nothing going on in this place that ain't legal. I'm an honest man.   690

GERRY: Gerald Fisher is my name. I'm part owner here. What's the
   trouble?

REYNOLDS: There's no trouble with either of you.

LOCKHART: We're looking for a Mister Dominick Athemus Skorpios.

JOE: Dominick? What's he done?   695

LOCKHART: He's in the country illegally.

GERRY: That's not true! He's an American citizen . . . by marriage.

REYNOLDS: We know of his marriage to one Carmen de Jesus—also
   known as Iris Morales-Milagros Ramirez. She has a list of aliases that
   can go on for a couple of days and we don't have much time.   700

JOE: Well, I don't know how many names she has, nor do I care if she is
   an American citizen by birth.

JOE THE COP: Easy, Joe. Will ya hear them out first before you blow a
   fuse.

GERRY: She is a Puerto Rican—she's a citizen by birth.   705

JOE: Yeah, what ya mean! That Puerto Ricans aren't citizens of this country? They are one of the finest people to ever set foot in this God-
   given soil.

REYNOLDS: Puerto Ricans are citizens, sir.

LOCKHART: But not Mexicans, Mr. Scott.   710

JOE: Mexican?

GERRY: Mexican? What ya mean? She's a Mex? . . . She showed us her birth certificate.

LOCKHART: Phony. Most of her papers are phonies.

REYNOLDS: Where's Mister Skorpios now?   715

JOE: He's out making a delivery . . . He'll be back soon.

REYNOLDS: Good, we'll wait.

JOE THE COP: See, Joe, it's like this. This dame goes around posing as Puerto Rican so that she can hook fishes like Dominick into paying her to marry her so they can stay in the country through marriage.   720

LOCKHART: We have her in custody now. Mister Skorpios may have to face other charges of conspiracy. So his chances to have stayed here are less even with the help you may offer in his behalf.

REYNOLDS: Lockhart, call in.

LOCKHART: Will do.   725

GERRY: Oh, poor Dominick. *(Enter DOMINICK.)*

DOMINICK: Hell, Joe, here's the money. She gave me no tip. She's cheap, ain't she?

JOE: Isn't she. It's "isn't she." These two men are here to see you, Dom. They're from the government. They wanna talk to you about . . . hell,   730
Gerry, you tell him.

GERRY: They say you are here illegally and they . . . well, they . . .

DOMINICK: Illegally? No that's not true anymore. I'm married to an American. I got married to an American. I'm not . . .

JOE: That's just it. She's not an American. She's not a Puerto Rican.   735
She's a wetback Mexican scab who slipped into the country and took all of us in . . . goddamn it, Dominick . . . goddamn her soul.

DOMINICK: She not an American?

LOCKHART: I'm afraid not, Mr. Skorpios.

REYNOLDS: Let's go. We can talk about this downtown.   740

DOMINICK: Wait please! I just want to live here to make a life here, like your fathers did. Like Joe says, I would, if I work hard enough at it. I want to make my life here, to make a decent living here in America. Can't I stay? Can't I stay please! Let me stay here in this place. I work hard, ask Joe . . . ask Gerry . . . I'm never late, never did I miss a day   745
of work, always I work late and hard and very much. Never am I lazy.

REYNOLDS: Let's go.

DOMINICK: I do not ask for welfare or any kind of help from government . . . just to let me make a life here. I just want to be an American.

JOE THE COP: I'm sorry, Dominick.   750

JOE: It's not your fault, Joe. It's all our faults.

REYNOLDS: Come along, Mr. Skorpios. Good night, gentlemen.

LOCKHART: Good night, sorry, we're just doing out job . . . you understand.

JOE: We understand . . . yeah, we understand. *(Exit REYNOLDS,*   755
LOCKHART and DOMINICK.)

GERRY: Poor Dominick. He didn't even get laid . . . *(Lights out.)*

ACT II

Same scene. Three hours later, it is the height of the hour JOE *and* GERRY *are busy serving the customers.* ZULMA *enters during the scene and sips on a cup of chocolate. The scene as originally produced was improvised around the following set of characters:* MAN ONE, MAN TWO, HOOKER ONE, HOOKER TWO, COWBOY. *At the end of the scene, the* HOOKERS *exit with* COWBOY. GERRY *turns to* JOE.

GERRY: *(Pointing to* JUNKIE GIRL.*)* Hey, Joe.
JOE: She's pulling a Mary Hartman—Mary Hartman.
GIRL: Hey, wow, Mary Hartman. I look like Mary Hartman?
JOE: No.
GERRY: What he's saying is you're pulling a Mary Hartman.   5
GIRL: How's that?
JOE: Drowning in a bowl of soup.
GIRL: This soup is cold. I don't want it.
JOE: You pay for it just the same.
GIRL: Hey, yeah, wow, like I got bread. *(Throws her money on the counter*   10
        and stumbles out into the night. The SHOPPING BAG LADY *sits on a stool*
        mumbling to herself, hell, damn, fuck you, shit, bastard. Profanity is the
        only thing she says.)
LADY: Mumble mumble Damn you mumble mumble. *(Waving her hands*
        all the time, she takes the things from time to time and puts them inside
        her shopping bag. She exits during the song "Greasy Spoon Blues.")
GERRY: Goddamn it, wouldn't you know it, Joe, that today would I turn
        out to be busier than usual? Just our luck to have Dominick picked up
        at the height of the hour.
JOE: Poor Dominick. He should have called in sick.   15
GERRY: Aw, they would have turned up tomorrow or the next day. When
        the Feds are after you, forget it. You can run, but you can't hide.
        That's the old saying about them. Dillinger found that out. So did
        Babyface Nelson and Ma Barker and a host of others that fled the
        F.B.I. You just can't win. It's like playing a game of stud poker and   20
        knowing that the deck is stacked against you, but you sit down to play
        anyway, that's the philosophy of the criminal mind. They go out and
        play against a stacked deck. It's a means of ending the beginning of
        yourself.
JOE: Well, you know what they say about destiny.   25
GERRY: No, I don't. What is it they say about destiny?
JOE: How should I know? I thought you knew. *(Telephone rings.)*
JOE: There's a midnight moon at the greasy spoon tonight. Oh . . . hi,
        Ruth. What can I do for you? . . . Who? Oh, Dominick . . . naw, he
        ain't here anymore. They took him away today . . . Who? The F.B.I.,   30
        that's who . . . they found out he was a wanted killer . . . Yeah, they
        got wind of him from the C. I. A. They spotted him and turned him

over to the C. I. D., who turned him over to the B. C. I., who
called Scotland Yard, who called Interpol, who called the F.B.I.
and they came and took him away. . . . That's right. A born killer, 35
they said. . . . Yep, about twenty people with a rusty ax handle . . .
no motive. He did it for pleasure . . . what? . . . no . . . throughout
the nation, yep, been underground for years. Sure we knew about it.
Gerry thought he could rehabilitate him. . . . No, I'm not lying to
you. . . . You wanna ask Gerry? . . . Sure, it's the truth. . . . Yep, 40
twenty people . . . mostly late night working women. . . . Yep, late
night working women. . . . Naw, no men . . . just women . . . in
their late forties. Seems he had a kind of psycho thing about him,
always when he delivered coffee to them. You sure are lucky . . .
he's not going to be able to keep that date. Yeah, it's really a 45
shame. . . . Take it easy. . . . No, there's no chance of him escaping.
But if he does, you will be the first to know. . . . Yeah, he talked
about you a lot. Yeah, I think you should go to bed. Yeah, that's
not a bad idea. . . . Sure will. Good night. Pleasant dreams. . . .
Bye. . . . Chiao . . . hang up already, will you! . . . Damn, that 50
woman sure can be a pain in the lower back. . . . Boy, one of these
days. One of these days . . .

GERRY: I'll bet she'll dream of Dominick tonight.

JOE: I bet she will.

GERRY: Twenty people with a rusty ax handle . . . that's a good one. 55

JOE: Mostly late night working women . . .

ZULMA: *(Stands up slowly.)* You guys had a killer working here . . . trying
to rehabilitate a born killer. That guy Dominick was a killer? He sure
didn't look like a killer. He didn't look like a killer. He didn't act like
a killer. And he didn't talk like a killer. *(Pause.)* But then again, what 60
does a killer look like or what does a killer say to someone when they
first meet. Hi, I'm a killer.

JOE: Zelma, he was no killer. Believe me, I was joking with that women.

ZULMA: The name is Zulma, not Zelma.

JOE: Zulma out here and Zelma at home. 65

ZULMA: It's Zulma out here and Zulma at home and Zulma on stage and
Zulma in here.

JOE: Zulma. Zelma. Zulma. Zelma. Zelma. Zulma. What's in a name?

ZULMA: Plenty.

GERRY: So how's business? 70

ZULMA: Do you know what? This morning I went to five auditions.
Count them. Five. Since this morning I've been pounding the concrete, making the rounds and all I got is the same "don't call us, we'll
call you" routine.

JOE: Oh, how I know them words so well. 75

ZULMA: Oh, I bet you know the routine.

GERRY: But with a name like Zulma Samson, well you know, what you
can expect?

ZULMA: It has nothing to do with the name, Gerry. It's the age . . . the
         age. It's the age. *(She begins to weep.)*   80
JOE: Hey! Hey, look, don't do that. Come on now, pull yourself to-
       gether. Come on, Zulma, not in here. What if someone comes in?
       Look, stop crying, will ya? . . . please stop crying.
ZULMA: It's the age. It's the age. I'm a has-been . . . a has-been that
         never was. I was once so beautiful, to look at me you wouldn't think   85
         so, but I was. I was once so beautiful . . . what's happened to me . . . ?
JOE: You're still beautiful. You still got a lot of spunk left in you. Stop
       crying.
ZULMA: Oh, stop it. I know the truth. I know the truth, that's why I'm
         crying, 'cause I know the truth . . . I realize the truth. I can't hide 90
         from the mirror anymore. My time is over. My time is over and I
         never even got to look at the clock of success. . . . I'm passed the hour
         of life. . . . I can face the truth now . . . I can face all the wrinkles
         without all the make-up. I can face it now . . . I know that I'm all
         washed up . . . but what am I going to do? . . . What am I going to   95
         do . . . ? I know nothing else but show business . . . it's all I know
         since I was a child. And I am not going to end up in no old actors
         home to tell stories of glorious events that never took place . . . lay by
         the window all the time watching the sunrise . . . hoping that each ray
         of light will bring in a letter from Dino de Laurentis or a script hand- 100
         delivered from Joseph Papp saying that he needs me to play the lead
         in a new production at Lincoln Center . . . no . . . no . . . no actors
         home for me. . . . I was born on stage . . . well, not exactly on stage it
         was a traveling show in a tent. I was on stage when the final labor pain
         struck my mother . . . no, I know nothing else, and I never wanted to   105
         know anything else but what I know . . . and it's been grand and I
         want to remember it as being grand and I always, since the moment I
         was able to fend for myself . . . I've took care of myself and now I've
         reached the ebb of my tide . . .
GERRY: "The ebb of my tide" . . . . Zulma, you're really a ham.   110
ZULMA: Of the finest caliber.
JOE: So, now that you say you know what you think is the truth of your
       final years on the good earth, what do you plan on doing with them?
GERRY: How do you plan to support yourself?
ZULMA: I'll get me a steady job.   115
JOE: You have any place in mind?
ZULMA: Sure.
JOE: Where?
ZULMA: Here.
GERRY: Where?   120
ZULMA: Here.
JOE: Here!
ZULMA: Here.
GERRY: Did she say here?

ZULMA: What are you guys . . . a comedy team?   125

GERRY: She did say here.

ZULMA: I thought I was clear about that.

JOE: I know you sounded clear and I know that you think you sounded
clear, but I wanted to make sure that you sounded clear about being
clear about working here . . . I mean, I don't want to sound as if I   130
and Gerry were a large firm, but we feel somehow that since we are
going to have to pay wages to whoever spends hours here . . .

ZULMA: What's the problem? I mean, look, you like me and I like
you. . . . You do like me???

JOE: Sure.   135

GERRY: No one said that they didn't like you, at least I didn't.

JOE: I didn't say it either.

ZULMA: Okay, then what's the problem? You like me, I like you, we can
have a beautiful working relationship. And it's close to Broadway, you
know what I mean.   140

JOE: I know what you mean, more than you think.

GERRY: Well, it's okay with me if it's okay with Joe.

JOE: Well, if it's okay with you, then it's okay with me.

GERRY: When can you start?

ZULMA: Nothing like the present for doing what you have to do, right   145
fellas?!

GERRY: Right!

JOE: Go in the back and put on something that'll keep the grease off
your clothes.

ZULMA: Oh, by the way. I look ridiculous in a mini-skirt, so I hope you   150
don't require that your female workers wear one.

JOE: I wouldn't dream of asking you to wear one.

ZULMA: Look at that. Not even in your dreams can you see me in a mini-
skirt. Boy, I must look worse than I thought.

JOE: I didn't mean it that way.   155

ZULMA: No! In what way then?

JOE: Just go get somethin' on, will ya? (ZULMA *exits to the kitchen.*)

GERRY: She's okay, you know . . . a regular guy.

JOE: Yeah, she's all right. I'm glad that she's getting a little more sense
into her head nowadays. You know, I think we're going to have a nice   160
night tomorrow.

GERRY: Yeah, I think so too . . . though, I still feel sorry for poor old
Dominick.

JOE: Yeah, I think I'm going to miss him too.

GERRY: He would have made a great American citizen.   165

JOE: Just like you, huh?

GERRY: Yeah, just like me . . . What??!! You think that I'm not a great
American citizen?

JOE: No, I don't think you're a great American citizen.

GERRY: You don't?   170

JOE: No, I don't think you're a great American citizen.

GERRY: You're kidding.

JOE: No, I'm serious.

GERRY: What you think, I'm some kinda pinko fag commie or   175
something?

JOE: No, I don't think you're some kinda pinko fag commie or
something.

GERRY: Then what do you mean by saying that I'm not a great American
citizen?

JOE: Gerry, I think you're a good American citizen. I think you're a pa-   180
triotic American citizen. I think you're a loyal American citizen. But I
don't think you're a great American citizen. Greatness is reserved for
those who do not make their living being a short order cook.

GERRY: Greatness is not reserved, Joe. Greatness is there for all who wish
to claim it. I for one never had the passion to grab it and the responsi-   185
bilities that go along with it. I am a simple man . . . a humble man . . .
a man of wisdom, of worldly knowledge . . . of compassion . . . *(Enter
a* YOUNG MUSICIAN *and his* GIRLFRIEND.*)*

GIRL: You tell 'em.

BOY: You tell 'em.

GIRL: Why did you tell me you was going to tell 'em if you ain't going   190
to tell 'em?

BOY: I said I *might* tell 'em today.

GIRL: Well, tomorrow is the gig and we promised to tell 'em if we got
the job. Right! So tell 'em!

BOY: Yeah, if . . .   195

GIRL: No ifs, ands or buts about it . . . Joe . . .

JOE: Yeah.

GIRL: Can we see you for a sec?

JOE: Hey, Gerry, you wanna handle the old lady. I want to talk with the
kids.   200

GERRY: No skin off my nose . . .

JOE: Hey, kids, how's the business treating you?

BOY: Well, I think we got a gig.

JOE: No kidding.

GIRL: Well, it's not much of a gig . . .   205

BOY: It's in the West Village.

GIRL: But it's a start.

JOE: A start, no matter how big or small, it's a start. What'a ya wanna
eat?

BOY: Boy, I'm too excited to talk or sleep *or eat.*   210

GIRL: I never thought we could make it here in the concrete cold, metal
monster, but it looks like it might happen.

JOE: Yeah, no time at all you might be another Sonny and weird.

GIRL: You mean Cher.

JOE: That's just what I said, weird.   215

GIRL: I hope it happens soon. Our phone has been disconnected, the rent is due and we owe you almost twenty dollars.

BOY: We wanted you to know that we are singing at this place 'cause they're putting up posters announcing our appearance and we didn't want you to think that we are making money and eating for free.   220

JOE: Yeah, but you're playing for free.

GIRL: We wrote . . . well, he wrote a song for you and the place.

BOY: Yeah, we wanna dedicate this song to you and Gerry.

GERRY: For us?

BOY: Hunh, yeah.   225

GIRL: You've been so wonderful, we needed encouragement and you gave it.

GERRY: Hey, what time is the performance? Maybe we can make it.

JOE: You know those things happen at night.

BOY: Yeah, too bad 'cause we would really dig it if you showed up at the joint.   230

GIRL: Well, we better be going if we are going to be wide awake for the gig.

JOE: Not until we hear our song.

GERRY: Right, since you can't pay us the money you owe, ya gotta play Tommy Tucker and sing for your supper.   235

GIRL: You want me to sing?

BOY: You got the voice.

GIRL: Well, I don't know . . .

JOE: What's there to know? Look at it this way, it's a rehearsal before the performance tomorrow.   240

GIRL: All right.

BOY: Are you ready, Cher?

GIRL: Yes, Sonny.

LADY: Fuck you, mumble, mumble . . .   245

GERRY: *(To SHOPPING BAG LADY.)* Please sweety.

JOE: Forget about her, she isn't listening or talking to anyone here but herself. Go ahead, kids. *(The song, "Greasy Spoon Blues". Words and music by Charles Coker. During the song the SHOPPING BAG LADY exits, mumbling profanities to whomever is listening.)*

GIRL: Bye, Joe.

JOE: Bye, kids. Break a leg tomorrow. *(JAKE enters.)*   250

GERRY: Yeah, break a leg.

JAKE: Hey, nigger, what's happening?

JOE: Jake, why do you always call me a nigger?

JAKE: Because you are.

GERRY: Hi, Jake, how's the parlor business coming along?   255

JAKE: Great, can't do better if I try. I just got me two new girls.

GERRY: Black?

JAKE: Two tall Swedish blondes that are looking sweeter than a piece of watermelon on a hot sticky day in the city.

JOE: Two blondes, huh?   260
JAKE: Two blondes.
GERRY: Two tall blondes?
JAKE: Yep, two tall blondes.
JOE: Blondes, huh?
JAKE: Two tall big-tit blondes that are for real. I mean it ain't dye either.   265
That yellow goldness is for real . . . it's natural . . . I know cause they
got that yellow hair everywhere else too.
GERRY: Natural blondes, huh?!
JAKE: Natural blondes.
JOE: They got yellow hair everywhere else?   270
JAKE: All over!
GERRY: All over?
JAKE: Boy, I wish I had a tape recorder with me.
GERRY: A tape recorder, what in heavens name for?
JAKE: To get this all down for posterity. You guys sound like a couple of   275
typical out of town businessmen in a cathouse.
JOE: Well, we are a couple of businessmen, not from out of town, but
businessmen nevertheless. You know, Jake, we weren't exactly raised
with the same disadvantages that you had to endure.
JAKE: What disadvantages are you talking about?   280
GERRY: Yeah, cause I would also like to know.
JOE: You know what I mean . . . this whole production number that you
had to undergo since the curtain rose on your act . . . not having the
same education that I and Gerry were fortunate enough to have, even
though I never really finished high school, only because of the fact   285
that I was the oldest of the family, and when my father died in the war
I had to go out into the wide rushings of making a daily living for the
rest of the kids, not that I'm complaining, you know, I mean, I loved
doing what I did . . . show biz is my cup of tea, every penny that I
earned from hoofing it up, wherever the show boat stopped, went   290
back home . . . and . . .
GERRY: I thought you were an orphan, Joe.
JOE: There you go again, Gerry, everytime that I have this nigger by the
balls, hanging onto every word, there you go again breaking up the
story.   295
JAKE: Joe . . . fifteen years . . .
JOE: Yeah, it's been fifteen years. Well, what about it?
JAKE: Do you think that I was really going for that cock 'n' bull yarn you
were spinning?
JOE: I'm sure that if this klondike over here hadn't of interrupted, you   300
would've been standing there with your tongue hanging out, hanging,
yeah . . . yeah . . . and what happened next, Joe . . . ?
JAKE: Joe, come on off it.
JOE: Jake, I made my living spinning yarns to suckers like you.
JAKE: What kind of a car you drive, Joe?   305

JOE: You know what kind of a car I drive.

GERRY: Yeah, you gave it to him last Christmas.

JAKE: That's not what I'm saying, Gerry.

JOE: Well, if you are going to flaunt that present in my face and in front
of strangers . . .

GERRY: Strangers? Who's a stranger here?

JOE: Gerry, why don't you go in the back and do something?

JAKE: Yeah, Gerry, why don't you go take some meat in the back.

GERRY: Why don't both of you get yourselves a nice job in a balloon factory blowing . . . ?

JAKE: As you were saying, Joe.

JOE: If you are going to flaunt that present in my face in front of
strangers, then I suggest that you get me a Cadillac instead of that
cheap second-hand station wagon that I drive from Honest Harry.

JAKE: Joe, I drive a Cadillac on Tuesdays and Thursdays. On Fridays and
Sundays, while I relax in my country home, I fool around with my
Porsche and sometimes I even get a big kick by returning to this God-
forsaken city in my Honda. So you see, Joe, all that bull about my dis-
advantaged childhood is just a lot of hot air blowing out your mouth.
Actually, it's a substitute for the bottom part of your body. (GERRY
laughs.)

JOE: It ain't that funny, Gerry.

GERRY: You're big, Joe. The truth isn't always funny, but with you it's a
riot.

JOE: Careful how you use that word around Jake, 'cause you know what
they say . . . you can take the nigger out of the country but . . .

JAKE: You can't take the country out of the nigger and you know where
that comes from, Joe.

JOE: Sure, from where all sayings come from . . . wise thinking of a man
of wisdom.

JAKE: No. Not from any great man of wisdom, but from a truth that all
niggers know about this country.

GERRY: What truth, Jake?

JOE: Don't fall for it, Gerry, he's pulling the same routine I pulled on
him.

JAKE: It's not a routine, Joe, it's the real thing. Here we are reaching the
heights of our existing on this planet . . . two hundred years old . . .
we've just celebrated the birth of a freedom revolution that ceased
being a revolution for freedom twenty-four hours after its conception.
. . . As the years rolled by and the mentality of this country remained
stagnant, the niggers in this country became angrier and angrier as
they paid in blood in countless wars that cried out the words of liberty, justice and equality. We found ourselves being booed over and
over again, no matter how many times we fought and died and bled in
other lands for the sake of free enterprise and yet couldn't share in the
profits . . . a free nation, a free people dedicated to the thought that

all men are created equal up to the color of their skin, up to the
pattern of your speech. Freedom became a whore, just like my ladies
are. They're whores, but they're whores that admit they're whores and
when the time comes that they know it doesn't benefit them to be
whores any longer they change with the times and became respectable, 355
quote unquote, "working women" with a family to raise. . . .
Here . . . here we have a whore calling herself liberty-justice-and-
equality. Oh, yeah, she's a whore, I can see by the look in your face,
Joe, that you don't like what I am saying, but I am a spade who likes
calling it as it plays, liberty is a whore, justice is a whore and equality is 360
a faggot. How does that grab you? . . . She is a whore who spreads her
legs to the highest bidder. Justice is blind to everyone but to those
that spread over her eyelids the greed mercurochrome that heals all
wounds. She sees, and liberty is once again that night your sleeping
companion . . . the great average typical all-American dollar, that is 365
the miracle worker, that is the real equalizer. If your pockets are hungry, so is your stomach and so is your soul. All that to say what we
were saying: "You can take the niggers out of the country, but you
can't take the country out of the nigger." All the niggers, white as
well as black, the niggers who feel that they have a right to everything 370
that this country has to offer them, the white niggers who built the
railroads from the East, the yellow niggers who built the railroad from
the West, the black niggers who built this land from all over, the rest
of the niggers that died and crippled their lives so that all of us niggers
can be a part of this great concept called America, land of the free. 375
Death remembers the songs of false democracy. You understand what
I am saying . . . it's like this . . . I remember after that prison rebellion
in Attica . . . a politician said when Americans prefer to die than to live
one more day in this country, it's time we start examining ourselves. I
don't know if those were his exact words, but they had an effect on 380
me. Joe, I did just that. I started to examine what my responsibilities
were as a citizen of the greatest nation on the face of the earth. Am I
or am I not . . . if I am, then it's time that I behave like one . . . how
do you see yourself? . . .

JOE: I hope to see that I fulfill myself here everyday that the sun shines. 385
GERRY: So do I.
JOE: What brought this all about in you today, Jake?
JAKE: I don't know. Maybe it's reading that an eleven-year-old child
O.D.'d in Harlem while an eleven-year-old in Scarsdale won the
spelling bee for his district. Maybe it's age . . . maybe it's after know- 390
ing you fifteen years . . . you reacted pretty strange to the fact that I
hired two white blonde girls to work in the parlor.
JOE: Wait a second . . . you didn't take me seriously, did you?
JAKE: Maybe I did without realizing it, maybe I did.
JOE: Well, you shouldn't, 'cause you know that I don't give a damn 395
about who works for you or what their title of work is, as long as they
respect me and what's mine.

GERRY: Yeah, you should know Joe better by now . . . fifteen years, damn if you don't.

JAKE: Yeah, and he even had dinner with me once in his home, his very own home, though he never came to my house to eat.

JOE: You know it could be because you never invited me, ever thought of that?

JAKE: Hell, that's right, I never did, did I?

JOE: No, you never did.

JAKE: And you know what, I never will.

JOE: The hell with you, you nigger.

GERRY: Things are back to normal.

JAKE: They always were.

JOE: That's great to hear.

GERRY: Two big-tit blondes, huh?

JAKE: Yep, two real big-tit blondes.

JOE: Yellow everywhere, huh?

JAKE: Yep, everywhere.

JOE: And they let you see it, huh?

JAKE: Well, if they didn't, they wouldn't be working for me, Joe.

JOE: Well, have they got any sense of shame?

JAKE: Why? 'Cause they are working in a massage parlor that's a front for a you-know-what or because they let a big black ugly nigger like me see their private parts, heh?

JOE: As for the first part of your question, if they want that kind of work, that's their business, not mine. To each his own, right Gerry?

JAKE: Don't ask Gerry, because he's been up there.

JOE: You have?

GERRY: Yeah, well . . . sure, but just out of curiosity.

JAKE: Out of what?

JOE: He said out of curiosity.

JAKE: I heard what he said, it's just that I couldn't believe that I heard what he said.

JOE: Repeat what you said for the gentleman, Gerry.

JAKE: He don't have to because you don't believe him and you know that I know you don't believe him.

GERRY: Hey, the *News* is here.

JOE: I'll get it.

JAKE: That's okay, Joe, relax, I'll bring them in for you.

JOE: (*Handing* JAKE *a check.*) Here, Jake, give the driver this check for me.

JAKE: Sure . . . (*JAKE exits.*)

JOE: How come you didn't tell me you were up at Jake's place?

GERRY: Well, Joe, you see, I was passing by one late afternoon, not having anything to do and well, you know, knowing Jake all these years and not ever being up to his place of business, well, I figure . . .

JOE: I know . . . I know . . . since he's such a good and steady customer, you wanted . . .

GERRY: Exactly . . .   445

JOE: One hand washes the other.

GERRY: Just what I was thinking on that very day.

JOE: I bet.

GERRY: Well, you know Joe, there's still a lot of something in this old
         man.   450

JOE: How was the merchandise? *(JAKE enters.)*

JAKE: Here you are, Joe . . . let me take out five of these for my girls.
         They get bored after a while, you know, they need things, to read. I
         always believe that they should keep abreast of what's going on in the
         world . . . they need to have more to say to the customers.   455

GERRY: The merchandise is excellent, not like the rest of the trash out
         there.

JOE: Maybe I'll take a look-see.

JAKE: You should. That's always advisable at your age . . . see what you
         can handle before you get involved.   460

JOE: I don't remember asking for your advice, Mister Jake Andrews.

JAKE: Well, normally, Jake Andrews Esquire requires a small fee for ad-
         vice, but since we're such bosom buddies, I thought I'd give it to you
         free of charge, but don't make it a habit.

JOE: That's the mistake of your career, Jake, you think . . . *(ZULMA enters* 465
         from the kitchen in her waitress outfit. She has removed her wig and
         cleaned the make-up off her face.)

ZULMA: How's this, fellas?

JOE: Get back into the kitchen, there's talk going on in here that a
         woman shouldn't hear . . .

ZULMA: Oh, you got to be kidding. Hey, hi, Jake, how's the girls?

JAKE: Zulu baby . . . what're you doing in that get-up?   470

JOE: Zulu baby?

GERRY: Zulu baby?

ZULMA: There they go again.

JAKE: There who goes again?

ZULMA: The gold dust twins.   475

JOE: Zulu baby?

ZULMA: Yeah, Zulu! It's a nickname. Don't you guys have nicknames?
         . . . You know, like when you're a kid growing up and you get a name
         tagged on . . . Sinky . . . Tubby . . .

JAKE: These guys were born standing up.   480

JOE: But Zulu!

JAKE: And what's wrong with Zulu?

ZULMA: Yeah, what is wrong with Zulu? I like it, as a matter of fact.

GERRY: To each his own.

ZULMA: And what do you have?   485

JAKE: These guys haven't got nothing, but the lard in the frying pan to
         talk to.

JOE: At least if the lard is hot it tells you.

JAKE: It does, does it? . . . you talk to the lard? . . . little spoonfuls or big
    globs of it?   490

JOE: Oh, oh, oh very funny . . . very funny!!

GERRY: Five thousand comics out of work and he wants to be a
    comedian.

JAKE: I didn't think it was funny. I was asking a very serious question.

ZULMA: Yeah, he wasn't the one who said that he talks to the lard in the   495
    frying pan.

GERRY: You two should appear on stage at the Palace.

JOE: You two are really funny. I'll bet you'll be a regular hit with the
    drunks.

JAKE: I don't think we're funny. If I did, I would have tried the stage like   500
    you did.

JOE: Yeah, well I think that I am going . . .

JAKE: I saw you play the Lyric once when I was young.

JOE: You did? . . . you saw me on stage? . . .

JAKE: Sure did.   505

JOE: Really!

GERRY: Joe, he's trying to . . .

JOE: Be quiet, Gerry . . . can't you see the man is saying something
    important.

GERRY: Joe, he's only trying . . .   510

JAKE: No really, I did see him play on stage.

GERRY: Come on, you really expect me to believe that?

JAKE: He used to do a comic routine and then your partner would come
    on and do a soft shoe, right?

JOE: The Lyric . . . that was one of my favorite places.   515

JAKE: Am I right? You were billed as Jack and Jill.

JOE: That's right . . . gee, you remember . . . after all these years too.

JAKE: Oh, why wouldn't I remember. You were terrific.

JOE: Well, we was good.

JAKE: Good . . . you were great . . . everyone would just sit there after   520
    the movie and wait for you two to come on with the real show.

JOE: The real show?

JAKE: Yeah man, the real show.

GERRY: You really saw him play at the Lyric?

JAKE: Sure, just before the war, I think. You know it's been a long time.   525

JOE: You know, when I was a kid I was brought up in an orphanage.

GERRY: No, I didn't know that.

JOE: My parents were killed in an automobile accident at the age of
    three.

GERRY: Gee, I bet that was tough on you.   530

JOE: No, not really, being so young I really didn't feel the loss that great.

JAKE: I lost my folks too, at an early age . . . didn't go to no orphanage,
    though, my grandmother raised me . . . and with an iron hand and the
    cord.

JOE: The cord I remember only too well, the hurt it can inflict on a   535
       young child.
JAKE: Especially if it's in the hands of strangers.
JOE: Especially in the hands of strangers.
GERRY: You two got a lot in common. *(Telephone rings.)*
ZULMA: I'll get it . . . Joe's Diner . . . sorry, no deliveries tonight . . .   540
       can't be helped . . . sorry . . . tomorrow . . . bye . . . you were saying
       Joe?
JOE: I was in the place a few years, couldn't get adopted . . . every Sun-
       day in summer they would have an invited performer come to enter-
       tain the kids. Once these two black men came in and they were really   545
       funny, they made me forget all the heartaches that flowed inside my
       soul . . . I was never a cute kid, so no one would even take me home
       for the weekends . . . they came on stage and told some really funny
       stories and they did a song and dance number . . . I looked around me
       and saw all those smiling faces and I began to sing out loud with the   550
       two men on stage. They called me with them and I joined them in the
       song . . . not the dancing, though. I never seen anyone dance like
       those two guys did. Boy, they could really move . . . later that week
       they came back and visited with me. I was surprised, to say the least,
       when the administrator let them come in for the month they played in   555
       town and teach me their routine . . . that Fourth of July I went on
       stage with them and let me tell you, I was the happiest kid in the place
       . . . soon they left and I never saw them again . . . but I kept on prac-
       ticing how to dance and tried different jokes and stories at night on
       the other kids. Soon, I never wanted to be anything else but an enter-   560
       tainer . . . but life being what it is, I found myself drifting as a short
       order cook . . . not that there's anything wrong with being a short
       order cook, especially being part owner . . . I always dreamt that I
       would . . . well, so many dreams . . . never growing old . . . ahead of
       death by two yards . . . yet . . . here I am . . . I can't even remember   565
       the routine that I used to do, I . . . I, well . . . life sometimes leaves
       no room for a celebration . . . your greatest moments become objects
       of torment . . . but I guess I should thank the Lord for each dream,
       even if the dream never came true, at least I had the opportunity to
       have dreams . . . you reach a certain time in life . . . you find yourself   570
       wandering about in countless acres of flowers and one day it dawns on
       you . . . butterflies . . . thousands and thousands of butterflies . . .
       butterflies . . . and no more flowers are growing . . . *(ZULMA begins to
       sing "Moonlight Bay." JOE joins in. They do a vaudeville soft-shoe routine.
       JAKE and GERRY hum along.)*
JAKE: A bit rusty . . .
JOE: Go screw yourself . . .   575
GERRY: What'll it be, Jake?
ZULMA: I'll make it . . . you'll be my first customer.
JAKE: Great . . . two coffees regular and a bacon and egg sandwich to go.
ZULMA: Two coffees and a B&E to travel, coming right up.

GERRY: Got it?   580
ZULMA: *(Exiting to kitchen.)* Got it.
JAKE: Then get it, already.
JOE: Hold your horses.
JAKE: Hey, what happened to Dominick? . . . that funny Greek guy you
  had working here?   585
JOE: He got picked up by the Feds.
JAKE: When?
GERRY: Earlier this evening.
JAKE: No shh . . . really, what for?
JOE: Naw, I'm not going to tell you.   590
JAKE: Hey, come on . . . all right, don't tell me . . . come on, tell me,
  what for?
JOE: Seems Dominick was a top syndicate hit man. He was posing as a
  jerk to get closer to a certain psuedo-hip black, would-be king of the
  pimps.   595
GERRY: You know, Jake, you're the only man I know whose head is as
  pointed as his shoes.
JAKE: Okay. Enough! Hey, baby, don't burn the bacon. *(Goes to jukebox.)*
  Hey, you know my cousin Rufus . . . the one in the hospital?
JOE: Can't say I do.   600
JAKE: No, seriously speaking.
JOE: Still can't say that I do.
GERRY: Never mentioned him to me either . . . Rufus . . . Rufus . . . with
  a name like that I would have remembered him if you had said any-
  thing about him.   605
JAKE: Sure I did . . . well, anyway, he was in the hospital for an operation
  . . . I forgot what was wrong with him . . . but, anyway . . . the doc-
  tors gave him an operation all right, they cut off both of his legs and
  there was nothing wrong with his legs. They made a mistake on the
  chart. Anyway, that's what they are saying . . . they cut both of his legs   610
  right above the knees, so he can't even walk.
GERRY: He's going to sue, right?
JOE: Of course, he's going to sue, he's got an open-and-shut case.
JAKE: Well, that's what we all thought until last week when we went to
  court and the jury didn't vote in his favor.   615
JOE: They didn't what?
GERRY: What do you mean, they didn't vote in his favor! They cut off
  both of the poor slob's legs and they found him . . .
JAKE: Yeah, I know the way you feel, but the court was right.
JOE: The court was right, what kind of crap is that?   620
GERRY: Yeah, what kind of crap is that? He should have sued their asses
  off.
JAKE: Well, he lost the case because of one thing, only one little fault.
JOE: One little fault! The man doesn't have his legs anymore and you call
  that a little fault.   625
JAKE: That's why he lost the case.

GERRY: Why?

JAKE: Well, you see, he didn't have a leg to stand on.

ZULMA: *(From kitchen window.)* You two fell for the old·hokey dokey.

GERRY: He was pulling our leg all the time.   630

JAKE: Just like the doctor's pulled old Rufus' legs off. He didn't have a
leg to stand on.

JOE: *(To Zulma.)* Get back to the stove.

ZULMA: What's the matter, you can't stand being taken for a ride.
(ZULMA exits to the kitchen.)

JOE: You know that's one of my old routines.   635

JAKE: Sure, it is. I was surprised you didn't catch on sooner.

JOE: He didn't have a leg to stand on.

GERRY: You wanna hear a new Polish joke?

JAKE: Naw.

JOE: Have you got any nice nigger jokes?   640

JAKE: A Jewish joke.

ZULMA: *(Entering from kitchen.)* Here's your things, Jake.

JAKE: Thanks baby . . . you know I'm going to come here even more
than before. I only come here as a last resort, like when everything
else is closed. That's why he's open so late, if it closed any earlier no   645
one would come in here to . . .

JOE: Can it, Jake, can it.

JAKE: Give me a couple'a them donuts.

ZULMA: What kind, we got, jelly . . . chocolate and . . .

JAKE: Two jelly.   650

JOE: Jake, for you they're seventy-five cents apiece.

JAKE: Seventy-five cents apiece, are you for real?

JOE: Yes and so are the jelly donuts too.

ZULMA: Can't you see it in his baby-brown eyes that he is?

JAKE: Seventy-five cents apiece! That's highway robbery!   655

JOE: Seventy-five cents, take it or leave it.

JAKE: You got any matches, Joe?

JOE: It's a penny a book.

JAKE: *(Tossing a penny on the counter.)* Here, don't spend it all in one place.

JOE: Thank you . . . and I won't . . . pennies make dollars.   660

JAKE: So I've heard. *(ZULMA exits to pay phone.)*

GERRY: The phone is customers only, Zulma . . . no out calls except on
your break and then we would appreciate it if you'd go out and make
it on the corner.

ZULMA: What! No calls?   665

JOE: That's our policy . . . no calls except emergency. *(ZULMA exits to the
street.)* You got what you wanted, now what else can we serve you?

JAKE: That's what I like about this place, the hospitality that one receives.
Makes your eyes want to water with tears . . . just like . . . you know
what this place makes me remember . . . the night that I was invited   670

to a great outdoors party by the Ku Klux Klan and I was going to be
the guest of honor . . . I always felt guilty that I didn't make that
shindig, but you know a man of my importance just can't make every
party he's invited to . . .

JOE: I bet they were put off by your absence.   675

JAKE: Shit, I know they were.

GERRY: Why don't you two cut it out for a little while?

JOE: Cut what out?

JAKE: Cut what out?

GERRY: The bullshit. *(ZULMA enters.)*   680

ZULMA: My sister doesn't answer the phone . . . I get a little worried.

JOE: You wanna go over and see if she needs anything?

ZULMA: Naw . . . you know it's cold out there tonight . . . I couldn't believe it, a two-car accident happened as I walked from here to the
phone on the corner. What a place this town is . . . someday, I think   685
I'll leave this town for good, never come back.

GERRY: How many times in your life have you said that?

ZULMA: Since I first got off the train in 1954 . . . I wanted to go right
back, but I didn't, I stuck it out to reach the pedestals of failure. I
never set out to be a giant in the theatre world or in any world, for   690
that matter, I just wanted to be a part of wherever I was, to be noticed, to be recognized for what I brought to the atmosphere. I never
asked anyone to give me anything for my talent or for any type of
work that I put out there from my soul.

JOE: Do we have to go through your life history again?   695

JAKE: I kinda like listening to life histories.

GERRY: So do I, but once is enough for me.

JOE: You can say that again.

GERRY: So do I, but once is enough for me.

JOE: Really, Gerry, you're getting cornier by the day.   700

GERRY: It's the sun, Joe . . . the sun ripens me up.

JOE: It does something to you, all right.

JOE: The sun did something to me too.

GERRY: No shit, Sherlock.

JOE: Hey, Zulma, you wanna fix some fresh coffee?   705

ZULMA: Okay, Joe.

JAKE: Well, I think it's time that I be leaving or else the girls are going to
think that the earth swallowed me up.

JOE: Okay! Jake, take care of yourself and give the girls a hello for me.

GERRY: For me, too.   710

JOE: I knew you'd say that, Gerry.

ZULMA: Oh! So you guys know Jake's girls.

JOE: I don't know them personally, at least I mean, I don't *know them,*
but there's someone else here that does!

ZULMA: Who is that?   715

JOE: *(Imitating various movie villains.)* What you take me for, a squealer
         . . . a fink . . . a rat . . . a stool pidgeon, I won't talk, that's not my
         cup of tea . . . I won't talk, but if you took at the person I'll whistle
         Dixie.

JAKE: Yeah, you'll whistle Dixie all right when you drop in the parlor and   720
         see those two blondes.

JOE: Not me!

JAKE: Yep, you and Gerry. Joe, you're no different than any other man
         who lives alone and needs the companionship that a woman can give.
         They feel good and you'll feel good and I feel good . . . when people   725
         feel good I make money and that makes me feel extra good. You see
         in a way, it's like a therapy program and I'm Doctor Feelgood . . . I
         can probably pick up a master's degree on feelgood sometime in some
         college . . . what do you think, Joe, is there a course in college that
         trains men and women in my profession, making people feel good,   730
         making lonely men who can't seem to find the right kind of talk for a
         woman feel good, old men who can't make the grade anymore, give
         them a chance to feel like a man again?

JOE: I know you fifteen years, right?

JAKE: Yeah, fifteen miserable years. Hey, that's a real long time . . .   735

GERRY: *(Opening the cash register.)* Any more quarters in the box, Joe?

JOE: Naw, you're going to have to go to the bank later on today.

GERRY: Okay, will do.

JOE: Fifteen years, right?

JAKE: Right.   740

JOE: For fifteen years, just like tonight, you come in here and called me a
         nigger and you know something, Jake, I don't like it. I don't like it
         one bit. I don't like being called a nigger by you or any other nigger.
         Get that straight.

JAKE: I've been called a nigger all my life.   745

JOE: Well, Jake, I can't help it if you are one. *(GERRY breaks into a roar
         of laughter. ZULMA joins in on the joke. JOE begins to laugh too. JAKE
         starts to laugh. JOE begins to shake, to choke. He lets out a stifled yelp. He
         falls to the floor.)*

JAKE: Hey man, come on, don't joke like that man, come on man, be
         cool.

GERRY: Joe, Joe, come on Joe. He's right, don't joke like this.

ZULMA: Joe . . . Joe.   750

JAKE: Zulu, call the police . . . call an ambulance, hurry . . .

ZULMA: *(At phone.)* Right . . . Right . . . hello, operator . . . damn it to
         hell . . .

JAKE: Quick, go out and get a cop.

ZULMA: I'll go. Hold on, Joe, I'll be right back. *(ZULMA exits.)*   755

GERRY: Oh, Joe, please don't do this, Joe, don't you go and die on me.
         Joe . . .

JAKE: Joe, Joe, hang in there baby, hang in there, you can beat it.

JOE: Gerry . . . Gerry . . . Gerry!!

GERRY: I'm right here, Joe. I'm right here. I'm not going anywhere. I'm 760
right by your side.

JOE: Oh, Gerry, I thought I would be different.

GERRY: Save your energy, Joe. Don't talk . . .

JOE: Where's that nigger!

JAKE: Joe, baby, be cool man, Gerry's right, save your energy. 765

JOE: Two big-tit natural blondes, hey?

JAKE: Forget about that, Joe, save your energy man, be cool.

JOE: Two big-tit natural blondes, I bet that's something to see.

JAKE: You'll see them, Joe, you'll see them. I'll bring them around for
you. 770

JOE: Don't look like that, Gerry . . . leave. Gerry . . . go away.

GERRY: What are you talking about, Joe, I'm staying right here with you.

JOE: No . . . no . . . leave, Gerry 'cause I'm leaving soon . . . go away,
take a trip.

JAKE: *(Crossing to the door.)* Where's Zulu with the cop? 775

JOE: Forget about the cop, you can't ever get one when you need one.

GERRY: Please, Joe, take it easy, everything is going to be all right.

JOE: Jake, tell him about Europe.

JAKE: I don't know anything about Europe.

JOE: Damn it, nigger, you could lie. 780

JAKE: Yeah, I could lie, Europe is . . .

JOE: Listen to him, Gerry, listen to him and leave this place before it kills
you. Oh, look at this. I'm pissing in my pants. Gerry . . . Jake, don't
tell anyone about this.

JAKE: Oh, Joe, take it easy, please man. 785

GERRY: Please, Joe, don't die on me, please Joe, don't leave me alone. I
have nobody but you, Joe, please don't . . .

JOE: Gerry . . . Gerry . . . I'm tired of hanging in there . . . Jake . . . look
at this, I'm farting my life away . . . I feel like a baby . . .

GERRY: Oh, God, please help him, don't let him die on me, don't take 790
him away from me, please God, please.

JOE: Gerry . . . Gerry, . . . I can't think of anything famous to say . . .

(Fade to black.)

Discussion Questions

1. How is irony used in the play? Focus on Dominick's attitudes toward America in comparison to the other characters.

2. Examine the speeches by both Joe on page 469 and Gerry on page 471. What do those speeches reveal about Joe's and Gerry's lives and about modern American society?

3. Do any of these characters have any redeeming qualities? Who and what are they? Which of them is the most self-absorbed?

4. Compare the way Joe treats some of the patrons to the way Bernabé is treated in Luis Valdez's play on page 148. Also compare the fate of Bernabé with that of Joe. Are both of these characters equally *heroic* in the classical sense of the word?

Miguel Algarin and Tato Laviera

Olú Clemente *is a musical eulogy for Roberto Clemente, the Puerto Rican baseball player, who died in a plane crash while bringing aid to the victims of a Nicaraguan earthquake in 1972. The play opened the following year in New York and was an instant success. Focusing on Clemente's African heritage and set in Clemente's hometown of Piñones, the play transforms Clemente into an African deity. The heritage of Afro-Caribbean literature and music is a strong presence throughout the play, as congas, bongos, and maracas punctuate the play's dialogue.*

While the play is grounded in modern literary and musical traditions, it also relies on the classical element of the chorus to comment on the action. The chorus plays a dual role, both as a representative of the voice of the people and as individual characters who participate in the drama's plot. Some of the issues that these characters focus on go well beyond commenting on the qualities of the title role. The lighthearted music and dances often serve as a backdrop for the discussion of serious issues.

Olú Clemente*

CHARACTERS

A Poet
Sonero
Siete Potencias *(also serve as Coro)*:
   Maria Socorro, *madre*
   Ruth Maria, *hija*
   Irma Antonia, *hija*
   Vera Cristina, *hija*
   Jesus Abraham, *hijo*
   Miguel, *hijo*
   Tito, *hijo*
   Musicians: *piano, trumpet, trombone, tenor sax, percussion (congas, timbales, panderetas, claves)*

Editor's Note: The text contains many Spanish words and phrases. Since much of the play relies on the Latin musical forms such as *salsa*, entire songs are presented in Spanish. In some sections, providing literal translations as the play progresses would be both cumbersome and awkward. More importantly, it would detract from the overall tone of the text which relies on fluidity, especially during the musical numbers. Thus, I have elected to provide the reader with a glossary of terms, along with paraphrases of the musical numbers, rather than a word-for-word translation.

SCENE 1

The stage is a ballpark diamond. The first scene takes place in Piñones, Puerto Rico. The traditional "parrandas" are being celebrated. The news of Roberto Clemente's death reaches the people of Loíza. The parranda transforms into a frantic urgent musical evocation of the spirit of Clemente known as Olú, teacher and saviour.

POETA: It is 12 o'clock, las doce, in a new year. It is 12 o'clock, las doce. By strange circumstances there's an urgency in my soul.

POTENCIAS: Urgency! Urgency! Urgencia! Urgencia!

POETA: Clemente died inside the waters of Piñones. He died when I touched land in Puerto Rico.   5

POTENCIAS: Urgency! Urgencia! El agua se menea. Se ahoga.

POETA: The first time I touched your land, after living 30 years in New York.

POTENCIAS: El agua . . . Se hunde . . . Se muere . . . Clemente.

POETA: What are these voices? I hear the soul of street women crying,   10
diving, into the waters . . . I saw the plane fall, about an hour ago, I saw the plane fall . . . ¿Qué pasa? . . . Don't push me . . . ¿Qué me pasa? I feel like I'm being transformed. What's wrong? Clemente, tell me. Am I cursed? What kind of dream is this? Shall I come to cele-brate the New Year, to find myself alone among so many mourners.   15
Can't speak to anyone . . . There's no one I know. It is 12 o'clock.

POTENCIAS: Urgency . . . Urgency . . . Urgency, Urgencia . . . Rápido . . .
Rápido . . . Se ahoga . . . Un ríto . . . Nuevo Año . . . Penoso . . . El avión se cae . . . se cae . . . se cae . . . se cae.

POETA: I saw people in circles, they were praying, they were saying.   20

POTENCIAS: Promesas. Promesas.

POETA: This old lady saying . . .

POTENCIAS: EL ESPIRITU DE CLEMENTE.

POETA: I knelt down, and I prayed. Coño, it had to be Clemente. I wish it were me. Damn it.   25

POTENCIAS: Clemente . . . Clemente . . . Regresa . . . Regresa . . .
Clemente. ¡No! ¡No! ¡No! No puede ser, Clemente, Clemente.

POETA: I prayed hard, and I screamed, and the people gathered round me, and they prayed to Clemente. Una oración by the sea, by the sea, Clemente, vente inside of me, give me your beauty, help me trans-   30
form. I want to sing my negroid verses. What is this? ¿Qué . . . me . . . vie . . . ne . . . por . . . den . . . tro . . . I feel something coming out of me, shaking me, moving me, as swiftly as the waves. I feel a second voice coming out of me.

SONERO: Soy.   35

POETA: Coming out of me . . .

SONERO: Soy el . . .

POETA: Coming out of me, coming from inside of me.

SONERO: Soy el espíritu . . .
POETA: I feel a spirit, a great spirit.   40
SONERO:

> Soy el espíritu del poeta.
> Mi nombre es Martín Elegua.
>
> Soy su guía, soy su cuerpo.
> Estaba yo encarcelado
> Adentro del lenguaje del sajón.   45
>
> Soy el espíritu del poeta,
> Mi nombre es Martín Elegua.
> Le enseñaré su español
> Porque hoy Clemente murió, me liberó. *(Begins the*
> *first song: "Al Boricua y al Amor".)*
> *Mi Señor, Mi Gran Clemente, Señor,*   50
> *Usted hoy murió,*
> *Con los Dioses por delante,*
> *Lo llevaron a la gloria.*
> *Se sentó con el Señor. (Repeat Twice.)*

CORO: *Usted nos busca aquí, nos busca aquí, al boricua y al amor. (Repeat.)*   55

Instrumental interlude: First Song, "Al Boricua y al Amor"

SONERO: *Nos busca aquí, al boricua y al amor.*
CORO: *Nos busca aquí, al boricua y al amor.*
SONERO: *Con un vaso de diamantes, Clemente nos despidió.*
CORO: *Nos busca aquí, al boricua, y al amor.*
SONERO: *Lo llevaron a la gloria. Se sentó con el Señor.*   60
CORO: *Nos busca aquí, al boricua, y al amor.*
SONERO: *Con los brazos por delante, nos mandó su bendición.*
CORO: *Nos busca aquí, al boricua, y al amor.*
SONERO: *Todo el mundo se arrodilla, pide aquí la bendición.*

Instrumental interlude: First Song, "Al Boricua y al Amor"

CORO: *Al boricua y al amor.*   65
SONERO: *Con un vaso de diamantes.*
CORO: *Al boricua y al amor.*
SONERO: *Clemente nos despidió.*
CORO: *Al boricua y al amor.*
SONERO: *Con los brazos por delante.*   70
CORO: *Al boricua y al amor.*
SONERO: *Nos mandó su bendición.*

Instrumental interlude: First Song, "Al Boricua y al Amor"

POETA: I see this spirit coming out of me, coming out of me. I am en-
           thralled. My spirit sings. People can not see my spirit. They applaud
           me. But I can't sing. Estoy loco, estoy loco. It is as if I lived here.   75

CORO: Lo que tengo nunca se me fue.
            Lo que tengo nunca se me fue.
POETA: I feel tradition in my veins.

Instrumental interlude: Second song, "Nunca se me Fue"

CORO: *Lo que tengo nunca se me fue, se me fue*
            Lo que tengo nunca se me fue, se me fue   80
            Nunca, nunca, nunca, nunca, nunca, se me fue
            Lo que lengo nunca se me fue (Repeat Twice.)
SONERO: *Borinquen, Indios, Negros de Loíza están aquí*
            Pasado en mis ojos revive, yo soy feliz,
            Lo que tengo nunca se me fue, que otra vez.   85
CORO: *Lo que tengo nunca se me fue, se me fue . . .*
            (Repeat Once.)
SONERO: *Santos, estatuas, español, tradición,*
            Acepto todo lo que se llama Borinquen,
            Lo que tengo nunca se me fue, otra vez.
CORO: *Lo que tengo nunca se me fue, se me fue . . .*   90
            (Repeat Once.)
SONERO: *Melao, melamba, caña de cañaveral,*
            Pregón, hacia el pozo voy, a ver un Dios,
            Lo que tengo nunca se me fue.

Instrumental interlude: Second Song, "Nunca se me Fue"

CORO: *Lo que tengo nunca se me fue.*
SONERO: *Piñones ven.*   95
CORO: *Lo que tengo nunca se me fue.*
SONERO: *Aquí estaré.*
CORO: *Lo que tengo nunca se me fue.*
SONERO: *Un Indio Madamo.*
CORO: *Lo que tengo nunca se me fue.*   100
SONERO: *Negros Africanos.*
CORO: *Lo que tengo nunca se me fue.*
SONERO: *Español a mi lado.*
CORO: *Lo que tengo nunca se me fue.*
            Lo que tengo nunca se me fue.   105

Instrumental interlude: Second Song, "Nunca se me Fue"

CORO: *Nunca se me fue.*
SONERO: *Piñones ven.*
CORO: *Nunca se me fue.*
SONERO: *Lo tengo todo.*
CORO: *Nunca se me fue.*   110
SONERO: *Lo que tengo nunca se me fue. (Slow.)*
            Lo que tengo nunca se me fue.

POETA: There were so many voices in the air. They wanted me
         somewhere. There were so many voices in the air. They wanted me
         somewhere. There were so many voices in the air. They wanted me   115
         somewhere.
CORO: Hacia el pozo voy, a visitar la Diosa de la Aldea.
POETA: Piñones was tranquil. The heat of the moon was serene. It was
         magic. The night was taking me somewhere to cry or to be confessed.
         I sang to the night as the elders sang to the spirits.   120
CORO: Hacia el pozo voy, a visitar la Diosa de la Aldea.
POETA: I see a well in the sea. I see a well, over there in the sea, over there
         in the sea I see a well. I must get there, but how? I must have faith.

Instrumental Interlude: Third Song, "El Pozo"

CORO: *Hacia el pozo voy, a visitar la Diosa de la Aldea.*
         Mil ruidos me acompañan, entrando todos   125
         en mis entrañas. (Repeat twice.)
SONERO: *Estoy libre, estoy fuerte*
         Puerto Rico mi sola protección.
         Estoy libre, estoy fuerte
         Puerto Rico mi sola protección.   130
CORO: *Hacia el pozo voy . . . mis entrañas. (Repeat once.)*
SONERO: *El cántico alto sonero.*
CORO: *Hacia el pozo voy a pedir la bendición.*
SONERO: *El saludo, Madre, bendición.*
CORO: *Hacia el pozo voy a pedir la bendición.*   135
SONERO: *Las Potencias son espiritistas.*
CORO: *Hacia el pozo voy a pedir la bendición.*
SONERO: *El calor de las poesías de Palés Matos.*
CORO: *Hacia el pozo voy a pedir la bendición.*
SONERO: *La fuerza de los afligidos.*   140
CORO: *Hacia el pozo voy a pedir la bendición.*
SONERO: *El pensamiento humilde de sentir.*
CORO: *Hacia el pozo voy a pedir la bendición.*

Instrumental Interlude: Third Song, "El Pozo"

POTENCIAS: Allá en el mar hay un pozo,
           Un pozo allá en el mar,   145
           Piñones se abrió,
           Su mar recibió,
           El avión, el avión, el avión, el avión,
           Lo protegió, lo preparó,
           El Mar Caribe lo arropó.   150
           Hacia el pozo voy, hacia el pozo voy.

Instrumental Interlude: Third Song, "El Pozo"

SONERO: *Puerto Rico, mi sola protección.*

CORO: *Hacia el pozo voy.*
SONERO: *Puerto Rico, mi sola protección.*
   Puerto Rico, mi sola protección. 155
   Puerto Rico, mi sola protección. (Music fades.)
POETA: My only protection Puerto Rico, my island. Oh! Green goddess,
   Queen of the tropics and the sun, Mother of Agüeybana, Woman
   whose milk gave life to Roberto Clemente, I touch the holy waters of
   your sea tonight, María Borinquen. Give me a chant, give me a ritual, 160
   give me a Clemente prayer for my altar in New York.
CORO: *Oluko, Oluko, Oluko, Oluko*
   Nuestro Sabio Oluko.
POETA: What is this that I see? I see a woman's shadow over the sea. I see
   a woman's shadow coming from the tree, the palm tree. To get to the 165
   well, I must cross that shadow.
SONERO: El Espíritu de Clemente se llama Olú, Olú, Olú, Olú, Olú, Olú.
   El Espíritu de Clemente se llama Olú. Para cruzar por la sombra se
   dice "Olú."
POETA: A palm tree slowly dancing like a son montuno. I must go deep 170
   into the swaying of palm trees dancing salsa tunes in my reflection,
   overlooking the beach, stretching their shadows gently over the sea
   until their upper palm leaves touch the gleaming, gliding moon. I
   must go deep and climb the highest palm tree in the seas of Piñones. I
   must follow its shadows, its curvings, until all shadows meet and there 175
   will be the well of my baptism. SHADOWS, SHADOWS, SHAD-
   OWS, EIGHT SHADOWS, 7 POWERS, ONE NEW POWER, LA
   OCTAVA POTENCIA, OLÚ, OLÚ, OLÚ, OLÚ, OLÚ, OLÚ,
   OLÚ, OLÚ, OLÚ.
SONERO: El Espíritu de Clemente se llama Olú. 180
   Para cruzar por la sombra se dice "Olú"
   El Espiritu de Clemente se llama Olú.
   Para cruzar por la sombra de dice "Olú."

Instrumental Interlude: Fourth Song, "Olú"

SONERO: *El Espíritu de Clemente se llama Olú, Olú, Olú,*
   Olú, Olú, Olú. El Espíritu de Clemente se llama 185
   Olú, Olú, Olú, Olú, Olú, Olú.
   Viaje del fenómeno.
CORO: *Olú, Olú.*
SONERO: *Gritan las estrellas.*
CORO: *Olú, Olú.* 190
SONERO: *Aire nuevo baile.*
CORO: *Olú, Olú.*
SONERO: *Brisas espantosas.*
CORO: *Olú, Olú.*
SONERO: *Nace aquí en Piñones.* 195
CORO: *Olú, Olú.*

Instrumental Interlude: Fourth Song, "Olú"

POTENCIAS: El avión se fue y regresa para atrás,
El avión se fue y regresa para atrás.
Cuando se cayó era La Santa Trinidad.
El avión se fue y regresa para atrás,   200
El avión se fue y regresa para atrás.
Cuando se cayó era La Santa Trinidad,
Cuando se cayó era La Santa Trinidad.

Instrumental Interlude: Fourth Song, "Olú"

SONERO: *El Espíritu de Clemente se llama Olú.*
El Espíritu de Clemente se llama Olú.   205
El Espíritu de Clemente se llama Olú.
El Espíritu de Clemente se llama Olú.
Para cruzar por las sombras se dice "Olú."
Para cruzar por las sombras se dice "Olú."

CORO: *Se llama Olú.*   210
SONERO: *La luz de Olú.*
CORO: *Bendice Olú.*
SONERO: *Se dice Olú.*
CORO: *Orarle a Olú.*
SONERO: *Olú, Olú, Olú, Olú . . . (Fades.)*   215

POETA: While I searched for the tallest palm tree, as I walked deep into
the nocturnal solitude of my fears, I saw eight shadows from a distance.
I saw eight candles shining from afar. There it was, the tallest palm
tree, how beautifully curved. I stood there in amazement. I must climb
it. But I stopped. I looked around in the early morning solemnity. And   220
there it was. My family, mi familia. I saw mi familia from New York.
They were going to help me cross the shadow. Eight candles guiding
me from New York, eight candles guiding me from New York!

Instrumental Interlude: Fifth Song, "Ocho Velas"

SONERO: *Al pararme media noche en tus entrañas,*
Oí un ruido muy adentro entre las palmas,   225
Al mirar yo vi que mi familia me acompaña,
Ocho velas que me guían de mi casa,
Al mirar yo vi que mi familia me acompaña,
Ocho velas que me guían de mi casa.

CORO: *Al pararme media . . . . de mi casa.*   230
(CORO repeats above once.)

Instrumental Interlude: Fifth Song, "Ocho Velas"

CORO: *Qué dulces son, qué bellos son, qué gratos son,*
Qué amorosos son, qué sagrados son, son, son,
son, son, son, son, son, son. (Repeat twice.)

SONERO: *Ocho velas que me guían de mi casa.*
CORO: *Ocho velas que me guían de mi casa.*   235
SONERO: *Muy adentro en los palmares, me guiaban a mi bien.*
CORO: *Ocho velas que me guían de mi casa.*
SONERO: *La Potencias Africanas, Olú La Octava y el mar le habla.*
CORO: *Ocho velas que me guían de mi casa.*
SONERO: *Un saludo con respeto y a mi madre bendición.*   240
CORO: *Ocho velas que me guían de mi casa.*
SONERO: *La familia es la base, de toda tradición.*
CORO: *Ocho velas que me guían de mi casa.*
SONERO: *Un bautizo, un bautizo, el primero de Olú.*

Instrumental Interlude: Fifth Song, "Ocho Velas"

SONERO: *Al pararme medianoche en tus entrañas . . . (Slow.)*   245
CORO: *Ocho velas que me guían de mi casa.*
          Ocho velas que me guían de mi casa.
POETA: I was deeply touched. When I saw that the palm tree was crossing the sea. Then I saw the well, Clemente's final entry into the sea of the Mar Caribe. I gave my New Year's first kiss, towards the sea, to my   250
mother, and to papi. And I bit my tears, my deep, down, dry gutted tears. I could not contain them. As I climbed the palm tree, the tear fell. A tear of brilliance, but I could not climb.

Instrumental Interlude: Sixth Song, "Más gotas que Estrellas"

SONERO: *Me caí por lo que vi allí*
          Tuve que llorar allí   255
          Llorar hondo, humilde despojando
          Un llanto alto
          Llorar hondo, humilde despojando
          Un llanto alto
          Mil lágrimas con mil fuerzas,   260
          Caen más gotas que estrellas.
          Mil lágrimas con mil fuerzas,
          Caen más gotas que estrellas.

Instrumental Interlude: Sixth Song, "Más Gotas que Estrellas"

CORO: *Me caí por lo que vi allí.*
SONERO: *Yo vi, yo vi, yo vi.*   265
CORO: *Tuve que llorar allí.*
SONERO: *Yo vi, yo vi, yo vi.*
CORO: *Llorar hondo.*
SONERO: *Llorar, Llorar.*
CORO: *Humilde despojando un llanto alto.*   270
SONERO: *Que llora, llora como yo lloré.*
CORO: *Mil lágrimas con mil fuerzas.*

SONERO: *Me despojé.*

CORO: *Caen más gotas que estrellas.*
    Mil lágrimas con mil fuerzas.   275

SONERO: *Más gotas que estrellas.*
    Más gotas que estrellas.
    Más gotas que estrellas, más gotas.

CORO: *Caen más gotas que estrellas.*

SONERO: *Hacia el pozo voy, hacia el pozo voy, yo voy, yo voy.*   280

CORO: *Caen más gotas que estrellas.*

SONERO: *A contarles todas mis penas, bautizarme con la plena.*

CORO: *Caen más gotas que estrellas.*

SONERO: *Hacia el pozo voy, y después para el Ancón.*

CORO: *Caen más gotas que estrellas.*   285

SONERO: *Olú allí me espera, mi dolor, mi dolor, mi pena.*

CORO: *Caen más gotas que estrellas.*

SONERO: *Más gotas que estrellas, más gotas que estrellas.*

CORO: *Caen más gotas, caen más gotas, caen más gotas,*
    Caen más gotas que estrellas.   290

Instrumental Interlude: Sixth Song, "Más Gotas que Estrellas"

SONERO: *Me caí por lo que vi allí . . . Caen más gotas que estrellas.*
    (Repeat once.)

CORO: *Hacia el poza voy, a visitar la Diosa de la Aldea.*
    Mil ruidos me acompañan,
    entrando todos en mis entrañas. (Repeat twice.)

SONERO: *Estoy libre, estoy fuerte, Puerto Rico, mi sola protección.*   295
    (Repeat twice.)

SONERO y CORO: *Υ le canto a Puerto Rico en Piñones.*
    Υ le canto a Puerto Rico en Piñones.
    Υ obsequio mis inquietudes a Piñones.
    Diciendo alegremente, lo que tengo nunca se me fue.
    Lo que tengo nunca se me fue.   300

CORO: *QUE CANTE EL POETA, QUE NO TENGA MIEDO,*
    QUE CANTE EL POETA, QUE NO TENGA MIEDO.
    ESTAS CON TU GENTE, NO TE VAMOS A ENGAÑAR
    QUE CANTE, QUE CANTE, AQUI CON SU GENTE.

POETA: *Lo que tengo nunca se me fue.*   305
    Lo que tengo nunca se me fue, se me fue.
    Nunca, nunca, nunca, nunca, nunca se me fue.
    Lo que tengo nunca se me fue.

EVERYONE: *Lo que tengo nunca se me fue, se me fue.*
    Lo que tengo nunca se me fue, se me fue.   310
    Nunca nunca, nunca, nunca, nunca se me fue.
    Lo que tengo nunca se me fue, que otra vez.
    Lo que tengo nunca se me fue, se me fue.
    Lo que tengo nunca se me fue, se me fue.

> *Nunca, nunca, nunca, nunca, nunca se me fue.*   315
> *Lo que tengo nunca se me fue. (Slow.)*

SCENE 2

New York

MARIA SOCORRO: Le tenemos que rogar:
"oremos por nuestra Potencia,"
Olú we want to celebrate
our spirits, we want to
frame our presence in   5
New York. We want
to sing the stunning life
of our talents,
we want to bleed from
the stage the sweat   10
of our tortured days
in el barrio frío,
in the helpless
caminar de esta
máquina de intereses   15
which shares its goodies
in a circuit of interests
that Puerto Ricans
never see:
"oremos por nuestra Potencia,"   20
Olú, give us energy
with which we can fight.

TITO: Can you keep the energy clean?

JESUS ABRAHAM: Congas
necesitamos congas   25
las congas para crear.

TITO: Si, praise me with tambores.

JESUS ABRAHAM: Puerto Rico needs to have its people respected.

MIGUEL AND JESUS ABRAHAM: Si, si, si, si, si, si, si, si, si,
The city needs to have you   30
spread your beauty to
Staten Island, Queens, Brooklyn,
the Bronx. You need to lead
the people of New York
to spirtual cleanliness.   35

IRMA ANTONIA: *May all Puerto Ricans*
praise the
spirit of a hero-man

> *Clemente-man*
> *Roberto-baseball-player-man*   40

The SIETE POTENCIAS *tremble and shake to the conga music.*

RUTH MARIA: *Las llaves*
las claves,
el poder son
las llaves,
las que abren las   45
puertas, las que
te dejan entrar
sin que te llamen
PILLO,
las llaves son   50
la revolución
la rebeldia,
las llaves,
las claves,
las llaves are the key   55
to entrance and to power:
the key to not breaking into
600 Park Avenue
Son LAS LLAVES
porque sin las llaves   60
te llevan preso.

MIGUEL AND JESUS ABRAHAM: *Las llaves*
son el miedo,
son el miedo,
las llaves de   65
metal son el
miedo. Cójanlas
todas cójanlas.
No esperen,
inicien su acción.   70

JESUS ABRAHAM: *The people we*
want to create
a religion for
can not arrive
till they get out   75
of factorías,
WE MUST WORK AT NIGHT
we can't spend the day
exploring the ritual
presentation of the tribe   80
back to itself,
we first pay dues

FACTORIAS, FACTORIAS, FACTORIAS,
    FACTORIAS, FACTORIAS
Pay Dues, 85
Then Look,
Pay Dues,
Then Look,
Pay Dues,
Then 90
LOOK. (Congas go crazy playing.)
MIGUEL AND JESUS ABRAHAM: sí, sí, sí, sí, sí, sí, sí, sí, sí, sí, sí, sí.
MARIA SOCORRO:
    Clemente's family,
    la familia
    Clemente is present 95
    to the myth,
    to the creation,
    to the spirit
    of Roberto's
    force, to the spirit 100
    that we beat our
    drums for, la familia,
    is here to gather energy,
    to withstand its loss in
    our celebration of Roberto. 105
TITO: You must
    exhibit your
    passion for Roberto.
MIGUEL: We need a major
    prayer to a major 110
    god—Olú.
TITO: A rhythm from my drum
    will release it for you.
MIGUEL: Let us give thanks
    to Olú Clemente 115
    for our daily knowledge:
    Olú teach us to
    dance on high pitch
    fear, teach us to fight
    sleep, to want more wakedness. 120
    All will be done in
    Heaven as it is in el barrio.
    Olú, Olú
    teach us to dance
    on high pitch fear 125
    Olú, Olú,
    teach us to fight

on high pitch fear for
All will be done in
Heaven as it is in el barrio. 130

MARIA SOCORRO:
We, I, you, us,
we cannot help
the standing System of Justice
keep its course in declaring
us criminals, 135
beasts of loathing,
we cannot raise
the flag of contempt
against ourselves.

RUTH MARIA: My children are not 140
CRIMINALS,
mis hijos no son
CRIMINALES.

IRMA ANTONIA: Mi esposo no es
un pillo, 145
my husband is not a thief,
do not accuse me,
I am not the mother
of criminals.

VERA CRISTINA: I am the mother 150
of beautiful
children born of a
beautiful Puerto Rican union.

MARIA SOCORRO: A marriage bearing children
was not to be a curse 155
on society,
it was to be an offering,
IT IS AN OFFERING,
NO!
We reject all 160
Standing Systems of Justice.

IRMA ANTONIA: We are the mothers of
What is called
DEFIANCE.
Here I sit watching 165
Roberto run
around the diamond,
a black Spanish
speaking stallion:
running more than he 170
walks,
being free in

<pre>
                    his knowledge of always
                    expressing himself:
                    tirando para afuera.   175
MARIA SOCORRO: NO! to all external justice!
RUTH MARIA: We are at war
                    and our children are
                    the warriors of our nation:
                    A NATION OF BEAUTIFUL   180
                    WARRIORS.
VERA CRISTINA: We are the mothers
                    of salvation
                    for our
                    children have the   185
                    muscles of resistance,
                    they are the blood
                    of the promise,
                    they are not criminals
                    they are los dioses   190
                    of tomorrow.
MARIA SOCORRO: We, I, You, Us,
                    We are the mothers of the NEWNESS
                    We are the mothers of DEFIANCE.
</pre>

TITO: Y para continuar nuestro respeto al querido Roberto Clemente   195
queremos hacer homenaje a todas las madres que sufren por sus hijos,
los cuales están sometidos al peligro. Y lo hacemos asi porque sabemos
que tú, Roberto, desde allá donde estás sentado a la derecha de nues-
stros creadores, desde allá como Olú, el maestro, nos ayudarás para
que estos niños puedan ser el futuro de nuestra patria. Sabemos que   200
donde moras eres el ejemplo del hombre santo y bueno.

SOCORRO *and* IRMA *embrace. The two women walk towards shortstop.* RUTH
is touching VERA's *hair. As* SOCORRO *and* IRMA *arrive,* IRMA *looks towards
the fence around home plate, and the other women follow. They move slowly,
pointing towards the plate in an upward position.* MIGUEL *is on Third Base,
as he looks at the women. There is spiritual cleanliness, a concentrated
simplicity.*

<pre>
MIGUEL: There they are, the mother,
                    hablando del dolor,
                    pena que también Roberto
                    sufrió en su vida. Viviendo   205
                    entre dos razas.
                    They are
                    las madres de la tierra.
                    In Short—between two worlds
                    the calmness of trees   210
                    colliding with a jungle of buildings
</pre>

las madres,
In . . . between . . . they are the wired
fences that protect us.

VERA CRISTINA: Roberto tenia una mirada que me tumbaba los ojos.   215

RUTH MARIA: Tenia mucho poder. Roberto hacía todo lo que él queria.

MARIA SOCORRO: Las cosas son como Dios las dispone. Tú sabes que
Roberto no murió. *(Looking at JESUS ABRAHAM.)* ¡No! El está aqui en
el mundo haciendo milagros. *(Looking at MIGUEL.)* Roberto, yo
quiero que tú lo sepas. Vera. Roberto va a ser el próximo San Martin   220
de Porres.

VERA CRISTINA: El supo hacer todo lo posible con sus manos. Y también
sufrió. Siempre trató de traer a nuestro pueblo a su punto de máxima
fuerza. *(A little child, ROBERTO ENRIQUEZ, passes by playing a campana.
He is always moving about the mothers as they talk.)*

IRMA ANTONIA: El fue un gran padre. Te has dado cuenta como es que el   225
nene está interesado. El nene sabe que se habla de Roberto. El sabe
que se habla de su papá.

RUTH MARIA: *(To ROBERTO)* Ven acá.

VERA CRISTINA: Si, ése es Roberto Enriquez. Los de más edad ya saben o
mejor conocen lo que ha pasado. Pero el más pequeño, como que lo   230
espera por las noches. ¡El era su pasión!

RUTH MARIA: Qué lindo cuando son nenes y qué mucho peligro les
queda en este mundo. Y en Nueva York olvidate. Ahi, no se salva ni
uno. Todos llegan a lo mismo. Todos se pierden en el peligro.

VERA CRISTINA: Roberto siempre sufrió mucho por la juventud   235
puertorriqueña.

RUTH MARIA: Raymond el hermano de la esposa de Jesus Abraham
murió abandonado. Solo, sin nadie.

MARIA SOCORRO: ¿Por qué murió Raymond tan abandonado? Yo como
que lo veo *(Holds her forehead.)* con gente, con muchos amigos.   240

RUTH MARIA: El tuvo que morir solo, sin que nadie lo ayudara.

VERA CRISTINA: ¿Por qué?

RUTH MARIA: ¿Por qué murió buscando sueños? Murió buscando el futuro en el humo de la perdición. No le culpo. El buscaba lo que lo
balanceara.   245

VERA CRISTINA: Es que mueren tantos por ese gusto. Y es un gusto tan
lejos de la familia. Es un gusto que nos amenaza.

MARIA SOCORRO: Pero, ¿quién dice que la amenaza la producimos
nosotros? ¿Quién le vende a nuestros hijos este falso sueño de un balance quimico que cada ocho horas necesita más fuego?   250

RUTH MARIA: Las calles están llenas de vicio. La destrucción es tan fácil
de comprar como la aspirina.

MARIA SOCORRO: No, mi pregunta es ¿quién les vende el asunto ése que
necesitan para lograr su "High"?

RUTH MARIA: En las calles, en todos lados, en todas las esquinas, en   255
todas las bodegas del barrio.

VERA CRISTINA: Somos nuestros mismos destructores. Si son puertorriqueños los que la venden, somos nosotros los que nos matamos uno
al otro.

RUTH MARIA: ¿De qué parte del mundo es que sale la pestilencia esa?   260

IRMA ANTONIA: Sale de la China, Turkey, India, Sud América. Come on!
It comes from all around the world. De todas partes del mundo.

RUTH MARIA: ¿Y qué puertorriqueño tiene el poder de negociar la venta
a un nivel, tú sabes, un nivel internacional?

VERA CRISTINA: Hay mucho que nosotros no controlamos que nos de-   265
struye. Hay mucho que nos quiere tumbar pero que está fuera de
nuestro alcance.

MARIA SOCORRO: ¡Miren ustedes! ¿Qué es un puertorriqueño para un
chino, un indio, un africano? Para esa gente el puertorriqueño es un
alfiler en el panorama americano.   270

RUTH MARIA: Así que en cosas de negocios el puertorriqueño es una paja
en el horizonte.

IRMA ANTONIA: Ellos venden pero no son los que la traen. Yo tengo una
hermana que le dieron cinco años por venderia. Pero ella no era la
fuente, la fuente es la mafia, el gobierno, la policía.   275

VERA CRISTINA: Me dicen que se usa en las cárceles.

MARIA SOCORRO: Sí, ¡así es! ¡así es!

RUTH MARIA: ¿Y qué entonces? Somos todas madres, somos todas mujeres de hijos, somos todas la fuente de la sangre puertorriqueña.
Somos la sangre.   280

VERA CRISTINA: Bien dicho. Pero se nos mueren los hijos en los pasillos
de edificios fríos y estranjeros. Se nos mueren solos, sin ayuda, deses-
perados, se nos mueren sin MADRES, se nos mueren sin apoyo.

RUTH MARIA: ¿Y qué hacemos?

MARIA SOCORRO: No dejemos que eso pase. Yo no deseo ver a mi hijo   285
destruido; yo no quiero ayudarlo en su vicio. Pero, Señor Mío, Dios
querido, cuando me dicen que se nos mueren los hijos en pasillos sin
amigos, eso no lo tolero yo.

IRMA ANTONIA: ¡Ni yo tampoco!

RUTH MARIA: ¿Y qué hacemos?   290

VERA CRISTINA: ¡A la meta! Tenemos que ir a nuestra responsabilidad, a
nuestros sagrados hijos que están en peligro.

IRMA ANTONIA: Look! We are not free to set our own laws.

MARIA SOCORRO: ¿Y si no tenemos el poder de defender los nuestros,
qué tenemos?   295

IRMA ANTONIA: La ayuda del progreso.

MARIA SOCORRO: No lo creas. Nada es nuestro y el progreso es un em-
buste. Todos mienten.

RUTH MARIA: Si, nuestra responsabilidad es ayudarnos.

IRMA ANTONIA: Bueno, tú sabes que a mí nadie sacaría un hijo de mi   300
hogar.

RUTH MARIA: ¿Y si está en el vicio?

IRMA ANTONIA: No, a mí no, a mí no me lo llevarian.

MARIA SOCORRO: ¿Cómo que no? Ya tú, ella y yo sabemos que es la ley, que es la ley. Y con la ley no hay negocios.   305

IRMA ANTONIA: ¡A mí no! A mí no me lo llevarian.

MARIA SOCORRO: Con la policía a la puerta y el F. B. I. en la cocina ¿cómo te quedarías con tu nene en la casa?

IRMA ANTONIA: Con mis manos, con mis uñas, con mis dientes mordiría.

RUTH MARIA: Y yo te ayudaría.   310

MARIA SOCORRO: ¡Cálmense! Porque no he oido una proposición de acción. Ésta puede gritar su bravura pero cuando llegue la policía ellos se lo llevarán.

RUTH MARIA: Pero el punto es que no los dejaríamos llevárselo.

MARIA SOCORRO: ¿Qué proponen? . . . que todas nos unamos, que todas   315
nosotras gritemos: "no dejen que se los lleven lejos de su hogar?"

VERA CRISTINA: Que idea tan simple y bella.

RUTH MARIA: No podemos tirarle al que está sufriendo. Nuestros hijos sufren bajo fuerzas que los odian.

MARIA SOCORRO: Los curamos nosotras, nosotras mismas, la madre cura,   320
la madre de un hogar es la hoja verde tropical. Nosotras las madres tenemos que proteger a los hijos. Ellos bien lo saben. Desde ahora en adelante aquí no hay policía alguno que se me lleve a un hijo mío.

RUTH MARIA: ¡Que Dios que está en los cielos nos bendiga el momento!

IRMA ANTONIA: Que nos dé la fuerza del mañana de nuestra promesa.   325

MARIA SOCORRO: Mi casa es el humilde respaldo de mis hijos y en nues-tras casas serán protegidos. Roberto, tú, Clemente lleno de Clemencia, sálvanos, reza por nosotros. Protégenos. Ayúdanos a salvar a nuestros hijos.

RUTH MARIA: Tú has de hacer muchos milagros. (*RUTH MARIA and*   330
IRMA ANTONIA are alone. Center stage.) Yo como que necesito un aliento, un abrazo en el pecho.

IRMA ANTONIA: ¿Qué te pasa? ¿Tú buscas y no encuentras? ¿Ya el calen-tón abrazo se te olvidó?

RUTH MARIA: Eso lo manda Dios. Pero la seguridad, mi seguridad la   335
creo yo.

IRMA ANTONIA: Yo he dejado mucha "oportunidad" perderse por verme cerca de mis hijos.

RUTH MARIA: Verdad es. Es malo estar sola. Con los hijos pero sola sin un hombre que me traiga felicidad.   340

IRMA ANTONIA: A mí me acaba de llegar.

RUTH MARIA: Y a mí me llegará.

IRMA ANTONIA: Ruth, ¿qué es un hombre puertorriqueño?

RUTH MARIA: Roberto Clemente, Don Pedro, Emeterio Betances, mi padre, mi hermano.   345

IRMA ANTONIA: Nuestros hombres viven con mucho dolor.

RUTH MARIA: En Nueva York lavan platos.

IRMA ANTONIA: No es eso, es otra cosa.

RUTH MARIA: ¿Cómo? ¿Qué?

IRMA ANTONIA: No tienen seguridad.   350

RUTH MARIA: ¿Cómo? ¿Qué?

IRMA ANTONIA: ¿Qué le pasa al check de cada semana?

RUTH MARIA: Se gasta.

IRMA ANTONIA: Y ¿cómo se van a levantar si se nos ahogan con cada paso?   355

RUTH MARIA: Ellos viven nadando.

IRMA ANTONIA: Los tenemos que respaldar en su lucha.

RUTH MARIA: Tenemos que darle orgullo que respetar a su lucha.

IRMA ANTONIA: Pero qué dolor, qué dolor, qué dolor el que trabaja tanto y le pagan tan poco. Qué dolor, la humillación de ganarse una miseria   360
cuando se necesita mucho más.

RUTH MARIA: No podemos resignarnos.

IRMA ANTONIA: Pa' trás con el que me humilla al esposo. Pa' trás con el que me humilla al hijo. Pa' trás con el que me ultraje la hija—pa' trás, pa' trás.   365

RUTH MARIA: Basta ya con la humillación, está bien, ¡basta! Pero lo que cuenta es resistir la humillación. Lo que importa es que nos respeten
(MARIA SOCORRO enters.)

MARIA SOCORRO: Nuestros hombres nos han dado respaldo, cariño, y sobre todo nos han dado orgullo.

IRMA ANTONIA: Pero nosotras siempre hemos luchado con nuestros hom-   370
bres: Lola Rodríquez de Tió, Mariana Boracetti, a la que llamaban brazo de oro durante el grito de Lares, Lolita Lebrón que vive aún y no hablemos de la gran Vera Clemente.

RUTH MARIA: A Lolita la están matando por su dignidad.

MARIA SOCORRO: Esa dignidad y esa hombría nutrimos nosotras y le   375
damos aliento.

IRMA ANTONIA: ¿Es que ustedes no ven que nosotras somos el futuro de nuestros hombres.

RUTH MARIA: ¡Eso es! Los hay, los tenemos. Mi hermano, mi Jesús Abra-ham es bravo. Tito es bravo. Miguel es fuerte.   380

MARIA SOCORRO: *(All the women join her.)* Tenemos poder. Nosotras vamos hacia adelante, pero necesitamos unirnos para darle respaldo a nuestros hombres.

TITO: *(The men at homeplate.)* That's Piñones. That's where the plane crashed. They looked for him for hours.   385

MIGUEL: ¿Dónde está Piñones? Over there?

TITO: That's Piñones!

MIGUEL: Tito, Piñones is directly in front view of the house. Roberto died within sight of his family.

TITO: ¿Ella lo sabrá?   390

MIGUEL: ¡Y cómo lo sabrá!

TITO: There's a current out there that's deep, very deep. If you dive here, when you surface you're there. It's that powerful.

MIGUEL: Ayer estuvimos en Piñones and the rocks were espina sharp. I
          didn't sit down because my pants would have been torn. Espina sharp,   395
          lo juro! Imagínate el cuerpo del pelotero.
TITO: Tons of food were being hauled to Nicaragua. Roberto estaba dis-
          puesto a ir. Nada lo aguantaba. Y habian tratado de salir tres veces
          pero el avión no podía.
MIGUEL: The news today reported that the plane was overloaded with   400
          two thousand tons of food and clothing.
TITO: It was an inexperienced flight engineer.
MIGUEL: Salió, voló, captó lo que tenía que captar y resultó en su
          muerte.
TITO: Un pelotero hecho líder, con sangre para todo el mundo.   405
MIGUEL: Puerto Rico is in a state of civil war. Los fuegos no los apagan.
          Quitan el agua y la ponen. La isla sufre bajo un self-contemp, un odio
          contra su propia imagen. ¡Que todo Nueva York lo sepa! Nuestras fa-
          milias están muertas de miedo.
TITO: Look here brother, we need strength.   410
MIGUEL: Roberto is the living proof of la pureza del Caribe.
TITO: Our children sharpen their wits. But is it a nation they construct?
MIGUEL: It is in this world of savage criticism that Clemente was judged
          a quirky, odd Spanish-speaking black man who got more attention
          paid to him than any other Puerto Rican in history. He pained for it   415
          though. He was a one to one bet. The odds never lowered with
          Clemente; he was a bargaining point: "nobody can get near him."
JESUS ABRAHAM: *(Enters with MARIA SOCORRO and IRMA ANTONIA.)* The
          trabajo that we have in mind is to talk with Vera this morning about
          Roberto's spiritual transformation at Piñones.   420
MARIA SOCORRO: Queremos hablar de la pureza, de Clemente, la mar-
          avilla de haber creado una imagen que llegó más allá del universo,
          pero MURIO. Se lo tragó el Caribe. Las mujeres lloran y saben que
          está muerto. Lloramos todas, y aquí, tú vas a cantar.
JESUS ABRAHAM: Clemente, the new rhythm of tomorrow in the realities   425
          of today, a poem of the present.
MARIA SOCORRO: Yo, como que veo un niño, un Robertito: a bat, a hat,
          and our newness in this world. The course of Clemente's life: the
          travel, the meandering of his being, his beginning in Carolina where
          his Maestra fue la que supo señalarle a Roberto quién iba a ser su   430
          esposa.
IRMA ANTONIA: Qué mucho tú ves, porque yo, como que veo a Vera, a la
          mujer que le daría luz, la que le enseñó an eventual road to the
          INTERNATIONALITY OF BEING: a place where he can dance.
JESUS ABRAHAM: Roberto had reached a place from which he struggled.   435
MARIA SOCORRO: Roberto's energies will rise to help not yet born Puerto
          Rican men to stop our constant loss of blood . . .
IRMA ANTONIA: The connection of Puerto Rico to Clemente's blood
          being spilt at Piñones is that we've lost a protector, that while the sea

drank Roberto's blood in New York City, war is being declared against   440
us: a chemical warfare eats up our youth.

JESUS ABRAHAM: El mundo entero le suplicaba no te vayas, no nos dejes
en el nuevo año. Pero tenía que ir. Tenía que salir. Tenía que subir al
cielo para bajar un hombre totalmente espiritual.

Bright green lights, the SIETE POTENCIAS *go to different positions on the dia-*
mond. IRMA ANTONIA *is at home plate. This is done quickly, almost inaudibly.*
IRMA ANTONIA *with her hands up in the air twirls twice to the left, twice to*
the right. She stops. Her muscles quiver. She feels a change coming on ROBERTO.
MARIA SOCORRO *possesses her.* IRMA ANTONIA *puts her hand up to her squint-*
ing face. She is stooping, holding her back. She is looking. She talks to first base.

IRMA ANTONIA: Oye, ¿tú has visto a Roberto, tú has visto a Roberto?   445
Dime, dime, dime. Tú sabes que ese negrito es bueno, ¿verdad? Tú
sabes que ayer me dio los chavos pa la comía, tú sabes que sin él me
hubieran botao, yo bien sé que tú sabes, que sin él el horno no tuviera
fuego, no tuviera carne en la caserola. (IRMA ANTONIA *looks to outfield*
but quickly turns back to first base. Slowly she begins to walk toward sec-
ond base.) Oye, ¿tú has visto a Roberto? Me dijeron que salió pa Nica   450
yo no sé qué a llevarle comía a la gente. (IRMA ANTONIA *moves to-*
wards third base.) Me dijeron que no pudo salir tres veces ya. Oye, ¿y
Robertito, tú lo has visto? (*She gazes out towards left field.*) Estará en la
pista o jugando pelota. Tú sabes lo mucho que le gusta jugar pelota.
¡Oye! (*She turns towards home plate again. All the other potencias move*   455
towards her. The light is very, very bright again.) ¡Tú! ¿Has visto a
Robertito? Estará jugando bola porque a esta hora él siempre me llama
pa decirme si ganó: no habrá ganao, ¿verdad? Porque no ha llegao, no
ha venío. Se habrá perdío ¿qué crees?

By the time all las Siete Potencias reach home plate IRMA ANTONIA *is done.*
She begins to shake. Las Siete Potencias are all in front of the house. They wait.
VERA CRISTINA *enters center backstage. She stops at pitcher's mound. She*
reaches out. She walks a few steps from the pitcher's mound and gestures for
Las Potencias to come in. The contact is immediate. The circuits are set off by
RUTH MARIA's *first vision of El Indio, la energía in people's lives.*

RUTH MARIA: ¿Se ha dado cuenta del Indio que está en la esquina del   460
sofá?
VERA CRISTINA: Mira, de veras es un Indio.
MIGUEL: Yo vi la cara en el tronco del árbol al entrar.
VERA CRISTINA: ¿Dónde?
MIGUEL: ¡Ahí!   465
VERA CRISTINA: La veo.
MIGUEL: Yo veo al Indio claramente.
MARIA SOCORRO: Lo vemos todos. El Indio es omnipotente y está en
todos lados agobiado. Su realidad es la potencia divina del ahora, del
ahora de este mundo.   470

VERA CRISTINA: Perdonen ustedes, pero hay mucho que hacer desde la
    muerte.
RUTH MARIA: Usted es una mujer de poder, una mujer llena de santos
    sentimientos, llena de angustia, llena de amor doliente, llena de miedo.
MARIA SOCORRO: Estamos adoloridas al haber perdido tanto, al haber   475
    sufrido la verdad de la muerte.
VERA CRISTINA: Roberto did not want to stay at home while other peo-
    ple risked their lives to bring aide to Nicaragua.
MIGUEL: Was the trip planned?
VERA CRISTINA: No, no existía, el viaje no existía.   480
MIGUEL: From the window in his room Roberto could see Piñones, the
    place he was to meet his death.
IRMA ANTONIA: I can see in the horizon the actual sight of the tragedy,
    the point at which he would begin again in death.
MARIA SOCORRO: De la carne al espíritu sin presencia en la materia fisica   485
    que los hombres del planeta reconocen como la realidad.
MIGUEL: *(To VERA)* Roberto's death surprised us, but we do not think
    his presence has left us.
JESUS ABRAHAM: *(To VERA)* This is a humble family. You have not lost
    nor will you lose your humility.   490
MARIA SOCORRO: You are filled with pride over Roberto's triumph. You
    are proud of his struggle, his attaining fame without selling out his
    honor.
IRMA ANTONIA: Inside your home there is the spirit of love and
    contemplation.   495
TITO: La obra de Clemente fue la obra más grande de Puerto Rico: él,
    Roberto, supo darle su presencia a los niños, a los muchachitos
    peloteros de la isla. El no se olvidaba de el que lo necesitaba; su
    grandeza era su bondad y eso lo hizo inolvidable. El mundo lo quería
    porque él supo querer.   500
VERA CRISTINA: *(To IRMA ANTONIA.)* Sometimes his fame would scare
    those he wanted closest to him.
RUTH MARIA: Roberto was insulted by the lack of attention paid to ef-
    forts; his teammates looked on in awe. He stood at home-plate, sure
    of his footing; the only one that came through in a clutch. His team-   505
    mates marvelled.
MARIA SOCORRO: America made him into a smooth bronze thrill for its
    people. He wasn't black, but that's America's holdback. It deceives
    itself.
RUTH MARIA: America lies to itself: Clemente was black, not bronze. You   510
    hear that? He was not a new skin color. Black, not bronze!
VERA CRISTINA: Roberto was proud to be a Puerto Rican man close to
    his people.
TITO: Imagine when at first he couldn't understand el inglés del coach, an
    English-speaking disciplinarian talking about the action of the game.   515

VERA CRISTINA: The press reported his ailments as Roberto's psychosomatic ritual.

MIGUEL: He complained that his body hurt in all the vital parts, but he played in Pittsburgh. He played sin parar, pana sin parar, sin dejar de empujar hasta el extremo de su poder.   520

TITO: For years and years he played and heard multitudes cheer and feel proud in his presence, orgullosos de su presencia.

JESUS ABRAHAM: *(To VERA.)* Roberto emerged as a brilliant symbol in the sun, a leader, a model for our struggling youth.

RUTH MARIA: He started every world series he played by looking forward   525
to playing ball back in Puerto Rico.

MIGUEL: The cancerous problem is that America saw him as bronze; it was easier to see you as exotic ROBERTO! *(A pantomime baseball game starts.)*

TITO: While America saw him as a bronze, colored man batting balls, no matter what the curve. He was a lump of muscular earth that hit any   530
ball.

VERA CRISTINA: Qué agilidad tenía Roberto, qué disposición.

TITO: You never really knew where the bat came from.

JESUS ABRAHAM: He just hit all the pitches.

MIGUEL: All the challenges that came at him.   535

VERA CRISTINA: He hit the balls that came at him.

MIGUEL: Balls coming at him.

TITO: Balls pitched at him.

RUTH MARIA: Balls flying towards him.

MARIA SOCORRO: All the balls they pitched at him were curve balls.   540

MIGUEL: *(Aggressive, angry.)* Balls at him.

MARIA SOCORRO: *(Confident at Roberto's capacity for batting them all.)* Balls at him.

RUTH MARIA: *(Clear statement to the audience.)* Curve balls at him.

TITO: *(Shields himself with his arms.)* At him, balls at him.

VERA CRISTINA: Balls at him.   545

ALL OF THE POTENCIAS TOGETHER *(Repeat four times)*:   Balls at him.

MARIA SOCORRO: I hear him say *(She grabs her forehead.)* "I die alone, no one knowing cómo me dolía la espalda, cómo me arropaba para calentar el cuerpo, para que el calor me llegara hasta la espina dorsal donde se reciben tantas penas, tantos accidentes de hueso penetrando hueso.   550
(Deep silence, then MIGUEL continues.)

MIGUEL: He always had reserved energy for his public. Each time he played he knew each game was a judgment on his people.

JESUS ABRAHAM: He timed every move at the plate; it was a matter of looking at the ball and being ready.

TITO: He is not our only hero.   555

MARIA SOCORRO: No! There are more; let them through. Let them come all the way through. *(All of the* THROUGH *is said in unison by* LAS

SIETE POTENCIAS.*) THROUGH, THROUGH, THROUGH,
THROUGH, THROUGH, THROUGH.

RUTH MARIA: *(Moving towards third base.)* Roberto committed his body   560
to a discipline: to the daily torture of his muscles batting curves, to
the daily pouring of his sweat, to the daily bending of his body energy
into catching balls, balls of fire worth hundreds, hundreds, hundreds
of thousands of dollars and millions of faces.

MARIA SOCORRO: Había muchos puertorriqueños among those faces who   565
worshipped his form. But then el Caribe te tragó en buche.

MIGUEL: Te tragó en buche.

RUTH MARIA: Te tragó en buche.

IRMA ANTONIA: Te tragó en buche.

TITO: The blacks of Loíza played all night. Their congas searched while   570
all the people waited, the poets described the happening, the searching
for him, the over-all look leading to tears because we couldn't find
him, we couldn't liberate him from the water, we couldn't get more
time for the hombre-adult Clemente to stay on the planet. The waters
claimed him. The poets talked of him in the duet of a controversia.   575
Every one sought him; we had not yet realized death would teach us
that dying is the next stage toward the fullest realization of where we
are. What bothered Roberto, and what bothers me, is a hopeless
Rican, the type that doesn't see outside of el barrio apartment that's
got him trapped. The Rican who gets created por lo de afuera, by the   580
outside, and forgets to fight.

MIGUEL: Yes, the one who ignores confrontations that would release
anger, who struggles for restriction rather than release.

TITO: Few people manage to penetrate to the loco part of their mind,
where a point of view can be changed.   585

MIGUEL: I hate hermanos who educate themselves into docility.

TITO: What is docility? *(A high pitched guaguancó begins. The rhythms become sharper, more intense. Each definition is accurate. Nothing is
thrown away.)*

MIGUEL: Docility is acting on what has been learned rather than fighting
back for having to pay 10¢ for a lavatory in the subway.

TITO: Docility es una situación donde las necesidades se tratan como si   590
no existieran.

MIGUEL: Docility is too many people tucking their energies deep into
their spines.

TITO: Don't let the Ph.D. behavioral psychologist put your children to
sleep in New York schools and everywhere else.   595

MIGUEL: Docility is passive peace.

TITO: Docility drums pain.

MIGUEL: Docility is sleeping with despair.

TITO: Docility fears action.

JESUS ABRAHAM: Docility is paying 50¢ bus fare *(LAS POTENCIAS begin to*   600
walk towards third base.)

MIGUEL: Docility empties out lungs.

JESUS ABRAHAM: Docility is believing Nixon.

TITO: Docility devours our minds.

MIGUEL: Docility is believing in standards.

RUTH MARIA: Docility bites at your muscles.   605

IRMA ANTONIA: Docility is eating your tongue.

MIGUEL: Docility atrophies hearing.

MARIA SOCORRO: Docility is depression.

MIGUEL: Docility shapes you.

MARIA SOCORRO: Docility is letting it happen to you.   610

RUTH MARIA: Docility stimulates withering.

MARIA SOCORRO: Docility puts sleep into our cells.

TITO: Docility fights our energies.

MARIA SOCORRO: Docility attacked by us is docility defeated by us.

MIGUEL AND POTENCIAS: When we become the tongue, eyes, nose, touch   615
of all action that awakens our minds, then docility will be defeated by
our being, a fighting, talking center of consciousness.

JESUS ABRAHAM: Clemente was the people. He put everything into his
baseball. He beat rhythms with his ringers on the bat and made the
ball sound like a conga.   620

TITO: Roberto aimed his hits into the Gods' dining room where he woke
the witch that concocted his death.

VERA CRISTINA: His batting average was political. In baseball he had the
straightest ball, right into the center of the diamond of our being.

MARIA SOCORRO: Poeta, Poeta, Poeta, much charged the space between   625
Roberto's adulthood and his son's childhood was filled by his intense
manifestation, by his being a field of electricity.

RUTH MARIA: He was a field of action on the diamond, on the sparkling
sun-filled diamond that working people pack with their bodies.
Roberto, they came to see your spiritual hits, your metaphysical han-   630
dling of a bat and ball, your striking out twice, waiting 'til the very
moment of need.

MIGUEL: The moment of the hit, tiene que salir el hit, the hit. Your
metaphysical batting is the pitch of truth.

TITO: *(To JESUS ABRAHAM.)* Fuera del béisbol, Olú Roberto, el maestro,   635
era un hombre humilde del pueblo.

JESUS ABRAHAM: Pero nunca, nunca olvidó que lo queríamos, que lo
protegíamos, que sería respetado por el mundo. Y nunca buscó nada
más que su respeto por medio de sacrificios, por medio de ese don de
ser disciplinado, de adquirir la gracia que lo elevó al nivel del amor   640
puro.

VERA CRISTINA: Olú maestro,
Roberto tú eres
el filósofo del béisbol,
tú, Roberto, tú eres,   645
la filosofía realizada,

           tú, Roberto, tú serás la gracia del futuro
           del ahora puertorriqueño.

MIGUEL: Roberto Olú, help us.

Lead us.   650

Teach us

the future wisdom

of death.

JESUS ABRAHAM: We are the body,

we are the head,   655

we have to right on one front,

one fist,

one people.

MIGUEL: Roberto Olú maestro

teaches we are one.   660

Clemente's sangre

changed the Caribbean

waters into crimson

rage, the Caribbean

burned in anger,   665

the Caribbean sea

hate swallowing Roberto's energy,

there was a revolution

in the waters

of a sea made   670

of blood that fed

our teacher's mind.

JESUS ABRAHAM: The Caribbean was

in convulsions of despair

as Roberto live hero: 675

our best pelotero humanist

tragaba el agua que arrancaba el fuego

para llevarlo at cielo:

fire from above,

el fuego del cielo, Clemente,   680

el sol Roberto

shines on las calles

de Nueva York,

el sol caribe,

pelotero sol,   685

Roberto, tú ardes,

tú eres la llama del mañana,

tú, Roberto, el mañana

del ahora y del pasado:

tú fuego eres: 690

tú agua quemas:

tú luna y sol

alumbras con tu ser.

LAS POTENCIAS *bow to* VERA. *She takes their hands. A circle of hands above the heads.* MIGUEL *goes out left center field.* JESUS ABRAHAM *goes out front stage right.* IRMA ANTONIA *goes out right center field.* MARIA SOCORRO *walks out from the pitcher's mound to the back of center field.* RUTH MARIA *leaves from front stage left.* TITO *stands with* VERA *out in left field. Lights out. Los Pleneros de Loíza play. The musicians play.*

Discussion Questions

1. What is the role of the "Poeta" in the play?
2. How does the chorus function in the play?

Glossary
Olú Clemente

adentro inside
adolorido in pain
agobiado deeply concerned
agua water
ahoga drown
aldea village

bondad generosity

caer fall
caminar walk
carne flesh
cójanlas grab them
coño common vulgar expression which has many uses; similar to "damn"
cosas things
cruzar cross
cuerpo body

dejar allow
dime tell me
dispuesto willing
dolor pain

edad age
empujar push
encarcelado inprisoned
enseñar teach
esperar wait
espina dorsal spinal cord

espíritu spirit
esposa wife

frío cold
fuego fire
fuerza strength; force
futuro future

ganar win
guía guide

hablar speak
humo smoke
hunde sink

indio indian
interesado interested

juventud youth

lenguaje language
liberar free
llaves keys
llorar cry

maestro master
máquina machine
manos hands
mañana tomorrow
menea move
miedo fear
milagros miracles

mirar look
mismo same
muere die
mundo world

necesitar need
nene young men
noche night
nombre name
nuestra our

ojos eyes
oración prayer
orar pray

padre father
pasado past
pasión passion
pelotero baseball player
pena shyness; suffering
pequeño small
poder power
poner put; place
pozo ditch; grave
preso imprisoned
promesas promises
próximo next
puerta door
pureza purity

querer want; desire
quitar remove

rapido quickly
raza race
rebeldía rebellion
revolución revolution
rito rite
rogar plead

sajón Saxon
salió left
salvar save
sombra shadow
sufrir suffer
suplicar beg

tambien also
tenemos have to
tierra earth
trabajo job
tragar swallow
tragó en buche swallowed whole

viaje trip
visitar visit
voló flew

Tito's speech on page 507: And to continue with our respect to dear Robert Clemente we want to pay tribute to all the mothers who suffer for their children who have to place themselves in danger. And we do it because we know that you, Roberto, from the place where you are seated at the right hand side of our creators, from there like Olú, the master, will help us so that our children will be the future of our country. We know that you are the example of a saintly and good man.

Conversation between Vera Cristina, María Socorro, Irma Antonia, and Ruth Maria on page 508–511: The thrust of the conversation is surrounding the possible reason(s) behind Clemente's death. Clemente, it is argued, died trying to save the lives of future generations of Puerto Ricans. These generations are in jeopardy because of the ills of modern society. Irma Antonia argues that a child is to be protected even if he or she has done something illegal because the reponsibility behind that child's vice lies with the system. Poverty, drug use, poor working conditions, are all a result of a society that turns a deaf ear to the plight of Puerto Ricans, something that Clemente, of course, did not do. The conversation concludes with the belief that women must band together and serve as a force to support their husbands and children against society's oppression.

First, Second, and *Third* Songs: "*Al Boricua y al Amor*", "To the Boricua and to Love"
                                    "*Nunca se me fue*", "It never left me"
                                    "*El Pozo*", "The Grave"

Boricua, a derivation of Borinquen, the name the indigenous inhabitants of Puerto Rico, Taínos, named the island. Thus, a boricua is another name for Puerto Rican, but with a patriotic connotation. Taken together, the songs are a tribute to the island and the chorus affirms that what a boricua has can never be taken away. It is also an acknowledgment that a Puerto Rican is an amalgam of Spanish, African, and Taino blood. The conclusion in the third song is therefore that when the speaker dies he will be protected by both traditional Catholic saints and *las potencias,* or African deities. The songs thus reflect the focus of the play on Clemente as a deity.

Fourth Song: "*Olú*"

The song describes the death and spiritual resurrection of Clemente by combining both Catholicism and African pagan belief. When Clemente fell into the ocean, the song claims, he was the Trinity. His spirit, however, has been resurrected in the form of Olú, an African god.

Fifth Song: "*Ocho Velas*" "Eight Candles"

Now fully realized, the spirit of Clemente, Olú, is the eighth Power of African deities. The traditional "*Siete Potencias,*" or Seven Powers, now have an addition to the pantheon. Thus, eight candles now have to be lighted by those who seek protection by the gods.

Credits

Jack Agueros, "One Sunday Morning" from *Dominos and Other Stories from the Puerto Rican.* © 1993 by Jack Agueros. Reprinted with the permission of Curbstone Press. Distributed by Consortium.

—, "Sonnet: Waiting in Tompkins Square Park," and "Sonnets for the Four Horsemen of the Apocalypse: Long Time Among Us" from *Sonnets from the Puerto Rican.* © 1996 by Jack Agueros. Reprinted with the permission of Hanging Loose Press.

Miguel Algarin, "Nuyorican Angel" and "August 21" from *Love Is Hard Work: Memories of Loisada* (New York: Scribner, 1997). © 1997 by Miguel Algarin. Reprinted with the permission of Susan Bergholz Literary Services, New York.

—, and **Tato Laviera,** "Olu Clemente" from *Nuevos Pasos: Chicano and Puerto Rican Drama.* © 1989. Reprinted with the permission of Arte Publico Press.

Rene Aloma, " A Little Something to Ease the Pain" from *Cuban American Theater,* edited by Rodolfo Cortina. © 1991. Reprinted with the permission of Arte Publico Press.

Rudolfo Anaya, excerpt from *Bless Me Ultima* (New York: Warner Books, 1994). © 1994 by Rudolfo Anaya. Reprinted with permission of Susan Bergholz Literary Services, New York.

Gloria Anzaldua, "To Live in the Borderlands Means You" from *Borderlands/La Frontera.* © 1987 by Gloria Anzaldua. Reprinted with the permission of Aunt Lute Books.

Jimmy Santiago Baca, "Roots," "Accountability," and "A Daily Joy to Be Alive," from *Black Mesa Poems.* © 1986 by Jimmy Santiago Baca. Reprinted with the permission of New Directions Publishing Corporation.

Teresa Bevin, "City of Giant Tinajones" from *Havana Split.* © 1998 by Terersa Bevin. Reprinted with the permission of Arte Publico Press.

Ana Castillo, Chapter 1 from *So Far From God.* © 1998 by Ana Castillo. Reprinted with the permission of W. W. Norton & Company, Inc.

—, "Women Are Not Roses" and "Not Just Because My Husband Said" from *Women Are Not Roses* (Houston: Arte Publico Press, 1984). © 1988 by Ana Castillo. Reprinted with the permission of Susan Bergholz Literary Services, New York.

Lorna Dee Cervantes, "To We Who Were Saved By the Stars" from *From the Cables of Genocide.* © 1991 by Lorna Dee Cervantes. Reprinted with the permission of Arte Publico Press.

Denise Chavez, "Willow Game" from *The Last of the Menu Girls* (Houston: Arte Publico, 1986). © 1986 by Denise Chavez. Reprinted with the permission of Susan Bergholz Literary Services. New York.

Sandra Cisneros, "My Wicked Wicked Ways" and "For All Tuesday Travelers" from *My Wicked Wicked Ways.* © 1987 by Sandra Cisneros. Reprinted with the permission of The University of Georgia Press.

Jesus Colon, excerpt from *A Puerto Rican in New York and Other Sketches.* © 1975 by Jesus Colon. Reprinted with the permission of International Publishers.

Victor Merced Hernandez, "African Things" and "Bi-Lingual Education" from *By Lingual Wholes* (San Francisco: Momo's Press, 1982). © 1982. Reprinted with the permission of the author.

Margarita Engle, excerpt from *Singing to Cuba.* © 1993 by Margarita Engle. Reprinted with the permission of Arte Publico Press.

Martin Espada, "Niggerlips" from *Rebellion Is the Circle of a Lover's Hands.* © 1990 by Martin Espada. Reprinted with the permission of Curbstone Press. Distributed by Consortium.

—, "Thanksgiving" from *A Mayan Astronomer in Hell's Kitchen.* © 2000 by Martin Espada. Reprinted with the permission of W. W. Norton & Company, Inc.

Sandra Maria Esteves, "In the Beginning" and "A la Mujer Borrinquena"

Roberta Fernandez, "Esmerelda" from *Intaglio: A Novel.* © 1990 by Roberta Fernandez. Reprinted with the permission of Arte Publico Press.

Roberto Fernandez, "Et Tu, Delfina?" and "Conversation" from *Holy Radishes!* © 1995 by Roberto Fernandez. Reprinted with the permission of Arte Publico Press.

Gustavo Perez Firmat, "Bilingual Blues" and "Dedication" from *Bilingual Blues.* © 1995 by Gustavo Perez Firmat. Reprinted with the permission of Bilingual Press/Editorial Bilingue, Arizona State University, Tempe, AZ.

Cristina Garcia, excerpts from *Dreaming in Cuban.* © 1992 by Cristina Garcia. Reprinted with the permission of Alfred A. Knopf, a division of Random House, Inc.

Rodolfo Gonzales, excerpt from *I Am Joaquin* (New York: Bantam, 1972). © 1972 by Rodolfo Gonzales. Reprinted with the permission of the author.

Oscar Hijuelos, excerpt from *The Mambo Kings Play Songs of Love.* © 1989 by Oscar Hijuelos. Reprinted with the permission of Farrar, Straus, & Giroux, LLC.

Rolando Hinojosa, "Becky" from *Becky and Her Friends.* © 1990 by Rolando Hinojosa. Reprinted with the permission of Arte Publico Press.

Carolina Hospital, "Dear Tia" from *Cuban American Writers: Los Atrevidos,* edited by Carolina Hospital (Princeton: Ediciones Ellas/Linden Lane Press, 1988). Reprinted with the permission of the author.

Tato Laviera, "My Graduation Speech," "Savorings, from Pinones to Loiza," and "Against Munoz Pamphleteering" from *La Carreta Made a U-Turn.* © 1981 by Tato Laviera. Reprinted with the permission of the author.

Pablo Medina, "The Birthmark" from *The Marks of Birth* (New York: Farrar, Straus, & Giroux, 1994). © 1994 by Pablo Medina. Reprinted with the permission of the author.

—, "The Exile" and "Winter of a Rose" from *Pork Rinds and Cuban Songs* (Washington: Nuclassics, 1975). © 1975 by Pablo Medina. Reprinted with the permission of the author.

Nicholasa Mohr, excerpts from *Nilda* (Houston: Arte Publico Press, 1986). © 1986 by Nicholasa Mohr. Reprinted with the permission of the author.

Pat Mora, "Sonrisas," "Bilingual Christmas," and "The Grateful Minority" from *Borders.* © 1984 by Pat Mora. Reprinted with the permission of Arte Publico Press.

Carlos Morton, "El Jardin" from *The Many Deaths of Danny Rosales.* © 1983 by Carlos Morton. Reprinted with the permission of Arte Publico Press.

Elias Miguel Munoz, excerpt from "Little Sister Born in This Land" from *En Estas Tierras/In This Land.* © 1997 by Elias Miguel Munoz. Reprinted with the permission of Bilingual Press/Editorial Bilingue, Arizona State University, Tempe, AZ.

Himilce Novas, excerpt from *Mangos, Bananas, and Coconuts: A Cuban Love Story.* © 1996 by Himilce Novas. Reprinted with the permission of Arte Publico Press.

Americo Paredes, excerpts from *George Washington Gomez.* © 1990 by Americo Paredes. Reprinted with the permission of Arte Publico Press.

Ricardo Pau-Llosa, "Foreign Language" from *Bread of the Imagined.* © 1992 by Ricardo Pau-Llosa. Reprinted with the permission of Bilingual Press/Editorial Bilingue, Arizona State University, Tempe AZ.

—, "Minas de Cobre" from *Cuba.* © 1993 by Ricardo Pau-Llosa. Reprinted with the permission of Carnegie-Mellon University Press.

Pedro Pietri, "Puerto Rican Obituary" from *Puerto Rican Obituary.* © 1971 by Monthly Review Press. Reprinted with the permission of the Monthly Review Foundation.

Miguel Pinero, excerpt from *A Midnight Moon at the Greasy Spoon.* © 1984 by Miguel Pinero. Reprinted with the permission of Arte Publico Press.

Dolores Prida, "Beautiful Senoritas" from *Beautiful Senoritas and Other Plays.* © 1991 by Dolores Prida. Reprinted with the permission of Arte Publico Press.

Abraham Rodriguez, Jr., "The Boy Without a Flag" from *The Boy Without a Flag and Other Sketches.* © 1992, 1999 by Abraham Rodriguez, Jr. Reprinted with the permission of Milkweed Editions.

Esmeralda Santiago, excerpt from *When I Was Puerto Rican.* © 1993 by Esmeralda Santiago. Reprinted with permission.

Gary Soto, "Black Hair" from *Living Up the Street* (New York: Dell, 1992). © 1985 by Gary Soto. Reprinted with the permission of the author.

Gary Soto, "Who Will Know Us?" from *Who Will Know Us?* © 1990 by Gary Soto. Reprinted with the permission of Chronicle Books, San Francisco.

—, "Moving Our Misery" from Junior College. Originally published in *The Massachusetts Review* 36:4 (Winter 1995 – 1996), Special Latino/Latina Poetry Section. © 1995 by Gary Soto. Reprinted with the permission of Chronicle Books, San Francisco.

Virgil Suarez, "Spared Angola" and "La Ceiba: The Tree of Life" from *Spared Angola.* © 1977 by Virgil Suarez. Reprinted with the permission of Arte Publico Press.

Caridad Svich, "Gleaning/Rebusca" from *Shattering the Myth: Plays by Hispanic Women,* edited by Linda Feyder. © 1992. Reprinted with the permission of Arte Publico Press.

Piri Thomas, "Hung Up Between Two Sticks," "Hey Barrio—I'm Home," and "I Swears to God and the Virgin" from *Down These Mean Streets.* © 1967 by Piri Thomas. Reprinted with the permission of Alfred A. Knopf, a division of Random House, Inc.

Estela Portillo Trambley, "Sor Juana" from *Sor Juana and Other Plays.* © 1983 by Estela Portillo Trambley. Reprinted with the permission of Bilingual Press/Editorial Bilingue, Tempe, AZ.

Luis Valdez, "Bernabe" from *Zoot Suit and Other Plays.* © 1992 by Luis Valdez. Reprinted with the permission of Arte Publico Press.

Ed Vega, "The Barbosa Express" from *Mendoza's Dreams.* © 1987 by Ed Vega. Reprinted with permission of Arte Publico Press.

Victor Villasenor, Chapter 15 from *Rain of Gold.* © 1991 by Victor Villasenor. Reprinted with the permission of Art Publico Press.

Jose Antonio Villreal, excerpts from *Pocho.* © 1959 by Jose Antonio Villareal. Reprinted with the permission of Doubleday, a division of Random House, Inc.

Helena Maria Viramontes, excerpts from *Under the Feet of Jesus.* © 1996 by Helena Maria Viramontes. Reprinted with the permission of Dutton, a division of Penguin Putnam Inc.

Jose Yglesias, "the Place I Was Born" and "Celia's Family" from *The Guns in the Closet.* © 1996 by Jose Yglesias. Reprinted with the permission of Arte Publico Press.

Bernice Zamora, "Luciano" from *Releasing Serpents.* © 1983 by Bernice Zamora. Reprinted with the permission of Bilingual Press/Editorial Bilingue, Tempe, AZ.

Selected Bibliography

Books

Borland, Isabel Alvarez, *Cuban-American Literature of Exile: From Person to Persona.* Charlottesville (VA): University P of Virginia, 1998.

Christie, John S. *Latino Fiction and the Modernist Imagination: Literature of the Borderlands.* New York: Garland, 1998.

Fabre, Genvieve. *European Perspectives on Hispanic Literature in the United States.* Houston: Arte Publico, 1988.

Flores, Juan. *Divided Borders: Essays on Puerto Rican Identity.* Houston: Arte Publico, 1993.

Hernandez, Carmen Dolores. *Puerto Rican Voices in English: Interviews with Writers.* Westport (CT): Praeger, 1997.

Herrera-Sobek, Maria, ed. Beyond Stereotypes: *The Critical Analysis of Chicana Literature.* Binghamton: Bilingual Press, 1985.

Herrera-Sobek, Maria and Helena Maria Viramontes, eds. *Chicana Creativity and Criticism: New Frontiers in American Literature.* Albuquerque: U of New Mexico P, 1996.

Horno-Delgado, Asunción et al., eds. *Breaking Boundaries: Latina Writing and Critical Readings.* Amherst: U of Massachusetts P, 1989.

Kanellos, Nicolas, ed. *Biographical dictionary of Hispanic literature in the United States: the Literature of Puerto Ricans, Cuban Americans, and other Hispanic Writers.* New York: Greenwood 1989.

———. *A History of Hispanic Theater in the United States: Origins to 1940.* Austin: U of Texas P, 1990.

Lee, Joyce Glover. *Rolando Hinojosa and the American Dream.* Denton: U of North Texas P, 1997.

Limón, José Eduardo. *Mexican Ballads, Chicano Poems: History and Influence in Mexican-American Social Poetry.* Berkeley: U of California P, 1992.

Luis, William. *Dance Between Two Cultures: Latino Caribbean Literature Written in the United States.* Nashville: Vanderbilt UP, 1997.

Neate, Wilson. *Tolerating Ambiguity: Ethnicity and Community in Chicano/a Writing.* New York: Peter Lang, 1998.

Maitino, John R. and David R. Peck, eds. *Teaching American Ethnic Literatures: Nineteen Essays.* Albuquerque U of New Mexico P, 1996.

Perez-Firmat, Gustavo. *Life on the Hyphen: The Cuban-American Way.* Austin: U of Texas P, 1994.

Portales, Marco. *Crowding Out Latinos: Mexican Americans in the Public Consciousness.* Philadelphia: Temple UP, 2000.

Rebolledo, Tey Diana. *Women Singing in the Snow: A Cultural Analysis of Chicana Literature.* Tucson: U of Arizona P, 1995.

Rodriguez de Laguna, Asela, ed. *Images and Identities: The Puerto Rican in Two World Contexts.* New Brunswick (NJ): Transaction, 1987.

Saldívar, Ramón. *Chicano Narrative: the Dialectics of Difference.* Madison: U of Wisconsin P, 1990.

Shirley, Carl R. and Paula W. Shirley. *Understanding Chicano Literature.* Columbia (S.C.): U of South Carolina P, 1988.

Vigil, Evangelina, ed. *Woman of Her Word: Hispanic Women Write.* Houston: Arte Publico, 1987.

Articles

Aranda, Jose F., Jr. "Contradictory Impulses: Maria Amparo Ruiz de Burton, Resistance Theory, and the Politics of Chicano/a Studies." *American Literature* 70.3 (1998): 551–79.

Acosta Belén, Edna. "The Literature of the Puerto Rican Minority in the United States." *Bilingual Review* 5 (1978): 107–16.

Alvarez-Borland, Isabel. "Displacements and Autobiography in Cuban-American Fiction." *World Literature Today* 68 (1994): 43–53.

Casal, Lourdes and Andrés R. Hernández. "Cubans in the U.S.: A Survey of the Literature." *Cuban Studies* 5 (1975): 25–52.

Castells, Ricardo. "Next Year in Cuba: Gustavo Perez Firmat and the Rethinking of the Cuban-American Experience." *Secolas Annals* 30 (1999): 28–35.

Cruz-Malave, Arnaldo. "What a Tangled Web!: Masculinity, Abjection and the Foundations of Puerto Rican Literature in the United States." *Differences: a Journal of Feminist Cultural Studies* 8.1 (1996): 132–51.

Fernandez Olmos, Margarite. "Growing Up Puertorriquena: The Feminist Bildungsroman and the Novels of Nicholasa Mohr and Magali Garcia Ramis." *Centro.* 2.7 (1989–90): 56–73.

Figueredo, Danilo H. "Ser Cubano (To Be Cuban): The Evolution of Cuban-American Literature." *Multicultural Review* 6.1 (1997): 18–28.

Flores, Juan. "Back Down These Mean Streets: Introducing Nicholasa Mohr and Louis Reyes Rivera." *Revista Chicano-Riqueña* 8 (1980): 51–56.

———. "Puerto Rican Literature in the United States: Stages and Perspectives." *ADE Bulletin* 91 (1988): 39–44.

Franco, Dean. "Ethnic Writing/Writing Ethnicity: The Critical Conceptualization of Chicano Identity." *Post Identity* 2.1 (1999): 104–22.

Gutierrez Spencer, Laura. "The Desert Blooms: Flowered Songs by Pat Mora." *The Bilingual Review* 20.1 (1995): 28–36.

Hernandez Cruz, Victor. "Mountains in the North: Hispanic Writing in the U.S.A." *Americas Review* 14 (1986): 110–14.

Klein, Dianne. "Coming of Age in Novels by Rudolfo Anaya and Sandra Cisneros." *English Journal* 81.5 (1992): 21–26.

Murphy, Patrick D. "Conserving Natural and Cultural Diversity: The Prose and Poetry of Pat Mora." *MELUS* 21.1 (1996): 59–69.

Myers, Inma Minoves. "Language and Style in *Pocho*." *The Bilingual Review* 16.2,3 (1991): 180–87.

Newkirk, Glen A. "Anaya's Archetypal Women in *Bless Me, Ultima*." *South Dakota Review* 31.1 (1993): 142–50.

Perez-Torres, Rafael. "Chicano Studies at the Millennium." *Contemporary Literature* 39.4 (1998): 675–86.

Requeña, Gisele M. "The Sounds of Silence: Remembering and Creating in Margarita Engle's *Singing to Cuba*." *MELUS* 23.1 (1998): 147–57.

Saldívar, Ramón. "Americo Paredes, the Border Corrido and Socially Symbolic Chicano Narrative." *Critical Exchange* 22 (1987): 11–22.

Vallejos, Thomas. "Ritual Process and the Family in the Chicano Novel." *MELUS* 10.4 (1983): 5–16.

Viera, Joseph M. "Matriarchy and Mayhem: Awakenings in Cristina Garcia's *Dreaming in Cuban*." *The Americas Review: a Review of Hispanic Literature and Art of the USA* 24.3 (1996): 231–42.

Walter, Roland. "The Cultural Politics of Dislocation and Relocation in the Novels of Ana Castillo." *MELUS* 23.1 (1998): 81–97.

Wiley, Catherine. "Teatro Chicano and the Seduction of Nostalgia." *MELUS* 23.1 (1998): 99–115.

Index